# Cannons' Bibliography of Library Economy, 1876-1920:

## *An Author Index with Citations*

edited by
Anne Harwell Jordan
and
Melbourne Jordan

The Scarecrow Press, Inc.
Metuchen, N.J.    1976

**Library of Congress Cataloging in Publication Data**

Jordan, Anne, 1924-
    Cannons' Bibliography of Library Economy,
1876-1920:  An Author Index with Citations.
    1.  Library science—Bibliography.  2.  Bibliography
—Bibliography.  3.  Cannons, Harry George Turner.
Bibliography of library economy.  I.  Jordan,
Melbourne, joint author.  II.  Cannons, Harry George
Turner.  Bibliography of library economy.  III.  Title.
Z666.J67          016.02          76-3711
ISBN 0-8108-0918-4

# TABLE OF CONTENTS

Cannons', H. G. T. Bibliography of Library Economy: a
classified index to the professional periodical literature in
the English language relating to library economy, printing,
methods of publishing, copyright, bibliography, etc., from
1876 to 1920 (Chicago, A L A, 1927) was the first of several
comprehensive compendiums in the field of library literature.
As its name implies, it listed articles published in the leading periodicals devoted to librarianship in the United States
and Great Britain, as well as a few monographs. These citations were presented in a classed arrangement, many appearing
under several different subject headings. Among the contributors to this literature were such eminent figures as Dewey,
Putnam, Pollard, Certain, Billings, Dana, Cutter, and Spofford.
It is the intention of the editors of this supplementary publication to provide further access to this material.

All the entries in Cannons', H. G. T. Bibliography of
Library Economy which bore a personal author's name are
presented in the work in hand. Entries taken from the classed arrangement have been examined, consolidated, and arranged
alphabetically under the names of the authors. The user need
not refer back to Cannons', H. G. T. Bibliography of Library
Economy to obtain all available information about the article
desired. Listings in this volume include the author's surname,
initials, title of the article or monograph, name of the periodical in which it appeared, volume number, and pagination.
In the case of government reports, yearbooks, and monographs
the year of publication is included. Whenever possible, doubtful entries have been checked in the sources cited, to insure
accuracy. A list of periodicals indexed in the Bibliography,
together with the abbreviations of their names used in this
work, follows this preface.

The Compilers

Introduction

It is not surprising, since librarians are charged with
keeping track bibliographically of the rest of the world,
that they do something less than a good job in their own
special field. The basic document of library history, Harry
George Turner Cannons' Bibliography of Library Economy, amp-
ly testifies to this fact. Cannons' is the document which
records the beginning of scientific scholarship in librarianship. Since it is a classified bibliography with quite dated
subject access, it is a Byzantine task to find what Rider,
Dewey, Cutter and other historically important figures in
librarianship have written about a particular topic. It is
for this reason that library historians will be grateful to
Anne and Mel Jordan. These compilers have taken the information in Cannons' and used it to produce an index to the
individuals who have shaped library history, and whose scholarship has been buried in this bibliography for decades.
    The Jordans, furthermore, have improved upon the index-
ing of this important bibliography. Corrections were made,
whenever possible, to the existing material appearing in
Cannons', and a considerable number of incomplete and blind
entries were rescued with appropriate changes. This book
as a result, is a genuine supplement to Cannons' Bibliography
of Library Economy, as well as a tool which makes Cannons'
indexing accessible to the profession.
    It is the historian's challenge to interpret the past
so that its relevance can be determined in the present. This
index now makes that task genuinely feasible. The data are
laid bare, and the profession, which has not had access to
this historical material for decades, can now see it first
hand. It's time for systematic analysis in the history of
librarianship, and one need only pick a name now that this
indexing project is complete. It is as simple as that.


                                            John Gordon Burke

| Abbreviation | Title |
| --- | --- |
| A L A Bull | Bulletin of the American Library Association |
| Am Lib Annual | American Library Annual |
| An Leab | An Leabharlann |
| B A R | Book Auction Records |
| B Q R | Bodleian Quarterly Record |
| Bib Soc Amer Proc | Bibliographical Society of America: Proceedings |
| Bib Soc Chic Yrbk | Bibliographical Society of Chicago: Yearbook |
| Bib Soc Trans | Bibliographical Society of London: Transactions |
| Bull Bib | Bulletin of Bibliography |
| Cal News Notes | News Notes of California Libraries |
| | Carnegie United Kingdom Trust: Annual Reports |
| | Colorado Library Association: Occasional Leaflets |
| Conn P L D | Connecticut Public Library Document |
| Del L C Hdbk | Delaware Library Commission Handbook |
| 1st Int Conf | First International Library Conference: Proceedings. London |
| | Greenwood's "Public Libraries" |
| | Greenwood's "Year-book," 1897, 1900-01 |
| Ia L C Q | Iowa Library Commission Quarterly |
| Ind L C Rept | Indiana Public Library Commission: Biennial Report |
| | Irish Book Lover |
| Kans City L Q | Kansas City (Missouri) Library Quarterly |
| L | Library |
| L (ns) | Library (new series) |
| L (3d ser) | Library (3d series) |
| L (4th ser) | Library (4th series) |
| L A | Library Assistant |
| L A M N | Library Association Monthly Notes |
| L A of Austral Proc | Library Association of Australasia: Proceedings |
| L A R | Library Association Record |

Publications Indexed--Continued

| Abbreviation | Title |
|---|---|
| L A U K | Library Association United Kingdom: Transactions |
| L A Yrbk | Library Association Year-book |
| L C | Library Chronicle |
| Libn | Librarian |
| Lib Occ | Library Occurrent (Public Library Commission of Indiana) |
| Lib Work | Library Work |
| Lit Yrbk | Literary Year-book |
| L J | Library Journal |
| | Library Miscellany (Baroda, India) |
| L N (U S) | Library Notes (U.S.) Boston |
| L W | Library World |
| Maine Lib Bull | Maine State Library Bulletin |
| Mass L C Bull | Massachusetts Library Club Bulletin |
| Med Lib and Hist Journal | Medical Library and Historical Journal |
| | Michigan Board of Library Commissioners: Report |
| Mich Lib Bull | Michigan State Library Bulletin |
| Minn, Ia and Wis L C Hdbk | Minnesota, Iowa and Wisconsin Library Commission Handbook |
| Minn P L C N | Minnesota Public Library Commission Notes (Title since 1919: Department of Education Library Notes and News) |
| N C Bull | North Carolina Library Bulletin |
| Nat Educ Assn | National Education Association: Proceedings (Library Section) |
| Neb Lib Bull | Nebraska Library Commission Bulletin |
| New Hamp Bull | New Hampshire Library Bulletin |
| N J Lib Bull | New Jersey Public Library Commission Bulletin |
| N Y L | New York Libraries |
| N Y S L Rept | New York State Library Report |
| Ohio Lib Bull | Ohio State Library Bulletin |
| | Pacific Northwest Library Association: Proceedings |
| Penn Lib Notes | Pennsylvania Library Notes |
| P L | Public Libraries |
| Rept of Libn of Congress | Library of Congress: Report of Librarian |

Publications Indexed--Continued

| Abbreviation | Title |
| --- | --- |
| 2nd Int Conf | Second International Library Conference Proceedings, London |
| | South Dakota Library Bulletin |
| | Special Libraries |
| Sub L | Subscription Libraries |
| U S Govt Rept | United States Commissioner of Education: Report |
| Vt L Bull | Vermont Library Commission Bulletin |
| Wash L A Bull | Washington Library Association Bulletin |
| | Wilson Bulletin |
| Wis Lib Bull | Wisconsin Library Bulletin |

Abbot, Alderman. The financial position of our public libraries. L A R 21: 129-36.

Abbot, Councillor. On rate limitation. L A R 6: 489-90.

Abbot, E. Ancient papyrus and the mode of making paper from it. L J 3: 323-4.

--- E. Reading list on the history of the latter half of the 15th century. N Y S L Rept 81, Bibliography No 10, 1898.

--- E. The Studebaker library and its work. Special Libraries 1: 66-8; P L 15: 416-8; Lib Occ 2: 158, 175.

Abbot, G. M. Some recollections of Lloyd P. Smith, Librarian of the Library Co., Philadelphia. L J 12: 545-7; Bull Bib 9: 37-8.

Abbott, A. An experiment in high school English. School Review 12: 550-8.

---- A. High school course in periodical literature. English Journal 2: 422-7.

---- A. Reading for high school students. School Review 10: 585-600.

Abbott, E. L. Bibliography in a small library. P L 7: 8-12.

Abbott, J. H. Stock privilege: a layman's experience. L J 44: 371-2.

Abbott, S. A. B. History of the Boston public library. L J 16: 173.

Abbott, T. C. Commercial libraries. L A R 19: 472-6.

---- T. C. Relation of the public libraries to other educational institutions. L 8: 428-34.

Abernathy, J. W. Literature in the school program. Education 22: 10-4.

Abrahams, V. Use of pictures in schools: Bibliography. Wilson Bulletin 1: 447.

Abrams, A. W. Libraries and visual instruction. N Y L 1: 235-7.

Ackerman, A. School library as a public library. Minn P L C N 3: 203.

Ackerman, C. W. Book-worms of New York: how the public libraries satisfy the immigrant's thirst for knowledge. In dependent 74: 199-201.

Ackley, G. Librarian's reading. Wis Lib Bull 6: 43.

Acland, H. W. Foundation and progress of the Radcliffe Library. L A U K Trans 1: 29-31.

---- H. W. Radcliffe iron bookcases. L A Trans 1: 75.

Acland-Troyte, J. E. Harmonies of the gospels and other words made at Little Gidding by Nicholas Ferrar. L 2: 317-27.

Adams, A. F. The combining system of notation. L J 23: 52-4.

Adams, C. F. Fiction in public libraries. L J 4: 330-8.

--- C. F. Problems of the small library. L J 29: 365-7.

--- C. F. Sifting as a library policy. L J 18: 118-9.

Adams, C. F., Jr.  Public library and schools.  L J 1: 437-41.

Adams, E. L.  Book exhibits at Plainfield (N. J.) public library.  L J 27: 763-5.

--- E. L.  Bulletin work of the Plainfield (N. J.) public library.  L J 31: 23-4.

--- E. L.  Children's library methods as determined by the needs of the children.  P L 2: 395.

--- E. L.  Instruction in the use of reference books and libraries in normal schools.  L J 23: Conf No 84-6.

--- E. L.  Library work with schools.  L J 23: 137-41.

--- E. L.  Methods of children's library work as determined by the needs of the children.  L J 22: Conf No 28-31.

--- E. L.  Work accomplished by various state library associations.  L J 20: 380-2.

Adams, H. B.  Library facilities at Harvard.  U S Bureau of Education, Circular of Information 1887 No 2: 43-6.

--- H. B.  Library facilities for the study of history at the University of Michigan.  U S Bureau of Education.  Circular of Information 1887 No 2: 119-23.

--- H. B.  Library facilities in history at Cornell University.  U S Bureau of Education.  Circular of Information. 1887 No 2: 164-70.

--- H. B.  Library of history and political science at Columbia University.  U S Bureau of Education, Circular of Information 1887, No 2: 82-4.

--- H. B.  Public libraries and popular education.  Univ of State of New York Home Education Bulletin No 31, 1900.

--- H. B.  Seminary libraries and university education. Johns Hopkins University Studies in Historical and Political Science 5: 437-69.

--- H. B.  Seminary library of the Johns Hopkins University.  U S Bureau of Education, Circular of Information, 1887, No 2: 179-91.

--- H. B.  Suggestions for the Forbes library.  L J 12: 512.

Adams, J. R. C.  Registration of colonial publications. 2d Int Conf 194-6, 1897.

Adams, J. R. G.  What local literature should be preserved in a public library.  L A of Austral Proc XLV-XLVII.

Adams, M. B.  Open access lending departments.  L A R 7: 229-32.

--- M. B.  Public libraries, their building and equipment.  L A R 7: 161-77, 220-36.

Adams, R. W.  Binding: historic and artistic.  P L 11: 289-99.

Adams, W. G. S.  Report on library provisions and policy to the Carnegie United Kingdom Trust, 1915: 104p.  Statistics compiled from Prof. Adams' report.  Carnegie United Kingdom Trust, Second annual report, 1915: 37-44.

Adams, W. H. Ways of making a library useful. L J 28: 286-90.

Adams, Z. F. Practical hints on organizing. P L 4: 58-9, 143, 198-9.

Addison, C. Libraries and education: address at L. A. conference. L A R 19: 430-4.

Adler, C. International catalog of scientific literature. L J 20: Conf No 58; L J 29: Conf No 97-9.

--- C. London International conference on a catalogue of scientific literature. L J 22: Conf No 58-60, 168.

--- C. Museums of art and science. L J 23: Conf No 95-6.

--- C. Relation of the publishing department of a university to its library. L J 23: Conf No 106.

--- C. and L. C. Gunnell. The international catalogue of scientific literature. Bib Soc Amer Proc 3: 109-15.

Adler, E. N. Gazeteer of Hebrew printing. L W 19: 200-4, 231-4, 264-6, 290-5, 314-6.

Agg, R. Over the loan desk. P L 21: 355-7.

Ahern, M. E. A. L. A. news from overseas. A L A Bull 13: 309-12, 348, 385.

--- M. E. Business side of a woman's career as a librarian. L J 24: Conf No 60-2.

--- M. E. Co-operation between libraries and schools. P L 7: 99-111.

--- M. E. Debits and credits of twenty years. P L 20: 474-7.

--- M. E. Discusses library unions. A L A Bull 13: 385-6.

--- M. E. Library institute. A L A Bull 2: 312-3.

--- M. E. Library instruction in normal schools. Nat Educ Assn 1903: 976-83.

--- M. E. Library legislation--California. U S Commissioner of Education Report 1913: Vol 1: 319.

--- M. E. Library legislation for Illinois. P L 13: 353.

--- M. E. Library legislation--Indiana. U S Commissioner of Education Report 1913 Vol 1: 320.

--- M. E. Library legislation--Minnesota. U S Commissioner of Education Report 1913, Vol 1: 320-1.

--- M. E. Library legislation--Montana. U S Commissioner of Education Report 1913 Vol 1: 321.

--- M. E. Library legislation--Texas. U S Commissioner of Education Report 1913 Vol 1: 322.

--- M. E. Library of Congress and printed cards. P L 10: 294-6.

--- M. E. Library work in the United States and Canada. L A R 12: 559-61.

--- M. E. Need of balance in library work. Wis Lib Bull 7: 110-1.

--- M. E. Overseas library service. N Y L 6: 188-90.

--- M. E.  Professional training for school libraries.
New York State Teachers' Assn Proceedings 1912: 220-5.
--- M. E.  Reading for young people.  Ia L C Q 1: 44-5.
--- M. E.  Reference work with the general public.  P L
9: 55-65.
--- M. E.  States authorizing county libraries.  U S Com-
missioner of Education, Report 1913, 1: 315-6.
--- M. E.  Unsolved problems of the library commissions.
A L A Bull 1: Conf No 231-6.
--- M. E.  What state supervision does in other states.
P L 13: 430.
--- M. E.  Women as librarians in the business world.  P
L 4: 257-61.
--- M. E. and W. H. Brett.  Library instruction in the
normal school.  Nat Educ Assn 1903: 692-702.
Ahern, S. M.  Bringing together business men and library ser-
vice.  P L 21: 312-4.
Aiken, W. E.  Some poets of the war.  Vt L Bull 14: 1-8.
--- W. E.  Study of English literature.  Education 26: 36-9.
Aiken, W. F.  Unique library plan.  American Agriculturist 67:
420.
Aitken, G. A.  Notes on the bibliography of Matthew Prior.  Bib
Soc Trans 1915-17: 39-68.
---- G. A.  Notes on the bibliography of Pope.  Bib Soc
Trans 12: 113-43.
Aitken, P. H.  Some notes on the history of paper.  Bib Soc
Trans 13: 201-17.
Aitken, V.  Junior work of classification.  L A 6: 330-3.
Aitken, V. A.  Stamping books.  L W 10: 155-6.
Akin, S. M.  The Frederick County free library in Maryland.
P L 21: 313-4; Am Lib Annual 1916-17: 41.
-- S. M.  Good book week at Conshohocken.  Penn Lib Notes
9: 4-5.
Albee, H. H.  Relation of the school and library.  New Hamp
Bull (ns) 6: 231-3.
Aldis, H. G.  Organization and methods of the Cambridge Univ-
ersity Library.  L A R 7: 625-36; Discussion 545-7.
Aldred, T.  Book selection and rejection.  L A R 3: 143-56.
---- T.  Cataloguing rules: a letter re revision.  L A R
1: 756-8.
---- T.  Discursive jottings on novels.  L W 2: 295-8.
---- T.  Expansive classification.  L A R 7: 207-19, Dis-
cussion 196-201.
---- T.  Formation of an advisory board on cataloguing and
classification.  L A R 9: 167-72.
---- T.  Law for the prevention of spreading disease.  L
W 2: 198.
---- T.  Linotype in catalogue printing.  L W 1: 226-7; 2:
58-9.
---- T.  Monthly meetings.  L A R 10: 6-8.

---- T.  Notes on matters connected with the organization
of libraries.  L A 12: 188-96; L A R 18: 1-20.

---- T.  On the formation of an advisory board on cataloguing and classification.  L A R 9: 167-72, Discussion 201-6.

---- T.  Perpetual catalogues--Linotype.  L 8: 189-90.

---- T.  Provision of ballad music, ancient and modern.  L
W 2: 42-5.

---- T.  Sequel stories.  L W 2: 327-30; 3: 14-7, 40-3, 69-
71.

---- T.  Shelf arrangement.  L 10: 184-5.

---- T.  Stocktaking: a note.  L A R 8: 244-7.

Aldrich, C.  Iowa library legislation.  L J 17: 163-4.

Aldrich, G. I.  Children's reading.  Educational Review 14:
96-100.

Aldrich, S. J.  Augsburg printers of the 15th century.  Bib
Soc Trans 2: 25-47.

----- S. J.  Incunabula.  Bib Soc Trans 1: 107-19, Discussion 119-21.

----- S. J.  Procope Valdfoghel, goldsmith and printer
(French 15th century printer).  L 2: 217-9.

Alexander, C. B.  The library in the economy of the state.  N
Y L 5: 153-6.

------- C. B.  The library's part in war service.  N Y L
6: 92-3.

Aley, R. J.  Books and high school pupils.  Nat Educ Assn
1909: 844-8; Educator-Journal 15: 1-5.

-- R. J.  High school student and the book.  Nat Educ Assn
1918: 454-7.

Alford, D. P.  Notes on the Tavistock public library.  L C:
81-6.

Allchin, A.  Communal Library of Abbeville on the Somme.  L A
M N 4: 75-81.

Allen, E.  Value of myths for story telling.  Kind M 22: 85-7.

Allen, E. E.  Departments for the blind in free libraries.  P
L 4: 171-3.

--- E. E.  Library work for the blind.  L J 31: 8-11.

Allen, E. W.  The librarian as an aid to agricultural research.
Special Libraries 10: 30-1.

--- E. W.  Needs and opportunities of libraries of the State
agricultural colleges and experiment stations.  A L A Bull
8: 200-1.

Allen, F.  Selected list of Bible stories for children.  Wis
Lib Bull 15: 98-9.

Allen, F. L.  Children and patriotism.  Wis Lib Bull 14: 46-7.

Allen, P. S.  Erasmus' relations with his printers.  Bib Soc
Trans 13: 297-321.

--- P. S.  Some sixteenth century manuscript letter-books.
Bib Soc Trans 12: 65-85.

Allen, W. H.  Bureau of municipal research.  L J 33: 401.

--- W. H.  How may a public library help city government?
P L 17: 160-1; L J 37: 186-7; Wis Lib Bull 8: 138-9.
--- W. H.  The Municipal research library and publicity
in public affairs.  L J 38: 228.
Allnutt, W. H.  James Gaver, a newly discovered English prin-
ter in 1539, and other printers at the Sign of the Sun in
Fleet street.  L (ns) 2: 384-8.
----- W. H.  Notes on the introduction of printing presses
into the smaller towns of England and Wales, after 1750
to the end of the 18th century.  L (ns) 2: 242-59.
----- W. H.  Printers and printing in the provincial towns
of England and Wales.  L A Trans 1: 157-64.
----- W. H.  The King's Printer at Shrewsbury, 1642-1643.
L (ns) 1: 355-64.
Almack, J. C.  Reading interests of junior high school stu-
dents, with special emphasis on history.  American School-
master 13: 5-14.
Almirall, R. F.  Design and construction of branch library
buildings.  L J 31: Conf No 46-9.
Altgelt, H. W.  The intermediate reader.  Texas Libraries 1,
Nos 10-11: 103-4.
Alton, R.  Arts of illuminating and binding in the Middle
ages.  Arts and Decorations 13: 46-50.
Alvord, C. W. and Pease, T. C.  Archives of the State of Ill-
inois.  Am Hist Assn Rept 1909:  379-83.
Alvord, J. W.  How to use the technical library.  Special Li-
braries 5: 130.
Amann, D.  Treatment of book covers.  P L 23: 425.
Ambrose, L.  A conception of librarianship.  P L 9: 439-40.
----- L.  Dr. Dziatzko on German libraries.  L J 21: 53-9.
----- L.  German library exhibit at the World's fair.  L
J 18: 499-503.
----- L.  How many languages? how many cards?  P L 20: 4-
7.
----- L.  Orrington Lunt library, Northwestern university.
L J 19: 338-40.
----- L.  Staff meetings.  L J 33: 16-7.
----- L.  Study of college libraries.  L J 18: 113-9.
----- L.  Use of books in one library by readers of an-
other.  L J 15: 68.
----- L.  Use of government documents in the university
library.  L J 30: Conf No 86-91.
----- L.  Use of printed cards in the Northwestern univ-
ersity library.  L J 31: 257-9.
Ames, A. S.  Instruction in the use of reference books and
libraries in high schools.  L J 23: Conf No 86-7.
-- A. S. and E. P. Andrews.  Reading list on renaissance
art of the 15th and 16th centuries.  Bulletin No 9, N Y
S L Rept 81.
Ames, C. W.  National materialism and the public library.
Minn P L C N 9: 4-13.

Ames, E., and Walkley, R. L.   "All in the day's work."   L J
   43: 159-63.
Ames, J.   Index to Dibdin's edition of the "Typographical an-
   tiquities," with some references to the intermediate edition by William Herbert.   Bibliographical Society Publication, 1899.
Ames, J. G.   Index to public documents.   L J 18: Conf No 72-
   4.
   -- J. G.   Public documents.   L J 8: 107.
Ames, S.   Subject headings for children's books.   P L 8: 461.
Amin, M. N.   How to popularize the library.   Lib Miscellany
   1: 45-8.
Amundsen, A.   Social center in a small town.   Wis Lib Bull 8:
   129-30.
Anderson, A.   Inter-library loans in Sweden.   L J 29: Conf No
   83.
------ A.   Research libraries of Sweden.   L J 20: Conf No
   79-81; L J 29: Conf No 71-84.
------ A.   Swedish catalogue of accessions--Sveriges Offen-
   tliga Bibliothek: Stockholm, Uppsala, Lund, Goteberg acces-
   sions katalog.   L J 29: Conf No 112-3.
Anderson, E. H.   Bases of computation of cost of circulation.
   P L 22: 187-8.
------ E. H.   Branch libraries: planning and equipment.
   L J 27: Conf No 38-41.
------ E. H.   Co-operative catalog cards for children's
   books.   L J 28: Conf No 165-6.
------ E. H.   Library's position in our modern equipment.
   P L 13: 365-6.
------ E. H.   Linotype work at the Carnegie library of
   Pittsburgh.   L J 23: 273-6.
------ E. H.   On resignations from the New York public li-
   brary.   L J 43: 464.
------ E. H.   A plea for fairer support.   P L 22: 56-7.
------ E. H.   The tax on ideas.   A L A Bull 5: 73-7; L J
   39: 499-503; P L 19: 271-2.
------ E. H. and M. Dewey.   Librarianship--what it implies.
   Ia L C Q 2: 54.
Anderson, H. C. L.   A cataloguing guide.   P L 4: 19.
------ H. C. L.   A guide to cataloguing--a guide to the
   system of cataloguing the Reference library of New South
   Wales, Sydney, with relative decimal classification and
   headings used in the subject index.   P L 8: 171-2.
------ H. C. L.   Library work in New South Wales.   2nd
   Int Conf 93-6.
------ H. C. L.   National library in relation to country
   libraries and students.   Lib Assn of Australasia Proceed-
   ings XVI-XVIII.

Anderson, J. M.  Note on book-tags.  L J 2: 200-1, 271.
------ J. M.  Selection and selectors of books.  1st Int
Conf 57-8; L J 2: 151-2.
Anderson, J. P.  Estimate of the contents of the british Mu-
seum library.  L C 1: 65-6.
Anderson, J. R.  A general circulating library.  L J 1: 441-3.
Anderson, P. J.  University library, Aberdeen.  L A R 9: 81-3.
Anderson, P. L.  Author and work marks.  L W 3: 278-80.
Anderson, Mrs. R. E.  Preliminary study of the reading tastes
of high school pupils.  Pedagogical Seminary 9: 438-60.
Anderson, R. R.  Library methods at the Community clearing
house.  L J 44: 34.
Anderson, W. T.  The library and the school.  Wis Lib Bull 8:
193-5.
Anderton, B.  Best books of 1902--Science books in English.
L A R 6: 40-6.
------ B.  Books brought into relation and made operative.
L A R 4: 382-9; 7: 443-58; 8: 129.
------ B.  Continuity in library work: some preliminary
difficulties.  L A R 3: 551-61.
------ B.  Notes on some of the printers and libraries of
Newcastle-upon-Tyne.  B A R 7: I-XII, 1909-10.
------ B.  On planning a printed catalogue of local liter-
ature.  L A R 15: 542-52, Discussion 635-9.
------ B.  On the learning of librarians.  L A R 2: 630-40.
------ B.  On the place of specialization in library work--
a general review.  L 8: 536-48.
------ B.  The recent conference: views and reviews.  L A
R 19: 399-401.
------ B.  Selection of science books.  L A R 6: 85-93.
------ B.  Struggle for a public library in Newcastle-
upon-Tyne.  L A R 7: 259-71, 307-8.
------ B.  Summer schools and provincial library assist-
ants.  L A R 10: 378-80.
------ B.  Thomas Berwick, the Tyneside engraver.  L (3d
series) 6: 365-84.
Anding, I. M.  Our state documents.  South Dakota Lib Bull 6:
8-10.
Andrews, C. M.  Lessons of the British archives.  Am Hist
Assn Rept 1909: 349-50.
----- C. M.  List of the journals and acts of the councils
and assemblies of the thirteen original colonies, and the
Floridas, in America.  Am Hist Assn Rept 1908, 1: 399-509.
Andrews, C. W.  A. L. A. General review of its work.  Wis Lib
Bull 5: 39-45.
----- C. W.  Acquisition of books.  P L 5: 195-202.
----- C. W.  Address to the Wisconsin library school class
of 1909.  Wis Lib Bull 5: 37-45.
----- C. W.  Co-operative cataloguing--estimate of cost.
L J 25: Conf No 78-80; L J 26: 146; P L 6: 229.

----- C. W.  Co-operative lists of periodicals and transactions.  L J 24: Conf No 29-32.

----- C. W.  Co-operative work of the A. L. A. publishing board.  A L A Bull 4: 774-5.

----- C. W.  Co-operative work of the John Crerar library. L J 28: Conf No 166-7.

----- C. W.  Economics of library architecture.  A L A Bull 10: 18-21, Discussion 37-8.

----- C. W.  Field of co-operation between libraries of learning.  L J 41: 319-22.

----- C. W.  International bibliography of scientific literature.  L J 20: Conf No 25-7, 87.

----- C. W.  The John Crerar Library.  Wis Lib Bull 12: 124-8.

----- C. W.  Librarian's official relations to his colleagues.  Wis Lib Bull 5: 39-41.

----- C. W.  The library and the university.  Univ of Chicago Magazine 2: 238-51.

----- C. W.  Library work in the United States and Canada. L A R 12: 555-9.

----- C. W.  Maps in public libraries.  P L 8: 22-5.

----- C. W.  A model law for the distribution of state documents.  A L A Bull 3: 327-9.

----- C. W.  A plan for a census of research resources. A L A Bull 11: 221-2.

----- C. W.  Principles of classification.  A L A Bull 11: 195-7, 340.

----- C. W.  Printed card catalogues.  2d Int Conf 126-8, Discussion 242-3; L 9: 293.

----- C. W.  Problems arising from the size of card catalogs.  A L A Bull 3: 372-5.

----- C. W.  Report of the co-operation committee.  L J 23: Conf No 43-5.

----- C. W.  Report on union list of serials.  A L A Bull 10: 44.

----- C. W.  Staff meetings: their organization, methods and results.  L J 32: 547-8.

----- C. W.  Technical collections in public libraries. L J 20: 6-9.

----- C. W.  Union list of periodicals.  A L A Bull 12: 303.

----- C. W.  Use made of the printed catalogue cards for articles in current periodicals.  L J 23: Conf No 110-2, 176.

----- C. W.  Use of books: Presidential address.  A L A Bull 1: Conf No 7-12; L J 32: 249-53.

Andrews, E. P.  Book selection.  L J 22: Conf No 70-4.

----- E. P.  Report on gifts and bequests to libraries. L J 23: Conf No 52-5.

----- E. P. and A. S. Ames.  Reading list on Renaissance
art of the 15th and 16th centuries.  Bulletin No 9, N Y S
L Rept 81.
Andrews, E. V.  Reference list of fables, fairy tales, etc.,
noticed in.  P L 24: 452.
Andrews, G. E.  How the library is meeting the changing con-
ditions of child life.  A L A Bull 7: 188-93.
----- G. E.  Special features of library work with child-
ren.  Lib Occ 3: 77-82.
Andrews, G. W.  Agricultural literature in a reference libra-
ry.  A L A Bull 4: 789-90.
Andrus, G.  Buying books for a children's department.  A L A
Bull 14: 176-9, 330-1.
---- G.  Children's reading.  Vt L Bull 13: 18-9.
---- G.  Education and the cash register.  Pacific North-
west Library Assn Proceedings 1920: 49-52.
---- G.  The outlook in the children's department for schools.
Pacific Northwest Library Assn Proceedings 1919: 27-30.
Andrus, G. E.  How to select and advertise children's books.
Pacific Northwest Library Assn Proceedings 1909: 15-7.
Angell, J.  Use of the library.  L J 29: 592-3.
Angell, J. B.  Literature and life.  P L 17: 355-57.
Ansteinsson, J.  The library history of Norway.  L J 45: 19-
24, 57-62.
--------- J.  Library of the Museum at Bergen.  L J 45: 57.
--------- J.  Monastic libraries of Norway.  L J 45: 19-21.
--------- J.  University library, Kristiania.  L J 45: 23-
4.
Anstruther, E.  The camps' library and public libraries.  L W
18: 278-9.
Anthony, F. W.  Bradford high school library.  Massachusetts
Board of Education Report 1883-4: 257-9.
Anthony, J. B.  Books as tools.  Chautauquan 31: 143-6.
Antin, M.  The immigrant in the library.  A L A Bull 7: 145-
50.
Antrim, E. I.  Books for the rural population.  Penn Lib
Notes 10: 21-2.
Antrim, E. I.  First county library of Ohio.  P L 6: 282-3.
---- E. I.  The latest stage of library development.  For-
um 31: 336-40.
---- E. I.  Library development beyond the Mississippi.
L J 39: 832-4.
---- E. I.  Library privileges for rural districts.  Dial
30: 36.
Appleton, A. I.  Simple lessons in cataloguing.  L J 12: 115,
123.
Arber, E.  Recovery of lost English books: a suggestion.  Bib
Soc Trans 3: 227-30.
Archer, F. R.  Publicity work: aims and methods.  N C Bull 3:
47-50.

Archer, W.  American cheap magazines.  Living Age 265: 579-
87.
---- W.  Classification and the library building of the
National library of Ireland.  L J 10: 11-2.
---- W.  Essential features of a library building.  L A
M N 4: 46-8.
---- W.  Library building of the National library of Ire-
land.  L J 10: 11.
---- W.  Remarks on classification.  L C 3: 86-96.
---- W.  Some remarks on classification, preliminary to
a forthcoming scheme in alphabetical series of subject
headings for a classed dictionary catalogue.  L C 3: 86-
96.
---- W.  Suggestions as to public library buildings.  L
A Trans 4: 51-8.
Ardsley, H.  Confessions of a reporter.  Pacific Monthly 26:
26-33.
Armstrong, E.  One "Time saver": statistical records.  Ia L
C Q 7: 250-1.
Armstrong, E. L. T.  Model library from a librarian's point
of view.  L A of Austral Proc: XIII-XV. 1901.
Armstrong, I.  Public documents in a small library.  Wis Lib
Bull 10: 275-7; Ia L C Q 7: 103-5.
Armstrong, J.  Benefits of library training.  L J 41: 16-22.
Armstrong, M. E.  List of titles suitable for starting a mu-
sic collection in a library.  Wis Lib Bull 13: 79-80; L J
42: 761-2.
Arnold, E. C.  Injurious insects.  L J 6: 40.
---- E. C.  Solecisms in cataloguing.  L J 10: 132.
---- E. C.  Suppression of boys.  L J 10: 107.
Arnold, G. F.  German libraries and librarians.  L J 5: 131-
3.
---- G. F.  Value of the public library to the working man.
P L 12: 4-7.
Arnold, G. U.  Charging by day-books.  L J 11: 167.
Arnold, L. B.  Library advertising.  Lib Occ No 8: 1-3.
---- L. B.  Our present problem.  Ia L C Q 7: 113-7.
---- L. B.  Publicity, or, library advertising.  Ia L C Q
6: 69-73.
Arnold, S. L.  Nature study and literature.  Nat Educ Assn
1895: 570-2.
Aronovici, C.  Americanization: its meaning and function.
Minn P L C N 5: 181-2.
Asbury, G. B.  Book selection at the Indiana reformatory li-
brary.  Lib Occ No 9: 1-2.
Ashbee, H. G.  Iconography of "Don Quixote."  Bib Soc Trans
1: 123-44, Bib Soc Illustrated Monograph No III, 1895.
Ashbee, H. S.  Some books about Cervantes.  Bib Soc Trans 5:
13-38.

Ashe, Mrs. M. L.  A new fairy ring.  Cal news Notes 14: 286-7.
Ashhurst, J.  On taking ourselves too seriously.  L J 26: 265-
8.
Ashley, F. W.  Size marks and class numbers.  L J 26: 22.
Ashley, G.  Helps for the modern library.  P L 7: 20-2.
Ashley, M.  Some war books of the past year.  Pacific North-
west Library Assn Proceedings 1918: 16-22.
Ashley, R. E.  A systematic scrap-book: loose-leaf binders
for clippings, etc.  Machinery 17: 205-7.
Ashmun, M.  Library reading in the high school.  School Re-
view 17: 618-22, 701-4; 18: 196-9, 270-3.
---- M.  Reading of high school students.  Nat Educ Assn
1910: 999-1000.
---- M.  Study of English masterpieces.  Education 27:
628-33.
---- M.  Training class at Springfield.  Mass Lib Club Bull
5: 112-4.
Ashton, H.  Use of the library as compared with the reduction
of hours.  L W 2: 226.
Ashton, R.  Withdrawal of stock.  L A R 20: 223-5.
Ashurst, J.  Children's room in free libraries.  P L 4: 168-
70.
Askew, S. B.  How a library woke up a town.  Suburban Life
9: 177-8.
--- S. B.  Jersey roads and Jersey paths.  A L A Bull 3:
352-4.
--- S. B.  Library heresies.  P L 19: 191-6.
--- S. B.  Library work in the open country.  Annals Amer-
ican Academy 67: 257-66.
--- S. B.  The place, the man and the book.  A L A Bull
2: 150-7; N Y L 1: 163-9.
--- S. B.  Problems of a small town library.  L J 31: 705-
8.
--- S. B.  Public libraries and school libraries.  L J 37:
363-8.
Atkinson, F. W.  Reading of the young people.  L J 33: 129-
34.
Atkinson, Mrs. J. S.  Bibliography of modern drama.  N C Bull
4: 104-11.
Atkinson, W. A.  Is the encyclopaedia doomed? or The passing
of the encyclopaedia.  Libn 7: 1-3, 23-5.
Atkinson, W. P.  An address opposing sensational fiction.  L
J 4: 359-62.
Atteridge, A. H.  Literature of the war; histories and des-
criptions of operations.  L A R 17: 453-60.
Atwood, C. L.  Women's clubs in the recreation movement.
Minn P L C N 4: 129-30.
Aunspaugh, J. G.  A Virginia high school library,  Maury High
School of Norfold, Va.  L J 43: 222.

Austen, W.  Card catalogues, suggestions for making them us-
able.  L J 23: 655-7.
---- W.  Congressional bills and reports in libraries.
A L A Bull 1: Conf No 153-6.
---- W.  Dependence of reference department on catalogu-
ing and classification.  L J 23: Conf No 108-10.
---- W.  Educational value of reference-room training for
students.  A L A Bull 1: Conf No 274-7.
---- W.  Efficiency in college and university work.  L J
36: 566-9.
---- W.  Facts and fancies about the bookworm.  L A R 1:
496-7; L J 24: 266.
---- W.  Principles governing the selection of a reference
collection in a university library.  A L A Bull 3: 375-8.
---- W.  Pamphlets--what to do with them.  L J 18: 143-4.
---- W.  Reference, seminary and departmental libraries
at Cornell university.  L J 18: 181-3.
---- W.  Rights of the users of a college or university
library and how to preserve them.  A L A Bull 6: 275-7;
P L 18: 6-10.
---- W.  The university branch library.  L J 28: 220-2;
33: 220-2.
Austen, W. H.  Educational value of bibliographic training.
National Education Assn 1917: 660-5; L J 42: 489; Am Lib
Annual 1917-18: 15-6; L J 34: 427-30.
---- W. H.  Report on aids and guides.  L J 19: Conf No
77-80.
Austin, E. T.  The relation of literature in the grades to
that in the high school.  School and Home Education 27:
628-33.
Austin, E. W.  National Library for the blind.  L A R 12:
304-13; Discussion: 351-3.
---- E. W.  News from the blind world.  Libn 4: 30, 111,
175, 218, 308, 317; 5: 81, 165-6.
---- E. W.  Present conditions and possibilities of pub-
lic library service to the blind.  L A R 13: 450-60, 519-
24.
---- E. W.  Public libraries and the blind.  Libn 3: 102,
178, 223, 257, 305, 384, 422, 467-71.
Austin, G. J.  Simple book-plates for children's libraries.
School Education (Minneapolis, Minn) 29: 347-8.
Austin, I.  What the school needs from the library.  L J 34:
395-8.
Austin, R.  Gloucestershire collection: order of arrangement.
L (3d series) 8: 330-8.
---- R.  Notes on printing in Gloucestershire, with an ac-
count of the Gloucester cathedral library.  B A R 16: I-
VIII, 1919.

---- R.  The printed catalogue of a local collection. L.
(3d series) 8: 315-38.
---- R.  Robert Raikes, the elder, and the "Gloucester
Journal." L (3d series) 6: 1-24.
---- R.  Samuel Rudder. L (3d series) 6: 235-51.
Austin, W.  Banking method of charging books. L J 30: 144-6.
Austin, W. H.  Combination order and shelf list slips. L J
20: 49-50.
Averill, M. E.  Collaboration of the Thompson free library
and the public schools. Maine Lib Bull 4, No 1: 6-7.
----- M. E.  Co-operation of the library and the school.
Maine State Teachers' Assn Proceedings 1911: 76-7.
Axon, E.  Alphabetisation of names beginning Ff or ff. L A
R 20: 131.
-- E.  Cataloguing association books. L A R 20: 232.
-- E.  Cataloguing section opened in "L. A. R." L A R 20:
12-3.
-- E.  Change of name. L A R 20: 92.
-- E.  Classification and cataloguing. L A R 20: 12-3.
-- E.  Forename entry. L A R 20: 47.
-- E.  Graded registration. L A R 11: 92.
-- E.  Japanese names. L A R 20: 231-2.
-- E.  Notes on classification and cataloguing: Co-opera-
tive cataloguing cards versus books. L A R 20: 131-2.
-- E.  Prefix. L A R 20: 46.
-- E.  Public records and public libraries. L A R 2: 142-
50.
-- E.  Registration--why chief librarians? L A R 11: 90-1.
-- E.  Weeding out at Manchester library. L 8: 264-7.
Axon, W. E.  Thomas Greenwood. L A R 10: 683-5.
Axon, W. E. A.  An appreciation of the "Bibliotheca Linde-
siana." L A R 14: 4-13.
-- W. E. A.  "The athiest-converted": the first book print-
ed at Lincoln. L (3d series) 2: 319-22.
-- W. E. A.  Authorship of the "Summe of the Holy Scrip-
ture," etc. L A R 10: 81-4.
-- W. E. A.  The Autocrat as a book-lover. L (3d series)
2: 356-62.
-- W. E. A.  Bibliography of the writings of W. S. Jevons.
L A M N 4: 155-62.
-- W. E. A.  Books, ancient and modern. L C 5: 73-7, 111.
-- W. E. A.  Books and reading. L C 4: 23-5, 44-9.
-- W. E. A.  British Museum in its relation to provincial
culture. L J 2: 125-8, Discussion 246-7.
-- W. E. A.  Church library at Michelstadt in Odenwald. L
(ns) 2: 405-12.
-- W. E. A.  Cornaro in English. L (ns) 2: 120-9.
-- W. E. A.  Danjou's scheme of a universal bibliography.
L J 5: 205-6.

-- W. E. A.  De Quincey and T. F. Dibdin.  L (ns) 8: 267-74.

-- W. E. A.  De Quincey collection at Moss Side.  L A R 2: 410-24.

-- W. E. A.  Dewey system of classification.  1st Int Conf 166-7.

-- W. E. A.  Early history of the public library movement. Greenwood's library Yr Bk: 16-27.

-- W. E. A.  Edward Edwards, 1812-1886.  L (ns) 2: 298-307.

-- W. E. A.  In memoriam: Nicholas Trubner.  L C 1: 42-6.

-- W. E. A.  Is a printed catalogue of the British Museum practicable?  L A Trans 1: 65-7.

-- W. E. A.  James Amphlett and Samuel Taylor Coleridge. L (3d series) 2: 34-9.

-- W. E. A.  Juvenile Library.  L (ns) 2: 67-81.

-- W. E. A.  The Lady Margaret as a lover of literature. L (ns) 8: 34-41.

-- W. E. A.  Legislation for free public libraries.  L A Trans 4: 31-3, 74.

-- W. E. A.  Libraries of Lancashire and Cheshire.  L A U K Trans 2: 47-53; L J 4: 35-8, 412.

-- W. E. A.  Library in relation to knowledge and life. L J 29: Conf No 16-22.

-- W. E. A.  Library lectures.  L J 3: 47-9.

-- W. E. A.  Licensing of Montagu's "Miscellanea spiritualia."  L (ns) 2: 269-73.

-- W. E. A.  London circulating library in 1743.  L (ns) 1: 377-8.

-- W. E. A.  Michael, the bishop, in praise of books.  L (ns) 4: 367-72.

-- W. E. A.  Notes on Chinese libraries.  L J 5: 6-10, 35-7.

-- W. E. A.  On Christian captive indulgencies in the British Museum, Lambeth palace and John Rylands library.  L (ns) 7: 275-86.

-- W. E. A.  On the distribution of documents printed at the expense of the nation.  L J 4: 81-3.

-- W. E. A.  Place of libraries in relation to elementary, secondary and higher education.  L 5: 265-9.

-- W. E. A.  A plea for adequate description in cataloguing books and pamphlets.  L (3d series) 4: 171-85.

-- W. E. A.  Poetry of the bibliomaniac.  L A M N 1: 50-6.

-- W. E. A.  Professorship of bibliography.  L A Trans 1: 104-7.

-- W. E. A.  Projected universal catalogue.  L J 3: 175-7.

-- W. E. A.  Robert Copland and Pierre Gringoire.  L (3d series) 3: 419-21.

-- W. E. A.  A seventeenth century lament on "Too many books." L (3d series) 3: 33-7.
-- W. E. A.  Sir John Chesshyre's library at Halton in Cheshire. L J 4: 35-8.
-- W. E. A.  Some twentieth century Italian chapbooks. L (ns) 5: 239-55.
-- W. E. A.  Spenser society and its work. L 7: 201-10.
-- W. E. A.  Statistics of British publishing and the need of an official bibliography. L 10: 65-7.
-- W. E. A.  Statistics of printed literature of the world, and the need of an official record of British publications. L A R 14: 509-12.
-- W. E. A.  Subsidised indexing. L (ns) 6: 281-303.
-- W. E. A.  Sunday use of libraries. L J 3: 258-9.
-- W. E. A.  Thomas Greenwood library for librarians at Manchester. L A R 9: 302-6.
-- W. E. A.  "Visio Fulberti". L (3d series) 4: 409-16.
-- W. E. A.  Where was Sommariva's "Batrachomyomachia" printed? L A R 14: 317-20.
-- W. E. A.  A year's use of the "Encyclopaedia Britannica." L (3rd series) 3: 221-9.
Ayer, C. W.  Shelf classification of music. L J 27: 5-11.
Ayer, J. Y.  Literature in the rural school. Educational Foundations 25: 101-8.
Ayer, T. P.  Administration of library binding. Oversewed versus straight sewed books. L J 39: 28-31.
-- T. P.  Duplication of titles for required undergraduate reading. L J 42: 356-8.
-- T. P.  The value of a university bindery. L J 38: 518.
Ayers, C. E.  The normal school English teacher and the library. English Journal 4: 60.
Ayres, G. G.  Theological literature in libraries. L J 28: 601-3.
Ayres, L. P., and McKennie, A.  Inadequate salaries of school librarians. L J 41: 752-4.
Ayres, S. G.  The librarian: requirements and duties. L J 27: 309-11.
--- S. G.  On the exchange of duplicates. A L A Bull 12: 311.
B. J. R.  Account of the Harris collection of American poetry. L J 9: 180.
Babbitt, G. E.  Pamphlets and clippings in reference work. L J 39: 353-5.
Babcock, C. E.  Columbus memorial library of the Pan-American union. L J 44: 710-1; Special Libraries 5: 147-8.
----- C. E.  Danish West Indies: a list of English references. L J 42: 422-3.
Babcock, H. S.  Directory of high school librarians. L J 44: 447-54.

----- H. S.  The high school library.  P L 22: 252-4.
Babcock, J. G.  How to handle slides and records.  P L 24: 377.
----- J. G.  Special material in libraries.  Cal News Notes 14: 155-6.
Babcock, Mrs. J. G.  The branch library building of Kern county free library.  Cal News Notes 15: 289-94.
Babcock, K. C.  Bibliographical training in college.  L J 38: 133-6.
Babcock, L. E.  Reference library in a manufacturing plant.  Special Libraries 2: 13-5.
Babine, A. V.  Libraries in Russia.  L J 18: 75-7.
---- A. V.  Problems of a college library.  P L 13: 340-2.
Bach, R. F.  On classification.  L J 43: 807.
Bache, L. F.  The call of the Pied Piper.  P L 24: 308-10.
--- L. F.  An exhibit which connected dolls with books.  L J 42: 971-2.
Backus, T. J.  Methods of teaching English literature.  Univ of State of New York Annual Report 1888-89: 55-71.
Bacon, C.  Card index of the library: modern methods by which the reader most surely and quickly secures the book he needs.  Wis Lib Bull 8: 165-6.
--- C.  Duplicate pay collections.  N Y L 1: 76-8.
--- C.  Fiction as reference material.  L J 41: 379-81.
--- C.  I want a library catalog that I can take home.  N Y L 4: 205-7.
--- C.  A librarian's reading.  N Y L 1: 136-9.
--- C.  A library that's alive.  P L 18: 50-5.
--- C.  Present tendency of public library service.  P L 20: 241-7.
--- C.  Principles of book selection.  N Y L 1: 3-6; Vt L Bull 3, No 3: 1-5.
--- C.  Reading for citizenship: ten books for boys and girls from ten to sixteen.  Wilson Bull 1: 484-6.
--- C.  Reference work from the librarian's standpoint.  L J 27: 927-32.
--- C.  Relation of the library school to the school and college library.  P L 19: 396-8.
--- C.  Report of the A. L. A. Committee on library administration.  A L A Bull 2: 222-31.
--- C.  Reserving books.  N Y L 1: 53-4.
--- C.  Some important books.  Wis Lib Bull 16: 106-30.
--- C.  Subject headings for use in dictionary catalogs of juvenile books.  P L 21: 236-7.
--- C.  What it means to be a librarian.  Vt L Bull 11: 19-21.
--- C.  What makes a novel immoral.  Wis Lib Bull 6: 83-95; L W 13: 129-40; Minn P L C N 3: 4-11; N Y L 2: 4-12.
--- C.  What novels?  P L 18: 55-6.

--- C. "What the public wants." L J 38: 251-5; New Hamp
Bull 9: 179-83.

Bacon, C. C. Co-operation of libraries with library schools.
A L A Bull 7: 347-50.

Badger, H. C. Floundering among the maps. L J 17: 375-7.

---- H. C. New catalogue drawer. L J 17: 168-9.

---- H. C. Our card catalog: what to do with it. L J 17:
161-3.

Baechtold, E. L. The Famous players-Lasky corporation library,
Los Angeles. Special Libraries 11: 45-6.

------- E. L. Pacific mutual life insurance company library. Special Libraries 11: 46.

------- E. L. Southern California Edison Co. library,
Los Angeles. Special Libraries 11: 89-90.

------- E. L. Special libraries in Los Angeles: the furniture library of Barker Brothers. Special Libraries 11:
44-5.

Baensk, E. Division of labor. Wis Lib Bull 7: 27-8.

Bagguley, W. H. Education and the diploma. L A R 10: 289-94.

Bagley, H. A. After the war, what? P L 25: 559-60.

Bailey, A. H. Book cloths. L A R 11: 44.

Bailey, A. L. Bibliography of Biography of musicians in English. Bulletin No 17, N Y S L Rept 81, 1898.

---- A. L. How shall the library help the working man?
L J 32: 198-201.

---- A. L. More about reinforced binding. P L 14: 380-1.

---- A. L. Notes from the A. L. A. Committee on binding.
P L 14: 302-3.

---- A. L. What people read. L J 38: 387-91; Penn Lib Notes
5, No 4: 3-10.

Bailey, E. Concerning the library assistant. L A R 11: 229-
36.

---- E. How the municipal libraries assist. L A R 16:
429-37.

Bailey, H. T. Present and future of printing. Printing Art
15: 273-9.

---- H. T. Public libraries and art educational work.
L J 25: 641-2.

Bailey, J. B. Classification for scientific and medical libraries. L C 3: 109-14.

---- J. B. Index to scientific bibliographies. L A Trans
3: 116, 169-73.

---- J. B. Library of the Royal college of surgeons in
England. L 1: 249-61.

---- J. B. Medical bibliography. L C 2: 63-5.

---- J. B. On classification for scientific and medical
libraries. L C 3: 110.

---- J. B. Proposal for making the continuation to Poole's
Index of use in library catalogs. L J 4: 187-91.

---- J. B.  Some points to be considered in preparing cata-
logues of transactions and periodicals.  L A M N 1: 12-6.
---- J. B.  Subject index to scientific periodicals.  L
A Trans 1: 85-7.
Bailey, J. E.  Historical and descriptive accounts of the
Manchester libraries.  L A U K Trans 2: 113-29.
Bailey, J. J.  Catalogue of the St. Louis public school li-
brary.  U S Rept 660-2, 1876.
Bailey, L. C.  Library opportunities in the junior high school.
Nat Educ Assn 1917: 576-81.
Bailey, L. E.  Branch library and her neighboring schools.
School and Society 7: 306-9.
---- L. E.  Library work for rural communities.  New Hamp
Bull (ns) 7: 45-9.
---- L. E.  Vacation reading.  Pacific Northwest Library
Assn Proceedings 1910: 54-60.
Bailey, L. H.  Human interest in old agricultural books.  Spe-
cial Libraries 10: 31.
---- L. H.  Library work in rural communities.  L J 33:
381-5; N Y L 1: 169-72.
---- L. H.  Rural communities.  Journal of Education 65:
411.
---- L. H.  Rural development in relation to social wel-
fare.  National Conference of Charities and Correction,
Proceedings 1908: 83-91.
---- L. H.  Some relations of library work to rural bet-
terment.  N Y L 2: 52-4.
Bailey, L. J.  Gary (Ind.) library exhibit.  Lib Occ 2: 172.
---- L. J.  The Gary (Ind.) public library shelf-list re-
cord and order card.  Bull Bib 8: 61-2.
---- L. J.  Library use of lantern slides.  Lib Occ Jan
1918: 12-5; L J 43: 204-5.
---- L. J.  Qualifications of librarians.  P L 17: 172-3.
---- L. J.  Seven million books are not enough.  World
Outlook 5: 25-6.
---- L. J.  Social functions of the public library.  P L
19: 385-8; L J 40: 292; New Hamp Bull (ns) 11: 68-71.
Bailey, W. B.  Kind of books we read: Enoch Pratt free library
circulation.  Independent 77: 303.
Bailey, W. H.  Bookbinder's leather.  L A R 8: 467-8.
---- W. H.  Free libraries and education.  L A R 8: 467.
---- W. H.  The ideal librarian.  L A R 8: 471-4.
---- W. H.  Lectures in connection with libraries.  L A
Trans 2: 34-7; L J 4: 410.
---- W. H.  Libraries for children.  L A R 8: 475-6.
---- W. H.  Novel reading.  L A R 8: 465-7.
---- W. H.  On public libraries.  L A R 15: 124-9.
---- W. H.  Presidential address.  L A R 8: 461-76.

Baillie, H.  Library work in New Zealand.  L J 29: Conf No
89-91.
----- H.  Short account of work of New Zealand libraries:
Wellington public library as an example.  A L A Bull 2:
143-6.
Bain, G. G.  The Congressional Library at Washington.  Amer-
ican Architect and Building News 48: 95-7.
Bain, J.  Libraries of Canada.  L 7: 241-9; L J 25: Conf No
7-10.
-- J.  Library movement in Ontario.  L J 26: 269-73.
Bain, J., Jr.  Books in branch libraries.  L J 23: Conf No
100-1.
-- J., Jr.  Brief review of the libraries of Canada.  L
J 12: 406-9, 450.
-- J., Jr.  Museums, art galleries and lectures in connec-
tion with public libraries.  U S Rept 850-61 1892; L J 18:
214-5.
-- J., Jr.  Public Libraries in the Dominion of Canada.
L J 12: 217-20.
-- J., Jr.  Supplying of current newspapers in free library
reading rooms.  L J 19: Conf No 49.
Bakeless, O. H.  What are the normal schools doing in train-
ing their students in library work?  Penn Lib Notes 4: 37-
46; P L 16: 454-5.
Baker, C.  On a survey of agricultural libraries.  A L A Bull
14: 325-6.
Baker, C. A.  Documents for an agricultural library.  Colorado
Lib Assn Occasional Leaflets 1: 581.
Baker, E. A.  Advertising dodges.  L A R 10: 430-1.
--- E. A.  Anonymous attacks upon public libraries.  L A R
13: 89-90.
--- E. A.  Arrangement of periodicals.  L W 2: 9-11.
--- E. A.  Best books of 1903: Fiction.  L A R 6: 617.
--- E. A.  Best books of 1904--Literature.  L A R 8: 53-7.
--- E. A.  Book annotation in America.  L W 4: 253-5.
--- E. A.  Book reviews: their help and their hindrance
in selection.  L A R 4: 28-36.
--- E. A.  Book selection: fundamental principles and some
applications.  Discussion.  L A R 12: 538-42; L A R 13: 17-
29.
--- E. A.  British Museum monthly catalogue of accessions.
L A R 18: 233-4.
--- E. A.  Classes at the London School of Economics.  L
A R 14: 371-2.
--- E. A.  Classification of fiction.  L W 1: 198-200, 216-
20; 2: 177-83.
--- E. A.  Compilation of a complete card catalogue from
old printed catalogues.  L W 1: 141-2.
--- E. A.  Conference on the interchange system.  L A R
10: 212-5.

--- E. A.  Co-operation.  L A R 10: 1-4.
--- E. A.  Co-operation with elementary schools.  L A R
11: 145-7.
--- E. A.  Co-operative annotation and guides.  L A R 7:
272-82, Discussion 298-302.
--- E. A.  Co-operative schemes for libraries in London
area.  L A R 11: 12-6, Discussion 31-6.
--- E. A.  The correspondence classes and the public.  L
A R 14: 247.
--- E. A.  Coruscations at the examinations.  L A R 14:
369-71.
--- E. A.  Crank literature.  L A R 12: 80, 226.
--- E. A.  A descriptive guide to best fiction: a reply
to Mr. Jast.  L W 5: 295-7.
--- E. A.  Education and the diploma.  L A R 10: 146-7,
254-6, 372-3.
--- E. A.  Education and training of librarians.  L A R
19: 509-15.
--- E. A.  Education in the provinces.  L A R 10: 320-2.
--- E. A.  Education of the assistant in the provinces.
L A R 9: 292-4, 708-9.
--- E. A.  Education of the Librarian: advanced stage.
L A R 8: 573-86, Discussion 504-9.
--- E. A.  Educational matters.  L A R 11: 381-4.
--- E. A.  Essayists and critics from 1870 to 1900.  L A
R 12: 43-5.
--- E. A.  Examinations in literary history: hints to can-
didates.  L A R 9: 390-4, 443-51.
--- E. A.  Fee for the diploma.  L A R 10: 426-7.
--- E. A.  Fiction nuisance and its abatement: a sequel,
Reply to Mr. Nield, author of "Guide to historical novels."
L W 5: 318-20.
--- E. A.  French fiction in public libraries.  L W 2: 68-
71, 79-81.
--- E. A.  Gift horses.  L A R 11: 422-3.
--- E. A.  Historians, philosophers, and others.  L A R
12: 45-6.
--- E. A.  Inquiry circulars.  L A R 12: 301-3.
--- E. A.  Inter-change of borrowing facilities.  L A R
10: 484.
--- E. A.  The late Mr. Peter Cowell.  L A R 11: 89-90,
136-7.
--- E. A.  Letter re co-operative annotation.  L A R 7:
428.
--- E. A.  Librarians and the N. H. R. U.  L A R 10: 5-6.
--- E. A.  Library of the University of London.  L W 6: 207-
9; L A R 14: 1-31; L A R 16: 32-4, 38.

--- E. A.  Library of the University of London and the report of the Royal commission on university education in London.  L A R 16: 28-38.

--- E. A.  Literary history classes.  L A 6: 219.

--- E. A.  Literary training of the librarian.  L A 5: 313-5; 333-5.  L A R 10: 529-30.

--- E. A.  Literature of the war; pure literature.  L A R 17: 472-7.

--- E. A.  Local effort.  L A R 13: 85-6.

--- E. A.  Maps in the lending department.  L W 1: 54-5.

--- E. A.  Means of education for assistants in the provinces.  L A 6: 180-1.

--- E. A.  Metallic filament lamps versus carbon lamps.  L A R 11: 149-51.

--- E. A.  Modern fiction and the public library.  L A R 10: 4-5.

--- E. A.  Mutual loans of lantern slides.  L A R 12: 614.

--- E. A.  The need of two associations.  L A R 16: 26-7.

--- E. A.  The new education bill.  L A R 19: 309-12.

--- E. A.  Next examination in literary history, some hints.  L A R 9: 390-4, 443-51.

--- E. A.  A non-municipal librarian's club.  L A R 16: 25-7.

--- E. A.  Note on Mr Rye's "Guide to the libraries of London."  L A R 10: 257-8.

--- E. A.  The novel from 1870-1900.  L A R 12: 80-3.

--- E. A.  On government examinations for librarianship.  L A R 11: 94.

--- E. A.  On local collections and local documents.  L A R 11: 96-8.

--- E. A.  On the transference of libraries to the board of education.  L W 20: 40-2.

--- E. A.  Opportunities for students.  L A R 10: 427-9.

--- E. A.  Ordnance maps in public libraries.  L W 2: 155; L W 4: 144-7.

--- E. A.  Possibility of a library school.  L A R 10: 531.

--- E. A.  Practical literary history.  L A R 11: 473-5.

--- E. A.  Public libraries and literature.  L A R 10: 374-5.

--- E. A.  Public libraries and the press.  L A R 10: 423-5.

--- E. A.  Recent developments in library co-operation.  L A R 10: 660-77.

--- E. A.  Registration.  L A R 10: 425-6.

--- E. A.  Registration scheme.  L A R 11: 345-6.

--- E. A.  Reply to Mr. Philip.  L A R 13: 231.

--- E. A.  Reply to Mr. Stephen.  L A R 10: 523-4.

--- E. A.  Royal commission on university education in London.  L A R 15: 252-4.

--- E. A.  Rural public libraries.  L 8: 298-303.

--- E. A.  Sectional interests and the Library association. L A R 16: 25.
--- E. A.  Some recent developments of library co-operation. L A R 10: 660-77, Discussion 593-6.
--- E. A.  Special period of literary history. L A R 11: 562-5.
--- E. A.  Standard of fiction in libraries. L A R 9: 70-80, Discussion 98-103.
--- E. A.  A standardised examination for juniorships. L A R 11: 470-3.
--- E. A.  Thefts from libraries. L A R 11: 204.
--- E. A.  Thomas Hardy and the cultivation of pure literature. L A R 14: 285-6.
--- E. A.  University library and public libraries. L A R 14: 3.
--- E. A.  Wanted--a guide book to books. L A R 2: 89-97.
--- E. A.  Wanted--a new scheme of culture. L A R 10: 373-4.
--- E. A.  Wanted--Real branch associations. L A R 10: 638-9.
--- E. A.  Work of the Library association Education committee. L A 8: 193-5; L W 14: 70-2.
Baker, F. F.  High school reading: compulsory and voluntary. English Journal 4: 1-8.
Baker, F. T.  The teacher of English. English Journal 2: 335-43.
Baker, G. A.  The "Poisonous literature" scare. L A R 12: 1-2.
Baker, G. H.  Relation of seminary and department libraries in the general university library. L J 23: Conf No 103-6.
--- G. H.  Special collections in Columbia College library. Columbia Literary Monthly 2: 6-14, 158-70, 357-63.
Baker, M.  The town library and the country club. Minn P L C N 4: 128-9.
Baker, M. E.  Prevocational training for librarianship. L J 45: 446-9.
--- M. E.  The reasons anent cataloging. P L 22: 138-40; L J 42: 567.
Baker, M. M.  Story of library extension in Elwood and Pipe Creek township, Indiana. Lib Occ 2: 224-5.
Baker, T.  Employment of young women as assistants in public free libraries. L A Trans 2: 32-3.
--- T.  Presidential address. L A Trans 2: 17-20.
Baker, T. P.  The public library and the Sunday school: address delivered at the Maine library association. Maine Lib Bull 7: 69-70.
Baker, W. H.  Printer's ink, art and clothing. Printing Art 15: 33-9.

Balcarres, Lord.   Public libraries at home and abroad.   L A
   R 3: 80-6.
Baldwin, C. F.   Better support for libraries, aims of library
   commissions.   Wis Lib Bull 3: 30-2.
----- C. F.   Commissions and the local library.   Wis Lib
   Bull 7: 112-7.
----- C. F.   State examinations and state certificates for
   librarians.   L J 31: 806-8.
----- C. F.   Summer library schools.   L J 42: 120-1.
Baldwin, E. G.   Bryson library of Teachers college, Columbia
   university.   Columbia University Quarterly 13: 205-11.
----- E. G.   Report of the joint committee representing
   the A. L. A. and the N. E. A. on instruction in library
   administration in normal schools.   Nat Educ Assn 1906:
   215-81.
----- E. G.   Some old forgotten school libraries.   L J 29:
   175-9.
----- E. G.   The special student's reading.   Household
   Arts Review Ap 1913.
Baldwin, E. V.   Order department of a branch library.   P L
   11: 509-11.
----- E. V.   Order routine in the Brooklyn public library.
   P L 11: 560-1.
----- E. V.   Staff meetings: their organization, methods
   and results.   L J 32: 543-6.
----- E. V.   Training of professional librarians.   L J 44:
   574-6; P L 24: 160-2.
Balheim, C. H.   Trustee's view of the book-buying problem.
   Ia L C Q 5: 177-8.
Ball, F. D.   The librarian's share in vocational guidance
   through the high school library.   N Y L 3: 272-3.
-- F. D.   Summer schools and short courses.   Mich Lib Bull
   7: 24-5.
Ball, S.   What any library can do for the business interest
   of its town.   N J Lib Bull 3, No 2: 9-12.
Ball, S. B.   Maps and atlases: their selection and care.   P
   L 15: 11-5.
Ballard, H. H.   In the matter of book selection.   Wis Lib
   Bull 3: 94.
----- H. H.   Public documents in small libraries.   L J 34:
   91-2; P L 14: 84-6.
----- H. H.   Why readers select books.   Wis Lib Bull 15:
   103 4.
Ballard, J. F.   Classification scheme of the Boston Medical
   library.   Bull Med Lib Assn Jan 1918: 33-63.
Ballard, T. P.   How to use Mr. Tilden's bequest.   L J 12: 72.
Ballin, D.   Library schools in the United States.   L A 10:
   147-54.
Ballinger, J.   Admission to public libraries in Great Britain.
   L (ns) 2: 210-7.

------- J. An artist topographer: James Baker. L (3d series) 7: 116-43.

------- J. The Bible in Wales (a review). L A R 9: 192-4.

------- J. Cardiff free public libraries. L 7: 300-17.

------- J. Children and public libraries. Greenwood's Year-Book 1900-1901: 46-52.

------- J. Children's reading halls. L A R 5: 552-8, Discussion, 488-9.

------- J. Free libraries and the photographic survey of counties. L 3: 436-40.

------- J. Gladstone's translation of "Rock of ages." L (3d series) 6: 183-5.

------- J. Jottings from my note-book. L A M N 3: 2-6.

------- J. Library extension movement. L A R 12: 550-4.

------- J. Library politics. L A R 7: 482-93: Discussion 564-8.

------- J. Library work with children in Great Britain. L J 29: Conf No 46-9.

------- J. Milton Tercentenary. L A R 10: 317-8.

------- J. Municipal library and its public--Lending libraries and branches. L (ns) 9: 66-79, 173-85, 309-22, 353-68.

------- J. Municipal library and its public. L (ns) 10: 188-200.

------- J. The National library of Wales. L (3rd series) 1: 113-43, 276-88.

------- J. Newsrooms. L 5: 66.

------- J. Planning and equipment of the Roath (Cardiff) branch library. Plan il. L A R 3: 181-8, 277-8, Discussion 227-8.

------- J. On the Public libraries bill. L A R 9: 291-2.

------- J. Public libraries and the school: an experiment. L 9: 239-50.

------- J. Rate limit and the future of public libraries. L A R 5: 16-27

------- J. Report on the constitution of Library committees. L 7: 1-9.

------- J. School children in public libraries. L A R 1: 64-72.

------- J. Shakespeare and the municipal libraries. L (ns) 7: 181-91.

------- J. Some general considerations arising out of the Report to the Carnegie United Kingdom Trust by Prof. W. G. S. Adams. L A R 17: 510-6.

------- J. The Trevecca press--Wales. L (ns) 6: 225-50.

------- J. Variations of the public libraries acts by private legislation. L A R 3: 198-204.

------- J. Welsh Bible printed at Trevecca. L (ns) 6: 243.

Ballinger, J. and Chapple, C. R. Report on the summer school of library service. L A 14: 106-8.

Balzani, Una Count. Regulations of Italian public libraries. L J 4: 183.

Bancroft, E. H. Problems of foreign registration. L J 40: 402-5.

Bancroft, F. A. Relation of the public library to technical education from the viewpoint of organized labour. Ontario Lib Assn Proceedings 1911: 96-9.

Bancroft, J. A famous library: St. Gall, Switzerland. L J 12: 289-91.

Banff, H. E. Library of the University of Sydney. 2nd International Conference Proceedings. 196-8.

Banks, M. Reference work in a small library. Wash L A Bull 2: No 1: 5-7.

--- M. Seattle public library. Wash L A Bull 1 No 2: 8-10 il.

--- M. Specialization in libraries. Wash L A Bull 1, No 1: 10-1.

Banks, M. H. Books in New England colonies. P L 15: 382-3.

Banning, P. W. Some special methods with genealogical material. L J 42: 807-8.

Bannister, H. M. Human element in a manuscript (M.S. Hatton 113). B Q R 1: 163-4.

Banta, J. E. Library and the school. Nat Educ Assn 1909: 863-70.

--- J. E. The school's point of view. A L A Bull 3: 184-91.

--- J. E. Use of the dictionary in the grades. Univ of State of New York, Education Dept Bull 457: 292-3.

Banting, L. Fabre's 'Life of the spider" in the high school. Wis Lib Bull 15: 256-7.

Barbour, O. F. Library and the school. P L 6: 86-7.

Barchtold, E. L. Special libraries of Los Angeles. Special Libraries 11: 43-6, 89-90.

Barden, B. R. A clerical course for library assistants. A L A Bull 13: 171-3, 396.

Bardwell, D. L. The duties of the high school librarian. New York City Department of Instruction Report on high schools submitted to the Superintendent of Schools. 1914: 47-8.

------ D. L. A tentative budget for high school libraries in schools of 1,000, 2,000 and 3,000 pupils in New York city. New York city Department of education: Reports on high schools submitted to the City superintendent of schools, 1914: 43-50.

Bardwell, W. A. How we choose and buy new books. L J 14: 338.

------ W. A.  Library of music--Brooklyn public library
collection. L J 12: 159.
------ W. A.  Library work. L J 13: 5-7
------ W. A.  Newspaper history in the library. L J 14:
117.
------ W. A.  Reference work in libraries. L J 16: 297-
300.
------ W. A.  Report on scrap books. L J 14: 195-202.
------ W. A.  Scrap books. U S Rept 999-1010. 1892-93.
------ W. A.  Scrap books, clippings, etc. L J 18: 258-
9.
------ W. A.  Scrap books in libraries. L J 13: 243-4,
L J 14: 107.
------ W. A.  Selection of books. L J 19: Conf No 37-8.
------ W. A.  Wanted--an index to illustrations. L J 13:
173.
------ W. A.  What should librarians read? L J 25: 58-9.
------ W. A.  What we do about duplicates. L J 14: 370.
------ W. A.  What we do with pamphlets. L J 14: 470.
Barette, E. E.  Use of the library as an aid in school room
work. Nat Educ Assn 1917: 570-2; School and Society 7:
309-12.
Barker, K. C.  Story hour for older children. Wis Lib Bull
9: 43-4.
Barker, T. A.  Taxation and apportionment of proceeds to
respective needs of the library. A L A Bull 11: 350.
Barker, T. D.  The library and vocational progress. N C
Bull 3: 67-70.
---- T. D.  Reading list on Paul Ernest Hervieu (1857-).
Bull Bib 8: 40.
Barlow, H.  Book war: another comment. L W 9: 189-201.
---- H.  Future of the catalogue. L A 5: 239-43.
---- H.  Net book system. L W 9: 397-402.
---- H.  Smoking in public libraries. L A 5: 105-7.
---- H.  Thoughts on the reference department. L A R
8: 647-53.
Barlow, H. M.  Medical library association: a few observa-
tions. L A R 12: 174-89.
Barmby, M.  Bookplate of the Alameda county library. Cal
News Notes 15: 146.
---- M.  Special material in libraries. Cal News Notes
14: 152-3.
Barnes, C. P.  Re-registration--a plan. Wis Lib Bull 2: 8-
9, 17.
Barnes, Mrs. H.  Learning patriotism from books. P L 23:
416-9.
Barnes, W.  The continuation school of the book. Normal
Instructor and Primary Plans Jan 1917: 13-4; L J 42:
841; Am Lib Annual 1917-18: 73.

---- W.   Libraries in the city high schools of West Virginia.   West Virginia School Journal and Educator   June, 1916: 77-9; L J 42: 638; Am Lib Annual 1917-18: 48-9.

---- W.   The school and the boy's books and reading.   Wilson Bull 1: 251-6; L J 43: 202-3.

Barnes, W. E.   School libraries in London.   L A R 11: 7-8.

Barnett, Rev. Canon.   On Sunday labour in national public libraries, museums and art galleries.   Greenwood's Yr-Bk: 102-6, 1897.

Barnett, C. R.   Agricultural library work and the new epoch.   P L 24: 73-9.

----- C. R.   Co-operation of libraries with the county agents.   U S Food Administration.   Food News for Public Libraries 1 No 6: 14-7, Mch 1918.

----- C. R.   Government libraries--old and new.   Special Libraries 9: 214-9.

----- C. R.   The Library of the United States Department of agriculture.   Special Libraries 10: 40-3.

----- C. R.   Relation of the agricultural college and experiment station libraries to the library of the federal Department of agriculture.   A L A Bull 9: 156-9.

----- C. R.   Some opportunities and problems of the agricultural libraries.   A L A Bull 8: 190-2.

Barney, K. W.   Collections of local historical material.   Vt L Bull 3, No 2: 1-3.

---- K. W.   Liberal rules for borrowers.   Vt L Bull 7, No 3: 1-3.

---- K. W.   Library discipline.   New Hamp Bull 9: 175-6; P L 18: 103-4.

---- K. W.   Stories for girls.   Vt L Bull 9, No 2: 6.

Barnett, M. M.   Suggestions by which public libraries could be of increased assistance to community.   L A 14: 151-5.

Barnett, P. A.   English literature and English schools.   Journal of Education (London) 24: 208-10.

Barnett, T. A.   Libraries and welfare work.   L A 14: 86-91.

----- T. A.   University libraries and their arrangement.   L A 13: 37-41.

Barnish, E.   Co-operative libraries of Lancashire, Yorkshire and Durham.   L A U K Trans 2: 61-4, 149.

Barnstead, W. G.   Expansion of the Dewey decimal system for Canada.   Ontario Lib Assn Proceedings April 1912: 76-80.

Barnum, M. F.   Opportunities for college women in the library profession.   Bostonia, April 1913: 1-7.

Barnwell, J. G.   Library commission of Philadelphia--a correction.   L J 12: 152.

------ J. G.   Universal catalogue: its necessity and practicability.   L J 1: 54-8, 106.

Baron, J.   Bibliography of Blackburn.   B A R 12: LV-LIX.

Barr, C. J.  Bibliographical aids to the use of the current literature of science.  A L A Bull 1: 129-32.

-- C. J.  Relations of the greater libraries to the lesser. P L 10: 276-9.

-- C. J.  Some bibliographical aids to the use of the current literature of science.  A L A Bull 1: Conf No 129-32.

Barr, J.  Information boards for public libraries.  L W 10: 76-8.

-- J.  Library and the assistant: Staff organization.  L W 13: 4-9.

-- J.  Organization of a library service.  L A 6: 5-8, 25-8.

Barr, M.  Sick leave in college libraries.  L J 43: 95.

Barraud, L. M.  Some advice to directors of popular libraries as to the best method of distributing their books.  P L 5: 239-40.

Barrett, F. T.  An address delivered at the opening meeting of 2nd session of West of Scotland association of assistant librarians.  L A 14: 3-7.

----- F. T.  Alphabetical and classified forms of catalogues compared (favours dictionary form).  2d Int Conf 67-71, Discussion 234; L 9: 290. 1897.

----- F. T.  Book notation and an indicator.  L W 4: 281-6.

----- F. T.  Branch libraries: administration and relations with the central library.  L A R 6: 78-84, Discussion 5: 505-7.

----- F. T.  Form of stock book, or accessions catalogue. L A U K Trans 1: 79-81, 155-6.

----- F. T.  A great catalogue, being an appreciation of the catalogue of the Peabody institute, Baltimore.  L 6: 69-73.

----- F. T.  Notes on the manner of binding adopted by Mitchell library.  L A Trans 5: 185-6.

----- F. T.  Planning and arrangement of branch libraries. L A R 5: 301-6; Discussion 336-7.

----- F. T.  Presidential address.  L A R 9: 541-8.

----- F. T.  Selection of books for a reference library. L 8: 473-81.

----- F. T.  Selection of books for branch libraries: with select list.  L A R 6: 179-91.

----- F. T.  Significance of public libraries.  L A 6: 247-9.

----- F. T.  Sketch of a public library establishment for the City of Glasgow.  L C 5: 141-5.

**Barrett, M. M.**  Suggestions by which public libraries could be of increased assistance to the community.  L A 14: 152.

Barrett, R. C.  Few brief words about libraries.  Ia L C Q
1: 26.
Barrow, D. C.  Library as a form of extension work.  L J 36:
285-8.
Barry, J.  Some aspects of library administration in Ireland.
An Leab 1: 144-8.
Barry, R.  Melbourne library system of traveling libraries.
L J 2: 216-8, 279.
--- R.  On binding.  1st Int Conf 119-23, Discussion 167-
8; L J 2: 205-7, 271.
Barter  A.  The school library.  Journal of Education (Lon-
don) 29: 710-2.
Bartholomew, A. T. and Gordon, C.  On the library at King Ed-
ward VI school, Bury St. Edmunds.  L (3d s) 1: 1-26, 329.
Bartholomew, P. A.  Selling the service of the special li-
brary.  Special Libraries 11: 164-5.
Bartleson, M.  Some recent books on useful arts for boys and
girls.  Minn P L C N 3: 62-3; P L 16: 12-4.
Bartlett, E. K. N.  Efficient assistants.  L W 7: 344.
Bartlett, H. C.  The mirror for magistrates.  L (3d series)
3: 22-32.
------ H. C.  Quarto edition of "Julius Caesar." L (3d
series) 4: 122-32.
Barton, E. M.  Best use of duplicates.  L J 10: 231-4.
Barwick, G. F.  Book bound for Mary Queen of Scots, being
a description of the binding of the copy of the "Geo-
graphica of Ptolemy," printed at Rome, 1490, with notes
on other books bearing Queen Mary's insignia.  Bib Soc
Illustrated Monographs No IX, 1901.
----- G. F.  Books printed at sea.  L (ns) 1: 163-6.
----- G. F.  Copy of Ptolemy bound for Mary Queen of
Scots.  Bib Soc Trans 6: 5-8.
----- G. F.  Corantos.  L (3d series) 4: 113-21.
----- G. F.  A day's work in the reading room of the Bri-
tish Museum: L (ns) 6: 304-8.
----- G. F.  The formation of the Harleian library.  L
(3rd series) 1: 166-71.
----- G. F.  Humphrey Wanley and the Bodleian in 1697.
B Q R 1: 106-12.
----- G. F.  Humfrey Wanley and the Harleian library.  L
(ns) 3: 24-35, 243-55; L J 39: 744.
----- G. F.  The laws regulating printing and publishing
in Italy.  Bib Soc Trans 14: 311-23; 15-17: 69-107.
----- G. F.  Lutheran press at Wittenburg.  Bib Soc Trans
3: 9-25.
----- G. F.  Magazines of the 19th century.  Bib Soc Trans
11: 237-47.
----- G. F.  Notes from the first French translation of
"Vicar of Wakefield." L (ns) 5: 134-45.

----- G. F.   Presidential address.  L A R 21: 377-9.
----- G. F.   Recent English literature in Spain.  L (ns)
8: 275-9.
----- G. F.   Some early guide-books.  Bib Soc Trans 7: 191-
207.
----- G. F.   Some magazines of the eighteenth century.  Bib
Soc Trans 10: 109-40.

Barwick, F. G.  War prophecies.  L (3rd series) 6: 142-4.

Bascom, E. L.  Book selection department.  Wis Lib Bull 10:
25, 55, 85, 124, 161, 187, 257, 300; 12: 39, 88, 142, 182,
224, 268, 318, 407, 450; 13: 23, 59, 122, 153, 182, 213,
278, 309; 14: 29, 60, 78, 109, 168, 194, 251, 265.

---- E. L.  Books and bulletins on food conservation.  Wis
Lib Bull 14: 115-7.

---- E. L.  Books on vegetable gardening for the small library.  Wis Lib Bull 14: 82-3.

---- E. L.  Child welfare.  Wis Lib Bull 13: 87-98.

---- E. L.  Community taste in literature.  Wis Lib Bull
10: 133.

---- E. L.  Economical cookery: a selected list of books
and pamphlets.  Wis Lib Bull 13: 129-31.

---- E. L.  The European war.  New Hamp Bull 10: 55-63;
Wis Lib Bull 10: 226-32.

---- E. L.  How shall we select our books?  Ia L C Q 7:
65-9.

---- E. L.  The library and the "Runabout."  P L 24: 195-
6.

---- E. L.  Library work for college women.  Kappa Alpha
Theta.  May 1910: 321-8.

---- E. L.  The library's part in child welfare work.  L
J 44: 143-5.

---- E. L.  Modern drama: a reading list.  Wis Lib Bull
11: 17-20.

---- E. L.  The place of the commission in child welfare
work.  A L A Bull 13: 133-7.

---- E. L.  Problem of current fiction selection.  Wis
Lib Bull 7: 144.

---- E. L.  Safeguarding the welfare of mother and child:
the library's part.  Lib Occ 5: 154-6.

---- E. L.  Selected list of books-- Birds.  Wis Lib Bull
6: 34-6.

---- E. L.  Selection of fiction.  Wis Lib Bull 9: 34-40.

---- E. L.  The small library and modern poetry.  Wis Lib
Bull 13: 37-41.

---- E. L.  Work for child protection in our libraries.
Minn P L C N 6: 5-6.

---- E. L.  and M. T. Wheeler.  Indexing, principles,
rules and examples.  N Y S L Rept. 88: Bull No 94. 1904.

Bascom, J. A plea for the central library. Educational Review 38: 139-49.

Baskette, G. H. The library as a factor in education. Southern Education Assn Proceedings, 1908: 641-5.

Basset, E. Classification of foreign law books. L J 45: 751-2.

Batchelder, W. J. An experiment in the fairy tale. Temple Bar (ns) 3: 358; Living Age 249: 491.

Bates, A. J. Development of the Leominster library. L J 10:5.

--- A. J. High school library work in Quincy. L J 44: 149-51.

--- A. J. School library movement in New England. L J 43: 498; P L 23: 351-2.

Bates, E. W. Books and the child. Harper's Weekly Ap 10, 1909, 53: 15.

Bates, F. G. Municipal ordinances and documents. Special Libraries 5: 12-21.

--- F. G. Village government in New England. American Political Science Review 6: 367-85.

Bates, H. How to teach a masterpiece. School Review 11: 655-64.

--- H. Questions discussed at a round table meeting on the reading of high school students. L J 37: 393.

--- H. The schools and current fiction. N Y L 3: 43-7; English Journal 1: 15-23.

Bates, K. L. Literature in the schools. Journal of Education (Boston) 55: 329.

--- K. L. New ideas in teaching literature. Poet Lore 8: 563-7.

Bates, W. H. Library as an aid to school work. School Review 7: 179-82.

Batsford, H. Some suggestions on the formation of a small library of reference books on ornament and decorative arts. L 9: 257-69.

Batt, M. Library work in Great Britain and Germany. P L 15: 51-5.

Battis, M. M. Children and the public library. P L 5: 451-3; Ia L C Q 1: 10.

Battle, R. H. Olivia Raney library at Raleigh, N. C. N C Lib Bull 1: 27-30.

Battye, J. S. Bookbinding in public libraries. L A of Austral Proc XXI-XXIII, 1901.

Baxter, R. M. The legislative reference library. Arena 39: 674-81.

Baxter, W. E. Early editions of Milton. Bib Soc Trans 7: 152-5.

---- W. E. First edition of "Paradise lost." L A 2: 19-33.

--- W. E.  Stoke Newington and English literature.  L A R
16: 183, 193-205.
Bay, J. C.  A British criticism.  P L 14: 95-6.
- J. C.  Classification.  A L A Bull 11: 199-200, 340.
- J. C.  Contributions to the theory and history of botan-
ical bibliography.  Bib Soc Amer Proc 1: 75-83.
- J. C.  Inspiration through cataloging.  A L A Bull 10:
237-41, 406; L J 41: 547-51.
- J. C.  Nature study in the small libraries.  P L 11:
315-6.
- J. C.  A photographer photostat expert.  P L 22: 101.
- J. C.  Practical hints on the conservation of books.
P L 20: 53-4.
- J. C.  Reply to Mr. Voge's refutation.  P L 22: 11-2.
- J. C.  Review of the decimal classification, ninth edi-
tion.  P L 21: 267.
- J. C.  Some thoughts on classification occasioned by the
publication of Brown's Subject classification.  P L 12: 8-
10.
Bayles, M. B.  Results of elementary school class reference
work in public libraries.  Nat Educ Bull 1910: 1022-6.
Bayley, D. J.  Counter work.  L A 5: 30-4.
Bayley, H. A.  After the war, what?  P L 25: 559-60.
Bayley, W. C.  Entrance requirements and college domination.
School Review 19: 73-84.
Bayliss, A.  The function of the school superintendent in
procuring libraries for and their proper use in public
schools.  Nat Educ Assn.  1899: 1136-42.
----- A.  The library in relation to the school.  School
and Home Education 21: 113-9, 167-74.
----- A.  Some co-operative suggestions for schools and
libraries.  Nat Educ Assn 1903: 938-43.
Beach, F. N.  Literary haunts and shrines of Herefordshire.
B A R 5: LV-LVIII.
Beach, H. P.  Consolidation of the libraries.  Yale Literary
Magazine 29: 193-8.
Beach, W. G.  Opportunity and social action.  Pacific North-
west Library Assn Proceedings 1913: 7-16.
Beady, H. J.  Libraries of Alaska.  L J 30: Conf No 141-3.
Beal, W. H.  Statistics of experiment station libraries.
Association of American Agricultural Colleges and Exper-
iment Stations Proceedings, Columbus 1911: 162-71.
-- W. H. and E. L. Ogden.  The contribution of the U. S.
Department of agriculture to the bibliography of science,
with a list of the bibliographical publications of the
department.  Bib Soc Amer Proc 3: 135-52.
Bean, M. A.  Evil of unlimited freedom in the use of juve-
nile fiction.  L J 4: 341-3.
-- M. A.  Report on the reading of the young.  L J 8:
217-27.

Bear, L.  Publishers of music material for schools.  Illinois
    University High School Conference Proceedings 1920: 281-3.
Beardsley, I. L.  Fiction in libraries.  L J 7: 175-6, Dis-
    cussion 204-5.
Beazeley, M.  History of the Chapter library of Canterbury
    cathedral.  Bibliographical Soc Trans 8: 113-85.
Beck, F. G. M.  New Ipswich book of 1548.  L (ns) 10: 86-9.
Beck, F. M.  The school library, Charleston, Illinois.  East-
    ern Illinois State Normal School Bulletin No 7.
Beckley, A. M.  Pictures in libraries.  Cal Lib Assn Hdbk 54-
    7.
Beckley, J. M.  Proper organization of the school library.
    Minn P L C N 2: 73-5.
Bedwell, C. E. A.  Law libraries.  L A R 22: 253-6.
Beebe, W. L.  Disinfection of books.  Vt L Bull 12: 22.
Beecher, M. L.  Practical value of a taste for literature.
    Nat Educ Assn 1888: 78-86.
Beeching, H. C.  Library of the Cathedral church of Norwich,
    with an appendix of priory manuscripts now in English li-
    braries by Montague Rhodes James.  Norfolk Archaeology 19,
    Pt 1: 67-116.
------ H. C.  Some notes on an examination.  Longman's
    Magazine 38: 350-8.
Beeman, Mrs. A.  Imperial county library at the fair.  Bin-
    dery Talk 2: 13.
Beer, O.  Methods for use of newspapers and magazines in the
    high school English.  Illinois University High School Con-
    ference Proceedings 1920: 196-9.
Beer, W.  Fisk free library.  L J 22: Conf No 32-4.
    -- W.  Libraries in the Gulf States (Florida, Alabama,
    Mississippi, Louisiana, Texas).  L J 24: Conf No 6-7.
    -- W.  Library floors and floor covering.  L J 19: Conf
    No 100-1.
    -- W.  Louisiana.  A L A Bull 1: 76-7.
    -- W.  New Orleans academy of science.  Bib Soc Chic Yr-
    Bk 1902-3: 44-6.
    -- W.  Newspapers in libraries.  P L 16: 195-6.
    -- W.  Report on aids and guides.  L J 15: Conf No 73-4.
Beers, F. M.  Libraries essential to public schools.  South-
    ern Educ Assn Proceedings 1899: 311-4.
Beets, F. W.  Public libraries and American civilization.  P
    L 25: 504-5.
Behrend, F.  German manuscripts of the Middle Ages.  L A R
    14: 47-9.
Belden, C. F. D.  Civil service inadequacy.  P L 22: 143-4.
    ---- C. F. D.  Libraries.  New Hamp Bull (ns) 8: 62-9.
    ---- C. F. D.  Library commission work in Massachusetts.
    L J 42: 5-10.
    ---- C. F. D.  Library service for Boston department store
    employees.  Special Libraries 11: 96-7.

Bell, B. W.  The colored branches of the Louisville free public library.  A L A Bull 11: 169-73, 343; Discussion, 344.

-- B. W.  Library beginners.  P L 21: 224-5.

-- B. W.  Relation of the public library to the public school.  Southern Educational Assn Proceedings 1914: 333-4.

Bell, E. J.  Public libraries in New Zealand.  L A R 16: 145-55.

-- E. J.  Punctuation of catalogues.  L W 11: 38-9.

Bell, H. I.  Dafydd ab Gwilym.  L 10: 44-61.

-- H. I.  Early codices from Egypt.  L (ns) 10: 303-13.

Bell, J. C.  Hygiene of reading.  The Child May 1915: 464-7.

Bell, L.  List of historical novels dealing with English history.  Wis Lib Bull 13: 116-7.

Belloc, H.  Catalogue of Danton's library.  L (ns) 1: 67-70.

Bembridge, C.  Printing without ink.  Technical World 14: 573-7.

Benedict, L. E. W.  Hints on classification.  L J 24: Conf No 65-7.

------ L. E. W.  Suggestions to beginners in cataloguing.  P L 1: 266-7, 302-3.

Benguiat, F.  On the making of books.  Pacific Monthly 26: 335-40.

Bennett, A.  Book selection.  P L 17: 6-8.

Bennett, C.  State university library work.  Education 14: 152-9, 298-304.

Bennett, C. E.  Responsibilities of a library trustee.  Mich Lib Bull 11: Sept-Oct 1920: 26-8; P L 25: 487-9.

Bennett, C. K.  Librarian of a small library.  Minn P L C N No 1: 2-5.

Bennett, F. A.  Note on the national library of Chile.  L J 29: Conf No 92-3.

Bennett, N.  Advertising the library to the public.  N J Lib Bull 2, No 3: 12.

Bennett, W. Z.  Circulating books of scientific societies by mail.  L J 19: 176.

Bennington, A.  Books to read at different periods of life.  Van N 6: 100-6.

Benson, A. C.  The place of classics in secondary education.  Educational Foundations 22: 282-3.

Benson, R. T.  High school libraries.  Maine Lib Bull 9: 44-6.

Bensusan, S. L.  The Eragny press.  Booklover's Magazine 8: 119-25.

Berdam, J. N.  American literature and the high school.  Arena 29: 337-44.

Bergengren, R.  Art and craftsmanship in printing of books.  Outlook 90: 203-9.

Berger, L. J.  Comparative legibility of printing type.  Printing Art 14: 109-11.

Berger, Mrs. V. L.   How the library can serve the worker.
Wis Lib Bull 12: 381-2.

Berkey, M. L.   Primary schoolroom libraries.   P L 6: 77-9.

Berolzheimer, D. D. and F. M. Turner, Jr.   The chemical engineering catalog.   Special Libraries 10: 105-7.

Berry, I. R.   Relation of the school and library.   New Hamp
Bull (ns) 6: 229-31.

Berry, M. E.   Teacher's use of the public library.   Ia L C Q
6: 81-2.

Berry, S. H.   About reading room tables.   L J 27: 82-3.
--- S. H.   How to prevent fines.   L J 16: 207.
--- S. H.   How we choose and buy new books.   L J 14: 338-9.
--- S. H.   How we made the change from groups to classes.
L J 13: 283-4.
--- S. H.   Library versus libraries: advantages of large
collections of books in a metropolitan organization.   L
J 15: 337-8.

Berry, W. J. C.   Law classification under the author arrangement.   A L A Bull 1: 257-8.

Berry, W. T. and F. W. T. Lange.   Books on the Great War:
supplement.   L W 17: 263-6, 332-4, 367-9; 18: 17-20, 45-8,
139-44, 173-6.

Bethell, G.   An account of the library of the Medical society
of London.   L A R 16: 217-29.

Betteridge, G. L.   Province of the traveling library as a
part of the state library system of New York.   N Y L 1:
70-3.

Betterly, H. G.   The story hour.   Penn Lib Notes 6, No 4: 32-
6.

Beust, N.   Some children's books for first purchase.   1918-
19.   Wis Lib Bull 16: 60-2.

Biagi, G.   Inter-library loans in Italy.   L J 29: Conf No 58.
--- G.   International printed catalogue cards.   L J 27:
319.
--- G.   Note on Italian library affairs.   L J 29: Conf No
57-61.
--- G.   Title-pages in ancient manuscripts.   Printing Art
17: 17-23.

Bicknell, P. F.   College library and the college paper.   L
J 20: 387.
------ P. F.   New library building of the University of
Illinois.   L J 22: 303-4.
------ P. F.   University and college libraries and their
relation to the library movement of to-day.   P L 2: 301-
10.

Bigelow, J.   New York City Hall and the Tilden library.   L
J 18: 77-80.
----- J.   The Tilden trust library; what shall it be?   L
J 17: 378-83.

Bigley, W. H.   Special material in libraries.   Cal News Notes
14: 156-7.
Billings, J. S.   Card catalog of a great public library.   L
J 26: 377-83.
------ J. S.   Librarians in Washington.   L J 8: 199-200.
------ J. S.   Medical libraries in the United States.   U
S Rept: 171-82. 1876.
------ J. S.   National catalog of medical literature.   L
J 3: 107-8.
------ J. S.   New York's public library.   Century 81: 839-
52; L J 36: 233-42; L A R 1: 210-5.
------ J. S.   Presidential address.   L J 27 Conf No 1-16.
------ J. S.   Public library, its usefulness to the muni-
cipality.   L J 28: 293-4.
------ J. S.   Public library system of Greater New York.
L J 36: 489-92.
------ J. S.   Report relating to suggestions for consoli-
dating libraries of New York.   L J 25: 634-8, 741; 26: 21-
2.
------ J. S.   Some library problems of tomorrow.   L J 27:
Conf No 1-9; P L 7: 292-7.
------ J. S.   Suggestions for consolidating New York li-
braries.   L J 25: 634-8, 741; 26: 1-22.
Billingsley, M. P.   U. S. public documents as Christmas gifts.
P L 20: 105-6.
Billstein, N.   Linotyping library catalogues.   L J 19: 257-8.
(See also L J 19: 255, 259-61)
Bingham, C. S.   Library of an historical society.   American
Historical Assn Rept 1911 1: 255-61.
Bingham, J.   Danger line in fiction.   P L 3: 9.
Bircholdt, H. N.   Care of war literature and other books.
P L 24: 237-9.
Bird, G. W.   Governor Doty's public-private library.   Wis Lib
Bull 3: 67.
Birdsong, J. C.   Insect pests.   L J 12: 152.
Birge, A. E.   The small library and foreign fiction.   Lic Occ
5: 401-4.
Birge, A. G.   Selected list of current books.   Wis Lib Bull
16: 25-7.
Birge, E. A.   Books and life.   L J 31: 203-11; Minn P L C N
9: 37.
--- E. A.   Effect of the two-book system on circulation.
L J 23: 93-101.
--- E. A.   Home libraries.   P L 10: 165-6.
--- E. A.   Library extension.   P L 10: 163-7, 215-7, 259-
61.
--- E. A.   What may be done for libraries by the state.
L J 26: Conf No 7-8.
Birtwell, C. W.   Home libraries.   L J 19: Conf No 9-13.

Bisbee, M. D.  Place of bibliography in the equipment of a cul-
tivated man.  L J 22: 429-32.
Biscoe, E. D.  Bookbinding of our American publishers.  L J
24: 561-3.
---- E. D.  Ideals in children's work.  L J 25: 171.
Biscoe, N. S.  Public documents.  L J 1: 10.
Biscoe, W. S.  Cataloguing pamphlets.  U S Rept 826-35. 1892-
93.
---- W. S.  Chronological arrangement of books on shelves.
L J 10: 246-7; L N (US) 3: 424-9.
---- W. S.  Improvement of Poole's Index.  L J 1: 279-81.
---- W. S.  Pamphlets.  L J 18: 236-8, Discussion Conf No
66-7.
---- W. S.  Time numbers.  N Y S L Rept 88: 623-5.
---- W. S. and M. Dewey.  Comments on Dieserud's sugges-
ted classification.  L J 23: 609-11.
Bishop, E. W.  Moral effect of war stories on children.  P
L 20: 354-6.
Bishop, W.  Training in the use of books.  Sewanee Rev July
1912, 19 p.
Bishop, W. W.  The American library association at the cross
roads.  A L A Bull 13: 99-105; L J 44: 489-95.
---- W. W.  Amount of help to be given to readers (College
and reference section).  A L A Bull 2: 327-32, Discussion
332-4; L J 33: 264-8.
---- W. W.  A call to service.  A L A Bull 12: 185; L J
43: 547; Cal News Notes 13: 283-4; Ia L C Q 8: 100-1.
---- W. W.  Changing ideals in librarianship.  L J 44: 5-
10.
---- W. W.  Considerations of the cost of cataloguing.
L J 30: 10-4.
---- W. W.  A decade of library progress in America.  Popular Science Monthly 66: 131-8.
---- W. W.  Encouragement of serious reading through bib-
liographical enterprise.  L J 28: 235-7.
---- W. W.  Estimating the necessary seating capacity of
the reading room.  L J 45: 732-4.
---- W. W.  Further notes on the number of catalogue cards
to a book.  L J 31: 270-1.
---- W. W.  How the Library of Congress serves the people
of several states.  A L A Bull 8: 348-53; P L 19: 331-4.
---- W. W.  How to order and use the printed catalogue
cards from the Library of Congress.  N Y L 1: 145-6; Lib
Occ 2: 31-2.
---- W. W.  Inter-library loans.  L J 34: 527-32; P L 15:
56.
---- W. W.  Leadership through learning.  A L A Bull 10:
155-61, 381; Discussion 397.
---- W. W.  Library and post-school education.  School and
Society 11: 1-10.

---- W. W.  New library building of the University of Mich-
igan.  L J 44: 633-7; P L 25: 78-9.
---- W. W.  Printed analytical cards.  P L 23: 77.
---- W. W.  Printed cards from the Library of Congress, and
how to order them.  P L 12: 101-2; N Y L 1: 145-6.
---- W. W.  Problems of the departmental system in univer-
sity libraries.  L J 26: 14-8.
---- W. W.  Review.  L J 31: 836-8.
---- W. W.  School libraries and public libraries.  P L 1:
94-5.
---- W. W.  Should the librarian be a bibliophile.  L J 27:
126-9.
---- W. W.  Some considerations on the cost of cataloguing.
L J 30: 10-4.
---- W. W.  Some library gains from the war.  Bookman (N Y)
49: 353-5.
---- W. W.  Subject headings in dictionary catalogues.  L
J 31: Conf No 113-23, 236, Discussion P L 11: 449.
---- W. W.  The theory of reference work.  A L A Bull 9:
134-9.
---- W. W.  The true significance of library work.  L J 42:
385-6.
---- W. W.  Two unsolved problems in library work.  L J 37:
7-11.
---- W. W.  Vatican library: some notes by a student.  L J
25: 110-2.
---- W. W.  Zapon as a paper preservative.  L J 25: 284-5.
Black, C. E.  Card system in medical practice.  P L 10: 98.
--- C. E.  Medical literature in public libraries.  P L 14:
180.
--- C. E.  Story of one medical library.  P L 13: 397-401.
Black, J. E.  Courses in literature for children.  Nat Educ
Assn 1912: 1281-4.
Black, M. J. L.  Concerning some library fallacies.  P L 23:
199-204.
--- M. J. L.  An important aspect of the present time: hu-
morous fiction.  P L 22: 215-8.
Black, W.  Biographical notices of some Edinburgh librarians.
L A Trans 3: 30-48.
Black, W. M.  Value of a library commission.  P L 16: 53-6.
Blackall, C. H.  Some smaller Paris libraries.  L J 10: 82-4.
Blackburn, C. F.  Hints on catalogue titles and index entries.
Reviewed in L C 1: 78.
Blackburn, F.  Library exhibits.  P L 22: 8.
Blackmar, F. W.  Social degeneration in towns and rural dis-
tricts.  National Conference of Charities and Corrections
Proceedings 1900: 115-24.
Blackwalder, P.  Books on the war for the small library.  Wil-
son Bull 1: 51-4.

Blades, R. H.  Who was Caxton?  L (ns) 4: 113-43.
Blades, W.  Account of proposals made nearly two centuries
    ago to found public libraries.  L 11: 9-12.
    ---- W.  Development of books and their size notation.  L
    A M N 1: 2-5, 9-12.
    ---- W.  On chained libraries.  L 1: 412-5.
    ---- W.  On paper and paper marks.  L 1: 217-23.
    ---- W.  On signatures in old books.  L 1: 121-31.
    ---- W.  On the present aspects of the question, who was
    the inventor of printing.  L C 4: 135-43.
    ---- W.  Water-marks.  il.  L J 14: 129-31.
Blair, E. H.  Indexing and indexers.  A L A Bull 5: 234-8.
Blair, F. G.  Study and use of books.  Nat Educ Assn 1909:
    852-9.
Blair, R.  Public libraries and public schools.  L A R 11:
    195-7.
Blaisdell, T. C.  Dramatizing the story.  Nat Educ Assn Pro-
    ceedings 1907: 485-91.
Blake, K. E.  Americanization.  Minn Lib Notes 5: 150-1.
Blakeslee, M. F.  Personal reading of the librarian.  P L
    22: 188.
Blanchard, A.  One hundred of the best non-fiction for child-
    ren.  Vt L Bull 5, No 4: 5-6; 6, No 2: 6. 1910.
Blanchard, A. A.  Lincoln's birthday.  Wash L A Bull 3, No 1:
    9.
    ------- A. A.  Story telling as a library tool.  Child
    Conference for Research and Welfare Proceedings 1909, 1:
    39-44; Pedagogical Seminary 16: 351-6.
Blanchard, C. A.  Using other people's bulletins.  L J 24:
    476-8.
Blanchard, C. A. and F. M. Crunden.  Reading of school child-
    ren and college students.  L J 13: 89-90.
Blanchard, G.  Against the publication of books in series.
    New Hamp Bull 11: 139-41.
    ------- G.  The child and the public library.  P L 12: 91.
    ------- G.  A sermonette.  New Hamp Bull (ns) 15: 148-9.
    ------- G.  What a library worker can do.  New Hamp Bull
    (ns) 12: 217-20.
Blanchard, L. R.  Some catalogers' reference books of re-
    cent years.  A L A Bull 11: 203-7, 341.
Blanton, M. L.  How to meet the library needs of the farmer.
    L J 43: 10-3.
Blanton, Mrs. M. L.  Library needs of North Carolina.  N C
    Lib Bull 4: 42-6.
Blathwayt, R.  Romance of the sale room.  Fortnightly 98:
    939-50.
Blease, W.  Co-operative cataloguing.  L A R 16: 513-24.: Am
    Lib Annual 1915-16: 25-6; L J 40: 708-13.
Blessing, C. W.  What changes should be made in the library
    books or the selections for memorizing given in the var-
    ious grades in the New York state syllabus.  Univ of New
    York Education Dept Bull No 457: 296-306.

Bleyer, Prof. W. G.   Publicity for public libraries.   Wis Lib
  Bull 13: 49-50.
Bliss, H. E.   Accession records again.   L J 29: 19-20.
  --- H. E.   Accession records economized and systematized.
  L J 38: 255-63.
  --- H. E.   Better bookbinding for libraries.   L J 30: 849-
  57; P L 11: 294-9.
  --- H. E.   Conservatism in library classification.   L J 37:
  659-68.
  --- H. E.   Departmental libraries in universities and col-
  leges.   Educational Review 43: 387-409.
  --- H. E.   Economy in accession record.   L J 28: 711-3.
  --- H. E.   Headings for government publications.   L J 29:
  475.
  --- H. E.   A modern classification for libraries with simple
  notation, mnemonics and alternatives.   L J 35: 351-8, 544-7.
  --- H. E.   The problem and theory of classification.   A L
  A Bull 11: 200-2, 340.
  --- H. E.   A simplified alphabetic order table.   L J 37:
  71-4.
  --- H. E.   Some practical considerations regarding classi-
  fication for libraries.   A L A Bull 7: 309-15.
Bliss, R., Jr.   Alphabetization versus classification.   L J
  7: 104-5.
  --- R., Jr.   Bonazzi's scheme for a classed catalogue.   L
  J 16: 5-8.
  --- R., Jr.   Communication.   L J 9: 177.
  --- R., Jr.   Logical classification: Schwartz's scheme.   L
  J 7: 251.
  --- R., Jr.   Quarterly versus monthly indexes.   L J 13: 70.
  --- R., Jr.   Report on classification.   L J 14: 240-6.
Bliss, R.P.   Why a county library?   Penn Lib Notes 10: 22-3.
Block, L J. Study of English literature.   Educational Bi-month-
  ly 5: 215-9.
Blodgett, E. M.   The spirit of cataloging.   L J 44: 176-8.
Blood, E.   Music and the library.   Pacific Northwest Library
  Assn Proceedings 1920: 30-1.
Bloomfield, M.   How the librarian can assist in vocational
  guidance and training.   Mass Lib Club Bull 2, No 1: 9.
Blount, A.   Ways of European libraries.   Western Journal of
  Education 3: 348-56, 1910.
Blue, T. F.   Colored branches of the Louisville free library.
  Special Libraries 11: 145-7.
Bluemner, O.   Planning for small library buildings.   P L 3:
  3-4.
Blumenthal, W.   Copying process for printed matter without the
  use of photography.   Zentralblatt fur Bibliothekwesen,
  Leipzig Oct-Nov 1915: 321-6.
Boardman, A.   Traveling libraries in Ohio.   L J 23: 104.

Boas, F. S.  Selling the nation's heirlooms.  Nineteenth Century 86: 262-5.
-- F. S.  A seventeenth century theatrical repertoire.  L (3d series) 8: 225-39.
Bobbitt, J. F., Boyce, A. C., and Perkins, M. L.  Literature in the elementary curriculum.  Elementary School Teacher 14: 158-66.
Bodwell, W. P.  Treatment of the vignette.  Printing Art 16: 357-60.
Boggan, E. L.  Sidelight in the museum department of a library.  P L 8: 11-2.
Bogle, S. C. N.  Preparedness to meet new educational demands.  A L A Bull 11: 153-6, 343.
--- S. C. N.  Training for high school librarianship.  A L A Bull 13: 277-8, 396.
Bolton, A. T.  Robert Adam, architect to King George III and to Queen Charlotte, as a bibliographer, publisher and designer of libraries.  Bib Soc Trans 1915-17: 243-310.
Bolton, C. K.  As they do in Vermont, Pomfret library.  L J 36: 633-4.
---- C. K.  Bettering the circulation in small libraries.  L J 19: 161.
---- C. K.  Bulletin boards and special lists.  P L 5: 47-9.
---- C. K.  Charging systems and statistics.  L J 19: 225-6.
---- C. K.  Free public libraries as promoters of subscription libraries.  P L 12: 175.
---- C. K.  Harvard university library: a sketch of its history and its benefactors, with some account of its influence through two and a half centuries.  New England Magazine 15: 433-9.
---- C. K.  The librarian's canons of ethics.  P L 14: 203-4.
---- C. K.  Librarian's duty as a citizen.  L J 21: 219-22.
---- C. K.  Librarian's future.  L J 43: 3.
---- C. K.  Library examinations in schools.  L J 20: 122-3.
---- C. K.  Planning libraries.  P L 6: 620.
---- C. K.  The present trend.  A L A Bull 8: 154-8; L J 39: 503-7; N Y L 4: 98-101.
Bolton, F. E.  Special state aid to high schools.  Educational Review 31: 141-66.
Bolton, G. H.  History of the Bodleian library.  L W 12: 241-6.
---- G. H.  Library work with children.  Mass Lib Club Bull 7: 15-7.
Bolton, G. R.  Anglo-American joint code of cataloguing rules, 1908.  L W 12: 382-90.

---- G. R.  The newsroom as a department of the public
library.  L A R 12: 335-43.
---- G. R.  Practical book selection.  L A 10: 71-8; L
A R 15: 160.
---- G. R.  Work at the shelves: a day in an open access
library.  L A 5: 110-1.
Bolton, H. C.  Bad features of periodicals.  L J 21: 317-
20.
---- H. C.  Bad features in good books: imperfections
and absurdities in the "make-up."  L J 21: 265-7.
---- H. C.  Dated book marks.  L N (U S) 2: 216.
---- H. C.  Library check list of scientific literature.
L J 11: 189.
---- H. C.  Plea for a library of science in New York
City.  L J 19: 12-7.
---- H. C.  Russian transliteration.  L J 17: 383-4.
---- H. C.  Statistics of libraries in New York city and
vicinity.  L J 19: 14-7.
Bolton, H. E.  The Bancroft collection at Berkeley, Califor-
nia.  L J 44: 227.
Bond, E. A.  Presidential address.  L C 4: 1-10.
Bond, H.  The best Bible commentaries.  Expository Times
1903: 153-5, 203-5.
-- H.  Classified versus dictionary--a comparison of
printed catalogues.  L A R 2: 313-8.
-- H.  Criticisms and suggestions relating to Carnegie
library benefactions in the past and future in the Report
to the Carnegie United Kingdom trust by Prof. W. G. S.
Adams.  L A R 17: 522-9.
-- H.  Discussion of Mr. Willcock's paper "Is the printed
catalogue doomed?"  L A R 9: 402.
-- H.  Fiction anotation.  L W 2: 239-42.
-- H.  Government publications and public libraries.  L
A R 5: 444-51, Discussion 480-1.
-- H.  Monthly meetings in London.  L A R 10: 376-7.
-- H.  Question of overbuilding in the report to the
Carnegie United Kingdom trust by Prof. W. G. S. Adams.
L A R 17: 529-32.
-- H.  Quinn-Brown classification (a letter).  L 9:
131-2.
-- H.  Some features of recent library practice in Great
Britain.  L A R 17: 227-43; L J 29: Conf. No 28-33.
Bonnefoy, A.  Women as librarians: a French viewpoint.  L
J 40: 657-8.
Bonner, M. F.  Index to reference lists published in li-
brary bulletins.  Bull Bib 7: 84-8.
---- M. F.  Index to reference lists published in li-
brary bulletins, 1913.  Bull Bib 8: 7-10; 124-9.
---- M. F.  Index to library reference lists, 1916.
Bull Bib 9: 115-9.

---- M. F. Index to library reference lists, 1917. Bull
Bib 10: 10-5; 87-90.
---- M. F. Index to library reference lists 1919. Bull
Bib 11: 6-10.
Bonney, C. C. Bibliography of World's Congress publications.
U S Rept 1893-4, vol 2: 1756-60.
Boody, D. A. Public library as part of our educational sys-
tem. A L A Bull 10: 440-2; Discussion 442-3.
--- D. A. Relation of libraries to municipal government.
L J 31: Conf No 28-30.
Boose, J. R. Best books of 1903--Travel. L A R 6: 614-7.
--- J. R. Best books of 1904--Travel. L A R 8: 97-100.
--- J. R. Colonies in relation to public libraries, with
classified list of works. L A R 2: 589-99.
--- J. R. Constitution of Colonial public libraries. L
6: 391.
--- J. R. Libraries of Greater Britain. L (ns) 1: 123-8;
179-86. L (ns) 2: 183-9; 1902 L (ns) 3: 214-21.
--- J. R. Library of the Royal Colonial institute. L 6:
191-206.
--- J. R. Principal libraries of the British colonies.
Library Association Year-Book 1901: 65-7. L A Year-Book
1902: 67-9. L A Year-Book 1903: 70-2. L A Year-Book 1904:
76-8. L A Year-Book 1905: 78-80. L A Year-Book 1907: 103-
5.
--- J. R. Progress of Colonial libraries. L C 2: 81-9,
109-19.
--- J. R. Registers of colonial publications. L 8: 15-21.
Booth, H. K. A layman's biblical library. Cal News Notes 5:
384-90.
Booth, M. J. A debtor to his profession. L J 42: 567-8; P
L 22: 5-8.
--- M. J. Geographical and industrial material. N J Lib
Bull 2, No 4: 9-14.
--- M. J. The high school library and home economics.
Journal of Home Economics 8: 118-21.
--- M. J. Index to material for the study of poems and
stories. Bull Bib 8: 66-69, 100-2, 137-8, 163-4, 197-8,
223-6; 9: 16-7, 98-100, 163-6, 193-8.
--- M. J. Material on geography which may be obtained
free or at small cost. Journal of Geography, Jan 1914:
129-51.
--- M. J. Subject bibliographies appearing regularly in
periodicals. Bull Bib 5: 199-202; 6: 5-6, 41-2, 81-3,
113-6.
--- M. J. A suggestion for a bulletin board for periodicals. P L 19: 11.
Bosanquet, H. Cheap literature. Contemporary Review 79:
671-81.

Boss, H. R.   Chicago historical library.  L J 12: 72.

Bostwick, A. E.   Acknowledgment: discontinuance at St. Louis public library.  L J 44: 418.

------ A. E.  An adequate library survey.  A L A Bull 13: 366-7.

------ A. E.  Administration of a public library, especially its public or municipal relations.  L J 36: 342-5.

------ A. E.  Advertisement ideas.  Minn P L C N 3: 190-7.

------ A. E.  American libraries.  IV.  Some American libraries which we should know.  Wis Lib Bull 12: 158-65.

------ A. E.  The American public library: a review.  Nation 91: 78.

------ A. E.  Attitude of authors towards libraries.  P L 25: 565-6.

------ A. E.  Bailment in the library.  P L 18: 275-7.

------ A. E.  Book annotation.  P L 24: 87-90.

------ A. E.  Books for foreign population.  L J 31: Conf No 67-70.

------ A. E.  Books for tired eyes.  Yale Review Jan 1917: 358-68; Am Lib Annual 1917-18: 21-2.

------ A. E.  Branch libraries.  L J 23: 14-8.

------ A. E.  Business service in St. Louis.  Special Libraries 11: 184-5.

------ A. E.  Card catalogue for blind readers.  L J 30: 475.

------ A. E.  Club women's reading.  L J 40: 413-4.

------ A. E.  The companionship of books.  Pacific Northwest Library Assn Proceedings 1910: 8-23.

------ A. E.  Conflicts of jurisdiction in library systems.  L J 39: 588-91.

------ A. E.  Co-operation with municipal authorities.  L A R 13: 208-9.

------ A. E.  The day's work: some conditions and some ideals.  L J 28: 704-7.

------ A. E.  Discusses the question of library unions.  A L A Bull 13: 377.

------ A. E.  Duties and qualifications of assistants in open shelf libraries.  L J 25 Conf No 40-1.

------ A. E.  Economic features of libraries.  L J 34: 48-52.

------ A. E.  The educated librarian.  Nat Educ Assn 1912: 1262-7.

------ A. E.  Efficiency records in libraries.  L J 38: 131-3.

------ A. E.  Efforts to improve the character of reading in New York City.  L J 28: 229-33.

------ A. E.  The encouragement of good reading.  New Hamp Bull (ns) 14: 104-9.

------ A. E.  Exchange of assistants:  St. Louis public library experiment.  L J 42: 874.

------ A. E.  Exploitation of the public library.  P L 16: 294; A L A Bull 5; 60-5.

------ A. E.  Free mail transmission of library books.  L J 31: 124.

------ A. E.  The future of library work.  A L A Bull 12: 50-7.

------ A. E.  General principles involved in the administration of high school libraries.  Nat Educ Assn 1916: 660-4; L J 41: 646-7.

------ A. E.  Good will.  Lib Occ 5: 415-6.

------ A. E.  Historical stories.  A L A Bull 3: 269-70.

------ A. E.  How can central and branch work best be coordinated.  L J 23: Conf No 98-100, Discussion 164.

------ A. E.  How libraries choose books.  P L 8: 137-41.

------ A. E.  How the community educates itself.  A L A Bull 10: 115-22, 381; P L 21: 356-7; N Y L 5: 113-8; L J 41: 541-7.

------ A. E.  How to raise the standard of book selection.  P L 14: 163-7.

------ A. E.  Improving the standard of reading.  L A R 13: 207-8.

------ A. E.  Internal working of a public library.  P L 21: 56-7.

------ A. E.  James Hulme Canfield, 1847-1909, an appreciation.  L J 34: 143-4.  A L A Bull 3: 131.  L J 35: 273.

------ A. E.  Labor and rewards in the library.  P L 15: 1-5.

------ A. E.  Librarian as a censor.  L J 33: 237-44; 257-64; A L A Bull 2: 114-21; Ia L C Q 5: 226-31.

------ A. E.  The library and commercial art.  Special Libraries 10: 61-4.

------ A. E.  The library and its locality: how far it should be standardized and how far localized.  Mass L C Bull 9, No 2: 4-5.

------ A. E.  The library and the business man.  L J 42: 259-64.

------ A. E.  The library and the child.  P L 19: 337.

------ A. E.  The library and the school.  P L 17: 9.

------ A. E.  Library as the educational centre of a town.  P L 12: 171-4.

------ A. E.  Library circulation at long range.  L J 38: 391-4.

------ A. E.  Library extension movement in American cities.  Annals American Academy 67: 250-6.

------ A. E.  Library statistics.  L J 29: 58.

------ A. E.  Library work with children.  A L A Bull 10: 209-10, Discussion 411-21.

------ A. E.  Love of books as a basis for librarianship.
L J 32: 51-5; Ia L C Q 5: 143-4.
------ A. E.  Making an American's library.  Bookman (N Y)
38: 115-20, 278-83, 399-404, 531-7  618-23.
------ A. E.  Mal-employment in the library.  Ia L C Q 6:
247-52.
------ A. E.  Municipal reference libraries.  Am Lib An-
nual 1917-18: 62.
------ A. E.  Net book prices from the library standpoint.
P L 10: 292-4.
------ A. E.  A new kind of inventory of books at St. Louis
public library.  L J 42: 369-71.
------ A. E.  The new library day.  Lib Occ 5: 267-74.
------ A. E.  New York library civil service examinations.
L J 26: 391
------ A. E.  Open shelves and book theft.  L W 3: 62-4;
L J 25: 280-1.
------ A. E.  An oral speed test in mental response.  L J
35: 555-6.
------ A. E.  Pains and penalties in library work.  L J
27: Conf No 29-34.
------ A. E.  The people's share in the public library.
L J 40: 227-32.
------ A. E.  Poets, libraries and realities: address at
the dedication of the Indianapolis public library.  L J
42: 944-50.
------ A. E.  Popularizing music by the library.  Musician
24: 15-6 Feb 1919.
------ A. E.  The public library, the public school and
the social center movement.  Nat Educ Assn 1912: 240-6.
------ A. E.  Purchase of current fiction.  L J 28: Conf
No 31-3.
------ A. E.  The quality of fiction.  A L A Bull 7: 253-
6; Minn P L C N 4: 39-40; N Y L 3: 307-8; Ia L C Q 7: 69-
70; P L 19: 211.
------ A. E.  Reference work in small circulating libraries.
P L 5: 419-22.
------ A. E.  School libraries and mental training.  School
Review 23: 395-405; New Hamp Bull 11: 118-24.
------ A. E.  Service systems in libraries.  L J 37: 299-
304.
------ A. E.  Social work of the St. Louis public library.
L J 36: 461-3; L A R 13: 206-7.
------ A. E.  Socialization of the library.  Bookman (N Y)
51: 668-73.
------ A. E.  Some administrative problems of special li-
brarians.  Special Libraries 6: 97-100.
------ A. E.  Some economic features of libraries.  L J 34:
48-52.

------ A. E.  Some terse and pertinent suggestions regarding book selection for village libraries. N Y L 1: 238-9.
------ A. E.  Special field of work of libraries in close proximity. P L 15: 107.
------ A. E.  Statement concerning the Copyright conference. A L A Bull 1, No 1: 4-5.
------ A. E.  Symposium on recent books for boys. A L A Bull 3: 263-7.
------ A. E.  System in the library. L J 34: 476-82.
------ A. E.  Three kinds of librarians. P L 20: 1-4, 47-50.
------ A. E.  Truth in fiction. P L 7: 178-82.
------ A. E.  'Twixt library and museum. P L 21: 298-300.
------ A. E.  Two kinds of books. L J 45: 919-21.
------ A. E.  Two tendencies of American library work. L J 36: 275-8.
------ A. E.  Uses of fiction. A L A Bull 1: Conf No 183-7.
------ A. E.  Value of associations. L J 33: 3-9.
------ A. E.  Views of library school directors. P L 23: 14-5.
------ A. E.  Volume of children's work in the United States. A L A Bull 7: 287-91.
------ A. E.  What a library may do for a small town. N Y L 1: 172-3.
------ A. E.  What adults and children read. L J 21: 444-6.
------ A. E.  What should librarians read? L J 25: 57-8.
------ A. E.  The what, why and whither of the library. P L 8: 397-401.
------ A. E.  Whole duty of a library trustee from a librarian's standpoint. L J 31: Conf No 40-4, Discussion 239-40.
------ A. E.  Work of some states for library advancement. L J 33: 213-8.
------ A. E.  The work of the Missouri Library Association. Texas Libraries 1, July 1916: 28.
------ A. E.  Work of the small public library. L J 28: 596-600.
Bostwick, A. L.  Applied science department of the St. Louis public library. L J 37: 671-2.
------ A. L.  The relation between the municipal library and the legislator. Special Libraries 4: 163-5.
------ A. L.  The relation of the library to the city government through its municipal reference department. A L A Bull 8: 253-4.
Bottomley, G.  Hand printing and the Peartree press. Booklover's Magazine 7: 182-94.

Bottomley, H. T.   The private library.   Brickbuilder April
1914: 75-80.
Booth, W. M.   On the monetary value of book facilities to
readers offered by the public library.   P L 25: 194.
Borchard, E. R.   Recent development in international and muni-
cipal law.   A L A Bull 11: 412.
Borden, F.   Monopolies and trusts in America, 1895-1899.   N Y
S L Rept 85, Bulletin No 67, Bibliography No 31. 1902.
Borden, W. A.   Baroda and its public libraries.   Library Mis-
cellany (Baroda) 1: 187-94.
----   W. A.   Baroda, India, and its libraries.   L J 38: 659-
63.
----   W. A.   Classification of photographic collections.
L J 17: 195-7.
----   W. A.   How to popularize the library.   Lib Miscellany
1: 41-5.
----   W. A.   Library book stack.   Official Gazette U S Pat
Off Dec 28, 1915: 1112-3; Am Lib Annual 1916-17: 123-4.
----   W. A.   Library situation in Baroda.   Library Miscel-
lany (Baroda) 1: 1-3.
----   W. A.   Newspaper file.   L J 10: 313-4.
----   W. A.   On classifying fiction.   L J 34: 264-5.
----   W. A.   Organization of the free public library sys-
tem in the United States.   P L 22: 177-80.
----   W. A.   Pij free public library.   Library Miscellany
(Baroda) 2: 1-3.
----   W. A.   Sub-classification of J 7 (or whatever class
sign may be used: Photographic collection).   L J 17: 195-
7.
----   W. A. and W. K. Stetson.   Printed cards for catalo-
gues.   L J 16: 209.
Borrajo, E. M.   Books for the reference library: some selec-
ted lists and a suggestion.   L A R 1: 770-80.
-----   E. M.   Guildhall library: its history and present
position.   L A R 10: 381-95; Discussion: 406-9.
Bouick, J. B.   Summary of the history of the Sandeman public
library, Perth, 1898-1908.   L A R 13: 322-9.
Bourdillon, F. W.   Addenda and corrigenda.   Bib Soc Trans 8:
229-32.
--------   F. W.   The early edition of the "Roman de la
Rose."   Bib Soc Trans 7: 95-6, Bib Soc Monographs No XIV.
--------   F. W.   Early printing at Lyons.   L (ns) 6: 257-
64.
--------   F. W.   Some notes on two early romances: Huon
de Bordeaux and Melusine.   L (4th series) 1: 21-39.
--------   F. W.   Theseus de Cologne: notes on a fragment
of a lost edition, and an unknown version of the romance.
L (3d series) 9: 73-83.
Bourland, B. P.   A beginner's list in modern Spanish.   P L
21: 23.

Bowen, H. C.  English literature in schools.  Educational
    Times 44: 174-8.
--- H. C.  Use of fact and fiction in the early education
    of the young.  Educational Foundations 15: 93-104.
Bowerman, E. F.  Some notes on binding pamphlets.  L J 33:
    258-9.
Bowerman, G. F.  The business man and the public library.
    Special Libraries 11: 181-4.
------ G. F.  Co-operation between the library and the
    bookstore.  L J 38: 324-31; Lib Miscellany (Baroda) 2:
    9-21.
------ G. F.  Co-operation between the library and the
    book-store: how the librarian can aid the bookseller.
    Wis Lib Bull 10: 42-4.
------ G. F.  Co-operation between library workers and
    publishers.  P L 20: 79-80.
------ G. F.  Costs versus expenditure.  P L 22: 222-3.
------ G. F.  How far should the library aid the peace
    movement and similar propaganda?  A L A Bull 9: 129-33;
    L J 40: 477-81; P L 20: 296-301.
------ G. F.  Librarians' salaries in the District of Colum-
    bia.  L J 45: 63-6.
------ G. F.  Library advertising.  P L 10: 335-9.
------ G. F.  Library discounts.  L J 40: 370-1.
------ G. F.  Municipal popular libraries in Paris.  P L
    12: 395-6; L J 33: 9-13.
------ G. F.  Net prices and public libraries.  L J 27:
    134-6.
------ G. F.  Principles governing choice of religious
    and theological books for public libraries.  L J 30: 137-
    140.
------ G. F.  Public library an investment--not an expense.
    P L 18: 182-6; N C Bull 2: 19-22.
------ G. F.  The public library of the twentieth century
    in small and medium sized towns.  N C Bull 3: 59-66.
------ G. F.  Salaries in government department libraries.
    A L A Bull 13: 82-5.
------ G. F.  School work of the District of Columbia.  L
    J 31: 165-6.
------ G. F.  Some libraries in the farthest northwest.
    P L 12: 120-2.
------ G. F.  Some notes on binding. L J 35: 258-9.
------ G. F.  The spirit of the war literature: Prose.
    A L A Bull 12: 60-72, 287.
------ G. F.  A suggested salary schedule.  L J 44: 510-
    2.
------ G. F.  Survey of religious and ethical work of li-
    braries.  L J 29: 289-93.
------ G. F.  Unionism and the library profession.  L J
    44: 364-6.

------ G. F.  Washington library reclassification substitute.  L J 45: 687-90, 701.
------ G. F.  The Washington public library situation.  A L A Bull 13: 378, 385.
Bowker, R. R.  American book trade.  L J 22: 383.
---- R. R.  American library association and the Library Journal.  L J 19: 191-2.
---- R. R.  American National Library.  L J 21: 357-8.
---- R. R.  Being a librarian.  L J 15: 232.
---- R. R.  Bibliographical endeavours in America.  2d Int Conf 150-3, 1897; L J 22: 384-7.
---- R. R.  Bibliographies of U. S. government publications.  L J 10: 236, 335.
---- R. R.  Co-operative scheme of subject entry with a key to catalogue headings.  L J 3: 326-9.
---- R. R.  Current magazine check lists--another method. L J 14: 404-5.
---- R. R.  Discusses the question of unions and salaries. A L A Bull 13: 383-5.
---- R. R.  Events incident to the organization of the American Library Association.  L J 41: 569-70.
---- R. R.  Formation and organization of public libraries. L J 12: 117-9, 152.
---- R. R.  Heating.  A L A Bull 1: Conf No 121.
---- R. R.  Index to documents to 54th congress.  L J 22: 43, 270 770.
---- R. R.  Index to newspaper, or annual register of events.  L J 18: 506.
---- R. R.  Institut international de bibliographie, Brussels.  L J 25: 273-4.
---- R. R.  Learning to read in college.  L J 2: 60-2.
---- R. R.  Libraries and the century in America: retrospect and prospect.  L J 26: 5-7.
---- R. R.  Libraries and the library problem in Greater New York.  L J 21: 99-102.
---- R. R.  Library conditions in Russia.  A L A Bull 11: 328-9.
---- R. R.  Library Journal and library organization: a twenty years' retrospect.  L J 21: 5-9.
---- R. R.  Library service with respect to salaries, organizations and civil service control.  L J 44: 627-32.
---- R. R.  Literature of copyright.  L J 36: 492-6.
---- R. R.  Making the most of a small library.  L J 40: 173-5.
---- R. R.  Memories among English librarians.  L J 11: 405-9, 437-41.
---- R. R.  Music selection for public libraries.  L J 40: 579-82.
---- R. R.  National Library as the central factor of library development in the nation.  L J 37: 3-6.

---- R. R.   Order of imprint data.  L J 13: 86.
---- R. R.   Poore's catalogue.  L J 11: 3-4.
---- R. R.   Position of women.  In his discussion of the
question of unions.  A L A Bull 13: 384-5.
---- R. R.   The province of the public library.  A L A
Bull 9: 147-50 Discussion 243-4; New Hamp Bull (ns) 12:
177-9.
---- R. R.   Report of committee on public documents.  L J
24: Conf No 100-2; L J 25: Conf No 91-2; L J 29: 121-5.
---- R. R.   Report on index to portraits.  L J 14: 174-5.
---- R. R.   Resolution of A. L. A.  Appreciation for Com-
missioner of education's support of rural extension.  N Y
L 3: 13.
---- R. R.   Schwartz's new method of size notation.  L J
10: 396.
---- R. R.   Should librarians be under municipal and state
civil service?  A L A Bull 8: 246-7.
---- R. R.   Some libraries of the Northwest.  L J 20: 77-
80.
---- R. R.   Stockbridge.  L J 30: 954.
---- R. R.   Trustees' relation to the library.  L J 18:
227.
---- R. R.   Women in the library profession.  L J 45: 545-
9, 587-92, 635-40, 647, 658.
---- R. R.   Work of the 19th century librarian for the li-
brarian of the 20th.  L A Trans 5: 149-52; L J 8: 247-50.
---- R. R.   The work of trustees in a small library.  L J
38: 3-7; 663-6; New Hamp Bull 10: 1-4.
---- R. R.   U. S. government publications.  L J 10: 236-
41, Discussion 335.
Bowles, G. S.  History of the Waynesville library.  N C Lib
Bull 4: 75-7.
Bowman, J. C.  Use of magazines in English.  English Journal
5: 332-40.
Bowman, J. N.  Report on the archives of the State of Wash-
ington.  Am Hist Assn Rept 1908, 1: 365-98.
Boyd, A. M.  Contemporary poets: a classified list.  Bull Bib
10: 136-9; 11: 10-2, 28-9.
Boyd, C. N.  Care of the choir library.  Musician 18: 204-5.
Boynton, P. H.  Suggestions for the English literature sec-
tion of a high school library.  School Review 20: 111-6;
25: 111-6.
Boys, R. D.  Public lending library of Victoria.  Lib Assn
of Australasia Proceedings XXXIX-XLIV, 1901.
Brace, M. C.  Child welfare station, Waterloo, Iowa, public
library.  Ia L C Q 8: 140-1.
Brace, W.  F. A. Ebert's view of a librarian's education.
L A M N 2: 30-6.
Bradbury, L. A.  Difficulties found in cataloguing portraits.
L J 29: 588-90.

Braddon, Mary Elizabeth--bibliographies.  Notes & Queries
    Ap 1915: 282-4.
Bradley, E. J.  Application vouchers.  L W 19: 279.
Bradley, H.  Letter of Dr. Gregg's review of Dr. Bradley's
    work.  L (4th series) 121-2.
Bradley, J. W.  Books before printing.  L C 5: 30-7.
Bradley, L. S.  Bibliographies published by historical soci-
    eties of the United States.  Bib Soc Amer Proc 1: 146-57.
Bradley, W. A.  Design in make-up.  Printing Art 16: 455-8.
----- W. A.  Early watermarks.  Printing Art 16: 176-80.
----- W. A.  Typography in magazine make-up.  Printing
    Art 16: 345-8.
Bradley, W. T.  Wandsworth public library.  L A 1: 26-7.
Bradshaw, H.  Letters to officials of the British Museum.  L
    (ns) 5: 166-92, 431-42.
------ H.  Note on local libraries as considered museums
    of local authorship and printing.  L A Trans 5: 237-8.
------ H.  Size notation as distinguished from form nota-
    tion.  L W 5: 204.
------ H.  Some account of the organization of the Cam-
    bridge university library.  L A U K Trans 5: 229-37.
------ H.  Word on size notation as distinguished from
    form notation.  L A Trans 5: 238-40.
------ H.  Presidential address.  L A Trans 5: 107-15.
Bragg, C. W.  Library work in a rural community.  N Y L 4:
    141-4; New Hamp Bull 11: 95-7.
Bragg, P. W.  Purpose of story telling in the library.  Vt L
    Bull 6, No 2: 4-5.
Brainard, J. M.  "Coming out of Egypt."  Ia L C Q 2: 42-3.
------ J. M.  Fiction question again.  Ia L C Q 3: 45.
------ J. M.  Public libraries for farmers.  Ia L C Q 1:
    27.
Brainerd, C.  Libraries of the Young men's Christian assoc-
    iations.  U S Govt Rept: 386-8. 1876.
------ C.  Library or libraries: arguments against branch-
    es.  L J 16: 112-3.
Brainerd, E.  Newspapers in pamphlet form.  L J 12: 152.
Brainerd, E. W.  Reading at the front.  Independent 93: 103.
Brainerd, J.  Evolution of a high school librarian.  P L 24:
    143-5.
Brainerd, J. F.  Picture work in the New Rochelle public li-
    brary.  P L 11: 255-6.
------ J. F.  What one student council does for its li-
    brary.  P L 25: 413-5.
------ J. F.  Work with schools in New Rochelle, New York.
    N Y L 1: 108-9.
Brainerd, M.  A library survey of Maine.  Maine Lib Bull 6,
    No 1: 18-9.
Brannon, M. A.  Some functions of the library.  Pacific North-
    west Library Assn Proceedings 1914: 6-10.

Branson, E. C. The Georgia club--for the study of rural soc-
iology. U S Bureau of Education Bulletin 1913 No 23.
Brassington, W. S. Additional notes to Blades' "Bibliograph-
ical Miscellanies" Nos 3, 4, 5. Books in chains. L 3:
270-3, 441-5.
--------- W. S. Thomas Hall and the old library founded
by him at King's Norton. L C 5: 61-71.
Brauer, H. G. A. Municipal information and research in the
Pacific Northwest. Special Libraries 6: 112-4.
Brazier, A. W. Principles and practice of library classifi-
cation. L A of Austral Proc XXIX-XXXIX.
Breck, E. J. The efficient high school library. American
School Master Dec 1915: 453-6; Catholic Educational Re-
view Jan 1916: 45-7; English Journal 5: 10-9.
--- E. J. A new task for the English teacher. English
Journal 1: 65-71.
Bredvold, L. I. Suggestions for reconstruction in high school
English. Education 33: 492-8.
Breedlove, J. P. Reference work in a college library. N C
Bull 2: 107-9.
------- J. P. A service our libraries may render. N C
Bull 1: 116-8.
------- J. P. Some effects of the European war on college
libraries. N C Bull 3: 75-7.
------- J. P. Standardization: service and salary. N C
Bull 4: 62-7.
------- J. P. Trinity college library. North Carolina
Lib Bull 1: 76-8.
Breene, M. L. The mission of the small library. Penn Lib
Notes 3, No 2: 2-9.
Brett, G. P. Book publishing and its present tendencies.
Atlantic 111: 454-62; Discussion, Dial 54: 401-3.
Brett, W. H. Access to the shelves in Cleveland public li-
brary. L J 16: Conf No 34-5, Discussion 108-9.
--- W. H. Advances in methods of assistance to readers.
L J 23: Conf No 174-5.
--- W. H. Better evaluation of books. A L A Bull 10:
107-8; L J 41: 456.
--- W. H. Books for the youth. L J 10: 123, 127-8.
--- W. H. Cataloging children's books. P L 7: 304.
--- W. H. Certification of librarians. Ia L C Q 8: 17-9.
--- W. H. Cleveland library examinations. L J 15: 327-8.
--- W. H. Cleveland public library. L J 27: 27-8.
--- W. H. Comments on library legislation. A L A Bull
10: 319-24.
--- W. H. Expenditure of library funds. P L 7: 367.
--- W. H. Freedom in public libraries. 2d Int Conf 79-
83, Discussion 243-6.
--- W. H. Improper books: methods employed to discover
and exclude them. L J 20: Conf No 36-7.

--- W. H.   The library and the book trade.   A L A Bull 10: 402-5; L J 41: 750-2; P L 21: 405-8.
--- W. H.   Library architecture from the librarian's point of view.   L J 31: Conf No 49-52.
--- W. H.   Library in vacation days.   L J 23: 279.
--- W. H.   Library instruction in the normal school.   Nat Educ Assn 1903: 971-6.
--- W. H.   Ohio county library law.   P L 22: 140.
--- W. H.   The open library.   L J 17: 445-7.
--- W. H.   Periodical library bulletins.   L J 19: Conf No 55-6.
--- W. H.   Presidential address.   L J 22: Conf No 1-5.
--- W. H.   President's address on the work of the A. L. A. L J 22: Conf No 1-5.
--- W. H.   Public library of the future.   L J 25: 69-70.
--- W. H.   Re-arrangement of Cleveland public library for open access.   L J 15: 136-7.
--- W. H.   Regulations for readers.   U S Rept 939-43, 1892-3; L J 18: 230-2.
--- W. H.   Relation of library and school.   P L 6: 84-5.
--- W. H.   Relation of the public library to the public school.   Nat Educ Assn 1892: 692-702.
--- W. H.   School and the library.   P L 10: 225-7.
--- W. H.   Selection of books.   L J 19: Conf No 38-9.
--- W. H.   Sending books "over there." A L A Bull 12: 183.
--- W. H.   Some notes on book selection.   Ia L C Q 2: 1-4.
--- W. H.   Some other book.   L J 12: 505-7.
--- W. H.   Use of periodicals.   L J 20: Conf No 12-6.
--- W. H.   Use of the public library in the Cleveland schools.   L J 16: Conf No 30-1.
--- W. H.   War library service.   Nat Educ Assn 1918: 461.
--- W. H.   What we do about duplicates.   L J 14: 369.
--- W. H.   Work of the dispatch office at Newport News. L J 43: 575-7.
--- W. H. and Ahern, M. E.   Library instruction in the normal school.   Nat Educ Assn 1903: 692-702.
Brewer, F. M.   Library work: choosing an occupation.   Board of Education, Poughkeepsie 1911: 77-9.
Brewer, H. J.   A good word for the card index.   Special Libraries 5: 131.
Brewer, W. A.   Book plates.   Cal News Notes 4: 266-92.
Brewster, E.   An ideal.   New Hamp Bull (ns) 12: 169.
------ E.   Our work with children.   New Hamp Bull (ns) 14: 128-9.
Brewster, W. L.   Library conditions in Oregon.   L J 30: 785-6.
------ W. L.   Main purpose of a library is the education of the people.   Pacific Northwest Library Assn Proceedings 1911: 31-5.

‑‑‑‑‑‑ W. L.  A model library law‑‑city and county.  Pacific Northwest Library Assn Proceedings 1917: 20‑3.

‑‑‑‑‑‑ W. L.  On the selection of a librarian.  Pacific Northwest Library Assn Proceedings 1911: 32‑5.

‑‑‑‑‑‑ W. L.  Responsibility of library trustees.  P L 17: 205‑7.

Bricker, G. A.  Rural libraries.  American Education Jan 1918: 251‑61; Nebraska Teacher Jan 1918: 199‑201.

Bricker, G. H.  High school agricultural library.  L J 41: 38.

Brickford, I. A.  Use and importance of rural libraries.  New Hamp Bull (ns) 14: 126‑8.

Bridges, A.  Story telling to children.  P L 24: 372.

Bridgman, M.  Libraries and schools.  School and Home Education 20: 507‑8.

Briggs, I.  Concerning the juvenile library.  L A 6: 172‑9.

‑‑‑‑ I.  The need of "English" in the examinations.  L A 11: 30‑6.

‑‑‑‑ I.  Should children's reading be restricted?  L A R 13: 194‑5, 201‑5.

Briggs, M. J.  The A. L. A. List of subject headings.  A L A Bull 6: 227‑31.

Briggs, W. B.  Maps: their value and availability.  N Y L 3: 59‑61.

‑‑‑‑ W. B.  Public library and the city government, or what public libraries should do for municipal departments and officials.  L J 33: 385‑90.

‑‑‑‑ W. B.  Reference work in public and in college libraries: a comparison and a contrast.  L J 32: 492‑5.

Brigham, C. S.  Need of a bibliography of American colonial newspapers.  Bib Soc Amer Proc 1: 160‑4.

Brigham, H. O.  Co‑operation between special libraries.  L J 35: 12‑4; Special Libraries 1: 6‑7.

‑‑‑‑‑ H. O.  Indexing and care of pamphlets.  L J 37: 668‑71.

‑‑‑‑‑ H. O.  Library efficiency under new conditions.  L J 35: 302‑9.

‑‑‑‑‑ H. O.  Statistics of state libraries.  A L A Bull 1: Conf No 216‑20; A L A Bull 2: 270‑6.

Brigham, J.  Co‑ordination‑‑not competition: our responsibility to the Commonwealth‑‑the call to service and a note of warning.  A L A Bull 8: 328‑32.

‑‑‑‑‑ J.  Duties of a librarian.  P L 13: 81.

‑‑‑‑‑ J.  How can co‑ordination best serve the library' interests of the state?  A L A Bull 4: 725‑31.

‑‑‑‑‑ J.  Iowa in the world's literature.  Ia L C Q 5: 1‑8.

‑‑‑‑‑ J.  Legislative reference work without appreciation.  A L A Bull 1: Conf No 200‑12.

‑‑‑‑‑ J.  Library extension in the state of Iowa.  Ia L C Q 2: 17‑8.

----- J. Literary Iowa. Iowa L C Q 7: 228-34.

----- J. Model library commission law. L J 30: Conf No 46-50; P L 10: 83-7.

----- J. State librarian's outlook. L J 24: Conf No 81-4.

----- J. The state library. Ia L C Q 6: 34-5.

----- J. Synopsis of laws authorizing library commissions. P L 10: 83-7.

----- J. Text of the Oregon Library commission law. L J 30: Conf No 49-50.

----- J. Union-co-operation. Ia L C Q 1: 23-34.

----- J. A world of books. Ia L C Q 3: 56-62.

Brindley, J. E. Legislative reference movement. Iowa Journal of History and Politics 7: 132-41.

Brindley, S. How may the teacher help the library. Neb Lib Bull 1, No 4: 5-7.

Briscoe, J. P. Bergen public library. L 10: 20-24.

----- J. P. Book music in public libraries. L C 5: 146-7.

----- J. P. Half-hour talks about books with library readers. L 7: 18-20.

----- J. P. How to extend the library movement. L 8: 73-6; Libn 3: 88-90.

----- J. P. Libraries and reading circles. L A R 5: 219-24.

----- J. P. Libraries for the blind. L C 4: 68-71.

----- J. P. Libraries for the young. L C 3: 45-8; Discussion L A Proceedings 1885: 17.

----- J. P. Public libraries and emigration. L A R 1: 294-6.

----- J. P. Subscription libraries in connection with free public libraries. L A U K Trans 1: 19-23.

----- J. P. A well-equipped library. L A 1: 49-52.

Briscoe, W. A. Library publicity methods. L W 16: 353-60.

----- W. A. Our war aims. L A R 20: 114-6.

----- W. A. Public libraries and the coming trade war. L W 19: 205-7.

----- W. A. Recent development in library work amongst the young. L A R 11: 264-7.

----- W. A. Selection of periodicals for a public reading room. L W 12: 215-6.

----- W. A. Uses of advertisement in library administration. L A R 15: 604-10.

Brittain, W. H. Presidential address. L A R 11: 424-34, 508-9.

Britton, J. The library's share in Americanization. L J 43: 723-7.

Broadhurst, H. P. Enquiry desk: its usefulness. L W 15: 32.

-------- H. P. A note on distinctive bindings. L W 16: 303-5.

Brockett, P.  International exchanges.  L J 35: 435-7.

Bromley, W. T., pseud of W. B. Thorne.  Our new war service.
L W 20: 125-8.

Bronson, W. C.  English literature in secondary schools.  Academy (Syracuse) 4: 384-95.

Brooks, A. A.  What I expect of an index.  L J 35: 51-5.

Brooks, C. S.  On buying old books.  Yale Review (ns) 7: 120-
8.

Brooks, E. A.  Public library and the school.  L J 18: 185.

Brooks, M. H.  Sunday school libraries.  L J 4: 338-41.

Brooks, M. S.  The library as an agency in Americanization.
New Hamp Bull (ns) 16: 20-2.

Broughton, J. M., Jr.  Rural school library.  N C Bull 1: 78-
80.

Brouse, J. P. W.  The library as seen by the state.  Southern
Education Assn Proceedings 1912: 397-400.

Brower, K. W.  Value of a series number in registration.  L
J 36: 578.

Brown.  Village libraries.  P L 16: 118.

Brown, A. N.  Collation.  L J 12: 184.
    --- A. N.  Library and the newspaper.  Wash L A Bull 3,
    No 1: 1-3.
    --- A. N.  National library of Mexico.  L J 10: 248-9.
    --- A. N.  United States Naval academy library: a sketch.
    Special Libraries 9: 40.

Brown, B. M. and M. F. Williams.  Furnishing of children's
libraries.  Ia L C Q 1: 21.
    --- B. M. and M. F. Williams.  Reading list for children's
    librarians, 1899-1900.  Bibliography No 27, N Y S L Rept
    84, 1901.

Brown, C.  Shakespeare and the horse.  L (3d series) 3: 152-
80.

Brown, C. E.  Museum auxiliaries in libraries.  Wis Lib Bull
2: 31-2.
    --- C. E.  Publications of the Wisconsin archaeological
    society.  Wis Lib Bull 10: 157.
    --- C. E.  Screen bulletins in the State historical soci-
    ety's museum.  Wis Lib Bull 4: 89-90.

Brown, C. H.  Libraries and the Stevens Bill.  L J 41: 112-3.
    --- C. H.  Limitations of the branch librarian's initia-
    tive.  A L A Bull 5: 105-9; L J 36: 333-6.
    --- C. H.  Naval libraries.  L J 45: 169-70.
    --- C. H.  Naval libraries: present and future.  L J 44:
    235-41.
    --- C. H.  Public documents in technical libraries.  A L
    A Bull 1: Conf No 156-7.
    --- C. H.  Use of scientific and technical books.  A L A
    Bull 1: Conf No 163-5.

Brown, C. M.  Handling books for collateral reading.  L J
38: 675-6.
Brown, D.  Relation of the state library to other libraries
of the state.  A L A Bull 4: 699-702.
Brown, D. C.  Librarian a scholar or not?  P L 13: 169.
--- D. C.  Scope of book purchases in a state library.
A L A Bull 1: Conf No 227-30.
--- D. C.  State libraries.  Wis Lib Bull 12: 371-4.
--- D. C.  The state library.  A L A Bull 5: 215-6; L J
36: 447-51.
--- D. C.  State-wide influence of the state library.  New
Hamp Bull 9: 215-8.
Brown, F. C.  Architectural illustration.  Printing Art 16:
109-15.
Brown, F. H.  India office library.  L (ns) 5: 256-65.
Brown, G. A.  State libraries, their management and support.
L J 8: 245-7; Discussion, 295-6.
--- G. A.  Students' preferences in literature.  School
and Home Education 31: 164-5.
Brown, G. P.  On the teaching of English in elementary and
high schools.  National Society for the Scientific Study
of Education, Year Book 5, pt 1.
Brown, G. S.  Wastefulness in primary reading.  Western Jour-
nal of Education 5: 111-6.
Brown, J. D.  Adjustable catalog holder.  L J 18: 299-300.
--- J. D.  American library statistics--a query.  L W 10:
113-4; L J 33: 395.
--- J. D.  Annotation of fiction.  L W 2: 150-4.
--- J. D.  Arrangement of large subject headings in a dic-
tionary catalogue.  L C 5: 170-6.
--- J. D.  Best books of 1903--Music.  L A R 6: 559-62.
--- J. D.  Best periodicals.  L A R 6: 430-2.
--- J. D.  Bibliographical aids.  L W 5: 197-205.
--- J. D.  Bibliographical lantern slides.  L A R 10: 147-
8, 215-7.
--- J. D.  Bibliography of library science.  L W 6: 236-
45, 265-73.
--- J. D.  Book description.  L W 8: 87-90, 145-7.
--- J. D.  Book exhibitions: proposal for a publisher's
permanent book exhibition on systematic lines.  L W 10: 201-
4.
--- J. D.  Book museum at Brussels.  L W 10: 337-8.
--- J. D.  Books for very young readers.  L W 9: 282-9.
--- J. D.  British, Colonial, and American library legis-
lation.  L W 8: 201-7.
--- J. D.  British library itinerary.  L W 15: 99-105, 130-
6, 170-7; L A 10: 118.
--- J. D.  British municipal libraries.  L (ns) 9: 218-24.
--- J. D.  Catalogue annotations.  L A 4: 106-14.
--- J. D.  Cataloguing appliances.  L 3: 392-4.

--- J. D.  Cataloguing of music. L 9: 82-4.
--- J. D.  Charging systems. L 3: 390-2.
--- J. D.  Checking of periodicals. L 9: 35-6.
--- J. D.  Classification and cataloguing. L 9: 143-56.
--- J. D.  Classification scheme for music libraries. L
9: 82-4.
--- J. D.  Clerkenwell open access library. Greenwood's
Yr-Bk: 82-3.
--- J. D.  Clerkenwell open lending library. L J 20: 51-
4.
--- J. D.  Current views on registration. L A R 11: 203-
4.
--- J. D.  Descriptive cataloguing. L (ns) 2: 135-40.
--- J. D.  Discussion of Mr. Willcock's paper "Is the print-
ed catalogue doomed?" L A R 9: 405-6.
--- J. D.  Editorial 1898-1910, a retrospect. L W 13: 1-
4.
--- J. D.  Fiction classification. L 8: 22-31.
--- J. D.  Formation of public libraries. Greenwood's Yr-
Bk: 61-77, 84, 1897.
--- J. D.  History and description of charging systems.
L W 1: 3, 33-5, 75-6, 110-3, 187-90, 242-7.
--- J. D.  History of charging systems. L W 2: 3-5, 29-
31, 57-62, 113-8. L W 3: 3-4, 18-20, 33-5, 75-6, 110-3.
L W 4: 187-90, 242-7.
--- J. D.  In defence of Emma Jane. L W 11: 161-6.
--- J. D.  Indicators. L 3: 386-90.
--- J. D.  Lecture in Belgium on work of British Municipal
libraries. L (ns) 9: 218-24.
--- J. D.  Library appliances. L 3: 382, 386-392, 395.
Greenwood's Yr-Bk: 94-101.
--- J. D.  Library classification and cataloguing: review.
Libn 3: 3-4.
--- J. D.  Library lighting. Illuminating Engineer 4, No
2; Libn 1: 195-6.
--- J. D.  Library of the Library association. L A R 5:
183-7, 238-9, 313, 630-1.
--- J. D.  Library progress. L (ns) 1: 5-11.
--- J. D.  Library progress, 1898-1910. L W 13: 1-4.
--- J. D.  Limitation of newspapers in public libraries.
L W 9: 153-7.
--- J. D.  Mechanical methods of displaying catalogues.
L 6: 45-66.
--- J. D.  Methods of filing pamphlets, etc. L 3: 394.
--- J. D.  Miscellaneous appliances. L 3: 394-6.
--- J. D.  Music subject list. L 3: 147-51.
--- J. D.  Note on an "Index to general literature," issu-
ed by the American library association. L 5: 209-16.
--- J. D.  Open access in public libraries exposed: a re-
ply to Mr. Foskett's pamphlet. L W 2: 282-3.

--- J. D.  Open access libraries from a British standpoint.
L J 20: 9-12.
--- J. D.  Out-of-print books.  L W 3: 141-2, 215-9, 235-
7, 287-90.
--- J. D.  Outline of classification of library science.
L A R 5: 183-5.
--- J. D.  The philosophy of cataloguing.  L W 6: 319-24.
--- J. D.  Plea for select lists of books on important sub-
jects.  L 7: 363-6.
--- J. D.  Practical bibliography.  L (ns) 4: 144-51.
--- J. D.  Principal rate-supported libraries.  L A Yr-Bk:
61-102.
--- J. D.  Procedure in formation of public libraries.
Greenwood's Yr-Bk 60-78, 1897.
--- J. D.  Public utilization of existing libraries.  L
(ns) 5: 93-102.
--- J. D.  Racks and stands for periodicals and newspapers.
L 3: 383-6.
--- J. D.  Recent developments in library practice.  Green-
wood's Yr-Bk 1897: 79-101.
--- J. D.  The reference library.  L W 3: 201-5.
--- J. D.  Report of the librarian of Clerkenwell on his
visit to American libraries: and criticism thereon.  L 5:
282-90.
--- J. D.  Report on library appliances.  L 3: 382-3.
--- J. D.  Reprints of standard works.  L W 6: 8-10, 39-41,
71-3, 130-3, 162-5, 210-2.
--- J. D.  Revolving catalogue holder.  L 3: 393.
--- J. D.  Roberts, Henry David.  L W 11: 219-21.
--- J. D.  Select list of books on photography.  L W 1:
174-7.
--- J. D.  Select list of books on special subjects--music.
L W 1: 227-31, 256-9.
--- J. D.  Select lists of books on important subjects.
L W 7: 363-6.
--- J. D.  Selection of current periodicals.  L A R 6: 591-
7.
--- J. D.  The shy enquirer.  L W 13: 365-8.
--- J. D.  The small library, its formation, equipment and
management.  L W 4: 309 et seq (Published in book form,
1907).
--- J. D.  Some Cornish libraries.  L W 3: 57-62.
--- J. D.  Subject classification, criticisms, revisions
and adjustments.  L W 12: 41-5, 81-6, 121-4, 153-60.
--- J. D.  Subject indexes and bibliographies.  L W 3:
155-8.
--- J. D.  Suggestions for a new form of library indicator.
L 8: 96-101.
--- J. D.  Thomas Greenwood.  L A R 10: 633-6, L W 11: 201-4.

   --- J. D.  Training of assistants.  L 10: 94.

   --- J. D.  The tyranny of the catalogue.  L W 11: 1-6.

   --- J. D.  Village library problem.  L 6: 99-105.

   --- J. D.  Where do we get our librarians?  L W 3: 124-7.

   --- J. D.  Women as librarians in Clerkenwell.  L W 1: 219.

   --- J. D.  Working of the Clerkenwell library.  L 5: 109-19.

   --- J. D. and Fincham, H. W.  Clerkenwell open lending library.  L 6: 344-55; L J 20: 51-4.

   --- J. D. and L. S. Jast.  Compilation of class lists.  L 9: 45-67.

   --- J. D. and J. H. Quinn.  Classification of books for libraries in which readers are allowed access to the shelves. L 7: 75-82.

Brown, J. W.  How to deal with books from their accession to their delivery to the borrower (Prize essay).  L A 2: Supplement.

   --- J. W.  Village libraries: the Westmorland scheme.  L A R 10: 644-7, Discussion, 698-9.

   --- J. W. and H. Farr.  Cataloging and otherwise preparing books for the use of the public.  L A R 3: 226-7.

Brown, L. F.  Trials of a new assistant.  L J 24: 55-6.

Brown, M. J.  Trials and tribulations of an assistant.  P L 21: 76-7.

Brown, Mr.  An English librarian on American libraries.  L J 19: 88-90.

Brown, R.  Glasgow and the Public libraries acts.  L C 5: 123-33.

Brown, R. W.  Commercial libraries.  L A R 19: 157-9.

   --- R. W.  Co-operation between the Education committee and the Public libraries committee.  L A R 17: 141-50; L W 17: 313-6.

   --- R. W.  Northamptonshire printing, printers and booksellers.  B A R 14: XXIX-XXXVI, 1917.

   --- R. W.  Public libraries and national conditions.  Libn 7: 224-6.

   --- R. W.  Symposium on public libraries after the war.  L A R 19: 157-9.

Brown, T. H.  Art of programme making.  Wis Lib Bull 3: 73-5.

Brown, W.  Chivers' indicator adapted as an author indicator for fiction.  L W 11: 243-4.

Brown, W. H.  Possibilities of contagion in the circulation of books.  Mass L C Bull 6: 82-3.

Brown, W. L.  Breadth and limitations of book-buying.  A L A Bull 6: 124-7.

   --- W. L.  The changing public.  A L A Bull 11: 91-5, 314; L J 42: 587-91; P L 22: 299-301; School and Society 6: 1-6.

--- W. L.  Educational unity.  A L A Bull 6: 1-3; L J 37: 70-1.

--- W. L.  Staff meetings: their organization, methods and results.  L J 32: 546-7.

Brown, Z.  What to do with pamphlets.  L J 32: 358-60.

Browne, F. F.  American publishing and publishers.  Dial 28: 340-3.

---- F. F.  Eternal "or" of the librarian.  A L A Bull 5: 112-9; N Y L 3: 5-8; P L 16: 233-7.

Browne, J. S.  A few hints on Medical library administration.  Med Lib and Hist Journal 1: 33-4.

Browne, L.  How a bibliomaniac binds his books: verses.  L J 13: 70.

Browne, M. W.  Traveling library statistics.  A L A Bull 2: 306-9.

Browne, N. E.  Another charging system.  L J 20: 168, Discussion Conf No 127-8, 130.

---- N. E.  Another chargind system.  L J 20: 168.  For Discussion see Conf No 127-8, 300.

---- N. E.  Comparison of charging systems--a correction.  P L 13: 402-3.

---- N. E.  Library fines.  L J 23: 185-8.

---- N. E.  One librarian's way of keeping notes.  L J 20: 306-8.

---- N. E.  Proposed classed catalog.  L J 27: Conf No 184.

---- N. E.  Shelf department.  L J 18: Conf No 82-4.

Brownbill, J. Science and art: a theory of library classification.  L C 3: 133-6.

Browning, E. G.  How women's clubs may help the library movement.  L J 24: Conf No 18-20.

Browning, E. W.  "Manifest pleasure?"  L J 44: 440-2.

------ E. W.  Some statistics from the middle west.  L J 45: 741-2.

------ E. W.  What libraries can learn from salesmanship.  N Y L 6: 128-9.

Browning, W.  Medical history repositories: a suggestion.  Med Lib and Hist Journal 5: 287-91.

Brownscombe, F. J.  Library as a factor in education.  Vt L Bull 7, No 2: 3.

Brubaker, L.  Hours of service, vacations, etc.  Mich Lib Bull 8: 84-7.

Bruce, Charles.  Althorp library.  L A U K Trans 7: 51-60; L C 2: 6-15.

Bruce, H. A.  Fairy-tale and your child.  Good Housekeeping 61: 325-31.

Bruce, W. G.  Schoolroom temperature and humidity.  Scientific American Sup 1901, 52: 214, 36-7.

Brumbaugh, M. G.  Educational principles applied to the teaching of literature.  Nat Educ Assn 1900: 169-74.

Brunner, M. A. R.  The library as a place for women (in Germany).  L W 10: 137-9.

Bruncken, E.  California's county library law.  P L 15: 329-30.

------ E.  Defective methods of legislation.  American Political Science Review May 1909.

------ E.  The Legislative reference bureau.  Cal News Notes 2: 96-105.

------ E.  New county library system of California.  P L 15: 81-2, 226-9; Library Work 1912: 139.

------ E.  Scheme of classification for books on forestry.  L J 33: 313-4.

Brunius, A.  The art of the book in Sweden.  Studio, spring number 1914: 253-5.

Brush, M. C.  Librarian in a business house.  Special Libraries 8: 83-4; P L 22: 454.

--- M. C.  The so-called librarian's real duties.  Special Libraries 8: 83-4; Am Lib Annual 1917-18: 56.

Brushfield, T. N.  Bibliography of "The history of the world," and the "Remains" of Sir Walter Raleigh.  L C 3: 8-15, 120-1.

Brusie, C. F.  Literature as a means of moral training in the schools.  Education 14: 129-37.

Bryant, S. C.  Children's reading on the use of "How to tell stories" in the home.  Home Progress Oct 1912: 42-6.

---- S. C.  Story telling.  P L 8: 167.

Bryant, W. W.  Co-operation and duties of trustees.  Mass L C Bull 3: 126-9.

Bryce, Viscount.  Guides to books: Address at L. A. U. K conference.  L A R 19: 459-62.

Brydon, J. M.  Public library architecture.  L A R 1: 258-62.

Buchanan, H.  What New Jersey is doing for public libraries.  L J 25: 173-6, 180.

Buck, G.  Children's literature course at Kansas state normal school, Emporia.  L J 41: 647-8.

-- G.  Jersey City typographic library and museum.  Printing Art 15: 189-94.

Buck, S. J.  Historical preparedness.  Minn P L C N Dec 1917: 109-12; L J 43: 293-4.

Buckland, A.  Uses of educational stories.  Educational Foundations 15: 105-12.

Buckley, A. McC.  Pictures in libraries.  Cal News Notes 4: 272-6.

Buckley, J. P.  Library and the workers.  Minn P L C N 2: 83-7; No 4: 48-9.

Bucklin, W.  A choice of modern poetry.  Minn P L C N 4: 180-3.

Buckstaff, G. A.  The business man's reading room.  Wis Lib
   Bull 8: 192-3.
Buddy, L.  Aldus Manutius and the influence of his letter.
   Printing Art 16: 459-60.
Budington, E. H.  Book selection in the university library.
   Columbia Univ Q 13: 218-23.
Budlong, M. C.  A plan of organization for small libraries.
   New Hamp Bull (ns) 12: 195-212; 13: 2-11.
   ----- M. C.  What can the League of library commissions
   do for its members?--Evaluation.  A L A Bull 13: 286-91,
   406.
Buell, D. C.  Library as an efficiency tool.  Special Libra-
   ries 6: 105-8.
   --- D. C.  Sources of information for business men.  Spec-
   ial Libraries 7: 142-4; L J 42: 223; Am Lib Annual 1917
   18: 80-1.
Buell, H. C.  Library and its functions.  Wis Lib Bull 3: 17-
   21.
Burger, P.  Retrospect of fifty years' work in German second-
   hand bookselling.  B A R 2: I-III, 1905.
Buhre, M. E.  Charging systems.  P L 1: 133.
Bull, S. B.  What any library can do for the business inter-
   ests of the town.  A L A Bull 7: 336-9.
Bullard, F.  The awakening of the young print-collector to a
   sense of beauty.  Print Collector's Quarterly 1, No 5:
   573-86.
   ----- F.  The print collection of the Museum of fine arts,
   Boston.  Print Collector's Quarterly 2, No 2: 183-206.
Bullard, F. L.  Widener memorial library.  Harper's Weekly
   56: 14  Oct 5, 1912.
Bullard, J. F.  Uniformity in library statistics.  Medical
   Lib Assn Bull Oct 1915: 21-6; L J 40: 918-9.
Bullard, M. A.  Book thieves.  L J 10: 380.
Bullard, W. I.  Women's work in war-time.  Special Libraries
   9: 2-3.
Bullen, A. H.  The Appledore private press, U. S. A.  L 1:
   13-4, 51-5.
Bullen, G.  The executives of a library--their qualifications,
   functions, vacations, salaries.  1st Int Conf 176-8, 208.
   ---- G.  On the presumed earliest printed notice of Guten-
   berg as the inventor of printing.  L A Trans 7: 25-31.
Bullen, H. L.  Histories of printing and paper in China and
   Japan.  Facsimile of Chinese woodcut printed A.D. 1331:
   portrait of Motogi, introducer of printing into Japan.
   Far Eastern Review Oct 1915: 195-7.
   ---- H. L.  Keeping the plant young.  Printing Art 14: 105-
   8.
   ---- H. L.  Typographic library and museum of the American
   type founders company.  L J 42: 279-81.

Bullen, R. F.   Library catalogues: their effects and defects.
    L A 5: 235-9.
---- R. F.   Library loans.   L A 8: 170-4.
---- R. F.   Symposium on public libraries after the war.
    L A R 19: 234-5.
Bullitt, W. M.   Suggests a Handbook of state commissions.   A
    L A Bull 11: 365.
Bullock, E.   Problems in classification.   P L 5: 6-8.
Bullock, E. D.   First county library in Nebraska.   P L 18: 16.
----- E. D.   Practical cataloguing.   P L 6: 134-8.
Bullock, E. F.   Inquisitiveness.   P L 13: 311.
Bullock, R. W.   Some observations on children's reading.   Nat
    Educ Assn 1897: 1015-21.
Bullock, W. I.   Encouragements in library work.   P L 11: 500-
    2.
Bumstead, F. M.   The equity of the service basis of charge for
    periodical indexes.   L J 42: 304-5.
Bunker, F. F.   Instruction in library administration in nor-
    mal schools.   Nat Educ Assn 1907: 363-70.
Bunn, R.   Best editions of Shakespeare for a library.   Wis
    Lib Bull 2: 21-4.
Bunnell, A.   Medical serials with bibliography of cerebro-
    spinal meningitis.   Bulletin No 99, Additions 6, N Y S L
    Rept 88.
----- A.   New York state medical library.   Med Lib and
    Hist Journal 2: 195-7.
----- A.   Practical work--New York state library school.
    N Y S L Rept 88: 591-2.   1905.
Bunting, H. M.   Reference room in a public library.   L J 28:
    115.
Burbank, C. H.   Amateur annotation.   L J 12: 254-5.
Burdick, E. E.   Educational work of the Jersey City free li-
    brary.   L J 21: 359-61.
Burgess, C. F.   Selection of technical and scientific books.
    L J 27: Conf No 56-60.
Burgess, F. W.   Cambridge College bookplates.   Connoisseur
    25: 172-3.
Burgess, G.   Battle of the books fought by collectors over
    the rare volumes of the Hoe library.   Collier's 48: 17.
Burgess, R.   The library at the School for the blind.   Minn
    P L C N 4: 4-5.
Burgess, T. C.   Means of leading boys from the dime novels to
    better literature.   L J 21: 144-7.
Burgoyne, F. J.   Choice of books for a small library.   L A R
    3: 189-97, 225-6.
------ F. J.   Library architecture from librarian's stand-
    point.   2nd Int Conf 103-5, Discussion 236-7, 1897.
------ F. J.   Library planning.   L A R 8: 178-86.
------ F. J.   On the choice of books for small libraries--
    Select list, L A R 3: 189-97, Discussion 225-6.

------ F. J.  Planning of branch libraries.  L A R 6: 72-7.

------ F. J.  Printers of England--Richard Pynson.  L A 4: 146-9.

------ F. J.  Public library architecture from the librarian's standpoint.  2nd Int Conf: 103-5, Discussion 236-7. 1897.

------ F. J.  Select list of books on electricity.  L W 2: 22-8, 53-5.

------ F. J.  Selection and purchase of books.  L W 1: 136-8, 157-9.

------ F. J.  Some points in library planning.  Greenwood's Yr-Bk: 12-20. 1900-01.

------ F. J. P.  Display and filing of periodicals.  L A 4: 197, 203-4.

------ F. J. P.  Origin of movable types.  L A 4: 130.

Burlingame, L. J.  County extension law--Wisconsin, L J 43: 83.

-------- L. J.  County library law--Indiana.  L J 43: 76-82.

-------- L. J.  Digest of library legislation.  A L A Bull 12: 261; L J 43: 74-83, corrections p. 182.

-------- L. J.  General library law--Pennsylvania.  L J 43: 81-2.

-------- L. J.  Library legislation during 1917.  L J 43: 74-83.

Burnite, C.  The beginnings of a literature for children. L J 31: 107-12.

----- C.  Book buying for a small children's library.  Lib Occ 2: 60-1.

----- C.  Good and poor books for boys and girls.  New Hamp Bull 8: 74-7; P L 11: 360-2.

----- C.  Instruction in work with children in library schools and summer schools.  A L A Bull 3: 420-7.

----- C.  Library work with children in war time.  A L A Bull 12: 95-8; L J 43: 705-7; N Y L 6: 96-8.

----- C.  Sequences in children's reading.  P L 20: 160-5; New Hamp Bull (ns) 11: 124-8.

----- C.  Standard of selection of children's books.  L J 36: 161-6.

----- C.  Values in library work with children.  A L A Bull 7: 282-7.

----- C.  The youngest children and their books.  L J 28: Conf No 215-7.

Burnite, C. M.  Tables for the reading use of boys and girls. L J 41: 447-8; Am Lib Annual 1916-17: 104-5.

Burns.  Card catalog versus printed bibliographies.  P L 7: 35.

Burns, A. L.  The empasse (sic) in library work.  Bulletin, League for Business Opportunities for Women, June 1917: 3, 9; L J 42: 838-9; Am Lib Annual 1917-18: 57.

Burns, W. S.   "Acid to casks," a few words on indexing.  L
  J 28: 664-5.
--- W. S.   Law relating to United States public documents.
  L J 32: 206-7.
Burpee, L. J.   Are reviews reliable?  L J 33: 101-2.
---- L. J.   As others see us.   Ontario Lib Assn Proceed-
  ings Ap 1912: 50-63.
---- L. J.   Bibliography in Canada.  L (ns) 6: 403-11; P
  L 10: 111-3; P L 12: 401-5.
---- L. J.   Canadian libraries and Mr. Carnegie.  P L 10:
  87.
---- L. J.   Canadian libraries of long ago.  A L A Bull
  2: 136-43; P L 13: 255-6.
---- L. J.   Canadian library news.  P L 8: 75-6, 125-6,
  175-6, 287-8, 333-4, 439-40; 9: 186.
---- L. J.   Canadian parliamentary library fire loss.  P
  L 21: 176.
---- L. J.   Canada's national library.  L J 37: 123-4.
---- L. J.   Modern methods in small libraries.  P L 9:
  217-21.
---- L. J.   On the Aberdeen association, founded for the
  distribution of good literature to settlers in isolated
  parts of Canada.  A L A Bull 4: 680-3.
---- L. J.   A plea for a national library.  Univ M 10:
  152-63.
---- L. J.   Restrictions on the use of historical mater-
  ials.  Am Hist Assn Rept 1914: 314-27.
Burr, G. L.   Special collections at Ithaca.  L J 12: 369-72.
Burrell, C. B.   The child's reading.  Harper's Bazar 33:
  1532-3.
Bursill, P. C.   Public and its libraries.  L A 4: 275-9.
----- P. C.   Staff time sheets and routine books.  L A 5:
  333-5.
----- P. C.   Treatment of periodical publications.  L A
  5: 98-101.
Burt, A.   Booksellers' catalogues.  L A R 9: 49-55.
Burt, A. G.   Newspapers.  L A R 8: 296-302.
-- A. G.   Newsroom arrangement.  L W 4: 256-64.
Burt, M. E.   Experiments in the teaching of reading.  Dial
  14: 172-3.
-- M. E.   Literature for children to the front.  Nat Educ
  Assn 1889: 253-65.
-- M. E.   The muses in the common school.  Atlantic Month-
  ly 67: 531-7.
-- M. E.   On teaching children to read.  New England Mag
  (ns) 1: 426-9.
Burton, C. P.   The ministry of books.  Lib Occ 3: 150-1.
Burton, E. D.   Library building as a memorial to President
  Harper.  Univ of Chicago Magazine 2: 251-6; Popular Science
  Monthly 77: 513-5; Univ of Chicago Magazine 4: 249-62.

---- E. D. Relation of the departmental or group libraries to the main library. L J 28: Conf No 19-23.

---- E. D. Treatment of books according to the amount of their use: relation of departmental and group libraries to the main library. L J 28: Conf No 19-23.

Burton, R. Literature for children. North American 167: 278-86.

Bush, G. G. Harvard college. U S Bureau of Education, Circular of Information 1891 No 6: 104-7.

Bushnell, C. J. The great divide: a study of present social tendencies in the United States. Wis Lib Bull 8: 190-2.

Bushnell, G. H. Ambition and library assistants. L W 22: 376-8.

Bushnell, G. H. Books, and a phase of education. L A R 22: 198-201.

Bushy, M. J. Cataloguing. P L 8: 148-50.

Butler, A. J. The Gioliti and their press at Venice. Bib Soc Trans 10: 83-107.

---- A. J. Some Elizabethan cipher books. Bib Soc Trans 6: 127-35.

Butlin, I. M. Honor system in college libraries. L J 34: 162-4.

Butz, R. H. Reading for business efficiency. Special Libraries 11: 155.

Byrne, M. J. Coloured cards for ephemeral literature. L A R 20: 46.

Byrne, M. St. C. Anthony Munday and his books. L (4th series) 1: 225-6.

--- M. St. C. The date of Anthony Munday's "Journey to Rome." L (3d series) 9: 106-15.

Byrnes, P. R. The new library of the National Bank of commerce in New York. L J 42: 976.

C. G. The Foulis exhibition. L (3d series) 4: 306-23.

C. H. B. Suggestions for a working library in religious pedagogy. Bulletin of the General Theological Seminary Oct 1915: 100-4.

Cabell, E. D. Some points on teaching literature. Educational Bi-Monthly 5: 453-9.

Caddie, A. J. Co-operation of adjoining towns for the establishment of reference libraries. L A R 3: 562-6.

---- A. J. Some further remarks on co-operation for the establishment of reference libraries. L A R 4: 237-40.

Cade, R. Carlyle's Lectures on literature: a note respecting the various manuscripts. L 4: 225-7.

Cadwallader B. A national library system with a universal catalogue. L J 1: 369-71.

--------- B. Record blanks of books loaned. L J 1: 254-5.

Cady, H. M. "Again"--The American college girls' ignorance of literature. Journal of Pedagogy 19: 231-9.

Caffin, C. H.  Instruction in printing: the use of prizes.
Printing Art 15: 349-53.
---- C. H.  Relation of printing to photography.  Printing Art 14: 253-6.
---- C. H.  Stimulating of advancement of printing by
awards.  Printing Art 15: 265-8.
Cahill, E. D.  An aspect of the work of the teacher of English.  School Review 13: 560-6.
Caine, Hall.  On public libraries.  L 8: 368-70.
Caldwell, B. D.  Greensboro public library, Carnegie building.  L J 31: 718-9; N C Lib Bull 1: 35-8.
Caldwell, G. C. and White, A. D.  What a university library
ought to be.  L J 15: 205-6.
Caldwell, Mrs. I. P.  Reaching Jeffersonville business men.
Lib Occ 5: 367-9.
Caldwell, M. H.  Gold ink marking.  P L 11: 105.
Caldwell, M. R.  Preparing books for binder.  P L 11: 302-3.
Caldwell, R. D.  State history illustrated: story hour of the
Greensboro, N. C., public library.  P L 18: 294-7.
Caldwell, W. R.  Gold ink marking.  P L 11: 24, 105.
Calhoun, A.  Development of the library movement in Alberta.
Pacific Northwest Library Assn Proceedings 1911: 59.
----- A.  Library progress in western Canada.  Pacific
Northwest Library Assn Conference Proceedings 1914: 41-3.
Calhoun, A. H.  Some phases of art work in the public library.
Pacific Northwest Library Assn Proceedings 1915: 45-9.
Calkins, M. J.  The library and its branches.  Wis Lib Bull
8: 37.
Callahan, J.  Educating all the people all the time.  Wis Lib
Bull 9: 88-92.
Cameron, A. W.  Provincial library system.  Ontario Lib Assn
Proceedings 1911: 46-54.
Cameron, M. S.  After the war: the opportunity of the Junior
Red Cross.  Wilson Bulletin 1: 347-8.
Cameron, W. H.  What does library service do for you and your
business?  P L 23: 256-7.
Camp, W. R.  Annual wild flower show at Olivia Raney library,
Raleigh, N. C.  N C Bull 4: 17-8.
Campbell, A. A.  Irish provincial printing.  Irish Book Lover
Aug 1915: 6-7.
Campbell, F.  Battle of bibliography.  L 5: 120-4.
------ F.  Bibliography of periodical literature.  L 8: 49-64.
------ F.  Education committee and the selection of textbooks (a letter).  L A R 3: 339-40.
------ F.  Need of endowed scholarships in the training
of librarians.  L 10: 115-9.
------ F.  Printed slips.  L A R 1: 755-6.
------ F.  Training of library assistants.  L A R 1: 272-3.

Campbell, F. B. F.   Bibliography of the future.  L 7: 33-48.
------ F. B. F.   L'Institut international de bibliographic.
L 7: 341-6.
------ F. B. F.   Introduction to the theory of a state
paper catalogue.  L 3: 126-43.
------ F. B. F.   Past and future papers of L. A.--our aims
and objects.  L A R 1: 4-15.
------ F. B. F.   Plea for annual lists and annual reviews
of state papers, as being essential preliminaries in state
paper catalogues.  L 4: 175-83.
------ F. B. F.   Printed catalogue slips.  L A R 1: 755-6.
Campbell, G. L.   Grouping of places for library purposes.  L
J 4: 409-10.
------ G. L.   Grouping of populous places for library pur-
poses.  L A Trans 2: 28-31.
Campbell, J. M.   Americanizing books and periodicals for im-
migrants.  A L A Bull 19: 269-72.
------ J. M.   Books for foreign population.  L J 31: Conf
No 70-2.
------ J. M.   An educational opportunity and the library.
L J 32: 157-8.
------ J. M.   Foreign periodicals.  Mass L C Bull 4: 62-9.
------ J. M.   Public library and the immigrant.  N Y L 1:
100-5, 129, 132-6.
------ J. M.   Small city library.  L J 28: Conf No 50-2.
------ J. M.   Supplying books in foreign languages in pub-
lic libraries.  L J 29: 65-7.
------ J. M.   What the foreigner has done for one library.
Mass Lib Club Bull 3: 100-6; L J 38: 610-5; New Hamp Bull
(ns) 10: 44-8.
Campbell, R. A.   Legislative and municipal reference depart-
ment.  Cal News Notes Oct 1910.
Canby, H. S.   Current literature and the colleges: for the
production of good literature intelligent readers are nec-
essary.  Harper's Mag July 1915: 230-6.
Canfield, A. C.   Book numbering without labels.  P L 3: 377.
Canfield, J. H.   Basis of taxation for public libraries.  L
J 31: Conf No 36-40.
------ J. H.   Benefits of library institutes.  L J 27: Conf
No 241-5, Discussion 242-9.
------ J. H.   Library in relation to special classes of
readers: books for foreign population.  L J 31: Conf No
65-7.
------ J. H.   Library methods in business world.  P L 11:
244-6.
------ J. H.   Library of the American university.  P L 9:
385-8.

------ J. H.  Library's part in education.  P L 14: 120.
------ J. H.  Methods of administering public libraries
for benefit of public schools.  Nat Educ Assn 1908: 1095-9.
------ J. H.  The modern college library.  Education 27:
129-35.
------ J. H.  The need for specialized libraries.  Inde-
pendent 61: 155-7.
------ J. H.  Preparation for library work.  P L 13: 351.
------ J. H.  Public libraries and the public schools.
Nat Educ Assn 1901: 836-41.
------ J. H.  Special students' reference room.  P L 12:
217-8.
------ J. H.  Specialization of libraries.  L J 28: 820-2.
------ J. H.  Treatment of books according to their use in
Columbia university.  L J 28: Conf No 170-2.
------ J. H.  The value of trained librarians.  P L 11: 64.
Cannon, C. L.  After-war needs of reference librarians.  L J
43: 387-9.
Cannons, H. G. T.  Library lectures.  L W 13: 113-4.
----- H. G. T.  Pseudonyms and real names.  L W 1: 234-5;
2: 216-7.
----- H. G. T.  Select list of books of shorthand.  L W 2:
76-9.
----- H. G. T.  Select list of books on practical and his-
torical printing, book illustration and paper manufacture.
L W 2: 245-8, 270-2.
----- H. G. T.  Selection of books and editions for child-
ren.  L A R 20: 68-73.
Canon, E. T.  How to get the best books read.  P L 19: 96-8;
New Hamp Bull 10: 21-3; Wis Lib Bull 10: 140-1.
Cansler, Charles W.  Lawson McGhee library: opening address
by Charles W. Cansler.  P L 24: 5-8.
Capek, A. V.  The immigrant's contribution to American culture.
A L A Bull 13: 387.
Capelli.  Circulating library in every Commune: Capelli library
law.  P L 20: 131-2.
Capes, W. P.  The Bureau of municipal information of New York
state conference of mayors, etc; its functions and accom-
plishments.  A L A Bull 12: 321-9.
Carabin, M. A.  Detroit Edison company's library.  Special Li-
braries 7: 123-40; Am Lib Annual 1917-18: 35-6.
----- M. A.  Looking forward with the S. L. A.  L J 45: 391-5.
Carey, M. E.  From camp to camp: the work of a field representative.  A L A Bull 12: 225-6.
--- M. E.  In the land of counterpane: books for crippled
children's library.  The Nurse Dec 1916: 389-91.
--- M. E.  Libraries and their management in state hospitals.  Modern Hospital 1915, Vol 5, No 6: Am Lib Annual
1916-17: 61-2; L J 41: 854-5.

--- M. E.  Libraries in state institutions.  A L A Bull 1: Conf No 101-8; P L 12: 127-8; Minn P L C N 2: 67-70.

--- M. E.  Libraries in state laboratory, Woods Hole, Mass. Special Libraries 8: 160, 170.

--- M. E.  A library in Nebraska state hospital.  P L 25: 203.

--- M. E.  A new phase of library work.  P L 12: 127-8.

--- M. E.  A note about a library in a prison.  L J 41: 779; P L 21: 317.

--- M. E.  Possibilities of library work in state institutions.  N Y L 3: 222-7.

--- M. E.  What men read in hospitals.  A L A Bull 12: 222; L J 43: 565-7; P L 23: 364-5.

Cargill, J. V.  Seven-day book: why not transfer it?  Wis Lib Bull 2: 44-6.

Carleton, E. F.  Public school libraries of Oregon.  School and Home Education 28: 207-9.

Carlile, W. B.  To keep faith with the fallen.  P L 25: 321.

Carlin, J. W.  Advertising a public library.  American City (Country ed) 17: 122-3.

Carlton, P. H.  Relation of the college library to the student. Educational Review 33: 202-6.

Carlton, W. N. C.  The American library institute and the research problem.  L J 44: 203-6.

----- W. N. C.  The child's world of books:  papers presented at the conference held during the Chicago welfare exhibit.  Chicago Sch Civics and Philanthropy, 1912 part 7.

----- W. N. C.  College libraries and college librarians: views and comments.  L J 31: 751-7.

----- W. N. C.  College libraries in the mid-nineteenth century.  L J 32: 479-86.

----- W. N. C.  The Newberry library children's room. Educational Bi-Monthly 4: 296-300.

----- W. N. C.  Prestige.  A L A Bull 8: 169-79.

----- W. N. C.  Universities and librarians.  P L 20: 451-6.

Carman, B.  Poetry and the spoken word.  N Y L 5: 11-4.

Carman, F. A.  Our archives and the national spirit.  Canadian Mag 40: 307-16.

Carnahan, H. L.  Library publicity.  Cal News Notes 5: 379-81.

Carnegie, A.  Library as a field for philanthropy.  L J 15: 42-3.

------ A.  On dead books.  L J 37: 74.

------ A.  The public library as a social force.  Wis Lib Bull 11: 181-2.

------ A.  On public libraries.  L 8: 501-4.

Carney, F.  Some problems of a shelf department.  L J 33: 433-7.

Carpenter. How best the rare books in private libraries may be made available for students. L J 25: 26.

Carpenter, F. O. The library the centre of the schools. Education 26: 110-4.

Carpenter, H. F. Picture and clipping collections. Wis Lib Bull 9: 10-3; New Hamp Bull 10: 6-9.

Carpenter, M. F. Disinfecting books. Wis Lib Bull 7: 35.
------- M. F. The librarian's hours. Wis Lib Bull 10: 74-5.
------- M. F. Notes for librarians: Reading clubs. Wis Lib Bull 13: 55-6; Vt L Bull 13: 2-3.
------- M. F. Picture and clipping collections. Wis Lib Bull 9: 10-3; New Hamp Bull (ns) 10: 6-9.
------- M. F. Picture collections. Wis Lib Bull 7: 123-7.
------- M. F. Picture exhibits. Wis Lib Bull 11: 280-1.
------- M. F. Pictures of the Scott country. Wis Lib Bull 10: 118, 212-3.
------- M. F. Publicity in college and school libraries. Wis Lib Bull 13: 14-7.
------- M. F. Shakespeare pictures. Wis Lib Bull 12: 112-5.
------- M. F. Some recent German books. Wis Lib Bull 9: 198-201.
------- M. F. Vacation privileges. Wis Lib Bull 12: 239.
------- M. F. Wisconsin documents. Wis Lib Bull 7: 143-4.

Carpenter, W. H. Latin-Americana in the library of Columbia university. L J 44: 224.

Carr, B. E. Formation of a financial library. Special Libraries 10: 125-7.
-- B. E. Some aspects of a financial library. L J 35: 10-2.

Carr, F. F. Publicity through exhibits. Minn P L C N 4: 212-4.
-- F.F. Re-registration of borrowers. Minn P L C N 4: 13-4.

Carr, H. J. Being a librarian. P L 6: 459-61.
-- H. J. Book storage and shelving. U S Rept: 735-8.
-- H. J. Book trucks. U S Rept: 742, 1892-3.
-- H. J. Buying books by library boards. L J 14: 41-2.
-- H. J. Classification and notation of the book arts. L J 9: 172.
-- H. J. Counters and delivery desks. U S Rept: 738. 1892-93.
-- H. J. Disinfection by formalin at Scranton public library. L J 25: 71-2.

-- H. J.  Fixtures, furniture and fittings.  U S Bureau of Education Report 1892-93: 742.

-- H. J.  Index to some recent reference lists.  L J 8: 27-32.

-- H. J.  Necrological records of A. L. A. members.  A L A Bull 1, No 5: 65; 2: 107, 123-5; 3: 113.

-- H. J.  Office and catalogue desks.  U S Rept: 739, 1892-93.

-- H. J.  Pamphlet boxes.  U S Rept 1892-3: 742.

-- H. J.  Preservation and care of newspaper clippings.  L J 26: 872-3.

-- H. J.  Presidential address.  L J 26: Conf No 1-5.

-- H. J.  Reading desks.  U S Rept: 738. 1892-93.

-- H. J.  Registration of book borrowers.  L J 12: 340-4.

-- H. J.  Report on charging systems (Bibliography).  L J 14: 203-14.

-- H. J.  Report on collections of the minor literature of local history.  L J 19: Conf No 67-9.

-- H. J.  Revised list of members.  L J 34: 219-20.

-- H. J.  Tables.  U S Rept: 738-9. 1892-3.

Carr, J. F.  Books in foreign languages and Americanization.  L J 44: 245-6.

-- J. F.  A greater American Library Association.  L J 45: 775-8, 979, 981-2.

-- J. F.  The library and the immigrant.  A L A Bull 8: 140-7; New Hamp Bull 10: 41-4; P L 19: 276-9.

-- J. F.  Library work for immigrants.  A L A Bull 10: 273-6, 402.

-- J. F.  "Making Americans": a preliminary and tentative list.  L J 45: 209-12.

-- J. F.  The nation's need and the library's opportunity.  N Y L 5: 192-4.

-- J. F.  Shall public libraries buy books in foreign languages?  Minn P L C N 6: 8-9.

-- J. F.  Some of the people we work for.  L J 41: 552-7.

-- J. F.  What the library can do for our foreign born.  Penn Lib Notes 7, No 3: 2-6.

-- J. F.  What the library can do for our foreigners.  Mass Lib Club Bull 3: 94-9; L J 38: 566-8.

Carrick, A. V.  "Bequest on wings": Howe library, Hanover, N. H.  House Beautiful 41: 77-9.

----- A. V.  Library that is the life of a town: Howe library, Dartmouth, N. H.  Country Life 37: 54-5.

Carrington, F.  The appreciation of prints.  Mass L C Bull 6: 16-8; L J 41: 513-4.

Carrington, J. T.  Scientific books in public libraries.  L 6: 80-1.

Carroll, M.  Paul Bartlett's decorative sculptures for the New York public library.  Art and Archaeology 3: 34-9.

Carruth, W. H.  College credit for browsing.  School and Society 1: 660-4.

Carson, J. M.  The children's share in a public library.  L J 37: 251-6.

Carson, M. D.  The case against the librarian: Pennsylvania compensation rating and inspection bureau.  Special Libraries 11: 68.

Carson, V.  Library at the Home school for girls.  Minn P L C N 4: 3-4.

Carson, W. O.  Revised Public libraries act for the Province of Ontario.  L A R 22: 284-5.

---- W. O.  Status and training of the public librarian.  Ontario Library Association Proc. April, 1912: 106-14.

Carter, A. F.  Cataloguing pictures.  P L 9: 116.

---- A. F.  A few notes on book selection.  Colorado Lib Assn Occasional Leaflet 1: 84-6.

Carter, A. H.  The polytechnic and public libraries of London.  L A 1: 16-9.

Carter, B.  Discussion on the principles and practice of reference library work.  L A R 8: 181-3.

---- B.  Military libraries.  L W 2: 233-5.

---- B.  Naval libraries.  L W 2: 290-2.

---- B.  School libraries.  L W 8: 29-34.

Carter, E.  Township library extension.  P L 15: 175-80.

Carter, Mrs. E. S.  Gates memorial library.  Port Arthur, Texas.  L J 43: 400-2.

---- Mrs. E. S.  The high school library and its possibilities.  Texas Libraries 2: 68-71; P L 22: 43-4.

---- Mrs. E. S.  Relation of the high school library to the modern educational movement.  Texas Libraries 2: 103-6.

Carter, G. H.  Letter from U. S. Congress Joint-committee on printing.  A L A Bull 11: 350-2; Resolution, 353.

---- G. H.  The printing bill.  A L A Bull 10: 3012, 444, Discussion 446.

---- G. H.  Purpose and scope of the codification of the printing laws as contained in the printing bill.  A L A Bull 8: 255-62; L J 39: 815-23.

Carter, H. J.  Travelling libraries of illustrations.  L J 22: 293.

Carter, S. J.  Library work: its penalties and perquisites.  Wis Lib Bull 15: 224-9.

Carter, W. T.  In defence of the public library.  Libn 1: 72-4.

---- W. T.  Library legislation: a provincial point of view.  L A R 12: 221-3.

Carver, E.  Library advertising.  Penn Lib Notes 2, No 3: 2-5.

Carver, M. L.  Twenty years of library work.  Maine Lib Bull
   3, No 4: 6-8.
Cary, C. P.  Educating all the people all the time.  Harper's
   Weekly May 22, 1909.  53: 72-81.
   -- C. P.  Libraries and library privileges for village and
   rural communities.  Nat Educ Assn 1905: 854-7.
   -- C. P.  Qualifications for librarian.  Wis Lib Bull 7:
   134.
Case, C. M.  The child and the book.  Ia L C Bull 8: 177-83.
Case, F. M.  Basis of selection of an elementary school li-
   brary.  Nat Educ Assn 1915: 1075-8.
Cashmore, R. M.  A provincial point of view.  L A 11: 14-7.
Caspar, C. N.  Hints for finding the author, title, publisher,
   place of publication, size or price of books.  L J 10:
   180-1.
Castro, J. P. de.  Henry Fielding's last voyage.  L (3d series)
   8: 145-59.
   ---- J. P. de.  The printing of Fielding's works.  L (4th
   series) 1: 257-70.
Catlin, G. B.  Library of the Detroit News.  Special Libraries
   11: 161-3.
   ---- G. B.  A live newspaper library: The Detroit News Li-
   brary.  L J 42: 287-8.
Catlin, M.  Library club-room for men.  Wis Lib Bull 2: 29-
   30.
Cattell, S. W.  Work in Young women's Christian association
   libraries.  L J 17: Conf No 91-2; L J 19: 121-4.
   ----- S. W. and A. B. Kroeger.  Aids to book selection.
   Penn L Comm Bull 1: 7-9.
Catterall, R. C. H.  Some recent literature on Oliver Crom-
   well.  Bib Soc Chic Yr-Bk 1900-1: 32-50.
Cavannagh, A. B.  Literature in the primary grades.  School
   and Home Education 28: 330-2.
Cavannaugh, J.  A plea for the classics.  P L 18: 1-6, 45-9.
Cawthorne, A.  Lecture work in connection with libraries.  L
   A 12: 40-2, 52-8; L A R 17: 128-9.
Center, M.  Walla Walla public library.  Wash L A Bull 2 No
   1: 8-9 il.
Certain, C. C.  Public school libraries.  L J 42: 359-65.
   ----- C. C.  School library situation in the South.  A L
   A Bull 10: 295-9, 432.
   ----- C. C.  A standard high school library organization
   for accredited secondary schools of different sizes.  Edu-
   cational Administration and Supervision.  June 1917: 317-
   58; Educational Review 54: 76-82.
   ----- C. C.  Standard library organization and equipment
   for secondary schools of different sizes.  Nat Educ Assn
   1918: 691-719.
   ----- C. C.  Status of the library in southern high schools.
   L J 40: 632-7.

Chadburn, I.   Book selection committee for juvenile literature in Germany.  L A R 9: 56-69.

Chadsey, C. E.   What does each library and public library
contribute to the making of an educated man?  Nat Educ
Assn 1909: 860-3.

Chadwick, J. R.   The Boston medical library.  il. Med Lib and
Hist Journal 1: 127-35.

Chamberlain, A. D.   Work with schools.  Vt L Bull 4, No 2:
1-4.

Chamberlain, A. H.   Increasing the efficiency of the library
as an educational factor.  A L A Bull 5: 154-63; N Y .L 3:
8-11.

Chamberlain, E. J.   Displaying wild flowers.  Vt L Bull 14:
10-1; L J 43: 690-1.

--------- E. J.   A new plan for high school libraries.
Vt L Bull 16: 27.

Chamberlain, F. W.   Sunday school library charging system.
P L 5: 58-9.

Chamberlain, J. P.   Legislative drafting and reference bureaus.
Survey 37: 386-8.

Chamberlain, L. T.   Sunday school libraries: charging system.
L J 6: 159-60.

Chamberlain, M.   An address on the danger of sensational fiction.  L J 4: 362-6.

--------- M.   Public library and public school.  L J 5:
292-302.

Chamberlain, M. C.   State library for the blind.  N Y L 1:
142-4.

Chamberlain, M. J.   Fiction in libraries.  L J 4: 362-6.

--------- M. J.   Report on fiction.  L J 8: 208-10.

Chambers, R. W.   Library of the University college, London.
L A R 11: 350-8, 361-3.

Chambers, W. G.   Anomalies of library nomenclature ( a letter).
L A 6: 4 See also 185-6.

------ W. G.   Branches.  L A R 10: 211-2.

------ W. G.   Catalogue annotations.  L A 5: 116-7.

------ W. G.   Dress in the library.  L W 11: 242.

------ W. G.   Hours of library assistants.  L W 2: 310-1.

------ W. G.   Library assistants association.  Greenwood's
Yr-Bk: 614. 1900-01.

------ W. G.   The new Public libraries bill.  L A 10: 25-
6.

------ W. G.   Registration: an urgent need.  L A 6: 41-2.

------ W. G.   Registration of librarians.  L W 10: 241-3.

------ W. G.   Registration: the classification difficulty.
L A R 11: 1-2.

------ W. G.   Should library appointments be put out to
tender?  L A R 10: 375-6.

------ W. G.  Staff time sheets.  L A R 10: 218-20.
------ W. G.  Value of the linotype for catalogue printing.
L A R 9: 402-3.
------ W. G.  Wanted--a binding cloth.  L A R 10: 482-3.
Champkins, A. W.  Indexing of lantern slides: some brief notes.
L W 17: 79-80.
Champlin, G. C.  Camp library at Plattsburg.  N Y L 6: 12-3.
Chance, F.  Preservation of bookbindings.  L J 12: 71.
Chandler, A. C.  Library art club.  L J 24: 521-3.
Chandler, A. E.  Woman's education association.  L J 20: 305-
6, 310.
Chandler, A. G.  The country library versus the donor and the
architect.  Mass Lib Club Bull Mch, 1915: 10-7; Am Lib An-
nual 1916-17: 26-7.
------ A. G.  Duties and opportunities of library trustees.
Mass L C Bull 2, No 5: Oct 1912: 106-16.
------ A. G.  Helping the small library in Massachusetts.
New Hamp Bull (ns) 12: 153-9.
------ A. G.  Library art club--co-operative work of New
England libraries.  L J 24: 521-2.
Chandler, E. M.  "Do," advice based on experience of librarians.
L J 21: Conf No 43-6.
Chapin, A. M.  Cataloging in a small city library.  A L A Bull
5: 218-20; N Y L 3: 13-4.
---- A. M.  Charging system without borrower's card.  L J
44: 545.
Chapin, M.  How the Owatonna, Minn., library gets publicity.
Wis Lib Bull 8: 139-40.
Chapin, W. O.  The print collection of the Albright art gal-
lery, Boston.  Print Collector's Quarterly 2, No 1: 50-5.
Chapman, C. E.  South America as a field for an historical
survey.  Am Hist Assn Rept 1916, 1: 203-9.
Chapman, J. J.  Children's books.  A L A Bull 10: 122-5, 381.
Chapman, S. J.  Some thoughts on the value of public libraries.
L A R 3: 233-8.
Charlton, H. B.  A textual note on "Love's labour's lost."
L (3d series) 8: 355-70.
Chartres, W. W.  Changing fashions in dime novel substitutes.
L J 43: 215-7.
Chase, C. H.  Changes in lighting at Lynn (Mass.) public li-
brary.  L J 29: 562.
--- C. H.  Government collection of reconstruction infor-
mation offered to the business world.  L J 44: 456.
Chase, S. F.  The choice of reading for the early adolescent
years.  Nat Educ Assn 1898: 1011-9.
Chauvin, V.  What a bibliography should be.  L J 17: 87-8.
Checketts, H. W.  The encyclopaedia, iconographic and general
record work of the Brussels institute; with possible application of the institute's work in Great Britain.  L A 9:
49-54.

Checketts, H. W.  The library in utopia.  L A 7: 193-4, 207.
------- H. W.  Non-municipal side of the library profes-
sion; its scope and prospects.  Libn 1: 161-5, 204-6.
Cheeseman, J.  Harmony in type.  Printing Art 16: 350-1.
Cheever, W. H.  Use and abuse of school libraries.  P L 2:
349-51.
Chenery, W. H.  A librarian's papers: Review of Dr. Bostwick's
two books.  L J 45: 933-4.
Cheney, C. P.  Association of Sunday school libraries.  L J
10: 123, 125.
Cheney, F. E.  Mental deficiency and eugenics.  Mass L C Bull
3: 130-5.
Cheney, J. V.  Method of cataloguing U.S. public documents
and the periodicals in the San Francisco public library.
L J 16: Conf No 61-2.
Chennell, F. E.  Few words on the censor in the library.  L
W 2: 316.
------ F. E.  Foreign section in the public library.  L
W 2: 33-5.
------ F. E.  The lady assistant--a rejoinder.  L W 4:
319-22.
------ F. E.  Lady assistants in public libraries.  L W
4: 245-8.
------ F. E.  Public library age limit.  L W 2: 175-7.
------ F. E.  Woes of a librarian.  L A 3: 56-61.
------ F. E.  The woman assistant again.  L W 5: 40-3.
Chesney, L. D.  Picture collections.  Vt L Bull 3, No 2: 3-
4.
Child, G. A.  Mounted pictures and picture bulletins.  Conn
P L D No 8: 47-52.
Child, M.  Mr. Spectator and Shakespeare.  L (ns) 6: 360-79.
Child, W. B.  Reference work at the Columbia College library.
L J 16: 298.
Chiles, R. P.  National archives: are they in peril?  Rev of
Revs 45: 209-13.
Chitham, F.  Libraries in business houses.  L A 12: 172-5;
Special Libraries 7: 98-9.
Chittenden, G. E.  Official library at Railway administra-
tion headquarters, South Africa.  Special Libraries 11:
9-12.
Chivers, C.  Binding and paper of library books: review.  L
A 7: 218-9.
----- C.  How to open a book.  L (ns) 1: 323-6.
----- C.  Library bookbinding.  L A R 7: 559-62.
----- C.  Materials and methods in bookbinding.  A L A
Bull 5: 164-79, Discussion 179.
----- C.  Methods of preserving old or valued bindings.
L (ns) 6: 208-11.
----- C.  Nature and value of good binding.  Wis Lib Bull
9: 204.

----- C. The other side of the bookbinding controversy in New York. L J 33: 444-5.

----- C. Paper and binding of lending library books. A L A Bull 3: 231-9; L J 34: 350-4; P L 15: 192-3; L (3d series) 1: 222-4.

----- C. Practical bookbinding. L A 1: 171, 302.

----- C. Relative value of leather and other binding materials. L A R 13: 415-30, 508-9.

Choate, C. W. The library's opportunity to interest young people in better things. Ia L C Q July 1912: 209-12.

---- C. W. Reading the indicator. Ia L C Q 7: 193-5.

Cholmeley, R. F. Bad books. L (ns) 5: 225-38.

------- R. F. A book of snobs. L (ns) 6: 391-402.

------- R. F. Boys' libraries. L (ns) 4: 11-21.

Chorton, J. Rating of public libraries--a letter. L A R 4: 477-8.

Christie, R. C. Catalogue of the library of the Duc·de la Valliere. L C 1: 153-9.

------ R. C. A dynasty of librarians. L 1: 97-101.

------ R. C. Elzevir bibliography. L C 5: 117-23; L 10: 56-7.

------ R. C. An Incunabulum of Brescia, hitherto ascribed to Florence. Bib Soc Trans 4: 233-7.

------ R. C. Old church and school libraries of Lancashire. L A U K Trans 6: 45-7; L C 13: 15-7.

------ R. C. Presidential address. L 1: 353-66.

------ R. C. Special bibliographies. Bib Soc Trans 1: 165-77.

------ R. C. Work and aims of the Library association: an address. L 1: 360-1.

Christison, J. Factors contributing to the success of a public library. L W 17: 102-8; L A R 13: 438-43, 509.

Christopher, K. M. Use of the library in the Julia Richman high school library. L J 44: 146-8.

Chubb, P. Reading of high school boys and girls. P L 16: 134-8.

--- P. Value and place of fairy stories in the education of children. Nat Educ Assn 1905: 871-9.

Church, A. J. Gaslight and bindings. L J 3: 64-5.

Church, H. O. The use of scientific material in the high school course in English. School Review 21: 461-6.

Churchill, J. A. Relation of the high school library to modern educational aims. Nat Educ Assn 1918: 457-9.

------- J. A. State supervision of school libraries. Nat Educ Assn 1917: 572-6; P L 23: 146-9.

Churchill, W. Mission of the public library. L J 28: 115-6.

Chute, G. What a library can mean to an institution child. Minn P L C N 4: 1-3.

Claflin, A. B. Financial institutions. Special Libraries 11: 79-81.

Clapp. Advantages of a dictionary catalog to the public.
Minn P L C N 3: 187.

Clapp, C. B.  Arrangement of cards under place names in a dictionary catalog.  L J 38: 73-7.

--- C. B.  The Group system: or, Catalog at the shelves.
L J 39: 430-5.

--- C. B.  Handling library of Congress card orders in the
average library.  L J 41: 463-8.

--- C. B.  Sources of commercial information.  L J 36: 461-
2.

Clapp, J. M.  Bibliography of English fiction in the 18th century.  Amer Bib Soc Papers 6: 37-56.

Clapworthy, L. M.  Cataloguing.  P L 9: 107-8.

Clark, A.  Librarian and the public.  Lib Occ 2: 70-1.

Clark, A. W.  Review of F. Madan's "Books in manuscript," 2d
edition.  L (4th series) 1: 123-8.

--- A. W.  The story hour.  L J 34: 164-5.

Clark, B. H.  The Drama league and the libraries.  Bull Bib
8: 182-3.

--- B. H.  Some unusual experiences in the work of a blind
librarian.  L J 33: 393-4.

Clark, C. H.  Hibbing's traveling library.  Minn P L C N 6:
57-9.

Clark, E.  Early books on agriculture.  Bib Soc Trans 3: 160-
2.

Clark, E. E.  Considerations on the card catalogue and library
construction.  L J 17: 229-32.

Clark, E. M.  Relation of the library to the country life problem.  Vt L Bull 7, No 4: 4-6.

Clark, G. M.  Children's literary club of Muncie, Indiana.
Lib Occ 1, No 8: 4-5.

Clark, G. T.  The child in the public library.  P L 1: 310-1,
312.

--- G. T.  Lessons from destruction of San Francisco libraries.  A L A Bull 1: Conf No 121-3.

--- G. T.  Letter on his Japanese experiences. Cal News Notes 15: 147-8.

--- G. T.  Method of school circulation of library books.
L J 31: 155-7.

--- G. T.  New library building at Leland Stanford Junior
University.  L J 44: 714-7.

Clark, H.  Does a small library need the Harvard classics?
Ia L C Q 8: 103-6.

Clark, H. C.  Publication of Revolutionary military records: report.  Am Hist Assn Rept 1915: 191-9.

Clark, J. A.  Agricultural college libraries.  Association of American Agricultural Colleges and Experiment Stations. 15th Proceedings, Washington, 1901: 35-7.

Clark, J. T.  Employment of young women in public libraries. L J 4: 410.

--- J. T.  Notes on the early printing in Scotland, 1507-1600.  L A Trans 3: 22-9.

Clark, J. W.  Evolution of bookcases.  L A R 7: 555-8.

Clark, L.  Pictures for children's rooms in libraries and schools.  Mich Lib Bull 7: 154-7.

Clark, M.  How one township library sends out books.  Lib Occ 2: 55-6.

--- M.  Literature for agricultural reference work.  P L 21: 120-1.

Clark, M. C.  Literature in the high school.  Nat Educ Assn 1889: 265-74.

--- M. C.  Ministration of literature.  Nat Educ Assn 1887: 417-27.

Clark, M. V.  Books by the yard.  Nation 106: 398-9.

Clark, N. A.  Bulletin boards from the decorative point of view.  P L 8: 313.

Clark, O. E.  Book labelling.  L W 10: 67-9.

Clark, S. H.  University libraries.  P L 15: 120-1.

Clark, S. N. and S. R. Warren.  Common school libraries.  U S Govt Report 38-58, 1876.

--- S. N. and S. R. Warren.  Libraries in prisons and re-formatories.  U S Govt Rept 218-29, 1876.

Clark, S. T.  Lessons as to library construction and equipment from the San Francisco fire.  L J 32: 258-9; P L 12: 255-7.

Clark, V. E.  An index to agricultural periodicals.  A L A Bull 9: 162-3.

--- V. E.  Technical books for public libraries.  Ia L C Q 7: 11-2.

Clark, W. B.  Book thieving and mutilation.  L J 4: 249-50, 377.

Clark, W. S.  What the district superintendent can do for school libraries.  New York State Teachers' Assn Proceedings 1912: 125-33, Discussion 134-7; N Y L 3: 269-71.

Clarke, A.  Examination of library assistants.  L 9: 130-1.

---- A.  Lessing as a librarian.  L (ns) 2: 376-83.

---- A.  The philosophical classification of literature as compared with practical schemes of classification.  L A R 2: 347-56.

---- A.  Reputed first circulating subscription library in London.  L (ns) 1: 274-89.

---- A.  Scientific text-books and the disposal of editions out-of-date.  L 6: 164-7.

---- A. Some old treatises on libraries and librarians'
work. L 10: 327-9, 385-95.

---- A. Work of academies of literature and their connection with libraries. L A R 1: 286-93.

Clarke, A. B. The library and higher education. Library Miscellany (Baroda) 1: 74-7.

---- A. B. Situation between the schools and the library
from the school standpoint. P L 19: 119.

Clarke, A. E. On Allibone's "Critical dictionary of English
literature." L (ns) 5: 419-30.

Clarke, A. L. Abstracts and extracts in general and professional literature. L A R 13: 37-54.

---- A. L. Arrangement of place-name entries in subject
catalogues, indexes and directories. L (3d series) 4: 221-
34; L A R 15: 270-81.

---- A. L. Essays on indexing. L W 5: 265-7, 286-91; L
W 6: 67-70, 123-6, 156-8, 181-90; L W 7: 2-8, 29-31, 60-5,
123-5.

---- A. L. Leland and Henry VIII. L (3rd series) 2: 132-
49.

---- A. L. Public lending libraries for the city of London. L (ns) 3: 135-40.

---- A. L. Reference, in its relation to literature, to
bibliography, to subject indexes and to systems of classification. L A R 14: 73-95.

---- A. L. Reform in indexing methods. L W 9: 317-20.

---- A. L. Reputed first circulating library in London.
L (ns) 1: 274-83.

---- A. L. Some aspects of military bibliography. L A R
18: 438-58.

---- A. L. Some points in practical bibliography. L A R
6: 192-205.

---- A. L. Subsidised indexing. L (ns) 6: 274-80.

Clarke, C. P. Access to museum material. P L 13: 214-5.

Clarke, D. E. and J. D. Stewart. Terminological dictionaries.
L W 12: 87-92.

Clarke, E. Departmental libraries: Division of labour within
the library. L J 16: 264-8.

---- E. Family letters of Oliver Goldsmith. Bib Soc Trans
15: 11-58.

---- E. New lights on Chatterton. Bib Soc Trans 13: 219-
51.

Clarke, E. C. Government publications as seen in libraries:
with a program of betterment in the public printing. A L
A Bull 10: 312-9, 444.

Clarke, E. E. Boards of library trustees. Vt L Bull 2, No
3: 1-3.

---- E. E.  Corporate entry.  L J 22: 434-5.

---- E. E.  Departmental arrangement of college libraries.
L J 11: 340-3; L J 14: 340-3; L J 16: 264-8.

---- E. E.  Good and bad points of the printing bill.  P
L 22: 19-21.

---- E. E.  Guide to the use of United States government
publications: Review by F. R. Curtis.  P L 23: 429.

---- E. E.  Library of the library school: an index of its
work.  L J 23: Conf No 125-7.

---- E. E.  Proposed public document legislation.  P L 20:
262-3.

---- E. E.  Signor Chilovi's plan for new Library of Florence.  L J 17: 483-4.

---- E. E.  United States public documents and their catalogues.  L J 31: 317.

---- E. E.  Woman in literature at the fair, from the
standpoint of a librarian and cataloger.  L J 19: 47-9.

Clarke, E. F.  Auburn, New York, State prison library.  L J
44: 188.

---- E. F.  Books for the prison library.  N Y L 3: 235-6.

Clarke, E. P.  Advertising the library.  L W 22: 312-3.

---- E. P.  Browne charging system--a further word.  L J
24: 478-9.

---- E. P.  The library and the school.  P L 4: 116-8.

---- E. P.  The library in industry.  L W 21: 152-3.

---- E. P.  Periodicals: their selection and purchase.  N
Y L 4: 108-10.

---- E. P.  Story telling, reading aloud, and other special
features of work with children.  L J 27: 189-90.

Clarke, G.  Libraries and books.  Lib Miscellany 1: 17-20.

Clarke, G. G.  Birmingham university library.  L A R 18: 404-
5.

---- G. G.  Bristol university library.  L A R 18: 405-6.

---- G. G.  Durham university library.  L A R 18: 406-7.

---- G. G.  Leeds university library.  L A R 18: 407-8.

---- G. G.  Liverpool university library.  L A R 18: 409-
11.

---- G. G.  London university library.  L A R 18: 411-4.

---- G. G.  Sheffield university library.  L A R 18: 417-
8.

---- G. G.  University libraries of England (Oxford and
Cambridge excepted).  L A R 18: 403-8.

Clarke, G. M.  Nature study as a phase of library work.  Vt
Lib Bull 12: 13-18.

Clarke, G. T.  Improper books: methods employed to discover
and exclude them.  L J 20: Conf No 33-5.

---- G. T.  Methods of school circulation of library books.
L J 31: 155-7.

Clarke, J. F.  Address on reading.  L J 4: 355-7.

Clarke, M.  How one township library sends out books.  Lib Occ
2: 55-6.

Clarke, O. E.  The aim and foundation of the Institut international de bibliographie.  L A 9: 42-6.

---- O. E.  Book labelling.  L W 10: 67-9.

---- O. E.  Diary of an Easter pilgrimage.  L A 8: 92-5,
141-5.

---- O. E.  The Easter school in Holland.  L A 10: 85-9,
110-5, 143-7.

---- O. E.  English publishing trade bibliographies.  L W
13: 197-201.

---- O. E.  Impressions of the international congresses.
L W 13: 107-9, 141-2.

---- O. E.  Learning to catalogue.  L A 6: 116-21, Discussion 122-3.

---- O. E.  Librarianship for women.  L A 8: 24-5.

---- O. E.  The modern book.  L A 7: 266-70.

---- O. E.  Our second great adventure.  L A 9: 99-105, 111-
9.

---- O. E.  The signed article.  L W 18: 106-7.

---- O. E.  Story telling.  L W 13: 168-70.

---- O. E.  The unborn to-morrow.  L W 14: 18-20.

---- O. E.  Women assistants and the war.  L W 17: 240-1.

---- O. E. and J. D. Stewart.  Book selection.  L A 7: 115.

---- O. E. and J. D. Stewart.  Guides to book selection.
L W 11: 409-17, 445-50.

---- O. E. and J. D. Stewart.  Terminological dictionaries.
L W 12: 87-92.

Clarke, W. S.  What the district superintendent can do for
school libraries.  N Y L 3: 269-71.

Clatworthy, L. M.  Cataloging.  P L 9: 107-9.

-------- L. M.  Library course given to city normal school
students.  L J 31: 160-3.

-------- L. M.  Ohio libraries in the flood.  L J 38: 594,
602-7.

-------- L. M.  Reference work.  L J 31 Conf No 263-5.

Claude, L. W.  Some recent development in small library design.  Wis Lib Bull 4: 9-11.

Claudin, A.  On the first Paris printing press: an account of
the books printed for G. Fichet and J. Heynlin in the Sor-
bonne, 1470-1472.  Bib Soc Trans 3: 162-5.  Also issued
as the Bibliographical Society's Illustrated Monograph No
6, 1896.

Clawson, C. R.  Departmental libraries.  P L 17: 363-4.

Claxton, P. F.  Teacher-librarian courses in normal schools.
L J 41: 521.

Claxton, P. P.  Books for those who need them most.  N Y L 3:
130; L J 37: 585.

----- P. P. County libraries, U S Commissioner of Education Report 1913, pt 1: XXXVIII-IX.

----- P. P. For "Good collections of the best books." L J 45: 273.

----- P. P. Libraries for rural communities. A L A Bull 8: 147-52; New Hamp Bull (ns) 11: 93-4.

----- P. P. A plea for the establishment of county libraries throughout the United States. N Y L 3: 139-41.

----- P. P. The right arm of the prison school. N Y L 3: 238.

----- P. P. Some needed extension of the public library. L J 37: 201-2.

Clayton, R. H. The public technical library. L A R 21: 5-8.

Cleland, E. Indiana legislative reference work. Special Libraries 1: 58-60.

----- E. Indianapolis business branch birthday party. P L 24: 127.

----- E. A sociology seminar. L J 45: 397-8.

Cleland, T. M. The fine art of printing. A L A Bull 9: 104-11.

Clemens, H. Dr. Crowther and the librarian. P L 16: 371-3.

----- H. Statement of A. L. A. representative in Siberia. A L A Bull 13: 221-3.

Clement, C. B. What about fiction in our public libraries? New Hamp Bull 11: 158-9.

Clement, C. H. Libraries for state institutions. Vermont Lib Bull 8 No 1: 4-5.

Clifford, F. W. Library of the Chemical Society. L A R 18: 228-31.

Clizbe, J. A church library. L J 7: 86.

Cloud, E. Children's work in a small library. P L 25: 65-7.

Cloud, J. Renewals, transfers and sevenday books. Minn P L C N No 9: 28-9.

Clough, W. G. Directing the reading of the young. Wis Lib Bull 1: 50-1.

---- W. G. Library and the schools. Wis Lib Bull 7: 138-42.

---- W. G. Progress of library extension in a small library. P L 10: 168-9.

---- W. G. Window display at Portage. Wis Lib Bull 10: 117-8.

Clouston, W. A. Hieroglyphic Bibles, their origin and history: a hitherto unwritten chapter of bibliography (Review). L 5: 260-2.

Clowsley, W. F. San Joaquin county free library's large circulation. Cal News Notes 6: 431.

Coatsworth, N. L. The female assistant from her own standpoint. L A 7: 217-8.

Cobb, M. A.   Scope and function of the state library of Georgia.  Special Libraries 11: 31-3.

Cobb, M. B.   Law and legislative reference as part of the state
library.  A L A Bull 11: 365-7.

Cobden-Sanderson, T. J.   The book beautiful.  P L 14: 384.

Coburn, L. H.   More liberal rules for borrowers.  N Y L 2:
231.

---- L. H.   Reader and the library.  P L 15: 219-23; N Y
L 2: 231.

Cochran, A.   Purpose of the normal school course.  Penn Lib
Notes 5, No 4: 44-7.

Cochran, H. B.   Poster bulletins at the May day fete of the
Wisconsin library school.  Wis Lib Bull 12: 261-4.

Cochran, H. R.   An argument for library support.  Wis Lib Bull
13: 303-4.

----- H. R.   Book repairing.  Wis Lib Bull 13: 102-7.

----- H. R.   The service the library performs for children.
Wis Lib Bull 14: 20-8.

Cochran, M. R.   State institution libraries in Ohio.  L J 43:
486-8.

Cochrane, J. M.   Arranging pamphlets.  P L 14: 254-5.

Cock, F. W.   "The Kentish Post or the Canterbury Newsletter."
L (3d series) 4: 285-90.

Cockerell, D.   Fine bookbinding in England.  Studio, Spring
number, 1914: 69-126.

Cockle, M. J. D.   Short list of some standard military works
of reference.  L W 2: 272-3.

Cocks, O. G.   Libraries and motion pictures: an ignored educational agency.  L J 39: 666-9.

--- O. G.   Motion pictures and reading habits.  L J 43: 67-
73.

--- O. G.   Public film libraries needed.  L J 40: 656-7.

Cody, E. V.   Catalogue cards numbered from rubber type.  P L
5: 94.

Cody, H. J.   State recognition of public library work in Canada.  L A R 21: 12.

Cody, S.   The ideal course in English for vocational students.
English Journal 3: 263-81, 371-80.

Coe.   A modification of the Dewey classification.  L J 39: 450-
1; P L 19: 118.

Coe, E. M.   Common novels in public libraries.  L J 19: Conf
No 23-4.

- E. M.   Fiction: List of questions submitted to American
librarians.  L J 18: 250-1.

- E. M.   Fiction (with bibliography).  U S Rept 933-9. 1892.

- E. M.   Relation of libraries to public schools.  L J 17:
193-4.

- E. M.   Should American literature be specially favoured
in (American) libraries.  L J 15: 101-4.

- E. M.  What can be done to help a boy like good books
after he has fallen into the "Dime novel habit." L J 20:
118-9.

Coffin, E. E.  Reference work in a small library.  New Hamp
Bull 5: 147-9.

Coffin, H. L.  What is a public library?  Everybody's Magazine 26: 634-5.

Coffin, W. A.  The decorations in the new Congressional Library.  Century 31: 694-711.

Coffman, H. C.  How may state history be best conserved?
Wash L A Bull 2: 5-8.

Cohen, J.  Value of libraries.  L J 16: 174-5.

Cohen, L. M.  Free libraries in New York.  L J 11: 480-2.

Cohen, M.  Differentiation of libraries: a criticism of P. L.
Ford's paper.  L J 15: 70-1.

--- M.  The librarian an educator, and not a cheap-john.
L J 13: 366.

Cohn, A. M.  A few notes upon some rare Cruikshankiana.  B A
R 12: XXV-XXXI. 1914.

Colby, C. W.  The library and education.  A L A Bull 3: 179-
84; L J 34: 340-5.

Colby, J. R.  Literature in the high school.  National Her-
bart Society Year-Book 2: 145-64.

--- J. R.  Reading for girls.  Educational Bi-Monthly 2:
17-24.

Cole, F. C.  Card charging and appliances.  L W 10: 26-30,
188-94.

-- F. C.  What is the value of the public library as an
educational force.  L A R 15: 100-7.

Cole, F. C. P.  Library extension work.  L A R 16: 511.

Cole, G. W.  American bibliography: general and local.  L J
19: 3, 5-9, 41.

-- G. W.  Bibliographical ghosts.  L J 44: 752.

-- G. W.  Bibliography: a forecast.  L J 45: 465-6.

-- G. W.  Branches and deliveries.  U S Rept 709-18; L J
18: 45-7, 220-3, Discussion, Conf No 26-8.

-- G. W.  Cataloguing in the future.  L J 20: Conf No 24,
72.

-- G. W.  Cataloguing married women's names.  L J 13: 80-
1.

-- G. W.  Compiling a bibliography.  L J 26: 791-5, 859-
63.

-- G. W.  Delivery stations or branch libraries.  L J 17:
480-2.

-- G. W.  An early French general catalogue.  L J 25: 329-
31.

-- G. W.  An easy method of measuring books by the A. L.
A. rules.  L J 10: 49-50.

-- G. W.  The extra gill and the full quart pot: a bibliographical study.  L (3d series) 10: 157-67.

-- G. W.  Fiction in libraries: a plea for the masses.  L J 19: Conf No 18-21.

-- G. W.  First folio of Shakespeare: a further word regarding the correct arrangement of its preliminary leaves.  Bib Soc Amer Proc 3: 65-83; L (3d series) 1: 211-7.

-- G. W.  The future of cataloguing.  L J 15: 172-6.

-- G. W.  Good words for the Library Journal.  L J 10: 404.

-- G. W.  How teachers should co-operate with librarians.  L J 20: 115-8.

-- G. W.  Library extension.  U S Commissioner of Education, Report, 1892-93: 715.

-- G. W.  Local cartography (with rules for cataloguing them).  L J 23: 102-3.

-- G. W.  Matters bibliographical: a review of various schemes for general bibliographies.  L J 19: 333.

-- G. W.  Missions and mission pictures: a contribution towards an iconography of the Franciscan missions in California.  Cal News Notes 5: 390-412.

-- G. W.  Periodical library bulletins.  L J 19: Conf No 50-2.

-- G. W.  A quicker method of measuring books, with practical illustrations.  L J 12: 345-9.

-- G. W.  Report on gifts and bequests to American libraries.  L J 26: Conf No 87-102.

-- G. W.  Report on gifts and bequests to American libraries.  L J 27: Conf No 97-119.

-- G. W.  Some thoughts on close classification.  L J 12: 356-60.

Cole, T. L.  Plan for a union catalogue of American colonial laws.  Bib Soc Amer Proc 1: 172-3.

Colegrove, M. E.  Material of current value: its collection and care.  L J 44: 295-8.

Coleman, C. H.  Books for little children.  Wis Lib Bull 14: 123-5.

Coleman, N. F.  The Bible as literature in the high school.  School Review 21: 246-9.

Colerick, M. M.  Fort Wayne (Ind) children's department.  Lib Occ No 12: 3-4.

Collar, M. A.  Children's books: subject headings.  L J 28: Conf No 65-8.

---- M. A.  Classification and cataloging of children's books.  L J 28: Conf No 57-61.

Collier, B. G. Curtis.  Local records in public libraries.  L A R 13: 268-75.

----- B. G. Curtis.  The public library towards an ideal.  Athenaeum, Oct 1917: 512-4.

----- B. G. Curtis.  The public library towards reconstruction.  Libn 8: 142-5.

----- B. G. Curtis.  A rational accession method.  Libn 9: 1-8.

Collier, R. G. Curtis.  Libraries of government departments
in England.  L W 14: 85-9.
Collins, J. H.  Literature on the job.  Special Libraries 7:
1-2.
Collins, V. L.  Princeton preceptorial system and the univer-
sity library.  L J 31: 165-7.
----- V. L.  Universities and the encouragement of serious
reading.  L J 28: 233-5.
Collman, S. M.  Books for the young people's shelf.  P L 18:
420-6.
----- S. M.  Pictures in the children's room.  Ohio Lib Bull
3, No 11: 1-3.
----- S. M.  Some standard novels for the small library.
New Hamp Bull 9, No 1: 4-5; P L 18: 91-6.
Collyer, R.  Influence of good books.  L J 14: 380-3.
Colt, A. M.  Ferguson library, Stamford, Conn.  L J 38: 342-
4.
Colville, A. P.  Value of fairy tales in teaching courage.
Home Progress 4: 1123-6.
Comings, M. E.  Arrangement of children's books.  Ohio Lib
Bull 4 No 3: 1-2.
Commin, F. M.  Development of the printed book.  B A R 16:
XIII-XVII, XXV-XXIX, 1919.
Commons, J. R.  One way to get sane legislation.  American
Review of Reviews 32: 722-3.
Compton, C. H.  Adventures in library advertising.  L J 42:
515-9.
----- C. H.  Best methods of familiarizing college students
with the use of the library.  Pacific Northwest Library
Assn Proceedings 1910: 61.
----- C. H.  Co-ordination of reference work.  P L 20: 107-
9.
----- C. H.  Letter on publicity.  A L A Bull 10: 40-1.
----- C. H.  Library advertising: a field of practical co-
operation.  New Hamp Bull (ns) 15: 135-6.
----- C. H.  Library babies.  P L 19: 9-10.
----- C. H.  The library in relation to the university.
L J 35: 494-503.
----- C. H.  Library publicity.  Pacific Northwest Library
Assn Proceedings 1914: 11-20.
----- C. H.  A publicity expert for libraries.  A L A Bull
11: 133-4, 331.
----- C. H.  A publicity expert for public libraries.  P
L 20: 469-71.
----- C. H.  Staff meetings in a reference department.  P
L 18: 281-2.
----- C. H.  The use of free publications.  Pacific North-
west Library Assn Proceedings 1913: 67-72, 76-7.
----- C. H.  What then?  A L A Bull 13: 6-11; L J 44: 99-106.

Comstock, M. E.   The library as an educational factor.   L J
21: 147.

Comstock, S.   Byways of library work.   Outlook 106: 200-5.

Comstock, Sarah.   Eight million books a year: activities of
New York public library, including work with foreigners.
World's Work 26: 100-8.

Conat, M. L.   List of periodical publications relating to
municipal affairs.   Special Libraries 6: 129-39.

Condon, J.   Short bibliography of Irish history.   An Leab 1:
40-52, 85-95; 2: 48-63, 148-59; 3: 47-69.

Cone, K. M.   Children and literature.   Education 18: 290-8,
365-9.

Congdon, M. L.   How one library serves the townspeople.   Vt
L Bull 5: 3-4.

Conklin, W. J.   Library flotsam and jetsam.   P L 12: 1-4, 45-
7.

----- W. J.   Union of library and museum.   P L 8: 2-8, 47-
9.

Connelly, Miss.   The librarian's boot straps.   P L 19: 214.

Conner, F. C.   Public library and the public school.   Minn
P L C N 1, No 9: 22-5.

Conner, M.   Charging system for a college library.   L J 44:
616.

---- M.   Dust in libraries.   L J 45: 562.

Connolly, E.   Remarks on the art of using a library.   L J 31:
308-11.

Connor, R. D. W.   Aids in the study of state history.   N C
Bull 1: 90-8, 153-4.

Conover, M.   What can the library best do for the children?
P L 4: 317-20.

----- M.   Work with children.   P L 12: 92-3; Michigan
Board of Library Commissioners Report 1907: 129-35.

Converse, M. L.   Professional reading.   Mich Lib Bull 11:
Sept-Oct p 11-3.

Conway, M.   High school reading at Kilbourn, Wisconsin.   Wis
Lib Bull 13: 108-9.

Cook, A. S.   The teaching of English.   Atlantic Monthly 87:
710-22.

Cook, E. B.   Fiction as reference material.   L J 41: 249-51.

Cook, E. L.   Elementary library training in a high school.
P L 20: 155-7.

Cook, G. L.   Arranging and classifying trade catalogs.   L J
44: 558.

-- G. L.   A library of trade catalogs.   L J 44: 307-8.

Cook, M. W.   Magazines on special subjects for a town library.
N Y L 5: 89-91.

Cooke, E. B.   Fiction as reference material.   L J 41: 249-51.

Cooley, A. W.   Literature in the grades and how to use it.
Nat Educ Assn 1903: 198-213.

Cooley, Mrs. A. W.  Story telling and the teaching of literature.  Story Hour 1: 3-8.

Coolidge, A. C.  Plans, resources and tasks of the library.  Harvard Graduates Magazine 24: Sept 1915.

Coolidge, J. R.  Achievement thru conviction: an enlarged program for the American Library Association.  L J 45: 103-4.

Coolidge, J. R., Jr.  Architectural character of small libraries.  P L 16: 119.

------ J. R., Jr.  Functions of libraries in village improvement.  L J 33: 240-1.

------ J. R., Jr.  Ideals versus technical efficiency.  Mass Lib Club Bull 5: 133-4.

Coolidge, O. P.  Records necessary for the small library.  P L 14: 10-3.

Cooper, A. B.  Fairy tale in art.  Canadian Magazine 38: 181-8.

Cooper, A. C.  Library maintenance tax.  P L 14: 381.

Cooper, C.  Leading children to love books.  American Education, 9: 399-403.

Cooper, E. J.  Problem of the junior assistant.  L A 10: 200-1.

Cooper, F. B.  Is there a need for instruction in library methods by normal schools and universities?  L J 31: 157-60; Wash L A Bull 2, No 2: 1-5.

Cooper, L. M.  What is a librarian?  Journal of Assn of Collegiate Alumnae Jan 1918: 294-7; L J 43: 450-1.

Cooper, O. H.  The superintendent and good literature in schools.  Nat Educ Assn 1887: 530-8.

Cooper, T. E.  Library architecture.  Libn 2: 231-2, 271-2, 305, 470-2; 3: 24-5, 72-3, 119-20.

Cooper, T. P.  The city of York: some of its literary associations.  B A R 10: XLI-XLIX.

Copinger, W. A.  Corrections and additions to the Mazarine catalogue of incunabula.  Bib Soc Trans 1: 210-5.

------ W. A.  A few words on fifteenth century Latin Bibles.  L 3: 161-9.

------ W. A.  Incunabula Biblica.  L 4: 154-5.

------ W. A.  Incunabula Virgiliana: a list of editions of Virgil printed during the 15th century.  Bib Soc Trans 2: 127-226.

------ W. A.  Necessity for the formation of a bibliographical society.  L 4: 1-7.

------ W. A.  Notes on catalogues of incunabula.  Bib Soc Trans 2: 87-90.

------ W. A.  Presidential address.  Bib Soc Trans 2: 103-22.

Coray, G. Q.  Library and reading room.  University Chronicle
    Mch 1894 2: 221-2.
Corey, D. P.  Some trustees.  A L A Bull 1: Conf No 278-82.
Corneford, M.  Some account of Dundalk public library, being
    the first established in Ireland under the Libraries acts.
    L 7: 359-62.
Cornelius, C. O.  Two New England libraries.  Architectural
    Record 44: 225-36.
Corning, C. R.  Address at opening of the Baker Free Library,
    Bow, N. H. Oct 29, 1914.  New Hamp Bull 11: 129-36.
Corns, A. R.  Bibliotheca imperfecta.  B A R 9: I-XXIX.
    --- A. R.  Lincolnshire libraries and literature.  B A R
    7: XLI-XLV.
    --- A. R.  Some insufficiently developed points in library
    practice (Indexing contents of collected works).  L A R
    11: 257-63.
    --- A. R. and Sparke, A.  Bibliography of unfinished books
    in the English language: Review.  L W 18: 319-20.
Corwin, E. F.  Bibliography of Louisiana.  P L 8: 267-70.
    ---- E. F.  Charging system in use at Elkhart (Ind.).  Lib
    Occ 5: 112-3; L J 44: 333.
    ---- E. F.  Fads and fallacies in library work.  L J 27:
    821-2.
    ---- E. F.  Organization of small libraries.  P L 4: 195-
    7.
    ---- E. F.  Use of library bulletins.  P L 9: 326-8.
Cost, M. L.  Oriental libraries: Bangkok, Siam.  L J 12: 256.
Cotgreave, A.  Comments on an article concerning library in-
    dicators, by A. K. Gill.  L W 9: 402-5.
    ------- A.  Disadvantages of two-ticket system.  L 8: 260-
    3.
    ------- A.  Extension of time for reading works of fiction
    from 7 to 14 days.  L W 4: 155-6.
    ------- A.  Index to contents of general and periodical
    literature.  L 9: 270-5.
    ------- A.  An indicator-book.  L A U K Trans 2: 71-2.
    ------- A.  Library indicator: pro and con.  L A R 4: 333-
    9, 360-1.
    ------- A.  Library indicator versus book-keeping.  L J
    5: 51-2.
    ------- A.  Library publications with special references
    to subject indexes.  L A 1: 129-35.
    ------- A.  Modified Kennedy indicator.  L W 11: 363.
    ------- A.  Open access.  L W 13: 255-6.
    ------- A.  Open access versus indicators.  L W 10: 196-
    200.
Cotton, F. J.  School furniture for Boston schools.  American
    Physical Education Review 9: 267-84.
Cotton, K.  Staff exchanges in public libraries.  Libn 3: 137-8.

Coulson, T.  Are newsrooms a desirable adjunct to libraries.
L A 4: 157.
----- T.  Outline of the theory of classification.  L W
14: 37-42, 67-70.
----- T.  Situation of branch libraries.  L W 12: 201-4.
Coult, M.  How can we best direct the reading of high school
pupils?  N Y L 3: 52-5.
--- M.  Use of pictures in high school English.  P L 21:
449-51.
Coulter, S.  Rural community and the library.  Lib Occ 2: 167-
77; P L 16: 1-6, 49-52.
Coulter, V. C.  Redistribution of the contents of some high
school courses.  English Journal 3: 490-9.
Countryman, G.  Community studies.  Minn P L C N 4: 53-4.
-------- G.  How far should the selection of books for bran-
ches be uniform?  L J 23: Conf No 101-2.
-------- G.  Library as a social centre.  Minn P L C N No
5: 3-5; P L 11: 5-7.
-------- G.  Opportunities.  L J 26: Conf No 52-4.
-------- G.  Shall public libraries buy foreign literature.
L J 23: 229-31.
-------- G.  State aid to libraries.  L J 29: Conf No 148-
52.
-------- G.  Summary of work in various states.  P L 10:
55-60.
-------- G.  Whence and whither: an appraisal.  Minn P L
C N 5: 46.
-------- G.  How far should the selection of books for bran-
ches be uniform?  L J 23: Conf No 101-2, Discussion Conf No
164-6.
Countryman, G. A.  Librarianship.  University of Minnesota.
Vocations open to women.  Bulletin No 1, Extra Series, Minn
1913: 18-9.
--------- G. A.  Lines of work which a state library com-
mission can profitably undertake.  L J 25: Conf No 51-4.
--------- G. A.  State aid to libraries.  P L 10: 55-60.
--------- G. A.  Traveling libraries as a first step in dev-
eloping libraries.  L J 30: Conf No 56-8, Discussion 159-63.
Couper, W. J.  Watson's "History of printing."  L (3d series)
1: 424-36.
Coupland, W. B.  Brief description of the parts of a modern
book.  L W 16: 193-5.
------ W. B.  Difficulties of the provincial library assis-
tant.  L W 14: 60-1.
------ W. B.  Irregularities in the make-up of early print-
ed books.  L W 16: 118-9.
------ W. B.  Methods of book illustration.  L W 15: 356-62.
------ W. B.  Notes on the arrangement and compilation of
bibliographies.  L W 15: 180-5.

------ W. B.  Some aids to provincial library assistants.
L W 14: 151-2.

------ W. B.  Some difficulties of the provincial library
assistant.  L W 14: 60-1.

Cousin, J.  A French librarian on librarianship.  L A M N 3:
194-8.

Coutts, H. F.  Are newsrooms a desirable adjunct to libraries.
L A 4: 169-71.

Coutts, H. T.  Affirmative: discussion on library extension:
do lectures forward library work.  L A 7: 64-8.

---- H. T.  Bookbinding orders and checking.  L W 10: 113-
8.

---- H. T.  Colour question in bookbinding.  L W 14: 323-
4.

---- H. T.  Education of the assistant.  L A 6: 56-9, Discussion 59-60.

---- H. T.  Edward Edwards: a brief memorial oration.  L
A 10: 16-8.

---- H. T.  Home binderies.  L W 9: 233-6; 10: 150-4.

---- H. T.  Modern library bookbinding.  L A 10: 89-96.

---- H. T.  Overdue books and the treatment of defaulters.
L W 14: 241-6.

---- H. T.  Public library as an advertisement agency.  L
W 14: 97-9.

---- H. T.  Reading, libraries and the war.  L W 17: 234-
5.

---- H. T.  Sir Thomas Bodley: a tercentenary note.  L W
15: 225-6.

---- H. T.  Some steps toward a more perfect organization
of the library profession.  L A 9: 151-5.

---- H. T.  Specialization in library work.  L W 9: 393-5.

---- H. T.  The Subject classification.  L A 6: 304-14,
Discussion 315-8.

---- H. T.  Wilful damage: the general reader's responsibility.  L W 15: 206-7.

---- H. T.  Work amongst children in the library.  L A 5:
34-8, Discussion 38-40.

---- H. T. and Stephen, G. A.  Manual of library bookbinding: review.  L A 8: 72-3; L W 13: 363-4.

Cowell, A. L.  Library war publicity.  Cal News Notes 13: 172-
4.

Cowell, P.  Admission of fiction in free libraries.  1st Int
Conf 60-7; L J 2: 152-9, Discussion 255-8.

---- P.  Experientia docet: or, thoughts and experiences
of a public librarian.  L C 5: 157-66.

---- P.  Free public library lectures.  L A R 1: 146-50.

---- P.  How to popularize a free library.  L J 18: 461-
5.

---- P.  Lectures at the Liverpool library.  L A M N 3: 53-
6.

---- P.  Library work forty years ago: circulation of music and its advantages. 2d Int Conf 99-102. 1897.

---- P.  On electric light in public libraries. L A Trans 5: 153-7; L J 7: 43.

---- P.  Origin and history of some Liverpool libraries. L A U K Trans 6: 31-9.

---- P.  Public library work forty years ago (Free lectures as aids to library work). 2d Int Conf 99-102, Discussion 236, 1897.

---- P.  Reminiscences of library work in Liverpool during 40 years. 2nd Int Conf Proceedings: 99-102.

---- P.  Report of the chief librarian of Liverpool on his visit of inspection to some of the principal libraries of the United States and Canada. L 5: 277-82.

Cowgill, T. W.  Teaching literature. Nation 83: 326-7.

Cowing, A.  Some experiments in work with elementary school children. L J 43: 210-4.

Cowing, H.  The intermediate collection for young people in the library. L J 37: 189.

Cowley, A.  Hospital library service at Fort Sheridan, Illinois. Minn P L C N 6: 4; Hospital libraries. Minn P L C N 6: 65-6.

Cox, E. M.  Ballads of Francois Villon. L (3d series) 8: 53-74.

- E. M.  Lyons as a literary centre in the fifteenth and sixteenth centuries. Bib Soc Trans 1915-17: 23-37.

- E. M.  Notes, critical and bibliographical on Louise Labe. L (3d series) 6: 293-307.

- E. M.  Notes on the bibliography of Herrick. L (3d series) 8: 105-9.

- E. M.  Some of my books. L (3d series) 7: 144-62.

Cox, E. S.  English in American schools. Nat Educ Assn 1885: 181-91.

Cox, H. T.  London school borad libraries. L C 4: 169-71.

Cox, M. D.  The case against the librarian. American telephone and telegraph company. Special Libraries 11: 68-70.

Crafts, L. M.  President's address. Minn P L C N 2, No 4: 37-9.

---- L. M.  Reading of our youth. P L 7: 117-9.

Cragg, F.  Book indexes. L J 27: 819-21.

Cragin, E. F.  Work with the schools at the New York free circulating library. L J 23: 194-5.

Craig, E. L.  Library legislation. A L A Bull 11: 226-8, 349.

Craig, F. M.  The education of librarians: a fantasy. L J 44: 577.

Craig, H.  Effectual culture. Minn P L C N 4: 57-61.

--- H.  "Faust." P L 15: 111-2.

Craigie, J.  Constitution, rules, regulations, etc. L A R 11: 19-22, 339-41; L J 34: 61, 407.

Cramer, K. D.   Methods of keeping books clean.   Wis Lib Bull
    1: 66.
Crandall, F. A.   Library of public documents in the office of
    superintendent of documents.   L J 32: 203-6.
------ F. A.   Official titles of government publishing of-
    fices.   L J 27: 938-9.
------ F. A.   Public documents and proposed new public doc-
    uments bill.   L J 21: Conf No 20-5.
Crandall, M. I.   Art element in library work.   L J 13: 365.
------ M. I.   Full fornames in catalogues.   L J 18: 4.
------ M. I.   Reference notes on catalogue cards.   L J 22:
    180.
Crandall, M. S.   What can be done by a small library in a
    small town.   P L 19: 1-4.
Crane, F.   The ten points of Americanism.   L J 45: 214-5.
Craver, H. W.   Library in relation to special classes of read-
    ers--supply and use of technological books.   L J 31: Conf
    No 72-5.
Crawford, E.   Cataloguing: review by C. A. Cutter.   L J 25:
    596-7.
------ E.   New edition of the "A. L. A. Subject Headings."
    L J 32: 25-6, 435-6, 500-1, 560-1 (questions and answers);
    Illinois, Discussion 136-9; P L 12: 39-40, 312-5, 343-4,
    384-5, 398-9.
------ E.   Shelf list.   P L 4: 381-3.
------ E.   Some essentials of co-operative cataloguing.
    P L 13: 201-6.
Crawford, Earl of.   Presidential address.   L 10: 267-9.
------ Earl of.   Private library and the individual col-
    lector: Presidential address.   L A R 1: 572-6.
Crawford, M.   Laboratory equipment for the teacher of English.
    English Journal 4: 145-51.
Crawford, Ruth.   Immigrants in St. Louis.   P L 21: 327.
Crawford, W. R.   The book when bound.   P L 9: 263-4.
Credland, W. R.   County councils and village libraries.   L
    A R 1: 763-9.
------ W. R.   Free libraries in 1882.   L A M N 4: 18-22.
------ W. R.   Free public libraries of Manchester.   L A
    U K Trans 2: 118-25.
------ W. R.   Rating and the taxation of Public libraries.
    Greenwood's Yr-Bk: 45-51, 1897.
------ W. R.   Starved free libraries.   L A Trans 6: 71-8.
Creighton, J. B.   Honolulu library.   L J 23: 575-6.
Creighton, M.   On the training of the library assistant.   L
    10: 101-11.
Crenshaw, M. V.   Public library exhibit.   L J 43: 139-40.
------ M. V.   Public libraries in the South (Virginia,
    West Virginia, North and South Carolina, Georgia, Florida,
    Alabama, Mississippi, Louisiana, Texas, Kentucky, Tennessee,
    Arkansas and Oklahoma)   L J 42: 163-74.

Crittenden, Mrs. E.  Reading of college men.  N C Bull 3:
    100-2.
Crocker, R.  Bringing the library to the rural population.
    Multnomah Co., Oregon.  A L A Bull 9: 198-9.
Croft, J.  The library story hour.  Vt L Bull 12: 10-2.
Cropton, F. B.  A hint in cataloguing.  2d Int Conf 146-7.
Cross, J. A.  Universal index of subjects.  1st Int Conf 104-
    7, Discussion 161-4; L J 2: 191-4.
Cross, L. M.  Library work with high school pupils.  P L 21:
    117-20.
Crous, E.  Co-operation among German libraries by mutual loans
    and the information bureau.  L (3d series) 5: 113-39, 337-
    44.
Crous, E.  The general catalogue of incunabula.  Bib Soc Trans
    12: 87-99.
    --- E.  Inventory of incunabula in Great Britain and Ire-
    land.  Bib Soc Trans 12: 177-209.
Crowell, J. F.  The financial and statistical bureau.  Spec-
    ial Libraries 2: 96-8; Discussion 98-101.
Crowell, M.  The school library in the school-room.  P L 4:
    51-3.
Crowther, E.  Combined indicator and card catalogue.  L W 1:
    170-2.
Crowther, W.  Chatsworth and its library.  L 8: 439-45.
Crum, F. S.  Library and statistical work with the Prudential
    insurance company of America.  Special Libraries 10: 159-
    62.
Crunden, F. M.  Books and text-books: the library as a factor
    in education.  2nd Int Conf 46-54.  1897.
    ----- F. M.  Business methods in library management.  L
    J 12: 335-8, 435-6.
    ----- F. M.  Classification and cataloguing.  L (ns) 1:
    295-8.
    ----- F. M.  Closing a library for stock-taking.  L J 18:
    Conf No 37-8.
    ----- F. M.  Executive department: general super-vision,
    including building finance, etc., U S Rept 1892-93, 795-
    809; L J 18: 232-4.
    ----- F. M.  Functions of trustees and their relations to
    librarians.  L J 21: Conf No 32-7.
    ----- F. M.  How things are done in one American library.
    L (ns) 1: 147-52, 290-8, 384-406, 450-2; 2: 20-43, 296-8.
    ----- F. M.  Humour of book titles.  L J 16: 75.
    ----- F. M.  Librarian as administrator.  L J 19: 44-7.
    ----- F. M.  The library: a plea for its recognition.  L
    J 29: Conf No 1-7.
    ----- F. M.  Library advertising.  L J 21: 327.
    ----- F. M.  Library in education.  International Congress
    of Arts and Sciences.  St. Louis 1904, 8: 195-202.

----- F. M.  Library reports. L J 15: 198-200.
----- F. M.  Library stations. L J 24: 153.
----- F. M.  Most popular books. L J 16: 277-8.
----- F. M.  New novel problem and its solution. L (ns)
1: 92-100.
----- F. M.  Presidential address. L J 29: Conf No 1-7.
----- F. M.  President's address on the work of the A. L.
A. L J 15: Conf No 1-5.
----- F. M.  Public libraries. Univ of State of New York,
Regents' Report, 1900: 234-7.
----- F. M.  Public library as a factor in industrial pro-
gress. L (ns) 7: 384-96.
----- F. M.  Reading lists: general and special. L (ns)
2: 37-9.
----- F. M.  Report on aids and guides. L J 11: 309-30.
----- F. M.  Report on periodicals. L J 14: 254-6.
----- F. M.  The school and the library: value of litera-
ture in early education. Nat Educ Assn 1901: 108-18.
----- F. M.  Self-supporting collection of duplicate books.
L J 4: 10-1.
----- F. M.  Selection of books. L J 19: Conf No 41-2.
----- F. M.  Some thoughts on classification. L J 11: 418,
468.
----- F. M.  Special training for children's librarians.
L J 23: Conf No 82.
----- F. M.  Supplying of current daily newspapers in free
reading rooms. L J 19: Conf No 46-7.
----- F. M.  Value of a free library. L J 15: 79-81.
----- F. M.  What is a public library? L J 26: 141.
----- F. M.  What of the future? L J 22: Conf No 32, 5-11.
----- F. M.  Work between libraries and schools in St. Louis.
U. S. Bur of Educ Rept 1897-98, pt 1: 674-5; L J 22: 182.
----- F. M. and Blanchard, C. A.  Reading of school child-
ren and college students. L J 13: 89-90.
Culin, S.  Book collecting in India and the Far East. P L
20: 195-7.
Cullingworth, C. J.  Manchester medical society's library.
L A U K Trans 2: 127.
Culver, E. M.  Special material in libraries. Cal News Notes
14: 154.
Cummings, R. R.  How to interest children in classed books.
Ia L C Q 5: 96.
Cummins, A. E.  The position of the junior assistant. L A
15: 19-20.
Cummins, G. D.  The evolution of the rural library in Ireland.
L (3rd series) 8: 120-7.
Cundall, F.  Insect enemies of books. 2nd Int Conf 1897: 178.
----- F.  Library work in Jamaica. 2nd International Con-
ference Proceedings 173-8, 1897.

Cunningham, A.  Departmental libraries.  P L 17: 114-7.
-------- A.  Training of teachers in library work.  Ind S L Bull No 10: 1-2; P L 8: 85-9.
Cunningham, J.  Problems discovered in cataloging the library of the Missouri school of mines.  A L A Bull 10: 234-7.
-------- J.  Progress report of the committee investigating the use and methods of handling and filing newspaper clippings.  Special Libraries 6: 116-7.
-------- J.  Service of St. Louis public library to the city government.  L J 37: 506-8.
Curran, H. E.  Acceptable free library catalogues.  L 7: 21-8.
---- H. E.  Public lectures in relation to public library work.  L A R 13: 313-21.
Curran, M. G.  What shall I read next?  P L 20: 171-6.
Currey, J. S.  Library trustee.  P L 2: 319-22.
Currier, A. F.  Sterilization of books by vapour of formalin.  L J 27: 881-3, 964.
Currier, C. A. M.  A library in Constantinople.  P L 20: 257-8.
Currier, C. W.  Archives of old Seville.  Bulletin Pan Am Union 35: 1162-9.
Currier, F. F.  Graduate training for college library assistants.  L J 44: 378.
Currier, F. T.  Cost reduction in cataloging.  A L A Bull 12: 243-5, 300.
Currier, T. F.  Change of name of corporate bodies: a suggestion for the cataloger.  L J 35: 202-5.
----- T. F.  Harvard rules for counting volumes and pamphlets.  L J 43: 241-5.
----- T. F.  Reorganizing a card catalog.  Mass L C Bull 6: 14-5; L J 41: 708; Am Lib Annual 1916-17: 29-30.
----- T. F.  Result of poster questionnaire sent out by American library institute.  A L A Bull 13: 392-3.
----- T. F.  Too many cards under a subject heading.  L J 35: 412-3.
Curtin, W. H.  Disinfection of books and papers.  L A R 4: 316.
Curtis, C. B.  Tariff on books by mail.  L J 15: 180-1.
Curtis, F. R.  Annual report of a small public library.  Lib Occ 2: 115-7. 1910.
---- F. R.  The assistants' professional and cultural reading.  Lib Occ 5: 326-8.
---- F. R.  The collection of social survey material.  L J 40: 76; Am Lib Annual 1915-16: 72.
---- F. R.  Selection of books for prison libraries.  P L 18: 367-70.
---- F. R.  Survey of institution libraries.  Conference of National Charities and Correction, Proceedings, 1916: 355-60; L J 41: 475-8.

---- F. R.  What prison library catalogs show.  N Y L 3: 236-7.

Curtis, G. T.  Letters on the Congressional building.  L J 11: 17, 50-8, 111.

Curtis, H. S.  Educational extension through the rural social center.  Education 34: 291-4.

Curzon, F.  Yorkshire village libraries.  L 10: 29-30.

Cushman, R.  The library on Sunday.  L J 15: 235.

Cust, L.  Originals of the designs of the block book "Ars Moriendi."  Bib Soc Trans 4: 141-4.

-- L.  Portraits of Shakespeare.  Bib Soc Trans 9: 117-9.

Cuthbertson, D.  The protest against the burning of John Huss.  L (3d series) 4: 146-56.

Cutler, C. A.  Photographs and photoprints.  L J 25: 619-25.

Cutler, M. S.  Catalogs and classification.  L J 16: Conf No 50-1.

---- M. S.  Charging systems in foreign libraries.  L J 16: Conf No 51-2.

---- M. S.  Home libraries.  L J 19: Conf No, 13-4; 21: 60-2.

---- M. S.  Hours of opening: evening, Sunday, holiday and vacation.  U S Rept 771-94; L J 18: 431; Discussion, Conf No 44-6, 1892-3.

---- M. S.  Impressions of foreign libraries--catalogs and classification.  L J 16: Conf No 50-1.

---- M. S.  Library opening.  L J 18: 431; Discussion, Conf No 44-6; U S Rept: 771-94, 1892-93.

---- M. S.  Official names of legislative bodies of states of the Union.  L J 11: 141.

---- M. S.  Principles of selection of books.  L J 20: 339-41.

---- M. S.  Sunday opening of libraries.  L J 14: 176-90, 279.

---- M. S.  Use of the imprint.  L J 16: 102.

---- M. S.  What a woman librarian earns.  L J 17: Conf No 89-91.

Cutler, W. P.  Card index of department of agriculture.  L J 25: 42.

Cutler, W. P.  Expansive classification.  A L A Bull 5: 224-7.

Cutter, A. S.  Report of Elementary school committee on library co-operation with the Junior Red Cross.  Nat Educ Assn 1918: 452-4.

Cutter, C. A.  Abbreviations for feminine names.  L J 5: 176.

---- C. A.  Abbreviation of Christian names.  L J 1: 405-6.

---- C. A.  Adversaria--Cole on close classification.  L J 13: 79.

---- C. A.  Another charging system.  L J 4: 17-8.

---- C. A. Another plan of numbering books. L J 3: 248-51.

---- C. A. Arrangement and notation of Shakespeariana. L J 9: 137-9.

---- C. A. Arrangement of biography by Cutter's author-table. L J 12: 544.

---- C. A. Arrangement of the parts of the U. S. in historical and geographical system of classification. L J 8: 205-10.

---- C. A. Author catalogues in classified shelf systems. L J 3: 371-2.

---- C. A. Book arts. L J 7: 168-72, 271.

---- C. A. Brass guide-boards for card catalogues. L J 5: 215-6.

---- C. A. Buffalo public library in 1983; an excursion in the land of dreams. L J 8: 211-7.

---- C. A. Cataloguing. 1st Int Conf 82-3; L J 2: 174-5.

---- C. A. Charging simplified. L J 28: 664.

---- C. A. Charging systems. L J 4: 445-6.

---- C. A. Classification. L J 11: 158.

---- C. A. Classification for the natural sciences. L J 5: 163-6.

---- C. A. Classification of education. L J 16: 330-2.

---- C. A. Classification of philosophy. L J 10: 79-30.

---- C. A. Classification of the recreative and athletic arts. L J 10: 6-8.

---- C. A. Classification on the shelves. L J 4: 234-43; 6: 64-9.

---- C. A. Clearing house for public documents. L J 11: 19-24.

---- C. A. Close classification. L J 11: 167, 180-4.

---- C. A. Close classification of folklore. L J 9: 136.

---- C. A. Common sense in libraries: presidential address L J 14: Conf No 141-54.

---- C. A. Co-operative entries. L J 1: 403-4.

---- C. A. Corporate entry: further consideration. L J 22: 432-4.

---- C. A. Cost of cataloguing. L J 17: 192.

---- C. A. Dr. Hagen's letter on cataloguing. L J 1: 216-20.

---- C. A. European Libraries--British Museum. L J 19: 289-92.

---- C. A. Exhibits of photographs, posters, engravings, etc. L J 22: 256.

---- C. A. Expansive classification: with a scheme for a Shakespeare collection. 2d Int Conf 84-7.

---- C. A. Franklin society of Paris. L J 1: 3-5.

---- C. A. Government pamphlet on college libraries. L J 5: 179-82.

---- C. A.  Greek and Latin authors.  L J 11: 280-9.
---- C. A.  Harvard college library.  North American Review, 107: 568-93.
---- C. A.  How to use Cutter's decimal and author table. L J 12: 251-2.
---- C. A.  Inconveniences of library cards.  L J 10: 48.
---- C. A.  Large base notation.  L J 4: 88-90.
---- C. A.  Last word on cataloguing.  P L 10: 17.
---- C. A.  Length of symbols.  L J 4: 47.
---- C. A.  Libraries and disease.  L J 8: 336-7.
---- C. A.  Library architecture.  L J 10: 35.
---- C. A.  Library associations in France and America. L J 1: 389-91.
---- C. A.  Library catalogues.  U S Rept 552-60. 1876.
---- C. A.  Library discipline--rules affecting the public. L J 28: 65-7.
---- C. A.  Library furniture, fixtures and appliances. L J 21: Conf No 127-9.
---- C. A.  Library statistics.  L J 8: 7.
---- C. A.  Mechanical arrangements for a card catalogue. U S Rept 556-60. 1876.
---- C. A.  Minute classification of philosophy.  L J 16: 5.
---- C. A.  Need of apprenticeship for students.  L J 23: Conf No 135-6.
---- C. A.  A nomenclature of classification.  L J 9: 115-6.
---- C. A.  Notation for small libraries.  L J 12: 324-6, 430-1.
---- C. A.  Notes on the Bibliotheque Nationale.  L J 19: 193-4, 289-92.
---- C. A.  Numbering: rejoinder to Mr. Schwartz.  L J 3: 340, 453.
---- C. A.  Numbers.  L N (US) 3: 421-4.
---- C. A.  On collecting local literature.  L J 14: Conf No 151-2.
---- C. A.  On Mr. Larned's new notation.  L J 9: 115-6.
---- C. A.  On mixing letters and figures.  L J 7: 195-6.
---- C. A.  On the suitability of the expansive classification to college and reference libraries.  L J 24: Conf No 41-9, 154-6.
---- C. A.  Photographs and photo prints.  L J 25: 619-25.
---- C. A.  Place of folk-lore in a classification.  L J 9: 136.
---- C. A.  Plan for numbering books.  L J 4: 17, 88-90.
---- C. A.  Preservation of pamphlets.  L J 1: 51-4, Discussion 104-6.
---- C. A.  Presidential address.  St. Louis conference. L J 14: 148.

---- C. A.  Proposed reform in public documents.  L J 21:
217-8.
---- C. A.  Proprietary libraries and their relation to
public libraries.  L J 18: 247-8.
---- C. A.  Remarks on Mr. Adams' paper on the combining
system.  L J 23: 55-6.
---- C. A.  Review of J. C. Rowell's scheme of classifica-
tion of books in the library of the University of Califor-
nia.  L J 20: 214-5.
---- C. A.  Rules for a dictionary catalogue, 4th ed: a re-
view.  L J 30: 42-3.
---- C. A.  Rules for a printed dictionary catalogue.
Printed separately as pt 2 of the U S Rept. 1876.
---- C. A.  School of library economy.  L J 8: 293-5.
---- C. A.  Schwartz's classification and notation.  L J
11: 3, 8.
---- C. A.  Search for a guide (cardboard class guides to
denote the position of various books on shelves).  L J 7:
44-5.
---- C. A.  Shelf classification of music.  L J 27: 68-72.
---- C. A.  Should libraries buy only the best books?  L
J 26: 70-2.
---- C. A.  Some thoughts on classification.  L J 15: Conf
No 100-1.
---- C. A.  Suitability of the expansive classification to
college and reference libraries.  L J 24: Conf No 41-9.
---- C. A.  Supervision of children's library use.  L J 23:
149-50.
---- C. A.  Thirty-five versus ten.  L J 7: 62-3.
---- C. A.  Time of loans.  L J 3: 79.
---- C. A.  Titles: examples of difficulties.  L J 12: 355.
---- C. A.  Use of capitals.  L J 1: 162-6.
---- C. A.  Visit of the New York state school to Boston.
L J 15: 176.
---- C. A.  What we do with pamphlets.  L J 14: 433-4.
---- C. A.  Why and how a dictionary catalogue is made.
L J 15: 143-4, 165.
---- C. A.  Wonders of bibliography.  L J 7: 87.
---- C. A.  Wooden book supports.  L J 3: 192.
---- C. A.  Word to starters of libraries.  L J 1: 1-5.
---- C. A. and J. Schwartz.  Scraps from script.  L J 7: 6.
---- C. A. and W. C. Lane.  Schwartz's classification and
notation.  L J 11: 8-9.
Cutter, M.  Developing a children's room.  P L 19: 242-5.
---- M.  Pioneer library work in Labrador.  L J 41: 102-4.
Cutter, W. P.  Acme of co-operation.  P L 13: 217-8; A L A
Bull 2: 183-90.
---- W. P.  Binding of library books.  P L 10: 307.
---- W. P.  Card index of the department of agriculture.
L J 25: 42.

---- W. P.  Classification of an agricultural library.  A L A Bull 4: 793-4.

---- W. P.  Classification of technical literature: report of meeting creating a permanent body for the preparation of a scheme on the subject.  L J 40: 419-21; P L 20: 324-5.

---- W. P.  The Engineering society's library.  L J 39: 894-7.

---- W. P.  The facts in the copyright case.  P L 11: 436-7.

---- W. P.  An international technical index.  Special Libraries 2: 69-71, 83, Discussion 84-6.

---- W. P.  Let the large help the little.  L J 37: 593-6.

---- W. P.  The library.  U. S. Dept of Agriculture, Yearbook, 1897: 220-4.

---- W. P.  New copyright law.  A L A Bull 3: 26; P L 14: 37-8, 133-4, 184-5.

---- W. P.  Notes on book purchasing for small libraries. L J 30: 518-20; Vt L Bull 1: 13-5.

---- W. P.  Report of A. L. A. committee on bookbuying. A L A Bull 4: 506-9.

---- W. P.  Report of the bookbuying committee.  A L A Bull 2: 183-90.

---- W. P.  Selection of technical books.  P L 13: 86.

---- W. P.  The technical library's field of service.  Special Libraries 6: 150-2.

Cutter, W. R.  Genealogical research in public libraries.  L J 21: 222-3.

---- W. R.  Local collection in the Woburn public library. L J 17: 420-2, 428-9.

Cuttle, A. H.  Library publicity.  Ontario Lib Assn Proceedings 1911: 109-11; P L 16: 285-6.

Dacus, I. J., and Martin, M. E.  Elementary library rules for school libraries.  Winthrop Normal and Ind College Bulletin Dec 1912.

Dadachanji, B. M.  The child and the library (in India) Lib Miscellany (Baroda) 1: 203-14.

-------- B. M.  Public libraries for public education.  Library Miscellany (Baroda) 1: 33-40, 81-8.

Daggett, M. P.  Library's part in making Americans.  Delineator 77: 17-8.

Dalal, C. D.  Scheme of classification for Sanskrit libraries. Lib Miscellany 1: 3-8.

Dalal, V. S.  Select bibliography of the history of ancient India.  Lib Miscellany (Baroda) 1: 195-202.

Dale, A. W. W.  Library lectures.  L J 8: 338.

Dale, M.  Notes from a base hospital library (Camp Kearny, California).  Cal News Notes 14: 1-5.

Dall, C. H.  Fiction in public libraries.  L J 6: 158.

Dallimore, F.  Branch libraries.  L A 5: 111-3.

------- F.  Library association examinations.  L A 11: 195-8.

------- F.  Object lessons to school children in the use of libraries.  L A R 11: 49-68.

Damon, F.  A library crusade.  P L 24: 51.

Dana, J. C.  A. L. A. primer.  P L 1: 6-130.

-- J. C.  About small public libraries.  American City 9: 132-4.

-- J. C.  Advertising a library.  L J 20: 88.

-- J. C.  American library association constitution.  P L 14: 64-5.

-- J. C.  Anticipations, or what we may expect of periodicals.  P L 12: 381-3.

-- J. C.  As others see us: civil service and librarians. P L 22: 105-6.

-- J. C.  Book preparation.  P L 1: 43-4.

-- J. C.  Book service in small libraries.  L J 44: 621-2.

-- J. C.  Book using skill in higher education.  A L A Bull 3: 191-5; P L 14: 306.

-- J. C.  Bookbinding.  L J 31: 182-3.

-- J. C.  Bookbinding for libraries.  P L 11: 287-9.

-- J. C.  Bookbinding for public libraries.  P L 7: 147-8.

-- J. C.  Building up directories as advertising mediums: address before Philadelphia convention A. A. C. of the W., June 27, 1916.  Printer's Ink June 29, 1916: 33-6; L J 42: 74-5; Am Lib Annual 1917-18: 36-7.

-- J. C.  The business man and the special library.  Special Libraries 10: 1-2.

-- J. C.  The business man's branch of the Newark (N.J.) library.  Associated Advertising Oct 1914: 25-8.

-- J. C.  Business men's branch.  Wis Lib Bull 7: 190.

-- J. C.  The changing character of libraries.  Atlantic Monthly 12: 481-5, Apr. 1918; L J 43: 452-3.

-- J. C.  Children's reading: what some of the teachers say.  U S Bur of Educ Rept 1897-98: 680-4; L J 22: 187-90.

-- J. C.  A clearing-house for pamphlet literature.  L J 44: 299-301.

-- J. C.  The college and university library.  P L 16: 143.

-- J. C.  Commercial and industrial libraries.  L J 44: 309-10.

-- J. C.  Cost of library bulletins.  A L A Bull 9: 462-3.

-- J. C.  The country church and the library.  N Y L 3: 106-7; Outlook 98: 34-5.

-- J. C.  Discusses the A. L. A. enlarged program.  A L A Bull 13: 368-70.

-- J. C.  Establishment of a library.  L J 36: 189-90.

-- J. C.  The evolution of the special library.  Special Libraries 5: 70-6; Newarker 3: 439-50.

-- J. C.  Exhibition of Ralph Ruzicka's engravings.  P L 22: 149.

-- J. C.  Fiction in libraries.  Ia L C A 2: 47-9.

-- J. C.  Fiction in public libraries.  L J 24: 670-1; P L 3: 12-3.

-- J. C.  Filing pamphlets by the color-band method.  L J 43: 747-8.

-- J. C.  Harvard university course in printing.  Graphic Arts March 1911; National Printer-Journalist 29: 262-3; Lib Work 5: 1-3.

-- J. C.  Hear the other side: president's address at the A. L. A. Conference, Cleveland.  L J 21: Conf No 1-5.

-- J. C.  Helpful state of mind.  P L 10: 178-9.

-- J. C.  How to meet arguments against libraries.  L J 21: Conf No 3-5.

-- J. C.  Insurance libraries.  Reprinted from The Independent, Dec 30, 1909, L J 35: 61-2.

-- J. C.  Learning one's own library.  P L 23: 461-2.

-- J. C.  The legitimate field of the municipal public library.  The Newarker Aug 1914: 559-68; L A R 16: 465-82.

-- J. C.  A letter on publicity.  A L A Bull 10: 31; P L 21: 310.

-- J. C.  Lettering the backs of books when rebound for libraries.  P L 12: 306-7.

-- J. C.  Librarian's pastime reading.  L J 21: 22.

-- J. C.  The librarian's spirit and method in working with schools.  Nat Educ Assn 1899: 515-25; U S Bur of Educ Rept, 1899-1900: 710-7.

-- J. C.  Libraries and museums for business.  Bull Bib 10: 52-4.

-- J. C.  Libraries and schools as art educators.  L J 21: 150.

-- J. C.  Libraries and teachers.  L J 21: 133; P L 1: 81-2.

-- J. C.  The library as a practical aid in the world of affairs.  N Y L 5: 8-10; New Hamp Bull Nov 1915: 8-16.

-- J. C.  Library associations and clubs.  L J 30: Conf No 21-6.

-- J. C.  Library building.  P L 7: 406-7.

-- J. C.  Library law.  A L A Primer.  P L 1: 5.

-- J. C.  Library movement in the Far West (Montana, Idaho, Wyoming, Utah, Arizona, Colorado, New Mexico, Texas).  L 8: 446-50.

-- J. C.  Library opportunities.  P L 9: 1-5.

-- J. C.  Library primer.  P L 1: 4-10, 39-45, 79-82, 115-33, 167-74, 212-5, 263-4.

-- J. C.  Library printing.  Printing Art 6: 284-90; P L
13: 35-7.
-- J. C.  Library promotion.  Wilson Bulletin 1: 379-81.
-- J. C.  Library training in forty-two American libraries.
P L 6: 533.
-- J. C.  Magazines for small libraries.  P L 1: 116-7.
-- J. C.  Making a library useful.  Wash L A Bull 2, No 2:
6-7; Vt L Bull 1: 18-22.
-- J. C.  The making of an insurance library.  Independent
67: 1523; L J 35: 61-2.
-- J. C.  Many sided interest: how the library promotes it.
School Journal 73: 563-5.
-- J. C.  Materials and features of books.  Printing Art
14: 97-104.
-- J. C.  Meaning of the public library in a city's life.
L J 27: 755-7.
-- J. C.  Misdirection of effort in reference work.  P L
16: 108-9.
-- J. C.  Missionary work--What does the free library do
for a community, A. L. A. Primer.  P L 1: 5-6.
-- J. C.  Municipal legislative reference, commercial, tech-
nical and public welfare libraries.  A L A Bull 3: 223-4.
-- J. C.  A national bureau of municipal information.  Spec-
ial Libraries 5: 104-6.
-- J. C.  New York public library service.  L J 44: 621-2.
-- J. C.  Newark's business branch: a pioneer in the field.
L J 42: 265-6.
-- J. C.  Notes on bookbinding for libraries.  P L 11: 287-
9.
-- J. C.  Notes on figures about the circulation of novels
in Newark library.  L J 28: 616.
-- J. C.  Notes on pictures for school rooms and the Biblio-
theca Paedogogica.  L J 34: 15-6.
-- J. C.  On the establishment of a library.  L J 36: 189-
90.
-- J. C.  Our youngest readers.  2nd Int Conf 118-9.
-- J. C.  The pamphlet-library.  Special Libraries 10: 77-8.
-- J. C.  Periodical library bulletins.  L J 19: Conf No
54-5.
-- J. C.  Periodicals for a small library.  P L 11: 367.
-- J. C.  Physical side of books: suggestions for the for-
mation of a collection of material employed in the making
of a book.  L J 32: 351-8.
-- J. C.  Picture bulletins from another point of view.
Wis Lib Bull 3: 75.
-- J. C.  Place of fiction in the library.  P L 8: 352-4.
-- J. C.  Place of fiction in the public library.  L J 28:
Conf No 36-7.
-- J. C.  Presidential address.  L J 21: Conf No 1-5.

-- J. C.  Print collections in small libraries.  Print Collector's Quarterly 3: 61-9; P L 18: 279-81.

-- J. C.  Printing exhibit for libraries.  L J 35: 191.

-- J. C.  Printing presses in museums and libraries.  L J 42: 538-9.

-- J. C.  Public libraries as censors.  Bookman ( N Y) 49: 147-52.

-- J. C.  The public library and publicity in municipal affairs.  L J 38: 198-201.

-- J. C.  Purposes of library associations.  L J 28: 776.

-- J. C.  Qualities and training necessary for a business librarian.  P L 22: 362-4.

-- J. C.  Relations of the library to the city.  American City 7: 314-7.

-- J. C.  School libraries and their value.  P L 11: 435.

-- J. C.  Schools and museums.  P L 23: 60-3.

-- J. C.  Selection and rejection of books.  P L 13: 177-8; L J 33: 148-9.

-- J. C.  Some French libraries.  P L 13: 344-7; P L 14: 19-21.

-- J. C.  Story of the made in Newark material.  Special Libraries 2: 93-6.

-- J. C.  Story telling in libraries.  P L 13: 349-51.

-- J. C.  Summary of the library associations and clubs of the world.  L J 30: Conf No 21-6.

-- J. C.  Things children should know.  P L 6: 98-9.

-- J. C.  Things every one should know.  Ia L C Q 1: 33-5.

-- J. C.  Three factors in civilization.  P L 14: 43-5.

-- J. C.  The use of print in the world of affairs.  L J 35: 535-8; Special Libraries 2: 2-3.

-- J. C.  What next.  P L 21: 3-7.

-- J. C.  What state and local associations can do for library interests.  L J 30: Conf No 17-21.

-- J. C.  What the modern library is doing.  Independent 70: 193-6; Outlook 97: 301-2; P L 16: 143.

-- J. C.  What the work of the state library associations should be.  L J 26: Conf No 183-5, Discussion 186-8.

-- J. C.  Women in library work.  Independent 71: 244-50.

-- J. C.  Work in certain typical libraries.  U S Govt Rept, 717-8, 1899.

Danenbaum, R.  Expanding the usefulness of the public library, Minneapolis.  World To-Day, 20: 743-5.

Danforth, G. F.  Co-operation in lending.  P L 4: 275-6.

Daniel, R. M.  Libraries and education.  L A 7: 35-6.

---- R. M.  Problem of the junior assistant.  L A 10: 177-8.

Daniels, J.  Americanization by indirection.  L J 45: 871-6.

Daniels, J. F.  Agricultural bulletins: their indexing and use.  L J 30: 930-1.

----- J. F.  Author and title marks in fiction.  P L 7: 143-4.

----- J. F.  The county free library service as operated at Riverside, California.  A L A Bull 11: 125-7, 328.

----- J. F.  The empty heart: a paper on the educational future of libraries.  L J 34: 4-8.

----- J. F.  Indeterminate functions of a college library. L J 32: 487-92.

----- J. F.  Library conditions and a plan for their betterment.  P L 8: 100-1.

----- J. F.  Library handicraft.  P L 7: 405-6.

----- J. F.  Library work at the State normal school, Greeley, Colorado.  P L 3: 167-8.

----- J. F.  Net price system in operation.  P L 8: 54-5.

----- J. F.  New phase of net price controversy.  P L 7: 222-3.

----- J. F.  People: a modern emphasis in library training. L J 33: 173-6.

----- J. F.  Prospective view of catalog training.  A L A Bull 9: 267-70.

----- J. F.  To the normal school librarians who need it. P L 6: 197-200.

----- J. F.  Typewriter and catalogue cards.  P L 6: 537.

----- J. F.  What I believe about library schools.  P L 23: 18-9.

Danielson, C. L.  What the teacher wants of the library.  P L 8: 97-8.

Danton, G. H.  Required reading and company.  Educational Review 41: 510-5.

Darch, J.  Library lighting.  Illuminating Engineer 4, No 2; Libn 1: 198, 227-31.

Darling, G. R.  Stout institute library and its method of reaching technical students.  Wis Lib Bull 4: 90-1.

Darlow, G.  The municipal section of a public library.  P L 13: 4-6.

Davenport, C.  Bagford's notes on bookbindings.  Bib Soc Trans 7: 123-59.

------- C.  Bookbinding and book production.  L A R 7: 553-5.

------- C.  Bookbinding in England.  L A R 9: 19-23.

------- C.  English and Scottish heraldry in books.  L A R 10: 149-52.

------- C.  English embroidered bindings.  Bib Soc Trans 4: 144-8.

------- C.  Forgeries in bookbinding.  L (ns) 2: 389-95.

------- C.  Heraldry of English royal bindings.  Bib Soc Trans 8: 73-6.

------- C.  King Charles I.'s embroidered Bible.  L (ns) 1: 373-7.

------- C.  Leather used in bookbinding.  L 10: 15-9; Bib
Soc Trans 5: 161-2.
------- C.  Library bookbinding.  L A R 5: 5-15, Discussion
50-3.
------- C.  Notes on bookbinding.  L 5: 217.
------- C.  On bookbindings at the British Museum.  Bib
Soc Trans 2: 93-6.
------- C.  Some popular errors as to old bindings.  L
(ns) 2: 231-7.
------- C.  Three bindings with Little Gidding stamps.  L
(ns) 1: 205-12.
------- C. and E. W. Hulme.  Deterioration of binding lea-
ther.  L A R 6: 276-8.
Davenport, C. J.  Bookbinding in France.  L A R 13: 98-104.
------- C. J.  Bookbinding in Germany.  L A R 12: 49-51.
David, A. C.  New York public library.  Architectural Record
28: 144-72.
Davidow, A. D.  Medical libraries.  Med Lib and Hist Journal
3: 45-99.
Davidson, A. T.  Big possibilities of the little library.  New
Hamp Bull (ns) 15: 132-4.
Davidson, C.  Library work in schools.  L J 24: 150.
------ C.  Use and abuse of aid in research.  L J 23: Conf
No 110-1.
Davidson, H. A.  Special needs of study clubs.  L J 23: Conf
No 158.
Davidson, J. W.  Club and the library.  Ia L C Q 3: 17-20.
Davis, A. O.  Libraries and the new food program.  P L 24:
20-1.
Davis, B. M.  The rural school as a community centre.  Nation-
al Society for the Scientific Study of Education, Year Book
10, pt. 2: 1-16. 1911.
Davis, C. T.  Fire prevention and insurance.  Greenwood's Yr-
Bk: 52-6. 1900-01.
--- C. T.  Indicators versus card charging.  L 5: 291-304.
--- C. T.  Insurance of public libraries.  L W 2: 121-2.
Davis, E. C.  Story telling and the poem.  National Education
Assn Journal of Proceedings & Addresses, 1893: 351-5.
Davis, E. M.  Adapting the Dewey classification to the needs
of school work.  P L 20: 8-9.
Davis, J. B.  The high school library of the next decade.  A
L A Bull 13: 126-30, 353; L J 44: 593-6.
--- J. B.  Outline of work in vocational guidance in the
Central high school.  A L A Bull 7: 297-300.
--- J. B.  Use of the library in vocational guidance.  Nat
Educ Assn 1912: 126-73.
Davis, J. F.  Special bibliographic or library course in univ-
ersities, colleges and libraries.  L J 23: Conf No 139-40.
Davis, L.  Literature in primary schools.  Southern Education
Assn Proceedings 1900: 255-60.

Davis, M. G.  Latin-America in the children's room.  L J 44: 234.

Davis, M. L.  Necessity of staff meetings.  L J 33: 398; 34: 299-301.

--- M. L.  Promoting efficiency in the smaller libraries. N Y L 4: 5-9, Nov 1913.

--- M. L.  Reading list on Harley Granville Barker.  Bull Bib 7: 130-2.

Davis, O. C.  Experience overseas.  A L A Bull 13: 302-6, 348.

Davis, O. S.  Traveling libraries for New Hampshire.  New Hamp Bull (ns) 12: 220-4.

--- O. S.  Y.M.C.A. library, Albany, charging system.  L J 16: 232.

Davis, R.  Traveling library service on the Mexican border. Ia L C Q 8: 120-1.

Davis, R. C.  An over use of books.  P L 9: 435-9.

--- R. C.  Preliminary parts of a book.  P L 21: 255-8.

--- R. C.  Teaching bibliography in colleges.  L J 11: 289.

--- R. C.  The unselfish nature of bibliographical labor in the last century.  P L 21: 1-3.

Davis, R. L.  Some library reminiscences.  P L 22: 180-2.

Davis, T. K.  College library and the college.  L J 10: 100-3.

Davis, W. L.  Summer school course for teacher-librarians. Wis Lib Bull 15: 250-2.

Davison, J. L.  Paper making and book production.  L A R 17: 326.

Dawley, F. F.  Library boards under the commission plan of city government.  Ia L C Q 6: 150-2.

Dawson, A.  The most artistic book.  L 3: 433-5.

Dawson, G. E.  Prose writers of Canada.  L J 25: Conf No 11-24.

Day, L. F.  Type set book ornaments.  Printing Art 14: 333-8.

Day, M. B.  At your service: Five safety libraries.  Special Libraries 11: 206-7.

- M. B.  Bringing the library to its members.  L J 45: 935-6.

- M. B.  Library and information bureau of the National safety council, Chicago.  Special Libraries 10: 212-4.

Daykin, J.  Village libraries.  L A R 9: 365-74.

---- J.  Village libraries, with special reference to York-shire.  L A R 8: 485-7.

Dayton, G. W.  The County library law: its purposes and pro-visos.  Texas Libraries 1: 94-5, October 1915.

Dayton, H. I.  Books for the browsing corner of a high school library: some illustrated editions of classics in English and world literature.  Wilson Bulletin 1: 325-7.

Dayton, I.  Words you ought to know.  L J 43: 885.

Dean, M.  Games for use in libraries.  Wis Lib Bull 5: 15-6.

Dean, M. W.  A word of protest.  School Review 4: 686-9.

Deane, T. N., and T. M.  Notes descriptive of plans of new
    buildings in Dublin for National library of Ireland.  L
    A Trans 7: 125-7.
Dearholt, H. E.  Frank Avery Hutchins, 1850-1914, an appre-
    ciation.  Wis Lib Bull 9: 195.
Deas, C.  Sunderland public libraries: open access plans.  L
    W 10: 367-9, 416-7.
Deas, J. A. C.  How we may show our museums and art galleries
    to the blind.  L W 16: 76, 216-7.
DeBernardi, T.  Child welfare.  Cal News Notes 14: 24-40.
DeCastro, J. P.  The printing of Fielding's works.  L (4th
    series) 1: 257-70.
Deeds, M. L.  Bulletin boards.  Lib Occ 5: 213.
    --- M. L.  Library housekeeping: The reading room.  Lib
    Occ 5: 202.
Deffenbaugh, E.  History and description of the Spokane pub-
    lic library.  Wash L A Bull 1 No 1: 8-9.
    --------- E.  Spokane picture bulletin.  Wash L A Bull 3,
    No 1: 8.
    --------- E.  Value of intelligent criticism.  Wash L A
    Bull 2, No 3: 3-5.
DeGarmo, C.  Value of literature in moral training.  Nat Educ
    Assn 1894: 388-97.
Delamarter, E.  The reading of high school students.  Michigan
    State Board of Library Commissioners, Report 1909: 52-4.
Dalannoy, P.  Library of the University of Louvain: its his-
    tory, description and contents.  By the Librarian.  Nine-
    teenth Century 77: 1061-71; Living Age 286: 265-72.
DeLaughter, N. M.  The German story-hour at Carondelet branch,
    St. Louis public library.  P L 21: 255.
    -------- N. M.  Printed children's catalogs: review of
    Corinne Bacon's "Children's catalog," published by H. W.
    Wilson Co.  P L 22: 148-9.
DeLaughter, Mrs. N. M.  Reaching the readers in war-time: an
    account of publicity work of the St. Louis public library.
    St. Louis Public Library Annual Report 1917-18: 73-124
    (also published separately)
Delisle, L.  Discovery of the long missing pictures stolen
    from an illuminated MS. in the library of Macon.  L (ns)
    1: 45-9.
    ----- L.  Souvenirs de jeunesse.  L (ns) 9: 201-11, 245-
    56.
Dellenbaugh, F. S.  Library of the American geographical so-
    ciety.  L J 36: 625-8.
DeMontmorency, J. E. G.  Place of libraries in national educ-
    ation.  L A 8: 222-6, 230-5.
    --- J. E. G.  Public libraries and national education.
    Contemporary 100: 881-5.
De Morgan, A.  Difficulty of correct description of books.
    L A R 4: 247-73.

Denie, L.   How to make the most of a small library.  L N (U
  S) 3: 469-74.
Deniker, M. J.  London bibliographical conference.  L J 21:
  499-500, 522.
Denne, G. E.   Donations.  L A 5: 226-9.
--- G. E.  Show cases for books.  L W 10: 70-1.
Dennis, A. L. P.  Abstract of a paper on the European histor-
  ians of the Turks in the 16th and 17th centuries.  Bib Soc
  Amer Proc 1: 103-4.
---- A. L. P.  Special collections in American libraries--
  The Oriental collection of Count Paul Riant at Harvard
  university.  L J 28: 817-20.
Dennis, H. J.  Duties of a state librarian.  L J 12: 184.
---- H. J.  Library garment.  L J 15: 293.
---- H. J.  Statutory laws: official lists by states and
  territories.  L J 13: 36, 277.
Dent, R. K.  Amendment of by-law as to meetings and discus-
  sion of contentious business.  L A R 10: 579-84.
-- R. K.  Birmingham: its libraries and its book-sellers.
  B A R 4: I-IV.
-- R. K.  Children's books and their place in reference
  library.  L A R 1: 216-21.
-- R. K.  Classification of local literature.  L A R 9:
  107-8.
-- R. K.  Curious catalogue--some notes on the catalogue
  of William Drummond of Hawthornden.  L A R 2: 427-9.
-- R. K.  Elementary bibliographies.  L A R 15: 99.
-- R. K.  Formation of a small reference library.  L 8:
  531-5.
-- R. K.  Free lectures in connection with libraries.  L
  6: 354-60.
-- R. K.  Free libraries of Birmingham and its neighbour-
  hood.  L C 5: 1-6.
-- R. K.  "Gnats."  L 3: 408-13.
-- R. K.  Introduction to discussion on blacking out of
  sporting news in libraries.  L 6: 127-9.
-- R. K.  John Baskerville and his work.  L A R 5: 109-18.
-- R. K.  Librarian as a collector.  L A R 10: 11-8.
-- R. K.  Librarian as a help to the reader.  L A R 3: 609-
  15.
-- R. K.  Library extension work: Lectures.  L W 1: 162-4,
  220-1.
-- R. K.  New cataloguer and some of his ways.  L 9: 173-
  8.
-- R. K.  Notes on the formation of a small reference li-
  brary.  L 8: 531-5.
-- R. K.  Shakespeare--Bacon question.  L A R 13: 191-2.
-- R. K.  Some of the institutions of Birmingham and the
  neighbourhood.  L A R 4: 371-81.

-- R. K.  Titles; or, traps for the unwary.  L 10: 165-9.
Denton, A.  Early parochial libraries.  L A 1: 200-7.
De Perolt, J.  Libraries and the scholar.  Nation 97: 162-3,
    Aug 21, 1913.
Depping, G.  Action of gas on bindings.  1st Int Conf: 50.
----- G.  Note on co-operative cataloguing.  1st Int Conf
    100; L J 2: 188, 264-5.
----- G.  Notes on library buildings.  1st Int Conf: 50;
    L J 2: 145, 251-5.
----- G.  Suggests a committee of chemists and librarians
    to consider question of action of gas on bindings.  1st Int
    Conf: 50. 1877.
DePuy, A. R.  Social activities.  Mich Lib Bull Jan-Feb 1916:
    22-3.
Derr, Mrs. E. G.  Motion pictures and the library in Cleve-
    land.  L J 43: 157-8.
Derthick, E. L.  Children's books: what constitutes a good
    edition?  P L 17: 120.
Deubner, L.  The art of the book in Germany "Studio" spring
    number 1914: 127-60, 161-76.
Deutsch, B.  The public library and the public need.  Dial 64:
    475-7, May 23, 1918, L J 43: 537-8.
Deveneau, G. A.  Agricultural extension work and the opportun-
    ities it offers to agricultural college libraries.  A L A
    Bull 11: 140-8, 328.
------ G. A.  Libraries and the United States Boys working
    reserve.  Special Libraries 10: 66-7.
DeVinne, T. L.  Types of Giambattista Bodoni, with examples.
    Printing Art 17: 277-86.
Dewar, J. A.  Presidential address to the L. A. U. K. at Perth.
    L A R 12: 367-72.
--- J. A.  Presidential address.  L A R 13: 367-72.
--- J. A.  Value of libraries.  L A R 13: 368-72.
Dewey, A. C.  Library training of children.  Educational Bi-
    Monthly 3: 17-25.
Dewey, F. K. W.  On an order record by funds.  L J 38: 22-3.
Dewey, H. B.  County circulating school libraries.  Washington
    Lib Assn Bull 1, No 2: 5-7; Cal New Notes 3: 130.
--- H. B.  Postal rates on books.  P L 23: 471.
Dewey, J.  Primary education fetich.  Forum 25: 315-28.
Dewey, M.  A. L. A. catalog.  L J 10: 73-6; P L 9: 78; Minn P
    L C N 1: 6: Ohio Lib Bull 2, No 3: 1-2.
--- M.  A. L. A. Standard accession book.  L N (U S) 2: 17-2
--- M.  Abridged decimal classification and the relative
    index.  L N (U S) 4: 1-200.
--- M.  Accession book.  L N (U S) 1: 27-9.
--- M.  Accession book, card shelf-list and full names.
    P L 9: 281-2.
--- M.  The accession catalog again.  L J 3: 336-8.
--- M.  Accession order.  L N (U S) 3: 422.

--- M.  Accession rules. L J 1: 316-20.
--- M.  Albany library school graduates. L J 3: 459.
--- M.  Alphabeting catalog cards. L J 5: 176-7.
--- M.  American library association. L J 1: 245-7.
--- M.  The Amherst classification. L J 3: 231-2.
--- M.  Apprenticeship of librarians. L J 4: 147-8.
--- M.  Arrangement on the shelves. L J 4: 117-20; 191-2.
--- M.  Bindery in building. P L 8: 405.
--- M.  Book braces, supports and props. L N (U S) 1: 214-23; 2: 38.
--- M.  Book marking. L N ( U S) 3: 426-9.
--- M.  Book numbers. L J 10: 296-300; L N (U S) 3: 419-21.
--- M.  Book plates. L N (U S) 1: 23-5; 2: 39-41.
--- M.  Book selection. L J 1: 391-3.
--- M.  Books and readers' accounts. L J 4: 131.
--- M.  British Museum catalogues. L N (U S) 1: 179-82.
--- M.  Broadening of state libraries. P L 11: 22.
--- M.  Buckram and Morocco. L J 11: 161-2.
--- M.  Capacity of book stacks. P L 7: 28-9.
--- M.  Card catalog drawer. L N (U S) 1: 39-40.
--- M.  Card pockets. L N (U S) 1: 282-5.
--- M.  Card shelf list. P L 9: 281-2.
--- M.  Catalogues and cataloguing. U S Rept 632. 1876.
--- M.  Changing catalog rules. L J 27: Conf No 196, Discussion 196-202.
--- M.  Changing the size of catalogue cards. L J 25: 350.
--- M.  Charging system: a new combined plan and various details. L J 3: 359-65.
--- M.  Charging systems based on an account with borrowers. L J 3: 252-5, 285-8.
--- M.  Cheap library post movement. L J 27: 754.
--- M.  Chronologic order. L N (U S) 3: 423-4.
--- M.  Civil service examination (with questions) for New York state library. L J 14: 118-21.
--- M.  Classification scheme. L J 4: 117-20, 191-4.
--- M.  Clearing house for duplicates. L J 5: 216-7.
--- M.  Close classification versus bibliography. L J 11: 350-3.
--- M.  College course in bibliography. L J 18: 422.
--- M.  Colors in typewriting. P L 10: 467.
--- M.  Coloured guide blocks. L J 3: 192.
--- M.  Combining administrative departments. P L 14: 21.
--- M.  The coming catalogue. L J 1: 423-7.
--- M.  Competition of architects on library plans. P L 8: 63-4.
--- M.  Consulting librarianship. L J 5: 16-7.
--- M.  Co-operative cataloguing. L J 1: 170-5.
--- M.  Cost of duplicate card catalogue of National library. P L 7: 240-1.

--- M. Cost of library equipment. L N (U S) 1: 22-3.
--- M. Criticism of Shurtleff's scheme. L J 4: 61, 120.
--- M. Decimal classification: a reply to Messrs. Schwartz and Perkins. L J 11: 100-6, 132-9.
--- M. Decimal classification and subject index. U S Rept 623-48. 1876.
--- M. Decimal classification beginnings. L J 45: 151-4.
--- M. Decimal classification of the great war. L J 44: 98; L W 21: 160-2.
--- M. Defacing books. L J 2: 327.
--- M. Delinquent notices and check boxes. L J 3: 370-1.
--- M. Designating sex in registration. L J 3: 311; 4: 174.
--- M. Detailed classification in course of preparation. L J 43: 497.
--- M. Duplicate clearing house. P L 3: 255-6.
--- M. Duplicating processes. L J 4: 165.
--- M. Eclectic book numbers. L J 11: 296-301; L N (U S) 3: 419-21.
--- M. The educational trinity. L N (U S) 1: 44-5.
--- M. Embossing stamps. L N (U S) 1: 26-7.
--- M. F. Jackson. L J 11: 435.
--- M. Factors of successful administration. L N (U S) 1: 45.
--- M. The faculty library. L (ns) 2: 238-41.
--- M. Field and future of traveling libraries. Univ of State of New York, Home Education Department Bulletin No 40.
--- M. Field libraries. Dial 40: 75-7.
--- M. Function of the library as a bookstore. L J 23: Conf No 152-3.
--- M. Functions of a state library association. L J 27: Conf No 236-8.
--- M. Future of library commissions. L J 31: 27, 328, Conf No 204.
--- M. Future of library schools. P L 10: 435-8; N Y S L Rept 85, Bull No 78: 216-22.
--- M. The growth of librarianship. P L 21: 270.
--- M. Heating libraries. L J 6: 93-6.
--- M. Hunting for full names. P L 9: 281.
--- M. Ideal relations between trustees and librarian. L J 31: Conf No 44.
--- M. Importance of using standard sizes. L N (U S) 2: 46-52.
--- M. Impressions of the fourteenth annual conference. L J 17: 56-7.
--- M. In Memoriam. L J 11: 478.
--- M. Inexperienced card makers. P L 8: 460.
--- M. Inter-library loans. L N (U S) 3: 405-7.

--- M.  James Duff Brown, 1862-1914.  L W 14: 161-2.
--- M.  Labour-savers for readers and writers.  L N (U S)
1: 55-6.
--- M.  Large base notation.  L J 4: 7-10, 75-8.
--- M.  Lecture outline course and problems.  N Y S L Rept
85, Bull No 75.
--- M.  Librarian as educator.  L J 11: 165.
--- M.  Librarianship--what it implies.  Ia L C Q 2: 54.
--- M.  Libraries as bookstores.  L J 45: 493-4.
--- M.  Libraries as educational forces.  P L 1: 268-9.
--- M.  Libraries as related to the educational work of
the state.  L N (U S) 3: 333-40; U S Bureau of Education
Report 1887-88: 1031-9.
--- M.  Libraries the true university for scholars as well
as the people.  Library Notes 1: 49-50; L N (U S) 1: 49-50.
--- M.  Library abbreviations for fore-names, headings,
imprints and notes; book titles, places of publication,
titles, states, etc., months, days and size notation.  L
N (U S) 1: 206-11.
--- M.  Library as an educator.  L N (U S) 1: 43-4.
--- M.  Library conditions in America in 1904.  P L 9:
363-5.
--- M.  Library co-operation and the index to periodicals.
L J 11: 5; L N (U S) 1: 195-7.
--- M.  Library hours.  L J 4: 449.
--- M.  Library notes.  P L 7: 70-1, 153, 191-2, 239-40,
371, 461-2; 14: 261.
--- M.  Library notes: long hours of work.  P L 8: 323.
--- M.  Library pictures.  P L 11: 10-1.
--- M.  Library progress.  L 1: 367-82.
--- M.  Library schools of doubtful value.  P L 7: 119-20.
--- M.  Library shelving--definitions and general princi-
ples.  L N (U S) 2: 95-122.
--- M.  Man-a-month volunteers.  A L A Bull 1, No 2: 1-3.
--- M.  Massachusetts state library bill.  L J 4: 130.
--- M.  A model accession catalogue.  L J 1: 315-20.
--- M.  Monthly versus quarterly indexes.  L J 13: 172.
--- M.  National headquarters for the A. L. A.; some sug-
gestions and opinions.  L J 28: 757-64.
--- M.  New library development of the National education-
al association.  P L 1: 183.
--- M.  New York library association.  L J 15: 267-8.
--- M.  Newspaper print.  P L 6: 433.
--- M.  Notation system.  L N (U S) 3: 421-2.
--- M.  Note on American and state library associations.
L J 16: 169-70.
--- M.  Notes on some continental libraries.  L J 17: 121-
2.
--- M.  Notes on the articles on fixtures, furniture and
fittings.  U S Rept 739-40. 1892-93.

--- M. Numbering books. L J 6: 53.

--- M. On fines. L J 3: 359-62, 370-1.

--- M. On library progress. L 1: 367-76.

--- M. On the revision of the decimal classification. L J 25: 684-5.

--- M. On the suitability of the Dewey scheme for college libraries. L J 24: Conf No 154.

--- M. Origin of the motto of the A. L. A.: "The best reading for the largest number at the least cost." P L 11: 55.

--- M. Our cheap and effective catalogue of sale duplicates. L J 12: 140-1.

--- M. Past, present, and future of the A. L. A. L J 5: 247-76.

--- M. Perkins' classification. L J 7: 60-2.

--- M. Photographic facsimiles. P L 14: 22.

--- M. The place of the library in education. Nat Educ Assn 1901: 858-64.

--- M. Plans for numbering. L J 4: 43.

--- M. A plea for collections of lantern slides in public libraries. P L 11: 10-1.

--- M. Principles underlying charging systems. L J 3: 217-20.

--- M. Printed catalogue cards from a central bureau. L (ns) 2: 130-4.

--- M. The profession. L J 1: 5-6.

--- M. Proportional expenditures. P L 10: 137-8.

--- M. Public documents. L J 1: 10-1.

--- M. Qualifications of a librarian. L W 2: 96-8; N Y S L Rept 85: 91-6, Bulletin 75.

--- M. Relation of school libraries to public library system. P L 10: 224-5.

--- M. Relation of state to the public library. 2nd Int Conf 19-22. 1897.

--- M. Relation of the colleges to the modern library movement. Assn of Colleges and Preparatory Schools of the Middle States and Maryland, Proceedings 1891, 4: 78-83.

--- M. Relation of the school libraries to the public library system. P L 10: 224-5.

--- M. Revolving shelf pin. L N (U S) 1: 134.

--- M. Rubber stamps. P L 14: 21-2.

--- M. Salaries of librarians. P L 8: 323.

--- M. Sale duplicate slip catalog. L J 13: 283-6; L N (U S) 3: 350-3.

--- M. School of library economy. L J 8: 285-91; 9: 117-20.

--- M. Schwartz's new method of size notation. L J 10: 396.

--- M. Science in printing: being experiments with various size types. P L 6: 110-1.

--- M.  Scope and functions of the state library.  N Y S L Rept 87: 7-18.

--- M.  Selecting a library system.  L N (U S) 1: 21-2.

--- M.  Shelf lists.  U S Rept 645. 1876.

--- M.  Should the local library have a museum.  P L 7: 148.

--- M.  Simplified library school rules.  L N (U S) 4: 246-315.

--- M.  Size marks.  L N (U S) 3: 428-9.

--- M.  Size versus decoration.  P L 7: 121.

--- M.  Slip indicator.  L J 5: 320-1.

--- M.  Special topic cards in catalogues.  P L 7: 461-2.

--- M.  Standard sizes for printed books.  L N (U S) 2: 243.

--- M.  Subject blanks.  L N (U S) 2: 220-1.

--- M.  Subject catalogues.  U S Rept 647-8. 1876.

--- M.  Take books to readers.  P L 19: 154-5.

--- M.  Too many organizations.  P L 4: 56-7.

--- M.  Traveling A. L. A. Exhibit.  P L 5: 324.

--- M.  Use of colours in libraries.  L J 3: 65.

--- M.  Useless words.  L J 5: 321.

--- M.  Van Everen numbers.  L J 5: 316-8.

--- M.  Waste in trifles.  P L 3: 348.

--- M.  What the A. L. A. was intended to be and to do. Wis Lib Bull 13: 41-9.

--- M.  What the Canadian government is doing for Canadian libraries.  L J 33: 17-8.

--- M.  Why a library does or does not succeed.  L N (U S) 1: 45-7.

--- M. and C. A. Cutter.  Numbering.  L J 3: 339-40.

--- M. and W. S. Biscoe.  Comments on Dieserud's suggested classification.  L J 23: 609-11.

De Yoe, F. E. and Thurber, C. H.  Where are the high school boys? School Review 8: 234-43.

Dhar, K. N.  Critical account of the literature of the Indian mutiny.  L A R 13: 165-77.

Dial, S. T.  The Cincinnati public library.  Harper's Weekly 53: 27 March 13, 1909.

Dickerson, L. L.  Beaune university A. L. A. library.  A L A Bull 13: 322-4; L J 44: 763-5; P L 24: 255-8.

------- L. L.  The college librarian and his community. L J 40: 318-9.

------- L. L.  The library and changing Iowa.  Ia L C Q 7: 184-5.

------- L. L.  Why not your town also?  Ia L C Q 8: 8.

Dickey, H. L.  The bulletin beautiful.  Educ Bi 'Monthly 4: 201-6.

---- H. L.  Chicago school children: good books and good reading.  Harper's Weekly June 5, 1909, 53: 24-5.

Dickinson, A. D.   Anti-librisection: a reply to Mr. Foster.
   P L 15: 158-9.
------- A. D.   By Flanders bridge: the adventures of an
   A. L. A. man overseas.  A L A Bull 13: 157-65, 348.
------- A. D.   The days work in Hoboken.  A L A Bull 12:
   200-2, 280.
------- A. D.   Magazine campaign.  P L 14: 215-6.
------- A. D.   A national library for the blind.  L J 31:
   218; P L 11: 308-9.
------- A. D.   On His Majesty's service only.  P L 21:
   132-5, 179-80, 226-7.
------- A. D.   Opportunities abroad: a suggestion to li-
   brary school students.  L J 42: 427-30.
------- A. D.   Organizing the library of Lahore university
   on modern American lines.  L J 41: 329-31.
------- A. D.   Periodicals for the blind.  L J 31: 218; P
   L 11: 308-9.
------- A. D.   Sending books "over there"--the day's work
   in Hoboken.  L J 43: 572-4.
Dickinson, M.   List of articles on children's schools and li-
   braries.  P L 3: 245.
Dickson, F. S.   The chronology of "Tom Jones." L (3d series)
   8: 218-24.
----- F. S.   The early editions of Fielding's "Voyage to
   Lisbon."  L (3d series) 8: 24-5.
----- F. S.   Errors and omissions: "Tom Jones." L (3d ser-
   ies) 9: 19-26.
Dickson, W. P.   Address to the Library association.  L C 5:
   107-9.
----- W. P.   Glasgow university library: its growth by do-
   nations.  L 8: 381-93.
----- W. P.   How to procure full names for author entries.
   L 5: 16-9, Discussion 82-3.
----- W. P.   John Small, 1828-1868.  L C 4: 166-8.
----- W. P.   Presidential address.  L C 5: 103-10.
Diephius, A.   Library and the wage earner.  L J 37: 366-70.
Dieserud, J.   Classification of anthropology: a review by J.
   C. Bay.  P L 13: 326-7.
------ J.   A classification of psychology.  P L 4: 53-4.
------ J.   Decimal classification: a reply to Messrs. Dewey
   and Biscoe.  L J 23: 657-8.
------ J.   Suggestion towards an improved decimal classifi-
   cation.  L J 23: 607-9.
Dietrichson, Mrs. M. W.   Discusses municipal reference library.
   A L A Bull 10: 48-9.
Dietz, J. W.   Corporation school movement: training men dur-
   ing business hours.  A L A Bull 11: 114-20, 328.
Dill, M. A.   Essentials of a good loan system (review of var-
   ious systems).  Ia L C Q 2: 7-10.

Dill, M. E.  Don'ts in reference work.  P L 9: 283-5.

Dillard, J. H.  Literary tastes of pupils and their vocabu-
lary.  Nation 71: 189.

Dimmitt, L.  The package library and its increasing popular-
ity.  L J 43: 390-3.

Dimmitt, L. N.  Cataloguing and classification for small libraries.  Texas Libraries 2: 73-4.

Dinsmore, K. E.  Trials and tribulations of an assistant.  P
L 21: 76-7.

Dippy, A. W.  Typographical designing.  Printing Art 18: 93-
100.

Diven, L. G.  Traveling libraries of Washington.  Wash L A
Bull 2, No 1: 15-6.

Dix, E. R. McC.  Earliest Belfast printing.  Irish Book Lover
May 1915: 157-8.

- E. R. M.  Earliest Dublin printers and the Company of
stationers of London. Bib Soc Trans 7: 78-85.

- E. R. McC.  History of Irish printing.  Irish Book Lover Mar 1915: 124-5.

- E. R. M.  Irish librarians and Irish bibliography.  An
Leab 1: 28-34.

- E. R. M.  Irish printed editions. An Leab 2: 67-77.

- E. R. McC.  Irish provincial printing.  Irish Book Lover Dec 1915: 90-1.

- E. R. McC.  Irish provincial printing prior to 1701. L
(ns) 2: 341-8.

- E. R. McC.  An old Dublin stationer's will and inventory.
L (3d series) 2: 379-83.

- E. R. McC.  Printing in Athlone in the nineteenth century.  Irish Book Lover Feb 1915: 106-8.

- E. R. McC.  Printing in Boyle.  Irish Book Lover Sept
1915: 24-6.

- E. R. McC.  Printing in Cashel in the nineteenth century.
Irish Book Lover Oct 1915: 46.

- E. R. McC.  Printing in Loughree, 1825-62.  Irish Book
Lover June 1915: 105-6.

- E. R. McC.  Printing in Mullingar 1830-1900, continued
from Vol II, p22.  Irish Book Lover Mar 1915: 127-8; Ap
140-1; May 160-1.

- E. R. McC.  Printing in Sligo in the nineteenth century,
Part III.  Irish Book Lover Jan 1915: 89-90.

- E. R. McC.  Printing in Strabane, 1825-1900.  Irish Book
Lover Nov 1915: 68-9.

- E. R. McC.  Printing in Tuam, 1825-1900.  Irish Book
Lover Oct 1915: 40-1.

Dixon, H.  Adventures of books.  L W 17: 201-4.

--- H.  The bespoken file.  L W 15: 316-7.

--- H.  Corporation of Dublin: its public libraries committee and the Bible in Irish.  An Leab 2: 184-90.

--- H.  Library as a holiday bureau.  L W 11: 480-1.
--- H.  Objects of Cumann na Leabharlann.  An Leab 1: 1-4.
--- H.  Select list of early printed books.  L W 16: 209-
11.
Dixon, J.  Bibliography of works written, translated, or edit-
ed by John O'Donovan.  An Leab 2: 1-39, 160-83, 195.
Dixon, M. A.  Sunday school libraries.  P L 5: 211-2.
Dixon, P. E.  Charles Lamb: the man and his work.  L A R 14:
399-405.
Dixon, V. M.  Agricultural library of the Iowa state college
of agriculture and mechanic arts.  Special Libraries 10:
44.
--- V. M.  Library extension in agriculture and home econ-
omics.  A L A Bull 12: 299: Special Libraries 9: 226-9.
--- V. M.  A plan for library extension work in agricul-
ture and home economics.  A L A Bull 12: 299; Special Li-
braries 9: 226-8.
Dixon, W. H.  A discussion of the public library.  Wis Lib
Bull 9: 163-5.
Dixon, W. McN.  Address inaugurating the course of lectures
at the London School of economics.  L A R 5: 597-614.
--- W. McN.  Presidential address.  L A R 5: 431-3.
--- W. McN.  Presidential address.  L A R 4: 479-91.
--- W. McN.  Shakespeare the Englishman.  L A R 18: 273-4,
324-6.
--- W. McN.  World of books: Presidential address.  L A R
4: 479-91.
Dixon, W. W.  Library work: some personal experiences with
the continuation school pupils in Eau Claire, Wisconsin.
Wis Lib Bull 9: 202-3, 1912-13.
Dixson, Mrs. Z.  Denison University library, Granville, Ohio.
L J 15: 15-6.
Dixson, Z. A.  Departmental libraries of the University of
Chicago.  L J 20: 375-7.
---- Z. A.  Library of the Chicago university.  L J 17: 50-
1.
---- Z. A.  Teaching library science by University exten-
sion methods.  P L 2: 285-9.
---- Z. A.  Traveling libraries of University of Chicago.
P L 2: 50.
Dobbins, E. V.  American telephone and telegraph company li-
brary, New York City.  L J 42: 284-5.
----- E. V.  An outline of the work of the Accounting li-
brary of the American telegraph and telephone company.
Special Libraries 3: 166-7.
Dobson, A.  Fielding and Andrew Miller.  L (3d series) 7: 177-
90.
---- A.  Horace Walpole's printing press.  L 1: 313-9.
---- A.  On certain quotations in Walton's "Angler."  L (ns)
2: 4-11.

---- A.  On some books and their associations.  L (ns)
9: 132-42.

Dock, G.  Medical library of the University of Michigan.
Med Lib and Hist Journal 3: 165-73.

Dockery, E. J.  How a library commission was secured in Idaho.
L J 26: Conf No 188-90.

Dodd, C.  Books for children.  National Magazine 45: 846-52.

-- C.  Some old school books.  National Review 45: 1006-14.

Dodd, H. P.  Care of books in a children's room.  P L 12:
83-6.

-- H. P.  Schoolroom libraries in Newark, N.J.  P L 8:
317-8.

-- H. P.  Undistinguished authors: their use in the children's room.  L J 33: 138-41.

Dodd, N. E.  Library versus the white slave traffic.  L J
37: 508-9.

Dodd, W. F.  Bibliography of political science.  Bib Soc Amer
Proc 1: 217-22.

Dodds, M. H.  The date of "Albion Knight."  L (3d series) 4:
167-70.

--- M. H.  "Lover,' vows": an adaptation by Mrs. Inchbald
of a German play "The love child," by Kotzebue.  L (3d
series) 8: 1-23.

Dodge, D. K.  What can be done by Illinois libraries for Shakespeare year.  P L 20: 460-2; Wis Lib Bull 12: 103-5.

Dodge, V.  The library and the school.  P L 3: 353.

--- V.  Loan system at Cedar Rapids.  P L 3: 259-61.

Dodge, V. R.  Librarians' aids.  L J 22: Conf No 67-70.

Dodgson, C.  Some Augsburg books illustrated by Hans Wieditz.
Bib Soc Trans 8: 1-3.

Donnelly, J. R.  The library school and the library.  L J 35:
109-11.

------ J. R.  Library school graduates.  P L 21: 259-61.

------ J. R.  Looking forward.  Special Libraries 10: 5-6.

------ J. R.  Views of library school directors.  P L 23:
15-7.

Donovan, A.  The blacksmith's story: what owning books meant
to him.  Wis Lib Bull 10: 38-42.

Doolittle, L.  Use of the library in teaching history in the
elementary school.  Missouri State Teachers' Assn Proceedings 1909: 313-5.

Doran, J. E.  Doing our bit.  P L 22: 273-5.

Doren, E. C.  Action upon bad books.  L J 28: 167-9.

--- E. C.  How to use the library in making a bibliography.
P L 7: 17.

--- E. C.  Library and the school: work now done.  L J 29:
Conf No 153-7.

--- E. C.  The organization of the Camp Denvers (Mass).
A L A library.  Bull Bib 10: 5-6.

--- E. C.  Public library work for public schools.  Nat
Educ Assn 1903: 943-8.

--- E. C.  School libraries.  U S Bur of Educ Rept 1897-
98, pt 1: 684-5; L J 22: 190-3.

--- E. C.  Special training for library work.  P L 4: 3-8.

--- E. C.  Standardization of library service: with discu-
sion, at midwinter meeting of the A. L. A. council in Chicago, Dec 28-29, 1916.  A L A Bull 11: 19-24; L J 42: 115-
6; P L 22: 68-9.

--- E. C.  Statistics and reports.  L J 24: 57-9.

--- E. C.  The war hospital library service at Dayton, Ohio.
Bull of Bibliog 10: 3-4.

Dorey, M.  What are the high school pupils reading?  School
Review 15: 299-300.

Doring, F. W.  How we use the library.  P L 8: 104-6.

Dorr, C. H.  Lure of old books.  Art World 9: 340-2.

Doubleday, W. E.  American library association conference at
Niagara Falls.  L (ns) 4: 424-31.

------- W. E.  Book buying scheme.  L A R 10: 525-7.

------- W. E.  Cinemas and libraries.  L A R 19: 41-2.

------- W. E.  Class lists, or dictionary catalogues?  A
defence of the latter, in reply to papers on class lists
by Messrs. Jast and Brown.  L 9: 179-80.

------- W. E.  Defects of mechanical type-setting.  L A R
12: 37.

------- W. E.  Dictionary versus classified catalogues for
lending libraries--The dictionary catalogue.  L A R 3: 521-
31, precis and discussion 486-7.

------- W. E.  Fiction nuisance and its abatement.  L W 5:
206-8.

------- W. E.  Home reading union and children.  L A R 11:
206-7.

------- W. E.  Letters on annotated catalogues, etc.  L 10:
36, 145-6, 190-1.

------- W. E.  Liability for accidents to children on library premises.  L A R 13: 117-8.

------- W. E.  Library association summer school.  L 8: 207-
12.

------- W. E.  Local records and the public libraries.  L
A R 2: 131-41, Discussion, 171; Correspondence 288, 345.

------- W. E.  Methods of co-operation.  L A R 9: 205-6;
11: 205-6.

------- W. E.  New Library bill.  L W 3: 1-3.

------- W. E.  New method of printing catalogues--Monotype.
L W 5: 281-3, 309-12.

------- W. E.  Open access question from a librarian's
point of view.  L (ns) 1: 187-95.

------- W. E.  Public libraries and the public.  L A R 14:
533; L J 37: 681-2.

------- W. E.  Public libraries and the war: a record.  L
A R 17: 1-9.
------- W. E.  Question of "net books."  L A R 4: 140-6.
------- W. E.  Review of the catalogue of the Bishopsgate
institute.  L W 4: 288-91  Boston Library Catalogue.
------- W. E.  The war and libraries.  L A R 18: 96-7.
------- W. E.  Weeding out the kindred problems.  L A R 6:
327-35, Discussion 356-8.
------- W. E.  A year's development of the public library
movement in Greater London.  L 4: 142-6.
Doubt, T. E.  Use and abuse of the library in the teaching of
physics.  School Science and Mathematics 15: 757-62.
Doud, M.  The inarticulate library assistant.  L J 45: 540-3.
Dougan, J. L.  Braille library at Oxford.  L A R 7: 178-9; L
J 30: 283-4.
Dougherty, H. Brest.  A. L. A. war service.  A L A Bull 13:
319-20.
Dougherty, H. T.  Use of the checker-board.  P L 20: 252-3.
Douglas, M. H.  Aids to reference work in a small library.
P L 9: 72-5, 121-3; New Hamp Bull 5: 157-60.
----- M. H.  Suggestions regarding future of the Iowa li-
brary association activities.  Ia L C Q 5: 118-20.
Douglas, M. M.  Old tales and modern adaptations.  Ia L C Q
6: 134-40.
Douglas, R. K.  Chinese libraries.  L A U K Trans 6: 40-4.
----- R. K.  Libraries in the Far East.  L C 4: 63-8.
Douglas, R. W.  Book selection for public libraries.  Pacific
Northwest Library Assn Proceedings 1912: 35-41.
Douglas-Hamilton, W. J.  Finance in public libraries.  L W
21: 200-2, 218-9; L W 22: 237-9.
Douglas-Lithgow, R. A.  Boston, Mass. public library.  Mass
M 4: 3-22.
Dousman, M. E.  Books for the play-ground.  Wis Lib Bull 3:
83-4.
----- M. E.  Children's departments.  L J 21: 406.
----- M. E.  Children's room of Milwaukee library.  L J
23: 664.
----- M. E.  How to organize girl's clubs.  Wis Lib Bull
7: 132-4.
----- M. E.  Methods of inducing care of books.  L J 25:
Conf No 60-2.
----- M. E.  Pictures and how to use them.  P L 4: 399-400.
----- M. E.  The public library and the public school at
Milwaukee, Wisconsin.  U S Bur of Educ Rept 1897-98, pt 1:
678-9; L J 22: 185-6.
Douthwaite, W. R.  Humfrey Wanley and his diary.  L C 1: 87-
94, 110-3.
-------- W. R.  Libraries of the Inns of Court.  L A U K
Trans 4: 27-30.

-------- W. R.  Notes on the Gray's Inn library.  L A M N
2: 2-7.

Dow, J. J.  Libraries and reading for the blind.  The Outlook
for the Blind Jan. 1909 2: 168-72; L J 34: 189.

Downey, J. A. L.  Are children taught the proper use of libraries?  L W 13: 319-20.

---- J. A. L.  Children and the use of libraries.  Libn 3:
60-2.

Downey, M. E.  Bird's-eye view of Utah libraries.  New Hamp
Bull (ns) 12: 179-82; Texas Libraries 1, July 1916: 24-8.

---- M. E.  Collecting magazines for reference files.  Wilson Bull 1: 83-6; L J 41: 98-102.

---- M. E.  Developing a public library.  L J 37: 128-33.

---- M. E.  Duties of a library organizer.  L J 40: 156-7.

---- M. E.  Libraries in Utah.  P L 25: 523-4.

---- M. E.  Library and school co-operation in Utah.  A L
A Bull 10: 254-7.

---- M. E.  Literature and culture.  L J 40: 163-8; New
Hamp Bull 11: 109-14.

---- M. E.  Pioneering in Utah.  A L A Bull 9: 139-44.

---- M. E.  Purpose of the visits of an organizer.  Am Lib
Annual 1915-16: 70-1.

---- M. E.  Relation of the public schools to the various
library agencies.  L J 45: 883-6.

---- M. E.  Renting of books from commercial libraries for
public library use.  Ia L C Q 4: 11-2.

---- M. E.  State library extension.  A L A Bull 11: 43-4;
L J 42: 122-3.

---- M. E.  Teaching the use of the library.  L J 40: 637-
40.

---- M. E.  What the League of library commissions can do
for states without organized commissions.  A L A Bull 13:
292-3, 405-6.

Downing, W.  Free public libraries from a bookseller's point
of view.  L C 3: 194-7.

Dracass, C. E. T.  An experiment in library training in the
high school.  English Journal 1: 221-31.

----- C. E. T.  Growth of the high school library in Chicago.  Educational Bi-Monthly 7: 153-6.

----- C. E. T.  Plans for the future of Chicago high school
libraries.  Educational Bi-Monthly 7: 295-304.

----- C. E. T.  Some high school library topics.  Educational Bi-Monthly 7: 411-34.

----- C. E. T.  Study of some libraries in high schools.
Cook County School News 7: 12-3.

Drake, J. M.  Elimination of the use of readers' cards in a
public library.  A L A Bull 12: 219-20, 308.

--- J. M.  How to increase your tax levy.  Wis Lib Bull
11: 310-2; L J 41: 785.

--- J. M.  Publicity.  Wis Lib Bull 6: 4-14.
--- J. M.  Relation of the public library to social better-
ment.  Ia L C Q 7: 1-9.
--- J. M.  Students' privileges in a public library.  P L
12: 221-3.
--- J. M.  Talks on timely books.  L J 45: 203.
--- J. M.  What can the public library do for men employed
in car shops.  Wis Lib Bull 6: 14-6.
Drake, M.  Method of getting non-fiction read.  Wis Lib Bull
5: 1-5.
Draper, A. S.  Rural supervision in New York.  Educational
Review 43: 193-8.
Draper, M. S.  Children's museum in Brooklyn.  L J 35: 149-54.
Draper, S. A.  Literature for the blind.  P L 9: 147-9.
Driggs, H. R.  Connecting the public schools with public li-
braries.  Nat Educ Assn 1913: 727-30.
Druar, M.  The public library as an aid to the school room.
L J 24: 143-4.
Drury, F. K. W.  Affiliation of the State association with
the A. L. A.  P L 19: 436-7.
--- F. K. W.  Care of maps (College and reference section)
A L A Bull 2: 347-55.
--- F. K. W.  Do we need a short story index?  A L A Bull
6: 277-8.
--- F. K. W.  Labor-savers in library service.  L J 35:
538; P L 15: 393-4.
--- F. K. W.  On college and university library committees.
L J 45: 551-2.
--- F. K. W.  On making signs.  L J 33: 315.
--- F. K. W.  On protecting pamphlets.  L J 35: 118-9.
--- F. K. W.  160 of the best foreign novels in English
translation.  N Y L 2: 196-8.
--- F. K. W.  Publicity for college libraries.  L J 45:
487-90.
--- F. K. W.  Recreations of a librarian.  P L 12: 339-43.
Du Bois, I.  A library game that has been tried at the Adriance
memorial library, Poughkeepsie, New York.  P L 20: 119.
Duckworth, T.  Local and county photographic surveys.  L A R
7: 19-30.
Dudgeon, M. S.  Administrative units in library extension:
State, county, township, city.  A L A Bull 5: 130-8: Libra-
ry Work 1912: 247-8.
----- M. S.  Charging country borrowers.  Wis Lib Bull 9:
32-3.
----- M. S.  Civic improvement and development.  Wis Lib
Bull 7: 60-4.
Dudgeon, M. S.  Creation of farmer country public libraries,
Texas.  P L 18: 205-6.
----- M. S.  Few books versus many books.  Wis Lib Bull
11: 97-9.

----- M. S. Function of state library commissions in war-
time. A L A Bull 11: 324-5.

----- M. S. Function of the library in the modern school.
Minn P L C N 4: 80-1.

----- M. S. General reading for men. P L 17: 399-401.

----- M. S. The law that stands the test. A L A Bull 7:
206-10; Wis Lib Bull 9: 119-24.

----- M. S. Librarian and bookseller: comparison and co-
operation. Publishers' Weekly May 27, 1916: 1741-5; Am
Lib Annual 1916-17: 23-4.

----- M. S. The library and the municipality. Wis Lib
Bull 7: 105-6.

----- M. S. Library appropriations. Wis Lib Bull 6: 113-
7.

----- M. S. Presenting the financial needs of the library.
Wis Lib Bull 8: 147-51.

----- M. S. Rural library extension. P L 18: 204.

----- M. S. Scope and purpose of special libraries. Special Libraries 3: 129-33.

----- M. S. What men read in camp. A L A Bull 12: 221-2.

----- M. S. The Wisconsin legislative reference library.
Yale Review 16: 288-95.

Dudley, A. T. The library commission. New Hamp Bull (ns) 13:
42-3; L J 42: 465.

Dudley, C. R. Library architecture. P L 12: 267-9.

---- C. R. Library editions of popular fiction. L J 21:
Conf No 41-2.

---- C. R. Report of Committee on architecture. A L A Bull
1: Conf No 119-23.

Dudley, R. C. Pamphlets: their care and use. New Hamp Bull
(ns) 16: 13-8.

Duff, E. G. Adrian Kempe van Bouchhout and the quarto new
testament of 1536. L (ns) 7: 376-83.

-- E. G. The "Assertio septem sacramentorum." L (ns) 9:
1-16.

-- E. G. The bindings of Thomas Wotton. L (3d series) 1:
337-47.

-- E. G. Booksellers accounts, circa 1510. L (ns) 8: 256-
66.

-- E. G. A century of English book trade: short notices
of all printers, stationers, bookbinders and others connected with it from the issue of the first dated book in 1457
to the incorporation of the Company of stationers in 1557.
Bibliographical Society Publication 1905.

-- E. G. Early chancery proceedings concerning members of
the book trade. L (ns) 8: 408-20.

-- E. G. An early stationer in England. L A R 1: 441-2.

-- E. G. English book trade before the incorporation of
the Stationers' company. Bib Soc Trans 8: 10-4.

-- E. G.  English fifteenth century broadsides.  Bib Soc
Trans 9: 211-27.

-- E. G.  Frederick Egmondt, an English 15th century stationer.  L 2: 210-6.

-- E. G.  Library of Richard Smith.  L (ns) 8: 113-33.

-- E. G.  A new English 15th century printer.  L 1: 102-5.

-- E. G.  Notes on stationers, from the "Lay subsidy rolls"
of 1523-4.  L (ns) 9: 257-66.

-- E. G.  Printer of Borde's "Introduction to knowledge."
L (ns) 8: 30-3.

-- E. G.  Printers of York.  Bib Soc Trans 5: 87-107.

-- E. G.  Printers, stationers and book-binders of York up
to 1600.  Bib Soc Trans 5: 87-107.

-- E. G.  Richard Pynson and Thomas Bercula.  L (ns) 298-
303.

-- E. G.  Scottish bookbinding, armorial and artistic.  Bib
Soc Trans 15: 95-113.

-- E. G.  H. R. Plomer, and R. Proctor.  Hand-list of English printers, 1501-1556.  Plates.  2 parts in 1.  Bibliographical Society Publication, 1895.

Duff, I. J.  Story telling in the Brooklyn public library.
A L A Bull 3: 415-7.

Dufferin and Ava, Marquess of.  Presidential address.  L 6:
295-8.

Duffield, D. W.  Binding of pamphlets and rebacking and rein-
forcing of books.  L J 43: 315-9.

------ D. W.  Formula for paste for binding pamphlets, etc.
L J 43: 319.

Duggan, S. P.  Exchange of librarians.  A L A Bull 14: 32.

---- S. P.  Proposed co-operation between A. L. A. and the
Institute of inter-national education.  A L A Bull 14: 31-3.

Dumenil, R.  Defaulters.  L A 12: 12-3, 35-40.

Dumenil, R. L.  Do exhibitions develop the reading habit?  L
A 7: 68-72.

----- R. L.  Manuscripts.  L A 6: 266-9, Discussion 272.

----- R. L.  Preparation of magazines for the tables.  L
W 10: 353-4.

Dunbar, A. M.  Training of a teacher of English.  Education
29: 97.

Dunbar, R.  Traveling library work in factory and store.  P
L 21: 18-9.

Duncan, B.  Music in the Boston public library.  L J 40: 592-
4.

Duncan, G.  Information.  Bookman (N Y) 31: 583-4.

Duncan, R.  Standardization in accession methods.  L W 9: 83-
7.

Dungan, W. S.  County historical societies.  Iowa L C Q 2: 60-
1.

Dunham, F. G.  The talking machine in the public library: a
new method of rendering greater service to the community.
P L 24: 154-5.

Dunlop, H. W. D.  New invention which renders slip catalogues available for reference.  L J 2: 160-1.
---- H. W. D.  On a new invention which enables slip-catalogues to be available for reference libraries.  1st Int Conf 68-9; L J 2: 160-1.
Dunlap, R. B.  Minnesota historical society--Genealogy.  Minn P L C N 4: 8-10.
Dunn, J. P.  Tainted money.  P L 18: 186-7.
Dunn, L. M.  The reading of the adolescent girl.  A L A Bull 11: 162-7, 344.
Dunn, P.  Literature of the war; medicine and hygiene.  L A R 17: 466-71.
Dunnack, H. J.  Library reconstruction in Maine.  Special Libraries 11: 33-6.
Dunne, J. P.  Detective stories.  Lib Occ No 10: 3-4.
Dupuis, M. S.  Woman's club and the traveling library.  L J 26: Conf No 194-5.
Durbin, E. C.  Reference libraries for ancient history in the high school.  School Review 12: 109-19.
Duren, F.  Co-operation of teacher and librarian in establishing standards for the reading public.  Iowa State Teachers' Assn Proceedings 1908: 74-80.
--- F.  Creating a demand and supplying it.  Ia L C Q 6-113-7.
--- F.  Library boys club: an experiment.  Ia L C Q 5: 129-31.
--- F.  Public libraries.  Ia L C Q 6: 14.
--- F.  Why should a small library be organized.  Ia L C Q 4: 5-10.
Durfee, C. A.  Scrap.books in libraries.  L J 2: 65-6.
Du Rieu, W. M.  Card catalogue of the Leiden University.  L J 10: 206-8, Discussion 315-6.
Durlin, M.  Picture bulletins.  Wis Lib Bull 3: 57-9.
Durrant, W. S.  Influence of William Morris.  Westminster Review May 1908.
Dutton, S. T.  Place and function of the high school library.  Education 18: 587-96.
Duval, L. M.  Library hours.  P L 5: 379-81.
Dwight, T. F.  Library of the Department of State.  U S Govt Rept: 262-7, 1876.
Dyer, B. L.  Claim of the library assistant upon the county educational funds.  L A R 2: 58-64.
-- B. L.  How best to increase the usefulness of the L. A. A. (Prize Essay) L A 2: 155-8.
-- B. L.  The L. A. and educational facilities.  L A 1: 107-8.
-- B. L.  Literature at the Cape seventy years ago.  L A R 1: 366-70.
-- B. L.  Occasional notes.  L A 6: 185.

-- B. L.  On special rates for carriage of library books.
P L 11: 342.

-- B. L.  Public library conditions in South Africa.  P
L 9: 109-12.

-- B. L.  Technical training and a Royal charter for librarians.  L A 1: 28-9.

-- B. L.  Training of library assistants.  L A R 1: 206-
8.

-- B. L.  War and the library: stray notes.  L A 3: 97-
101.

-- B. L. and J. Lloyd.  Women librarians in England.  L
A 1: 219-22.

Dyer, M. C.  Beginnings of public libraries supported by taxation.  P L 10: 458-60.

Dyer, W. A.  Feeding the book hungry.  Country Gentlemen April
1, 1916; L J 41: 448.

-- W. A.  Spread of county libraries.  World's Work (N Y)
30: 609-13; L J 40: 836; Am Lib Annual 1915-16: 39.

Dziatzko, C.  Instruction für die ordnung der titel im alpha-
betischen zettelkatalog der königlichen und universitäts-
bibliothek zu Breslau.  Noted in L J 11: 172, 192; L C 3:
62; L (ns) 1: 354.

------ C.  On the aids lent by public bodies to the art
of printing in the early days of typography.  2d Int Conf
72-8, 1897.

------ C.  Present state of libraries and librarianship
in Germany.  L C 4: 57-63.

Dziatzko, K.  International mutual relations of libraries.
L J 18: 465-8.

------ K.  Library and Reading Room of the British Museum.
L A M N 3: 10-5, 26-35, 46-53; L J 7: 79-84.

------ K.  Prof. Dziatzko on his cataloguing rules: a rejoinder.  L C 5: 194-5.

E. F. G.  Our small difficulties: application vouchers at
public libraries.  L W 19: 235.

E. F. G.  Our small difficulties: English, foreign and translated fiction.  L W 19: 285-7.

Eakins, W. F.  Public documents of dominion of Canada and
province of Ontario.  L J 27: 248-51.

Eames, W.  Care of special collections.  L J 22: Conf No 48-
52.

--- W.  Lenox library and its founder.  L J 24: 199-201.

--- W.  What should librarians read?  L J 25: 59-61.

Earhart, F. E.  Aids and methods in reference work.  Minn P
L C N 4: 54-5.

----- F. E.  How Duluth women learn to use the library.
Wis Lib Bull 10: 78.

Earl, E. C.  Extending library privileges to rural communities.
A L A Bull 13: 367.

-- E. C.  Indiana library trustees' association: president's message.  Lib Occ 4: 70-2.

-- E. C.  Library trustees obligation to the state.  A L A Bull 10: 293-5; L J 41:786-7.

-- E. C.  Library commission publicity.  A L A Bull 11: 132-3, 348.

-- Mrs. E. C.  Indiana library trustees' association; President's message.  Lib Occ 4: 70-2.

-- Mrs. E. C.  privileges and responsibilities of trusteeship.  Wis Lib Bull 13: 254-6.

Earle, C. C.  How to build a library.  L J 17: 124-5.

Earle, E. L.  Analysis of the principal systems of reading.  Kindergarten Mag 24: 31-3.

Earle, H.  Outline for study of twentieth century art.  Mich Lib Bull 7: 104-14.

Eason, A. B.  Co-ordination of libraries and abstracts.  Special Libraries  11: 201-3.

East, M. B.  Conditions of libraries in Virginia.  P L 9: 9-11.

Eastman, C. W.  Educational ideals in school and library.  Ia L C Q 3: 25-8.

Eastman, F. V.  Creating a reading public and directing aimless or purposeless readers.  Ia L C Q Ap-June 1914: 81-3.

----- F. V.  Loan desk, the point of contact between the library and the people.  Ia L C Q 5:211-4.

Eastman, L. A.  Aims and personal attitude in library work.  L J 22: Conf No 80-1.

----- L. A.  The child, the school and the library.  L J 21: 134.

----- L. A.  The children's room and the children's librarian.  P L 3: 417-20.

----- L. A.  Exchange of librarians.  L J 45: 326.

----- L. A.  The library and the children: an account of the children's work in the Cleveland public library.  L J 23: 143-4.

----- L. A.  Library equipment.  P L 16: 344.

----- L. A.  Lists helpful to librarians of small libraries.  P L 9: 66-8.

----- L. A.  Methods of work with children: The Cleveland library league.  L J 22: 686-8; P L 2: 268.

----- L. A.  Work between libraries and schools at Cleveland.  U. S. Bur of Educ Rept 1897-98, pt 1: 675-6; L J 22: 686-8.

Eastman, W. R.  Bookstacks in theory and practice.  L J 41: 235-8.

----- W. R.  By-laws suggested for a board of library trustees.  U S Rept: 705-6, 1899.

----- W. R.  The county library.  L J 41:8.

----- W. R.  Essentials of a good library law.  L J 25: Conf No 49-51.

----- W. R.  Evolution of library fittings: a review of The care of books.  L W 4: 141-3.

----- W. R.  First county library again.  P L 6: 405.

----- W. R.  The first ten years of the New York library association.  L J 40: 855-60.

----- W. R.  Hints for cataloging small libraries.  U S Rept 706-7, 1899.

----- W. R.  How to catalogue a small library.  P L 11: 314.

----- W. R.  Library building plans collected by W. R. Eastman.  N Y S L Rept. 90,  Bulletin 107, Library School 22; P L 12: 56-7.

----- W. R.  Library buildings.  L J 26: Conf No 43; P L 6: 475.

----- W. R.  Library buildings of moderate size.  L J 27: 80-1.

----- W. R.  Library legislation of 1907.  N Y L 1: 85; L J 33: 180.

----- W. R.  Library legislation in 1908.  L J 34: 106.

----- W. R.  Library legislation in 1911.  L J 37: 256-9.

----- W. R.  Library legislation in 1913.  L J 39: 3-9.

----- W. R.  Library legislation, 1914.  L J 40: 27-8.

----- W. R.  Library legislation in 1915.  L J 41: 5-11.

----- W. R.  Library legislation in 1916.  L J 42: 11-2.

----- W. R.  Library work of the University of the State of New York.  L J 20: 267-70.

----- W. R.  Public library buildings.  L J 26: Conf No 43.

----- W. R.  Recent library legislation.  A L A Bull 3, No 3: 30-1; L J 34: 106; P L 14: 239.

----- W. R.  Report of the A. L. A. Committee on library administration, W. R. Eastman and others.  L J 27: Conf No 86-91; 30: Conf No 102-6; 31: Conf No 146-53.

----- W. R.  Rural extension.  L J 39:6-7.

----- W. R.  Shelf capacity.  N Y L 4: 23.

----- W. R.  Summary of library legislation for 1909.  L J 35: 117-8.

----- W. R.  Value and work of a state library organizer.  P L 10: 67-72.

----- W. R.  The village library and the farm.  N Y L 1: 37-40; Cal News Notes 3: 130; Library Work 1912: 256.

----- W. R.  What can the state do for the public library.  L J 24: 619-20.

----- W. R. and C. B. Lester.  Library legislation of 1910.  L J 36: 66-7.

----- W. R. and C. Marvin.  Report of Committee on library administration.  L J 28: Conf No 71-6.

----- W. R. C. Marvin, and H. C. Wellman.  Report of the Committee of library administration.  L J 29: Conf No 163-7.

----- W. R., H. C. Wellman and N. D. C. Hodges. Report
of the Committee on library administration. L J 27: Conf.
No. 86-91.

Eastwood, M. E.  Advance titles of "Best Books." N Y L 3:
188-9.

------ M. E.  Books Worth buying.  N Y L 6:33-4, 69-72,
101-2.

------ M. E.  Children's books of 1912: vote of children's
librarians.  N Y L 3: 310-1.

------ M. E.  The how and why of "best books." N Y L 5:
194-8.

------ M. E.  The librarian's present dilemma in book-
buying.  N Y L 6: 163-5.

------ M. E.  One hundred books of popular non-fiction
for small libraries.  N Y L 7: 103-4.

------ M. E.  Recent books worth buying.  N Y L 7: 41,
74-5, 102, 134; 6: 169-70, 230-1; 5: 24; 4: 180, 211, 215.

------ M. E.  Some recent books worth buying.  N Y L 4:
46, 79, 110, 148.

------ M. E.  Some recent popular books worth buying for
a small library.  N Y L 3: 308-9.

Eaton, A. T.  Anthologies.  Wis Lib Bull 8: 85-93.

--- A. T.  For a book mark.  Vt L Bull 3, No 2: 7.

--- A. T.  Illustrations for children's books.  N Y L 2:
128-30, 1910.

Eaton, W. P.  Literature and Miss Lizzie Cox.  N Y L 7: 7-12.

Eddy, H. G.  California county free libraries.  A L A Bull 5:
138-44; L J 36: 336-42; Journal of Education 43: 193-8;
Nat Educ Assn 1911: 1026-9; Sierra Educ News 7: 38-9;
Library Work 1912: 135-6.

-- H. G.  California free libraries: how the state library
service is being brought close to the people.  California
Outlook 12: 13 (March 2, 1912).

-- H. G.  County library: report of progress.  California
Lib Assn Proceedings 1910: 29-31; L J 35: 274-5; P L 15: 250-2

-- H. G.  County library service: its purpose, plan, present
and prospects.  Everywoman 10: 29.

-- H. G.  Elk Grove station of the Sacramento county library.
Cal News Notes 4: 264-6; California Lib Assn Proceedings
1909: 46-8.

-- H. G.  How the libraries and the U. S. Department of
agriculture in extension work can work together.  Cal News
Notes 14: 141.

-- H. G.  Progress in county library work.  Cal News Notes
8: 293; California Lib Assn Proceedings 1913: 24.

-- H. G.  Relation between schools and libraries.  California Library Assn Proceedings 1910: 21-3; Cal News Notes
5: 867-9.

Edgerton, F. W.  A recent experiment with magazine literature.
English Journal 1: 278-83.

Edmands, J.  About title pages.  L J 28: 156.
----- J.  Annual American catalog.  L J 12: 216.
----- J.  Co-operative cataloguing report.  L J 1: 290-1.
----- J.  First use of catalogue cards.  L J 26: 850.
----- J.  How we choose and buy new books.  L J 14: 339.
----- J.  Lettering of books.  L J 12: 322-3.
----- J.  Library bureau card catalogue system again: comment on Mr. Parsons' reply to criticism.  L J 19: 256, 329.
----- J.  Library classification.  P L 20: 176-7.
----- J.  On Mr. Cutter's classification.  L J 6: 118-9.
----- J.  The origin of Poole's Index.  P L 19: 341.
----- J.  Periodical library bulletins.  L J 19: Conf No 54.
----- J.  Plan for numbering Congressional documents.  L J 8: 250-1.
----- J.  Plan of numbering.  L J 4: 38-40, 56.
----- J.  Report of Committee on exchange of duplicates, L J 4: 289-90.
----- J.  Report on library architecture.  L J 8: 201-3, 269-75.
----- J.  Rules for alphabeting.  L J 12: 326-31, 431-2.
----- J.  Table in his new system of classification and his article in L J 4: 38-40, 56.
----- J., and others.  Plan for numbering with especial reference to fiction.  L J 4: 38-47, 49.
Edmond, J. P.  Cataloguing of fifteenth century books.  L A R 1: 297-300; L J 24: 252-4.
---- J. P.  Description of books printed between 1501 and 1640.  L A R 3: 133-42.
---- J. P.  Method of treating broadsides.  L A R 3: 115-6.
---- J. P.  On the use of capital letters in cataloguing.  L A R 5: 77-80.
---- J. P.  Plea for private libraries.  L 7: 211-5.
---- J. P.  Suggestions for the description of books printed between 1501 and 1640.  L A R 3: 133-42.
Edmonds, C.  Town library as a war tribute: photographs.  Ladies' H J 36: 3.
Edmunds, A. J.  A short and easy method with pamphlets.  L J 39: 449-50.
Edward-Jones, T.  Ipswich libraries and book clubs.  B A R 11: xxxvii-xli.
Edwards, E.  Proprietary and subscription libraries of the United States.  In his Memoirs of Libraries  1859 2: 182-201.
----- E.  Researches for manuscripts in the Levant and more especially in the monasteries of Mount Athos: Giovanni Aurispa to Spyridion Lambros ( A. D. 1425 to 1880).  L C 1: 57-64, 81-6, 105-9.

Edwards, E. E.  Scrapping.  L J 5: 225.

Edwards, G. O.  Circular to principals and teachers.  Wis Lib Bull 2: 10-1.

Edwards, H. H.  An introduction to classification.  L A R 17: 57.

Edwards, L. B.  The literary cult of the child.  Critic 39: 166-70.

Edwards, R. G.  Musical library for violinists.  Musician 18: 343.

Edwards, W. A.  How can the librarian aid the teacher.  Nat Educ Assn 1907: 978-82; School Journal 75: 321.

Edwards, W. H.  Books as gifts for our friends in the country. P L 20: 203-4.

Egremont, G.  Libraries and children.  Westminster Review 173: 175-82.

Ehrle, F.  Preservation of manuscripts.  L J 35: 64.

Eichler, F.  Central cataloguing, the bureau of information and inter-library loans in Austria.  L J 33: 506-7.

----- F.  Inter-library loans in Austria.  L J 33: 506-7.

Elder, V.  Libraries in the Duplicate schools of New York City. L J 42: 725-7.

Eliot, C. W.  The differentiation of the high school course in English.  Education 31: 639-45.

--- C. W.  Division of a library into books in use and books not in use, with different storage methods for the two classes of books.  L J 27: Conf No 51-6; P L 7: 158-9, 219-21, 261-2, 296-7.

--- C. W.  Fundamental assumptions in the report of the Committee of ten (1892).  Educational Review 30: 325-43.

--- C. W.  Living books and dead.  L J 27: 256-7.

--- C. W.  On the storage of books.  P L 7: 158-9.

Eliot, Mrs. W. G.  Children's reading from the mother's standpoint.  Pacific Northwest Library Assn Proceedings 1910: 49-54.

Elliot, G. H.  Irish branch of the L. A. A.; Inaugural address by G. H. Elliot, President.  L A 6: 18, 28-30.

---- G. H.  Methods of popularizing standard books other than novels.  L A R 7: 155-60.

---- G. H.  Our readers and what they read.  L 7: 276-81.

Elliot, J.  Extinction of betting evil.  L J 19: 51.

---- J.  Extinction of betting evil in newsrooms.  L 5: 193-4.

Elliot, T. C.  Relation of the library board to the library. Wash L A Bull 2 No 1: 10-2.

Elliott, E. C.  State school systems.  U S Bureau of Education Bulletin 3: 124-6.

Elliott, J. E.  Catalog notes.  Wis Lib Bull 4: 32-3.

----- J. E.  Indexing and other unorganized forms of library work.  L J 35: 198-201.

---- J. E.  Library conditions which confront library
schools.  A L A Bull 3: 427-36.

---- J. E.  Relation of the librarian to the assistant.
R L 19: 463-5.

---- J. E.  Some catalogue notes.  Wis Lib Bull 4: 52-3.

---- J. E.  Use of children's book marks in libraries.
Wis Lib Bull 1: 49-50.

Elliott, R. B.  Directed home reading in grade IX at Milton,
Mass.  School Journal 73: 539; Journal of Education (Boston) 65: 18.

Ellis, A. C.  Reading and literature.  Texas State Teachers'
Assn Proceedings 1898: 67-73.

Ellis, E.  Instruction of school children in the use of library catalogs and reference books.  P L 4: 311-4.

Ellis, H.  First library in Indiana (Circulating library of
Vincennes) P L 10: 509-12.

--- H.  Some things the Madison (Wisconsin) library does.
Wis Lib Bull 1:45.

Ellis, H. C.  Children's reading and the family.  Penn Lib
Notes 8: 47-51.

Ellis, V.  Library co-operation with women's missionary
societies.  P L 19: 251.

Ellison, H. M.  Library work with children.  Libn 6: 91-5.

----- H. M.  Newspapers and periodicals: methods of public
display, filing, preservation and disposal in other ways.
L W 17: 129-37.

Ellison, J. B.  Book illustration.  L A 7: 277-8.

----- J. B.  Reading lists.  L A R 11: 379.

Elmendorf, H. L.  Access to a selected library.  L J 25:
Conf No 38-9.

------- H. L.  Assistants' opportunity.  L 9: 137-42.

------- H. L.  Books much in use and books that are least
used.  L J 27: Conf No 174-5.

------- H. L.  The greater school.  Nat Educ Assn 1900:
643-8.

------- H. L.  School department of the Buffalo public
library.  L J 28: 157-60.

------- H. L.  Some things a boy of seventeen should have
had an opportunity to read.  American Monthly Review of
Reviews 28: 713-7.

------- H. L.  Suggestive list of books and periodical
articles for both general and professional reading.  N Y L
2: 136.

Elmendorf, Mrs. H. L.  Buffalo system of public library and
school library co-operation.  N J Lib Bull Jan 1915: 9-14;
Bull Bib 9: 38-40.

------- Mrs. H. L.  Children's right to poetry.  Wis Lib
Bull 7: 119-20.

------- Mrs. H. L.  The public library: "a leaven'd and
prepared choice."  A L A Bull 6: 67-71; L J 37: 419-22;
Lib Miscellany (Baroda) 1: 54-5; P L 17: 299-302.

------- Mrs. H. L.  Public library books in public schools.
L J 25: 163-5.
------- Mrs. H. L.  School and library co-operation.
N Y L 3: 55-6.
Elmendorf, T.  Mutual help between libraries.  P L 7: 73-4.
------- T.  Periodicals for the staff.  P L 3: 45.
Elmendorf, T. W.  The things that matter; an attempt at a
study in values.  P L 14: 281-9.
Elmendorf, Mrs. T. W.  Some books of special importance to
libraries in the present crisis.  N Y L 4: 149-51.
Elrod, J.  How to interest children in good literature.
P L 5: 56-7.
--- J.  What critical magazines give best aid in select-
ion of books.  P L 7: 22-4
Ely, D.  A new substitute for picture bulletins.  Wis Lib
Bull 9: 111-2.
Ely, M.  The book that teacher says is good.  Nat Educ Assn
1912: 1253-8; P L 18: 133-5.
- M.  Our present problem.  A L A Bull 8: 219-23; P L 19:
284-5.
- M.  The story hour.  Ohio Lib Bull 4, No 1: 1-2.
Ely, M. E.  High school library as a vocational aid.  Mich
Lib Bull 10: 11-2; P L 24: 145.
Ely, R.  Reference work in school libraries.  Minn P L C N
No 2: 75-7.
Ely, T.  Corporate Maecenas.  New Republic 5: 244-6, Jan. 8,
1916.
Embury, A., Jr.  Make your town attractive:  Town halls and
libraries.  House Beautiful 38: 22-4, June 1915.
Emerson, M. F.  Making books available in the college library.
New Hampshire Lib Bull (n s) 14: 110-1.
Emerson, S. F.  The library and the school.  Vt Lib Bull 13:
10.
Emley, F.  Newcastle-on-Tyne library, reclassification and
cataloguing.  L J 13: 91.
Encking, L.  Teaching library methods in normal schools.
Western Journal of Education 5: 209-13.
Endicott, G.  What makes a juvenile book harmful or mediocre?
N Y L 7: 97-101; N J Lib Bull 1, No 4: 8-12; Penn Lib Notes
4: 30-6; P L 16: 454.
Endicott, L.  Washington union of library employees.  A L A
Bull 13: 379.
Endicott, W. E.  Library of the Massachusetts horticultural
society.  Massachusetts Horticultural Society Transactions,
1892 Part I: 174-89.
England, G.  Goldsmith's "Prospect of society."  L (n s) 3:
327-38.
England, G. A.  Obligations and opportunities of the city
library: the need for municipal reference libraries.
Special Libraries  11: 84-7.

Englander, E. S.  Library instruction: course in use of the
library for pupils in public schools from second through
eighth grade.  P L 18: 60-1, 110-1.

Engle, E. R.  Club work with boys and girls.  Penn Lib Notes
Oct 1913: 36-8.

--- E. R.  What children read in the library.  Pen Lib
Notes 7: 175-82; L J 41: 437-8.

English, M. F.  Classification of school libraries.  P L
2: 351.

Eno, J. N.  Name-making and cataloging of names.  L J 35:
553-5.

Eno, S. W.  Joseph Conrad: a contribution toward a bibliography.  Bull Bib 9: 137-9.

Ericson, C. J. A.  How shall co-operation between township
and public libraries be secured?  Ia L C Q 6: 64.

Erskine, E.  Co-operation between the library and the science
departments in the Carter Harrison high school.  A L A
Bull 13: 398.

----- E.  Library and the science department.  P L 24:
337-8.

Erskine, J.  Learning to read.  New Hamp Bull 11: 97-9; N J
Lib Bull 4, No 1: 10-2.

----- J.  Reading for young people.  N Y L 3: 30-43; New
Hamp Bull (n s) 8: 71-4.

----- J.  Teaching a love of literature.  Dial 47: 278.

Erwin, M. L.  Bankers trust company library.  Special Libraries 10: 129-30.

Esdaile, A.  "An apology of private mass," 1562.  L (4th
series) 1: 161-4.

----- A.  Public schools and their libraries.  L (n s)
7: 366-75.

----- A.  Shakespeare literature.  L (n s) 7: 169-80.

Esdaile, A. J. K.  Bibliography of the writings in prose and
verse of George Meredith.  Lit Yr-Bk i-lxx.

Esdaile, K. A.  An early appreciation of William Blake.  L
(3d series) 5: 229-56.

----- K. A.  The small house and its amenities in the
architectural handbooks of 1749-1827.  Bib Soc Trans 15:
115-32.

Eshelman, J. T.  Public library of Tacoma, Wash.  Wash L A
Bull 2 No 3: 8-9. il

Estabrook, C.  More about charging systems.  L J 5: 72-7,
108, Discussion 74-5.

Estee, J. A.  Correlation of library and school on the part
of the school.  Univ of State of New York, Regents'
Bulletin 36: 109-15.

Estey, H. G. Select bibliography on cost of living in the
United States.  Special libraries 9: 203-9, 231-2.

Euren, A. D.  Books and bookmen of Norwich.  B A R 10:
xxi-xxix.

Eustis, G. H.  Hints on library accounts.  P L 10: 7-8.
Evans, A. G.  Putting out new books.  P L 11: 499.
Evans, C.  Public documents in small libraries.  P L
12: 315-7.
--- C.  Sizes of books.  L J 1: 58-61, Discussion 106-9.
Evans, C. E.  Gifts: what to accept and what to refuse.
Penn Lib Notes 5, No 4: 30-1.
Evans, C. L.  Tax commission library.  Minn Lib Notes 4:
10-11.
Evans, G. H.  Aids to the technical and industrial work.
L J 34: 100-3.
--- G. H.  Experiments in library extension.  L J 38:
13-5.
--- G. H.  The remittance of fines.  L J 38: 405-6.
Evans, G. W.  Public library and the high schools in Boston.
Academy (Syracuse) 4: 125-9.
--- G. W.  Special libraries and special students.  L J
13: 180.
Evans, H. R.  Library instruction in universities, colleges,
and normal schools.  U S Bur of Educ Bull 1914, 34: 1-38.
Evans, J. T.  Reading room methods.  L W 12: 373-8.
Evans, L. B.  What the library can do for the boy.  P L
16: 120.
--- L. B.  Workings of the Massachusetts constitutional
convention.  A L A Bull 12: 314-21, 366.
Evans, M. J.  How much work is done in American literature
in the high school, and by what methods?  School Review
11: 647-54.
--- M. J.  Most valuable contribution of the small
library.  Minn P L C N 2, No 4: 84-5.
Evans, S. C.  The high school library.  Pen Lib Notes 5,
No 4: 35-7.
--- S. C.  Reading of high school students and how to
improve it.  P L 22: 123-6; L J 42: 569.
Evans, W. E.  Welsh publishing and bookselling.  L 7: 391-7.
Everett, E.  The need for adequate libraries.  L J 43: 223-4.
Everhart, E.  Dumas' series.  P L 13: 168, 211-2.
------ E.  Ways and means of popularizing government
documents.  A L A Bull 2: 382-5.
Ewart, S. T.  Descriptive annotation.  L A 5: 208-11.
--- S. T.  "For contents see books": a short discourse
upon the existence of annotation and annotation.  L W
9: 158-60.
Ewing, A. A.  Play element in dramatic reading.  Wis Lib
Bull 9: 54-5; 11: 9-10.
Ewing, C.  The school library as a part of the county system.
Pacific Northwest Library Assn Proceedings 1920: 33-5.
Faber, C.  The value of a library in teaching history.  P L
16: 139-41.

Faber, C. A.   A history teacher's use of a library.   New
    York State Teachers' Assn Proceedings 1910: 315-9; N Y L
    2: 228-30; P L 16: 139-41.
Faber, R. S.   Christopher Plantin.   L 2: 12, 38, 87, 133, 201.
    --- R. S.   The Musee Dobree at Nantes.   L (n s) 5: 206-24.
    --- R. S.   Printing in Sicily (1478-1554).   Bib Soc Trans
    5: 183-211.
    --- R. S.   Some Durham book-lovers.   Bib Soc Trans 8: 77-
    83.
Fagg, C. C.   Regional surveys and public libraries.   L A
    13: 64-71; L W 19: 32-4.
Fagge, E. H.   County free library service to high schools.
    Nat Educ Assn 1911: 1019-26.
    --- E. H.   High school libraries.   Nat Educ Assn 1911:
    1019-25.
Faguet, E.   The art of reading, summarized by T. W. Koch.
    P L 25: 557-9.
Fairchild, C. B., Jr.   The opportunities of a special lib-
    rarian.   Special Libraries 6: 91-2.
Fairchild, E. M.   Lantern slides for lectures in library
    work for children.   L J 28: 156.
    ------- E. M.   Methods of children's library work as
    determined by the needs of the children.   L J 22: Conf
    No 19-27, Discussion 156-8.
Fairchild, E. T.   Status of rural schools.   U S Bureau of
    Education, Bulletin 1912, 15: 18-20.
Fairchild, S. C.   American libraries: a method of study and
    interpretation.   L J 33: 43-7.
    ------- S. C.   American notes.   L (n s) 1: 100-8, 218-24,
    350-6, 434-8.
    ------- S. C.   Book selection.   P L 8: 281.
    ------- S. C.   Book symposium at Lake George.   P L 11:
    343-4.
    ------- S. C.   Chronological outline of modern library
    movement in America, with most important foreign events.
    N Y S L Rept 85, Bull 75: 111-6.
    ------- S. C.   Directions for original bibliography.
    Bulletin No 75, N Y S L Rept 85.
    ------- S. C.   Functions of the library.   P L 6: 527-32.
    ------- S. C.   James Lyman Whitney, 1835-1910.   L (n s)
    1: 220-1.
    ------- S. C.   Melvil Dewey, 1851- L (n s) 1: 221.
    ------- S. C.   Miniature standard library.   Minn P L C N
    4: 3-4.
    ------- S. C.   The one thing needful.   N Y L 1: 196-8.
    ------- S. C.   Periodicals useful for reviews.   N Y S L
    Rept 85, Bulletin No 75, 131-4.   1902.
    ------- S. C.   Presidents of the American library assoc-
    iation, 1876-1902.   New York State Library Report 85,
    Bulletin No. 75; 117-29.

------- S. C.  Principles of book annotation.  N Y S L
Bull 75: 135-8, N Y S L Rept 85.
------- S. C.  Putnam, Herbert.  L (n s) 1: 100-3, 220,
352.
------- S. C.  What American libraries are doing for child-
ren and young people.  L A R 5: 541-51, Discussion 486-8.
------- S. C.  Women in American libraries--salaries of
male and female librarians.  L J 29: 160-1.
Fairfax, V.  Pamphlets and clippings in a business library.
Journal of Electricity 45: 330-1, 426-8, 484-5, 531-4,
584-5; 46: 31-3, 78-80.
Fairlie, J. A.  State supervision in New York.  Political
Science Quarterly 15: 50-74.
Fairweather, L.  The grading of library positions.  L A 11:
225-6.
--------- L.  How to cut the leaves of a book.  L W 10:
159-60.
Falconer, R.  What a public library can do for the develop-
ment of a community.  N Y L 6: 57-8.
Falkner, R. F.  Report of A. L. A. Committee on public
documents.  L J 27: Conf No 92-6, L J 28: Conf No 112-6,
L J 29: Conf No 168-9.
Falkner, R. P.  Report on the exhibit of the Library of
Congress at the Louisiana Purchase exposition, St. Louis,
Missouri.  il. Rept of Libn of Congress, 1904: 227-87.
Fallon, J. F.  Well-chosen architectural library, with
illustration from books in the library of Messrs. McKim,
Mead, and White.  American Architect, 10 May 1915: 161-8,
171-3.
Fanning, C. E.  Some popular war books.  Minn P L C N 5: 183-4.
Faraday, J. G.  Weeding out.  L A 5: 46-50.
Fargo, L.  Library training course.  P L 24: 279-80.
Fargo, L. F.  High school library administration by School
boards.  Pacific Northwest Library Assn Proceedings 1914:
28-34.
--- L. F.  Self-government in a high school library.  L J
39: 938.
Fargo, Lucile F.  High school problem: Branch library in high
school library.  Pacific Northwest Lib Assn Proceedings
1911: 27-8.
--- Lucile F.  The place of the library in high school
education.  Education 33: 473-7.
--- Lucile F.  Magazine study for literature classes.
Education 36: 50-4.
--- Lucile F.  Training high school students in the use of
the library.  Nat Educ Assn Proceedings (Library Section)
1913: 756-60.
Farley, C. A.  New library building at Radcliffe college.
L J 33: 440-1.

---- C. A.  Radcliffe college library and its classification.  L J 21: 498-9.

Farley, M. M.  The Marshall Field & company employes' library.  Special Libraries 10: 68-9.

Farlow, J. W.  Medical library and its contents.  The Aesculapian 1 No 1: 43-52; L J 34: 401-5.

Farnell, W. J. C.  Duties of a library assistant.  L A 2: 188-90.

Farnham, M.  German propaganda work in children's library books.  P L 24: 14-7.

Farquhar, E.  Current index work.  L J 13: 333.

------ E.  Quarterly versus monthly indexes.  L J 13: 70.

------ E.  Specialization of libraries.  L J 15: 100.

Farr, A.  Library house-keeping.  Minn P L C N 9: 34-5.

Farr, A. N.  Correlation of school and public library.  Minn P L C N 3: 52-5; P L 15: 401-2.

Farr, H.  Libraries and the counties.  L A R 8:169-77;  Discussion 207-16.

-- H.  Libraries in the rural districts.  L A 6: 389-94.

-- H.  Library work with children.  L J 36: 166-71.

-- H.  Public libraries and the world of business.  L A R 12: 612-4.

-- H.  School library problem.  South Dakota Lib Bull 6: 10-4.

Farr, H. and J. W. Brown.  Cataloguing and otherwise preparing books for the use of the public.  L A R 3: 226-7.

Farr, M. P.  A library in a reform school.  P L 12: 234-5.

Farrar, Mrs. C. H.  Personal qualifications of a business librarian.  Special Libraries 8: 139-40; L J 43: 60-1.

Farrar, I. F.  Handwork of all nations.  P L 24: 253.

---- I. F.  How should the programme of a state library association meeting be made up to be of the most use to the librarians of small libraries?  L J 27: Conf No 239-41.

---- I. F.  Library and local history.  P L 17: 164-6.

Farrington, E. I.  Washington county, Maryland, library wagon.  Suburban Life 9: 299-300.

Farrington, J. L.  How the trustee may best keep in touch with the conduct of the library.  Ia L C Q 5: 81-3.

Farrow, P. E.  Children's rooms.  L W 10: 103-6.

---- P. E.  Rules and regulations for lending libraries.  L W 13: 36-41.

---- P. E.  Stock book.  L W 10: 33-5.

Farrow, P. F.  Staff conferences.  L W 10: 154-5; L J 32: 559.

Farrow, T. E.  The Graham indicator.  L W 11: 29-31.

Faunce, W. H. P.  Library as a factor in modern civilization.  L J 31: Conf No 18-20.

Faville, F. F.  Farmer's rest-rooms.  Ia L C Q 6: 78-80.

----- F. F.  The "Rest Room" in Storm Lake.  Ia L C Q 5: 201-2.

Faxon, F. W.  English drawing-room annuals.  Bull Bib 6:
110-3, 147-9.
--- F. W.  The irritation of the loose title-page and
index.  Bull Bib 8: 132-4.
--- F. W.  Lantern slide sorting and filing.  Bull Bib
8: 34.
--- F. W.  Literary annuals and gift books: American and
English.  Bull Bib 6: 7, 43-4, 77-81, 208-11, 243-5.
--- F. W.  Magazine deterioration.  Bull Bib April 1916:
34-5; Mich Lib Bull 7: 94-5.
--- F. W.  Periodicals in reference work.  P L 3: 207-9,
252-4.
--- F. W.  Times past--Twenty-four A. L. A. conferences
recalled.  A L A Bull 10: 286-93, 385.
Fay, L.  Development of the library in the high school.  N C
Bull 3: 32-6.
Fay, L. E.  Development of the library in high schools of
the South.  L J 42: 234-7.
- L. E.  Special work of college and normal school lib-
raries.  P L 19: 146-9.
- L. E.  Suggestive outline of a course for training
teachers in the use of books.  Southern Educ Assn Pro-
ceedings 1912: 393-7.
Fay, L. E., and E. M. Smith.  Library militant: a drama in
blank verse.  L J 33: 95-7.
Fazakas, C. A. S.  Library employees' union.  L W 21: 179.
Fearey, C. S.  Some reasons against purchasing subscription
books published in sets.  Lib Occ No 10: 9-10.
Fearing, D. B.  The making of an angling library and a short
account of some of its treasures.  Harvard Graduates
Magazine Dec 1915 263-74; Am Lib Annual 1916-17: 13-4.
Fearnside, K.  Co-operation between a town library and local
societies and bodies.  L A R 20: 140-9.
------- K.  Inspirational value of libraries.  L A 14:
227-8.
------- K.  Our libraries for boys and girls.  L A R
15: 702-4; Libn 4: 192-3; L W 16: 190-2.
------- K.  The proposed training school for librarians.
L W 19: 288-90.
------- K.  Voluntary assistants in public libraries.
Libn 5: 288.
Feather, W. A.  Advertising for readers.  P L 21: 19-20.
Feazel, E. A.  Foreign law in state libraries.  A L A Bull
4: 702-13.
Federer, C. A.  Bradford mechanics institute library.  L A R
8: 636-40.
Fegan, E. S.  American libraries: Discussion.  L A R 15: 659-
60.
--- E. S.  Modern fine printing since the Kelmscott press.
L A R 15: 301-27.

--- E. S.  Professional training.  L A 8: 53, 64-9.

--- E. S.  A short bibliography of fine printing.  L A R
15: 325-7.

--- E. S.  Some American Libraries.  L A R 16: 206-16.

--- E. S.  Some thoughts on professional training.  L A R
13: 237-42.

--- E. S.  Women Librarians.  L A R 12: 224-6.

Fegan, M.  Women assistants and the war.  L W 17: 197-200,
271.

Fegley, H. W.  Rural library service for millers.  American
Miller Feb 1916: 121-2.

Feipel, L. N.  A new scheme for card catalogs.  L J 35: 205-6.

---- L. N.  Primitive inter-library loan system.  L J
35: 370.

Feipel, L. W.  The rise and development of libraries on
board vessels of the United States navy.  L J 44: 638-44.

Fellows, D.  Accessioning, etc.  P L 4: 262-4.

Fellows, J. D.  Cataloguing, accessioning and shelf listing
for small libraries.  L J 24: Conf No 68-70; P L 4: 262-4.

----- J. D.  Concerning "Cataloging."  P L 21: 67.

----- J. D.  The decimal classification in the tenth
edition.  L J 45: 154-6.

----- J. D.  Some comments on the reply to her review of
T. Hitchler's "Cataloging for small libraries."  P L
21: 145-6.

Felmley, D.  How far should courses in normal schools and
teachers' colleges seek to acquaint all teachers with the
ways of organizing and using school libraries?  Nat Educ
Assn 1908: 1087-93: L J 33: 305-8.

Felsenthal, E.  The book symposium and its reason for being.
P L 22: 4-5.

Felter, F. A.  Bibliography of economic science.  Bib Soc
Amer Proc 1: 205-6.

Fennelly, C. M.  Winning friends for the library.  Wis Lib
Bull 9: 44-5.

Fenner, L. B.  Accounts with books and borrowers.  L J 16:
246.

Fergus, E. C.  Clippings for the library.  P L 6: 329-31.

Ferguson.  Book of secrets.  Bib Soc Trans 12: 145-76.

------  Lecture on Reisch's "Margarita philosophia," a
survey of the earliest editions of this compendium of
grammar, science and philosophy.  Bib Soc Trans 5: 180-2.

Ferguson, I. M.  Bird-house exhibit in Minneapolis.  P L
22: 231.

------  I. M.  Children and movies.  Minn P L C N 4: 139-42.

------  I. M.  Children's exhibition at Minneapolis public
library.  P L 21: 268-70.

Ferguson, J.  Brothers Foulis and early Glasgow printing.
L 1: 81-96.

Ferguson, M. J.  Books for the blind.  L J 44: 759-60.
------  M. J.  California County free library service:
success of the system demonstrates feasibility of
county unit.  County Commissioners Magazine 3: 161-2,
174.
------  M. J.  California libraries: a short review and
a look ahead.  Cal News Notes 13: 1-5.
------  M. J.  California state library school.  Cal News
Notes 12: 353-7.  California state library school discon-
tinued--and why.  Cal News Notes 15: 287-8.
------  M. J.  County free libraries.  Nat Assn of State
Libraries Proceedings 1917: 17-8; A L A Bull 11: 375-6.
------  M. J.  County free library system.  California
Weekly 2: 796, 799; Sierra Educ News 13: 445.
------  M. J.  The County library act.  Cal News Notes
4: 257-8; California Lib Assn Proceedings 1909: 39.
------  M. J.  Getting books to farmers in California.
A L A Bull 13: 137-40, 373, 405; L J 44: 599-602.
------  M. J.  Library war service in California.  Cal
News Notes 13: 9-16.
------  M. J.  Library work with the blind in California.
A L A Bull 11: 376.
------  M. J.  More about the enlarged program.  Cal News
Notes 15: 149-52.
------  M. J.  "Pikes Peak, or bust."  Cal News Notes
15: 300-3.  Precept and example.  L J 45: 779.
------  M. J.  Recent California library legislation and
its significance.  Cal News Notes 4: 253-9.
------  M. J.  School and library again: Proposed trans-
fer of libraries to education committees.  Cal News Notes
15: 40-1.
------  M. J.  Sutro Branch of the California state library.
Cal News Notes 12: 334-40; L J 42: 182-3.
------  M. J.  The Sutro library, San Francisco.  Cal News
Notes 8: 445-7.
------  M. J.  "There were they in great fear."  Cal News
Notes 15: 1-6.
------  M. J.  The trend toward county libraries.  Pacific
Northwest Library Assn Proceedings 1920: 40-5.
------  M. J.  Universal library service.  School and
Society 11: 703-5.
------  M. J.  Work with the blind.  A L A Bull 11:376.
Fernow, B.  Imperial public library at St. Petersburg.  L J
30: 860-1.
Ferree, B.  Work of the Brooklyn institute.  L J 23: Conf
No 144-5.
Ferrell, L. C.  Public documents of the United States.  L J
26: 671-4.
Ferris, W. N.  The library and the school.  Mich Lib Bull
7: 126-7.

Fetter, H. G.  Relation of the library to the study club.
P L 4: 78-80.
Fick, R.  Inter-library loans in Germany.  L J 33: 506.
-- R.  Prussian central catalogue, "Gesamtkatalog."
L J 29: Conf No 105-12.
Ficke, A. D.  Some recent poets of note.  P L 16: 9-12.
Field, C.  Book repairing.  Cal News Notes 2: 105-8.
Field, G. R.  Literature for little folks.  P L 6: 71-6.
Field, H. H.  Bibliographica zoologica.  L J 20: Conf No
29-30, 63.
--- H. H.  Concilium bibliographicum in Zurich.  L J
28: 661-3.  L J 29: Conf No 99-100.
Field, J.  The district schools in a county as educational
and social centres.  National Society for the Scientific
Study of Education, Year Book 10, pt 2: 17-9.  1911.
Field, P. I.  Expanding a branch system.  P L 16: 390-1.
--- P. I.  Libraries in business.  Wis Lib Bull 11: 183-6.
Field, W. T.  The illustrating of children's books.  Dial
35: 457-60.
--- W. T.  The problem of children's books.  Dial 27: 68.
--- W. T.  The public library and the children.  Dial
42: 67-9.
--- W. T.  Reading Shakespeare to children.  Dial 42: 279.
Fielding, H. G.  The medical library in wartime.  Medical
Lib Assn Bull Oct 1917: 29-32: L J 43: 454.
Figley, H. W.  Rural library service for millers.  The Ameri-
can Miller Feb 1916: 121-2; Am Lib Annual 1916-17: 41;
L J 41: 303.
Finch, W. L.  The librarian as a factor in community develop-
ment.  Wis Lib Bull 7: 64-6.
Fincham, H. W. and J. D. Brown.  Clerkenwell open lending
library.  L 6: 344-53; L J 20: 51-4.
Finley, J. H.  Address to graduating class of the New York
state library school.  N Y L 7: 96-7.
---- J. H.  The library of the future as an educational
institution.  N Y L 5: 6-8.
Finnegan, C.  How the library began to teach school in East
Canaan, Conn.  P L 19: 11-2; Mass L C Bull 4: 76-8; Vt
L Bull 10: 10-1.
Finney, B. A.  The "1516" edition of Gadesden's "Rosa Anglica."
Bib Soc Amer Proc 1: 71-4.
---- B. A.  High school instruction in the use of refer-
ence books.  P L 4: 315-7.
---- B. A.  Leopold DeLisle, 1826-1910.  P L 8: 465-6.
---- B. A.  Public libraries and local history.  P L
10: 3-6.
Finney, G. B.  The picture collection: sources, methods of
filing and use.  Wilson Bulletin 1: 441-4.
Firkins, I..T.  Dutch in the United States.  Bull Bib
9: 68-9.

----- I. T.  Irish in the United States.  Bull Bib
9: 22-4.

----- I. T.  Italians in the United States.  Bull Bib
8: 129-32.

----- I. T.  Japanese in the United States.  Bull Bib
8: 94-8.

----- I. T.  Scandinavians in the United States.  Bull
Bib 8: 160-3.

----- I. T.  Slavs in the United States.  Bull Bib 8:
217-20.

Firkins, O. W.  Teaching of literature.  Education 28:
306-18.

Firth, C. H.  Dispersion and destruction of archives and
works of art during the war: with bibliographical notes
of precedents for their restitution in 18th and 19th
centuries.  L A R 20: 29-33.

Firth, S. A. and W. Williams.  Should public libraries come
under the control of educational authorities?  L A R 15:
105-6; Libn 3: 279-80; L W 15: 253-4.

Fischer, W. H.  Developing the free county library: a new
conception of social service and how it is being worked
out.  California Outlook 15: 14-5.

Fish, C. R.  American history in Roman archives.  Catholic
World 91: 657-67.

-- C. R.  Lessons of the Italian archives.  Am Hist Assn
Rept 1909: 355-6.

Fish, D.  Lincoln collections and Lincoln bibliography.
Bib Soc Amer Proc 3: 49-64.

Fish, F. D.  What the Y. W. C. A. library means in Brooklyn.
L J 36: 181-2.

Fisher, B.  Studying for efficiency.  Special Libraries  5:
55-6.

Fisher, C. P.  How much is the library appreciated? Med Lib
and Hist Journal 5: 109-10.

---- C. P.  Medical libraries, medical publishers, and
the medical profession.  Med Lib and Hist Journal 2:
192-5.

---- C. P.  The photostat and the library.  Bulletin of
Med Lib Assn Oct 1917: 22-5; L J 43: 455-6.

---- C. P.  Remarks on library management.  Med Lib and
Hist Journal 1: 124-6.

---- C. P.  Should the size and growth of a medical
library be restricted?  Med Lib and Hist Journal 5: 34-5.

---- C. P.  Some points in the interior arrangement and
construction of a building for a special library.  Med
Lib and Hist Journal 4: 107-12.

---- C. P.  Typewriter in cataloguing and shelf-listing.
il. Med Lib and Hist Journal 1: 201-6.

Fisher, E. A.  Legislative reference.  American Political
Science Review  3: 223-6.

Fisher, F. M.   Individual work with children.   New Hamp
Bull (n s) 15: 136-8.
---- F. M.   Making the library more useful to the business
man.  L J 42: 276-7.
Fisher, N. M.   The library and the "Movies."   Pacific North-
west Library Assn Proceedings 1920: 27.
Fisher, R.   Taking care of books.   House and Garden   17: 56-8.
Fishwick, H.   Some Lancashire diaries.   L A R 16: 156-67.
Fiske, A. J.   Accessioning books.   P L 8: 146-7.
--- A. J.   Human interest in library work in a mining
district.  P L 13: 78-81.
Fiske, J.   Harvard College shelf-guide.   L J 6: 54.
--- J.   Harvard librarian's work.   Atlantic 38: 480-91.
--- J.   Librarian's work based on experiences in Harvard
university library.  Atlantic 38: 480-91.
Fison, H. W.   Country library.   L J 28: Conf No 47-50.
--- H. W.   Typewriter in small libraries.   L J 27: 35.
Fitch, A. W.   Ashtabula (Ohio) social library: list of early
members.  Old N W 12: 146-7.
Fitzgerald, E. M.   General use of the state library.   Ind
State Lib Bull No 9:2.
Fitzgerald, J. E.   A government system of filing commercial
information.  Special Libraries 8: 115-7.
Fitzgibbon, T. F.   Relation of superintendent of schools to
the library.  P L 8: 90-3.
Fitzpatrick, A.   Camp libraries in Ontario.   P L 9: 201-3.
--------- A.   Libraries in Canadian lumber camps.   L J
26: 141.
--------- A.   Libraries in the lumber camps of Canada.
A L A Bull 4: 683-4.
Fitzpatrick, E. A.   The special library and public efficiency.
Special Libraries 5: 89-92. Am Lib Annual 1915-16: 71-2.
Fitzpatrick, J.   Mnemonic numbering of books.   L J 7: 229-30.
Fitzpatrick, J. T.   Recent New York state publications of
interest to libraries.  N Y L 4: 47-8, 80-2, 181-5; 247-9.
Flack, H. E.   Municipal reference libraries.   National
Municipal League Proceedings 1908: 308-16.
--- H. E.   Municipal reference libraries and archives.
L J 37: 87-8.
--- H. E.   Present status of municipal reference work.
Special Libraries 2: 110-2.
Flagg, C. A.   Analyticals.   Am Lib Annual 1916-17: 13.
--- C. A.   Classification making.   A L A Bull 11: 198-9,
340.
--- C. A.   A librarian to his assistants.   P L 25: 516.
--- C. A.   Reference list on Connecticut local history.
N Y S L Rept 84, Bibliography No 23. 1901.
--- C. A.   Reinforced bindings.   Maine Lib Bull 8: 113-4.
--- C. A.   Treatment of biography.   L J 44: 622.

Flagg, G. A.  The pamphlet question.  Maine Lib Bull 4,
    No 2: 6-7.
Flagg, M. I.  State art society of Minnesota.  Minn P L C N
    3: 138.
Fleming, A. P.  Relation of the trustee to the librarian.
    P L 5: 3-5.
Fleming, M.  Reading: must it be a lost art?  Elementary
    School Teacher 4: 541:53.
Fletcher, E. W.  The Church House library.  L A R 18: 333-46.
Fletcher, F.  Place of literature in education.  Journal
    of Education (London) 24: 541-53.
Fletcher, F. B.  Publicity work in Vermont.  Vt L Bull 6,
    No 2: 7-8.
Fletcher, M. J.  Instruction to high school students in use
    of libraries.  L J 29: 481.
------  M. J.  The struggling high school library.  English
    Journal 4: 357-61.
Fletcher, O. J.  Libraries of Rome and the facilities for
    study which they offer.  Bibliographical Soc of Chicago
    Year Book 1902-3: 14-9.
Fletcher, R. H.  Progress of art in California.  Cal News
    Notes 3: 3-14.
Fletcher, R. S.  Amherst college dedicates Converse memorial
    library.  L J 42: 954-6.
------  R. S.  College library and research work.  A L A
    Bull 7: 321-5.
------  R. S.  Maps and charts in the public library.
    P L 4: 444-6.
------  R. S.  The new Amherst college library.  L J 41:
    649-51.
Fletcher, T. J.  Relation of the library to the study club.
    Ia L C Q 3: 63-4.
Fletcher, W. I.  Accessioning, classifying and cataloguing.
    L J 21: 129-30.
------  W. I.  Annotation.  L J 29: Conf No 144-7, noted
    in L (n s) 6: 74.
------  W. I.  Anticipations.  P L 14: 1-5; L J 33: 241.
------  W. I.  Apprenticeship as a means of library train-
    ing.  L J 23: Conf No 83.
------  W. I.  Architects and librarians.  L J 13: 331-40.
------  W. I.  Being a librarian.  L J 15: 264-5.
------  W. I.  Best library legislation.  L J 16: Conf No
    31-4.
------  W. I.  Biographical sketches of librarians and
    bibliographers: William Frederick Poole, 1821-1894.  Bull
    Bib 8: 30-1.
------  W. I.  Books for the young a century ago.  L J
    11: 477.
------  W. I.  Bull in the (library) china shop.  P L
    11: 549-55.

------ W. I.  Card catalogs.  Nation 99: 322, Aug 20,
1914.
------ W. I.  Cataloguing.  L J 21: Conf No 129-30.
------ W. I.  Chapters from an impossible autobiography,
Chapter xxiii.  The lost manuscript.  P L 19: 334-6.
------ W. I.  Classification from the reader's point of
view.  L J 15: Conf No 6-9.
------ W. I.  Close classification versus bibliography.
L J 11: 209-12, 250, 353.
------ W. I.  Collating of library books.  L J 20: 80-1.
------ W. I.  Co-operative cataloguing.  L J 11: 74-5.
------ W. I.  Co-operative index to periodicals.  Supple-
ment to L J 9, 99p; L J 10: 3, 24.
------ W. I.  Corporate authorship.  L J 21: 493-4.
------ W. I.  Durability of cloth bindings.  L J 18: 40.
------ W. I.  The duty of normal schools to provide library
training.  Southern Educational Review 4: 149-57.
------ W. I.  Economy of shelf room-dummies.  L J 15:
134-5.
------ W. I.  The "Essay index."  L J 11: 469-70.
------ W. I.  Few words to collaborators.  L J 9: 24.
------ W. I.  Future of the catalogue.  P L 10: 191-2;
L J 30: 141-4.
------ W. I.  General conditions respecting historical
research.  U S Govt Rept 1876: 325-32.
------ W. I.  Index prospects and possibilities.  L J 22:
Conf No 61.
------ W. I.  Indexes and indexing.  U S Rept 1010-4.
1892-93.
------ W. I.  Indexing.  L J 18: 358.
------ W. I.  Influence of library schools in raising the
grade of library work.  L J 23: Conf No 70-1.
------ W. I.  Library buildings.  L J 14: 39-40.
------ W. I.  Library classification.  L J 19: 238.
------ W. I.  Library classification: theory and practice.
L J 14: 22-3, 77-9, 113-6.
------ W. I.  Movable location plan of shelving books in
libraries.  L J 10: 316.
------ W. I.  Open shelves in a college library.  P L
12: 213.
------ W. I.  Poole, William Frederick, 1821-1894.  L J
12: 281; L J 19: 81-3, 233-4.
------ W. I.  Presidential address at Lakewood.  L J
17: Conf No 1-6.
------ W. I.  Promptness in supply of printed catalog
cards--a note.  L J 28: 802.
------ W. I.  Proper lighting of library rooms.  L J
15: Conf No 9-11.
------ W. I.  Proprietary libraries in relation to the
public library movement.  L J 31: Conf No 268-72.

------ W. I.  Public libraries and the young.  U S
Bureau of Education Report 1876: 412-8; P L 1: 412.
------ W. I.  Public libraries in manufacturing commun-
ities.  U S Govt Rept: 403-18, 1876.
------ W. I.  Public libraries in the 20th century.
P L 6: 379-84.
------ W. I.  Relation of the college library to the
local community.  A L A Bull 4: 767-9.
------ W. I.  Report of the Publishing board.  L J
27: Conf No 83-5; L J 28: Conf No 107-10; L J 29: Conf
No 169-72; L J 30: Conf No 107-9.
------ W. I.  Report on college libraries.  L J 10: 267-9.
------ W. I.  Serial stories: contributions toward an
index (alphabetical by authors) of serial stories con-
tained in bound volumes of leading periodicals.  L J
6: 42-4, 166-7.
------ W. I.  Some library superstitions.  L J 14: Conf
No 155-9.
------ W. I.  Some notes on classification.  A L A Bull
11: 340-1.
------ W. I.  Some points in indexing.  L J 4: 243-7.
------ W. I.  Some recollections of the Boston Athenaeum,
1861-66.  L J 39: 579-83.
------ W. I.  Supplement to Poole's Index.  L J 9: 61, 70.
------ W. I.  To make libraries more effective.  L J
34: 354-5.
------ W. I.  Value of old books.  L J 12: 292-3.
------ W. I.  Work of the Publishing section.  L J
19: Conf No 102.
------ W. I.  and W. F. Poole.  Supplement to Poole's
Index.  L J 9: 61, 70.
Fletcher, W. Y.  Collectors of broadsides.  L (n s) 2: 12-9.
------ W. Y.  English royal collectors.  L (n s) 1: 305-
14.
------ W. Y.  John Bagford and his collections.  Bib Soc
Trans 4: 185-201.
------ W. Y.  Rawlinsons and their collections.  Bib Soc
Trans 5: 67-84.
Flexner, A.  The preparatory school.  Atlantic Monthly 94:
368-77.
Flexner, J. M.  Choosing a librarian from the viewpoint of
the assistant.  P L 25: 429-32.
----- J. M.  Essential qualities of a good assistant.
Lib Occ 5: 286-91; P L 24: 405-10.
----- J. M.  The soldier in the Louisville free public
library.  L J 43: 404-6.
Flinn, A. D.  What the engineer expects from the library.
P L 24: 1-2.
Flint, W.  Croton bug as a library pest.  L J 4: 376.

--- W.  Libraries and the federal government: Report
on the library work of the U S Bureau of Education.
L J 15: Conf No 64-6, Discussion 114-5.
--- W.  Statistics of public libraries in the United
States and Canada.  U S Commissioner of Education,
Report, Circular of Information, No 7, 1893.
Flower, B.  Brian Born and the Irish manuscript tradition.
Bib Soc Trans 15: 133-5.
Flower, E.  Sounding the retreat.  Harper's Weekly 60: 417-8.
Flower, R.  Fate of the Baskerville type.  L (n s) 10: 251-2.
Flugel, E.  Bradshaw, Henry, 1831-1886.  L J 29: 409-13.
Focke, R.  Classification: general theory.  L J 29: Conf No
127-32.
Foerste, A. F.  Public school and the public library.  L J 22:
341-4
Foglesong, H.  Library work viewed from the byway.  P L 12:
293-7.
Foik, P. J.  Notre Dame university library.  P L 23: 174-5.
Foley, K. M.  Home teaching for the blind: a phase of state
library activities.  Cal News Notes 12: 479-83, 879-81;
Cal News Notes 13: 155-61.
--- K. M.  Prevention of blindness and conservation of
vision in adults and children.  Cal News Notes 14: 14-23.
Folger, H.  Insurance for libraries.  P L 12: 52-3; Cal News
Notes 2: 108-10.
Folkard, H.  Wigan: an historical sketch with a note on its
free public library.  L A R 1:357-68.
Folkard, H. T.  Obliteration of racing news.  L A R 9: 24-9.
Folsom, C.  How can and should the library assist the school?
P L 3: 164-6.
Folwell, W. M.  Library of the University of Minnesota.  L J
14: 412-3.
Foote, E. A.  Charging system for Sunday school libraries.
P L 5: 59.
--- E. A.  Strengthening the Sunday school library: hints
from a practical librarian.  Sunday School Times, Oct 19,
1901; Nov 9, 1901; Jan 11, 1902; Feb 2, 1902.
--- E. A.  Sunday school libraries again.  P L 6: 332-3.
Foote, E. L.  Instruction of the local librarian by organizers.
L J 23: Conf No 74; P L 3: 290-1.
--- E. L.  Some college libraries.  University Forum 1: 139.
--- E. L.  Those other qualifications.  P L 14: 342-3.
--- E. L.  Training for librarianship in Great Britain.
L J 35: 547-51.
--- E. L.  Women as organizers, directors, etc.  P L
3: 290-1.
Foote, F. R.  Cataloging for small college libraries.  A L A
Bull 5: 220-4.
Forbes, G. F.  Place of the library in the high school.
N Y L 3: 170-4.

Forbes, M. A.  Bulletin boards in the children's room.  Wis
    Lib Bull 4: 58.
---- M. A.  Children's books: what constitutes a good edit-
    ion?  P L 17: 118-20.
Ford, F. H.  Poster bulletins.  Wis Lib Bull 14: 87, 89-91.
Ford, G. S.  The library and the graduate school.  Educational
    Review 47: 444-56.
Ford, M. C.  School library question in New York city.  L J
    30: 211-4.
Ford, P. L.  Bibliography of private libraries.  L J 14: 306-7.
-- P. L.  Differentiation or specialization of libraries,
    with special reference to New York.  L J 15: 7-9.
-- P. L.  Index to bibliographies and portraits.  L J 17:
    85-6.
-- P. L.  Library from the reader's point of view.  L J
    18: 179-81, 218-9.
-- P. L.  Private libraries of Brooklyn.  L J 13: 296.
-- P. L.  Private libraries of New York.  L J 14: 20-2,
    83-4, 111-2.
-- P. L.  Reference list to bibliographies, catalogs and
    reference lists.  L J 13: 37, 82, 135, 174, 207, 244, 289.
Ford, W. C.  Manuscripts and historical archives.  Am Hist
    Assn Rept 1913, 1: 77-84.
-- W. C.  Public library and the state.  L J 25: 275-9.
Fordham, H. G.  Descriptive catalogue of maps.  Bib Soc Trans
    11: 135-64.
----- H. G.  Note on a series of early French atlases, 1594-
    1637 presented to the British Museum, 1920.  L (4th series)
    1: 145-52.
----- H. G.  Road-books and itineraries bibliographically
    considered.  Bib Soc Trans 13: 29-68.
Fordyce, C.  How the library may serve the school.  Neb Lib
    Bull 4: 8-9.
Fordyce, E. J.  Libraries and the schools.  Nat Educ Assn 1902:
    805-7; P L 7: 114-6; Ia L C Q 2: 18-9.
Foreman, M. J. and C. E. Merriman.  Proposed department of
    information and publicity.  City Club of Chicago Bulletin
    2: 165-70.
Forman, H. B.  Pleasures of a bookman.  Atlantic 105: 780-4.
Formby, T.  Donations and other aids to the library rate.  L
    1: 197-202.
---- T.  Proposed system of differential rating as applied
    to free public libraries.  L A Trans 6: 79-81.
Forrest, E.  How shall we interest and induce our faculty and
    students to more general cultural reading.  A L A Bull 9:
    159-62.
Forrest, G. E.  House-to-house delivery of books.  L J 30:
    338-40.
Forrest, M.  Suggestions concerning the new poetry.  New Hamp
    Bull (n s) 15: 160-4.

Forster, A. M.  Books and village children.  L A R 12: 566-72.

Fortescue, G. K.  British Museum and the compilation of the general catalogue of printed books.  L A R 3: 435-49.

------- G. K.  Comparison between the pamphlet literature of the English Civil war and that of the French revolution. Bib Soc Trans 9: 8-10.

------- G. K.  The library of the British Museum.  L A 9: 86-99.

------- G. K.  Presidential address.  L A R 3: 435-49.

------- G. K.  The Thomason tracts.  Bib Soc Trans 8: 7-10.

Foshay, F. E.  Twentieth century drama: English, Irish and American.  Bull Bib 8: 183-7, 221-2; Bull Bib 9: 18-9, 44-6.

Foskett, E.  Educational value of the public library movement, and a reply to some views advanced by Mr. C. Welch.  L 7: 110-9.

Foss, G. W.  The library as an inspirational force.  P L 4: 102-4.

Foss, S. W.  Government publications.  Lib Work 3: 15-6.

-- S. W.  The library alcove.  L J 34: 553.

-- S. W.  Library and industrial workers: carry the library to the workers.  P L 13: 82-3.

-- S. W.  Man more than machinery.  P L 12: 117-20.

-- S. W.  Some cardinal principles of a library.  P L 14: 77-81.

-- S. W.  Summer vacation cards.  L J 25: 683-4.

Fostall, E.  Junior work of annotation.  L A 5: 200-7.

Fostall, H.  Library bulletins.  L A 8: 54-5.

Foster, J.  The chronology of the Waverley novels.  L 4: 117-8.

Foster, J. E.  Open reference library at Cambridge.  L C 5: 71.

Foster, P. F.  Information service for the community: Motion picture bureau.  Special Libraries 9: 159-61; L J 43: 909-10.

Foster, P. P.  An American newspaper index.  P L 15: 240-1.

---- P. P.  The new encyclopedia.  P L 15: 236-7

---- P. P.  Reference libraries for busy men.  Independent 67: 1125-8.

Foster, W. E.  Aimless reading and its correction.  L J 4: 78-80.

---- W. E.  Annotations: "pro" and "con" in the catalog. L J 41: 726.

---- W. E.  Argument for public support of public libraries. L J 16: Conf No 39-47.

---- W. E.  Assistance to readers.  U. S. Rept 982-93, 1892; L J 18: 257-8.

---- W. E.  Being a librarian.  L J 15: 294-6.

---- W. E.  Bibliographical notes on historical composition. A L A Bull 1: 187-90.

---- W. E.  Charles Ammi Cutter.  L J 28: 697-704.

---- W. E.  Commercial organizations co-operate with the Providence public library.  L J 42: 301.

---- W. E.  Co-operation between schools and the library in Providence.  P L 3: 244.

---- W. E.  Co-operation in the Providence library.  L J 22: 344-6.

---- W. E.  Developing a taste for good literature.  L J 22: 245-51.

---- W. E.  Essentials of a library report.  L J 28: Conf No 76-81; P L 8: 355-6.

---- W. E.  Fiction at the Providence public library.  L J 27: 325-6.

---- W. E.  How to choose editions.  N Y L 2: 85-92.

---- W. E.  How to use the public library.  L J 4: 447.

---- W. E.  Industrial additions to the Providence public library.  L J 15: 144.

---- W. E.  Industrial catalogues in the Providence public library.  L W 7: 13.

---- W. E.  The information desk.  L J 19: 368-70.

---- W. E.  Information desk at the Providence (R. I.) public library.  L J 16: 263, 271-2.

---- W. E.  Justin Winsor.  Bull Bib 8: 2-3.

---- W. E.  Lectures.  L J 8: 244.

---- W. E.  Library bulletins: their possibilities.  L J 24: 474-6.

---- W. E.  Library's maximum of usefulness.  L N (U S) 2: 195-211; 271-85.

---- W. E.  Local exhibitions in public libraries.  P L 9: 317-8.

---- W. E.  Methods of inducing care of books.  L J 25: Conf No 63-4.

---- W. E.  Methods of securing the interest of a community. L J 5: 245-7.

---- W. E.  Necessity of giving name of state with that of city on library reports.  L J 13: 204.

---- W. E.  New charging system.  L J 5: 320.

---- W. E.  New Providence public library building.  L J 21: 355-6, 364-8.

---- W. E.  Photographic exhibitions in public libraries. L J 26: 139-40.

---- W. E.  Plan of systematic training in reading at school. L J 8: 24-6.

---- W. E.  President Eliot and discrimination in books. L J 27: 258-60.

---- W. E.  Progress towards intelligent ideals of the scope and method of public libraries.  L N (U S) 3: 319-33.

---- W. E.  Providence public library.  L J 25: 228-32.

---- W. E.  Reference lists on special subjects.  L J 5: 38-42.

---- W. E.  Relation of the libraries to the schools.  L J
5: 99-104.
---- W. E.  Report of Committee on proposed School of library
economy.  L J 10: 195.
---- W. E.  Report on aids and guides to readers.  L J 8:
233-45.
---- W. E.  Report on library buildings.  L J 23: Conf No
13-7.
---- W. E.  The school and the library.  Education Review
19: 279-89.
---- W. E.  School and the library: their mutual relation.
L J 4: 319-25.
---- W. E.  Some bibliographical notes on historical comp-
osition.  A L A Bull 1: Conf No 187-190.
---- W. E.  Some conpensations of a librarian's life.  L J
10: 195-200.
---- W. E.  Specializing of reading for general readers.
L J 6: 25-7.
---- W. E.  Standard library (Experiment at Providence).
L J 25: Conf No 36-8.
---- W. E.  Systematic training at school.  L J 8: 24.
---- W. E.  Treatment of books according to their use.
L J 28: Conf No 17-9.
---- W. E.  Use of a library by artisans.  L J 23: 188-9.
---- W. E.  Use of subject catalogues and subject lists.
L J 14: 236-9, Discussion 285-6.
---- W. E.  Week's work in the children's department of
Providence library.  L J 27: 1014-5.
---- W. E.  What our pupils read outside of school.  Journal
of Education 38: 347-8.
---- W. E.  What we do with pamphlets.  L J 14: 471.
---- W. E.  Where ought the emphasis to be placed in libra-
ry purchases?  L J 29: 229-37.
---- W. E.  Young writer's use of a library.  L J 9: 157-60.
Foster, W. T.  Your book, Sir.  Independent 103: 384.
Foucher, L. C.  Kinds of stories.  P L 14: 124-5.
----- L. C.  Story telling in public libraries.  Story Hour
1: 10-4.
Foulke, W. D.  Circulation of a public library.  P L 25: 321.
Foulton, B. S.  Department staff meetings.  L J 33: 398.
Fovargue, H. W.  Abandonment of adoption of Acts: Notes on
library law.  L A R 19: 192.
------ H. W.  Adoption of Acts by Parish councils.  L A R
22: 23-4.
------ H. W.  Balance of rate.  L A R 16: 426.
------ H. W.  Book clubs: Notes on library law.  L A R 21:
144.
------ H. W.  Book thefts: Police procedure.  In his Notes
and queries on library law.  L A R 20: 233-4.

------ H. W.  Can library committee sue in County court--
Notes and queries on public library law.  L A R 17: 183.

------ H. W.  Collection of rate.  L A R 22: 53.

------ H. W.  Cost of collecting library rate.  L A R 15:
449.

------ H. W.  Cost of lectures: notes and queries on public
library law.  L A R 15: 450; L A R 16: 428.

------ H. W.  Destruction of books exposed to infection
from infectious diseases.  L A R 18: 268.

------ H. W.  Disposal of old library building: Notes on
library law.  L A R 20: 264.

------ H. W.  Enforcement of rules: Notes and queries on
library law.  L A R 20: 130.

------ H. W.  Exemption from income tax--Notes and queries
on public library law.  L A R 14: 206.

------ H. W.  Exemption from rates: Notes on library law.
L A R 22: 310.

------ H. W.  Exemption of public libraries and museums
from rates and taxes.  L A R 10: 103-10.

------ H. W.  General rate surplus and the library rate.
L A R 21: 67.

------ H. W.  Gifts and income tax.  L A R 12: 385.

------ H. W.  Grants for technical books provided by
Education committee.  L A R 12: 386.

------ H. W.  Income of library museum expenditure.  L A
R 13: 158-9.

------ H. W.  Income tax.  L A R 21: 179.

------ H. W.  Income tax--Notes and queries on public library
law.  L A R 13: 158; L A R 15: 63.

------ H. W.  Income tax: Notes on library law.  L A R 20:
53-4.

------ H. W.  Irish library law.  L A R 20: 264-5.

------ H. W.  Lecture expenses: notes and queries on public
library law.  L A R 13: 495.

------ H. W.  Lectures and income tax: notes and queries on
public library law.  L A R 12: 384.

------ H. W.  Legal aspects of the recommendations and provisions required in any new Library Bill.  L A R 21: 304-9,
395.

------ H. W.  Legislation for County areas.  L A R 8: 492-4.

------ H. W.  Liability for local rates: Notes on library
law.  L A R 19: 188-90.

------ H. W.  Liability for rates and taxes--Notes and
queries on public law.  L A R 16: 424.

------ H. W.  Liability of public libraries to be assessed
for rates and taxes.  L A R 9: 642-3.

------ H. W.  Library rate balance.  L A R 14: 205-6.

------ H. W.  Library rate for museum--Notes and queries
on public library law.  L A R 16: 427-8.

------ H. W. Library rate under the Board of education.
L A R 21: 214.
------ H. W. Loans and the library rate. L A R 21: 180.
------ H. W. Loans for purchase of books. L A R 13: 155-6.
------ H. W. Local charges--Notes and queries on public
library law. L A R 15: 63, 64-5, 422, 450.
------ H. W. The McKnight lectures: notes and queries on
public library law. L A R 15: 63.
------ H. W. Museum Act: Notes and queries on library law.
L A R 22: 110-1, 213.
------ H. W. Museums and library rate: notes and queries
on public library law. L A R 12: 384-6.
------ H. W. Notes and queries on public library law.
L A R 12: 383-7; 13: 155-60; 493-6; 14: 205-7; 16: 421-8;
17: 181-3; 184-90; 19: 189-92; 20: 33-54, 130, 133, 233-4;
21: 37, 67, 144, 179-80, 214, 250, 293; 22: 23-5, 52-3, 109-
11, 172, 213, 310, 395.
------ H. W. Notes on library legislation. L (n s) 1: 89-
91.
------ H. W. Parish councils and the Libraries act. L 6:
307-13.
------ H. W. Parliamentary bill. L A R 15: 211-5.
------ H. W. Payment for lectures: notes and queries on
public library law. L A R 15: 449.
------ H. W. The power to close libraries: Notes on library
law: L A R 18: 189.
------ H. W. Profits on municipal undertakings transferred
to library. L A R 12: 385.
------ H. W. Proprietary libraries and income tax-- Notes
and queries on public library law. L A R 17: 181-2.
------ H. W. Public libraries act, 1919. L A R 22: 365-6.
------ H. W. Public library law. L 8: 435-8.
------ H. W. Public library legislation. Greenwood's
Library Yr Bk, 1897: 28-35.
------ H. W. Purchase of museum specimens--Notes and quer-
ies on public library law. L A R 15: 450.
------ H. W. Purchase of site for lecture hall. L A R
14: 203-4.
------ H. W. Rate limit. L A R 22: 24.
------ H. W. Rate limit--Notes and queries on public
library law. L A R 14: 206.
------ H. W. Rate limit removal--Notes and queries on
public library law. L A R 12: 384.
------ H. W. Reduction of library rate: Notes on library
law. L A R 18: 189-90.
------ H. W. Removal of reader: Notes on library law.
L A R 19: 191.
------ H. W. Resolution for promoting legislation to
enable county councils to put Libraries acts into operation
and to organize system for areas under their administration.
L A R 8: 208-9.

------ H. W.   Separate rating: Notes on library law.  L A R
22: 109-10.

------ H. W.   Suggested library legislation for counties.
L A R 9: 15-8.

------ H. W.   Surplus balance and Museum Act.  L A R 17:
182.

------ H. W.   Village libraries.  L A R 9: 365-74.

------ H. W.   War payments and the library rate: Notes
on library law.  L A R 20: 234; 21: 37, 144, 293.

Fowler, C. S.   New York civil service examination for library
organizer.  L J 32: 437.

Fowler, F.   The automobile industry.  Special Libraries  11:
79-81.

Fowler, J. H.   School libraries.  English Association Pamphlet
33, Nov 1915.

Fowler, M.   Autographs of Petrarch's "Rerurum vulgarium frag-
menta."  L (3d series) 2: 61-100.

Fox, N.   County library system, Portland, Oregon.  Pacific
Northwest Lib Assn Proceedings 1913: 24-9.

Foye, C. H.   Care of pamphlets.  L J 24: 13-4.

Frailay, P. L.   Every man his own textbook.  System (N Y) 25:
318-9.

Francis, C.   Libraries in state institions in Kansas.  P L
13: 25-9.

Francis, M. E.   Children's literature.  Littell's Living Age
247: 122-5.

Frank, M.   Mutual relations of large and small libraries.
Pacific Northwest Lib Assn Proceedings 1914: 64-8.

    --- M.   Report of New York public library staff association.
A L A Bull 13: 382.

Frank, P.   Bookbinding for government documents.  L J 33: 511-2.

    --- P.   Bookbinding for government libraries.  P L 14: 32-3.

Franklin, Mrs. V. P.   Making the public know the library.
Pacific Northwest Lib Assn Proceedings 1920: 29-30.

Fraser, A.   Ontario archives.  Am Hist Assn Rept 1911, 1: 353-
63.

Fraser, G. M.   Problems of juvenile reading in Aberdeen.  Libn
1: 295-7, 315-9, 343-50.

Fraser, M. C.   Children's magazines.  P L 16: 151-3.

Frayer, Mrs. A. M.   Relations between the public library and
the elementary school.  L A 14: 305; L A R 22: 64-70.

Frazer, N. L.   Choice of books for the high school library.
School World March 1916: 100-2.

Frear, W.   Indexing scientific literature.  L J 10: 377.

Frederick, J. G.   How a library might be advertised.  Printers'
Ink Ap 18, 1912: 22-7.

Frederick, J. T.   Iowa's contribution to middle western
literature.  Iowa L C Q 8: 1-5.

Freeland, A. M.   County libraries--value to schools.   L J
41: 147-8.
------ A. M.   Kent County.   Michigan Board of Library
Commissioners, 16th Annual Report 1915: 57-8; Am Lib Annual
1916-17: 41.
Freeman, J.   Canadian Pacific railroad co.'s library and read-
ing room.   L J 9: 115, 120.
Freeman, J. H.   Opportunity of developing a civic conscious-
ness through the traveling libraries.   P L 15: 396-7.
Freeman, M.   Library and the outside world.   L J 33: 488-92;
P L 13: 417-8.
Freeman, M. W.   Conditions and requirements for public library
assistants.   P L 21: 80-1.
----- M. W.   An experiment in library extension.   P L 15:
56-8.
----- M. W.   "Human interest" in the public library.   L J
42: 18-20.
----- M. W.   The joint work of the high school and the public
library in relating education to life.   Southern Education
Assn Proceedings 1912: 408-15; L J 38: 179-83.
----- M. W.   Library administration on an income of from
$1,000 to $5,000 a year; economics in plans and methods.
L J 30: Conf No 64-8; Discussion 177-8; P L 10: 394-7.
----- M. W.   Management of small libraries.   L J 23: 79-80.
----- M. W.   Management of small public libraries.   L J
24: Conf No 76-80.
----- M. W.   Professional standards.   P L 23: 156-61.
----- M. W.   Psychological moment.   L J 36: 55-62.
----- M. W.   Relation of the library to the outside world;
or, the library and publicity.   L J 33: 488-92.
----- M. W.   Scientific management and the reference as a
bureau of information.   A L A Bull 7: 331-6; N J Lib Bull
3, No 1: 9-14.
----- M. W.   Summer reading for children: an experiment.
Ia L C Q 1: 57-8.
----- M. W.   War and the library.   P L 23: 216-9.
Freeman, V. W.   The art of reading aloud.   Educational Bi-
Monthly 3: 39-45.
Freemantle, W. T.   Our local bibliography--Sheffield.   L A R
11: 435-55, Discussion 513-7.
French, C. W.   Some moral implications in the teaching of
literature.   Educational Bi-Monthly 2: 245-50.
French, E. E.   Rural school libraries.   Public School Journal
16: 429-30.
French, G.   Needed typographical reforms.   Dial 46: 395.
French, W. H.   The use of a high school library.   Michigan
State Board of Library Commissioners, Annual Report 1908: 57.
Fretwell, J.   Photographic copying in libraries.   L J 33: 223-4.
Freund, Mrs. C. W.   Some good stories that dignify work.   P L
23: 204-6.

Frey, A. R.   Catalog of anonymous and pseudonymous literature.
    L J 12: 192.
Fricker, F.   The library of chemical laboratories of the
    B. F. Goodrich Company, Akron, Ohio.   Special Libraries
    6: 82-3.
Friedel, J. H.   Aces for librarianship.   Special Libraries
    11: 15-6.
----- J. H.   Government documents.   Special Libraries   9:
    189-91.
----- J. H.   Hotel reference library of Lee-Huckins hotel,
    Oklahoma City.   Special Libraries   10: 75-6.
----- J. H.   International buyers' club library: The Bush
    Terminal sales company.   Special Libraries   10: 75.
----- J. H.   Looking back on the convention.   Special Li-
    braries 10: 151.
----- J. H.   Mortality among books: a study of the struggle
    for existence in the world of print.   Special Libraries 9:
    211-3, 225.
----- J. H.   A national library center.   Special Libraries
    11: 16.
----- J. H.   The need of the moment.   Special Libraries.
    10: 223-5.
----- J. H.   Qualities and training necessary for a business
    librarian.   P L 22: 361-2.
----- J. H.   Some unconsidered features of the enlarged
    program of the A. L. A.   Special Libraries 10: 253-4.
----- J. H.   Special libraries in the enlarged program.
    Special Libraries 11: 1-6, 14, 89-90.
----- J. H.   Training for librarianship.   L J 44: 569-74.
----- J. H.   Traveling libraries in the European War.   L J
    41: 662-4.
----- J. H.   We, our association, the future.   Special
    Libraries 10: 15-7.
Friedenwald, H.   Care of manuscripts.   L J 22: Conf No 52-5.
Friedley, G.   Work of a county library.   Lib Occ 2: 29.
Friepel, E. M. V.   United States Treasury Department library.
    Special Libraries 10: 127-8.
Frieze, H. S.   Art Museums and their connection with libraries.
    U S Rept 434.   1876.
Frost, A. J.   Duplicating processes.   L J 4: 51.
--- A. J.   Notes on the Ronalds catalog and library of works
    on electricity and magnetism.   L J 3: 283-4.
Frost, H.   Selection of technical books and periodicals.   A L A
    Bull 4: 663-6.
Frost, H. W. R.   Topics for nature study.   Wis Lib Bull 6: 36.
Frost, M.   Dress in the library.   il L W 10: 182-4.
Frost, S. T.   Why should teachers go beyond textbooks?   Educa-
    tion 12: 278-83.
Frothingham, M. A.   Staff meetings: their organization, methods
    and results.   L J 32: 551-2.

Fry.  Brief history of the development of the local library
  movement.  L A R 13: 307-8.
Fry, E.  Nature of libraries and the nature of books.  L A R
  2: 507-14.
  -  E.  Presidential address.  L A R 2: 507-13.
Fry, W. G.  Fines and penalties.  L W 17: 1-8.
  -  W. G.  Increasing facilities for borrowing books.  L A
  10: 12-5.
  -  W. G.  Practical professional education: a summary and
  notes on staff exchanges.  L W 15: 322-7.
  -  W. G.  Subject analytical cataloguing.  L W 18: 36-41.
  -  W. G.  Summer interchange of assistants: a suggestion.
  L W 15: 8-10.
Fudge, A. H.  Registration of borrowers.  L W 11: 118-20.
Fudge, A. L.  Literary aids.  L W 10: 345-6.
Fulcher, L. W.  Best books of 1903--Science.  L A R 6: 551-6.
  ----- L. W.  Best books of 1904--Science.  L A R 7: 658-63.
Fuller, C. H.  Indexing technical information.  Special
  Libraries 5: 131.
Fuller, E. D.  United States, state and town documents in
  small libraries.  L J 23: 564-6.
Fuller, G. W.  Status of the library in a commission form of
  government.  Pacific Northwest Library Assn Proceedings,
  1913: 42-7.
Fuller, H. B.  Office filing system for county agricultural
  agents in the northern and western states.  U S Dept of
  Agriculture, States Relations Service, Doc 4, Circular 2,
  Ext N, 1917.
Fuller, M.  Some books in the Yale collection of European war
  literature.  L J 40: 860-5.
Funnell, H. A.  Sketch of the history of the classified catalog
  in the British Isles.  L W 14: 197-200.
Furnas, M. M.  A chat about nature books.  Lib Occ 5: 339-42.
Furness, H. H., Jr.,  Shakespearean editors: past and present.
  L J 35: 112-3.
Furnish, A. H.  A public library a public necessity.  L A R 15:
  444-6.
  ----- A. H.  The small library and its financial limitations.
  L A R 12: 428-9.
Futternick, R. B.  Special methods of bookbinding for libraries.
  Pacific Northwest Library Assn Proceedings 1910: 23.
Gadd, J. B.  Libraries and school children.  L W 19: 4-6
Gaillard, E. W.  Beginning of museum work in libraries.  P L
  8: 9-11.
  ------ E. W.  The book larceny problem.  L J 45: 247-54,
  307-12.
  ------ E. W.  Book thieves: an incident and some suggestions.
  L J 29: 308-9.

------ E. W.  Charging desk problems.  L J 43: 462-3.

------ E. W.  Charging system wanted.  P L 3: 262.

------ E. W.  Difficulty of the high school library.  School Review 15: 245-50.

------ E. W.  Experiment in school library work.  L J 30: 201-4.

------ E. W.  Greater freedom in the use of books: hints on advertising books, and a criticism of existing regulations. L J 28: Conf No 38-9, 156.

------ E. W.  One way to popularize the library.  P L 11: 12-4.

------ E. W.  Outcome of the picture bulletin.  L J 26: 192-3

------ E. W.  Simple library simplification.  P L 11: 551-3.

------ E. W.  Trustees and library appropriations.  L J 30: 403-4.

------ E. W.  University education in two weeks.  L J 28: 8-10.

------ E. W.  Why public libraries should supply books in foreign languages.  L J 28: 67.

Galbraith, J. L.  William Purdie Dickson, an amateur librarian. Libn 5: 268-71, 295-7.

Galbraith, L. W.  Institute funds and a professional library. L J 10: 154.

Galbreath, C. B.  Bibliography of capital punishment.  Ohio Lib Bull 1, No 10: 1-16.

------- C. B.  Bibliography of corrupt practices.  Ohio Lib Bull 1, No 9: 5-6.

------- C. B.  Bibliography of elections and primaries.  Ohio Lib Bull 1: No 9: 1-8.

------- C. B.  Classification and cataloguing of a state library.  P L 4: 437-9.

------- C. B.  Co-operation of state librarians and state library commissions.  L J 25: Conf No 54-7.

------- C. B.  County library law in Ohio.  Ohio Lib Bull 3, No 1: 10.

------- C. B.  Library movement in Ohio.  Ohio Educational Monthly 58: 343-8.

------- C. B.  Ohio library legislation in 1902.  L J 28: 71-2.

------- C. B.  Ohio library legislation in 1906.  Ohio Lib Bull 2, No 7: 1-7.

------- C. B.  Traveling library department.  Ohio Lib Bull 3, No 2: 1-14.

Galbreath, L. H.  Books for various grades.  P L 2: 304-10.

Gale, F. W.  Classification of Christian Science literature. L J 30: 861.

Gale, S.  Function of the legislative reference bureau.  Special Libraries 5: 132-3.

Gallaudet, E. M.  National deaf mute college library.  U S Govt Rept: 270-1, 1876.

Gallaway, T. B.  Franklin county free traveling school library.
   In Galbreath, C. B. "Sketches of Ohio Libraries," 1902: 80-1.
Galleys, G. B.  Circular of information about library work.
   L J 15: 329-30.
Galloway, B.  A woman among ten thousand bluejackets.  A L A
   Bull 12: 223-5.
Galloway, J. H.  Work and read: does the artisan appreciate
   good literature--Yes!  L J 38: 143-4.
Gallup, F. L.  Library service in the chemical department
   laboratories of the Du Pont company.  Special Libraries
   10: 98-100.
Gallup, G. B.  Circular of information about library work.
   L J 15: 329-30.
Galt, H. R.  Library of autographed books.  World's Work (N Y)
   19: 12838-45.
Gamble, W. B.  Technology and patent division of the New York
   public library.  L J 36: 634-5.
Gamut, D.  Art of book buying.  L J 12: 293.
Ganley, M.  Some problems in cataloguing.  P L 6: 139-43.
Ganser, H. A.  Normal school course.  Penn Lib Notes 5, No 4:
   49-50.
Gantz, A. B.  An important insurance library in Chicago.  L J
   42: 288-9.
Gardiner, J.  The agricultural literature of Canada.  A L A
   Bull 12: 298-9.
Gardner, H.  The lending collection of slides of the Ryerson
   library, the Art institute of Chicago.  P L 24: 312-4.
Gardner, L. M.  Training children to read good literature.
   English Journal 4: 248-53.
Gardner, M. C.  The training of library apprentices.  L J 42:
   524-8; Texas Libraries 2: 63-8.
Gardner, R. B.  Competitors to books--Publishers co-operative
   bureau of New York.  P L 19: 329-30; N C Bull 2: 75-6.
Garland, C. H.  Common novels in public libraries.  L J 19:
   Conf No 14-6.
   ----- C. H.  Librarian's annual report.  L J 21: 65-6.
   ----- C. H.  Mounted pictures for circulation.  Minn Ia and
   Wil L C Hdbk 59-61.
   ----- C. H.  Photograph exhibition.  P L 1: 187.
   ----- C. H.  Pictures in a modest way.  New Hamp Bull (n s)
   2: 109-11.
   ----- C. H.  Some of the libraries at the exposition.  L J
   18: 284-8.
Garman, S. and Green, S. S.  Ravages of bookworms.  L J 19:
   230-1.
Garnett, R.  Books in the British Museum.  L J 10: 9-11.
   ----- R.  British Museum catalogue as a basis for a universal
   catalogue.  L A Trans 4: 120-8; L 5: 93-6.
   ----- R.  Card catalogue systems.  L N (U S) 1: 182-6.

----- R.  Case against the card catalogue.  L N (U S) 1:
186-7.
----- R.  Changes at the British Museum since 1877.  L C
4: 81-5.
----- R.  Co-operative cataloguing.  L 5: 252-4.
----- R.  Early Arabian paper-making.  L (n s) 4: 1-10.
----- R.  Early Spanish-American printing.  L (n s) 1: 139-
46.
----- R.  Edward Edwards, 1812-1886.  L A R 4: 1-9.
----- R.  Electric light at the British Museum reading room.
L J 4: 444; L J 5: 153, 171.
----- R.  In memoriam: Henry Stevens.  F. S. A. port.  L C
3: 65-9.
----- R.  Introduction of European printing into the East.
2d Int Conf 5-8, 1897.
----- R.  John Winter Jones, 1805-1881.  L A Trans 4: 59-67.
----- R.  Librarianship in the 17th century.  L C 1: 1-7.
----- R.  Manufacture of fine paper in England in the 18th
century.  L 9: 133-6.
----- R.  Memorandum by the late Rev. H. H. Baber on the
    removal of the British Museum library from Montague House.
    L C 2: 1-5.
----- R.  New book press at the British Museum.  L N (U S)
2: 97-100.
----- R.  New York and its three libraries.  North American
Review 193: 850-60.
----- R.  On printing the British Museum catalogue.  L J
10: 200-6, Discussion 314.
----- R.  On the "De Missione legatorum Japanensium," Macao,
1590.  L (n s) 2: 172-82.
----- R.  On the provision of additional space in libraries.
L 7: 11-7.
----- R.  On the publication of the British Museum catalogue.
L 5: 244.
----- R.  Photography in public libraries.  L A Trans 7:
66-73.
----- R.  Poole, William Frederick, 1821-1894.  L C 5: 53.
----- R.  Printing of the British Museum catalogue.  L A
Trans 5: 120-8.
----- R.  Prof. Dziatzko's cataloguing rules.  L C 5: 166-9.
----- R.  Sliding press at the British Museum.  L 3: 414-20;
L J 17: 422-4.
----- R.  Some colophons of the early printers.  L 2: 125-32.
----- R.  Some notes on ancient writing and writing materials
L (n s) 4: 225-35.
----- R.  Subject index to the British Museum.  L C 3: 119-
20.
----- R.  Subject indexes to transactions of learned
societies.  L J 4: 111-4.
----- R.  System of classifying books on the shelves at
British Museum.  L J 2: 198.

Garnett, R., and B. R. Green.  Mechanical book carriers in
the Library of Congress.  L (n s) 2: 282-97.
Garnett, Richard.  Presidential address.  L 5: 241-59.
Garoutte, E.  Study outline of California history.  Cal News
Notes 15: 13-29.
Garrett, E. H.  Illustration of books.  P L 7: 260-1.
Garrett, L.  The college and the library.  P L 4: 77-8.
Garrison, C. W.  "By-product" uses of technical journals.  L
J 42: 457-8.
Garrison, F. H.  Sketch of the library of the Surgeon-general's
office.  Med Lib and Hist Journal 4: 211-6.
Garrison, W. P.  Exchange of newspaper odds and ends.  L J 8:
148.
Garstang, A. H.  Co-operative specializing by municipal
libraries.  L A R 15: 633-5.
Garvin, E.  Use of the industrial collections at Providence
library.  L J 31: Conf No 76-8.
Gaselee, S.  Bibliography of Petronius.  Bib Soc Trans 10:
141-233.
----- S.  The incunabula of an Austrian Monastic library:
Review.  L (4th series) 1: 56-8.
Gaskins, E.  The library and the school.  New Hamp Bull Sept
1912: 116-8.
Gasquet, F. A.  Bibliography of some devotional books printed
by the earliest English printers.  Bib Soc Trans 7: 163-89.
----- F. A.  Books and bookmaking in the early chronicles
and accounts.  Bib Soc Trans 9: 15-30.
----- F. A.  Journal of 17th century: Revision of the
Vulgate.  Bib Soc Trans 10: 1-6.
Gatch, R. G.  Relation of the parent and librarian to child-
ren's reading.  Ia L C Q 5: 175-7.
--- R. G.  "Robinson Crusoe" in many renderings.  Ia L C Q
6: 130-4.
Gathany, J. M.  Using magazines in history classes.  Outlook
107: 1053-6; Wilson Bulletin 1: 4-6.
Gauss, C.  Popular education in literature.  L J 34: 391-4.
Gauss, E. F. L.  Some popular errors in the entering and
cataloguing of books.  L J 18: 6-7.
Gay, F. B.  How the binding of books began.  P L 11: 303.
Gay, H. K.  Reading list on Japan.  Bibliography No 6, N Y S L
Rept 80. 1897.
Gay, O. B.  Should a librarian cultivate hobbies of his own?
L J 29: 123-6.
Gay, T.  The librarian: a trustee's view.  Ia L C Q 5: 39-40.
Gayley, C. M.  On the reproduction of manuscripts.  L J 30: 929.
Gayley, J. G.  Classics for children.  Pedagogical Seminary
3: 342-6.
Gearhart, E. B.  List of pamphlets on present-day questions.
Special Libraries 9: 162-4, 192-3, 220-1.
------ E. B.  List of references on worshop committees.
Special Libraries 10: 203-8.

Gee, W. W. H.  Technical school libraries.  Libn 1: 339-42.
Geldert, J. M.  Public libraries in the Maritime Provinces.
    P L 9: 205-7.
George, A. J.  Translations of the ancient classics in the
    literary courses of secondary schools.  Academy (Syracuse)
    7: 195-201.
George, C. A.  Community libraries at Elizabeth, N.J.  P L 17:
    75-7.
Gerard, E.  Assistants' professional training: Presidential
    address, L A A.  L A 14: 207-15.
    ---- E.  Librarianship from a woman assistant's point of
    view.  L A 9: 164-71.
    ---- E.  Notes on some early printed maps of Sussex and
    their makers, with special reference to those in the
    Worthing reference library.  L (3d series) 6: 252-75.
    ---- E.  Presidential address: Library assistants' assoc-
    iation.  L A 14: 207-15.
    ---- E.  Some seventeenth century Sussex tracts.  L (3d
    series) 7: 227-38.
    ---- E.  Sussex book collectors past and present.  B A R
    15: xiii-xx.
    ---- E.  The woman's standpoint.  L A 10: 108-9.
Gerlinger, Mrs. G. T.  The library budget.  Pacific Northwest
    Lib Assn Proceedings, 1915: 7-11.
Gerould, J. T.  Care of serial publications.  L J 25: Conf
    No 44-5.
    ----- J. T.  Co-operation between the school and the library.
    Minn P L C N 2: 70-3.
    ----- J. T.  Departmental library.  L J 26: Conf No 46-9.
    ----- J. T.  How the librarian can help the Red Cross.
    Bull Bib 10: 28-9.
    ----- J. T.  Plan for the compilation of comparative univ-
    ersity and college library statistics.  L J 31: 761-3.
    ----- J. T.  University library statistics, 1915-16.  P L
    22: 22.
Gerry, M. S.  Library of Congress and the blind.  Scribner's
    Magazine Jan 1903: 101-8.
Gerstenber, C. W.  Financial library and the student.  Special
    Libraries 10: 122-3.
Gibbs, L. R.  Problem of the Union list.  L J 42: 95-9.
    --- L. R.  Student assistants in college libraries.  A L A
    Bull 4: 769-73.
Gibbs, W.  Deterioration of bindings.  L J 3: 229.
Gibson, A. A.  Recent books for children.  Lib Occ 5: 53-6.
Gibson, I.  On paying duplicate collections.  P L 5: 252-3.
Gibson, S.  Abstracts from the wills and testamentary docu-
    ments of binders, printers and stationers of Oxford.
    Bibliographical Society Publication, 1907.
    ---- S.  Bodley's library in 1697.  B Q R 1: 136-140.
    ---- S.  Early Oxford bindings.  Bib Soc Illus Monograph
    No x. 1903.

---- S. Localization of books by their bindings. Bib Soc
Trans 8: 25-38.

---- S. Oxford libraries. B A R 8: x-xviii.

Gifford, W. L. R. Difficulties in the Dewey classification
and their adjustments. L J 21: 494-8.

Gifford, W. S. Suggestions for making a business library
practical. Special Libraries 6: 100-4; Am Lib Annual
1915-16: 22-3.

Gilbert, C. Jewish children in the public library: their
love of reading and the books they read. American Jewish
Chronicle 1: 701-2.

Gilbert, C. B. Public library and public school. L J 29: 169-
73; Nat Educ Assn 1903: 948-53.

Gilbert, F. B. Free library, free to whom? N Y L 3: 20-1.

----- F. B. The law library. Law Library Journal 1: 6-10.

----- F. B. Special functions of a law library. A L A
Bull 1: 92-6.

----- F. B. Women's right to vote on library appropriations.
N Y L 3: 326-7.

Gilbert, M. Children's departments in municipal libraries.
L W 9· 289-92.

----- M. Education of the library assistant from the
standpoint of the woman. L A 6: 52-5, Discussion 59-60.

----- M. The Juvenile department. L A 13: 115-20.

----- M. Ladies' rooms. L W 10: 78-80.

----- M. Librarianship of the future. L A 15: 25-9.

----- M. Position of women in library work to-day. L A R
17: 131-2; L W 18: 100-5.

----- M. Sheaf catalogues applied to the shelves of a
classified library. L W 12: 161-6.

----- M. Talks and readings to children. L W 21: 120-4.

Gilbert, W. J. Indexing or cataloguing. L J 14: 246-8.

Gilburt, J. Fiction: some hard facts about it. L 10: 170-3.

----- J. In the lending library. L 6: 74-7.

----- J. Library surplusage. L C 2: 90-3.

----- J. Remainders. L 4: 324-8.

Gilchrist, D. B. Libraries for the new army. L J 42: 347-9.

Giles, L. Les Matinees du roi de Prusse. L (n s) 3: 148-63.

Gill, A. K. The annual report. L W 13: 360-3.

-- A. K. Best books of 1903--Poetry. L A R 6: 556-9.

-- A. K. Indicator considered as a modern library
appliance. L W 9: 313-7.

-- A. K. Staff time sheets. L W 10: 23-5.

Gill, B. Progress of the public library movement on the
South Coast. L A 13: 50-9.

Gill, C. W. Reading of our boys and girls. Chautauquan
70: 193-9.

Gill, F. H. Booklover's library: its organization and system
of distribution. P L 8: 257-61.

Gill, H. M.  Obstacles to a proper use of documents by
depository libraries.  A L A Bull 1: Conf No 149-53.
Gill, T.  Scientific libraries in the United States.  U S
Govt Rept: 183-217. 1876.
Gill, T.  Smithsonian system of exchange.  U S Rept 285-90.
1876.
Gillett, C. R.  Conglomerate in periodicals.  L J 11: 107-9.
----- C. R.  Notation for college libraries.  L J 23: 521.
Gilley, W. H.  Central filing in big corporations.  Filing
July 1918: 7-10.
Gilliam, E. L.  Library for business men: Newark public library
in business activities.  System (N Y) 24: 188-90. 1913.
Gillis, D.  Library publicity.  N C Bull 4: 86-8.
Gillis, J. L.  A. L. A. exhibit at the Panama-Pacific exposition.
L J 39: 898.
---- J. L.  California county free library service.  Pacific
Rural Press 91: 66, 95; Texas Libraries 1: 28-30.
---- J. L.  The California county library system.  A L A
Bull 3: 152-4.
---- J. L.  Co-ordination in library work in California.
A L A Bull 5: 72-5; Library work 1912: 136.
---- J. L.  Do you want the county free library?  Western
Journal of Education 15: 105-7.
---- J. L.  Free library service in rural schools.  Pacific
Rural Press 91: 170.
---- J. L.  How to improve the law in California.  National
Assn of State Librarians Proceedings 1910: 44-5.
---- J. L.  Inter-library loans.  A L A Bull 6: 99-101.
---- J. L.  The proposed new county library law.  Cal News
Notes 5: 377-8; California Lib Assn Proceedings 1910: 31-2.
---- J. L.  Relation of state libraries to other educational
institutions.  A L A Bull 2: 284-5.
---- J. L.  Shall the state library be the head of all
library activities of the state?  National Assn of State
Libraries Proceedings 1911: 12-3; Discussion 13-7; P L
16: 287-8.
---- J. L.  State library administration.  L J 30: Conf
No 34-7.
---- J. L.  State library for all the people.  Pacific Rural
Press 91: 226-7.
---- J. L.  A state library system for California: a suggest-
ion.  Cal News Notes 3: 227-8; L J 33: 316; Library Work
1912: 255.
Gillis, M. R.  California state library for the blind.  L J
34: 115-8.
Gilman, B. I.  Library docent service.  Mass Lib Club Bull
March 1915: 17-21; L J 40: 685-6.
Gilman, D. C.  Library of Yale college.  University Quarterly
3: 244-61.

Gilman, E. A.   How periodicals are illustrated.   P L 7: 83-4.
Gilman, S. W.   Business books recommended for purchase by
   libraries.   Wis Lib Bull 9: 196-8.
---- S. W.   The public library as an educator as viewed by
   the business man.   Wis Lib Bull 15: 221-4; L J 45: 204.
Gilmore, E. L.   Disappearance of books.   P L 15: 421-2.
Gilmount, E. L. L.   Co-operation with the teacher in the
   intermediate school library.   Wilson Bulletin 1: 455-6.
Gilruth, H. A.   Public library in the school: town service
   and school service.   Minn P L C N March 1915: 160-1.
Gilson, J. P.   Library of Henry Saville of Banke in Yorkshire.
   Bibliographical Soc Trans 9: 127-210.
Gilson, M. L.   Library and school work in Newark.   L J 31:
   167-8.
Givens, F. M.   The awakening of Fond du Lac.   Wis Lib Bull 7:
   73-5.
Gladstone.   On the growth of libraries in England.   L J 17:
   200-2.
Gladstone, E. J.   Cultural reading and arousing the interest in
   the library.   P L 22: 1-4.
------- E. J.   Cultural reading and ways of arousing inter-
   est in the library.   Minn P L C N 4: 177-80.
Gladstone, W. E.   On books and the housing of them.   L J 15:
   139-42.
Glasier, G. E.   Government documents exchanges.   A L A Bull
   12: 333.
Glasier, G. G.   Scope of the Wisconsin state library.   Special
   Libraries 11: 29-31.
Glasson, W. H.   Methods of book reviewing.   L J 37: 133-5.
Glavier, G. G.   Exchange of public documents.   A L A Bull 12:
   333.
Glazier, J. C.   Seamy side of indexing.   P L 2: 91-2.
Glazier, T. W.   Anticipated developments of library practice.
   L A 3: 221-6.
----- T. W.   Everyday work of an assistant in a library
   (prize essay).   L A 2: Supplement xv.
----- T. W.   Indicators and open access.   L W 11: 321-2.
Gleason, C.   What a county free library can do.   Sierra Educ
   News 13: 219-20.
Gleason, C. F.   A word on picture books: good and bad.   P L
   11: 171-5.
Gleason, E.   Psychology and the librarian.   P L 24: 415-6.
Gleaves, A.   Books and reading for the navy and what they have
   meant in the war.   A L A Bull 13: 155-7, 349.
----- A.   Libraries for the navy.   L J 44: 499-501.
Gleeson, C. F.   Word on picture books, good and bad.   P L 11:
   171-4.
Glenister, E. E.   Filing of periodicals.   L W 10: 350-1.
Glenn, E. R.   Standardization of book selection in high schools.
   A L A Bull 13: 397-8.

Glenn, F. M.  Technical training in librarianship in England
and abroad.  L A R 12: 118-29.
Glenn, M. R.  Library of the American bankers' association.
Special Libraries 5: 78-80; L J 12: 283-4.
Glick, G.  Have you a good love story?  P L 25: 432-3.
Glynn, P. M.  Works of Shakespeare as a key to the man.  L A
of Austral Proc lv-lviii. 1901.
Godard, G. S.  Development of the state library.  L J 30:
Conf No 37-40.
---- G. S.  History and progress of collecting material
for a bibliography of Connecticut.  Bib Soc of Amer Proc
3: 84-93.
---- G. S.  How shall states delinquent in their exchanges
be treated?  A L A Bull 1: Conf No 220-7.
---- G. S.  National legislative information service.
A L A Bull 10: 475-9, Discussion, 479-81.
---- G. S.  State and local historical societies.  A L A
Bull 2: 298-303.
---- G. S.  State and local historical societies--National
association of state libraries.  A L A Bull 3: 285-9.
Goddard, A.  County work with children.  A L A Bull 6: 248-50.
Goddard, E. N.  Classification of fiction.  L J 10: 55-6.
Goddard, W. D.  Classifying military literature.  L J 42:
804-6.
----- W. D.  Classifying the politics of war.  L J 44:
293-4.
----- W. D.  Some changes in D. C. for engineering.  P L
23: 266.
----- W. M.  Possibilities of public libraries in manu-
facturing communities.  L J 13: 40.
Goepp, P. H.  Musical libraries.  L J 23: 28; P L 3: 53-4.
Goethe, C. M.  Snowed in.  Cal News Notes 12: 461-5.
Goggins, R. B.  Paper and pulp industry and conservation.
American Forrestry 16: 415-18.
Gold, K. E.  Training of children's librarians.  P L 8: 223-7.
Goldberg, B.  Treatment of music in Chicago's new music room.
A L A Bull 9: 260-2; L J 40: 582-5.
Goldberg, J.  Liability of library authorities for injuries
to children.  Libn 2: 205-6.
Goldsmith, P. H.  Check list of important magazines and news-
papers of the Latin-American countries.  L J 44: 231-3.
Gollanez, I.  Librarians as students of literature and book-
lovers.  L A 6: 22-5, Discussion 20-1.
Gompertz, C. F.  Publishers and authors as cataloguers.  L J
10: 132.
Gooch, H. B.  New catalogue.  A L A Bull 1: Conf No 283-6.
Goodell, F.  A. L. A. service to the Merchant marine.  L J
44: 756-8.
----- F.  How the camp library reaches every man.  A L A
Bull 12: 236-7.

Goodoin, A. J.  Preservation of local history.  Mass L C Bull
    9, No 2: 10-3.
Goodrich, A. J.  Musical reminiscences of a California pioneer.
    Cal News Notes 3: 14-22.
Goodrich, F. L. D.  Responsibilities of librarianship.  P L
    14: 13-5.
Goodrich, J. E.  Library of the University of Vermont.
    Vermont Lib Commission, Biennial Rept 1895-6; 73-5.
Goodrich, N. L.  Classic fiction: a study and a comparison
    of 13 "Lists of best novels."  N Y L 1: 140-1.
------ N. L.  University of Texas library.  L J 36: 325-6.
Goodspeed, C. E.  Rare books: an address before the Massachu-
    setts library club.  L J 27: 320-3.
Goodwin, J. E.  Necessary red tape: college library classifi-
    cation.  A L A Bull 5: 253-8.
Gookin, F. W.  Improvements in type design.  Dial 47: 11.
Gordon, A.  How to use a library.  Woman's Home Companion 38:
    8, Jan 1911.
Gordon, C.  Books on accounting, 1494-1600.  Bib Soc Trans
    13: 145-70.
Gordon, P. D.  Open access.  L A 2: 137-43.
Gordon, R. J.  John Collier: the man and his work.  L A R 15:
    130-7.
---- R. J.  Library lectures.  L A R 16: 316-23.
Goree, E. S.  The county library.  Texas Libraries 1: 17-21,
    July 1916.
--- E. S.  A letter from another Texas librarian.  Cal
    News Notes 13: 40-1.
Goring, F. R.  Do exhibitions develop the reading habit?
    L A 7: 68-72.
Gosman, L.  The code as an efficient agent in library admin-
    istration.  A L A Bull 9: 253-4.
Goss, C. F.  Lewisham public libraries--open access.  L W 16:
    336-8; 17: 30-2.
Goss, C. W. F.  Daily press and libraries.  L A R 14: 437-8.
-- C. W. F.  Dates of Caxtons.  L A R 18: 90-1.
-- C. W. F.  Methods of producing and preserving prints.
    L A R 17: 265-94, 333-62.
-- C. F. W.  Mr. Burns and too many libraries.  L A R 14:
    245-6.
-- C. W. F.  Nasty literature.  L A R 14: 517-8.
-- C. W. F.  The reading-room loafer.  L A R 15: 69-70.
-- C. W. F.  "Tom Jones" and Doncaster.  L A R 15: 109.
Goudie, G.  Notes on the great libraries of Scandinavia.
    L A U K Trans 3: 91-4.
Gould, A. B.  Adventures of the missing fortnight.  Atlantic
    Monthly 124: 34-44.
Gould, C. H.  Co-ordination, or method in co-operation: address
    of President of A. L. A. at Bretton Woods conference.  A L A
    Bull 3: 122-8, Discussion 154-65; L J 34: 334, 335-40.

--- C. H.  Departmental libraries.  L J 28: Conf No 173-4.
--- C. H.  Description of important libraries in Montreal,
with remarks on departmental libraries.  2nd International
Conference of Librarians, Proceedings 1897: 154-7.
--- C. H.  Library matters in Montreal.  P L 9: 230-2.
--- C. H.  Regional libraries.  L J 33: 218-9.
--- C. H.  Report of A. L. A. Committee on co-ordination.
A L A Bull 4: 660-1.
--- C. H.  Short college course in bibliography.  L J 23:
Conf No 140.
Gould, F. J.  The child and the book.  Library Miscellany
(Baroda) 1: 89-90.
Gould, G. M.  Eye-strain and literature: an illustrative case.
Dial 60: 12-3.
--- G. M.  Union of medical and public libraries.  L J 23:
Conf No 157-8.
Gould, J. C.  Local records.  L W 5: 208-11.
--- J. C.  Local records: some notes and opinions of an
"Outsider."  L W 2: 231-3, 313.
--- J. C.  Planning of libraries.  L W 5: 60-1, 124-5.
Goulding, P. S.  Classification of literatures in the Univ-
ersity of Illinois library.  L J 39: 266-73.
------ P. S.  Co-operative cataloging.  A L A Bull 11:
342-3.
Gove, A. P.  Whole duty of a library trustee.  Minn P L C N
9: 17-9.
Gove, W. H.  How private gifts can supplement public expend-
iture.  L J 16: 221.
Gowen, R. H.  Librarian's service to the community.  Pacific
Northwest Library Assn Proceedings 1916: 13-22.
Gracie, H.  Bookbuying.  Pacific Northwest Library Assn
Proceedings 1910: 24-9.
Grady, E. A.  A novel exhibit: instruction in the care of
books.  L J 44: 154.
Graff, V. E.  The gentle librarian: a transcript from exper-
ience.  L J 30: 922-3.
Graham, A. B.  Rural school libraries.  National Society for
the Scientific Study of Education, Year Book 10, pt 2: 34-
43.
---- A. B.  Value of the traveling library in the district
schools.  Ohio State Lib Bull 3: 10-3.
Graham, A. R.  Library and continuation school at Racine.
Wis Lib Bull 11: 104-6.
Graham, C. C.  Library and the small college.  P L 12: 218-20.
Graham, E.  Co-operation between schools and libraries.  P L
6: 534-6.
Graham, H. A.  Publicity methods.  Minn P L C N 4: 214-6.
Graham, R. D.  A freemason's treasure house.  Iowa Masonic
Library Quar Bull April 1917: 35-43.

Graham, R. O.  Library and the small college.  P L 12: 218-20.
Graham, W.  Poets in the war.  Vt L Bull 14: 46-8.
Grainge, E.  An eighteenth century book room.  L (n s) 8: 63-8.
Granfelt, A. A.  Popular libraries in Finland.  P L 9: 396-400.
Granger, A. C.  Reference work in a small library.  P L 6:
    548-51.
----- A. C.  Selection of books for children.  P L 3: 409.
Granniss, R.  The John Carter Brown library and its catalog.
    L J 45: 67-9.
Granniss, R. S.  Grolier club typographical collection.
    Printing Art 16: 17-22.
------ R. S.  Typographic collection of the Grolier club
    and its classification.  L J 36: 501-4.
Grant, D. B.  Covering books in American cloth for lending
    libraries.  L A Trans 1: 96.
Grant, E.  Bradshaw, Henry, 1831-1886.  L C 3: 25-36.
Gratian, J.  Making Americans" how the library helps.  L J 44:
    729-30.
Graves, C. E.  Collecting local war records.  L J 44: 79-84;
    Minn P L C N 5: 176-7.
---- C. E.  Exchange records for medium sized libraries.
    L J 45: 495-7.
---- C. E.  A plan for a nature library.  L J 44: 707-10.
---- C. E.  Voting at meetings of the A. L. A.  L J 45: 82.
Graves, E. C.  Acknowledgment of gifts and exchanges.  L J 44:
    558.
Graves, F. B.  Printed forms for libraries.  P L 10: 218-20.
Graves, F. P.  The Maria Hosmer Penniman memorial library of
    education.  Journal of Education (Boston) 83: 6-8; School
    and Society 3: 236.
Graves, M.  Attractive editions of standard authors versus
    cheaper ones.  Ia L C Q 5: 65-6.
Gray, D.  Modern book illustration.  L A 11: 186-93.
    -- D.  Modern temple of education, New York's new public
    library.  Harper's 122: 562-76.
Gray, E. J.  Earlier Cambridge stationers and bookbinders.
    Bibliographical Society Monographs No xiii, 1904.
Gray, E. P.  Bookbinding.  Medical Library Assn Bull Oct 1915:
    26-32; L J 40: 919-20.
Gray, G. F.  Fisher's sermon against Luther.  L (3d series)
    2: 314-8.
    -- G. F.  Letters of Bishop Fisher, 1521-23.  L (3d series)
    4: 133-45.
Gray, G. J.  Earlier Cambridge stationers and bookbinders, and
    the first Cambridge printer.  Bibliographical Society
    Illustrated Monographs No xiii, 1904.
    -- G. J.  Queen Elizabeth and bookbinding.  L (3d series)
    7: 66-9.
    -- G. J.  William Pickering, the earliest bookseller on
    London bridge, 1556-1571.  Bib Soc Trans 4: 57-102.

Gray, G. J. and Palmer, W. M.  Abstracts from the wills and testamentary documents of printers, binders and stationers of Cambridge from 1504-1699.  Bibliographical Society Publication 1915.

Gray, J. C.  The perplexing personal name.  Special Libraries 11: 93-4.

Gray, L. F.  New public library of city of Boston.  L J 19: 365-6.

Gray, S. J.  Bibliography of the writings of Christopher Smart, with biographical references.  Bib Soc Trans 6: 269-303.

Gray, W.  Belfast public library: its character and object.  L 7: 231-40.

Graydon, S.  Commercial versus art printing.  Printing Art 14: 277-80.

Greathouse, C. H.  Development of agricultural libraries.  U S Dept of Agriculture, Yearbook, 1899: 491-512.

Green, B. R.  Building for Library of Congress.  Smithsonian Institution, Report 1897: 625-33.

--- B. R.  Library buildings and book stacks.  L J 31: Conf No 52-6.

--- B. R.  New building for the Library of Congress.  L J 21: Conf No 13-20.

--- B. R.  Planning and construction of library buildings.  L J 25: 677-83.

Green, C. H.  Union list of agricultural periodicals.  A L A Bull 13: 374.

Green, C. R.  Library extension work at the Massachusetts agricultural college.  L J 40: 331-2.

--- C. R.  Library of the Massachusetts agricultural college.  Special Libraries 10: 19-50

--- C. R.  List of references on women in agriculture.  Special Libraries 10: 138-45.

--- C. R.  Recent books on agriculture.  Mass L C Bull 3: 107-13.

--- C. R.  Relation of the experiment station library to the college library.  A L A Bull 4: 769-73.

--- C. R.  A union check-list of agricultural serials in agricultural libraries.  A L A Bull 10: 405.

Green, E.  Another kind of censorship.  L A R 13: 308-9.

--- E.  An available loan collection of pictures illustrating modern book illustration.  L A R 21: 376.

--- E.  Branch libraries and delivery stations.  L W 4: 88-90.

--- E.  Fiction issues in municipal libraries.  L A R 16: 81-2.

--- E.  A hospital library and some of its by-products.  P L 24: 240-2.

--- E.  Neglected factors in education.  L A R 15: 290-1.

--- E.  Notes on juvenile libraries.  L W 3: 129-30.
--- E.  The old order and the new.  L W 4: 38-41.
--- E.  On the improvement of old libraries.  L W 6: 204-7.
--- E.  Schools and libraries.  Athenaeum Nov 1917: 585-6.
--- E.  School libraries.  L A R 12: 227-41.
--- E.  Some elements of success in public library work.
   L W 6: 289-92.
--- E.  Value of annotation in cataloguing and book lists.
   L A R 8: 444-9.
Green, E. B.  Library architecture from the architect's stand-
   point.  P L 6: 599-602.
--- E. B.  Library buildings.  L J 26: 865-7.
Green, H.  School libraries: their organization and management.
   L A R 12: 227-41.
Green, H. C.  Henty versus the "Penny Dreadful."  L W 17: 41-3.
Green, H. E.  Card volumes versus card drawers.  L J 17: 5-6.
--- H. E.  Library experts: their rights and duties.  L J
   15: Conf No 15-9.
--- H. E.  Tabulated reports of state library associations.
   L J 16: Conf No 52-6, 112-3.
Green, H. R.  Card volumes versus card drawers.  L J 17: 5-6.
Green, S.  How to encourage the foundation of libraries in
   small towns.  L J 24: Conf No 14-5.
Green, S. A.  On the care of pamphlets.  L J 19: 198-9.
Green, S. S.  Adaptation of libraries to constituencies.  L J
   18: 219-20; U. S. Rept 698-703, 1892-93.
--- S. S.  Address at the A. L. A. Cincinnati conference.
   L J 7: 206.
--- S. S.  Aids and guides for readers.  L J 7: 139.
--- S. S.  Books for boys.  L J 6: 182-3.
--- S. S.  Capture of a notorious book thief.  L J 5: 48-9.
--- S. S.  Charles Ammi Cutter (1837-1903)  Bull Bib 8:
   59-60.
--- S. S.  Connection between libraries and schools.  Nat
   Educ Assn 1898: 1009-11.
--- S. S.  Desirableness of establishing personal inter-
   course and relations between librarian and readers in public
   libraries.  L J 1: 74-81.
--- S. S.  Discrimination regarding open shelves.  L J 24:
   Conf No 517-20.
--- S. S.  Distribution of U. S. Public documents.  L J 7:
   226-8.
--- S. S.  Duties of trustees and their relations to
   libraries.  L J 15: Conf No 24-7.
--- S. S.  Elevation in the Worcester (U. S.) public
   library.  L J 4: 201-2.
--- S. S.  Extent of operations: Presidential address,
   San Francisco conference.  L J 16: Conf No 7.
--- S. S.  How we choose and buy new books.  L J 14: 336-7.

--- S. S.  Inter-library loans.  L J 1: 15-6.
--- S. S.  Inter-library loans in reference work.  L J
23: 567-8.
--- S. S.  Lead us not into temptation--open shelves and
public morals.  L J 26: 137.
--- S. S.  Libraries and schools.  L J 16: Conf No 22-6.
--- S. S.  Libraries as bureaus of information.  L J 21:
324-6.
--- S. S.  Library aids.  L J 6: 104-11.
--- S. S.  Library and the school.  L J 12: 400-2.
--- S. S.  Library buildings: Presidential address.
L J 16: Conf No 1-2.
--- S. S.  Library in its relation to persons engaged in
industrial pursuits.  L J 14: 215-25.
--- S. S.  Opening libraries on Sundays.  L J 9: 83-6.
--- S. S.  Personal relations between librarians and
readers.  L J 1: 74-81, 123-4.
--- S. S.  Precautions against fire in the Worcester
public library.  L J 4: 201-2.
--- S. S.  Presidential address--San Francisco conference.
L J 16: Conf No 1-9.
--- S. S.  Printed lists of documents.  L J 7: 195, 216-8.
--- S. S.  Public documents.  L J 11: 482.
--- S. S.  Public libraries and schools.  Mass Board of
Educ Rept. 1884: 235-54.
--- S. S.  Relation of librarian to book committee.  L J
15: Conf No 116-7.
--- S. S.  Relation of the public library to the public
schools.  American Social Science Assn Journal 12: 13-28;
L J 5: 235-45.
--- S. S.  Remarks at conference of librarians, Philadel-
phia.  L J 1: 99-100.
--- S. S.  Remarks at London conference.  1st Int Conf:
L J 2: 256-7.
--- S. S.  Report of A. L. A. Committee on distribution
of public documents.  L J 6: 86-90, 130-1.
--- S. S.  Report on distribution of U. S. public documents.
L J 12: 445.
--- S. S.  Report on libraries and schools.  L J 8: 229-33,
281-5.
--- S. S.  Selection of books for Sunday-school children's
libraries.  L J 7: 250-1.
--- S. S.  Sensational fiction in public libraries.  L J
4: 344-55.
--- S. S.  Sunday opening.  L J 17: Conf No 45-6.
--- S. S.  Trustees and librarians.  L J 15: Conf No 24-7.
--- S. S.  Use of pictures in libraries.  U S Commissioner
of Education Report 1898, 2: 1725-31.
--- S. S.  What classes of persons, if any, should have
access to the shelves of large libraries?  L J 25: Conf
No 34.

--- S. S.  What we do about duplicates.  L J 14: 370-1.
--- S. S.  Work between the libraries and schools at
Worcester, Mass.  U S Bur of Educ Rept 1897-98, pt 1:
673-4; L J 22: 181-2.
--- S. S.  Work with library and school in Worcester.
L J 12: 119-21.
Green, S. S. and B. Samuel.  Mutual book lending between
libraries.  L J 18: 123.
Green, S. S. and S. Garman.  Ravages of bookworms.  L J
19: 230-1.
Green, T.  Obliteration of betting news.  L W 10: 32-3.
Green, T. O. E.  Description of the Sacconi binder.  L J
16: 185.
Green, W. C.  Library co-operation in a college town.  Penn
Lib Notes 6, Nl 4: 66-70.
Greenbank, W. H.  Library of the Ohio agricultural experiment
station.  Special Libraries 10: 48.
Greene, C. S.  Effects of earthquake and fire on San Francisco
libraries.  L J 31: Conf No 204-6.
---- C. S.  Libraries.  L J 30: Conf No 138-9.
---- C. S.  Relation between schools and libraries.  Cal
News Notes 4: 239-40.
---- C. S.  Report of Committee on relations between
schools and libraries.  Cal News Notes 2: 88-9.
---- C. S.  School and the library--wild flower day at
Oakland, Cal., public library.  L J 30: 344-5.
Greene, E. A.  To keep faith with the fallen.  P L 25: 443.
Greene, F. N.  State support for library extension.  South-
ern Educational Review 5: 219-27.
Greene, G. F.  Home reading in elementary schools.  Journal
of Education (Boston) 66: 403, 438, 468.
Greenhaigh, J. L.  Library accounting.  L J 43: 307-11.
Greenhough, W. H.  Ventilation, heating and lighting of public
libraries.  L 2: 426-33.
Greenman, E. D.  Better books on chemistry.  Special Libraries
9: 222, 230.
------ E. D.  Bibliographic work of the library of the
United States Bureau of education.  L J 36: 180-1.
------ E. D.  The chemist and his library.  Special
Libraries 9: 194-5.
------ E. D.  Development of secondary school libraries.
L J 38: 183-9.
------ E. D.  Functions of the industrial library--that
of Arthur D. Little, Inc. a type.  Special Libraries 10:
189-91.
------ E. D.  Housing an industrial library.  Special
Libraries 9: 138-40.
------ E. D.  Reading list on saccharin.  Special Libraries
11: 106-12.

------ E. D.  Selective bibliography on dehydrated foods.
Special Libraries 10: 108-18.

------ E. D.  State aid for public school libraries.  L J
37: 310-6.

------ E. D.  Technical literature and how to use it.
Special Libraries 9: 89-92, 93.

------ E. D.  Technical literature in reconstruction.
Special Libraries 10: 12-4.

Greenman, E. D. and C. J. West.  A reading list on industrial
research.  Special Libraries 11: 19-28.

Greenwood, J. M.  How to judge a school.  Educational Review
17: 334-45.

------- J. M.  What the school may properly demand of the
library.  Nat Educ Assn 1902: 811-8.

Greenwood, T.  Edward Edwards, 1812-1886.  L A R 4: 10-27.

Greer, A.  Sins of omission and commission in library work
with children.  Pacific Northwest Library Assn Proceedings
1911: 45-8.

Greer, A. F.  Lectures and night classes.  Penn Lib Notes 6,
No 4: 38-40.

Greer, A. F. P.  Library experiences in Mexico.  L J 44: 219-22.

--- A. F. P.  Professional ethics for the library worker.
L J 42: 891-2.

--- A. F. P.  Yale & Towne manufacturing company's library.
Special Libraries 11: 70-1.

Greeson, W. A.  Library branches in schools.  L J 37: 677.

Greg, W. W.  Another Baconian cypher.  L (n s) 10: 418-42.

-- W. W.  Bacon's biliteral cypher and its application.
L (n s) 3: 41-53.

-- W. W.  "Bad" quartos outside Shakespeare--"Alcazar"
and "Orlando."  L (3d series) 10: 193-222.

-- W. W.  The bakings of Betsy.  L (3d series) 2: 225-59.

-- W. W.  Bibliographical and textual problem of the
English miracle plays.  L (3d series) 5: 1-30, 168-205,
280-319, 365-99.

-- W. W.  Bibliographical history of the first folio.
L (n s) 4: 258-85.

-- W. W.  Cambridge, Beaumont and Fletcher: the facsimiles
of Shakespeare's poems and "Pericles": two reviews.  L
(n s) 7: 192-208.

-- W. W.  Facts and fancies in the Baconian theory.  il L
(n s) 4: 47-62.

-- W. W.  First edition of Ben Jonson's "Every man out of
his humour."  L (4th series) 1: 153-60.

-- W. W.  Henslowe, Collier and the latest German criticism.
L (n s) 5: 293-304.

-- W. W.  John Philip--notes for a bibliography.  L (3d
series) 1: 302-28, 395-423.

-- W. W.  John Philip--further notes.  L (3d series) 4:
432-6.

-- W. W.  List of masques, pageants, etc., supplementary
to the "List of English plays."  Bibliographical Society
Publications.

-- W. W.  List of the English plays written before 1643
and printed before 1700.  Bibliographical Society Publication, 1899.

-- W. W.  Notes on the types, borders, etc., used by
Thomas Berthelet.  Bib Soc Trans 8: 187-227.

-- W. W.  Old English poetical archetypes: a review of
Dr. Henry Bradley's work.  L (4th series) 1: 58-61.

-- W. W.  Old plays and new editions.  L (n s) 3: 408-26.

-- W. W.  On certain false dates in Shakespearian quartos.
L (n s) 9: 113-31, 381-409.

-- W. W.  Some points in the bibliography of the English
drama.  Bib Soc Trans 6: 8-11.

-- W. W.  Tottel's "Miscellany."  L (n s) 5: 113-33.

-- W. W.  The trial of treasure, 1567--a study in ghosts.
L (3d series) 1: 28-35.

-- W. W.  What is bibliography?  Bib Soc Trans 12: 39-53.

Greg, W. W., and A. W. Pollard.  Some points in bibliographical descriptions.  Bib Soc Trans 9: 31-52.

Gregory, W.  The engineer and the book.  Affiliated Engineering Societies of Minnesota Bulletin Dec 1917; 283-90; L J
43: 690.

Grierson, W.  Decline in the reading of fiction.  L J 37: 683.

Griffin, M. L.  Economic selection and processing of raw
materials.  American Forrestry 16: 177-9.

Griffin, Z.  Fiction in the library.  P L 8: 57-8.

Griffith, G.  A course of reading for children.  Educational
Review 17: 65-9.

Griffith, L. M.  Some things of general interest in the Bristol
medical library.  L A R 3: 285-97, 341-52.

Griffith, M. E.  A note on the preservation of order on the
shelves of an open library.  L W 16: 116.

Griffith, V.  List of books on useful arts.  Vt L Bull 8:
No 3: 7.

Griffiths, B.  The Chase bank library.  Special Libraries
10: 131.

Griffiths, M.  On overalls.  Libn 3: 18.

Griggs, L.  Rural library extension.  N C Bull 2: 95-7.

Grindle, H.  The fiction question.  L A 9: 6-16, 39.

----- H.  Impressions of the fourth Easter school.  L A
11: 86-90, 105-12.

----- H.  Parodies in the nineteenth century.  L A R 12:
52-6.

Grinling, C. H.  Libraries as workshops.  L A R 5: 403-5.

Griswold, C.  Lament of the library teacher: a poem.  L J
45: 162.

Griswold, S. B.  Law books desirable for town, village and
city libraries.  N Y S L Rept 85, Bulletin No 75: 103. 1902.

------ S. B.  Law libraries in the United States.  U S
Govt Rept 1876: 161-70.
Griswold, W. M.  Choice of books in public libraries, especially
at Cambridge.  L J 15: 110.
------ W. M.  Note on indexing.  L J 6: 186, 203.
Groesbeck, K.  Dignity of printing as a profession.  Printing
Art 17: 117-9.
------- K.  Effective but inexpensive printing.  Printing
Art 17: 393-5.
Grose, H. D.  How library work, field work and laboratory work
may be made mutually supplemental in the teaching of earth
science.  Journal of Geography 14: 253-6.
Grover, E. O.  Fundamental principles.  Printing Art 14: 18-23.
---- E. O.  Offset printing process.  Printing Art 14: 346-8.
Groves, C. E. and M. G. Wyer.  Index of New York governors'
messages, 1777-1901.  Bulletin 100, Legislation No 26,
N Y S L Rept 88, vol. 2.
Growoll, A.  Notes on co-operative or labour saving methods of
printing catalogues.  L J 13: 280-2; 17: 157-61.
Guernsey, R. S.  Legal bibliography--its importance and utility.
L J 1: 393-4.
Guerrier, E.  Bulletin boards.  N C Bull 3: 116-7.
------ E.  The child's first books.  P L 9: 6-7.
------ E.  Federal executive departments as sources of infor-
mation for libraries.  U S Bureau of Education Bulletin, 1919,
74: 1-204.
------ E.  Libraries and the U. S. food administration.
A L A Bull 12: 184.
------ E.  The library information service.  A L A Bull 14:
172-6.
------ E.  National library service, etc.  A L A Bull 14:
55-7; P L 24: 159; 25: 12-3, 74, 86.
------ E.  New program for library co-operation with the
food administration.  L J 43: 880-1; P L 23: 413-5.
------ E.  The social side of the library.  P L 25: 490-3.
------ E.  Work of the library in food conservation.
Journal of Home Economics.  10: 266-7.
Guggenheimer, A.  Frobel and the Kindergarten.  Bulletin No 60,
Bibliography No 26, N Y S L Rept 84.
---------- A.  Library methods for photographs.  L J 27:
324-5.
Guhin, M. M.  Americanization in South Dakota.  South Dakota
Lib Bull 6: 46-9.
Guild, R. A.  Bibliography as a science.  L J 1: 67-9.
--- R. A.  College libraries.  L J 10: 216-327.
--- R. A.  Memorial sketch of Professor C. Jewett, 1816-
1868.  L J 12: 507-11.
--- R. A.  Open shelves at Brown University.  L J 5: 210.
--- R. A.  Sunday opening.  L J 1: 443.

Gunnell, L. C.   Second international convention of the International catalogue of scientific literature, London, 1910.
Science (n s) 33: 713-8.

Gunnell, L. C. and C. Adler.   The international catalogue of
scientific literature.   Bib Soc Amer Proc 3: 109-15.

Gunsaulus, F.   The book and the people.   Wis Lib Bull 8: 183-4.

Gunter, J. B.   Library indexes.   Greensboro, N C Daily Record
Sept 4, 1911.

Gunter, L.   County libraries.   Texas Libraries   1: 14-7, July
1916.

---- L.   County libraries and the rural problem.   Texas
Libraries 1: 95-100, Oct 1915.

---- L.   County libraries and the rural problem.   Texas
Libraries 1: 11-2, Jan 1915.

---- L.   County libraries, with special reference to Texas
conditions.   Texas Libraries 1: 95-100, Oct 1915.

---- L.   Local historical research in one public library.
P L 20: 216-8; Texas Libraries 1, No 9: 7-9.

---- L.   Method of procedure in establishing a county
library.   Texas Libraries 2: 124-6, July 1917; 3: 17-9,
Oct. 1919.

---- L.   Pointers on County library bill.   Texas Libraries
2: 45-6, 76-7.

---- L.   A Texas librarian to the librarians of California.
Cal News Notes 12: 341-3.

Gunthrop, P.   What can the public library do for the college
library.   P L 8: 454-7.

Gunthorpe, E.   Association's cataloguing rules: a letter.
L A R 5: 57-8.

Guppy, H.   Analytical cataloguing for the reference library.
L A R 4: 539-40, 571-8.

--- H.   Best English books in philosophy and religion:
annotated list.   L A R 6: 438-55.

--- H.   Bibliography.   L A R 3: 109-13.

--- H.   Catalogue rules for anonymous literature.   L A R
22: 107-8.

--- H.   Cataloguing of anonymous literature.   L A R 3:
298-313.

--- H.   Co-operation: a necessary factor in library progress.
L A R 11: 518-21.

--- H.   Dewey classification at Sion College library.   L 8:
350-2.

--- H.   French fiction and French juvenile literature for
the public library.   L A R 2: 357.

--- H.   Librarian and his qualifications.   L A R 2: 53-7,
117-9.

--- H.   The librarian's equipment: an address.   L A 6: 66-74,
Discussion 75.

--- H.   New cataloguing code as a contribution to library
development.   L A R 11: 374-5.

--- H.  Notice of Augustus de Morgan.  L A R 4: 247-53.
--- H.  Rules for compiling a catalogue.  L A R 22: 47-51,
71-4, 103-8.
--- H.  Science of bibliography and what it embraces.
L A R 2: 171-5, 221-5, 263-9, 328-34, 384-91, 440-9.
--- H.  Some bibliographical tools.  L 10: 377-80.
--- H.  Special lectures for library students and others.
L A R 22: 19-23, 47-51, 71-4, 103-8.
--- H.  Steps towards the reconstruction of the library
of the University of Louvain: with list of contributions.
John Rylands Library Bulletin April 1915: 145-54: July 1915:
251-75; October 1915: 380-485.
--- H.  The work of the public library during and after the
war.  L A R 19: 236-49.
Gurd, N.  Free access in an Ontario library.  P L 9: 229-30.
-- N.  How to deepen public interest in the library.  P L
9: 222-4.
-- N.  Present problems of libraries in Canada.  P L 12:
176-80.
Guthketch, A. C.  "The tale of a tub, revers'd" and characters
and criticisms upon the ancient and modern orators, etc.
L (3d series) 4: 270-84.
Guthrie, W. N.  The vital study of literature.  Sewanee Review
8: 218-33.
Gymer, R.  Story telling in the Cleveland public library.
A L A Bull 3: 417-20.
Gymer, R. C.  Fifty school and college stories for young people.
Ia L C Q 1: 15-16.
--- R. C.  Juvenile court and the Cleveland public library.
L J 35: 159-60.
--- R. C.  Personal work with children.  P L 11: 191-3.
Hackett, I. A.  Administration of a small library.  Penn Lib
Notes 5, No 4: 28-30.
Hackley, F.  Book plates for a public library.  L J 28: 297-8.
Hadden, A.  Bookplate and mural decoration of the Monterey
county free library.  Cal News Notes 15: 145.
---- A.  The county historical department of the future.
California Lib Assn Proceedings 1912: 49-54.
---- A.  Library trails.  Cal News Notes 11: 581-8.
Hadley, A.  Outside cultural reading in high schools.  P L
18: 143.
Hadley, A. T.  Library in the university.  P L 14: 115-7.
Hadley, C.  A. L. A. plans.  P L 25: 9-11.
---- C.  Aim of library commissions.  P L 14: 306.
---- C.  The American library association and the library
worker.  A L A Bull 14: 135-41; L J 45: 535-40; P L 25:
357-62.
---- C.  Embarrassing publicity.  L J 43: 462.
---- C.  Internal affairs of a library.  P L 21: 57-9.

---- C.  Library progress in America.  Pacific Northwest
Library Assn, Conference Proceedings 1911: 7-15.
---- C.  Library training in Indiana.  P L 14: 217.
---- C.  Library war service and some of the things it has
taught.  A L A Bull 13: 108; P L 24: 287-92.
---- C.  Model commission law.  A L A Bull 3: 341-6.
---- C.  Municipal reference work.  P L 12: 232-4.
---- C.  Proposed enlarged program of the A. L. A.--A
statement by the President of the A. L. A.  A L A Bull 13:
362-3; L J 44: 753-4.
---- C.  Some recent features in library architecture.
A L A Bull 9: 125-8.
---- C.  State library associations.  P L 17: 37-9.
---- C.  The state library commissions.  Wis Lib Bull 12:
339-43.
---- C.  Tendencies in library architecture.  P L 21: 112-6.
---- C.  Trend of library commission work.  A L A Bull 3:
197-202.
---- C.  Two thoughts on instruction in library schools.
L J 44: 585.
---- C.  What library schools can do for the profession.
A L A Bull 6: 147-51; Discussion 151-8; P L 17: 401-5.
Hadley, C. H.  Library legislation in Indiana.  Indiana L C
Report 1908-10: 54-63.
Haebler, K.  Early printers of Spain and Portugal.  Biblio-
graphical Society Illustrated Monographs No iv, 1897.
Haferkorn, H. E.  The engineer school library.  Special
Libraries 10: 22-3.
------- H. E.  Searchlights: a short annotated bibliography
of their design and their use in peace and war.  Special
Libraries 9: 172-6.
Haffkin-Hamburger, L.  Russian libraries.  L J 40: 168-73.
Hagar, G. J.  Newspaper history in the library.  L J 14: 117-8.
Hagarty, L. D.  Formation of literary taste.  Educational
Review 33: 402-6.
Hagen, A. D.  Standard sizes of books.  L J 12: 544.
Hagen, H. A.  Insect pests.  L J 4: 251-4, Discussion, 292.
--- H. A.  Literature concerning injuries to books by
insects.  L J 4: 373-4.
--- H. A.  New library pest.  L J 11: 184-7.
Hagey, E. J.  A printed catalogue.  Neb Lib Bull No 4: 12-4.
Hagey, J.  Binding.  P L 9: 268-72.
Haggerston, W. J.  Newcastle-upon-Tyne card catalogue.  L J
11: 7.
Haigh, F.  An attempt to forecast some aspects of an education-
al control.  L W 23: 423-7.
--- F.  Home bindery: checking the processes.  Libn 4: 2-3.
--- F.  Improving the sheaf catalogue.  L W 15: 152-4.
--- F.  Librarianship in 2013: a study in tendencies.
L W 16: 22-6.

--- F.  The library column.  L W 15: 70-6.
Haight, R. W.  Fairy tales: an index.  Bull Bib 7: 3-5, 32-6,
    59-64, 88-92, 110-2, 135-8, 165-7; 8: 15-6, 42-6, 74-6,
    105-7.
Haines, H. A.  A commentary on catchwords.  L J 42: 939-43.
Haines, H. E.  California's new library law.  L J 35: 20-1;
    P L 15: 381.
---- H. E.  A commentary on catchwords.  L J 42: 941-2.
---- H. E.  Effect of civil service methods upon library
    efficiency.  L J 31: 699-704.
---- H. E.  A library exhibit for the Panama exposition.
    Bindery Talk Nov-Dec 1913: 3-4.
---- H. E.  Library legislation in California.  L J 34:
    167-8; Library Work 1912: 139.
---- H. E.  Library periodicals.  Bull Bib 6: 2-5.
---- H. E.  Library regulations.  L J 26: 880-1.
---- H. E.  The new county library system of California.
    P L 15: 294-5; Library Work 1912: 140.
---- H. E.  Place of the public library in the community.
    Dial 50: 483-5; L J 36: 426-8.
---- H. E.  Present-day book reviewing.  Independent 69:
    1104-6; Publishers' Weekly Jan 14, 1911: 48-9.
---- H. E.  Two aids in library work.  L J 36: 111-6.
Haines, H. K.  Notes on new books.  N Y L 5: 123-8.
Haines, J.  Work of a small school library.  L J 32: 159-60.
Haines, M. R.  Public library and the town history exhibit.
    Survey 32: 325, 1916.
Haines, W.  Notes on the bibliography of Monmouthshire.  L
    8: 239-47.
Hair, A.  Special vouchers for loan of books from reference
    department.  L W 20: 21.
Hale, W. G.  The annals of a country library.  L W 3: 35-7.
-- W. G.  Decimal classification as applied to small
    libraries.  L W 16: 263-8, 311-6.
-- W. G.  Museums--Local or educational?  L W 3: 335.
Hales, S.  Toynbee Hall.  L 5: 177-80.
Haley, J. M.  A successful library campaign.  P L 25: 268-9.
Haley, L.  Another apology: a consideration of the catalog.
    Pacific Northwest Lib Assn Proceedings 1915: 16-25.
--- L.  List of suggestions for story telling material on
    the war.  P L 24: 341.
Hall, A. G.  The library pilgrim.  N Y L 6: 166-8.
-- A. G.  The library pilgrim: Jaunt II.  N Y L 7: 38-40.
-- A. G.  Work with foreigners in a small factory town.
    N Y L 5: 159-61; L J 42: 410.
Hall, B. C.  One year in a small library.  Wash L A Bull 2,
    No 4: 6-9.
Hall, D. B.  Library rotation: method of popularizing books.
    L J 27: 934-6.

-- D. B.   Reference list on Maine local history.   N Y S L
Rept 84, Bulletin No 63, Bibliography No 28.

-- D. B.   Report on gifts and bequests to American libraries,
Jan 1-Dec 31, 1905.   L J 31: Conf No 159-74.

Hall, D. H.   Classified and condensed accession record.   L J
28: 830-2.

Hall, E. W.   Clearing house for duplicates.   L J 11: 118.

Hall, G. S.   Central pedagogical library and museum for
Massachusetts.   Pedagogical Seminary 12: 464-70.

-- G. S.   Children's reading: a factor in their education.
L J 33: 123-8.

-- G. S.   Psychology of childhood as related to reading
and the public library.   Pedagogical Seminary 15: 105-16.

-- G. S.   Reading differences in boys and girls.   N J Lib
Bull 1: 9-19.

-- G. S.   What children do read and what they ought to
read.   Nat Educ Assn 1905: 868-71; P L 10: 391-3.

Hall, H.   Bibliography of archives, palaeography and diplomatics.
L A 14: 113-5.

-- H.   National aspect of the Welsh records.   L A R 20: 197-
209.

Hall, M. E.   Books for the browsing corner of a high school
library.   Wilson Bulletin 1: 118-21.

-- M. E.   Children's reading as a factor in their education.
L J 33: 123-8.

-- M. E.   A day in a modern high school library.   P L 23:
51-9.

-- M. E.   The development of the modern high school library.
L J 40: 627-32.

-- M. E.   Helps in high school library work: some things
which have proved suggestive.   N Y L 2: 98-100.

-- M. E.   The high school library as a reinforcement of the
school.   New York State Education Department Bulletin 460;
Proceedings of the 47th Annual Convocation of the University
of the State of New York p 37-42.

-- M. E.   High-school library exhibit at the University of
Illinois library.   L J 44: 155-7.

-- M. E.   Librarian in the high school (abstract).   P L
14: 29.

-- M. E.   The library and the English teacher.   L J 40: 70.

-- M. E.   Library and the school: a program for constructive
work.   N Y L 6: 26-31; L J 44: 49-50.

-- M. E.   The library and vocational training.   P L 19:
161-3.

-- M. E.   The opportunity of the high school library.
Michigan State Board of Library Commissioners Annual Report
No 12: 44-56.

-- M. E.·  The possibilities of the high school.   A L A Bull
6: 260-8; L J 34: 154-9.

-- M. E.  Some inexpensive aids for vocational guidance. Mass L C Bull 4: 27-31.

-- M. E.  Suggestive list of references on high school libraries.  N Y L 3: 273-82.

-- M. E.  Vocational guidance through the library.  Mass Lib Club Bull 4: 13-27.

-- M. E.  What the librarian may do for the high school. L J 34: 154-9; P L 14: 29.

-- M. E.  Work accomplished by the high school library scrap books.  A L A Bull 11: 183-5, 348; L J 43: 32-4; P L 23: 317.

-- M. E.  Work with high schools.  L J 36: 509-11.

Hall, N. M.  A child's thoughts about books and libraries. L J 26: 731-5.

Hall, S. R.  The lay-out.  Printing Art 15: 30-2.

Hall, T. S.  Scientific periodicals in the Melbourne libraries. L A of Austral Proc LXVII-LXX.

Halleck, R. P.  Value of English literature in ethical training.  Nat Educ Assn 1900: 160-8.

Halsey, L. R.  Author and library work in schools.  Education 9: 390-5.

Halsey, Le R.  Practical methods of using literature.  Nat Educ Assn 1888: 70-8.

Hallsted, S.  The case against the librarian.  Special Libraries 11: 71-3.

------ S.  A library in a national bank: The National bank of commerce in New York.  Special Libraries 10: 137.

Halton, W. H.  The monetary question.  Wis Lib Bull 7: 177-80.

Hamel, F.  English books in the indexes "Librorum prohibitorum et expurgandorum."  L (3d series) 1: 351-83.

--- F.  Librarians of the Royal library at Fontainebleau. L (3rd series) 1: 190-9.

--- F.  Libraries of Louvain.  L W 17: 67-9, 124-5, 175.

--- F.  When is a novel immoral?  L W 17: 261-2.

Hamer, H.  Form classification.  L A 12: 129; L A R 17: 324-5.

--- H. and T. W. Wright.  A emendation of the Dewey classification, 790-799.  L W 17: 232-3.

Hamilton, C. M.  Story telling as a factor in education.  Educ Bi-Monthly 4: 172-4.

Hamilton, E.  Union county library, Liberty.  Lib Occ 5: 378-80.

Hamilton, E. A.  Show windows in a library.  P L 5: 422-4.

Hamilton, G. H.  Books for the blind.  L A R 4: 241-2.

Hamilton, M. D.  Literature in the intermediate grades.  School and Home Education 23: 313-7.

Hamilton, W. J.  County book wagon experience.  L J 45: 1024.

------ W. J.  The county library.  South Dakota Lib Bull 6: 64-6.

------ W. J.  County library laws in the United States.
A L A Bull 14: 341-2; L J 45: 727-31, 780-9.

------ W. J.  County library work in Indiana.  L J 45: 343-6.

Hamlin, A. D. F.  Library architecture abroad.  L J 31: 710-5.

---- A. D. F.  Views of a consulting architect.  L J 31:
Conf No 57-62.

Hammond, Anne.  The library league.  P L 4: 32-4.

Hammond, E. P.  Need of bibliographies in literary history.
Bib Soc Amer Proc 1: 65-70.

Hammond, L. M.  Reading for children.  Nation 83: 551-2.

Hammond, S. E. E.  Practical problems in bookbinding.  Industrial Arts Magazine 9: 465-72.

Hammel, W. C. A.  Little museum.  Greensboro (N.C.) Daily Record Sept 11, 1911.

Hanaway, E. S.  Children's libraries in New York.  L J 12:
183-5.

Hance, E.  Pamphlets and clipping collections.  Wilson Bull
1: 472-6.

Hand, T. W.  Inaugural address, Yorkshire branch of L. A. A.
L A 7: 16-8.

-- T. W.  Leeds booksellers, printers and libraries.  B A
R 8: XXXIII-XXXIX, 1910-11.

-- T. W.  Leeds public free libraries.  L A R 6: 1-28.

-- T. W.  Relation of the public library to the business
man.  L A R 16: 510.

-- T. W.  Relationship of the public library to our educational system.  L A R 13: 193-4.

Handley, W.  The expenditure of money for periodicals.  Am
Lib Annual 1917-18: 67-8.

Handy, D. N.  Insurance library at Boston.  Special Libraries
2: 34-6; L J 38: 399.

--- D. N.  John A. Lapp: an appreciation.  Special Libraries 8: 109-10.

--- D. N.  Library as a business asset: when and how.  A
L A Bull 6: 336-9; Special Libraries 3: 162-5, Discussion,
165-6.

--- D. N.  Selected list of references to recent publications of interest on fire insurance and related subjects.
Special Libraries 3: 186-8.

--- D. N.  Special libraries have earning power.  Christian
Science Monitor Jan 4, 1911: Lib Work 4: 1-3; Special Libraries 2: 5-6.

--- D. N. and Marion G. E.  The business library.  Special
Libraries 5: 133; System 26: 96-9.

--- D. N. and Marion G. E.  Responsibility districts.  Special Libraries 3: 194-6.

Haney, J. D.  How shall the public libraries help the high
schools.  P L 7: 224-7.

Hanna, B. S.   Reference work with small libraries.  P L 7: 149-51.

Hansen, A.   Work with foreigners.  A L A Bull 9: 196-8.

Hanson, F.   Net books and London booksellers (a letter).  L A R 9: 588.

Hanson, J. C. M.   Cataloging.  P L 23: 20-1.

---- J. C. M.   Catalogue of the library of Congress.  L J 25: 176.

---- J. C. M.   Cataloguing queries on L. C. cards.  P L 10: 261-2.

---- J. C. M.   The cataloging test in the University of Chicago library.  L J 40: 399-400.

---- J. C. M.   College and university catalogs, reports and announcements.  A L A Bull 13: 11-3.

---- J. C. M.   Departmental libraries of the University of Chicago.  A L A Bull 6: 280-92.

---- J. C. M.   Form of entry for institutions, associations, etc.  L J 31: 99-100.

---- J. C. M.   Library of Congress rules for Young men's Christian associations, etc.  L J 31: 44-5.

---- J. C. M.   Preliminary statement on collecting information in regard to early Scandinavian-American imprints. Bib Soc Amer Proc 3: 43-8.

---- J. C. M.   Questions in cataloguing rules.  L J 30: 278-9.

---- J. C. M.   Report of catalog rules committee.  A L A Bull 1: 47-52, 56-7, Discussion, etc., 282-3, 297-302.

---- J. C. M.   Rules for corporate entry.  L J 30: 72-80.

---- J. C. M.   Some observations on the departmental library problem in universities, with special reference to the University of Chicago.  A L A Bull 6: 280-92.

---- J. C. M.   Some points in cataloging.  P L 11: 62-3.

---- J. C. M.   Study of departmental libraries of the University of Chicago, 1912-17; observations and experiences. A L A Bull 11: 211-21.

---- J. C. M.   The subject catalogs of the Library of Congress.  A L A Bull, 3: 385-97.

---- J. C. M.   Subject catalogues or bibliographies for large libraries.  L J 29: 472-4.

---- J. C. M.   Wasteful duplication in cataloging.  L J 43: 97; L A R 20: 91-2.

---- J. C. M.   What the university library is doing to help win the war.  A L A Bull 12: 192-6, 282.

Hapgood, L.   Imperial library at St. Petersburg.  L J 14: 312-4.

Harbourne, J. W.   The guileless West on "weeding out": a reply to Mr. Stevenson's article.  L J 22: 251-2.

Harbrouck, M. K.   Thoughts on arranging a catalog.  P L 23: 469.

Hardman, E.   Helping children to know library tools.  P L 12: 299-300.

Hardy, A. M.  The "hows" and "whys" of admission slips.  L J
42: 692-6; A L A Bull 11: 185-90, 348.

Hardy, E. A.  How Ontario administers her libraries.  A L A
Bull 10: 181-5, 385; L J 41: 729-33; P L 21: 360-1.

--- E. A.  Outline programme of the work of the Ontario library association.  P L 6: 415-8.

--- E. A.  Training of librarians in the Province of Ontario.  P L 11: 143-5.

Hardy, G. E.  Art for children.  Nat Educ Assn 1892: 152-6.

--- G. E.  Function of literature in the elementary schools.
Educational Review 2: 140-50.

--- G. E.  School library as a factor in education.  L J
14: 343-7.

Hardy, R.  The use of the school library.  Nat Educ Assn 1898:
1007-9.

Hardy, W. J.  Book plates.  L 3: 47-53, 93-8.

Hare, H. T.  Some suggestions on planning public libraries.
L A R 7: 153-4.

Hare, W. T.  Suggestions on the planning of public libraries.
L A R 8: 148-54.

Hargreaves, R. T.  Possibilities of the high school library.
Nat Educ Assn 1915: 730-4.

Harlan, E. B.  Local historical material.  Ia L C Q 7: 149-50.

Harlan, E. R.  Library as collector of local war history material.  Ia L C Q 8: 38-9.

Harper, Mrs. G. F.  The child's library.  N C Bull 1: 64-6.

Harper, G. M.  Encouragement of serious reading, "profit you
in what you read?"  L J 28: 217-21.

Harper, R. M.  Suggestions for the development of scientific
libraries; with special reference to authors' separates.
Science (ns) 45: 315-8.

Harper, W. R.  The library in university and college work.  L
J 27: 179.

---- W. R.  Some university ideals: the library.  Athenaeum
of the West Virginia University 10 No 2: 19-23.

Harraden, B.  What our soldiers read.  Living Age 291: 651-6.

Harris, A. L.  Where the teaching of reading fails.  Educational Foundations 25: 212-8.

Harris, E. J.  The Library of Congress and the state libraries.
A L A Bull 8: 302-4.

Harris, G. W.  An adaptation of the British Museum scheme.  L
J 16: 138-9.

---- G. W.  British Museum system of press marking.  L J
12: 331, 435.

---- G. W.  Classification of the Cornell University library.  L J 16: 138-9.

---- G. W. College libraries: how best made available for college uses. Assn of Colleges and Preparatory Schools of the Middle States and Maryland, Proceedings 1892, 6: 40-4.

---- G. W. New library building of Cornell university. L J 14: 121-4.

---- G. W. Notes on the government and control of college libraries. L J 22: Conf No 55-7.

---- G. W. Some German publishing methods. L J 14: 250-4.

---- G. W. Willard Fiske, 1831-1904. L J 29: 534-5.

Harris, H. H. Richmond college library. U S Bureau of Education, Circular of Information 1888 No 1: 282.

Harris, H. J. Library of Congress and the state libraries. A L A Bull 8: 304-5.

Harris, J. H. Discussion of English masterpieces required for entrance to college. Michigan Schoolmasters Club, Proceedings 1902: 8-12.

---- J. H. Recent history and present status of English curriculum. School Review 10: 566-73.

Harris, J. R. Residual errors in great English authors. L A 10: 5-10.

Harris, N. Literature as a fine art. Texas State Teachers' Assn Proceedings 1898: 63-6.

Harris, R. D. The advantages of the colored branch libraries. Southern Workman July 1915: 385-91; L J 40: 683-4.

---- R. D. Work with children at the colored branch of the Louisville free public library. L J 35: 160-1.

Harris, W. J. Delimitation of the reference library, with a note on specialization. L A R 10: 85-95, Discussion 127-32.

---- W. J. Grading of the Islington libraries staff. Libn 7: 192.

---- W. J. How to popularize a public library (Cotgreave Prize Essay). L A 3: 49-51.

---- W. J. Indicators versus card charging. L W 7: 209-13.

---- W. J. J. P. Anderson, 1860-1901. Late clerk of the reading room of the British museum. L A 3: 7-8.

---- W. J. Modern work in modern libraries. L A 12: 85-7, 118-23.

---- W. J. The organization and conduct of reading circles: adult and junior. L W 17: 69-72.

---- W. J. Planning and arrangement of a public library. L A 4: 83-6.

---- W. J. Registration of borrowers. L W 5: 75-6.

---- W. J. Some recent developments in rating of libraries. L A 4: 304-5.

---- W. J. Suggestions on the planning of an ideal library: an utopian forecast. L A 5: 86-9.

Harris, W. T. Function of the library and the school in education. L J 15: Conf No 27-33.

---- W. T. The study of art and literature in the schools. U S Bur of Educ Rept 1898-99, 1: 687-706.

---- W. T. System of classification adopted in the public school library of St. Louis. U S Rept: 660-2. 1876.

---- W. T. What should teachers read. L N (US) 2: 11-4.

Harrison, H. M. How libraries advertise. L J 37: 389-90; Ia L C Q 6: 227-30.

Harrison, J. L. A. L. A. exhibit at Paris exposition. L J 25: 282-3, 331; P L 5: 326-7.

------ J. L. A. L. A. Publishing board. L J 26: Conf No 103-6.

------ J. L. Providence Athenaeum 1753-1911. New England Magazine (ns) 45: 47-60, 188-9.

------ J. L. Public library movement in the United States. New England Magazine 16: 709-22; L 8: 110-41.

------ J. L. Report on gifts and bequests to American libraries. L J 28: Conf No 111-26; 30: Conf No 110-20.

------ J. L. Report on gifts and bequests to American libraries, from 1881 to 1904. L J 29: Conf No 173-87.

Harrison, J. L. R. Library legislation. L J 23: Conf No 23-33.

Harrison, M. Southampton and the realm of books. B A R 11: XXI-XXV.

Harrison, R. County bibliography. L C 3: 49-54.

------ R. Dr. Priestley and his relations to proprietary libraries. L A M N 1: 17-21.

------ R. French clandestine press in Holland. L 5: 309-22.

------ R. On the elimination of useless books from libraries. L A Trans 4: 34-6.

------ R. Salaries of librarians. L A Trans 1: 90-5.

------ R. Selection of books for popular libraries. 1st Int Conf 51-6; L J 2: 145-50.

------ R. Stated minimum should be £250 per annum. L J 3: 359.

------ R. Stephen Gabriel Peignot. L C 5: 177-8.

Harrison, Robert. Presidential address. L 3: 353-64.

Harrison, S. E. and Dawes, A. J. Work with children. L A R 21: 205-13.

Harrison, W. H. Reading and some of its literary associations. B A R 8: LIII-LVIII.

Harron, J. S. Fifty biographies for a small library. N Y L 1: 206-9.

---- J. S.  The library and the holiday.  N Y L 1: 40-1.

Hart, H.  On the red printing in the 1611 Bible.  L (3d series)
2: 173-80.

Hart, J. W.  Heating, lighting and ventilating of public libraries.  Greenwood's Yr-Bk: 38-44, 1897.

Hart, M.  A tropical library, Port of Spain.  P L 14: 379.

Hart, S.  Co-operation in Hartford libraries.  L J 22: 95-6.

Harte, W. J.  Public library and the teacher of history.  L
A R 13: 119-22.

Hartham, D.  Lovely woman in the library.  L W 9: 360-3.

Harting, O.  Interchange of manuscripts between libraries.
L J 18: 505-6.

Hartley, J.  Book destruction.  L W 14: 7-10.

Hartley, M.  Concerning fairy tales.  Touchstone 8: 172-9.

Hartley, M. E.  Literary institutions of Bradford with notes
on the early printers, booksellers and newspaper press.
B A R 14: XXI-XXIII, 1917.

----- M. E.  Reading for the blind: a note and a suggestion.  L W 2: 203-5.

----- M. E.  Survey of the public library movement in Bradford.  L A R 8: 423-43.

----- M. E.  Time limit in the loan of books.  L W 3: 206-
7.

Hartman, E. V.  Project to aid German libraries.  L J 10: 47.

Hartshorn, W. H.  Maine library commission.  Maine Lib Bull
5, No 4: 15-6; 6, No 1: 20; No 2: 19-20.

Hartt, M. B.  Children's museum.  Outlook 111: 673-7.

Hartwell, E. G.  Magazine reading in the high school.  Independent 77: 457.

Hartwell, E. M.  Is there need of a downtown business and professional men's branch of the Boston public library?  Special Libraries 2: 4.

Hartwell, M. A.  Classification of federal documents.  A L A
Bull 9: 257-60.

------ M. A.  Thirteenth census, 1910 publications.  A L
A Bull 8: 265-8.

Harvey, C.  The dime novel in American life.  Atlantic 100:
37-45.

Harvey, H. P.  Pennsylvania: her county libraries.  Penn Lib
Notes 10: 20-1.

Harvey, W.  A peep into a prison library.  L W 2: 183-4.

Harwood, E.  An effective bulletin.  Wis Lib Bull 4: 41.

Hasbrouck, M. H.  Reinforced binding again.  P L 14: 349.

Hasbrouck, M. K.  Government documents and the small library.
P L 14: 52-3.

------- M. K.  War time service.  P L 23: 127.

------- M. K.  Why not tell?  P L 22: 9-10.

Hasse, A. R.  A bibliographical enterprise.  A L A Bull 8:
306-9.

--- A. R.  Bibliography of public documents.  L J 29: Conf
NO 116-20.
--- A. R.  Building up a public document collection.  L J
31: 661-5; P L 12: 48-51.
--- A. R.  Cataloguing annual reports.  P L 5: 319-20.
--- A. R.  Cataloguing of government documents.  L J 28:
Conf No 176-88.
--- A. R.  Cataloguing public documents: an editorial.  P
L 7: 413.
--- A. R.  Classification of numismatics.  L J 29: 461-8.
--- A. R.  Course on United States documents at Columbia.
L J 42: 309.
--- A. R.  Do libraries impede research?  Special Libra-
ries 9: 155-6.
--- A. R.  Documents for a small library.  P L 11: 511-3.
--- A. R.  Exhibit of trade papers at A. L. A. conference.
L J 42: 458-9, 629.
--- A. R.  Government documents and our foreign relations.
L J 41: 401-2.
--- A. R.  The great release.  Special Libraries 10: 2-3.
--- A. R.  How may government documents be made useful to
the public?  L J 26: 8-13.
--- A. R.  Libraries: why not?  New Republic 13: 341, Jan.
19, 1918.
--- A. R.  Library preparedness in the fields of economics
and sociology.  A L A Bull 10: 202-5; L J 41: 557-60.
--- A. R.  Making a market in libraries.  L J 42: 270-2.
--- A. R.  Municipal reference libraries.  L J 40: 699-703.
--- A. R.  New charging system of Los Angeles library.  L
J 19: 195-6.
--- A. R.  New York City records.  L J 32: 207-8.
--- A. R.  On a bibliography of public documents.  L J 29:
Conf No 116-20.
--- A. R.  A practical clipping collection for a public
library.  New Hamp Bull (ns) 11: 150-2.
--- A. R.  Public documents question.  P L 12: 251-4.
--- A. R.  Public libraries and businessmen.  L J 42: 185-
7; Special Libraries 8: 41-4.
--- A. R.  Public printing and records--legislation bull-
etin 29h, 135-9, N Y S L Rept 88 vol. 2.
--- A. R.  Public versus special libraries.  L J 42: 798-
800.
--- A. R.  Report of the A. L. A. Committee on public doc-
uments.  L J 30: Conf No 92-101; 31: Conf No 140-5.
--- A. R.  Socialized bibliography.  Lib Miscellany Baroda
2: 63-7; N Y L 4: 11-2.
--- A. R.  Subject headings for state documents.  L J 31:
Conf No 123-6, 236-7.
--- A. R.  Teaching of reference work in library schools.
L J 44: 582-4.

--- A. R.  This business of ours.  P L 23: 303-5.

--- A. R.  Training of library employees.  L J 20: 202-3, 239-41, 272-3, 304-5.

--- A. R.  Vexed question of public documents.  L J 27: 815-8; P L 7: 355-9.

--- A. R.  Women in libraries.  Journal of Assn of Collegiate Alumnae Oct 1917: 73-80; L J 43: 141-2.

Hassler, H. E.  Common sense and the story hour.  L J 30: Conf No 76-8.

----- H. E.  Instruction to school classes in the use of the catalog.  P L 21: 135-7.

----- H. E.  Notes on children's books taken at lectures. P L 14: 136-9.

----- H. E.  Work with children and schools in Portland, Oregon.  L J 30: 214-7.

Hastings, C. H.  Card distribution work of the library of Congress.  L J 27: Conf No 67-71, 156-7, Discussion 157-63; P L 7: 334-8; P L 8: 191-5.

------ C. H.  Distribution of library of Congress printed catalogue cards.  P L 8: 191-5.

------ C. H.  Proposed manual on the arrangement of cards in alphabetical catalogs.  A L A Bull 9: 270-3.

------ C. H.  Report on the card distribution work of the Library of Congress.  L J 28: 708-11; P L 8: 191-5.

------ C. H.  Some recent events and tendencies in bibliography.  Bib Soc Chic Yr-Bk 1889-1900: 10-8.

------ C. H.  Use of the printed cards of the Library of Congress by law libraries.  L J 37: 37.

Hatch, B.  Gradus ad Parnassum.  L J 44: 42.

--- B.  Reference work with school children.  Wis Lib Bull 15: 173-6.

Hatcher, A. F.  New method of indicator charging.  L A R 10: 419-20.

----- A. F.  Stock-taking methods.  L A 5: 43-6.

Hatcher, S. A.  Branch libraries.  L A 5: 113-6.

Hatfield, A. E.  Intensive and supplementary reading.  N Y L 3: 51-2.

Hathaway, C.  What shall we do with clippings?  Wash L A Bull 2, No 3: 9-10.

Hathaway, F. P.  Binding for a public library.  L J 4: 248-9.

Hathaway, G.  Everett library.  Wash L A Bull 1 No 2: 8-10 il.

Hathaway, H. K.  Mnemonic system of classification.  Industrial Management 60: 173-83.

Hathaway, M. A.  Accident prevention bureau and the library of the Portland cement association.  Special Libraries 10: 214-5.

Hatton, O. P.  Value of illustrations in books, etc.  Printing Art 17: 37-9.

Hatton, W. H.  Extracts from address delivered at annual meeting of the Fox River Valley association.  Wis Lib Bull 7: 160.

---- W. H.  Publicity for the sake of information: the public point of view.  A L A Bull 6: 72-5.

Haught, M.  Wilson Co. (Chicago) reference library.  Special Libraries 10: 71.

Havet, J.  National library of France.  L 4: 277-87.

Hawes, A. F.  Books on forestry.  Vt L Bull 5, No 4: 1-4.

Hawkes, A. J.  The alphabetization of catalogues.  L W 15: 262-6.

---- A. J.  Binding part music.  L W 10: 31-2.

---- A. J.  Dewey revision; a letter in answer to Mr. Sayers.  L A R 14: 119-20.

---- A. J.  Dewey's 760-799 schedule revision and elaboration.  Libn 3: 122.

---- A. J.  An extension and revision of the Dewey Africa schedule.  Libn 3: 242-5, 283-7.

---- A. J.  Functions of a central library and the problem of branches.  L A 6: 394-401.

---- A. J.  How to popularize reference libraries: a reply to Mr. Sayers.  L W 10: 62-3; 9: 433-7.

---- A. J.  Library of Congress classification.  L A R 16: 188-9.

---- A. J.  Notes on the classification of radium and radio-activity, according to Dewey's system.  L A R 11: 420-2.

---- A. J.  Open access to fiction.  L W 11: 404.

---- A. J.  Partisan literature in public libraries.  L W 12: 28-34.

---- A. J.  Points to Dewey's 790 schedule.  Libn 2: 247-9.

---- A. J.  Reply to Mr. Glazier.  L W 11: 404.

---- A. J.  Subject hunting: a reply to Mr. H. W. Wilson's criticism.  L W 10: 427-8; 156-8.

---- A. J.  Suggestions towards a constructional revision of the Dewey classification.  Libn 2: 5-8, 43-6, 83-7, 247-9.

---- A. J.  To popularize reference libraries.  L W 9: 433-7; 10: 328-31.

---- A. J.  Vain pursuits and their relation to public libraries: some thoughts on book selection.  L A 11: 45-51.

---- A. J.  Vice of consistency.  L W 12: 183-6.

Hawkes, E. B.  Catalog system of the Department of agriculture library.  A L A Bull 8: 204-6.

Hawks, E. B.  Printed cards for agricultural literature.  Special Libraries 10: 37-40.

Hawkins, E. E.  Analyzing books for a small library.  N Y L 2: 261-2; Lib Work 5, No 3.

Hawkins, J.  Printed guides for library catalogs.  N Y L 4: 23-4.

Hawkins, W. G.  Library association with examinations: a suggestion.  L W 15: 26-8.

----- W. G.  Some points in the upkeep of library buildings.  L A 10: 171.

Hawley, E.  Minnesota historical society publications.  Minn P L C N 4: 6-8.

Hawley, E.  Minnesota historical society publications.  Minn
    P L C N 4: 6-8.
Hawley, E. J. R.  Bibliography of literary geography.  Bull
    Bib 10: 34-8, 58-60, 76, 93-4, 104-5.
Hawley, F. B.  Some non-technical qualifications for library
    work.  L J 29: 360-2.
Hawley, M. E.  Swiss libraries.  P L 9: 392-5.
Haworth, F.  Social aspects of the public library movement.
    L W 7: 169-74.
Haworth, F. W. B.  Library assistants and education.  L W 6:
    36-9.
Hawthorne, H.  Books on the Lonesome Trail.  Bookman (N Y) 51:
    134-7.
------- H.  How to form a reading club.  St. Nicholas 41:
    734-6.
Haxby, R.  History, organization, and educational value of
    municipal library lectures.  L A R 13: 123-32.
Hay, J. T.  Note on classification used in recording statis-
    tics of issues.  L A Trans 2: 85-7.
Hayes, A.  List of bibliographies on woman suffrage.  Bull Bib
    8: 194-5.
--- A.  The woman movement: a short selected list on woman
    suffrage.  Bull Bib 8: 220-2.
Hayes, F. C.  Minimum wage and the wages paid to women.  Wis
    Lib Bull 9: 106.
Hayes, J. R.  Sixteenth century library rules.  L J 32: 74-5.
Hayes, L. B.  Chamber of commerce library and the facilities
    it offers.  Special Libraries 2: 3.
Hayes, R. P.  Library legislation and library commissions.  L
    J 23: 571-2.
Hayne, H. G.  The story of the almanac.  L A R 15: 389-407.
Haynes, E. S. P.  The taboos of the British Museum library.
    Eng Rev 16: 123-34.
Hays, A.  Staff meetings in library work: brief list of refer-
    ences.  L J 42: 497.
Hays, F. C.  Author headings for current Wisconsin state pub-
    lications.  Wis Lib Bull 11: 140-2.
Hayward, A. L.  Training of a librarian.  L J 17: 478.
Hayward, C. A.  Advertising libraries.  P L 14: 7-10.
----- C. A.  Reference work in a branch library.  P L 7:
    182-3.
----- C. A.  Women as cataloguers.  P L 3: 121-3.
Hazeltine, A. I.  Method of training children to use the li-
    brary intelligently.  P L 21: 160-2; L J 41: 855-6; Am Lib
    Annual 1916-17: 66-7.
------- A. I.  The St. Louis teachers room.  P L 24: 368-9.
------- A. I.  Select list of books and articles on teach-
    ing the use of the library in schools.  Wis Lib Bull 8: 33-4.
------- A. I.  Story telling in the Carnegie library of Pitts-
    burgh.  A L A Bull 3: 413-5.
Hazeltine, E.  Maintaining the public library by endowment.
    L J 21: 93-5.

Hazeltine, M.  Opportunities for college women in library work.
  Bookman ( N Y) Feb 1916, 685-91; Wis Lib Bull 12: 289-92.
Hazeltine, M. E.  Advertising a library.  L J 22: Conf No 74-
  9.
------- M. E.  The assistant and the book.  A L A Bull 6:
  134-8.
------- M. E.  Author entry in card catalogs.  Wis Lib Bull
  2: 44.
------- M. E.  Avon club at Jamestown, New York.  Wis Lib
  Bull 12: 107-8.
------- M. E.  Business administration; the budget.  Wis
  Lib Bull 8: 158-60.
------- M. E.  Checklist on library publicity methods.
  Wis Lib Bull 15: 91-4, 121-5.
------- M. E.  Children's room in the public library.  Chau-
  tauquan 39: 369-74.
------- M. E.  The co-operation of the librarian and kinder-
  garten.  L J 29: 468-72.
------- M. E.  Co-operative publicity.  Wis Lib Bull 15:
  135.
------- M. E.  Detail work in a small library.  L J 27:
  888-9.
------- M. E.  Exhibits.  Wis Lib Bull 15: 93-4.
------- M. E.  Fundamentals of reference service.  Wis Lib
  Bull 15: 85-90, 117-20, 148-53.
------- M. E.  Groups of books.  Wis Lib Bull 15: 92-3.
------- M. E.  How to conduct a dramatic reading.  Wis Lib
  Bull 11: 11-7; New Hamp Bull (ns) 11: 86-92.
------- M. E.  Inspirational reading for teachers.  Wis
  Lib Bull 7: 174-5.
------- M. E.  Lectures, book talks, poetry evenings.  Wis
  Lib Bull 15: 93.
------- M. E.  The librarian and his work.  P L 7: 402-4.
------- M. E.  List of books for foreigners.  Wis Lib Bull
  10: 122-3.
------- M. E.  Magazine day: an experiment.  P L 1: 51.
------- M. E.  Magazines for a small library.  Wis Lib Bull
  7: 147.
------- M. E.  Methods of training in one Library School.
  Wis Lib Bull 5: 49-54, 253-6.
------- M. E.  Newspaper publicity.  Wis Lib Bull 15: 121-2.
------- M. E.  Poster bulletins.  Wis Lib Bull 15: 92.
------- M. E.  Programme for an afternoon with Scott and
  Burns.  Wis Lib Bull 3: 98.
------- M. E.  Selected reading list on peace.  Wis Lib
  Bull 8: 66-76.
------- M. E.  Signs.  Wis Lib Bull 15: 92.
------- M. E.  Some recent reference books.  Wis Lib Bull
  11: 364-6.

------- M. E.  Suggestive list of reference books as a basis of purchase for a library of 2000 to 5000 volumes.  Wis Lib Bull 11: 235-8.

------- M. E.  Summer conference and summer school.  Wis Lib Bull 11: 135-6, 179-80.

------- M. E.  Technical notes for small libraries.  Wis Lib Bull 2: 44.

------- M. E.  War terms; their pronunciation and definition, where to find them and how to keep up-to-date.  Wis Lib Bull 14: 6-11; L J 43: 291.

------- M. E. and Humble, M.  Incidental tribute to libraries in popular books.  Wis Lib Bull 10: 195-9.

------- M. E. and Sawyer, H. P.  Problem of discipline.  Wis Lib Bull 4: 65-80.

Headicar, B. M.  Library of Congress classification--classes B. N. R. Z.  L A R 12: 515-6.

------ B. M.  The Sanskrit library association.  Libn 2: 326-30.

Healey, A. M.  A library exhibit in San Francisco.  Bindery Talk Nov-Dec 1913: 6-7.

---- A. M.  Training catalogers in public libraries by actual work.  A L A Bull 9: 267.

Heard, Mrs. E.  Relation between library and school.  Southern Education Assn Proceedings 1908: 636-40.

Heard, E. B.  The free traveling library: an aid to education and a factor in the national life.  Nat Educ Assn Proceedings 1900: 648-55.

--- E. B.  McKinley memorial libraries in public schools.  P L 7: 116.

Hearn, C. S.  Possibilities of library co-operation with farmers' institute and short course.  A L A Bull 8: 370-4.

Heath, E. J.  A system of classification for the libraries of colleges of pharmacy.  Bull Massachusetts College of Pharmacy Oct 1916: 13-24.

Heatwode, E. R.  Club work at the Goshen (Ind.) library.  Lib Occ 1, No 10: 5-6.

Hebbard, G. R.  Wyoming library activity.  P L 24: 417.

Heckman, F. B.  Bibliography of the Civil war (United States).  P L 7: 360-2.

----- F. B.  Libraries in the United States army and navy.  L J 32: 68-9.

Hedeler, G.  Projected list of private libraries.  L J 18: 475.

Heermans, J. W.  Teaching literature below the colleges.  Education 26: 474-85.

Hegeman, M. B.  Monthly catalog of United States public documents.  A L A Bull 8: 262-5.

Helliwell, F.  Local co-operative cataloguing.  L W 16: 99-102.

------- F.  Subject classification.  1400 expanded.  L W 16: 308-10.

Helmer, F. F.   Trademarks of printers.   Printing Art 15: 369-72.

Hempel, Rudolf.   Russell Sage foundation building: Social betterment organization building, lecture rooms, offices and library.   American Architect 20 Oct 1915: 267-9.

Hemphill, F.   Proposed centralization of Metropolitan libraries.   Lit Yr-Bk: 590-1.

Hempstead, E. A.   The new Congressional Library.   Chautauquan 23: 697-705.

Henderson, A.   Arthur Schnitzler (1862- ) a bibliography.   Translations, productions, and criticism in English.   Bull Bib 7: 155-6.

------- A.   August Strindberg (1849-1912) a bibliography.   Translations and criticisms in English.   Bull Bib 7: 41-2.

------- A.   Bjornstjerne Bjornson (1832-1910) a bibliography.   Translations, bibliographies and criticism in English.   Bull Bib 8: 69-71.

Henderson, A. G.   Dundee branch libraries: Langside branch.   Builder 25 June, 1915: 31.

Henderson, H.   Importance of parish registers.   L A 7: 271-6.

Henderson, R. W.   New York public library.   L A 9: 218-20.

------- R. W.   The New York public library as illustrating American methods.   L A R 15: 267.

------- R. W.   The outlook of the library assistant.   L A 7: 135-6.

------- R. W.   Prospects of the library assistant.   L W 12: 455-9.

Hendry, D.   An American observer in Leipzig.   P L 19: 423-9.

---- D.   Applied science reference department of Pratt institute library, Brooklyn (N. Y.)   Bull Bib 9: 64-5.

---- D.   The Deutsche Bucherei in Leipzig (Depository where the entire productions of books printed in Germany, German-Austria, German-Switzerland and German books printed in other countries are stored).   L J 41: 885-7.

---- D.   Library instruction at Pratt Institute.   L J 39: 211-2.

---- D.   List of technical and scientific books for boys.   Lib Occ 5: 343-5.

---- D.   Select list of technical books published in 1916.   N Y L 5: 172-3.

---- D.   Technical books for small and medium sized libraries.   Wis Lib Bull 15: 46-52.

Henley, D.   Picture bulletin at Wabash, Indiana, Library.   Lib Occ 1, No 11: 5-6.

Henley, L.   Public affairs information service: a practical application of the co-operation principle.   Special Libraries 8: 54-8.

Henman, W.   Free library buildings: their arrangement and fittings.   L A Trans 5: 100-4.

Henneberry, K. M.   Preparation of printed lists for circulat-
ing libraries.   L J 19: 9-11.
Hennessey, A. L.   Picture in typography.   Printing Art 14:
425-8.
Henrotin, E. M.   Children's literature.   National Magazine 7:
373-5.
Henry, F. P.   Bookworms.   Med Lib and Hist Journal 1903: 18.
Henry, N. E.   School libraries.   Education 32: 474-7.
Henry, W. E.   Academic standing of college library assistants
and their relation to the Carnegie foundation.   A L A Bull
5: 258-63; P L 16: 294-5.
---   W. E.   Certification of librarians.   L J 44: 762-3.
---   W. E.   Comparative cost of library buildings.   P L 8:
64-7.
---   W. E.   Conservation of library materials: a problem in
required reading.   A L A Bull 9: 176; P L 20: 395-9.
---   W. E.   Discipline and furniture.   P L 19: 238-41.
---   W. E.   Librarianship as a profession.   L J 42: 350-5.
---   W. E.   Library as an educational equipment.   P L 13:
291-4.
---   W. E.   Library reading course.   P L 11: 306-7.
---   W. E.   A library school at the University of Washing-
ton.   Pacific Northwest Lib Assn Proceedings, 1916: 36-8.
---   W. E.   Living salaries for good service.   L J 44: 282-4.
---   W. E.   Military training camps and libraries.   L J 42:
533-4.
---   W. E.   Qualifications of the teacher in the library
school.   P L 23: 113-5.
---   W. E.   Re-collecting state documents.   L J 27: 29-30.
---   W. E.   The salary question.   P L 25: 121-3.
---   W. E.   Scholarship for the trained librarian.   P L 11:
103-5.
---   W. E.   Some thoughts on the establishment and control
of a public library.   P L 5: 43-7.
---   W. E.   State library in its mission of collection, dis-
tribution and exchange.   L J 24: Conf No 85-91.
---   W. E.   State's relation to the public library.   Wash L
A Bull 3: 2-4.
Henshall, M. D.   Reading in rural districts.   A L A Bull 9:
190-5.
------   M. D.   Summary of progress in school library service.
Western Journal of Education 24: 1-2.
Henshall, Mrs. M. D.   County free library progress with the
schools.   California Lib Assn Proceedings 1917: 68-73.
------   Mrs. M. D.   The county school and its library ser-
vice.   California Lib Assn Proceedings 1916: 88-92.
------   Mrs. M. D.   An organizing trip through Inyo county,
April 15-25, 1917.   Cal News Notes 12: 445-52.
------   Mrs. M. D.   The Pacific coast conference on rural
education and country life.   Cal News Notes 13: 38-9.

------ Mrs. M. D.  The rural high school and the county free library.  Sierra Educ News 12: 152-4.

------ Mrs. M. D.  The state library exhibit at the California state fair and the Oakland land show.  Cal News Notes 14: 6-13.

Henson, J. C. M.  Preliminary statement on collecting information in regard to early Scandinavian-American imprints.  Bib Soc Amer Proc 3: 43-8.

Henthorne, M. C.  Book service for our sailors and soldiers. L J 43: 324-7.

Henwood, E. D.  Binding.  P L 13: 227-8.

Hepburn, W. M.  Agricultural books of 1919.  Special Libraries 11: 104-5.

----- W. M.  Agricultural periodicals.  A L A Bull 8: 198-9.

----- W. M.  A few words from the president.  Lib Occ 2: 87-8.

----- W. M.  Influence of the agricultural college on the farmer's use of books.  L J 39: 435-8.

----- W. M.  Library extension work of agricultural colleges. A L A Bull 6: 213-6.

----- W. M.  Public and school libraries in Nova Scotia. P L 15: 229-33, 279-83.

----- W. M.  Select list of books on agriculture.  Special Libraries 10: 81-3.

----- W. M.  Selection and preservation of agricultural periodicals.  A L A Bull 4: 794-7; L J 35: 309-11.

----- W. M.  U. S. government documents for the small and medium sized library.  Lib Occ 2: 1-5.

Hepner, A.  Proposition for an American libraries' clearing house.  L J 21: Conf No 67.

Herbert, C. W.  Children's books for Sunday school libraries. L A 10: 39.

----- C. W.  Establishing relations between the children's library and other civic agencies.  L J 34: 195-6.

----- C. W.  An exhibit of library resources helpful to schools and teachers.  P L 18: 150-2.

----- C. W.  A junior training class: the experience of the Washington public library.  L J 43: 489-90.

----- C. W.  Juvenile court library in Washington, D. C. L J 35: 159.

----- C. W.  Recruiting a training class: an experience and some reflections thereon.  L J 44: 108-9.

Herbert, J. A.  A review of Shakespeare's handwriting by Sir Edward Maunde Thompson.  L (3d series) 8: 97-100.

Herschel, C.  Slip catalog.  L J 2: 19-20.

Herdman, D. W.  Place and treatment of fiction in public libraries.  L A.6: 375-80, Discussion 381-2.

Hereford, J. P.  Experiments in rural libraries for school and home.  Nineteenth Century 62: 751-7.

Hering, H. M.  The war and the mission field.  A L A Bull 12: 312.

Hering, H. W.  The missionary research library in New York City.  L J 42: 23-5.

Herman, J.  County libraries and catalog problems.  A L A Bull 14: 151-4, 329.

Herne, F. S.  Libraries of Leicester.  B A R 6: XXV-XXIX.

Herrick, A. R.  Indexing technical information.  Special Libraries 5: 131.

Herrick, C. A.  The early New-Englanders: what did they read? L (3d series) 9: 1-17.

Herring, B. F.  Storytelling in high schools.  Quarterly Journal of Public Speaking 3: 37-47.

Herring, P.  Notes on a collection of Nottinghamshire books. L 2: 338-40.

Herrman, J.  Book distribution: County libraries and their problems.  A L A Bull 14: 153.

----- J.  County librarians and their catalog problems.  A L A Bull 14: 151-5.

Hertzberg, E. C. J.  Specifications for library bookbinding. Lib Occ 2: 135-7.

Hervey, J. L.  Tribulations of an amateur bookbuyer.  Atlantic 112: 319-27.

Herzberg, M. I.  High school reading.  Home Progress 4: 625-6.

------ M. I.  Supplementary reading for high school pupils. English Journal 4: 373-82.

Hessels, J. H.  A bibliographical tour.  L (ns) 9: 282-308.

----- J. H.  The so-called Gutenberg documents.  L (ns) 10: 152-67, 253-87; (3d series) 2: 183-211, 289-313, 396-421; (3d series) 3: 64-88, 195-220.

----- J. H.  Some notes on the invention of printing.  Bib Soc Trans 9: 11-4.

Hetherington, A. L.  The late Dr. Andrew Carnegie.  L A R 21: 284-7.

---------- A. L.  Library statistics.  L A R 19: 3-16; L W 19: 194-5.

---------- A. L.  Rural libraries.  L A R 18: 195-211.

Hewins, C.  Historical novels and stories for a class of high school grade studying general history.  Bull Bib 6: 174-5.

---- C.  On book selection.  P L 20: 422-3.

Hewins, C. M.  Book reviews, book lists, and articles on children's literature: are they of value to the children's librarian?  L J 26: Conf No 57-62.

---- C. M.  Books that children like.  2nd Int Conf 111-7, Discussion, 237-40.

---- C. M.  Boys' and girls' reading.  L J 16: 278.

---- C. M.   Children's books.  P L 1: 190-1.
---- C. M.   Children's books of 1896.  L J 22: 194-6.
---- C. M.   Children's reading.  P L 16: 164.
---- C. M.   Children's room at Hartford public library.
L J 30: 82-3.
---- C. M.   Connecticut Public Library Commission.  L J 21:
267-9.
---- C. M.   Hartford public library holiday exhibit of child-
ren's books.  Bull Bib 8: 214-5.
---- C. M.   History lessons in vacation.  L J 38: 457-8.
---- C. M.   How library work with children has grown in
Hartford and Connecticut.  L J 39: 91-9.
---- C. M.   How to make a library attractive.  L J 24: Conf
No 23-6.
---- C. M.   How to make the most of a small library.  L J
11: 305-8.
---- C. M.   Library work for women: some practical sugges-
tions.  L J 16: 273-4.
---- C. M.   New and old books.  L J 21: Conf No 47-8.
---- C. M.   Our vacation book talks.  P L 5: 231-3.
---- C. M.   Periodical library bulletins.  L J 19: Conf No
52-3.
---- C. M.   Reading clubs for older boys and girls.  Child
Conference for Research and Welfare Proceedings 1909, pt 1:
13-8; Pedagogical Seminary 16: 325-30.
---- C. M.   Reading for the young.  U S Govt Rept 1892:
944-9.
---- C. M.   Relation of the Hartford public library to the
public schools.  L J 19: 292-5.
---- C. M.   Report on children's reading.  L J 23: Conf No
35-9.
---- C. M.   Report on gifts and bequests.  L J 15: Conf No
14-5; 16: Conf No 27-9; 21: Conf No 58-64; 22: 90-3.
---- C. M.   Report on list of children's books with child-
ren's annotations.  L J 27: Conf No 79-82; Discussion 223-5.
---- C. M.   Report on reading of the young.  L J 18: 251-3.
---- C. M.   Some things done in Hartford (Conn) public li-
brary.  P L 12: 86-9.
---- C. M.   What a country library and country school can
do for each other.  Connecticut Public Library, Document 8,
1901: 33-5.
---- C. M.   What you can get out of a Henty book.  Wis Lib
Bull 2: 69-70; 4: 15-6; N Y L 1: 6-8.
---- C. M.   Work of an eastern library commission.  L J 30:
Conf No 51-5.
---- C. M.   Work with children.  P L 10: 475-6.
---- C. M.   Yearly report on boys' and girls' reading.  L
J 7: 182-90.
Hey, S.  The place of the public library in our system of educ-
ation.  L A R 21: 386-7.

Heyliger, W.  The book for boys.  P L 23: 324.
Hickcox, J. H.  Catalogue of government documents.  L J 11:
    99, 12: 161.
----- J. H.  Serials, technical and scientific publications
    of United States government.  L J 22: 16-7.
Hicks, F. C.  Departmental libraries.  Columbia University
    Quarterly 13: 183-95.
--- F. C.  Inter-library loans.  L J 38: 67.
--- F. C.  Library of Congress classification and its print-
    ed catalogue cards.  L J 31: 255-6.
--- F. C.  Library problems in American universities.  Educa-
    tional Review 49: 325-36; L J 40: 307-12; P L 20: 29-30.
--- F. C.  The methods of newspaper libraries.  Educational
    Review 44: 179-87; L J 38: 148-50.
--- F. C.  The modern Medusa: Index to legal periodicals.
    A L A Bull 14: 145-51.
--- F. C.  Newspaper libraries: clippings.  Educational Re-
    view 44: 179-87; L J 38: 148-50.
--- F. C.  The public library as affected by municipal re-
    trenchment.  A L A Bull 10: 169-75, 385, 554; P L 21: 348-9.
--- F. C.  Relation of special libraries to public and univ-
    ersity libraries.  L J 35: 487-93.
--- F. C.  The teaching of legal bibliography.  Educational
    Review Sept 1917: 164-76; L J 42: 998; Am Lib Annual 1917-18:
    16-7.
Higgins, A. G.  Library work with children.  Simmons College
    Quarterly, Jan 1912.
Higginson, T. W.  Access to the shelves.  L J 16: 268-9.
------- T. W.  Address.  L J 4: 357-9.
------- T. W.  Cambridge library and its critic.  L J 15:
    110-1.
------- T. W.  A child's morning lessons.  Outlook 78: 836-7.
------- T. W.  Children's book selection.  L J 3: 357-9.
------- T. W.  Education and the public library.  P L 6: 433-
    4.
------- T. W.  Free public library.  L J 13: 87.
------- T. W.  Sensational fiction in public libraries.  L
    J 4: 357-9.
------- T. W.  Significance of the public library.  L J 13:
    87-8, 340.
Hilchen, G. F.  An east-end library.  L 2: 174-7.
Hill, A.  Public libraries and the National home reading union.
    L A R 5: 615-22.
-- A.  Public library and the people.  L J 27: 15-7.
-- A.  Responsibility for the public taste.  L (ns) 7: 257-62.
Hill, A. C.  Reading in prisons.  N Y L 2: 62.
-- A. C.  Use of books in prisons.  L J 34: 431-3.
Hill, F. P.  Address at dedication of the New Bedford free pub-
    lic library.  L J 36: 62-4.

-- F. P.  Administration of branch libraries.  L J 27: Conf No 49-50.
-- F. P.  Book storage for libraries: reservoir libraries. P L 14: 304-5.
-- F. P.  Books of fiction.  P L 3: 118.
-- F. P.  Branch libraries: administration.  L J 27: Conf No 46-50.
-- F. P.  Brooklyn scheme of library service.  L J 29: 363-7.
-- F. P.  Charging systems: The Newark system.  L J 21: Conf No 51-6.
-- F. P.  Dead stock: storage libraries.  A L A Bull 3: 140-5, Discussion 154-65.
-- F. P.  Decimal classification reminiscences.  L J 45: 157.
-- F. P.  Deterioration of newspaper paper.  A L A Bull 4: 675-8; L J 35: 299-301; P L 15: 323-5.
-- F. P.  Discusses the A. L. A. enlarged program.  A L A Bull 13: 368.
-- F. P.  Library and the community.  L J 36: 82-4.
-- F. P.  Library associations and library meetings.  L J 36: 487-9; P L 16: 369-71.
-- F. P.  Library buildings--some preliminaries.  L J 24: 563-9.
-- F. P.  Library service.  U S Rept: 753, 1892-93, L J 18: 228-9.
-- F. P.  Newark public library and schools.  L J 17: 486-7.
-- F. P.  One phase of library development.  L J 31: Conf No 3-9.
-- F. P.  Organization and management of library staff.  L J 22: 381-3.
-- F. P.  Preparing a book for issue.  L J 21: Conf No 51-6.
-- F. P.  Relations between trustees and librarian.  Mass L C Bull 5: 131-2.
-- F. P.  Relations of members of the staff with each other. Mass Lib Club Bull 5: 131-2.
-- F. P.  Report on library progress.  L J 19: Conf No 56-60.
-- F. P.  Saturday half holiday.  L J 21: 217.
-- F. P.  Staff vacations.  U S Rept: 1892-93, 750.
-- F. P.  Storage libraries.  A L A Bull 3: 142.
-- F. P.  Trustees and librarians.  New Hamp Lib Bull (ns) 12: 173-4; L J 41: 786.
Hill, G. P.  Follow-up system in serial records in the New York public library.  Bull Bib 8: 192-3.
-- G. P.  How periodicals are checked in the New York library.  L J 26: 390-1.
Hill, H. C.  Political parties and the presidential campaign. Historical Outlook 11: 272-6.

Hill, J. C.  Paste for mounting photographs.  L J 6: 52.

Hill, J. F.  School and library.  L J 27: 186-8.

Hill, M.  Aims and methods of instruction in literature.  Academy (Syracuse) 7: 84-9.

Hill, T. P.  Library service: series of questions sent to 210 libraries in U. S.  L J 18: 228-9.

Hill, W. D.  Importance of public school libraries and how obtained.  Michigan Board of Library Commissioners Report 1907: 143-50.

Hillebrand, H. L.  Libraries in Hawaii.  L J 30: Conf No 140-1.

Hillkowitz, A.  Story telling.  P L 18: 28-9.

Himelick, R. W.  Libraries and schools.  Lib Occ 3: 7-8.

------ R. W.  Silent reading in the schools.  Lib Occ 2: 206-8.

Hinchman, W. S.  Reading clubs instead of literature classes.  English Journal 6: 88-95.

Hind, A. M.  Arrangement of print collections.  Burlington Magazine 19: 204-8.

Hinkins, C. E.  Sears, Roebuck & Co's house library.  L J 42: 289.

Hinman, M. W.  Practical use of reference books.  Nat Educ Assn 1880: 194-203.

Hinton, M. H.  The influence of one library: The Olivia Raney library.  N C Lib Bull 3: 36-7.

Hirshberg, H. S.  Camp library work at a Naval training station.  A L A Bull 12: 240-1.

------- H. S.  Directory exchange.  P L 15: 291.

------- H. S.  Library week in Toledo.  P L 21: 220-3; Wis Lib Bull 12: 248-9.

------- H. S.  Main reference department and the branches in the Cleveland public library.  A L A Bull 3: 368-70.

Hirth, E.  Library work: Classified list of vocations for women.  New York Inter-Collegiate Bureau of Occupations March 1917: 22-3.

Hiss, S. K.  Treatment of ephemeral material in the public library.  A L A Bull 3: 404-8.

Hitchcock, G. A.  List of books on fine and decorative arts suggested for small public libraries.  P L 7: 25-7.

Hitchins, A. B.  The yellowing of paper: a study of the causes of principal factors producing the yellowing of paper.  Paper July 24, 1918: 11-5; L J 43: 911-2.

Hitchler, T.  The A. L. A. book service: a question.  P L 24: 310-2.

------ T.  Cataloging for a system of branch libraries.  A L A Bull 3: 397-400.

------ T.  Cataloguing for small libraries.  L J 29: 9-16.

------ T.  Cataloging for small libraries: anent its review in January "Public Libraries."  P L 21: 144.

------ T.  Children's reading.  N Y L 1: 105-7.
------ T.  Discusses the A. L. A. enlarged program.  A L A Bull 13: 362.
------ T.  Efficiency in library work.  L J 38: 558-61.
------ T.  Inspiration: address to an apprentice class. L J 29: 416-8.
------ T.  Krupp circulating library at Essen.  L J 27: 1005-7.
------ T.  Library school training versus practical experience.  L J 42: 931-8.
------ T.  Personal relations between librarian and staff. L J 23: 49-51.
------ T.  Personality.  Lib Miscellany (Baroda) 2: 56-61.
------ T.  Six months at Headquarters and in the field.  A L A Bull 13: 312-5.
------ T.  Successful loan-desk assistants.  L J 32: 554-9.
------ T.  Telling stories to children.  P L 12: 89-91.
Hitt, I. A.  Library aids to study clubs.  Wash L A Bull 2 No 4: 9-10.
Hitt, J. M.  Growth of library sentiment in the state of Washington.  Pacific Northwest Library Assn Proceedings 1910: 37-60.
-- J. M.  How to extend and develop new libraries in this state.  Wash L A Bull 2, No 4: 3-6.
-- J. M.  Indexing state papers.  Wash L A Bull 3: 3-4.
-- J. M.  Magazine clearing house.  Wash L A Bull 1, No 1: 9-10; No 3: 13.
-- J. M.  Progress of libraries in Washington.  Pacific Northwest Library Assn Proceedings 1911: 46-50.
Hjaltalin, J. A.  Remarks on rules for an alphabetical catalogue.  1st Int Conf 93-6, 159, 1877.
Hoag, J. P.  Co-operation of the public library and the public schools.  P L 9: 225-7.
Hoagland, Mercia.  Trained librarians.  P L 7: 375.
Hobert, E.  Special library of the A. W. Shaw company.  Special Libraries 10: 185-8.
Hobart, F.  Attractive books for children.  Vt L Bull 9 No 1: 6-7.
---- F.  The farmer, his book and heart.  A L A Bull 4: 739-42; P L 16: 6-9.
---- F.  Money making for the smallest libraries.  N Y L 1: 199-203.
---- F.  Present state systems of library work for rural communities.  A L A Bull 8: 367-70.
---- F.  Reaching the rural population.  P L 14: 373-6.
Hodge, C. B.  Work done by the Free library commission.  Penn Lib Notes 5, No 4: 27-8.
Hodge, G. B.  Library and the Young men's Christian association. L J 25: 733-6.

Hodges, A. D.  One librarian's joys.  Vt L Bull 4: 1-4.

Hodges, N. D. C.  An Anathema upon finger posts.  A L A Bull 4: 593-7; L J 35: 295-8.

---- N. D. C.  Bibliographies versus catalogs.  P L 7: 299-302.

---- N. D. C.  Bibliographies versus dictionary catalogs. L J 27: Conf No 178-80.

---- N. D. C.  Branch libraries-their development.  A L A Bull 3: 360-2.

---- N. D. C.  County libraries as units in a state library system.  L J 26: 178-81; Cal News Notes 3: 130.

---- N. D. C.  Dead stock: Reservoir libraries.  A L A Bull 3: 145-50, Discussion 154-65.

---- N. D. C.  Exchange of duplicates.  A L A Bull 5: 71-2.

---- N. D. C.  Increase in the use of auditoriums and club rooms.  Am Lib Annual 1916-17: 15-6.

---- N. D. C.  Is the public library a promptuary for the public schools?  Nat Educ Assn 1903: 957-60.

---- N. D. C.  Methods of picture circulation in Cincinnati. L J 42: 15-8.

---- N. D. C.  Notes on English public libraries.  L J 28: 593-6.

---- N. D. C.  Open shelves.  P L 12: 128-9.

---- N. D. C.  Selection of books.  P L 9: 311-5.

---- N. D. C.  Selection of scientific books for a public library.  P L 7: 330-3.

---- N. D. C.  Summary of remarks on extension of the Cincinnati public library privileges to Hamilton County, and the tax levy therefor.  A L A Bull 8: 253.

---- N. D. C. , H. C. Wellman, and W. R. Eastman.  Report of the Committee on library administration.  L J 27: Conf No 86-91; 29: Conf No 163-7.

Hodgkin, T.  Presidential address.  L A R 6: 403-15.

Hodgson, E.  The adolescent's prejudice against the classics. English Journal 4: 427-38.

Hodgson, J.  La Bibliothèque de la Ville de Bordeaux.  L J 44: 35-7.

Hodgson, N. F.  What a library means to a town.  N Y L 5: 60-1; P L 21: 116-7.

Hodnefield, J.  Checking of gift and exchange separates.  L J 37: 382-3.

Hoff, B. M.  Gas City book-wagon experience.  Lib Occ 5: 217-8.

Hoffman, F. L.  Insurance libraries.  Special Libraries 4: 171-4; L J 40: 159-60.

Hoffman, U. J.  What the library means to the school.  Harper's Weekly April 24, 1909, 53: 24-5.

Hogg, J. F.  Central control of libraries and its advantages. L A 9: 131-5, Discussion 136-8.

-- J. F.  Presidential address.  Library assistants' association.  L A 14: 75-82.

Hohoff, W. W. von, Municipal reference library in New York.
Special Libraries 4: 161-2.

Holbrook, D.  Reading for youth.  Connecticut Board of Education Report 1882: 36.

Holbrook, J. F.  Collection of state war service records.  Am
Hist Assn Rev 25: 72-8.

Holbrook, P. K.  Township extension and the Onawa library.  Ia
L C Q 6: 201-2.

Holden, A. H.  System of book-binding records of serial publications used at the American academy of arts and sciences,
Boston.  Bull Bib 8: 92-3.

Holden, Mrs. C.  Love stories for children.  P L 22: 53-5.

Holden, E. S.  Subject index for the publications of observa-
tories.  L J 3: 365-6.

---- E. S.  Treatment of pamphlets in special libraries.
L J 5: 166-7.

Holden, G. P.  Study in typography.  Printing Art 18: 21-30.

Holder, K.  On the history of printing in Friburg.  Switzerland.  L 10: 305-7.

Holding, A. L.  Books about America in foreign languages to
aid in the selection of books for foreigners.  N Y L 2: 92-
100.

----- A. L.  County library at a county fair.  P L 19: 336.

Holgate, C. W.  Account of libraries in Australia and Tasmania.
L A Trans 7: 74-116.

----- C. W.  Auckland free public library.  L C 3: 115-9.

Holgate, J.  Reference list on taxation.  Wash L A Bull 2, No
3: 15-6.

----- J.  Saint Valentine's day.  Wash L A Bull 3, No 1: 9-
10.

----- J.  State administration.  Wash L A Bull 1, No 2: 4-5.

----- J.  Washington state library.  Washington Lib Assn Bull
2 No 2: 8.

Hollabaugh, Mrs. A.  How the Merced county free library system
has been worked out.  L J 36: 347-8; Library Work 1912: 139.

Holland, E. O.  The library as an adjunct to the secondary school.
Nat Educ Assn 1903: 961-6.

Holland, G. E.  Examinations in war-time.  L W 18: 249-50.

Hollands, W. C.  Bookbinding.  P L 9: 260-2.

------ W. C.  Library binding prices.  L J 40: 328-30.

Holmes, D. T.  Another feature of doubtful literature.  L W 13:
236-7.

Holmes, E. A.  Books for children: Science.  L J 26: Conf No
69-70.

Holmes, F. L.. A parcel post library system.  Am Rev of Rev
Dec 1915: 729-30.

Holmes, H. E.  Civic duties of a public librarian.  Maine
State Lib Bull 2, No 2: 7-10.

Holmes, I. H.   American history in elementary schools.   Nat
    Educ Assn 1915: 1078-81.
Holmes, K. T.   History of the traveling library system of Wash-
    ington.   Wash L A Bull 1, No 2: 2-4.
Holt, H.   Commercialism of literature.   Atlantic 96: 577-600;
    Discussion, Bookman (N.Y.) 24: 134-9.
    -- H.   Editor as schoolmaster.   Independent 79: 169-71.
Holt, H. G.   Fire protection in buildings: a review.   Libn 4:
    68-9.
Homer, J.   Union list of current serials.   Special Libraries
    7: 129-30.
Homer, T. J.   Boston Co-operative information bureau.   L J 37:
    503-4.
Homer, H. A.   Deterioration of bindings.   L J 5: 213-5.
    --- H. A.   Historical societies in the United States.   U S
    Govt Rept 1876: 312-25.
    --- H. A.   Legislation for public libraries.   L J 4: 262-7,
    300-2.
    --- H. A.   Lettering of book titles.   L J 5: 315-6.
    --- H. A.   Libraries and museums.   L J 6: 81-6, 128-9.
    --- H. A.   Libraries with museums.   L J 10: 229-31.
    --- H. A.   Selection of books for popular libraries.   L J
    3: 50-1, 53-4.
    --- H. A.   Shelf arrangement of books in New York state li-
    brary.   L J 8: 203-5.
    --- H. A.   State and territorial libraries.   U S Govt Rept:
    292-311, 1876.
    --- H. A.   Subject indexes for popular libraries.   L J 1:
    81-4.
    --- H. A.   Unbound volumes on library shelves.   L J 11: 214-
    5.
Honey, A. G.   Examinations in war-time.   L W 18: 248-9.
    --- A. G.   Problem of the junior assistant: a suggestion.
    L A R 15: 584.
Honeycutt, A. B.   Free libraries for all Texas Libraries 1:
    4-5, July 1914.
Honeyman, J. R. C.   Possibilities of the traveling library in
    Saskatchewan.   A L A Bull 8: 332-5; P L 19: 470.
Hood, W. D.   Relation of the high school library to vocational
    and technical courses.   Nat Educ Assn 1916: 539-41.
Hood, W. R.   Libraries--California.   U S Commissioner of Educ-
    ation Report 1915, 1: 22.
    -- W. R.   Libraries--Texas.   U S Commissioner of Education,
    Report 1915, Vol 1: 22.
Hooker, B.   Narrative and the fairy tales.   Bookman ( N Y) 33:
    389-93, 501-5.
Hooker, D. A.   Some recent scientific and technical books.
    Mich Lib Bull 11: Sept-Oct 13-21; L J 45: 967-73.
    ---- D. A.   A technology department as a business invest-
    ment.   Special Libraries 10: 164-5.

Hooper, L. M.  Disadvantages of re-inforced binding.  L J 34: 437.

---- L. M.  Pictures for library use.  P L 16: 159.

Hooper, W. de M.  Dirt in the city library.  L J 12: 73.

---- W. de M.  Evolution of the hobby.  L J 11: 225-8.

Hoover, A. F.  What the library expects of the teachers.  P L 16: 391-2; 17: 80-3.

Hopkins, A. H.  Building plans are misleading.  P L 9: 15.

----- A. H.  A Handbook of library economy.  L J 20: Conf No 41-2.

----- A. H.  Link between the library and the museum.  P L 8: 12-5.

----- A. H.  Net price question.  P L 8: 274-5.

----- A. H.  Organization and administration of university libraries.  L J 27: Conf No 10-6; P L 7: 297-9.

Hopkins, F. M.  Is there a need for a course in the choice and use of books in our high schools?  Nat Educ Assn 1912: 1258.

----- F. M.  Library work in high schools.  P L 10: 170-1.

----- F. M.  Library work in school courses.  P L 24: 393-4.

----- F. M.  Methods of instruction in the use of high school libraries.  Nat Educ Assn 1905: 858-64; P L 10: 170-1.

----- F. M.  Place of the library in high school education.  L J 35: 55-60.

----- F. M.  A plea for instruction in the choice and use of books.  Michigan State Board of Library Commissioners, Annual Report No 8, 1911: 113-21.

----- F. M.  A plea for the library in public schools.  Education 37: 35-41; L J 41: 943-4.

----- F. M.  The study of reference books in high schools.  P L 25: 94.

----- F. M.  What the library can do for the high school pupil.  Michigan State Board of Library Commissioners Report 1909: 46-52; Michigan State Teachers' Assn Proceedings 1909: 264-6.

Hopkins, J. A.  Lesson on the card catalogue.  P L 8: 156-8.

----- J. A.  Music in libraries.  Wis Lib Bull 3: 89-93.

----- J. A.  A new plan for training library assistants.  A L A Bull 13: 167-71.

----- J. A.  Plans and scope of the new normal course in library training.  Pratt institute.  Nat Educ Assn 1912: 1246-52.

Hopkins, M. L.  Book wagon delivery.  A L A Bull 10: 248-50.

Hopper, F. F.  Basis of support of organizations for public library work.  A L A Bull 5: 148-54; L J 36: 406-10; P L 16: 238-44.

---- F. F.  A $5,000 branch library building at Tacoma.  L
J 36: 457-8.
---- F. F.  The order department of the New York public li-
brary.  Bull Bib 9: 88-90.
---- F. F.  Principles which govern amount of budgets.  Paci-
fic Northwest Lib Assn Proceedings 1913: 38-42.
---- F. F.  Report of committee on libraries in federal pri-
sons.  A L A Bull 6: 324-6.
Hopper, F. T.  Administration of the catalog department from
a librarian's point of view.  A L A Bull 7: 259-68.
Hopwood, H. V.  Best books.  L A R 11: 385-6.
----- H. V.  Best books of 1904--Useful arts.  L A R 8: 89-
97.
----- H. V.  Branches.  L A R 10: 74-5 L. A. branches.  Lit
Yr-Bk: 671.
----- H. V.  Brussels congresses, 1910.  L A R 11: 94-5, 386-
8, 565-6.
----- H. V.  Capitation grant again.  L A R 10: 636.
----- H. V.  The danger of brevity: starved libraries.  L
A R 12: 609-10.
----- H. V.  Dewey expanded.  L A R 9: 307-22, Discussion
340-5; L J 32: 362-7.
----- H. V.  Educational standard of librarianship in rela-
tion to technology.  L A R 19: 323-7.
----- H. V.  Institut de bibliographie.  L A R 11: 94-5,
386-8.
----- H. V.  Is librarianship a profession?  L A R 9: 358-
9.
----- H. V.  List of books in useful arts.  L A R 6: 603-11.
----- H. V.  Proposed institut of librarians.  L A R 9: 535-
6.
----- H. V.  Reference shelf placing: ideal and practical.
L A R 6: 241-60, Discussion 309-12.
----- H. V.  Registration for librarians.  L A R 9: 359-60.
----- H. V.  Report on the Library conference in Brussels,
August, 1910.  L A 8: 6-10.
----- H. V.  Some results of the Brussels congress.  L A R
13: 1-16.
----- H. V.  Technical libraries.  L A 5: 270-4.
Horace, L. N.  The operation of a model suburban library, Sum-
mit, N. J.  Suburban Life, Apr 1912: 239-41, 266-7.
Horne, L.  Nebraska publications.  Neb Lib Bull No 4: 9-12.
Horton, H. E.  Agricultural research.  A L A Bull 11: 338-9.
Horton, M.  Here in the land of promise.  L J 44: 139-42.
Horton, M. L.  How to raise the standard of literary apprecia-
tion in high schools.  A L A Bull 11: 175.
---- M. L.  Instruction for pages at Los Angeles public li-
brary.  L J 43: 402-3.
---- M. L.  Joy reading: how to increase literary apprecia-
tion in the high school.  L J 42: 688-91.

---- M. L.  The library, the school and patriotism.  New
Hamp Bull (ns) 14: 124-6.
---- M. L.  Periodicals in the high school library.  L J
41: 522-4.
---- M. L.  Relations of public and school libraries.  A L
A Bull 14: 179-80.
Hosie, J. F.  Conduct of a course in children's reading.  P L
18: 383-4.
--- J. F.  The conduct of a course of reading for children.
Nat Educ Assn 1913: 730-6; American Schoolmaster 6: 351-8.
--- J. F.  The importance of the library in the school.  L
J 43: 888; P L 23: 297-8.
--- J. F.  Place of the school library in modern education.
A L A Bull 10: 210-3, 432.
--- J. F.  Reorganization of English in secondary schools.
U S Bureau of Education Bulletin No 2, 1917.
--- J. F.  What teachers expect from the library.  P L 16:
391; 17: 79-80.
Hosmer, H. R.  Library of the research laboratory of the Gener-
al electric company at Schenectady, New York.  Special Li-
braries 4: 169-71.
Hosmer, J. K.  In praise of the novel.  L (ns) 1: 132-8.
---- J. K.  Libraries from reader's point of view.  L J 18:
216-7.
---- J. K.  Library assistant: his title, duties and rela-
tion to his chief.  L J 24: 54-7.
---- J. K.  On browsing.  L J 15: Conf No 33-7.
---- J. K.  Presidential address.  L J 28: Conf No 1-8.
---- J. K.  Some things that are uppermost.  L J 28: Conf
No 1-8.
Hotchkiss, C. W.  Literature, Grade VII.  Teachers' College
Record 8: 249-56.
Houchens, J. B.  High school library exhibit.  Illinois Univ-
ersity. High School Conference Proceedings, 1920: 36-8.
Houghton, C. C.  Federal trade commission library.  Special
Libraries 7: 41-3.
------ C. C.  Trade catalogs in public libraries.  P L 15:
275-8.
Houlbert, C.  Insect enemies of books.  L J 28: 637-8.
House, R. D.  Finding mis-filed index cards.  L J 38: 519-22.
Houssayes, J. B. C. des.  The qualifications and duties of a
Librarian, 1870.  P L 9: 129.
Hovey, E. C.  Headquarters opened.  L J 31: 665-6.
--- E. C.  Report of the Executive officer.  A L A Bull 1:
Conf No 116-9.
How, W. W.  Library exhibitions.  L A 7: 77-8.
Howard, C. E.  Branch library and its relation to the district.
A L A Bull 5: 109-12.
---- C. E.  The Carnegie library of Pittsburgh and the for-
eigner.  Penn Lib Notes 3, No 4: 12-6.

---- C. E.  The modern high school library.  Penn Lib Notes
9: 2-4.
---- C. E.  Organizing a new high school library.  A L A
Bull 11: 176-9, 348.
---- C. E.  Schenley high school library, Pittsburgh, Pa.
P L 23: 67-9.
Howard, F. T.  Regional survey work in schools and how the pub-
lic library can assist in the work.  L A R 22: 338-41.
Howarth, E. and Platnauer, H. M.  Directory of museums in Great
Britain and Ireland: review.  Libn 2: 350.
Howarth, F.  Social aspect of the public library movement.  L
W 7: 169-74.
Howarth, F. W. B.  Educational basis of the free library move-
ment.  L A 3: 242-6.
Howe, E. F.  County library situation in Washington.  Pacific
Northwest Lib Assn Proceedings 1920: 62-5.
Howe, H. E.  What of the summer library school as a factor in
professional education?  A L A Bull 14: 141, 334-5; L J 45:
583-7.
Howe, H. J.  Monograph on the Iowa library association.  Ia.L
C Q 4: 56.
Howe, P. P.  Circulating libraries: their complaint and cure.
Nineteenth Century 74: 612-20.
Howe, W. D.  The part of the state supported library activities
in the educational program of the state.  A L A Bull 11: 360.
Howe, W. W.  History of Library association.  L A R 12: 57-64.
Howell, G. A.  Library as an aid to technical education.  Onta-
rio Lib Assn Proceedings 1911: 92-5; L J 36: 451-4; P L 16:
303-4.
Howells, W. D.  Examination of library gift horses.  L J 26:
741-3.
----- W. D.  On the public library.  L W 4: 113-5.
Howland, F. A.  What the public library means to men.  Vt L
Bull 7, No 2: 3-4.
Howlett, M. H.  Traveling library and the country reader.  Wis
Lib Bull 1: 69-70.
Hoyle, W. E. and C. Nordlinger.  The "Concilium bibliographicum"
at Zurich and its work.  L A R 1: 709-18.
Hoyt, F. S.  Problems in the production of books for children.
A L A Bull 13: 282-5.
Hrbek, S.  The Library and the foreign-born citizen.  P L 15:
98-104.
Hubbard, A. G.  Catalogue cards for maps.  P L 9: 13.
----- A. G.  Cataloguing and preservation of maps in the
Indiana state library.  L J 28: 610-1; P L 8: 375.
Hubbard, J. M.  Are public libraries public blessings?  L J 14:
407-9.
----- J. M.  How to use a library.  L J 9: 25-9.
----- J. M.  Public library--how the interests of its pa-
trons may be best served.  L J 6: 11-3.

Hubbard, T.  O'B. and Phillips, W. J.  Books and periodicals on aeronautics: a buying list.  L W 12: 293-8.

Hubble, J. P.  Commission government as affecting libraries in cities outside of Illinois.  P L 19: 65-8.

Hubert, P. G.  World's greatest library: Bibliotheque Nationale.  Bookman (N Y) 38: 31-41.

Huck, T. W.  An account of the Foulis press.  Glasgow, with a short account of Glasgow's earliest printers.  L W 12: 333-9.

-- T. W.  The bibliography of London.  L (3d series) 3: 38-54.

-- T. W.  The birth of the various book trade catalogues.  Libn 1: 98-102, 130-5, 168-72, 199-202.

-- T. W.  Book pests and book and print restoration.  L A R 15: 165-77.

-- T. W.  Borrowing of new books from subscription libraries.  L A R 10: 475-6.

-- T. W.  Catalogues of the Bodleian library, Oxford.  (Bodleian catalogue rules).  L W 12: 413-8, 447-52.

-- T. W.  Check on the book fund.  L W 11: 116-8.

-- T. W.  Johann Gottlob Immanuel Breitkopf, the printer, 1719-1794.  L A R 14: 14-8.

-- T. W.  University library, Cambridge.  L W 13: 257-66.

Hudson, J. W.  The library and the modern university.  Univ of Missouri Bull 17, No 12: 4-17; P L 22: 295-7.

Hudson, O. C.  Estimate of annual expenditure for an established Carnegie library with an income of £ 220 from penny rate.  L W 10: 134-6.

Hudson, W.  Useless records.  L W 14: 179-80.

Hughes, H. S.  English literature and the college freshman.  School Review 20: 583-92.

Hughes, S. C.  Feature work in Terre Haute (Ind) library.  Lib Occ No 8: 3.

Huling, J. B.  Sizes of printed books.  L J 1: 168-9, 221-2.

Huling, R. G.  How English is taught in one high school.  Nat Educ Assn 1891: 632-40.

Hull, C. H.  Helps for cataloguers in finding full names.  L J 14: 7-20.

-- C. H.  Subject catalogues in college libraries.  L J 15: 167-71.

-- W. I.  Lessons of the Dutch archives.  Am Hist Assn Rept 1909: 357-60.

Hulme, E. W.  Best books of 1903--Useful arts.  L A R 6: 94-7.

--- E. W.  Church house, Westminster, library.  L A R 12: 431-2.

--- E. W.  Construction of subject catalogues.  L A R 3: 507-13, Precis 486.

--- E. W.  Co-operative index of technical literature.  L A R 12: 389-90.

--- E. W.  Decay in binding leathers (letter).  L A R 3: 231-2.

--- E. W.  English patent law, its history, literature and library.  L 10: 42-55.

--- E. W.  How to transfer a library without "shutting down." L A R 1: 175-6.

--- E. W.  Ideals: old and new.  L A 10: 209-18; L A R 15: 580-2.

--- E. W.  Insect book pests: a review of recent literature. L A R 1: 369-72.

--- E. W.  Librarians' aids.  L A R 3: 49; 5: 119-32.

--- E. W.  Library of the Library association.  L A R 9: 296-301.

--- E. W.  Machine book sewing.  L A R 10: 8-9.

--- E. W.  A new index to periodicals.  L W 17: 291-2.

--- E. W.  On a co-operative basis for the classification of literature in the subject catalogue.  L A R 4: 317-26.

--- E. W.  On the construction of the subject catalogue in scientific and technical libraries.  Precis and discussion. L A R 3: 507-13.

--- E. W.  On the Subject index to periodicals.  L A R 22: 372-7.

--- E. W.  Principles of book classification.  L A R 13: 354-8, 389-94, 444-9; 14: 39-46, 174-81, 216-21.

--- E. W.  Principles of cataloguing.  L A R 8: 31-45, Discussion 66-8.

--- E. W.  Principles of dictionary subject-cataloguing in scientific and technical libraries.  L A R 2: 571-6.

--- E. W.  Technical libraries.  L A R 19: 485-9.

--- E. W. and Kinzbrunner, C.  On current serial digests and indexes of the literature of science and some problems connected therewith.  L A R 15: 22-8.

Hulshof, Dr. A.  Study of palaeography in England since 1873. L A R 19: 43-68.

Hulsizer, S. H.  How to make a library useful to a small town. L J 34: 257-60; N Y L 1: 232-5.

Hulst, C. S.  Organization of the course in literature in secondary schools.  English Journal 1: 72-83.

Hulton, C. E.  What our country neighbors read.  Wis Lib Bull 9: 45-6.

Humble, M.  Advertising the library.  Wis Lib Bull 10: 185.

---- M.  Children's book week.  N C Bull 4: 101.

---- M.  Children's books for Christmas purchase.  Wis Lib Bull 9: 165-71; 10: 253-6.

---- M.  Children's books: the exercise of choice.  Ia L C Bull 7: 209-14.

---- M.  Picture bulletins at the May day fete, library schoo Wis Lib Bull 10: 142-3.

---- M.  The Prairie du Chien idea.  Wis Lib Bull 10: 68-70; L J 39: 893-4.

---- M.  Reading list for high school seniors.  Wis Lib Bull
11: 362-4.

Hume, J. F.  The dream of an organizer: a library phantasy.  L
J 38: 513-8.

-- J. F.  Humors and horrors of municipal civil service.
A L A Bull 5: 127-9.

-- J. F.  Queens Borough public library: a sketch of its
development.  L J 34: 209-14.

-- J. F.  Why not? Questions in cataloging.  L J 40: 180-1.

-- J. F.  Work with clubs at the Queens Borough public library.  Child Conference for Research and Welfare Proceedings 1909, pt 1: 228-9; Pedagogical Seminary 16: 548-9.

Hummerston, M. M.  The art and practice of story telling to
children, and its possible application in juvenile reading
rooms.  L A 9: 194-6.

Humphrey, A. M.  Some statistics on children's reading.  P L·
4: 320-1.

Humphrey, G. P.  Selection of books for a small library.  P L
8: 144-5.

Humphrey, G. R.  Librarians and the working classes.  L A M N
4: 58-61.

------ G. R.  Workmen's or factory libraries.  L A M N 2:
53-8.

Humphreys, A. M.  How the Merced County free library system
has been worked out.  L J 36: 347-8.

------- A. M.  The other side.  P L 14: 300.

Hunger, E. A.  A numerical classification of periodical literature.  L J 42: 366-8.

---- E. A.  A practical library for an industrial research
laboratory: Eastman Kodak Co. research library.  L J 42:
975-6.

Hungerford, E.  Are you too busy to read?  System 37: 486-7.

Hunt, C.  Making the library better known.  P L 23: 263-4.

-- C.  A program for library advertising.  A L A Bull 11:
127-30, 331; N Y L 5: 267-9.

Hunt, C. W.  Arousing an interest in the great classics for
children.  New York State Teacher's Assn Proceedings 1911:
81-861; N Y L 3: 47-51; New Hamp Bull (ns) 8: 101-7; P L
17: 16.

-- C. W.  Brooklyn opens the first children's branch.  L J
39: 761-2.

-- C. W.  The child and the book in wartime.  Nat Educ Assn
1918: 448-9.

-- C. W.  Children's books.  Wis Lib Bull 10: 179-81.

-- C. W.  Children's library: a moral force.  L J 31: Conf
No 97-103.

-- C. W.  Children's room: evening hours.  N Y L 1: 186.

-- C. W.  Classification of children's story books.  L J
27: 65-8.

-- C. W.  Easy books and picture books.  N Y L 1: 209.
-- C. W.  Fairy tales to read to children.  Home Progress
4: 854-7.
-- C. W.  First 100 books for a children's library.  N Y L
1: 9-10.
-- C. W.  Illustrative material for nature study in primary
schools.  N Y S L Rept 81, Bibliography No 16.
-- C. W.  "It did me no harm."  N Y L 4: 45.
-- C. W.  Library work with children.  Mass Lib Club Bull
6: 56-7; P L 21: 20-1.
-- C. W.  Maintaining order in the children's room.  L J 28:
164-7.
-- C. W.  Opening a children's room.  L J 26: Conf No 83-6.
-- C. W.  Picture work in children's libraries.  L J 25:
Conf No 66-7.
-- C. W.  Proposed classification for an engineering libra-
ry.  Proc Amer Soc of Civil Engineers 42: 2292-322; L J 43:
290-1.
-- C. W.  Reading habit of girls.  P L 14: 31-2.
-- C. W.  Relation between the public school and the library.
School Work 7: 52-60.
-- C. W.  Some means by which children may be led to read
better books.  L J 24: 147-9.
-- C. W.  Values in library work with children.  A L A Bull
7: 275-82.
-- C. W.  Work with children in the small library.  L J 28:
Conf No 53-6.
-- C. W.  What is to be done?  P L 24: 369-71.
Hunt, E. B.  Catalog of the public library of Boston.  L J 27:
Conf No 25-8, Discussion 190-2.
Hunt, F. R.  A classification and catalogue system for an engi-
neering library.  Amer Soc of Mechanical Engineers Trans
1895-96, 7: 422-38, Discussion 439-49; Engineering News 35:
348.
Hunt, L. P.  Library work with the blind.  Simmons College
Journal Jan 1912.
Hunter, E.  Technical training:  English and American methods.
L A 7: 19.
Hunter, G. L.  Collection of the Avery architectural library.
Architectural Record 33: 550-60.
Huntington, A. T.  Association of medical librarians: past,
present and future.  Med Lib and Hist Journal 5: 111-23.
-------- A. T.  Completing periodical files and the use of
card check lists.  Med Lib and Hist Journal 1: 281-4.
-------- A. T.  The medical library in the United States.
Med Lib and Hist Journal 2: 119-28.
-------- A. T.  Medical library movement in the United States.
Med Lib and Hist Journal 2: 43-6.
-------- A. T.  Practical system of classification for medi-
cal libraries, large or small.  Med Lib and Hist Journal 1:
27-32.

Huntington, S.  Library and the county schools.  Cal News Notes
2: 92-3.
Huntington, T. F.  English in the high school.  School Review
7: 92-6.
Huntley, L.  Burden of newsrooms.  L W 7: 121-3.
----- L.  Pressure of the out-of-date book.  L A R 15: 478-
82.
----- L.  Small town libraries (duties of librarian).  L W
11: 205-8.
Huntting, H. R.  Public library from the business man's stand-
point.  P L 13: 335-9.
------ H. R.  Some notes on bookbinding.  Mass L C Bull 6:
53-4.
------ H. R.  Use of shellac for preserving the covers of
books.  P L 21: 319-20.
Hurd, C. W.  The up-to-date office library.  Printers' Ink
May 1912: 32-6.
Hurlbert, D.  Libraries in rural communities.  Minn P L C N 6:
102-4.
------ D.  Moving pictures.  Minn P L C N Dec 1914: 139-42.
Hurlbut, J. L.  Sunday school libraries, past, present and fu-
ture.  P L 5: 398.
Hurley, L.  Criticism of Mr. Sayers' article.  L W 12: 120.
Hurst, F. L.  McKinley avenue intermediate school library.
Wilson Bulletin 1: 454-5.
Husted, H. F.  Open shelves in Y. W. C. A. library, New York.
L J 25: 115.
Hutchenrider, R.  Meeting the public at the loan desk.  Texas
Libraries, 1, No 10-1: 100-3.
Hutchins, F. A.  Educational needs of hamlets.  N Y L 1: 73-6.
------ F. A.  Enlarging field of the small library.  Minn
P L C N 2: 39-43.
------ F. A.  Establishing libraries in villages.  U S Bureau
of Education Report 1899: 696-700.
------ F. A.  Evolution of library buildings.  Wis Lib Bull
2: 57-8.
------ F. A.  Local supervision of traveling libraries.  L
J 22: Conf No 17-8.
------ F. A.  Present conditions of school libraries in ru-
ral schools and villages of less than 2,500.  Nat Educ Assn
1899: 501; U S Bureau of Education Report 1899: 703-4.
------ F. A.  Report on traveling libraries.  L J 23: Conf
No 56-8, 148.
------ F. A.  Rural extension.  Wis Lib Bull 8: 77-8.
------ F. A.  School work of a librarian.  P L 10: 167-8.
------ F. A.  Securing libraries for rural schools.  Nat
Educ Assn 1899: 503-10; U S Bureau of Education Report 1899:
700-3.
------ F. A.  Sunday afternoon lectures in libraries.  Wis
Lib Bull 3: 8.

------ F. A.  Township school libraries in Wisconsin.  L
J 21: 185-6.

------ F. A.  Traveling libraries in farming districts.  L
J 21: 171-3.

Hutchinson, A. A.  Library training and the librarian of a
small library.  New Hamp Bull (ns) 14: 76-7.

Hutchinson, L.  School library as a public library branch.
Minn P L C N 3: 203-5.

Huth, A. H.  On the supposed false dates in certain Shakespeare quartos.  L (3d series) 1: 36-45.

-- A. H.  Some supplementary suggestions to Mr. Wheatley's
paper on "An English bibliography."  Bib Soc Trans 2: 17-
24.

Hutt, J.  A continental monastic library:  Monastic library
at Quarr, near Ryde, Isle of Wight.  L A R 21: 176-8.

-- J.  Essentials of good book production.  L A 11: 219-24.

-- J.  Libraries and public opinion.  L A R 8: 231-43; Discussion 277-84.

-- J. and E. A. Savage.  Education of provincial assistants.
L A R 9: 491-2.

Hutton, A. W.  New size notation.  L 2: 182-7.

---- A. W.  A political club library: Gladstone library at
the National liberal club.  L 2: 77-86.

Hutton, F. R.  A classification and catalogue system for an
engineering library.  American Society of Mechanical Engineers Transactions, 1895-96, 17: 422-38; Discussion 439-49;
Engineering News 35: 348.

Hutton, G.  Bristol: its libraries and its booksellers.  B A
R 4: XV-XIX.

Hutton, H. D.  Impression of twelve years' cataloguing in a
great library.  L A Trans 7: 45-50.

Hutton, S.  Bristol and its booksellers.  B A R 4: XV-XIX.

Huxley, F. A.  A. L. A. work on Ellis Island.  L J 45: 350-2.

---- F. A.  Library facilities for our soldiers.  Current
History Magazine of New York Times 9 Pt 1: 261-5.

Hyamson, M.  Biblio-kleptomania and how to check it.  L W 8:
207-8.

Hyatt, B. E.  Biography for young people.  Bulletin No 67,
Bibliography No 32, N Y S L Rept 85.  1902.

Hyde, D. W., Jr.  Better citizenship via the civic library.
P L 24: 379.

-- D. W., Jr.  Business libraries and basic service.  L J
45: 550-1.

-- D. W., Jr.  A chamber of commerce filing system.  Filing
Sept 1918: 85-7.

-- D. W., Jr.  The house organ as a factor in library service.  L J 45: 199-203.

-- D. W., Jr.  A library of civic art for New York City.
L J 45: 29.

-- D. W., Jr.  Reconstruction facts for city officials.
Special Libraries 10: 7-8.

-- D. W., Jr.  Special libraries in street railway service.
Special Libraries 11: 165-6.

Hyde, M. E.  Comparison of charging systems.  P L 13: 342-4.

Hyett, F. A.  County bibliographies.  L 8: 394-400.

--- F. A.  County bibliographies: suggestions for increasing their utility.  Bib Soc Trans 3: 27-40.

Hynes, W.  Book collecting in Italy at the renaissance.  L A
R 16: 526-36.

--- W.  Ideal public library from the ratepayers' point of
view.  L W 19: 64-9.

--- W.  Reference libraries for business men.  L W 16: 289-
97.

Ibbotson, J. D.  War pamphlets in the small library.  N Y L 6:
73-4.

Ide, M. S.  Librarianship, its own reward.  New Hamp Bull (ns)
14: 113-4.

- M. S.  Work for children in a New Hampshire library.  New
Hamp Bull (ns) 13: 59-62.

Ifould, W. H.  The country reference section of the Public library of New South Wales.  L J 43: 476-80.

Iles, G.  Appraisal of literature.  L J 21: Conf No 26-8; P L
1: 225-6; 2nd Int Conf 166-72.

-- G.  Bibliography of fine art.  P L 2: 51-3.

-- G.  Book reviewing systematized.  L J 16: 208.

-- G.  A bureau of review.  L J 38: 319-24.

-- G.  Critical annotation of books.  L J 19: 43.

-- G.  Evaluation of literature.  L J 17: Conf No 18-22,
Discussion 63-5, 80-1.

-- G.  Expert annotations of book titles.  U S Rept 994-9.
1892-92.

-- G.  Good books cheaper than ever.  L J 37: 435-6.

-- G.  Headquarters for our association.  L J 28: Conf No
24-8.

-- G.  Indexing literature other than books.  U S Rept 994-9.
1892-93.

-- G.  James Hulme Canfield, 1847-1909.  P L 14: 176-7, 179,
266.

-- G.  Librarians as local biographers.  N Y L 3: 61-3.

-- G.  Libraries from reader's point of view.  L J 18: 217-8.

-- G.  Public libraries and the public schools.  World's
Work ( N Y) 2: 775-6.

-- G.  Trusteeship of literature.  P L 6: 484-8.

Imboden, S. M.  Practical teaching of children to study.  School
and Home Education 31: 26-32.

Imhoff, O. M.  Cataloging in legislative reference work.  A L
A Bull 6: 238-45; Special Libraries 3: 149-54.

---- O. M.  List of sociological material.  Wis Lib Bull 7:
7-16.

---- O. M.  Overlooked material in public documents.  Wis
   Lib Bull 7: 142.
Ingalls, E. L.  Public library and boys' and girls' club work
   in co-operation.  Vt L Bull 16: 2-3.
Inge, W. R., Dean.  Books: their use and abuse.  L A 9: 202-
   10; L W 15: 157.
Ingersoll, H. F.  Free reference material for the small library.
   P L 18: 25-6.
Ingersoll, T. G.  Professional man's use of the public library.
   Minn P L C N 2, No 4: 50-2.
Ingerson, M.  The library as a summer school.  P L 25: 322-3.
Ingram, J. K.  Presidential address.  L A Trans 7: 13-24.
Ingram, L. M.  Amateur photography exhibit.  Wis Lib Bull 11:
   320-1.
Inkster, L.  Co-operative schemes for libraries in London area.
   L A R 11: 9-12, Discussion 31-6.
----- L.  How libraries were described a hundred and fifty
   years ago.  L 3: 228-31.
----- L.  Library grouping.  L A R 7: 562-64; L A R 8: 46-52.
----- L.  "Poisonous books."  L A R 12: 3-4.
----- L.  Relative functions of the lending and reference
   departments of a public library.  L A R 3: 273-81.
----- L. and others.  Interchangeable tickets.  L W 4: 3-5,
   33-7, 63-5.
Iredell, H.  Eleanor learns to read.  Education 18: 233-8.
Irving, Sir Henry.  On public libraries.  L 8: 549-53.
Irwin, R.  Books read by English boys.  A L A Bull 3: 274-6.
Irwin, T. J.  Music in libraries.  Cal News Notes 5: 378-9.
Irwin, W.  Library trustees: their responsibility for the suc-
   cess of the library.  Ia L C Q 7: 89-91.
Isaacs, J. H.  On a new edition of Lowndes' "Bibliographical
   manual."  Bib Soc Trans 2: 1-4.
Isom, M. F.  County libraries in Oregon.  A L A Bull 5: 144-6;
   Library Work 1912: 137.
-- M. F.  County library system in Multnomah County, Oregon.
   Cal News Notes 4: 259-62; California Lib Assn Proceedings
   1909: 41-4; Library Work 1912: 137-8.
-- M. F.  Hospital libraries in France.  Pacific Northwest
   Lib Assn Proceedings, 1919: 11-9.
-- M. F.  The library and modern life.  California Library
   Assn Proceedings 1917: 40-4; L J 43: 695.
-- M. F.  The library as a civic center.  P L 19: 93-6.
-- M. F.  Library conditions in Oregon.  L J 32: 70-1.
-- M. F.  Multnomah county public library, Portland, Oregon.
   L J 39: 41-3.
-- M. F.  Staff meetings: their organization, methods and
   results.  L J 32: 552-3.
-- M. F.  To what extent should the library become a social
   center?  Pacific Northwest Library Assn Proceedings, 1913:
   54-7.

-- M. F.  Work of a county library.  Pacific Northwest Library Assn Proceedings 1909: 15; Cal News Notes 4, No 2.

Ittner, W. B.  Sketch plan for a university library.  L J 13: 10-1.

J. D.  Dream of a people's library.  L J 12: 260.

J. M. Y.  The cost of periodicals.  L W 20: 15.

Jack, E.  Children's literature.  Parents' Review 18: 180.

Jackson, A.  Periodicals useful in the children's room.  P L 24: 352-5.

Jackson, A. B.  Music and collections of art photographs in public libraries.  L N (U S) 3: 463-9.

----- A. B.  Transforming a dwelling-house into a library building.  L J 25: 105-9.

Jackson, A. H.  Report on library work with children.  L J 31: Conf No 89-97, Discussion 244-7.

Jackson, C. P.  Maps: their value, provision and storage.  L A 8: 184-91.

Jackson, F.  Systems of charging loans, and an improved slip case.  L J 3: 230-1.

Jackson, F. R.  Care of periodicals.  P L 11: 493-4

Jackson, G. A.  New England's present library problem.  L J 25: 574-6.

Jackson, H.  The Caradoc press.  Booklover's Magazine 8: 251-6.

----- H.  Children in the public library.  P L 9: 228-9.

----- H.  Stories for children of 6th and 7th grades.  Ia L C Q 7: 31-2.

Jackson, J.  Sport of money kings.  World's Work (N Y) 25: 80-4.

Jackson, K. M.  Book selection and buying.  L N (U S) 2: 5.

Jackson, M.  The library and the community.  Mass L C Bull 9 No 4: 13-9.

----- M.  "Many men, many minds."  N Y L 5: 156-9.

Jackson, Mrs. M. C.  Books for the blind.  Colorado Lib Assn Occasional Leaflet 1: 165-9.

Jackson, W. C.  Marvelous growth in library extension.  P L 15: 39-40.

----- W. C.  The modern library.  N C Bull 1, No 2: 3-6.

Jackson, W. J.  On the signs and symbols in cataloguing.  L W 13: 161-5.

Jacobi, C. T.  Ink used in ancient Irish manuscripts.  P L 11: 37.

---- C. T.  Modern book printing.  Journal of Society of Arts 52: 1904.

---- C. T.  Printing inks.  L (ns) 7: 70-7.

---- C. T.  Printing of modern books.  Bib Soc Trans 1: 187-204.

---- C. T.  Printing of modern illustrated or decorated books.  Journal of Society of Arts 50: 1901-02.

Jacobs, H.  More guides to reference books.  P L 14: 297-8.

Jacobs, S. M.  How to give yourself a graduate course.  L J 45: 499-500.

Jacobsen, S.  Book selection for branch libraries.  P L 10: 515-6.

Jacobson, K. M.  Book selection and buying.  Minn P L C N 5: 5-7.

------ K. M.  Utah's library development.  Utah Educ R May 1912: 14-6.

------ K. M.  What Minnesota does for its foreign citizens.  Minn P L C N 9: 31-2.

Jacobson, P.  Bringing light to the blind.  Cal News Notes 13: 155-61.

Jacobus, M.  How the teacher can help the librarian.  Nat Educ Assn 1907: 974-8.

Jacobus, S. M.  The California county library law.  P L 15: 15; Library Work 1912: 136.

----- S. M.  The nuisance of unsolicited books on approval.  L J 43: 784.

Jaggard, W.  False dates in Shakespearian quartos.  L (ns) 10: 208-11.

----- W.  Shakespeare bibliography: a review by A. W. Pollard.  L (3d series) 2: 331-5.

----- W.  Stratford-upon-Avon from the student's standpoint.  B A R 11: I-VII.

Jahr, J. and A. J. Strohm.  Bibliography of co-operative cataloguing, and the printing of catalogue cards (1850-1902).  Re-printed from the report of the Librarian of Congress, 1902.

James, A.  A plea for imperial copyright.  World's Work (London) 18: 43-7.

James, E.  Presidential address.  L A Trans 8: 12-3.

James, E. J.  Economic significance of a comprehensive system of national education.  American Economic Assn Proceedings 1910: 1-25.

James, F. S. C.  The Mayo clinic library.  L J 42: 43-4.

--- F. S. C.  The medical library.  L J 41: 882-4.

James, H.  Public libraries in the United States.  L J 32: 313.

--- H.  Remodeling old buildings.  Am Lib Annual 1916-17: 26-7.

James, H. P.  Co-operation of Newton library with the public school.  L J 11: 224-5.

--- H. P.  Current magazine check lists.  L J 14: 377-8.

--- H. P.  Libraries in relation to schools.  U S Govt Rept 1892-93: 697, L J 18: 213-4.

--- H. P.  Need of apprenticeship for students.  L J 23: Conf No 134-5.

--- H. P.  Public school use of public libraries.  L J 11: 418.

--- H. P.  Reading room and periodicals.  L J 21: Conf No 49-51.

--- H. P.   Report on reading of the young.  L J 10: 278-91.

--- H. P.   Selection of books for Newton library.  L J 9: 207-10.

--- H. P.   Simplicity in call numbers.  P L 1: 189.

--- H. P.   Special training for library work.  2nd Int Conf 34-9.

--- H. P.   Women in American and British libraries.  L W 1: 89-90.

James, L. A.   A children's handicraft exhibit in a public library.  Lib Occ 3: 175.

James, M. S. R.   American women as librarians.  L 5: 270-4.

--- M. S. R.   Assistants' associations and clubs for self improvement.  L J 23: Conf No 136.

--- M. S. R.   Assistants' associations and training classes in England.  P L 4: 107-9.

--- M. S. R.   Card catalogue guides.  P L 7: 229-30.

--- M. S. R.   Modern British libraries.  P L 9: 371-7.

--- M. S. R.   People's palace and its library.  L J 18: 427-30.

--- M. S. R.   People's palace library.  L 2: 341-51.

--- M. S. R.   Plan for providing technical training for library students and assistants.  L 4: 313-9.

--- M. S. R.   Printed catalogue slips and cards.  L A R 2: 70-1.

--- M. S. R.   Progress of the modern card catalogue principle.  P L 7: 185-9.

--- M. S. R.   Public libraries of Nassau, N. P., and the Bahama Islands.  L A R 3: 368-70.

--- M. S. R.   Special training for library work.  2nd Int Conf: 34-9.

--- M. S. R.   Women in librarianship at the late conference.  L A 2: 14-5.

--- M. S. R.   Women librarians.  L 4: 217-24; L J 18: 146-8.

--- M. S. R.   Women librarians and their future prospects.  L A R 2: 291-304; P L 7: 1-8.

--- M. S. R.   Women librarians at the People's palace library.  L 2: 342.

James, W. J.   What proportion of its funds is a college library justified in devoting to current periodicals?  L J 23: Conf No 107-8.

Jameson, J. F.   The need of national archive building.  A L A Bull 8: 130-6, Discussion 136-40.

Jameson, M. E.   Colonel X-requests: Work of the Medical intelligence bureau of the American red cross.  L J 45: 117-8.

Jasspon, Mrs. W. H.   Charlotte's public library.  N C Lib Bull 3: 20-1.

Jast, L. S.   Accessions: the checking of the processes.  L (ns) 1: 152-62.

-- L. S.   Address to the Northern Counties.  Library association on branch work.  L A R 14: 19-27.

-- L. S.  Area of the N. C. L. A.  L A R 14: 436.
-- L. S.  Binders' lettering.  L W 3: 232-5.
-- L. S.  Book production and the loose leaf principle.  L
A R 12: 500-5, 537-8.
-- L. S.  Book selection by central cataloguing bureau.  L
A 9: 149.
-- L. S.  Books and reading.  L A R 13: 257-67.
-- L. S.  Borrower's view of fiction reading.  L W 1: 172-4
( a reply to Mr. Turner).
-- L. S.  Branches.  L W 5: 57-60.
-- L. S.  Charging checks.  L W 1: 16-7; 2: 16-7.
-- L. S.  Checks on assistants.  L W 2: 39-40, 70-1.
-- L. S.  The class list.  L 9: 41-4.
-- L. S.  Classification and discovery--Mendeleeff's table of
the elements.  L W 13: 353-5.
-- L. S.  Classification in British public libraries.  L A
R 5: 175-82, Discussion 208-11.
-- L. S.  Classification in libraries, with special refer-
ence to the Dewey decimal system.  L 7: 169-78.
-- L. S.  Classification in public libraries, with special
reference to the Dewey decimal system.  L 9: 169-78.
-- L. S.  Classification of library economy and office papers.
L W 9: 406-8.
-- L. S.  Classified and annotated cataloguing: suggestions
and rules.  L W 1: 159-62, 213-5; 2: 5-9, 32-3, 118-21, 229-
31, 285-8; L W 3: 29-31.
-- L. S.  The commercial library.  L A 14: 45-6.
-- L. S.  Committee work.  L A 4: 43-5.
-- L. S.  Dewey classification.  L 8: 341.
-- L. S.  Dewey classification and some recent criticisms.
L 9: 340-5.
-- L. S.  Dewey classification in the reference library.  L
8: 335-50, Discussion 350-3.
-- L. S.  Discussion of Mr. Willcock's paper "Is the print-
ed catalogue doomed?" L A R 9: 404-5.
-- L. S.  Examination of library assistants.  L 9: 79-80.
-- L. S.  Fiction annotation.  L W 2: 206-9.
-- L. S.  Hindrances to progress in public library work.
L A R 2: 82; 347-56.
-- L. S.  How a reference issue was built up.  L A R 3: 603-
8.
-- L. S.  Immediate future of the Library association.  L
A R 13: 384-8, 501-8.
-- L. S.  Indexing library supplies.  L W 2: 13-4.
-- L. S.  Lantern lecture.  L A R 11: 517-8.
-- L. S.  Lantern lecture on "Municipal public libraries
and their work."  L A R 10: 585-6.
-- L. S.  Library association cataloguing rules.  L A R 4:
579-82, Discussion 540-2.

-- L. S.  Library classification.  Greenwood's Yr-Bk: 21-36. 1900-01.

-- L. S.  Library editions of standard works.  L A R 21: 406-7.

-- L. S.  Library extension work in Great Britain.  L J 29: Conf No 34-7.

-- L. S.  Library lighting.  Illuminating Engineer 4, No 2; Libn 1: 196-8.

-- L. S.  The library outlook: an address to municipal library assistants.  L A R 14: 28-38; L W 14: 253-5; L A 9: 27-28.

-- L. S.  Library work with children: with discussion.  L A R 21: 91-102.

-- L. S.  Library work with schools in the United States.  L W 8: 34-6.

-- L. S.  Local history in photographic record.  P L 17: 129-30.

-- L. S.  Local photographic records.  L W 15: 234-6.

-- L. S.  Mr. Baker's descriptive guide: a criticism.  L W 5: 253-8.

-- L. S.  Mr. Baker's "Descriptive guide" a reply.  L W 6: 33-6.

-- L. S.  New book number.  L W 3: 120-3, 150-2.

-- L. S.  Newsrooms: are they desirable.  L A R 3: 55-62.

-- L. S.  Non-professional membership of L. A.  P L 16: 396-7.

-- L. S.  A note on library readings.  L A R 18: 53-62.

-- L. S.  Note on open access in America.  L W 7: 141-3.

-- L. S.  Note on the classification of Kant.  L A R 15: 327-8.

-- L. S.  A note upon a special use of lantern slides.  L A R 18: 68-71.

-- L. S.  A novel catalogue: Select catalogue of the Islington libraries.  L W 13: 193-6.

-- L. S.  Open access.  L A R 4: 274-82, Discussion 306-14.

-- L. S.  The part of the Central library for students.  L A R 21: 393-4.

-- L. S.  Philosophical versus practical classification. Greenwood's Yr-Bk 23-4. 1900-01.

-- L. S.  Present conditions and tendencies of library work in Great Britain.  A L A Bull 7: 139-44.

-- L. S.  Problem of the printed catalogue with a possible solution.  L (ns) 2: 141-6.

-- L. S.  A proposal for a library association edition of standard novels.  L A R 21: 355-9; P L 25: 151-2.

-- L. S.  Public libraries and doubtful books.  L A R 16: 77-8.

-- L. S.  Public libraries and the war.  N Y L 5: 220-2; L A R 17: 10-7.

-- L. S.   Relation of libraries to education.   L A R 19: 435-41.

-- L. S.   Reply to Mr. Baker.   L W 6: 33-6.

-- L. S.   Review of Mr. Baker's "Descriptive guide." L W 5: 253-8.

-- L. S.   Revision of the cataloguing rules of the L. A. U. K.   L J 29: Conf No 231-5.

-- L. S.   Seeds and fruit.   L A R 20: 157-8.

-- L. S.   Select list of books on occultism and theosophy. L W 1: 201-2.

-- L. S.   Sheaf and card catalogues--a comparison.   L W 5: 129-31.

-- L. S.   Simple and economical plan for founding a catalo-guing bureau for public libraries.   L (ns) 5: 146-57.

-- L. S.   Social work and the written record.   L A R 18: 215-8.

-- L. S.   Some hindrances to progress in public library work. L A R 2: 81-8.

-- L. S.   Some impressions of American libraries.   L A R 7: 51-67; L J 30: 147-9.

-- L. S.   Superstition of the bound volume.   L A R 15: 540-7; 17: 540-7; 20: 540-7.

-- L. S.   Technical libraries.   L W 3: 258-60; L A R 5: 467-72, Discussion 493-6.

-- L. S.   Treatment of pamphlets.   L W 4: 60-3.

-- L. S.   Treatment of parliamentary papers.   L W 4: 147-51.

-- L. S.   Waste in the library field.   L A 9: 142-51.

-- L. S.   What libraries can do during and after the war. L A R 18: 589-93.

-- L. S.   What public libraries can do during and after the war.   L A R 17: 439-5.

-- L. S. and H. Bond.   Best books of 1904: juvenile liter-ature.   L A R 8: 7-9.

-- L. S. and J. B. Paton.   New proposals in regard to the public libraries by the National home reading union.   L A R 9: 637-42.

-- L. S. and J. D. Brown.   Compilation of class lists.   L 9: 45-69.

-- L. S. and W. C. B. Sayers.   Registration of librarians: a criticism and a suggestion.   L A R 10: 325-35, Discussion 356-65.

-- L. S. and W. C. B. Sayers.   Scheme of re-classification of members of the Library association.   L W 10: 302.

Jastrow, M.   The university libraries.   U S Bureau of Educa-tion, Circular of Information 1892 No 2: 389-93.

Jayne.   Development of rural extension.   Lib Occ 4: 76-80.

Jayne, N. W.   Township library extension at Alexandria.   Lib Occ 2, No 10: 221-4.

--- N. W.   Work outside the walls.   P L 20: 197-201; New Hamp Bull (ns) 11: 114-8.

Jeffers, L. R.  Associated mountaineering clubs of North America.  L J 43: 755.
----- L. R.  Editions suggested for a Circulating library. L J 33: 48-53.
----- L. R.  Purchasing cheaper reprint editions of popular copyright fiction.  Am Lib Annual 1916-17: 22.
----- L. R.  Selection and cost of editions.  L J 39: 669-72; N Y L 4: 102-5.
----- L. R.  Successful book purchase system.  L J 32: 65-7.
----- L. R.  Suggestions for economy in book purchasing. L J 33: 494-5.
Jefferson, T.  Novel reading.  L J 18: 154.
Jeffries, E.  The enquiry of the death of Richard Hunne.  L (3d series) 5: 220-2.
Jenkins, E. H.  The station library.  Association of American Agricultural Colleges and Experiment Stations Proceedings, Columbus 1911: 159-61.
Jenkins, F. W.  Bibliography in its relation to social works. Bib Soc Amer Proc 8, Nos 1-2, 43-50.
----- F. W.  Duplicates for distribution.  L J 40: 36-7, 262.
----- F. W.  Library supplies.  P L 18: 432-4; 19: 104.
----- F. W.  Prison libraries in New York state.  N Y L 3: 233-5.
----- F. W.  Rise and distribution of literature.  L J 36: 99-111.
----- F. W.  Russell Sage Foundation library, New York.  L J 41: 174-9.
----- F. W.  Social worker and the library.  L J 36: 499-500.
Jenkins, J. H.  Relation of the trustee to the librarian.  P L 4: 249.
Jenkins, R.  Early attempts at paper-making in England (1495-1586).  L A R 2: 479-88.
----- R.  Paper-making in England (1588-1680).  L A R 2: 577-88.
----- R.  Paper-making in England (1682-1714).  L A R 3: 239-51.
----- R.  Paper-making in England (1714-1788).  L A R 4: 128-39.
Jenkinson, A. J.  Policy of the Bodleian library: criticism of financial and general policy.  Oxford Magazine 14 May 1915: 287-91, 301-2.
Jenkinson, F. J.  Presidential address.  L A R 7: 469-81.
Jenkinson, F. W.  Biographical sketches of librarians and bibliographers: VII.  Marvin Davis Bisbee (1845-1913).  Bull Bib 8: 212-3.
Jenks, T.  At the book fair in Yuletide.  Independent 52: 2991-4.

--- T.  The modern child as a reader.  Book-Buyer 23: 17-9.
--- T.  Reference books for boys and girls.  St. Nicholas
   25: 405-8.
Jenn, A. H.  A few notes on popularizing public libraries.  L
   W 17: 143-5.
-- A. H.  Public libraries and the Workers' educational assoc-
   iation.  L W 19: 88-90.
Jenner, H.  Movable presses in British Museum.  L C 4: 88-90.
---- H.  Service books of the Latin church.  L (ns) 4: 292-
   319.
Jennings, A. O.  The duty of public libraries.  L A R 12: 8.
------ A. O.  Fiction in public libraries.  L A R 10: 534-
   41, Discussion 558-64.
------ A. O.  Public library as an educational force.  L A
   R 12: 544-50.
Jennings, I. G.  A bank library of one hundred books.  Special
   Libraries 8: 61-3.
Jennings, J. F.  Plea for advanced instruction in library
   summer schools.  School and Society 7: 156-60; L J 43:
   693-4; P L 25: 306-9.
Jennings, J. T.  Bibliography of New York colonial history.  N
   Y S L Rept 84, Bibliography No 24.
------ J. T.  Camp Lewis library.  P L 23: 116-9.
------ J. T.  Librarianship as a profession in college and
   university libraries.  L J 43: 227-33.
------ J. T.  Municipal civil service as affecting librar-
   ians.  A L A Bull 5: 119-26; L J 36: 399-406; P L 14: 209-12,
   250-4.
------ J. T.  Relation of the library to the municipality.
   Pacific Northwest Library Assn Proceedings 1913: 36-8.
------ J. T.  Should libraries be under municipal and state
   civil service?  A L A Bull 8: 247-50.
------ J. T.  With the A. E. F. in occupied German territory.
   Pacific Northwest Lib Assn Proceedings 1919: 19-22.
------ J. T.  With the A. L. A. service overseas.  A L A Bull
   13: 307-9, 348.
Jennings, Mrs. J. T.  State certification of librarians.  P L 23:
   463-6.
------ Mrs. J. T.  Statistics of women in library work.  L
   J 43: 737.
Jennings, O.  Some old initial letters.  L (ns) 2: 44-59.
Jennings, R.  Paper and publishing at the beginning of the
   eighteenth century.  L A R 14: 249-54.
Jerome, J.  Our concern.  P L 24: 371.
Jerome, J. G.  Bulletin board advertising in the New Haven pub-
   lic library.  L J 43: 758-9.
Jett, D.  That "Publick" spirit.  Minn P L C N 6: 27.
Jevons, H. S.  Libraries from the students' point of view.  L
   A 6: 246-7.
Jevons, W. S.  List of selected books on political economy.
   L A M N 3: 105-11.

Jewell, A.  The ideal trustee from the librarian's point of
    view.  Mich Lib Bull 11: Sept-Oct 1920: 29-31.
    ---- A.  The public library and the school problem.  P L 14:
    117-9; L J 33: 309-11.
Jewett, W. K.  Proportion of university library income which
    should be spent on administration.  A L A Bull 6: 292-4.
    ---- W. K.  Treatment of reserved books.  L J 35: 115-6.
Jewett, W. R.  Relation of the college library to the public.
    A L A Bull 4: 762-5.
Jillson, W. E.  College library as a center of influence.  North-
    western Monthly 8: 299-300.
Joeckel, C. B.  The field of the public library in a college
    town.  A L A Bull 9: 178-9.
John, E. H.  Diversions of a librarian: the library and the
    circus.  L J 43: 765-6.
Johnson, A.  Lessons of the Swedish archives.  Am Hist Assn Rept
    1909: 365-8.
Johnson, B. H.  Selection of fiction.  Vt L Bull 6, No 3: 2-7;
    P L 18: 121-2.
Johnson, C.  An experiment in teaching English.  School Review
    10: 666-74.
Johnson, D. D.  Preparation of librarians for public school li-
    braries.  Nat Educ Assn 1907: 962-7.
Johnson, E.  Business library on women's work.  P L 19: 446-7.
Johnson, E. M.  Library work as a vocation for women: a biblio-
    graphy.  Special Libraries 9: 99, 106-7.
    ----- E. M.  Literature of women in industry.  Special Li-
    braries 9: 109-12, 127.
    ----- E. M.  The special library and some of its problems.
    Special Libraries 6: 157-61; L J 41: 858-9.
    ----- E. M.  The training of a business librarian.  Special
    Libraries 8: 141-4.
    ----- E. M.  Vocational library on women's work.  Special Li-
    braries 5: 116-8; L J 40: 218.
    ----- E. M.  Vocational work through the library.  L J 39:
    27-9.
    ----- E. M.  War emergency courses.  Special Libraries 9:
    6-11.
    ----- E. M.  Women and war-time industries.  Special Libra-
    ries 9: 1.
    ----- E. M.  Women: war-time occupations and employment.
    Special Libraries 9: 12-6, 19-24, 51-2.
Johnson, F. B.  Mechanical aids in filing cards.  P L 6: 532.
Johnson, G. J.  Presidential address.  L C 4: 129-35.
Johnson, H.  English current writing and early printing.  Bib
    Soc Trans 13: 273-95.
Johnson, H. L.  American printing to-day.  P L 20: 26-8.
    ----- H. L.  Books on printing, lettering and designing.  Mass
    L C Bull 4: 109-10.

Johnson, Mrs. I. C.  The library budget.  Ia L C Q 8: 135.

Johnson, J. R.  Selling the library idea.  L J 45: 105-6.

Johnson, J. S.  A trustee's point of view.  P L 10: 468-9.

Johnson, L. S.  Advertising the children's room.  P L 17: 123.

Johnson, M.  Coordination of business information in the library of the Northwestern university school of commerce.  Special Libraries 8: 161.

Johnson, M. E.  Brief selected list of books on accountancy.  P L 23: 268.

Johnson, M. H.  Co-operation of public school and public library.  Southern Educ Review 5: 8-13.

----- M. H.  Library development in Tennessee.  A L A Bull 1: Conf No 79-82.

----- M. H.  School reading: the wider responsibility of the school as to the reading habit of children.  Religious Education 5: 472-5.

----- M. H.  Southern libraries.  L J 28: Conf No 69-71.

Johnson, R.  Clubable, and incidentally poetical, librarians.  L W 18: 83-8.

----- R.  General policy of book selection for municipal libraries.  L W 18: 13-6.

----- R.  In re cataloging and indexing: a protest.  L J 40: 175-6.

----- R.  Public libraries and Mr. Andrew Carnegie.  L J 32: 440-1.

Johnson, R. I.  The school and the library.  English Journal 6: 243-7.

Johnson, S. C.  Ten best books for farmers.  Wis Lib Bull 16: 32-3.

Johnson, W. D.  Book notes in card catalogues.  L J 29: 420-1.

Johnson, W. F.  Selling the public library to professional men.  L J 45: 207-8.

----- W. F.  Story hour as an activity of the public library.  American City 23: 379-80.

Johnston, C. D.  Modification of the Browne system.  L J 26: 873-4.

Johnston, C. H.  Facilities for teacher training in colleges and universities.  University of Illinois School Review Monograph No 6: 7-17; Am Lib Annual 1915-16, 43-4; L J 40: 374-5.

----- C. H.  Library work and the public schools.  School and Society 3: 408-11; P L 20: 457-60.

----- C. H.  Need for an aggressive campaign for better school libraries.  School and Society 4: 381-8; Nat Educ Assn 1916: 539-43; L J 41: 633-9.

Johnston, D. V. R.  Auction catalogue problem.  N Y S L Rept 85, Bulletin No 75, 97-100, 1902.

----- D. V. R.  Binding and binderies.  L J 16: Conf No 9-16, 62.

------ D. V. R.   Binding and repair.  L J 18: 246-7, Conf
No 82-3.
------ D. V. R.   Elements of binding.  U S Commissioner of
Education Report 1892-93: 907-16.
------ D. V. R.   Notes on binding.  L J 17: Conf No 13-5.
------ D. V. R.   Selection of books.  L J 19: Conf No 36-7.
Johnston, H. E.   On the proposed division of the N. C. L. A.
area.  L A R 14: 321-6.
Johnston, J.   The Education (Scotland) act 1918 and public li-
brary development.  L A R 22: 92-7.
------ J.   Open-access system in technical libraries.  L W
15: 208-9.
Johnston, R. H.   Bureau of railway economics library, Washing-
ton, D. C.   Special Libraries 9: 129-35; L J 42: 281-2; L
J 44: 108.
------ R. H.   Catalog cards for analyticals.  Reprinted
from "Special Libraries."  Am Lib Annual 1917-18: 13-4; L
J 42: 488-9.
------ R. H.   Library of the Bureau of railway economics in
its inter-library relations.  A L A Bull 10: 532-9; Special
Libraries 3: 1-4; 8: 1-8; L J 42: 567.  A correction. L A
13: 12.
------ R. H.   The man and the book.  Special Libraries 6:
162-3.
------ R. H.   Memorandum relative to the collection and dis-
tribution of books and periodicals for the mobilization
camps.  A L A Bull 11: 322-4, 414.
------ R. H.   A new note on parcel post for libraries.  P
L 18: 194.
------ R. H.   Special libraries.  L J 45: 439-46.
------ R. H.   Specialization: its advantages and disadvan-
tages.  Special Libraries 6: 93-7.
Johnston, R. I.   The school and the library.  English Journal
6: 243-7.
Johnston, T.   Replacement of "infected" books.  L W 4: 6-9.
Johnston, W. D.   Additions to special collections.  L J 38:
331-3.
------ W. D.   Administration of departmental libraries.  L
J 38: 25-7.
------ W. D.   Bibliographical guides.  P L 10: 117-8.
------ W. D.   Book annotation in England.  L J 29: 67-8.
------ W. D.   Business libraries.  The Credit World April,
1915: 26-7.
------ W. D.   City libraries and civil service.  A L A Bull
11: 84-5.
------ W. D.   Concerning branch libraries: an analysis and
tabulation.  A L A Bull 10: 685-6.
------ W. D.   Co-operation between a public library and ci-
vic organizations.  American City (C ed) 16: 357-8.

------ W. D.  Critical bibliography and book annotation.  L
J 27: 1002-4.

------ W. D.  Discusses library architecture.  A L A Bull
10: 37.

------ W. D.  Engineering library efficiency.  School of
Mines Quarterly Nov. 1912: 26-31.

------ W. D.  History of the Library of Congress, v. 1,
1800-1864 (contributions to American Library History v. 1)
plates Library of Congress.

------ W. D.  International catalogue of current literature
of social sciences.  Bib Soc Amer Proc 1: 177-92.

------ W. D.  The librarian as an educator.  L J 35: 437-41.

------ W. D.  The library and history studies.  History
Teachers' Magazine 6: 31-3; St. Louis teachers' library.  L
J 39: 677-9, 883-6; 40: 457-8.

------ W. D.  The library and history teaching, with special
reference to the reading of local history.  School and Society 2: 14-8.

------ W. D.  Library and the Bureau of education in its
relation to other pedagogical collections.  A L A Bull 2:
338-41.

------ W. D.  The library and the teaching of English.  English Journal 4: 21-7.

------ W. D.  The library as a reinforcement of the school.
New York State Education Dept Bull No 460; Proceedings of
the 47th Annual Convocation of the University of New York
State 1909: 27-42; P L 16: 131-4, 165; American Education
13: 208-11; N Y L 2: 67-8.

------ W. D.  The library as a university factor.  L J 39:
10-1.

------ W. D.  Library of the Bureau of education in its relation to other pedagogical collections.  A L A Bull 2: 338-
42; Educational Review 56: 452-7.

------ W. D.  Library resources of New York City and their
increase.  Columbia Univ Q 13: 163-72; L J 36: 243-6.

------ W. D.  Library service to the business man.  L J 42:
273-5.

------ W. D.  Library standards.  A L A Bull 12: 16-7.

------ W. D.  Library statistics.  L J 45: 352.

------ W. D.  Nationalization of libraries.  P L 24: 118.

------ W. D.  The newspaper morgue, the library and the
school.  Minn P L C N 4: 110-2.

------ W. D.  The possibilities of the library.  Am Lib
Annual 1915-16: 19; L J 40: 76.

------ W. D.  Present bibliographical undertakings in the
United States.  L J 26: 674-7.

------ W. D.  Principles governing the selection of a reference collection for a great public library.  A L A Bull 3:
378-80.

------ W. D.   Proposal for a catalog of university serial publications.  A L A Bull 7: 330.

------ W. D.   Public libraries and the drama.  Am Lib Annual 1915-16: Bull Bib 8: 180-2.

------ W. D.   Relation between special and general libraries. Special Libraries 4: 146-8.

------ W. D.   Relation of the library to the teaching of English.  English Journal 4: 21-7.

------ W. D.   Relations between general purchasing departments and libraries.  L J 41: 315-8.

------ W. D.   The school librarian: training and status. Minn P L C N 4: 157-60; P L 20: 151-4; L J 40: 459-60.

------ W. D.   Schools and libraries.  Alabama Educational Assn Proceedings 1909: 75-86.

------ W. D.   Should libraries be under the general civil service of the state, or have a separate civil service organization?  A L A Bull 11: 229-32, 349; L J 42: 870-1.

------ W. D.   Social surveys by libraries.  A L A Bull 9: 23-5.

------ W. D.   Special collections in libraries.  L J 37: 675.

------ W. D.   Statistics for city libraries for 1916: L J 42: 956; 45: 28.

------ W. D.   Suggestions for a yearbook of library literature.  L J 29: Conf No 126-7.

------ W. D.   A survey of rural literacy.  P L 19: 160.

------ W. D.   University bibliographies.  L J 37: 327-8.

------ W. D.   The use of books in business.  Special Libraries 8: 44.

------ W. D.   Work of the Division of bibliography, Library of Congress.  L J 27: Conf No 63-7.

------ W. D. and Mudge, I. G.   Special collections in libraries in the United States.  Bureau of Education Bulletin No 23, 1912: 1-140; P L 18: 21.

Johnstone, N. K.   An institutional library: an experiment. Brooklyn industrial school association and Home for destitute children.  L J 41: 754-6.

Jolley, R. W.   The Filing association.  L J 45: 268.

Jones, A. A.   Library as an educator.  L N (U S) 3: 367-79.

Jones, A. H.   Public libraries after the war: the need for immediate preparation.  L W 19: 228-31.

Jones, Mrs. A. W.   Portland library guild.  Pacific Northwest Library Assn. Proceedings 1920: 31.

Jones, C.   A. L. A. hospital service in New York state.  L J 45: 491-2.

Jones, Mrs. C. B.   General survey of library conditions in the fifth district of the federation of women's clubs.  Texas Libraries 1 July 1916: 3-5.

Jones, C. K.   A current Chilian bibliography.  L J 38: 616.

--- C. K. Latin-Americana collection in the Library of Congress. L J 44: 226.

Jones, D. L. H. The uses of literature in elementary schools. Nat Educ Assn 1892: 766-71.

Jones, D. R. State aid to secondary schools. University of California, Publications 3: 147-50.

Jones, E. K. Hospital libraries: their relation to patients and training schools. National League of Nursing Education 22d Annual Proceedings, 1916: 184-90; L J 42: 493-4; Am Lib Annual 1917-18: 49-50.

--- E. K. Importance of organized libraries in institutions. Conference of National Charities and Correction. Proceedings, 1916: 360-6; L J 41: 459-62.

--- E. K. Libraries for the patients in hospitals for the insane. L J 36: 637-9.

--- E. K. Library work among the insane. A L A Bull 6: 320-4; N Y L 3: 239-41.

--- E. K. On books and reading: outline of a course of lectures for nurses in hospitals. Am Journal of Insanity, Oct 1915: 297-303.

--- E. K. Some problems of the institution library organizer in the state hospitals. A L A Bull 7: 369-74.

--- E. K. State control of state hospital libraries. Am Journal Insanity Ap 1912: 709-14.

--- E. K. Wartime reading. Bull Bib 9: 166-7.

--- E. K. What a base hospital librarian should know. A L A Bull 12: 226-31, 308; L J 43: 568-72.

--- E. K. "What can I find to read aloud?": some books for the convalescent patient. The Nurse, Feb. 1916: 79-88.

Jones, E. L. An ideal hotel library. P L 13: 9.

--- E. L. Importance of a complete card catalogue. P L 8: 451-2.

--- E. L. Making of a card catalog. P L 9: 109-14.

Jones, F. L. Reference work with the schools in Indianapolis. Lib Occ 1, No 12: 4-6.

Jones, G. M. A L A rules: advance edition: a review. L J 27: 903-4.

--- G. M. Accession book. U S Rept, 1892-93: 820; L J 18: Conf No 51-2.

--- G. M. Accession department (with bibliography) U S Rept 1892-3: 817-26; L J 18: 234-5, Discussion Conf No 46-52.

--- G. M. Cards for the two-book system. L J 20: 168.

--- G. M. Contagious disease and public libraries. L J 16: Conf No 35-8.

--- G. M. Delivery book difficulties. L J 18: 86.

--- G. M. Library periodicals. L J 23: Conf No 137-8.

--- G. M. Periodical library bulletins. L J 19: Conf No 50.

Jones, H.  Concerted action as to local topographical collections: their arrangement, cataloguing, etc.  L A R 2: 200-8.

--- H.  Criticism of public libraries and their work.  L A R 13: 413-4.

--- H.  Library authorities: their powers and duties.  2nd Int Conf: 23-6, Discussion 230-1, 1897.

--- H.  Mr. John Burns and libraries.  L A R 14: 246.

--- H.  The newsroom.  L A R 14: 182-90, Discussion 270-3.

Jones, H. K.  A problem of the college and the school library.  L J 37: 22-3.

Jones, J. D.  The uses of literature in elementary education.  Nat Educ Assn 1892: 776-80.

Jones, J. W.  Inaugural address.  1st Int Conf 1-21; L J 2: 99-119, 1877.

Jones, K. E.  Children's halls.  L A 6: 334-5.

--- K. E.  Picture collections.  L A R 20: 73-6.

Jones, K. K.  A problem of the college and the school library.  L J 37: 22-3.

Jones, L. E.  Government library report.  L J 1: 7-10.

--- L. E.  Report on cataloguing.  L J 7: 177-8.

Jones, L. K.  Emotional poise in war time: how the libraries can help the public.  P L 22: 403-7; P L 23: 1-3; L J 43: 696.

Jones, M. H.  "Librarians" (poem).  L J 42: 897.

Jones, M. L.  The college and the library.  P L 4: 77-80.

--- M. L.  Organization of labour within libraries.  L J 33: 171-3.

--- M. L.  The relation of the library to the pupil teacher.  Nat Educ Assn 1899: 488-98; U S Bur of Educ Rept, 1899-1900: 689-96.

--- M. L.  School and the library: Pomona and Los Angeles.  Cal News Notes 2: 90-2.

--- M. L.  School reading through the public library.  Nat Educ Assn 1899: 1143-8.

Jones, O.  Agricultural collections of the Ohio state library.  Special Libraries 10: 43-4.

--- O.  Classification for college libraries.  L J 24: Conf No 36-41.

--- O.  Student service in Ohio state university.  P L 12: 227.

Jones, P.  Limitations of the small library.  Minn P L C N 3: 197-9.

Jones, R. K.  Problem of the college and school library.  L J 37: 22-3, 179-85.

Jones, R. T.  Aids to readers.  L W 13: 225-33.

Jones, S. K.  The authorship of "Nova Solyma."  L (3d series) 1: 225-38.

--- S. K. The history of a Hebrew lexicon. L (3d series)
5: 410-23.

Jones, T. F. Archives of the Venetian Republic. Am Hist Assn
Rept 1911, 1: 69-77.

Jones, T. L. What the public library can do for the high school.
Wis Lib Bull 8: 28-9; P L 17: 274-6.

Jordan, A. M. A chapter in children's libraries. L J 38: 20-
21.

---- A. M. Co-operation between the public libraries and
the high schools. Mass Lib Club Bull 5: 140-7; L J 41: 400-
2.

---- A. M. Co-operation with the schools. Nat Educ Assn
1910: 1016-22.

---- A. M. German principles for the selection of books
for children. P L 13: 1-3.

---- A. M. Use of children's books. A L A Bull 1: 175-9.

Jordan, D. S. Lane memorial library of medicine, Stanford University. Science (ns) 36: 763-1; L J 38: 28.

Jordan, F. P. History of printed catalog cards. P L 9: 318-
21.

Jordan, M. A. Facts and fiction in English. School Review
12: 361-4.

Joseph, G. A. Ola mss. and the Government Oriental library
of Ceylon. L 7: 269-75.

Josephson, A. G. Johann Gutenberg and the invention of printing. P L 9: 276-9.

Josephson, A. G. S. The A. L. A. at the National capital.
Dial 56: 484-7.

------- A. G. S. Books for the immigrants--1, Swedish. L
J 33: 505.

------- A. G. S. The cataloging test: results and outlook.
A L A Bull 10: 242-4, 411; L J 41: 654-7.

------- A. G. S. Classification of municipal literature.
L J 20: 279.

------- A. G. S. A correction. A L A Bull 11: 45-6; L J
42: 159.

------- A. G. S. Dewey decimal classification and scientific classification. L J 21: 475.

------- A. G. S. Echoes from the library press of 1910:
Dial 50: 77-9.

------- A. G. S. For the librarian's study: city planning
and surveying. L J 37: 673.

------- A. G. S. Foreign books in American libraries. L
J 19: 364.

------- A. G. S. Gleanings from the library press of 1908.
L J 34: 55-7.

------- A. G. S. The index office: its nearer purpose and
its larger aim. Special Libraries 5: 98.

------- A. G. S.  Institute for bibliographical research.
Science (ns) 38: 52-3.
------- A. G. S.  International subject bibliographies.  L
J 19: 226-7.
------- A. G. S.  Is librarianship a learned profession?
P L 1: 195-6.
------- A. G. S.  Johann Gutenberg and the invention of
printing exhibition, 1903.  P L 9: 276-9.
------- A. G. S.  Library catalogues.  Nation 104: 361-7,
Mch. 29, 1917.
------- A. G. S.  Library progress in Germany.  P L 3: 126-
8.
------- A. G. S.  Need of a bibliographical institute.  Scien-
tific American 108: 431.
------- A. G. S.  The new Hain.  L J 33: 182-3.
------- A. G. S.  A notable piece of professional literature:
a review of "Politik der Bucherie."  P L 19: 18-9.
------- A. G. S.  Notes on Spanish bibliography.  L J 27:
836-7; P L 10: 122-3.
------- A. G. S.  On the history of libraries.  L J 42: 680.
------- A. G. S.  Plan for the organization of an institute
for bibliographical research.  Bib Soc Amer Proc 1: 96-102;
Bib Soc Chic Yr-Bk 1901-2: 57-62; L J 27: Conf No 61-2.
------- A. G. S.  Preparation for librarianship.  L J 25:
226-8.
------- A. G. S.  Problems in library co-operation.  L J
26: 816-7.
------- A. G. S.  Proposed institute of business and agri-
cultural research.  Dial 53: 375.
------- A. G. S.  Review of F. Campbell's "Theory of Nation-
al and international bibliography."  P L 3: 27.
------- A. G. S.  Some bibliographical desiderata and the
ways and means to carry them out.  L J 27: 89-90.
------- A. G. S.  Some notes on the Bibliography of library
economy.  P L 10: 122-3.
------- A. G. S.  Training for librarianship.  P L 22: 223-
5.
------- A. G. S.  Treatment of biography.  P L 24: 418.
------- A. G. S.  Treatment of pamphlets in the John Crerar
library.  A L A Bull 3: 403-4; P L 14: 309.
------- A. G. S.  What is cataloguing?  A L A Bull 6: 245-
7.
------- A. G. S.  What the Carnegie Institution could do
for librarianship and bibliography.  L J 27: 1823-4.
Josephson, G. S.  Library in its relation with scholars and
learned societies.  P L 9: 322-3.
Joshi, N. M.  The public library as a factor of social life.
Library Miscellany (Baroda) 1: 4-9.
Josselyn, L. W.  A day in camp.  A L A Bull 12: 239-40, 283.

Joy, J. S.  Salvaging war library service for peace time.  A
   L A Bull 13: 265-7, 349.
Joyner, J. Y.  Rural school libraries.  Conference for Educa-
   tion in the South, Proceedings, 1905: 44-50.
Judd, C. H.  Children's reading and municipal libraries.  Chi-
   cago School of Civics and Philanthropy 1912, Part I.
   -- C. H.  Reasons for modifying entrance requirements.  Educ-
   ation 32: 266-77.
   -- C. H.  Relation of the library to the school.  P L 16:
   116-7.
   -- C. H.  The school and the library.  Nat Educ Assn 1910:
   1026-31; A L A Bull 4: 607-11; Elementary School Teacher 11:
   28-33.
Judge, M. C.  A library reading-aloud club.  L J 42: 863-5.
Judson, K. B.  Work of a periodical department.  P L 15: 144-
   50.
Julian, I.  Filing in a law office.  Filing Sept 1918: 81-4.
Kaiser, J.  Making the library serve your purpose.  Journal of
   American Society of Mechanical Engineers  March 1918: 185-6.
   ---- J.  Systematic indexing: a review.  Libn 2: 462-4.
Kaiser, J. B.  American municipal documents: a librarian's view.
   L J 38: 453-6; Special Libraries 4: 117-21, June 1913.
   ---- J. B.  The civics room.  A L A Bull 9: 163-9.
   ---- J. B.  Law and legislative library conditions in Texas.
   Law Library Journal  Jan 1912: 27-30.
   ---- J. B.  Law, legislative reference and municipal refer-
   ence libraries: reviews.  L J 39: 918-20; and J. A. Lapp in
   American Political Science Review 9: 170-2.
   ---- J. B.  Municipal reference libraries.  Nation 94: 109.
   ---- J. B.  A neglected phase of the salary question: the
   problem of retiring allowances.  L J 45: 111-6, 158-62.
   ---- J. B.  Preliminary list of the national bibliographies
   of the South American Republics.  Bull Bib 7: 138-41.
   ---- J. B.  Publicity for libraries.  Pacific Northwest Li-
   brary Assn Proceedings 1914: 20-4; P L 23: 165-7.
   ---- J. B.  Scope and plans of the Washington state library
   advisory board's survey.  Pacific Northwest Library Assn
   Proceedings 1916: 39-42.
   ---- J. B.  Some phases of reference work.  L J 36: 454-6.
   ---- J. B.  Special library and the library school.  L J
   37: 175-9.
   ---- J. B.  The trend.  Pacific Northwest Library Assn Pro-
   ceedings 1918: 7-9.
Kaltenbach, M.  School-room libraries.  Nat Educ Assn 1897:
   1025-32.
Kammerling, E.  A civics room in a modern-sized town.  A L A
   Bull 7: 339-42.
Kantavala, M. H.  Gujarati poets and the reformation.  Lib Mis-
   cellany (Baroda) 3: 9-14.
Karlake, Frank.  David White, 1824-1910.  B A R 7: XXV-XXX, 1910

Karney, T.  United States Naval academy library.  U S Govt
  Rept: 268-9. 1876.
Karsten, E. G.  A course in business methods.  P L 20: 103-4.
Kauffman, P. W.  How may a teacher lead children to good books?
  L J 31: 170.
------ P. W.  Public schools and public libraries.  Educa-
  tional Review 33: 306-12.
Kautz, F. P.  Bookseller's word.  P L 7: 236-7.
Kavana, J.  What are the best days and hours for a small li-
  brary to be open?  P L 6: 425-8.
Kay, C. de.  On halls that need color.  Art World and Art Deco-
  ration 2: 251-4.
Kay, J. T.  How to catalog books.  L J 19: 125-8.
  - J. T.  Novels in libraries.  L J 4: 411.
  - J. T.  Owens college library.  L A U K Trans 2: 116-7; L
  5: 20-33.
  - J. T.  Provisions of novels in rate-supported libraries.
  L A Trans 2: 42-6.
Keator, A. D.  Helps in meeting the demand for the day.  Minn
  P L C N 4: 142-5.
Keator, F. W.  The relation of the library board to the city
  government.  Pacific Northwest Lib Assn Proceedings 1916:
  42-7.
Kedder, I. A.  Twelfth night.  Wash L A Bull 3, No 1: 8-9.
Keeler, L. E.  Book selection.  New Hamp Bull (ns) 15: 134.
  ---- L. E.  Cobwebs in the family library.  Bookman (N Y)
  50: 573-6.
  ---- L. E.  Library's relation to local history.  P L 23:
  161-3.
Keen, A.  Village libraries as part of a system of technical
  education.  L 10: 31-2.
Keen, W. W.  Library book stacks without daylight.  P L 14: 290-
  1.
Keller, H. R.  Old fashioned virtues versus the ideal librar-
  ian.  L J 34: 295-8.
  ---- H. R.  Why not a special course for the special libra-
  ry?  Special Libraries 10: 192.
Keller, R. L.  Seeking safety.  Special Libraries 10: 215-7.
Kelley, G.  Library staff associations.  P L 24: 416-7.
Kelley, G. O.  European war classification.  L J 44: 704-6.
Kellicott, G.  Book buying for a college library.  P L 7: 416-8.
Kelliher, Mrs. C. L. B.  Experience with municipal reference
  work.  A L A Bull 10: 50-3.
Kellogg, M. D.  County free libraries: a selected list of book
  and magazine articles in the California state library.  Cal
  News Notes 13: 330-60.
Kelly, A.  Novel reading for high school girls.  Home Progress
  2: 34-40.
Kelly, B. M.  Selection of juvenile books.  P L 14: 308-9, 367-
  72.

--- B. M.   Work in a small library.   P L 14: 45-9.

Kelly, P. W.   How the state may aid school libraries.   Southern
   Education Assn Proceedings 1914: 329-33.

Kelly, R. W.   Science in the class room.   Scientific American
   110: 265, March 28, 1914.

Kelsey, J. W.   An up-to-the-minute geographical filing system.
   L J 43: 850.

Kelso, A. B.   Branch libraries.   Penn Lib Notes 5, No 4: 15-25.

Kelso, T. L.   Los Angeles public library training.   U S Rept
   1892-93: 764-6.

--- T. L.   Some economical features of public libraries.
   L J 18: 473-4.

Kemball, T.   Library of the School of landscape architecture at
   Harvard University.   Special Libraries 4: 165-8.

Kemp, A. W.   Village libraries: The Isle of Wight Scheme.   L
   A R 10: 647-8.

Kennedy, J. P.   Librarian as a factor in securing library appropriations.   A L A Bull 1: Conf No 237-8.

----- J. P.   Virginia libraries.   A L A Bull 1: 68-71.

Kennedy, R. McM.   Hagerstown model.   Bulletin of State Univ of
   Columbia No 37, P L 1: 7-12.

Kenner, A. R.   Indexing and filing technical literature.   Engineering and Mining Journal 99: 851-6; L J 40: 653-5.

Kenngot, A.   Outside reading in modern language instruction.
   School Review 22: 385-90.

Kent, H. W.   Better books, paper, type and illustrations.   A
   L A Bull 8: 166-8.

-- H. W.   Bibliographical side of librarianship.   L J 35:
   483-7.

-- H. W.   Co-operation between libraries, schools and museums.
   L J 36: 557-60.

-- H. W.   Librarians' books.   L J 37: 550-6.

-- H. W.   Librarianship.   L J 35: 483-7.

-- H. W.   Library book plates.   L J 27: 932-4.

-- H. W.   The love of the book.   A L A Bull 9: 94-101.

-- H. W.   Printing press of the Metropolitan museum of art.
   Printing Art 16: 369-71.

Kenwood, H. R.   Risks from tuberculous infection retained in
   books.   L A R 17: 409-15.

Kenyon, E. E.   How to teach literature.   Education 10: 544-6.

Kenyon, F. G.   Presidential address at L. A. U. K. conference
   at Exeter.   L A R 12: 436-45.

---- F. G.   Should librarians read?   L A 7: 243-56; L A R
   12: 601-2; P L 16: 43-9.

Keogh, A.   Advanced library training for research workers.   A
   L A Bull 13: 165-7; L J 44: 581-2.

--- A.   Bibliographic equipment of a university library for
   its greatest efficiency.   N Y L 3: 56-9.

--- A.   Bibliography.   A L A Bull 1: Conf No 35-9.

--- A.  English and American libraries.  P L 14: 131-2.
--- A.  English and American libraries: a comparison.  L W
5: 146-9; P L 6: 388-95.
--- A.  Librarian as unifier.  Am Lib Annual 1915-16: 64:
N Y L 4: 591-5.
--- A.  Need of bibliographic equipment.  P L 16: 374.
--- A.  New A. L. A. rules.  P L 13: 356.
--- A.  Our library resources as shown by some government
needs in the war.  L J 44: 504-7.
--- A.  Practical bibliography.  A L A Bull 1: 35-9.
--- A.  Technical books in English libraries.  P L 5: 321-2.
--- A.  Thoughts on cataloguing and cataloguers.  P L 13:
246-7; A L A Bull 2: 360-1.
--- A.  Training, employment and compensation of assistants.
L A 6: 402-4.
--- A.  Training of college students in bibliography.  L J
33: 241; P L 14: 124.
Keogh, T. L.  Our library resources as shown by some government
needs in the war.  A L A Bull 13: 270-3, 350.
Kephart, H.  Being a librarian.  L J 15: 330-2.
----- H.  Bindings in libraries.  L J 18: 82-3.
----- H.  Classification.  L J 17: 228; 18 240-2; U S Rept
861-97, 1892-3.
----- H.  Combined receipt and cash register.  L J 19: 86-7.
----- H.  Economics in cataloguing.  L J 19: 105.
----- H.  Fumagalli's rules for cataloguing.  L J 12: 547-8.
----- H.  A new library journal: Revista delle Biblioteche.
L J 13: 205-6.
----- H.  New York state law--outline of classification.  U
S Rept 881-8, 1892-93.
----- H.  Notation for books.  L J 22: 739-41.
----- H.  Paste for labels.  L J 18: 8-9.
----- H.  Proposed national library, Florence, Italy.  L J
13: 139.
----- H.  Reference list on classification.  U S Rept: 893-
7, 1892.
----- H.  Report on gifts and bequests to libraries.  L J
19: Conf No 61-3.
----- H.  The Sacconi binder.  L J 18: 184-5.
----- H.  Word about writing inks.  L J 18: 8-9.
----- H.  World's library congress.  U S Rept: 872, 1892-93.
----- H.  World's library congress report.  U S Rept 895,
1892-93.
Keppel, F. P.  How the army libraries have helped our fighting
men.  A L A Bull 13: 152-5, 346.
---- F. P.  Library service for the army.  L J 44: 501-3.
Kern, O. J.  Traveling libraries in country schools.  School
and Home Education 23: 177-84.

-- O. J. Use of the library in the Institute. School and Home Education 19: 346-50; Illinois State Teachers' Assn Proceedings 1899: 85-8.

Kernahan, C. Anonymity and pseudonymity. Living Age 277: 479-85.

Kerr, C. The business man and the public library. P L 16: 96-9.

Kerr, E. Building up the special library. Special Libraries 9: 95-6.

-- E. The case against the librarian: Imbrie & company statistical library. Special Libraries 11: 73-5.

-- E. The magazine index and clipping file. Special Libraries 9: 136-7.

Kerr, W. H. The child in the school and the library. A L A Bull 9: 144-7; P L 20: 307-9.

-- W. H. Developing a college library. P L 12: 214-7.

-- W. H. Educational co-operation of the A. L. A. P L 18: 196.

-- W. H. The gist of the A. L. A. library publicity survey. A L A Bull 11: 130-2, 311; Discussion 354; P L 22: 358-9.

-- W. H. Libraries and schools: educational co-operation. Nat Educ Assn 1914: 813-4.

-- W. H. The library and the community. P L 23: 251-4.

-- W. H. The library and the schools. P L 23: 193.

-- W. H. The library as an English laboratory. School and Society 2: 121-4; L J 40: 923-5.

-- W. H. Library promoting. School and Society 9: 79-83.

-- W. H. The library work that the normal school ought to do. L J 39: 447-9.

-- W. H. Making the library earn its salt. P L 19:150-3.

-- W. H. Normal schools and their relationship to librarianship. A L A Bull 7: 193-9; American Schoolmaster 6: 411-4.

-- W. H. Practical help offered to Kansas school libraries. L J 42: 242.

-- W. H. Problem method and its library: a librarian's reaction: Discussion of Dr. Lull's paper. L J 42: 686-7.

-- W. H. Psychology for librarians. P L 16: 425-30.

-- W. H. Public library co-operation with Y. M. C. A. organizations. P L 23: 422-3.

-- W. H. Publicity methods for libraries and library associations. A L A Bull 10: 14-7; Discussion 39-43.

-- W. H. What may the library do for the school? L J 41: 34-6.

-- W. H. Why school libraries? L J 42: 241-2.

Kershaw, S. H. Archbishop Parker, collector and author. L (ns) 1: 379-83

Ketcham, E. B. A social service library. L J 38: 406-7.

Kettle, B. Best books of 1903--Bibliography and library science L A R 6: 543-51.

---- B.  Best books of 1904--Bibliography and library science.
L A R 7: 637-9.

Keyes, R. K.  How we use our school library.  English Journal
3: 86-93.

Keyser, R. S.  Use of books of travel in teaching geography.
American Education 13: 21-3.

Kidder, Mrs. I. A.  The creative impulse in the library.  P L
24: 156-7.

---- Mrs. I. A.  How to increase the culture reading of college students.  Pacific Northwest Library Assn Proceedings
1910: 61; P L 15: 419-20.

---- Mrs. I. A.  Requisites of an agricultural library.  L
J 44: 367-9.

---- Mrs. I. A.  Some opportunities in agricultural library
work.  A L A Bull 10: 228-34, 406.

Kies, P. P.  Teaching of opera librettos.  English Journal 9:
71-9.

Kildal, A.  Library work in Norway.  L J 41: 741-6

Kilian, H. E.  "Your home": The Johnson City library.  L J 43:
495-6.

Kilman, H.  Traveling libraries in British Columbia.  P L 21:
107-8.

Kilmer, J.  Inefficient libraries.  Bellman 22: 157-9.

Kimball, A. R.  Binding advertisements in serials.  L J 28: 766-
7; Rept Libn of Congress 1903: 104-7.

----- A. R.  The care of books, with special reference to
fine bindings.  Medical Library Assn Bull Jan 1912, 7p.

Kimball, T.  Streets: their arrangement, lighting and planning.
Special Libraries 6: 42-8.

Kimball, W. P.  Library situation in California.  L J 27: 200-2.

Kimber, S. A.  Watermarking.  Printing Art 16: 257-66.

Kimble, K.  Discussion of the preceding paper.  L J 43: 248-9.

Kimmins, C. W.  Lectures under the public libraries acts.  L
A R 3: 6-12.

King, E.  Reference books found in the 55th and 56th Congresses.
P L 8: 263-266.

-- E.  Some of the necessary qualifications of a reference
library assistant.  L W 20: 91-4.

-- E.  Story hour on occupations.  P L 9: 75-7.

King, F. A.  The complete collector.  Bookman (N Y) 36: 510-23,
615-23.

King, H. H.  Classification system for the Federation library.
The Student World April 1919; L J 44: 618.

King, J. E.  Province of the state library when restricted to
the service of the legislature.  A L A Bull 3: 292-4.

King, R.  The system used by the library of the Retail credit
company to develop employees.  Special Libraries 7: 157-9.

Kingery, H. M.   Life of Bonaparte, by a citizen of the United States.   Nation 97: 559-60.

Kingsbury, N. C.   The library a necessity of modern business.   L J 38: 442-9; Special Libraries 4: 33-9.

Kingsland, L. D.   Report on libraries of Guatemala, etc.   L J 29: Conf No 91-2.

Kingsley, C. D.   College entrance requirements.   Report of Committee of nine on the articulation of high school and college.   Nat Educ Assn 1911: 559-67.

Kingsley, D. M.   Recent tendencies in state publications.   A L A Bull 13: 294-6, 403; L J 44: 725-7.

Kinkaid, M. H.   Book reviewing.   P L 7: 373-4.

Kinkeldey, O.   American music catalogs.   L J 40: 574-8.

------- O.   New York public library and its music division.   L J 40: 589-92.

Kinzbrunner, C. and E. W. Hulme.   On current serial digests and indexes of the literature of science and some problems connected therewith.   L A R 15: 22-8.

Kirby, S.   Co-operation: a suggestion.   L A 5: 265-7.

--- S.   Enquiry assistants: a suggestion.   L W 14: 354-8.

--- S.   Initiation of the borrower in an open access library.   L W 12: 339-40.

--- S.   Ought public libraries to advertise?   L W 14: 230-2.

--- S.   Question of censorship.   L W 14: 257-9.

Kirchwey, M. P.   Literature, Grade VI.   Teachers' College Record 8: 167-76.

Kirk, A. B.   Class in current events.   History Teacher's Magazine 6: 97-8.

Kirkpatrick, D.   The Camp fire girls and the library.   Lib Occ 3: 86-7.

Kirkwood, W. P.   Newspaper publicity.   Minn P L C N 4: 212.

Kitchener, S. W.   Cross references in card catalogues.   L A 6: 32.

Kite, W.   Book registry for small libraries.   L J 8: 40-1.

-- W.   Fiction in public libraries.   L J 1: 273-9.

Kittle, W. H.   Magazines and "The interests."  Wis Lib Bull 7: 145-6.

Klein, A. J.   The new Service bureau in Washington.   L J 43: 491-2.

Klink, J. S.   Libraries and schools.   L J 16: 104.

--- J. S.   Use of libraries by school children.   P L 2: 16-9.

Klotz, H. G.   Brief history of the Library of the physicians to the German hospital and dispensary of the City of New York.   Med Lib and Hist Journal 2: 43-6.

Klotz, O. J.   Trustee's duty to the library.   A L A Bull 6: 302-4.

Knapp, E.   Elaborations on the obvious.   P L 24: 371-2.

Knapp, W.   Select list of books in English about Scandinavia
or by Scandinavians.   Bull Bib 8: 187-92.
Knight, E. B.   Collecting and making use of local geography
material.   Elementary School Journal 20: 459-65.
Knight, J.   The public school and the public library.   L A 14:
9-10.
Knowles, N.   Training of women for salesmanship.   Special Li-
braries 5: 58-9.
Knowlton, L.   Care of leather bindings.   Lib Occ No 11: 5.
------ L.   Library mending kit.   Lib Occ No 10: 4-5.
Koch, T.   Equipment for a small high school with a reference
library.   Pennsylvania School Journal 57: 97-9.
Koch, T. W.   Apportionment of book funds in college and univ-
ersity libraries.   A L A Bull 2: 341-7.
-- T. W.   Bibliothèque Nationale: history, organization and
administration.   L J 39: 339-50, 419-30.
-- T. W.   The Bodleian at Oxford.   L J 39: 739-46, 803-10.
-- T. W.   Books and bullets.   Review of Reviews (N Y) 58: 503-
8.
-- T. W.   Books in camp, trench and hospital.   A L A Bull
11: 103-8, 334; L J 42: 507-14, 591-8.
-- T. W.   Books new, and nearly new.   P L 17: 124-6.
-- T. W.   British censorship and enemy publications.   L J
42: 696-705.
-- T. W.   The British Museum library.   L J 38: 499-509, 547-
56.
-- T. W.   Carnegie libraries.   L J 30: Conf No 78-81.
-- T. W.   Further report on the Liverpool meeting of the L.
A. U. K.   L J 37: 679-83.
-- T. W.   Imperial public library, St. Petersburg: mainly
a digest of a centenary volume in Russian by the present
Director Kobeko.   L J 40: 5-33, 93-108.
-- T. W.   A librarian at the Leipzig exhibition.   L J 39:
583-7.
-- T. W.   Library of Louvain university.   L J 44: 443-6.
-- T. W.   More about books in camps, trench and hospital.
L J 42: 778-90.
-- T. W.   Proposed meeting of college and university libra-
rians of the Middle West.   L J 34: 354.
-- T. W.   Purpose of the Carnegie gifts.   L J 30: Conf No
78-81.
-- T. W.   Review of Miss G. B. Rawlings.   "The British Mu-
seum Library."   L J 42: 398-400.
-- T. W.   Some old-time, old-world librarians.   North Amer-
ican Review 200: 244-59.
-- T. W.   Some phases of the administrative history of col-
lege and university libraries.   A L A Bull 6: 268-75.
-- T. W.   Student circulation in a university library.   L
J 31: 758-61.

-- T. W.  Suggested readings for library assistants in the new Encyclopaedia Britannica.  L J 37: 63-9.

-- T. W.  Summer library school.  L J 34: 548-50.

-- T. W.  The university library.  L J 40: 322-5.

Koehler, E.  Are you a phthisiophobist?  Special Libraries 11: 148-9.

Kofoid, C. A.  Cooperation in scientific bibliography: the work of the Concilium bibliographicum.  Science (ns) 27: 543-5.

Konkle, B. A.  Library restictions.  Nation 91: 32-3, July 14, 1910.

Koopman, H. L.  Advantages of the small library.  P L 18: 97-100.

----- H. L.  The amateur professional.  L J 42: 794-7.

----- H. L.  The Ann Mary Brown memorial, Providence (R. I.) Printing Art 13: 341-4.

----- H. L.  Astor library catalog.  L J 12: 123-4.

----- H. L.  Biographical sketches of librarians and bibliographers: V. Reuben Aldridge Guild.  Bull Bib 8: 119-20.

----- H. L.  The book of to-day and the book of to-morrow. Printing Art 14: 413-5.

----- H. L.  Book treasures of New York.  Printing Art 15: 21-3.

----- H. L.  Books as a librarian would like them.  Printing Art Dec 1912: 273-4.

----- H. L.  Breadth of view.  Printing Art 17: 461-2.

----- H. L.  The Chinese book.  Printing Art 16: 449-53.

----- H. L.  Collecting for the future.  P L 6: 133-4, 195-7.

----- H. L.  Criticism of bookmaking.  Printing Art 15: 354-6.

----- H. L.  Diffusion of 15th century printing.  Printing Art 16: 101-3.

----- H. L.  Essential elements in bookmaking.  Printing Art 17: 25-7.

----- H. L.  Exceptions to the rule of printing legibility. Printing Art 14: 338-40.

----- H. L.  Functions of a university library.  L J 19: Conf No 25-6.

----- H. L.  A "handy sized" library for students at Brown University.  L J 44: 30.

----- H. L.  Individuality in the library.  L J 25: 571-2.

----- H. L.  Isaiah Thomas typographical collection at American antiquarian society, Worcester, Mass.  Printing Art 15: 429-36.

----- H. L.  Lest we forget in the multitude of books, the few great books.  P L 13: 117-20, 163-5.

----- H. L.  The librarian, himself.  L J 41: 738-41.

----- H. L.  Library militant.  P L 10: 331-5.

----- H. L.  Library progress in Rhode Island.  L J 31: Conf No 14-5.

----- H. L.  Painstaking revision necessary.  Printing Art
15: 100-2.
----- H. L.  Poets' tribute to printing.  Printing Art 17:
287-92.
----- H. L.  Print in education.  Printing Art 14: 89-91.
----- H. L.  Printing problems to be solved.  Printing Art
16: 22-4.
----- H. L.  Problems of the printing page and solutions.
Printing Art 16: 353-6.
----- H. L.  The question of book storage.  L J 39: 24-7.
----- H. L.  Simplified spelling from the printer's stand-
point.  L (ns) 10: 78-85.
----- H. L.  Typography of text and comment.  Printing Art
16: 275-81.
----- H. L.  Vacations and holidays.  L J 40: 408-9; P L 21:
64-5.
----- H. L.  Value of books to the community.  Printing Art
16: 173-5.
----- H. L.  Value of printing in communication.  Printing
Art 14: 249-51.
Korstian, C. F.  A decimal classification for forestry liter-
ature.  Journal of Forestry 15: 449-62; L J 42: 835-6; Am
Lib Annual 1917-18: 31-2.
Krause, L. B.  The business library: what it is and what it
does.  P L 25: 159.
---- L. B.  Commercial libraries.  P L 15: 391-2.
---- L. B.  Contribution of library science to efficiency
in business.  P L 17: 357-60.
---- L. B.  Fisk free and public library.  P L 4: 54-6.
---- L. B.  Libraries in business organizations: their ex-
panding function.  A L A Bull 7: 215-9.
---- L. B.  Library of H. M. Byllesby & Co., Chicago.  L J
42: 289-90.
---- L. B.  Library science as an adjunct to engineering.
Engineering Record Mch 2, 1912: 233-4.
---- L. B.  Methods of increasing the use of technical lit-
erature.  Engineering Review 67: 544-5.
---- L. B.  Periodicals in business libraries.  Wilson Bull
1: 360.
---- L. B.  Practical value of a company library.  P L 23:
260-1.
---- L. B.  Relation of the library to business education.
Nat Educ Assn 1916: 379-83.
---- L. B.  Some business libraries of Chicago, small in
size but large in service.  Wis Lib Bull 12: 120-3.
---- L. B.  Some technical terms defined for reference li-
brarians.  P L 16: 5-6.
---- L. B.  Technical libraries of Chicago.  L J 41: 331;
P L 21: 184.

---- L. B.  Training for special library work in library schools.  A L A Bull 14: 335.

---- L. B.  Value of a library in an engineering office. Engineering Review  April 23, 1914: 479-80.

---- L. B.  What are special libraries.  P L 15: 413-5.

Krauss, H.  Information bureaus in libraries.  L A R 12: 14-22.

Krauss, W. C.  Need of a medical library in Buffalo.  Med Lib and Hist Journal 3: 127-40.

Krey, A. C.  Books on the war.  Minn P L C N 4: 221-4.

Kroeger, A. B.  A. L. A. cataloguing rules.  L J 29: 309-10; P L 9: 279-80.

----- A. B.  Age limit in public libraries.  L N (U S) 3: 386-90.

----- A. B.  Arrangement of entries in catalogs.  L J 30: 146-7; P L 10: 18-9.

----- A. B.  Care of books.  P L 8: 319-20.

----- A. B.  Cataloguing and the new A. L. A. rules.  L J 27: 1011-2; P L 8: 20-1.

----- A. B.  Co-operative cataloguing and the A. L. A. rules. L J 25: Conf No 73-7.

----- A. B.  Desk assistant.  L J 26: 801.

----- A. B.  Dictionary catalogs versus bibliographies.  L J 27: Conf No 180-2, Discussion 182-6.

----- A. B.  Encouragement of serious reading: a survey of the field.  L J 28: 222-5.

----- A. B.  Evolution of the cirriculum of the Drexel institute library school.  A L A Bull 2: 210-3.

----- A. B.  Glossary of library terms compiled from various sources.  P L 1: 167-72.

----- A. B.  Guide to reference books: a review.  P L 8: 119.

----- A. B.  Instruction in books in library schools.  L J 32: 395-401.

----- A. B.  Instruction in cataloguing in library schools. L J 32: 108-11.

----- A. B.  The place of the library in technical education.  L J 30: 393-9.

----- A. B.  Recent reference books supplementary to A. L. A. Guide.  L J 28: 823-8.

----- A. B.  Reference books for small libraries.  Penn Lib Notes 1, No 1: 4-9.

----- A. B.  Reference books of 1904.  L J 30: 5-10.

----- A. B.  Reference books of 1905.  L J 31: 3-7.

----- A. B.  Reference books of 1906.  L J 32: 11-3.

----- A. B.  Reference books of 1907.  L J 33: 13-16.

----- A. B.  Women librarians.  L J 21: Conf No 57-8.

----- A. B. and S. W. Cattell.  Aids to book selection.  Penn L Comm Bull 1: 7-20.

Krumbacher.  Photographic copying in libraries.  L J 33: 223-4.

Kruse, W. C.  Reading of library books.  Univ of State of New York Education Dept Bull No 457: 294-5.

Kudalkar, J. S.  Melvil Dewey: the Sage of Lake Placid, Lib.
    Miscellany (Baroda) 2: 68-70.
------ J. S.  A unique Jewish library in the United States.
    Lib Miscellany (Baroda) 2: 126-37.
Kudlecka, J.  Library work among foreigners.  P L 15: 375-6.
Kunze, W. F.  Public library and the public school.  Minn P L
    C N 1, No 9: 19-22.
Kuser, W. L.  The book and the boy.  P L 21: 271-2.
Kyte, E. C.  Osram lamps.  L A R 11: 287.
-- E. C.  Recent library legislation in England.  L J 45: 66.
L. A. A.  Easter school in Holland.  L W 15: 223-4.
L. A. A.  Report on the hours, salaries, training and conditions
    of service of assistants in British municipal libraries.  L
    A 8: 121-38.
Lacey, M. G.  Agencies working for agriculture.  L J 45: 922-7.
Lach-Szyrma, W. S.  Libraries in Penzance.  L C 3: 169-73.
Lacy, A.  Aids to library work: school libraries.  Michigan
    Board of Library Commissioners Report 1907: 136-8.
Lacy, E.  Reconciliation between the ideal and the real in lit-
    erature.  P L 17: 243-7.
Lacy, M. G.  The farmer and his tools.  Educational Review 51:
    268-74.
-- M. G.  List of references on agricultural libraries in
    the United States including their history, administration
    and problems in general.  Special Libraries 10: 53-60.
-- M. G.  The opportunity of the agricultural college li-
    brary.  South Atlantic Quarterly 9: 78-82.
-- M. G.  Sources of agricultural statistics.  L J 43: 859-
    66.
Ladd, M. B.  List of references on the right to strike.  Spec-
    ial Libraries 10: 255-68.
La Fontaine, H.  International institute of bibliography.  L
    J 29: Conf No 101-4.
Lahy, J. H.  Public library situation in France.  P L 24: 203-4.
Lamb, A. A.  Reading of the child.  Minn P L C N 2: 62-4.
-- A. A.  Sunday opening.  Minn P L C N 9: 32-3.
Lamb, G. H.  Mr. Carnegie and the free library movement.  Penn
    Lib Notes 10: 2-12.
-- G. H.  School libraries.  Penn Lib Notes 5, No 4: 33-5.
Lamb, S.  Method of registering "Bespoken books."  L A 4: 3-4.
Lamb, W. L.  Reading of the trustee.  Minn P L C N 2: 46-8.
Lambert, C.  How can a state library association best arouse
    interest in towns and villages which are totally without
    library facilities.  L J 27: Conf No 238-9.
Lambert, L. V.  Study of literature.  Journal of Education (Bos-
    ton) 55: 7.
Lamberton, G. M.  Traveling libraries in Nebraska.  P L 2: 51.
Lamm, E. N.  Suggestions on library buildings.  P L 6: 613.
Lamprey, C.  The boy and the book.  P L 16: 119-20.

Lamprey, M. L.  Some recent books worth while.  Mass L C Bull
 6: 50-3.
Lamprey, W. L.  Methods of book buying.  L J 31: 17.
Lancaster, A.  Advantage of occasional exhibitions of the more
 valuable books.  L 6: 19-22.
------- A.  Improper books.  L A R 12: 6-7.
------- A.  Provision of technical books in public librar-
 ies from the technical education fund.  L A R 2: 18-9.
------- A.  Public libraries and technical education.  L 2:
 103-10.
Lancefield, R. T.  Arrangement of fiction.  L J 18: 183-4.
-------- R. T.  Linotyping library catalogs.  L J 19: 261.
Landon, F.  The library and local material.  Ontario Library
 Review Feb 1917: 61; L J 42: 572.
Lane.  Pictures in the library.  P L 7: 481.
Lane, E. N.  Children's vacation reading.  P L 5: 425.
 -- E. N. and Farrar, I. F.  Methods of evaluating children's
 books.  L J 26: 194-7.
Lane, L. P.  Typewritten book labels.  P L 4: 443.
Lane, M. E.  Library ventures in the Kentucky mountains.  L J
 43: 393-4.
Lane, W. C.  A. L. A. analytical cards for periodical publica-
 tions.  L J 36: 632-3.
 -- W. C.  A. L. A. publishing section.  L J 23: Conf No 46-
 52; L J 24: Conf No 95-7, 579.
 -- W. C.  The appointment of a librarian of Congress.  L J
 24: 99-101.
 -- W. C.  Astor library catalog.  L J 11: 160-1.
 -- W. C.  Bibliography in America.  P L 10: 111-3.
 -- W. C.  Catalog cases.  U S Rept 1892-3. 840.
 -- W. C.  Catalog of the Harvard college library.  L J 27:
 Conf No 187-90; P L 7: 320-2.
 -- W. C.  Catalogs--card and printed.  L J 17: Conf No 71-2.
 -- W. C.  Cataloguing.  U S Rept 1892-93: 1892.  L J 18:
 238-40, Discussion 75-82.
 -- W. C.  Cataloguing--present tendencies.  L (ns) 6: 74-5.
 -- W. C.  Central bureau of information and loan collection
 for college libraries.  L J 33: 429-33, 506.
 -- W. C.  Classification.  L J 10: 258.
 -- W. C.  Entry of pseudonymous works.  U S Rept 844. 1892-
 93.
 -- W. C.  First report of librarian of Harvard university,
 1898: 2-5; see also 5th report, p. 215.
 -- W. C.  Greek and Latin authors.  L J 9: 50-1.
 -- W. C.  Harvard college library subject heading index.
 L J 11: 208-9, 349; 12: 548-9.
 -- W. C.  Inter-library loans of German government extended
 to United States.  L J 31 Conf No 222-3; P L 11: 518.
 -- W. C.  Justin Winsor, 1831-1897.  L J 23: 7-14

-- W. C.  Justin Winsor's administration of the Harvard li-
brary 1877-97.  Harvard Graduates Magazine 6: 182-8.
-- W. C.  Moving of the Harvard library.  L J 38: 31-4.
-- W. C.  New Harvard Library.  L J 38: 267-70; P L 18: 21.
-- W. C.  Object of the Bulletin of the A. L. A.  A L A
Bull 1, No 1: 1-2.
-- W. C.  Opportunities for bibliographical work.  Bib Soc
Amer Proc 1: 43-9; L J 31: 118-9.
-- W. C.  Present tendencies of catalog practice.  L J 29:
Conf No 134-43, Discussion 228-31.
-- W. C.  Presidential address.  L J 24: Conf No 1-5.
-- W. C.  Printed cards for current books.  P L 2: 8-9, 49-
131.
-- W. C.  Printed periodical cards.  L J 23: Conf No 176-7.
-- W. C.  Relation of author to subject cards.  U S Rept 842,
847-9. 1892-93.
-- W. C.  Report for entry of societies, etc.  U S Rept 845.
1892-93.
-- W. C.  Report of the Publishing board.  L J 31: Conf No
154-9.
-- W. C.  Report of the Publishing section.  L J 22: Conf
No 84-6; L J 23: Conf No 46-52; L J 24: Conf No 95-9; L J
25: Conf No 86-90; L J 26: Conf No 127.
-- W. C.  Report on adjustments and organization.  L J 25:
Conf No 80-2.
-- W. C.  Report on aids and guides.  L J 14: 256-9.
-- W. C.  Report on catalogues and aids.  L J 12: 414-22.
-- W. C.  Report on classification.  L J 10: 257-62, Dis-
cussion 316-7.
-- W. C.  Rules for entry of the German A. O. U.  U S Rept
846. 1892-93.
-- W. C.  Rules for transliteration.  U S Rept 847. 1892-93.
-- W. C.  Suggestions on the use of the college library.
P L 5: 341.
-- W. C.  Treatment of books according to the amount of
their use.  L J 28: Conf No 9-16, Discussion 170-2.
-- W. C.  Use of printed cards in the Harvard college li-
brary.  Am  Lib Annual 1915-16: 24-5.
-- W. C.  Widener memorial library.  L J 40: 485-6: P L 20:
427.
-- W. C. and C. A. Cutter.  Schwartz's classification and
notation.  L J 11: 8-9.
-- W. C. and Tillinghast, W. H.  Justin Winsor, librarian
and historian, 1831-1897.  L J 23: 7-14.
Lane, W. J.  A nomenclature of classification.  L J 10: 257-8.
Lane, W. L.  A central bureau of information and lending col-
lection for university libraries.  A L A Bull 3: 380-4.
Lang, A.  "Aucassin and Nicolette."  L (ns) 4: 22-7.
Lange, F. W. T.  Card system of registration  of borrowers.  L
W 10: 272-3.

--- F. W. T.   Extra facilities to students.  L W 11: 482-3.
--- F. W. T.   Fines and a fine chart.  L W 11: 31-2.
--- F. W. T.   Notes on war literature.  L W 19: 284-5, 322-3.
--- F. W. T.   Pamphlets and their value in regard to the
history of the war.  L W 20: 87-90, 120-4.
--- F. W. T.   Shelf classification and shelf marking.  L W
11: 76-7.
--- F. W. T.   Some notes on the literature of the war.  L
W 20: 256-9, 290-3.
--- F. W. T., trans.  War libraries: their proper constitu-
tion and extent.  L W 20: 9-12.
--- F. W. T. and Berry, W. T.  Books on the Great War: sup-
plement.  L W 17: 263-6, 332-4, 367-9; 18: 17-20, 45-8, 139-
44, 173-6.
--- F. W. T. and Venner, B. M.  Standard books on the war.
Libn 9: 59-62, 79-82, 93-8.
Lange, H. O.  Danish research libraries.  L J 29: Conf No 67-
70.
Langton, H. H.  Canada and public libraries.  L J 28: Conf No
43-6.
----- H. H.  Co-operation in a catalogue of periodical pub-
lications.  2d Int Conf 122-5, Discussion 242-3.
----- H. H.  System of shelf notation.  L J 21: 441-3.
----- H. H.  What a permanant library commission can do to
aid libraries.  P L 9: 213-6.
Langton, J. F.  Duplicate pay collections of popular novels.
L J 28: Conf No 41-2.
Langworthy, C. F.  State and municipal documents as sources of
information for institution managers and other students of
home economics.  Journal of Home Economics Feb 1912.
Lanigan, E.  The child and the library.  Atlantic 87: 122-5.
Lapham, J. A.  The imperialist.  Americana 5: 187-93.
Lapp, J. A.  American libraries.  VII.  The special library.
Wis Lib Bull 12: 284-9.
-- J. A.  Committee report on co-operation between legisla-
tive reference departments.  A L A Bull 8: 309-16.
-- J. A.  Current references.  Special Libraries 1: 38-40.
-- J. A.  The growth of a big idea.  Special Libraries 9:
157-9.
-- J. A.  How to organize a municipal reference bureau.
American City Sept 1914: 206-10; Special Libraries 5: 129-
30.
-- J. A.  Legislative reference department.  Public Offi-
cials Magazine July 1910.
-- J. A.  The library and vocational education.  Lib Occ 4:
174-5.
-- J. A.  Organized information in the use of business.
Special Libraries 6: 57-61; Am Lib Annual 1916-17: 27-8.
-- J. A.  Picket lines of progress.  Special Libraries 10:
64-5.

-- J. A. The Public affairs information service. Special Libraries 5: 86-8.

-- J. A. Public documents of Indiana. Lib Occ 2: 108-11, 130-3.

-- J. A. Special libraries. Lib Occ 2: 173-4.

-- J. A. and J. B. Kaiser. Law, legislative reference libraries: reviews. American Political Science Review 9: 170-2.

-- J. A. and Mote, C. H. Making the library serve the worker. Special Libraries 7: 8-11.

Lapp, J. G. Agricultural libraries as special libraries. A L A Bull 10: 405; L J 41: 595-6.

Larned, Richardson, Lane, and Coe. Close classification. L J 11: 352-3.

Larned, J. N. Advice on the reading of history. N Y L 1: 177-8.

---- J. N. Arrangement of maps. L J 17: Conf No 44-5.

---- J. N. Classification of philosophy. L J 10: 80-2.

---- J. N. Education of a reading public. L J 32: 147-53.

---- J. N. Experiment in university extension. L J 13: 75-6.

---- J. N. How we choose and buy new books. L J 14: 339.

---- J. N. Improper books: methods employed to discover and exclude them. L J 20: Conf No 35.

---- J. N. Library of "best books." L J 14: 127.

---- J. N. Literature of American history. Reviewed in L J 27: 784-6.

---- J. N. A nomenclature of classification. L J 9: 62-9.

---- J. N. On Sunday opening. L J 12: 230; L J 13: 135.

---- J. N. Organization of co-operative work among public libraries. 2d Int Conf 120-1, Discussion 242-3. 1897.

---- J. N. Plans for numbering. L J 4: 40.

---- J. N. Presidential address, Lake Placid conference. L J 19: Conf No 1-4.

---- J. N. Public libraries and public education. L J 9: 6-12.

---- J. N. Report on classification. L J 7: 125-30, Discussion 195-6.

---- J. N. Report on library architecture. L J 12: 377-95, Discussion 442-5.

---- J. N. Retrospect and prospect in the last years of the century. L J 21: Conf No 5-12.

---- J. N. Selection of books for a public library. L J 20: 270-2.

---- J. N. Some new devices. L J 11: 294-6.

---- J. N. What we do with pamphlets. L J 14: 433.

---- J. N. Yearly report on classification. L J 7: 129.

Larned, J. W. The school and the library. Wis Lib Bull 5: 61-2.

Lasby, J. B.   Literary magazines for librarians.  Minn P L C
    N 5: 42-3.
Laskey, J. H.   Catalog system of the Washington public libra-
    ry.  A L A Bull 8: 212-3.
Lathrop, H. B.   English translations of "Don Quixote."  Wis Lib
    Bull 2: 5-8.
    ----- H. B.   Some rogueries of Robert Wyer.  L (3d series)
    5: 349-64.
Lathrop, H. L.   Value of libraries to club women.  Texas Li-
    braries 1, Nos 10-11: 114-7.
Lathrop, O. C.   State publications.  Mich Lib Bull 7: 158-61.
Lathrop, R. M.   Poster bulletins at the May fete of the Wis-
    consin library school.  Wis Lib Bull 14: 149-54.
Latimer, C. W.   Girls' reading.  N Y L 2: 135-6.
Latimer, L. P.   Public library books for the children of Cath-
    olic schools.  Catholic Educ Rev Jan 1918: 45-9; L J 43: 59.
    ----- L. P.   School work of the Public library of the Dis-
    trict of Columbia.  L J 42: 715-8.
Lauder, E. L.   Change.  L J 42: 29-30.
Laurence, I.   Cultural value of books for children.  Minn P
    L C N 2: 77-80.
    ------ I.   How shall children be taught to love good books?
    Nat Educ Assn 1899: 1148-55; P L 11: 179-83.
    ----- I.   Service of folk-lore in education.  A L A Bull
    2: 381-2.
Laurie, C. F.   Museum in a small library.  P L 8: 154-5.
Laurson, E.   The busy librarian and the porter.  S Dakota Lib
    Bull 5: 134-7.
Lavell, R. A.   Reading of the librarian.  Minn P L C N 2, No
    4: 64-7.
Law, H. E.   Public library as a business proposition.  L J 30:
    405-8.
Law, T. G.   A co-operative catalogue of English literature up
    to 1640.  L 5: 97-101.
Law, W.   Applying for another post.  L W 12: 210-2.
    - W.   Committee work.  L A 11: 65-73; L A R 16: 88; L W 12:
    127-9.
    - W.   Influence of the public library.  L A 8: 208-11, 227-
    9.
    - W.   Issue of lantern slides.  L W 15: 136-8.
    - W.   Wild flower exhibition in libraries.  L W 16: 66-7.
Law, W. R.   The library as a municipal institution.  Ia L C
    Q 8: 115-8.
Lawrence, G. E.   How libraries can help the schools.  New Hamp
    Bull (ns) 6: 233-4.
Lawrence, H. M.   The added cubit.  Wis Lib Bull 12: 292-4.
    ------ H. M.   Adventures in contentment.  Wis Lib Bull 6:
    127-8.
Lawrence, I.   Cultural value of books for children.  Minn P L
    C N 2, No 4: 77-80.
Lawrence, I.   Cultural value of books for children.  Minn P
    L C N 2, No 4: 77-80.

Lawrence, P. M.  Public libraries in South Africa.  L 9: 1-16.
Lawton, D. G.  The library's responsibility towards national
    music.  A L A Bull 14: 180-2, 332.
Layard, G. S.  Pooling of private libraries.  L (ns) 1: 245-54.
Lea, E.  British workman in fiction.  L (ns) 8: 360-9.
Learned, J. C.  Library work from the trustee's standpoint.  L
    J 15: Conf No 23-4.
Learned, M. D.  Lessons of the German archives.  Am Hist Assn
    Rept 1909: 351-4.
Learned, W.  Line of exclusion.  L J 21: 320-3.
Lease, E. S.  Economy and timeliness in book-buying.  Vt L Bull
    8, No 2: 3-4.
--- E. S.  Instruction in the use of books.  Vt L Bull 13:
    11.
--- E. S.  What's what.  Vt L Bull 13: 10-1.
Leash, S. G.  Essentials of a library trustee.  L J 29: 524-7.
Leatherman, M. W.  The state as a unit for library extension.
    A L A Bull 11: 230-2, 360.
Leavitt, B.  How to get and how to use a historical library
    in schools.  L J 29: 180-1.
Leavitt, T. W. H.  Traveling libraries in Ontario.  L J 33:
    231-2.
Le Crone, S. E.  Library house-keeping.  Minn P L C N 9: 33-4.
Ledbetter, E. E.  Simple methods.  N Y L 1: 13-5.
Ledbetter, F.  The school library.  North Carolina Education
    6: 4-5.
Lee, C. H.  A model letter.  Wis Lib Bull 7: 53-4.
Lee, E.  French literature during the war.  L (3d series) 8:
    36-52, 136-44, 271-82, 339-54.
  - E.  Ideals in modern French literature.  L (3d series) 6:
    25-37, 115-32, 276-92, 346-64.
  - E.  Ideals in modern French literature: Andre Gide.  L (3d
    series) 7: 239-40; Charles Peguy.  L (3d series) 7: 53-65;
    Henri de Regnier.  L (3d series) 7: 304-17; Remy de Gourmont.
    L (3d series) 163-75.
  - E.  Recent foreign literature.  L (3d series) 1: 96, 152,
    260, 384; 2: 49, 150, 277, 422; 3: 90, 181, 322, 375; 4:
    72, 186, 324, 417; 5: 80, 155, 266, 400.  L(ns) 4: 85, 320,
    430; 5: 35, 210, 305, 359; 6: 45, 156, 288, 412; 7: 78, 209,
    287, 411; 8: 177, 239, 393; 9: 80, 186, 267, 369, 10: 62,
    134, 288, 371.
  - E.  Some recent French books.  L (3rd series) 9: 58-72,
    132-49, 200-14, 255-67; 10: 45-56, 73-85, 168-78, 248-55.
Lee, E. D.  A library of highway engineering.  Special Libra-
    ries 5: 106-7.
Lee, E. F.  The Greensboro public library.  N C Lib Bull 3:
    52-3.
Lee, G. M.  State aid to libraries.  L J 21: Conf No 68-71.
Lee, G. S.  This admirable plant to let.  Living Age 274: 522-
    31.

Lee, G. W.   Apportionment of specialties.  L J 40: 783-90.
- G. W.   Boston Co-operative information bureau.  L J 36:
644-5; Special Libraries 3: 5, 19; 5: 92-4.
- G. W.   Community catalog as an example of library co-or-
dination.  Special Libraries 10: 146.
- G. W.   (1) Conservation of thought: the difficulty of the
obvious. (2) The intangible "they" and what to do about it.
Stone & Webster Journal Dec 1917 & May 1918.
- G. W.   A few data toward a list of available directories
and other resources for addresses.  Boston Co-operative In-
formation Bureau Bulletin June-Oct 1912.
- G. W.   Hints on sponsors for knowledge.  A L A Bull 11: 25-
6; L J 42: 116.
- G. W.   Inter-library references.  P L 21: 12.
- G. W.   Inter-library worker and the exhibit of new books.
L J 38: 408-9.
- G. W.   The library and its facilities.  Public Service
Journal July 1911, No 9: 41-8.
- G. W.   Library and the business man.  A L A Bull 1: Conf
No 169.
- G. W.   Library developments and the information docket.
Stone & Websters Public Service Journal Jan 1914.
- G. W.   The library phalanx: a presidential address at a
phantom conference.  L J 44: 277-81.
- G. W.   The library system of Stone and Webster.  Engineer-
ing Record, Aug. 24, 1907: Special Libraries 1: 44-7.
- G. W.   Oneness in library work.  Special Libraries 9: 95.
- G. W.   Plea for a reference book commission.  L J 38: 615-
6.
- G. W.   A private business library and information bureau
(Library of Stone & Webster, Boston).  L J 29: 591.
- G. W.   Proposed revision of Dewey classification for eng-
ineering libraries.  Special Libraries 9: 52.
- G. W.   Public utilities references.  Special Libraries 1:
36-8.
- G. W.   Reference books as public utilities: some well-
known encyclopedias compared.  L J 37: 587-93.
- G. W.   Reference books as public utilities.  II.  Some well-
known dictionaries compared.  L J 39: 178-87; New Hamp Bull 10,
13-21.
- G. W.   Reference books as public utilities: III.  Some small-
er dictionaries compared.  L J 40: 387-92.
- G. W.   Special library service.  L J 38: 561.
- G. W.   The specialized library of yesterday, to-day, and
to-morrow.  Special Libraries 5: 54.
- G. W.   Sponsors for knowledge.  L J 40: 783; A L A Bull
10: 25-6, 83-5; Stone and Webster Public Service Journal
July, 1914: 47-53.
- G. W.   Sponsors for knowledge.  II.  Outline for a nation-
wide information service.  L J 39: 886-90.

- G. W.  Standardization by a library unit system.  Stone
& Webster's Journal, June 1916: L J 41: 705; Am Lib Annual
1916-17: 17-8.
- G. W.  Stone and Webster library, Boston.  L J 42: 278-9.
- G. W.  Suggestions for the A. L. A.  Convention.  P L 13:
305-6.
- G. W.  Using the technical journal.  Special Libraries 5:
131.
Lee, M.  Book selection and book buying.  P L 13: 24-5.
Lee, S.  Beginning of French translation from the English, read
before the society under the title "An episode of Anglo-
French bibliography."  Bib Soc Trans 8: 85-112.
- S.  Books in relation to national efficiency.  L A 4: 55-
65.
- S.  National biography and national bibliography.  2d Int
Conf 55-62.  1897.
- S.  Notes and additions to the census of copies of the
Shakespeare first folio.  L (ns) 7: 113-39.
- S.  Some bibliographical problems connected with the
Elizabethan drama.  Bib Soc Trans 4: 148-50.
- S.  Some undescribed copies of the first folio Shakespeare.
Bib Soc Trans 5: 166-74.
Leeland, C. G.  Work with schools in the Buffalo library.  L
J 24: 150-1.
Leeper, A.  Bradshaw, Henry, 1831-1886.  L A of Austral. Proc.
1901: lx-lxv.
---- A.  Qualifications for librarianship.  L J 24: 482-3.
Leeper, D.  Aspects of the public library movement in Russia.
L A 13: 21-6.
Leeper, R. M.  Rural libraries in Texas.  Texas Libraries 1,
No 5: 8-9.
---- R. M.  School libraries in Texas.  Texas Libraries 1,
No 5: 5-8.
Leete, J. H.  Children's work at the Carnegie library of Pitts-
burgh.  L J 45: 936-7.
--- J. H.  Dollars and ideals.  Wis Lib Bull 16: 163-70.
--- J. H.  Reaching all classes of the community.  A L A
Bull 13: 111-7, 353; P L 24: 292-4, 349-51.
Le Fevre, H.  How to make geography interesting.  Ia L C Bull
7: 251-2.
Leffmann, H.  On library management.  P L 14: 36-7.
------ H.  Some suggestions for improvement in library man-
agement.  L J 33: 519-20.
Le Gallienne, R.  Books I loved and lost.  Bookman (N Y) 50:
3-10, 129-35.
Legg, J. W.  An agreement in 1536 between certain booksellers
of Rome and Venice to bring out the second text of the re-
formed breviary of Cardinal Quignon with introduction, list
of editions, and bibliographical notes.  Bib Soc Trans 13:
325-48.

---- J. W.  Bibliography of the Thoughts of Marcus Aurelius Antonius.  Bib Soc Trans 10: 15-81.

Legler, H. C.  Chicago's reading and lecture course.  Wis Lib Bull 11: 323-4.

---- H. C.  Adequate appropriations for libraries and how to secure them.  Wis Lib Bull 5: 81-2.

Legler, H. E.  Advertising problems of a large city library. P L 22: 280-1.

---- H. E.  Advocates annual appropriation for library advertising.  Printers Ink Sept 20, 1917: 114, 116-7; L J 42: 920.

---- H. E.  Boys' best books.  Ia L C Q 7: 170.

---- H. E.  Certain phases of library extension.  A L A Bull 1: Conf No 96-101; L J 32: 303-7.

---- H. E.  The Chicago public library and co-operation with schools.  Educ Bi-Monthly 4: 309-20; Ia L C Q 6: 94-6.

---- H. E.  Civics room of the Chicago public library.  Bull Bib 9: 113-4.

---- H. E.  Dear and dumpy twelves: or, the librarian's shelf of books.  A L A Bull 2: 148-50.

---- H. E.  Educational by-products in library work.  Nat Educ Assn 1912: 1241-6.

---- H. E.  Extension work in Chicago.  Minn P L C N 4: 29-30.

---- H. E.  How the public library can help in developing effective high school libraries.  A L A Bull 10: 213-5.

---- H. E.  Library bulletins: state and public.  A L A Bull 3: 329-36; P L 14: 316.

---- H. E.  Library work with children.  A L A Bull 5: 240-9; 10: 205-8; Discussion 411-21; P L 21: 345-8; Ia L C Q 6: 94-6.

---- H. E.  Municipal reference work of the Chicago public library.  P L 19: 64-5.

---- H. E.  Mystery of the twenty-fifth book.  Wis Lib Bull 11: 341-5.

---- H. E.  Next steps.  L J 40: 777-83.

---- H. E.  Outline of the work of the Wisconsin library commission.  L J 33: 513.

---- H. E.  Phases of library extension.  A L A Bull 1: Conf No 96-101; L J 32: 303-7.

---- H. E.  Should there be a pension law?  A L A Bull 8: 250-2, Discussion 252-3.

---- H. E.  Social significance of the modern library movement.  Wis Lib Bull 7: 117.

---- H. E.  Talks about books.  P L 13: 258-60.

---- H. E.  Types of stories for boys.  Ia L C Q 6: 107.

---- H. E.  What more can the A. L. A. Publishing board do? A L A Bull 11: 94.

---- H. E.  What state library commissions are and what they are doing.  L J 30: Conf No 40-5, Discussion 154-8.

---- H. E.  The world of print and the world's work.  A L
A Bull 7: 73-82; L J 38: 435-42; N Y L 3: 301-7.

Leibbrandt, H. C. V.  Education and libraries of the Cape of
Good Hope.  2nd International Conference Proceedings 179-
93.

Leighton, F. H.  Ink for marking white letters.  P L 10: 223.

------ F. H.  Preparing new books and restoring old.  P L
10: 223-4.

Leipziger, H. M.  Lectures and classes.  L J 23: Conf No 145-
6.

Leland, C. G.  Class-room libraries in New York.  New York
State Teachers' Assn Proceedings 1910: 302-4; L J 36: 178-9;
P L 16: 160-1.

---- C. G.  How New York guides its children through good
reading.  Harper's Weekly Dec 26, 1908, 52: 12.

---- C. G.  The library hour.  School Library Bulletin,
New York City Nov 1912.

---- C. G.  The mission of the class library.  Nat Educ Assn
1903: 953-6.

Leland, W. G.  American archival problems.  Am Hist Assn Rept
1909: 342-8.

---- W. G.  Archive depot.  A L A Bull 10: 517-9.

---- W. G.  Librarians and history.  A L A Bull 11: 325-6.

---- W. G.  National archives: a programme.  Am Hist Assn
Rev 18: 1-28.

Lemcke, E.  The librarian and the bookseller.  L J 22: Conf
No 12-6.

---- E.  The librarian and the importer.  L J 22: Conf No
12-16; P L 2: 443-6, 487-9.

Lemon, C. H.  Linotype in catalogue printing.  L W 2: 28.

Leonard, G. F.  Reading list on the history of the 17th century.
N Y S L Rept 80.  Bibliography No 5.  1897.

Leonard, O.  Branch libraries as social centers.  Survey 25:
1038-9; L J 36: 299-300.

Lescohier, D.  Selected list on Americanization.  Wis Lib Bull
15: 237.

Lescohier, D. D.  The library in Americanization.  Wis Lib Bull
16: 3-6.

------- D. D.  What is Americanization?  With select bibliography.  P L 24: 378.

Leslie, F. J.  Presidential address at Liverpool.  L A R 14:
485-96.

---- F. J.  Public library's part in the life of a modern
city: The value of bibliographies.  Presidential address.
L. A. U. K.  L A R 14: 491-3; L J 37: 679-80.

Lester, C. B.  The A. L. A.  Books for everybody fund.  Wis
Lib Bull 16: 51-2.

---- C. B.  Legislative reference.  Indiana Lib Bull No 17:
1-2.

---- C. B. Legislative reference libraries. Special Libraries 11: 81-2.
---- C. B. Legislative reference work and the law library. Law Library Journal 1: 45-50.
---- C. B. Library legislation of 1918. L J 44: 17.
---- C. B. Present status of legislative reference work. A L A Bull 7: 199-202.
---- C. B. Recent state publications of interest to libraries. N Y L 3: 186-8; 247-8; 312-4; 4: 15-6.
---- C. B. Wisconsin librarians salaries: facts and figures. Wis Lib Bull 16: 177-9.
---- C. B. and W. R. Eastman. Library legislation of 1910. L J 36: 66-7.
Letts, T. Maps, from the romantic and prosaic standpoint. L J 25: 5-7.
--- T. Maps: handling, classifying, cataloging. Eighth international geographic congress, 1904. American Geographical Society Bulletin August 1905.
--- T. Notes on the care of maps. L J 26: 688-9.
--- T. Notes on the cataloging of maps. L J 27: 74-6.
Leupp, H. L. Moving the University of California library. L J 36: 458-60.
--- H. L. University of California library. L J 37: 259-62.
Lever, A. Cinematograph and chronophone as educators in public libraries. Libn 3: 195-200.
--- A. Symposium on public libraries after the war. L A R 19: 159-61.
Levetus, A. S. The art of the book in Austria. "Studio" spring number. 1914: 203-19.
Lewin, P. E. Ancient and modern writing materials: a chapter in bibliography. L A 3: 189-92, 210-3.
--- P. E. The Empire and the public library: the relations between the libraries of the Empire. L A 6: 280-98; Discussion: 299-301.
--- P. E. Enquiry department in the public library. L A R 5: 3-5.
--- P. E. Farringdon road book-stalls. il. L W 5: 88-92.
--- P. E. Fiction nuisance and its abatement: a suggestion. L W 5: 320-2.
--- P. E. Gesner and Savigny. L A R 4: 401-9.
--- P. E. Libraries and education. L A 7: 163.
--- P. E. Libraries and the custody of public records. L A R 2: 288-9.
--- P. E. Records and research work in their relation to municipal public libraries. L A 4: 95-103.
--- P. E. Short list of books of use to the student of public and local records, local history and genealogy. L A 4: 87-90.

--- P. E.  Some anticipated developments of Library practice.  L W 5: 16-8.

--- P. E.  Some systems of classification.  L A 3: 141-6.

--- P. E.  Titles of honour in catalogues.  L A 3: 69-72.

Lewis, A. A.  Exhibits at county fairs.  Minn P L C N 4: 216-
7.

--- A. A.  Library as a social center.  Minn P L C N 3: 151-
2.

--- A. A.  Library lessons for teacher training department,
High School.  Minn P L C N 6: 139-40.

--- A. A.  Relation of book selection to reference work.
Minn P L C N 3: 205-7.

--- A. A.  War economy in libraries.  Minn P L C N 5: 149-
50.

Lewis, C. M.  Methods of teaching English literature.  School
Review 11: 187-9.

Lewis, E. F.  An experiment in self-government.  P L 12: 304-
5.

Lewis, F. G.  Library of the American Baptist historical society.  L J 40: 486.

Lewis, G. L.  Teaching children how to use the library.  Mass
Lib Club Bull 4: 110-1; P L 20: 122-3.

Lewis, J.  President's address at the Norwich conference.  L
A R 22: 320-5.

Lewis, J. C.  Preservation of leather bindings.  Special Libraries 4: 116-7.

Lewis, O. F.  The library as a factor in the education of the
prisoner.  N Y L 3: 227-30.

Lewis, P. E.  Libraries and museums.  L A 3: 285-6.

Lewis, S. S.  Library of the Corpus Christi college.  L 3: 121-
5.

Lewis, S. V.  Our place in the sun and other platitudes.  Pacific Northwest Library Assn Proceedings 1920: 45-9, 53-7.

Lewis, St. E.  Value of the specialized library for the business man, the salesman, or the shop expert.  Special Libraries 4: 69-72.

Lewis, W. P.  College students and the library.  P L 25: 289-
90.

--- W. P.  History of libraries.  Texas Libraries 2: 16-
9, Oct. 1916.

--- W. P.  How one university library solved its bindery
problems.  L J 44: 320-1.

--- W. P.  The library and the community.  Texas Libraries 1 Nos 10-11: 123-4: Mich Lib Bull 7: 145-6.

--- W. P.  The library bindery: pro and con.  Texas Libraries 1, Nos 10-11: 105-7.

--- W. P.  Library growth and extension.  New Hamp Lib Bull
(ns) 16: 22-3.

Leypoldt, A. H.  Practical bibliography: notes on the making
of printed book lists.  L J 31: 303-7.
Lichtenstein, J.  Essentials and non-essentials in library
work.  L J 30: 399-403.
---------- J.  History of the California library associa-
tion.  Cal News Notes 1: 72-4.
---------- J.  Library conditions in California.  P L 10:
280-2.
Lichtenstein, W.  Book-buying experiences in Europe.  L J 38:
77-81.
---------- W.  A book-buying trip to South America.  L J
40: 717-8.
---------- W.  Possible results of the European war.  A L
A Bull 10: 200-2, 422; L J 41: 382-4.
---------- W.  The question of a graduate library school.
L J 43: 233-5.
Liebmann, E. L.  Accident prevention data as found in the li-
brary of the National workmen's compensation service bureau.
Special Libraries 10: 220-1.
------ E. L.  Industrial accidents and the library's part
in their reduction.  Special Libraries 10: 176-9.
------ E. L.  Library of the National workmen's compensa-
tion service bureau.  Special Libraries 10: 197-8.
Light, F. D.  Interesting the working man.  N Y L 2: 260-1.
Lighthall, W. D.  Canadian poets and poetry.  L J 25: Conf No
25-6.
Lillie, R.  Recent activities.  L A R 15: 291.
Lillie, W.  Merits of the classified and dictionary catalogues.
L W 17: 97-102.
Limbrick, C. H.  Best books of 1904--Philosophy and religion.
L A R 7: 494-501.
Lincoln, C. H.  Material in the Library of Congress for the
study of United States naval history.  Bib Soc Amer Proc
1: 84-95.
Lincoln, D. F.  Ventilation of libraries.  L J 4: 254-7, Dis-
cussion 292.
Lincoln, H. B.  Children's literature: the mother's point of
view.  Outlook 58: 1075-6.
Lindemann, A. S.  Free lecture system and libraries.  Wis Lib
Bull 2: 63.
Linderfelt, K. A.  Charging system.  L J 7: 178-82, Discus-
sion 205-6.
-------- K. A.  Classification of education.  L J 16: 329-
30.
-------- K. A.  Eclectic card catalog.  L J 14: 248-50.
-------- K. A.  Eclectic card catalog rules--author and
title entries based on Dziatzko's instruction; reviewed in
L J 16: 148-9.
-------- K. A.  Fifty of the best English novels.  L J 15:
67.

-------- K. A.  Historical novels of Alexandre Dumas arranged in chronological order.  L J 15: 270.

-------- K. A.  Report on catalogues and classification. L J 15: Conf No 67-73.

Linderman, E. C.  Study outline for bird clubs.  Mich Lib Bull 7: 150-2.

Lindholm, M. F.  Handling a large circulation in an office library.  Special Libraries 6: 61-3.

------ M. F.  A review of chief sources of material for special libraries.  Special Libraries 4: 139-46.

------ M. F.  Useful sociological books for debating clubs. P L 12: 354-6.

Lindley, H.  Report on the archives of Indiana.  Am Hist Assn Rept 1910: 315-30.

Lindsay, A. B.  The follow-up system of the Bureau of railway economics.  Special Libraries 9: 165-8; L J 44: 194.

Lindsay, Lord.  Dewey's classification scheme.  L J 4: 149-52.

----- Lord.  Proposed modification of the Amherst classification in methematics, astronomy and physics.  L J 4: 149-52.

Lindsay, M. B.  Commission government as affecting libraries in Illinois.  P L 19: 68-70.

----- M. B.  Music rolls for player-pianos in Evanston, Ill., Library.  Musician 19: 448.

----- M. B.  Some general principles of book selection.  P L 10: 267-71.

Lindsay, M. H.  Changing from a subscription library to a free library.  L J 24: Conf No 73-6.

Lindsay, V.  The library and moving pictures: Photo-plays.  P L 21: 455.

Linn, J. W.  What the university expects of high school students in English.  School Review 19: 96-102.

Linton, E. M.  A library view in a technical school.  P L 23: 70-1.

Lister, J. W.  Library oversight.  L W 9: 102-4.

Little, A. D.  Chemistry and the special library: a foreword. Special Libraries 10: 85-6.

---- A. D.  The special library for industrial workers. Special Libraries 4: 189.

Little, E. L.  List of references on the textile industry. Special Libraries 8: 174-6, 179; 9: 24-5.

Little, G. T.  Charging system for small libraries (A. L. A. paper).  L J 11: 212-3.

---- G. T.  Helping inquiers.  L J 20: Conf No 19-20.

---- G. T.  Instruction in the use of books in colleges. L J 23: Conf No 92.

---- G. T.  Library and the small college.  L J 24: 50-3.

---- G. T.  Library building for a small college.  L J 28: 290-2.

---- G. T.  School and college libraries.  U S Bur of Educ
Rept 1892-93: 916-33.

---- G. T.  Some problems in book numbers.  A L A Bull 5:
251-3.

---- G. T.  Special training for college librarians.  L J
23: Conf No 79.

---- G. T.  Teaching bibliography to college students.  L
J 17: 83-8.

---- G. T.  What should be done for an old library with a
limited income.  L J 10: 245-6.

---- G. T.  What the smaller libraries in Maine can do for
the larger ones.  Maine Lib Bull 5, No 2: 15-6.

Little, H.  Making of a great newspaper.  P L 11: 569-70.

Littman, E.  Special collections in American libraries: The
Garrett collection of Arabic manuscripts at Princeton university library.  L J 29: 238-43.

Liveright, A. F.  How may the use of books and library catalogues be made a subject of study in normal schools.  L J
34: 160-2.

Lloyd, A. C. G.  The birth of printing in South Africa.  L
(3d series) 5: 31-43.

Lloyd, A. S. G.  The library that Joab started.  L J 43: 320-
3.

Lloyd, J. and B. L. Dyer.  Women librarians in England.  L A 1:
219-22.

Lloyd-Jones, R.  The true librarian.  Wis Lib Bull 9: 85-6.

Lloyd-Jones, T.  What the public library can do for the high
school.  Wis Lib Bull 8: 29.

Locke, G. H.  Benches instead of chairs.  P L 19: 111.

--- G. H.  Canada in the D. C.  L J 37: 86.

--- G. H.  Canadian libraries and the war.  Canadian Magazine 52: 588-91; L W 21: 88-9; A L A Bull 12: 78-81, 282;
Lib Occ 5: 112-3.

--- G. H.  Canadian libraries in wartime.  P L 23: 357-60;
N Y L 6: 93-6.

--- G. H.  Duty of the hour.  P L 22: 227-8.

--- G. H.  How a public librarian hears of books and orders
books.  Ontario Lib Assn Proceedings April 1912: 121-5.

--- G. H.  Library work in Canada.  L A R 12: 561-2.

--- G. H.  A new library law for Ontario.  L A R 22: 270.

--- G. H.  Salaries of librarians in the Public library of
Toronto, Canada.  L A R 22: 271.

Lockhart, J. C.  Traveling library and the school.  N C Bull
2: 119.

Lockner, L. P.  The International peace movement.  Wis Lib
Bull 8: 57-66.

Lockwood, G. H.  "Joining the Club."  P L 20: 125-6.

------ G. H.  Some experiences in work with children.  Mass
Lib Club Bull 5: 8-10.

------ G. H.  Taking books to boys.  L J 40: 421-2.

Lodge, H. C.  The meaning of a great library.  Harvard Graduates Magazine 24: Sept 1915.

Loehl, G. E.  Reading to get results at the State training school.  Minn P L C N 4: 68-70.

Logan, H.  Duplication of books in the high school.  P L 25: 69-71.

Logasa, H.  Adapting the library to the school.  P L 24: 41-3.

---- H.  Duplication of books in the high school library. P L 25: 69-71.

---- H.  Some phases of library study room management. School Review 24: 352-8.

---- H.  Story of an "Ivanhoe" exhibit.  English Journal 6: 175-9.

---- H.  Study helps for students of the University high school, Chicago.  L J 40: 450.

Lomax, B.  On the classification of history.  L A Trans 3: 67-8, Discussion 127-8.

London, H. M.  Legislative reference library, Raleigh, N. C. N C Bull 4: 114-6.

Long, A. B.  New Standards: the librarian.  Wilson Bulletin 1: 509-10.

-- A. B.  State school library laws: a digest.  Wilson Bulletin 1: 505-13.

Long, Mrs. F. A.  County libraries: paper read at Nebraska library association meeting, Geneva, Nebraska, 1914.

Long, H. C.  Certification of librarians.  Wis.Lib Bull 16: 93-7.

-- H. C.  The county as a unit for library extension.  A L A Bull 11: 232-4; L J 42: 656.

Loomis, C. B.  A resurrected juvenile.  Bookbuyer 21: 201-4.

Loomis, C. C.  Library problem and the trustees' responsibility.  Ia L C Q 7: 49-52.

Loomis, M. B.  Medical libraries of Chicago.  L J 41: 331-2; P L 21: 184-5.

Loomis, M. M.  Libraries that pay; efficient business houses are systematically bringing managers and mill-hands into touch with classified information.  Special Libraries 5: 133; Independent 74: 1436-8.

Lord, I. E.  College library versus university library.  L J 25: Conf No 45-9.

-- I. E.  Fixing a purpose.  A L A Bull 2: 165-7.

-- I. E.  Library machinery.  P L 8: 227-33.

-- I. E.  On the purpose of library meetings.  L J 28: 764-5.

-- I. E.  Open shelves and public morals.  L J 26: 65-70.

-- I. E.  Open shelves and the loss of books--favours open access.  A L A Bull 2: 231-49, Discussion 253-4; P L 13: 241-3.

-- I. E.  A reply to Mr. Green.  L J 26: 138; Ia L C Q 1: 37-41.

-- I. E.  Some notes on the principles and practice of book-buying for libraries.  L J 32: 3-11, 56-64.

-- I. E.  Use and value of fiction in education.  L J 28: Conf No 28-31.

Lord, J. S.  The gift extremely rare.  L J 27: Conf No 34-7.

Lorenz, A.  Library extension at Clarinda.  Ia L C Q 6: 194-9.

Loring, K. P.  The King's English and the librarian.  P L 24: 111-3.

Loshe, L. D.  Early American fiction.  P L 14: 63-4.

Lounsbury, T. R.  Yale college library.  Yale Literary Magazine 51: 219-27.

Love, C. S.  Campaigning for books in a southern college town.  L J 43: 335-6.

Love, E. F. J.  Library facilities of scientific investigation in Melbourne.  2nd International Conference Proceedings 204, 1897.

Love, G. S.  Educational value of literature.  Education 32: 141-6.

Loveday, T.  Edgar Allen library of the University of Sheffield L A R 11: 567-71.

Lovell, J.  Functions and operations of the free library system.  L A Trans 6: 58-66.

Low, F. B.  The reading of the modern girl.  Nineteenth Century 1906: 278-87.

Low, J. A.  Personal contact through the catalogue.  L J 34: 265.

Lowe, J. A.  The library district as a unit for library extension.  A L A Bull 11: 234-5, 360; L J 42: 656.

-- J. A.  Permanent book marking.  L J 35: 15-6.

-- J. A.  Reading list on Willian Clyde Fitch.  Bull Bib 7: 30-1.

-- J. A.  Relation of public and college libraries.  L J 38: 394-9.

-- J. A.  Rural library building.  Architectural Record 46: 451-6.

-- J. A.  Small-town library building.  House Beautiful 47: 9-11.

-- J. A.  The use of cards for binding memoranda.  L J 37: 83-4.

-- J. A.  What can the League of library commissions do for its members?--Publications.  A L A Bull 13: 291-2.

Lowe, M.  Children's work in a small library.  P L 5: 382-4.

-- M.  Evolution applied to children's reading.  Education 19: 486-94.

Lowe, O.  The development of a taste for literature in children.  The Child (London) Dec 1915: 133-6.

Lowell, A.  Modern poetry, its difference, its aims, its ac-
complishments.  Mass L C Bull 9, No 4: 8-11.
Lowell, J. R.  Books and the public library.  L J 11: 10-4.
Lowes, F. E.  A classification problem and its solution.
Penn Lib Notes 6, No 4: 75-7.
Lowrey, C. E.  Library directions.  L J 17: 87.
---- C. E.  University library: its larger recognition in
higher education.  L J 19: 264-7.
Lowrie, S. G.  Function of the legislative reference bureau.
L J 39: 273-9.
Lowy, A.  On censorship and Jewish literature.  Bib Soc Trans
2: 8-11.
Luard, L. D.  Use of public documents in a small library.  L
J 38: 402-3.
Lubbock, Sir J.  Inaugural address.  2nd Int Conf 1-4.
Lucas, Councillor.  On the delegation of powers to Library
committee.  L A R 6: 388-93.
Lucas, S.  Traveling libraries in Pennsylvania.  P L 2: 49.
Luce, R.  The clipping bureau and the library.  Special Li-
braries 4: 152-7.
Lugg, C. H.  What the teacher may expect from the library.
South Dakota Lib Bull 3: 31-2.
Lull, H. G.  Problem method of instruction and its probable
correlation in library service and administration.  Nat
Educ Assn 1917: 562-72; L J 42: 685.
Lundstedt, B.  Swedish libraries.  P L 9: 382-4.
Lunt, H. G.  Financial side of library work: division of funds.
Colorado Library Association, Occasional Leaflet 1: 152-4.
Lupton, A. W.  Social activities of the library.  L J 39: 441-
3.
Luther, J. W.  Assistants for a small library.  Wis Lib Bull
10: 218-21; New Hamp Bull 10: 49-52.
---- J. W.  Filing government pamphlets.  Wis Lib Bull 10:
155-6.
Lutz, C. S.  A library tour.  English Journal 4: 531-3.
Lydenberg, H. M.  The classification of war books in the New
York public library.  L J 44: 514-5.
------- H. M.  Collection of war material: New York public
library.  A L A Bull 13: 390-1.
------- H. M.  Historical manuscripts and prints in the
New York public library and the method of cataloging them.
L J 24: 249-52.
------- H. M.  The Latin-Americana collection in New York
public library.  L J 44: 223-4.
------- H. M.  Moving the New York public library.  L J 36:
296-7.
------- H. M.  Present discontents with newsprint stock.
A L A Bull 12: 211-6; 303; L J 43: 912; P L 23: 365-6.
------- H. M.  Preservation of modern newspaper files.  L
J 40: 240-2.

------- H. M.  Reference work in the New York public library branches.  A L A Bull 3: 366-68.

------- H. M.  Right arrangement of war material.  P L 25: 507-8.

------- H. M.  Staff meetings: their organization, methods and results.  L J 32: 549-51.

Lyell, J. P. R.  Early English books: a review of E. Gordon Duff's "Fifteenth century English books."  L W 20: 176-7.

--- J. P. R.  An early Italian press--the first printers at Cagli.  L W 21: 32-6.

--- J. P. R.  A famous bull.  L W 20: 144-8.

--- J. P. R.  John Rylands library.  L W 19: 312-4.

--- J. P. R.  Notes on rare books.  L W 21: 60-3.

Lyell, J. R. L.  A fifteenth century bibliography.  L W 20: 284-7.

Lyman, A.  Reading list on Scotland.  Bulletin No 112, Bibliography No 42, N Y S L Rept 90, 1907.

Lyman, E.  "Arabian Nights."  Ia L C Q 6: 141-4.

--- E.  The child and the library.  Michigan Board of Library Commissioners Report 1907:  125-9.

--- E.  Children's room at Scoville institute library.  P L 4: 9-10.

--- E.  Editions of the classics for children.  Ia L C Q 6: 129-30.

--- E.  Principle of work with children.  P L 13: 125-6.

--- E.  Purpose and results of telling stories to children. Michigan State Teacher's Assn Proceedings 1909: 262-4.

--- E.  Selecting books for children.  Ia L C Q 5: 208-9.

--- E.  Story hour.  Wis Lib Bull 1: 4-6.

Lymburn, J.  Plan of suspended iron presses as a general system of book accommodation in large libraries.  L 4: 241-2; L J 18: 10.

Lynn, A.  The case against public documents.  N Y L 4: 172-4.

Lyons, J. F.  Theological libraries of Chicago.  L J 41: 332; P L 21: 185.

Lyster, T. W.  Best books of 1903--History.  L A R 6: 598-603.

---- T. W.  Best books of 1904--History.  L A R 8: 309-17.

---- T. W.  Bibliography of the writings of John Kells Ingram, with a brief chronology.  An Leab 3: 5-46.

---- T. W.  Brief list of some of the more important historical publications of 1902.  L A R 6: 139-47.

---- T. W.  Dead books in libraries.  L A R 13: 411-2.

---- T. W.  English and American cooperation for an index to general literature: Discussion.  L A R 15: 648-52.

---- T. W.  Examination system of the Dublin public libraries committee.  An Leab 2: 123-32.

---- T. W.  Idea of a great public library: an essay in the philosophy of libraries.  L A R 5: 161-74.

---- T. W.  An index to periodicals wanted.  L A R 16: 39-47.

---- T. W.  Ireland and public libraries.  An Leab 1: 15-24; L A R 8: 303-8.

---- T. W.  A letter re subject index to periodicals.  L A R 17: 223.

---- T. W.  Modern public library: its characteristics and work.  L A R 3: 26-8.

---- T. W.  Notes on shelf classification by the Dewey system.  L 9: 329-39.

---- T. W.  Observations of shelf classification.  L A R 2: 399-409.

---- T. W.  Review of Brown's Subject classification.  L A R 8: 384-6.

---- T. W.  Shelf classification by the Dewey system.  L 9: 329-39.

---- T. W.  Some observations on the Dewey notation classification as applied to the arrangement of books on shelves.  L 8: 482-90.

Lytle, M.  U. S. government documents in small libraries.  Pacific Northwest Library Assn Proceedings 1914: 57-64.

M---.  Women as state librarians.  L J 12: 195.

M. E. G.  The confessions of a school librarian.  L J 42: 687.

M. S. S.  Library school training: an after-thought.  P L 14: 291.

Mabie, H. W.  French circulating library.  Outlook 96: 316-20.

Mac, E. A.  Card cataloguing.  L J 12: 184.

- E. A.  Co-operation versus competition.  L J 10: 55.

- E. A.  On book sizes.  L J 10: 318-20.

- E. A.  Reference book making.  L J 10: 176.

- E. A.  A select bibliography.  L J 9: 136.

- E. A.  Shakespeariana.  L J 10: 179.

McAfee, G.  Home visiting.  Lib Occ July 1917: 201-2; L J 42: 839.

---- G.  What the school and library did for a bookless neighborhood.  Lib Occ 5: 123-4.

McAlister, J. Y. W.  Circulation of reference books.  L A R 16: 90-1.

------- J. Y. W.  Collection of books for the camps' library.  L W 18: 222-3.

------- J. Y. W.  Dawn of a new epoch.  L 6: 212-3.

------- J. Y. W.  Durability of modern book papers.  L 10: 295-304.

------- J. Y. W.  European war: significance to librarians: Presidential address.  L A R 17: 405-8.

------- J. Y. W.  Is the library rate limited?  L A R 20: 24-6.

------- J. Y. W.  Letter to subscribers and contributors to the "Library."  L (ns) 3: 440.

------- J. Y. W.  New ways of keeping down the issue of fiction.  L 6: 236-7.

------- J. Y. W.  Notes on binding, and a suggestion.  L A Trans 5: 187-9.

------- J. Y. W.  The Osler medical library.  L (3d s) 10: 139-56.

------- J. Y. W.  Partingtonian sociology: a review of Mr. O'Brien's article on "Free Libraries."  L 3: 103-8.

------- J. Y. W.  Plea for a closer connection between public libraries and other educational institutions.  L 6: 207-10.

------- J. Y. W.  Presidential address to the L. A. U. K. 1915.  L A R 17: 405-8; 19: 426-30.

------- J. Y. W.  Progress of the public library movement in London.  P L 9: 401-3.

------- J. Y. W.  Some tendencies of modern librarianship. 2nd Int Conf 9-12.

------- J. Y. W.  A startling discovery.  L A 14: 146-7.

------- J. Y. W.  Wanted, a librarian.  L C 5: 11-6.

------- J. Y. W. and W. G. Savage.  Investigation into the risk of contracting infectious diseases by the use of public library books.  L A R 2: 550-1.

McAndrew, W.  The high school librarian.  Nat Educ Assn 1910: 994-1002; N Y L 2: 163-6.

------ W.  One might laugh a little in the English class. Educational Bi-Monthly 3: 56-61.

------ W.  One remedy for education.  World's Work (N Y) 25: 72-9; Literary Digest 45: 789.

McAneny, G.  Municipal reference library as an aid in city administration.  A L A Bull 7: 219-24: L J 38: 509-13.

McArthus, D. N.  Dominion archives.  Am Hist Assn Rept 1911, 1: 343-52.

McCabe, L. R.  Luxuriant art in leather: work of Marguerite Duprez Lahey.  International Studio 63: Sup 45-8, Dec 1917.

McCarnes, M. F.  An effective library course in a normal school.  Penn Lib Notes 5, No 4: 41-4.

McCarthy, A. J.  Concerning county libraries.  Wis Lib Bull 14: 178.

------ A. J.  Forms for the small library.  A L A Bull 13: 400.

------ A. J.  How European travel interprets library work. Wis Lib Bull 6: 29-32.

------ A. J.  Library as a place of business.  P L 17: 173-4.

------ A. J.  Opportunity talks in a library.  Wis Lib Bull 11: 110-1.

------ A. J.  Preparing magazines for the bindery.  Wis Lib Bull 8: 198-200.

McCarthy, C.  City library as a business investment.  A L A Bull 2: 190-6.

------ C.  Federal legislative reference department.  Survey May 18, 1912, 28: 298.

------ C. How our city secured an increased appropriation. Wis Lib Bull 6: 122.

------ C. Preparation of bibliographic data for the American political science association. A L A Bull 1: 214-6.

McCartney, G. B. Cataloging economies: how Rochester economizes. A L A Bull 12: 247-8, 300.

McCartney, L. Library and the school as co-ordinate forces in education. Nat Educ Assn 1901: 864-7.

McCaughey, V. The one hundred most important books and files relating to the Hawaiian Islands. Bull Bib 10: 71-3.

Macualay, C. T. Literary associations of Bath. L A R 3: 70-9.

McCauley, P. Advertising a public library. L J 42: 294-5.

------ P. Library advertising: the public library. Texas Libraries 1, Nos 10-11: 110-4.

------ P. Library week conducted by the Public library, Waco, Texas. P L 22: 145-7.

McClellan, E. H. Work with technical literature. P L 15: 269-72.

McClelland, E. H. Books for industrial workers. L J 44: 761-2, 779-87.

-------- E. H. Indianapolis business branch. Special Libraries 11: 187-90.

-------- E. H. Notes on recent technical literature. Penn Lib Notes 6, No 4: 14-21.

-------- E. H. Poultry raising. Wis Lib Bull 15: 101.

-------- E. H. The public library in the service of the chemist. Special Libraries 10: 86-92.

McClelland, M. Administration of a high school branch of a public library. New Jersey Lib Bull 1: 6-8.

-------- M. Facts in fiction. L J 41: 169-73.

-------- M. Work of a high school branch. A L A Bull 7: 295-6.

McClenon, W. H. The science of indexing. L J 43: 467-71.

McClure, D. E. The Hesperia plan. Educational Foundation 16: 284-5.

McCollough, E. Vocational education and the public library. Special Libraries 8: 52-3; April 1917; L J 42: 842-3.

McCollough, E. F. Children and the library. Wis Lib Bull 7: 134.

-------- E. F. Directions for the care of cork carpets. Lib Occ 4: 58.

-------- E. F. Financial responsibility of the librarian. Wis Lib Bull 6: 120-1; 8: 153-5.

-------- E. F. Library smoking room. P L 11: 259; Ind L C Bull No 11: 2.

-------- E. F. Pamphlets and clippings. A L A Bull 14: 160-1, 332-3.

-------- E. F. Practice versus theory: a reply to Mr. Dickinson. P L 15: 186-7.

-------- E. F.  Reaching the reading public.  Wis Lib Bull
4: 88-9.

McCollough, E. F. M.  Book selection.  Wis Lib Bull 7: 41-2.

-------- E. F. M.  General principles of book selection.
Wis Lib Bull 7: 142.

McCollough, R.  Child labor.  Wis Lib Bull 14: 15.

McColvin, L. R.  Ralation between the library and the school.
L W 22: 360-2.

McConkey, B. W.  Literature in the primary grades.  Journal
of Pedagogy 17: 225-30.

McConn, C. M.  High school students' rankings of English classics.  English Journal 1: 257-72.

McCorkle, C. E.  Teaching of current events.  Pedagogical
Seminary 22: 413-23.

McCormack, H. S.  Duplicating processes.  Libn 4: 43-5, 159-
61.

McCormick, A. M.  Municipal reference work in a public library.
P L 20: 204-8.

McCormick. B. M.  Love stories for children.  P L 22: 55-6.

McCoy, L.  Books of myth and legend: why boys and girls should
read them.  Ia L C Q 6: 28-9.

McCoy, L. N.  Use of the library in teaching English.  Maryland State Teachers' Assn Proceedings, 1909: 126-8.

McCracken, E.  What children like to read.  Outlook 78: 827-
32.

McCrady, L. L.  The child and imaginative life.  Atlantic 100:
480-8.

Macray, W. D.  Singular recovery of missing leaves (Cranmer's
Bible in the Bodleian).  B Q R July 1915: 172.

McCroben, G.  How to train a taste for literature.  Educational Foundations 22: 527-37.

McCrory, H. L.  Discussion on children's work in small libraries.  L J 25: Conf No 130-1.

----- H. L.  Library work for children.  P L 6: 93-5.

----- H. L.  School and library: a practical paper on methods.  P L 5: 9-11.

McCulloch, C. C.  A check list of medical incunabula in the
Surgeon general's library, Washington, D. C.  Annals of
Medical History 1, No 3: 1918.

McCulloch, C. C., Jr.  Library of the Surgeon general's office,
United States War department.  Special Libraries 9: 39.

McCullough, A. W.  Children and poetry.  Outlook 58: 227-8.

McCullough, M. R.  An author's opinion of the library.  Wis
Lib Bull 4: 43-7.

McCunn, F.  Fairy tale "morals."  Sunday Magazine 28: 289.

---- F.  A plea for precocious children.  Littell's Living
Age 213: 544-8.

McCurdy, D. D.  Methods to be used by libraries working with
schools to encourage the use of real literature.  A L A Bull
1: 289-93.

McDermott, F. A.  Plea for the use of references and accuracy therein.  Science (ns) 33: 852-3.

McDermott, W. F.  Model newspaper library: The Indianapolis News efficient system of indexing.  Fourth Estate, Feb 6, 1915: 6; Feb 13: 17; Feb 27: 19.

MacDonald, A. A.  Advantageous use of public documents in a small library.  L J 35: 503-5.

------- A. A.  A plea for public libraries.  N C Bull 1: 128-31.

------- A. A.  St. Aignan.  A. L. A. war service.  A L A Bull 13: 320-2.

------- A. A.  Work of a traveling librarian.  P L 22: 219-22.

McDonald, E. B.  What the city librarian can do for country readers.  Wis Lib Bull 9: 45-8.

MacDonald, G.  Fairy tale in education.  Contemporary 103: 491-9; Living Age 277: 783-90.

Macdonald, H.  Some literary associations of Salisbury.  B A R 10: I-VIII.

------- H.  A vicar's library.  L (3rd series) 3: 277-82.

MacDonald, H. L.  Books and plays in pictures.  Moving Picture World July 17, 1915; L J 40: 620.

McDonald, K. I.  A. L. A.  Booklist.  A L A Bull 2: 197-9.

------ K. I.  Choice of books in traveling libraries.  Wis Lib Bull 2: 39-43.

------ K. I.  Magazines for the small library.  Wis Lib Bull 4: 1-9.

Macdonald, R. M.  Catalog system of the Bureau of fisheries.  A L A Bull 8: 211-2.

MacDonald, W.  Some bibliographical desiderata in American history.  American Antiquarian Society Proceedings 1911: 266-76.

McDonnell, E. P.  Cataloguing in a small library.  Wash L A Bull 2, No 1: 2-5.

McDonnell, R.  The story of Marsh's library.  Irish Book Lover Jan 1915: 91-3.

MacDowell, L. I.  A public school library system.  Educational Review 34: 374.

McEwen, E. J.  A phase of literature work in the high school.  Education 10: 606-14.

McFadden, P. W.  Literature in the elementary schools.  Texas State Teachers' Assn Proceedings 1898: 142-6.

McFarland, H. H.  Libraries of the American seaman's friend society.  U S Govt Rept: 276-8, 1876.

McFarland, J. H.  University training for printers.  Printing Art 15: 181-5.

Macfarlane, J.  Antoine Verard.  Bib Soc Trans 4: 11-35; additions and corrections 4: 241-2; Bibliographical Society Illustrated Monograph No VII, 1899.

-------- J.  Confiscated libraries of the French Revolution.
L 8: 102-4.
-------- J.  National libraries of Great Britain and France
and their catalogues.  L 10: 37-41.
-------- J.  Pamphlets, and pamphlets duty of 1712.  L (ns)
1: 298-304.
-------- J.  Paper duties of 1696-1713; their effect on the
printing and allied trades.  L (ns) 1: 31-44.
-------- J.  Philadelphia commercial museum.  L J 30: 412-
3; 42: 278.
-------- J.  Philadelphia commercial museum and the pre-
sent commercial crisis.  Special Libraries 5: 146-7.
-------- J.  Projected printed catalogue of the Bibliothe-
que nationale.  L 7: 49-50.
Macfarlane, J. J.  Bibliography of commerce.  Bib Soc Amer
Proc 1: 207-12.
Macfie, R. A.  Copyright in its relation to the supply of books
to libraries.  L A Trans 3: 107-13.
McGill, W.  Co-ordination of the various departments of an open
access library.  L W 10: 246-8.
---- W.  Dust in libraries.  L W 12: 204-7.
---- W.  A form of work sheet.  L W 13: 204-8.
---- W.  Leighton library at Dunblane and its founder.  L
W 14: 1-7.
---- W.  Library statistics necessary and unnecessary and
the purpose of statistics.  L A 8: 84-92.
---- W.  List of books published in reinforced, or in spec-
ial library bindings.  L W 14: 277-86, 311-7; L W 15: 231-
3.
---- W.  Thoughts on literature for children.  L W 22: 411-3.
---- W. and W. J. Phillips.  Terms and phrases used in li-
brary work.  L W 10: 354-60, 391-400, 429-40, 458-67.
McGirr, A. T.  Reading list on John Galsworthy.  Bull Bib 7:
113-5.
---- A. T.  Reading list on William Butler Yeats.  Bull Bib
7: 82-3.
MacGloskey, F.  Illustrative material for Dickens' "Tale of two
cities."  Wilson Bull 1: 483-4.
McGrachy, A. A.  Book and bonfires.  N C Bull 3: 43-6.
McGraw.  How to develop interest in the library.  P L 4: 27-30.
MacGregor, F. H.  Importance of the study of civics.  Wis Lib
Bull 5: 93-5.
------- F. H.  The municipal reference bureau of Wisconsin.
American City 2: 65-8.
Macgregor, J. C.  Famous Parisian book-binders.  Bibliophile
4: 9-12.
McIlvaine, C.  Museums in their relation to libraries.  P L
10: 6-7.
-------- C.  Special collections in small libraries.  P L
10: 271-3.

McIlwaine, B.  Irish literature.  Penn Lib Notes 6, No 4: 8-14.

McIlwaine, H. R.  Report of public archives committee.  A L A
Bull 10: 516-7.

------- H. R.  Substance of the laws in reference to the
Confederate states government publications.  Bib Soc Amer
Proc 3: 85-91.

McIntosh, M.  Fiction selection.  P L 19: 389-92; New Hamp
Bull 11: 73-6; Vt L Bull 11: 2-5.

McIntrye, E. R.  The farmer and the library.  Wis Lib Bull 11:
277-8.

McIntyre, R. B.  Cost of New York city libraries.  L J 32: 438-
9.

Mackail, J. W.  Life of William Morris (a review).  L (ns) 1:
112.

Mackay, H. W. R.  Suggested card book catalog.  L J 19: 160,
191, 196-7.

McKee, A.  Business methods in library work.  Neb Lib Bull No
4: 14-6.

McKee, Mrs. J. S.  The library from the trustee's point of
view.  Pacific Northwest Library Assn Proceedings 1913: 59-
63.

McKee, S.  American circulating library of Manila.  A L A Bull
2: 254-7.

--- S.  American library in Manila.  P L 10: 472-3.

--- S.  Library work: its opportunities and developments
in the Philippines.  L J 33: 438-40.

McKee, T. H.  Classes and printing of U. S. documents.  L J
10: 241-4.

McKennie, A. and L. P. Ayres.  Inadequate salaries of school
librarians.  L J 41: 752-4.

Mackenzie, D.  The public school and the public library.  P
L 2: 423-6.

Mackenzie, G.  Reference issues.  L W 11: 159-60.

Mackenzie, M.  Impressions of American libraries.  L W 15: 23-
6.

McKerrow, R. B.  Did Sir Roger Williams write the Marprelate
tracts?  L (3d series) 3: 364-74.

------ R. B.  Note on variations in certain copies of the
"Returne of Pasquill."  L (ns) 4: 384-91.

------ R. B.  Notes on bibliographic evidence for literary
students and editors of English works of the 16th and 17th
centuries.  Bib Soc Trans 12: 212-318.

------ R. B.  Some notes on the letters i, j, u and v in
sixteenth century printing.  L (3d series) 1: 239-59.

------ R. B.  The supposed calling in of Drayton's "Harmony
of the church," 1591.  L (3d series) 1: 348-50.

McKetrick, M.  The adaptation of the work in English to the
actual needs and interests of pupils.  English Journal 2:
405-16.

McKibben, J. A.   The Chamber's system in getting information
for its committees at work.   Special Libraries 5: 56-8.

McKillop, J.   On the present position of London municipal libraries, with suggestions for increasing their efficiency.
L A R 8: 624-33, Discussion 495-7.

------ J.   Public libraries in rural districts.   L A R 15:
639-44.

------ J.   The rural library problem.   L A R 16: 48-56.

------ J. and I. Taylor.   Best books of 1904--Sociology.
L A R 7: 640-57.

Mackinder, H. J.   Ideal librarian and his training.   L A R 10:
198-204.

Mackintosh, R. S.   Gardening for Minnesota.   Minn P L C N 5:
151-2.

McKirdy, J.   Bill drafting.   Special Libraries 3: 177-82.

McKnight, E.   Libraries and recreation.   L A R 7: 72-6.

------ E.   On Brunet's scheme of classification.   L A R 6:
416-21.

------ E.   Provincial view.   L A R 10: 636-7.

------ E.   Public libraries and higher education: Oxford
university extension conference.   L A R 5: 411-6.

------ E.   Public libraries and university extension.   L
A R 5: 270-5.

------ E.   Smoke-rooms.   L A R 3: 125-7.

------ E.   Weak points of library administration: absence
of exact classification.   L A R 8: 289-95, Discussion 344-
8.

------ E.   Workpeople and public libraries.   L A R 12: 79.

------ E. and E. A. Savage.   How the Branch associations
may help the Library association.   L A R 9: 109-19, Discussion 143-54.

McLachlan, H.   Value of the catalog to the new assistant.   Minn
P L C N 3: 187-8.

Maclauchlin, J.   How the free library system may be extended
to counties.   L A Trans 3: 58-66.

McLaughlin, E. T.   Developing library taste in students.   Educational Review 5: 17-26.

McLean, R. B.   What the school expects from the library.   Minn
P L C N 4: 55.

Maclehose, R.   Net books: Why it is not practicable to make a
reduction in their price to libraries.   L (ns) 5: 52-8.

McLellan, J. A.   Ethical elements in literature and how to make
the most of it in teaching.   Nat Educ Assn 1894: 71-84.

McLenegan, C. E.   From fiction to facts.   Wis Lib Bull 8: 202-
3.

------- C. E.   The Milwaukee county library system.   Wis
Lib Bull 15: 197-202.

------- C. E.   The open door, through the book and the library: opportunity for comparison and choice; unhampered

freedom of choice.  A L A Bull 6: 127-32; L J 37: 429-33.
------- C. E.  A public service library.  N Y L 3: 166-70.
------- C. E.  Salaries.  Am Lib Annual 1914-15: 213-4.
McLennan, W.  Coloured guide blocks.  L J 3: 192.
McLeod, H.  Relation of the library to the school from a teach-
    er's point of view.  Vt L Bull 8, No 3: 4-5.
McLeod, J.  An employee's library: its scope and its possibi-
    lities.  House library of Sears, Roebuck and company, Chi-
    cago.  A L A Bull 6: 250-4; L J 37: 597-600.
Macleod, R. D.  The Foulis press.  L (3d series) 1: 172-89.
    ----- R. D.  Personal element in public library work.  L A
    5: 3-5.
    ----- R. D.  Preservation of books in libraries.  L W 11:
    256-61, 331-5, 368-71, 417-22.
    ----- R. D.  Reviewing from a bookman's standpoint.  L W
    15: 353-5.
McMahan, J.  Amateur wireless club, Indianapolis public library.
    Lib Occ 3: 25-6.
McMahon, E.  Reference library in history.  Wash L A Bull 2,
    No 2: 15-6.
MacMahon, J. H.  Catholic literature for libraries.  L J 24:
    255-6.
    ------ J. H.  "Yellow journalism" and newspaper reading.
    L J 23: Conf No 146-7.
McManis, R.  Exhibit of the Library school at The Wisconsin
    University exposition.  Wis Lib Bull 11: 152-3.
McMaster, V.  Children's books for reference use.  Pacific
    Northwest Library Assn Proceedings 1916: 14-6.
McMerrow, R. B.  The red printing in the 1611 Bible.  L (3d
    series) 2: 323-7.
Macmillan, M.  Relation of librarian and assistant.  L J 28:
    717-8.
    ------- M.  Some causes of ill-health among library workers.
    P L 8: 412-4.
McMurry, C. A.  Relation of the school to libraries.  Nat Educ
    Assn 1899: 472; U S Bur of Educ Rept 1899-1900: 678-9.
McMurry, O. L.  Bookbinding should be taught in schools.  Educ
    ation Bi-Monthly 5: 24-5.
Macnair, M. W.  Library of Congress list of subject headings.
    A L A Bull 6: 231-4.
McNamara, J. P.  The starvation of Irish libraries.  L A R 22:
    98-102.
MacNamara, T. J.  One hundred best books.  L A 5: 17-20.
    ------- T. J.  Relation of the public library to Public
    education.  L A 5: 15-23; L A R 7: 620-3.
McNamee, J. H. H.  Binding for libraries.  L J 19: 172-3.
McNamee, W.  Book collectors of the Victorian era.  Libn 5:
    64-6, 71-4, 98-101, 129-31, 161-5.
McNaught, Mrs. M.  Appreciation of pictures.  Calif Blue Bull
    3: 20-1.

------ Mrs. M.  County free library service to elementary
schools.  Cal Blue Bull 2: 21, Sept 1916.

------ Mrs. M.  Facts concerning county free library service.  Calif Blue Bull 3: 15-6.

------ Mrs. M.  The "Incensio" tree.  Calif Blue Bull 2:
21-2.

------ Mrs. M.  Old and new in school libraries.  Calif
Blue Bull 2: 9-11, June 1916.

------ Mrs. M.  Progress in school library service.  Calif
Blue Bull 1: 21-2, Dec 1915.

McNeil, A. H.  What the normal school may do to provide library
work in schools.  P L 6: 80-1.

McNiece, J. S.  Labor saving in the lending department.  A L
A Bull 13: 175-6, 400.

McPherson, Mrs. G. B.  County extension.  Minn P L C N 1, No
5: 7-9; Library Work 1912: 136; Cal News Notes 3: 130.

Macpherson, M. K.  Conversation room, or a study alcove.  Wis
Lib Bull 3: 85.

McPike, E. F.  Bibliographic exchange.  L J 30: 18, 857-8.

---- E. F.  Intercommunication: national and international.
Special Libraries 5: 95-6.

---- E. F.  Intercommunication of useful information.  Illinois Central Mag Sept 1917: 81-4; Am Lib Annual 1917-18:
50-1.

---- E. F.  Inter-communication on the democratization of
knowledge: a plan for direct interchange of useful information.  Central Magazine Sept 1917: 81-4; L J 42: 1000.

---- E. F.  On the publication of special bibliographies.
P L 10: 140.

---- E. F.  Plans for an American federation for intercommunication.  L J 39: 329; P L 19: 113-4.

---- E. F.  Research and intercommunication.  Dial 53: 40-1.

---- E. F.  Serial bibliography of bibliographies.  P L 10:
123-5.

---- E. F.  Specialists and special collections.  Central
Magazine July 1917: 27-30; L J 42: 1002.

McPike, J. M.  The foreign child at a St. Louis branch.  L J
40: 851-5.

McQuilken, A. H.  Making printed matter easier to read.  Dial
47: 11.

Macray, W. D.  Mr. Coxe's work at the Bodleian.  L A Trans 4:
13-6; L J 39: 803-4.

McRea, E. M.  Influence of 8,000 school libraries in Indiana.
Harper's Weekly Jan 23, 1906, 53: 16-7.

McSurely, E. G.  Opportunities in library work.  Delineator
77: 521.

Macurdy, T.  Methods of book buying.  L J 31: 14-5.

McVety, M. A.  Co-operation between a public library and museum.
The Museum (Newark) May 1917 pp 31-3; Am Lib Annual 1917-18:
63-4.

Madan, F.  Bodleian binding: a reply to criticisms on the policy of the library as to binding.  Oxford Magazine 19 Feb
   1915: 207-8.
--- F.  Bodleian trash: a defence of the library's policy
   in collecting books of apparently little value.  Oxford
   Magazine 5 Mch 1915: 238-40.
--- F.  Bodleian in 1914: criticism of financial and gen-
   eral policy; by our Bodleian Critic.  Oxford Magazine
   30 April 1915: 271-2.
--- F.  Chart of Oxford printing, 1468-1900.  Bibliographi-
   cal Society Publications, No XII, 1904.
--- F.  Degressive bibliography.  Bib Soc Trans 9: 53-65.
--- F.  The duplicity of duplicates and a new extension of
   bibliography.  Bib Soc Trans 12: 15-24.
--- F.  List of Thomas Rawlinson's sale catalogues in the
   Bodleian library.  Bib Soc Trans 5: 85-6.
--- F.  Loan of reference books.  L J 6: 226.
--- F.  On method in bibliography.  Bib Soc Trans 1: 91-
   102, Discussion 103-6.
--- F.  Oxford press during the Civil war.  Bib Soc Trans
   9: 107-10.
--- F.  A quantitative survey of the Bodleian library.  L
   J 41: 808-10; reprinted from the B Q R Vol 1.
--- F.  Some curiosities of the Oxford press.  L 1: 154-60.
--- F.  Some experiences of a bibliographer: Presidential
   address delivered before the Bibliographical society.  L
   (4th series) 1: 129-40.
--- F.  Some notes on the Oxford press with references to
   the fluctuations in its issues.  Bib Soc Trans 6: 1-3.
--- F.  Statistical survey of the Bodleian library, with
   notes on book standards.  B Q R 1: 254-62, 297.
--- F.  A supposed Shakespeare autograph.  L (3d series)
   9: 97-105.
--- F.  Two lost causes, and what may be said of them.  L
   (3d series) 9: 89-105.
--- F.  What to aim at in local bibliography.  L C 4: 144-
   8.
Madeley, C.  Classification of office papers: with a scheme
   for museum and library work.  L A R 6: 367-87.
----- C.  "Demy" book scale.  L A Trans 1: 82-4.
----- C.  L. M. D.: The story of a club.  L A R 22: 221-8.
----- C.  Report on public library reports.  L 3: 398-9.
Maddison, A. R.  Lincoln cathedral library.  L 4: 306-12.
Maddison, F. R.  Dean Honeywood's library.  L A R 4: 390-3.
Maddox, H. A.  Fine book printing.  Printing Art 17: 293-300.
---- H. A.  Selection of paper.  Printing Art 18: 173-7.
Madison, E.  The teacher-librarian.  School and Society 11:
   469.
Madison, E. S.  A high school course in library use.  English
   Journal 5: 196-207.

----- E. S.  Some problems of school library administration.
L J 41: 642-5.

Maffett, R. S.  Irish provincial printing.  Irish Book Lover
Oct 1915: 45.

Magill, H. N. W.  Rural library in practice.  L J 43: 84-6.

Magnusson, E.  On the system of classifying books.  1st Int
Conf 165-7. 1877.

------- E.  Spiral library buildings.  L J 11: 331-9, Discussion, 359-63.

Maguire, J. H.  Plea for the preservation of newspapers.  An
Leab 1: 109-18.

Mahanna, C. G.  Filing and indexing of engineering data.  Machinery 17: 544.

Maher, M.  Relation of libraries to public schools from the
teacher's standpoint.  Cal News Notes 2: 93-4.

Maire, A.  A French classification and notation.  L J 22: 253.

--- A.  Moving large libraries.  L J 23: 538.

Malcolm, C. A.  Library of a Forfarshirelaird in 1710.  L (3rd
series) 2: 212-6.

Male, E.  The Provincial assistant and the L. A. A.  L A 8:
204-6.

-- E.  Staff exchange.  L A 9: 211-5, Discussion 240.

Malmesbury, Earl of.  Education and libraries.  Library Miscellany (Baroda) 2: 75-82.

-- ----- Earl of.  Presidential address to L. A. U. K. at
Bournemouth, 1913.  L A R 15: 493-501, 628-9.

Malone, E. M.  Some problems of cataloging in a college library.  N C Bull 2: 112-5.

Malone, M.  Library employees union of New York.  A L A Bull
13: 379-81.

Maltby, A. B.  Immigrants as contributors to library progress.
A L A Bull 7: 150-4.

---- A. B.  Library work with children.  Outlook 82: 360.

---- A. B.  Some recent books of merit for children's room
and school libraries.  N Y L 3: 189-90.

Maltern, J.  Union list of periodicals.  L J 37: 605-6.

Manager, W.  Can leather be preserved?  L J 45: 229.

Manchester, E.  Relation of the library to the boy scout and
camp fire movement.  L J 39: 752-60.

Mander, G.  The identity of Elisha Coles.  L (3d series) 10:
34-44.

Manier, C.  Libraries in the Indian schools.  P L 21: 123.

Mann, A. C.  Organization of a branch library by students of
the Illinois state library school.  P L 8: 68-9.

Mann, A. H.  An interesting department of library work.  Ia L
C Q 6: 91-3.

Mann, B. P.  Bibliography in general and especially the bibliography of science.  L J 11: 245.

-- B. P.  Cataloguing anonymous works by known authors.
L J 10: 213, 327.

-- B. P.  Dui-Decimal classification.  L J 11: 139-41.

-- B. P.  Library fines.  L J 5: 320.

-- B. P.  Standard covers for temporary binding.  L J 8:
6-7.

-- B. P.  U S Department of Agriculture library.  L J 12:
80.

-- B. P.  Zoological subjects partly classified by the Dewey system.  L J 5: 143-4.

Mann, C. R.  Histories and bibliographies of physics.  Bib Soc
Chic Yr-Bk 1901-2: 31-40.

Mann, E. P.  Care of pamphlets.  L J 10: 399-400; 11: 245.

Mann, F. J.  Eye-strain and retardation in school life.  School
and Society 3: 33-6.

Mann, M.  Analyticals for experiment bulletins.  P L 8: 151.

-- M.  Cataloging system at the Carnegie library of Pittsburgh.  L J 38: 23-4.

-- M.  Cataloguing.  P L 2: 298-9.

-- M.  Checking duplicate copies on shelf-list cards.  L
J 37: 142-3.

-- M.  Technique versus science: a suggested remedy.  L J
44: 683.

-- M.  What can be done over the loan desk to help readers
in the selection of good books.  Ia L C Q 1: 2-5.

Mann, P. B.  Library fines.  L J 4: 441-2.

Mann, R. P.  Bibliography in general and especially in science.
L J 11: 245-50.

Manney, B. M.  Stereographic views in school.  Vt L Bull 6,
No 1: 6.

Manning, W. M.  Mexican foreign office archives.  Bulletin
Pan Am Union 37: 657-61.

Manny, F. A.  Place of the library in educational work.  P L
3: 42-4.

Mansbridge, A.  Co-ordination of educational effort from the
point of view of public libraries.  L A 7: 141-6; Discussion 148-52.

Many, M. C.  Esthetic appreciation of literature in secondary
education.  School Review 15: 731-43.

Mar, H. F.  The standardizing of library reports.  Penn Lib
Notes Oct 1911: 1-11.

Marble, A. P.  Study of English in the public schools.· Nat
Educ Assn 1894: 279-93.

Marche, O. de la.  Le Chevalier Delibere.  The illustrations
of the edition of Schiedam, reproduced with a preface by
F. Lippmann, and a reprint of the text.  Bibliographical
Society Publication, 1898.

Marcosson, J. I.  Remarkable system of Carnegie in giving of
    libraries.  Minn. P L C N 3: 2-3.
Marion, G. E.  Interpreting the library movement.  Special Li-
    braries 10: 154-7; L J 44: 495-8.
    ---- G. E.  Library as an adjunct to industrial laborator-
    ies.  L J 35: 400-4.
    ---- G. E.  Resume of the Special libraries association,
    1910-1915.  Special Libraries 6: 143-6.
    ---- G. E.  The Special libraries association.  L J 45: 295-
    304.
    ---- G. E. and D. N. Handy.  The business library.  Spec-
    ial Libraries 5: 133; System 26: 96-9.
    ---- G. E. and D. N. Handy.  Responsibility districts.  Spec-
    ial Libraries 3: 194-6.
Marks, L. B.  Cautions with regard to illumination of libra-
    ries.  L J 34: 106-7.
    --- L. B.  Illuminating of public libraries.  L A R 10: 551.
    --- L. B.  Illumination in the New York public library.  L
    J 34: 16-7.
    --- L. B.  Library lighting.  A L A Bull 3: 5-6.
Marple, A.  Reference use of public documents.  Lib Work 2:
    107-10.
Marquand, F. E.  Reading list on Debussy and Puccini.  Bull
    Bib 6: 206.
    ------ F. E.  Reading list on Richard Strauss.  Bull Bib 6:
    238-40.
Marquis, J. C.  Free literature on farming.  Wis Lib Bull 7:
    16-9.
Marron, J. F.  The Legislative reference bureau as a bill re-
    vising agency.  Special Libraries 7: 44-6.
Mars, H. F.  How to keep up the summer circulation.  Penn Lib
    Notes 1: 5-8.
Marsden, H.  Decay of leather bindings.  P L 11: 312-3.
Marsh, C. O.  Close contact of library with the community.
    Wis Lib Bull 9: 48-50.
Marsh, H. A.  New aspect of child study.  Pedagogical Seminary
    5: 136-45.
Marsh, L.  School library exhibit at the Los Angeles Liberty
    fair.  Wilson Bulletin 1: 315-6.
Marshall, J.  Attempt at an improved system of press and shelf
    notation.  L A Trans 3: 77-86, 168.
Marshall, J. J. and Reid, B.  Donaghadu printing.  Irish Book
    Lover Oct 1915: 46.
Martel, C.  The cataloger in his own defence.  L J 40: 33-5.
    ---- C.  Classification: a brief conspectus of present-day
    library practice.  L J 36: 410-6.

---- C. Classification: present tendencies. L J 29: Conf No 132-4.

---- C. Common nouns in German: why they need not be capitalized. L J 30: 333-7.

---- C. Contributions to the literature of cataloguing. L J 25: 28-30.

---- C. Library of Congress classification. A L A Bull 5: 230-2.

Martin, A. Buying of foreign books for small libraries. Minn P L C N 9: 30-1.

---- A. Prompt service. A L A Bull 11: 354-5.

Martin, C. Intricacies of binding. L J 27: 312-3.

Martin, D. B. Books on Oliver Hazard Perry and the War of 1812. Wis Lib Bull 9: 60.

---- D. B. Branch libraries. Wis Lib Bull 7: 175-7.

---- D. B. Helpfulness among librarians. Wis Lib Bull 2: 94-5.

---- D. B. Local history story hour. Wisconsin State Historical Soc Proceedings 1908: 48-51.

---- D. B. Modern drama in the library. Wis Lib Bull 11: 3-9.

Martin, E. S. Relations between staff and readers. L W 10: 269-71.

---- E. S. Staff time sheets. L W 10: 236-9.

---- E. S. Supplementary tickets and facilities to students. L W 10: 313-4.

Martin, H. I. How advertising would make the library an educational center. P L 17: 364-5.

Martin, M. Libraries of South Carolina. A L A Bull 5: Conf No 1, 72-3.

Martin, M. L. Literature for the intermediate school. Texas State Teachers Assn Proceedings 1898: 139-41.

Martin, T. Novel reading. L J 17: 241-2.

Martin, W. Shakespeare in London. L A R 18: 298-307, Discussion 326-8.

Martin, W. E. The advertiser in the library. Penn Lib Notes Oct 1913: 21-6; P L 25: 305-8.

---- W. E. A model small college library. Lafayette 24: 164-5.

Marvin, C. A. L. A. Report on library administration. P L 11: 554-5.

---- C. Bookbinding made unnecessary--Chivers' books. Wis Lib Bull 1: 42.

---- C. Care of books. Wis Lib Bull 1: 35-7; Washington Lib Bull 1, No 1: 12-4.

---- C. Children's books in inexpensive editions. Wis Lib Bull 1: 54-6.

---- C.  County library law: Discussion needed.  P L 25: 498-9.
---- C.  History of library commissions.  L J 22: 26.
---- C.  Library commissions and rural schools.  A L A Bull 2: 314-6.
---- C.  Library extension work.  Pacific Northwest Library Assn Proceedings 1913: 17-8.
---- C.  Library legislation in Oregon, 1919.  P L 24: 167.
---- C.  No new fiction during the war.  P L 22: 409.
---- C.  No new fiction till after the war.  P L 23: 269.
---- C.  Notes for librarians.  Wis Lib Bull 1: 10-3, 42-4, 61-5, 103-4; 2: 17-20.
---- C.  Our library problems.  P L 25: 67-9.
---- C.  Progress of libraries in Oregon.  Pacific Northwest Library Assn Proceedings 1911: 41-6.
---- C.  Public documents again.  P L 22: 304.
---- C.  Public libraries and tuberculosis.  P L 11: 433-4.
---- C.  A public library survey: status and work of a public library.  P L 25: 179-82.
---- C.  Things needful in library training.  P L 11: 267.
---- C. and W. R. Eastman.  Report of Committee on library administration.  L J 28: Conf No 71-6; L J 29: Conf No 163-7; L J 30: Conf No 102-6.
Marvin, C. E.  Work of a public library commission.  Pacific Northwest Library Assn Proceedings, 1909: 9-10, Discussion 10-1.
Marvin, G. E.  Interpreting the library movement.  L J 44: 495-8; Special Libraries 10: 154-7.
---- G. E.  The special library field.  Special Libraries 9: 59-64.
Marx, B.  Library housekeeping.  Wis Lib Bull 9: 160-1.
Marx, H. F.  How we keep up the summer circulation.  Penn Lib Notes 1, No 3: 5-8.
-- H. F.  Indifference of the public to the library.  P L 21: 445-9.
-- H. F.  Value of a bindery in a small library.  L J 30: 796-7.
Mash, M. H. B.  Cataloguing codes.  Libn 4: 135-40, 155-8, 195-9, 239-41.
-- M. H. B.  Classification of technology.  L W 15: 1-5, 50-5.
-- M. H. B.  Foreign student assistants in English libraries.  L W 15: 270-2.
Mason, C. B.  Some school library experiments in Nebraska.  Nat Educ Assn 1903: 966-71.
Mason, J.  Business men and public libraries.  P L 12: 390-1.
Mason, T.  Fiction in free libraries.  L 2: 178-81: L J 15: 265-6.
--- T.  Free libraries in Scotland.  L A U K Trans 3: 49-57, 167.

--- T. The future of London's public librarians. L A 1:
38-41.
--- T. London Government act, 1899, as it affects London
libraries and librarians. L (ns) 1: 25-31.
--- T. New method of arranging a lending library. L 6:
263-5.
Mason, W. Living with books. L J 43: 275.
Masse, S. M. Internal publicity as an aid to the laboratory.
Special Libraries 10: 92-3.
Massee, M. The changing literary taste and the growing appeal
of poetry. A L A Bull 9: 111-8.
---- M. Libraries as bookstores and bookstores as libra-
ries. Publishers' Weekly May 27, 1916: 1737-41; L J 41:
856; Am Lib Annual 1916-17: 77-8.
---- M. Method of preparing the Booklist. A L A Bull 10:
58.
---- M. The spirit of the war literature: Poetry. A L A
Bull 12: 72-8, 283, 287.
Massey, A. P. Classification of fiction. L J 6: 7-9.
---- A. P. Coloured cards for recording loans. L J 6: 34.
Massey, O. Z. The library; a business man's means for develop-
ing his employes. Special Libraries 4: 190-1.
Masters, F. G. Early stamped leather bindings. L A of Austral
Proc xlix-li, 1901.
Mate, C. H. Some literary associations of Bournemouth and neigh-
borhood. L A R 15: 453-77.
Mateer, E. What shall I be? answered for girls. Mich Lib
Bull 11: 15.
Mather, F. J., Jr. Library teaching versus teaching of lit-
erature. Nation 83: 218-9.
Mathews, B. Boys and books. Independent 67: 117-9.
Mathews, E. R. N. A century ago: famous borrowers and the
books they borrowed. L 5: 323-8.
----- E. R. N. Female library assistants and competitive
examinations. 2nd Int Conf: 40-3.
----- E. R. N. History of the public library movement in
Bristol. L 8: 198-205.
----- E. R. N. Libraries and music. L 5: 190-2.
----- E. R. N. Library binderies. L A R 8: 73-8.
----- E. R. N. Public library bye-laws and regulations.
L A R 6: 281-9.
----- E. R. N. Some early printed books and manuscripts
at Bristol. L A R 1: 589-92.
----- E. R. N. Survey of the Bristol public libraries. L
A R 2: 641-50.
Mathews, F. K. Every boy's library. N Y L 4: 147-8.
Mathews, J. M. Some phases of state library administration.
A L A Bull 11: 402-5.
Mathews, S. Democracy and world politics. A L A Bull 11: 95-
103, 314.

Mathiews, F. K.  Blowing out the boy's brains.  Penn Lib Notes
    7: 140-8; Mich Lib Bull 7: 182-5.
------ F. K.  The influence of the boy scout movement in
    directing the reading of boys.  A L A Bull 8: 223-8; P L
    19: 274-5.
------ F. K.  Making worth while boys' recreational read-
    ing.  P L 21: 300-3.
Mattern, J.  National and international co-operation in the
    field of analytical cataloging.  L J 37: 370-6.
----- J.  Review of "Kie Stadtischen Bucherhallen zu Leip-
    zig," Harrassowitz 1914.  L J 40: 738-41.
----- J.  Shelf classification in German libraries.  L J
    40: 409-13.
----- J.  Uniform cataloguing rules as viewed by the 13th
    Convention of German librarians (the first convention of
    German, Austrian and Swiss librarians) L J 34: 556-62.
Matthews, C.  Growing tendency to over-emphasize the children's
    side.  L J 33: 135-8.
Matthews, C. G.  A new catalogue card.  L J 33: 233.
Matthews, E. H.  Modification of Dewey's class 371.3.  Libn
    1: 255-6.
------ E. H.  Problem of the junior assistant.  L A 10: 176-
    7.
Matthews, H. S.  Co-operation between the public library and
    parochial schools.  Wis Lib Bull 4: 26.
------ H. S.  Library accounting at Lynn, Mass.  Bull Bib
    8: 121-2.
Matthews, J.  Means of obtaining books required in a lending
    library.  1st Int Conf 136-7; L J 2: 218-9, Discussion 279-
    80.
Matthews, R. B.  Brussels expansion of Dewey.  L A R 22: 156-
    7.
------ R. B.  The technical library.  L A R 22: 141-57.
Matthews, W.  How to open a new book.  Vt L Bull 5, No 2: 8.
Mattice, H. A.  Co-operation among railroads.  Special Libra-
    ries 10: 242-3.
Mauran, J. L.  Housing of books.  P L 6: 603-6.
---- J. L.  Relation of architect to librarian.  L J 26:
    Conf No 43-6; P L 6: 475-7.
Maury, N. B.  The new Congressional Library.  Cosmopolitan 23:
    10-20.
Maw, T.  Village libraries.  L W 3: 143-5.
Maw, T. E.  Card catalogue as a substitute for the printed
    catalogue.  L W 1: 64-6.
  - T. E.  German library system.  L W 3: 113-7.
  - T. E.  German public libraries.  L W 365-7.
  - T. E.  Immoral fiction.  L A R 2: 453-4.
  - T. E.  More about arrangement of periodicals.  L W 2: 36-
    7.

- T. E.  Note on the education of the assistant.  L A R 2: 269-71.
- T. E.  Readings to the blind.  L W 19: 224.
- T. E.  Some objections to the card catalogue answered. L W 2: 209-11.
- T. E.  State aid to public libraries.  L A R 7: 99-104, Discussion 91-3.

Mawson, C. O. S.  Uncle Sam:  librarian.  Bookman ( N Y) 48: 200-7.

Maxwell, S. B.  Women as state librarians.  L J 12: 195-6.

May, H. R. D.  Immorality of the modern burglar story and burglar play.  Nineteenth Century Feb 1915: 432-44.

May, I.  Moving pictures: the library and the children.  Lib Occ 4: 24-7.

May, S. W.  Literature and libraries of Liverpool.  B A R 6: L-LII.

May, W.  Clase classification.  L J 12: 80.
- W.  Improved form of book shelving for branch libraries. L 8: 255-9.
- W.  Librarian's treasure trove: a new copy of the "Speculum Vile Christi," by Wynkyn de Worde.  L 8: 194-7.
- W.  Plea for classification.  L C 4: 85-8; L J 12: 80.
- W.  Printing of library catalogues.  L C 3: 70-3.

Mayes, O. A.  A visual presentation of library work.  L J 38: 671-2.

Mayhew, H. M.  Revolving extension press.  L 7: 10.

Maynard, K.  Twentieth century poetry: a list of references to the English and American poetry, 1900-1915.  Bull Bib 9: 71-3, 120-1, 142-3, 167-71, 188-91.

Maynard, M.  A visit to the story hour in Waterloo school. Ia L C Q 8: 92-3.

Mayo, C. B.  Library service for the permanent naval establishments.  A L A Bull 13: 267-9, 349.

Mayor, J. E. B.  Cambridge libraries in 1710.  L A U K Trans 5: 116-9.

Mead, C. H.  Notes on children's reading.  L J 29: 476-7.

Mead, H. R.  Care and disposal of duplicates.  L J 32: 202-3.
-- H. R.  Limiting access to shelves.  P L 12: 211-2.
-- H. R.  Reference work in public and in college libraries. L J 30: 284.
-- H. R.  Some problems in book numbers.  A L A Bull 5: 251-3.
-- H. R.  Subject headings.  L J 35: 505.
-- H. R.  Training of students in the use of books.  L J 30: Conf No 82-4.
-- H. R.  Value of the study of reference work in public schools.  P L 14: 258-9.

Meany, E. S.  Local history and the state.  Wash L A Bull 2, No 4: 1-3.

Mechlin, L.  Educational work of the American federation of
    arts.  A L A Bull 8: 168.
----- L.  The work of the American federation of arts in
    relation to public libraries.  L J 39: 19-21.
Medlicott, M.  Museums of art, history, and science.  L J 23:
    Conf No 96-7.
------- M.  Public schools and public library at Spring-
    field, Mass.  U S Bur of Educ Rept, 1897-98, pt 1: 679-80;
    L J 22: 186-7.
------- M.  Rice, William, 1821-1897.  L J 22: 437-8.
Mees, C. E. K.  Production of scientific knowledge.  Science,
    Nov 30, 1917.
Megee, L.  The Wrenn library at the University of Texas.  Spec-
    ial Libraries 11: 6-9.
Mehsana, Kadi District, Baroda.  First library exhibition in
    India.  Lib Miscellany 3: 16-9; L J 40: 874-5.
Meisoner, J.  A charging system for a university library.  Pac-
    ific Northwest Library Assn Proceedings 1910: 62-4.
------ J.  Library training for teachers.  Pacific North-
    west Library Assn Proceedings 1909: 12-3, Discussion 13-4.
Melcher, F. G.  The bookstore and the library.  Wis Lib Bull
    13: 5-6.
Meleney, C. B.  Place of the library in school instruction.
    Nat Educ Assn 1904: 924-30.
Melville, A. G.  Thirty years in a Melbourne library.  Lib
    Assn of Australasia Proceedings LXVI-LXVII, 1901.
Mendenhall, D. R.  Infant welfare.  Wis Lib Bull 12: 32-8.
Mendenhall, H. G.  Journalism as a school for clergymen.  Hom-
    iletic Review 61: 118-20.
Mendenhall, I. M.  Library and school co-operation.  Lib Occ
    1, Nos 1-4: 5-7.
-------- I. M.  Library instruction in normal schools.  P
    L 13: 38-40, 91-3, 124-5.
-------- I. M.  Library training in normal schools.  Mich-
    igan State Board of Library Commissioners Report 1907: 19-
    26.
-------- I. M.  A plea for the training of students in the
    use of a library as a laboratory.  New York State, Educa-
    tion Department Bulletin Dec 1, 1909: 460; N C Bull 1: 47-50.
-------- I. M.  Report of Committee on normal school li-
    braries.  Nat Educ Assn 1912: 1258-62.
-------- I. M.  The school library as a laboratory.  Wil-
    son Bulletin 1: 219-23; L J 42: 763: Am Lib Annual 1917-
    18: 72-3.
-------- I. M.  Training future teachers to know children's
    literature.  L J 41: 527-9.
-------- I. M.  Training in the use of books.  L J 38: 189-
    92.
-------- I. M.  Training of high school students in the use
    of the library.  N Y L 3: 138-40.

Mercer, M.  Relation of school and library.  P L 3: 405.
Mercer, M. B.  Catalog system of the Army war college.  A L A
    Bull 8: 202-4.
Merington, M. E.  How can we make the guiding of pupils' read-
    ing a part of the teacher's work.  L J 20: 119-21.
    ------- M. E.  Public libraries and public schools.  L J
    12: 156-9.
Merrill, J. W.  Factory deposit stations.  Wis Lib Bull 15:
    43-5.
    ----- J. W.  How to be a treasurer.  Wis Lib Bull 13: 295-
    7.
    ----- J. W.  How to establish a county library.  Wis Lib
    Bull 16: 67-76.
    ----- J. W.  Library appropriation and budget.  Wis Lib Bull
    16: 147-62.
    ----- J. W.  Rural library extension in Wisconsin.  Wis Lib
    Bull 15: 167-73, 186.
    ----- J. W.  Staff meetings.  Wis Lib Bull 14: 91-4.
    ----- J. W.  Wisconsin documents.  Wis Lib Bull 1: 85-7.
Merrill, W. A.  Cataloguing of public documents.  L J 16: 107.
Merrill, W. S.  An American view of the alphabetic-mnemonic
    classification.  L W 22: 328-30.
    ----- W. S.  A code for classifiers: its scope and problems.
    L J 37: 245-51, 304-10.
    ----- W. S.  General and national bibliographies.  Bib Soc
    Chic Yr-Bk 1899-1900: 19-25.
    ----- W. S.  How the Newberry library was moved.  L J 19:
    11-2.
    ----- W. S.  Problems of classification and an A. L. A.
    code.  A L A Bull 5: 232-4.
    ----- W. S.  Report of Committee on code for classifiers.
    A L A Bull 10: 389.
    ----- W. S.  Report on A. L. A. periodical cards.  A L A
    Bull 10: 374.
    ----- W. S.  Subject groups for illustrated works.  P L
    10: 173-4.
    ----- W. S.  Taking care of pamphlets.  P L 11: 502-3.
    ----- W. S.  Utilizing government documents.  L J 32: 361-
    7.
    ----- W. S.  What classifiers are saying about the code.
    A L A Bull 9: 251-3.
    ----- W. S.  The young man and library work.  America, April
    18, 1914: 11-2.
Merriman, C. E. and Foreman, M. J.  Proposed department of in-
    formation and publicity.  City Club of Chicago Bulletin 2:
    165-70.
Merryhue, O.  Reading and revolution.  The Public 22: 687.
Merton, W.  A new Bristol pamphlet.  L (3d series) 8: 162-4.
Messer, I. C.  How to direct the child's reading in the home.
    Teachers' College Record 5: 206-10.

Mestre, R.  Library of the Guaranty trust company of New York.
Special Libraries 8: 94; L J 42: 285-7.

Metcalf, R. C.  The library movement.  Nat Educ Assn 1901: 830-
5.

----- R. C.  Reading in the public schools.  L J 4: 343-5.

----- R. C.  Report on school libraries.  Boston School
Committee Annual Report 1896: 97-105.

----- R. C.  Supplementary reading.  U S Bur of Educ Report 1899-1900: 673-7.

----- R. C.  Supplementary reading in the public schools.
Nat Educ Assn 1904: 466-72.

Metta, V. B.  Rabindra Nath Tagore.  Lib Miscellany (Baroda)
2: 61-2.

Metz, C.  County library system of Wasco county.  Pacific Northwest Lib Assn Proceedings 1913: 18-21.

Metz, C. A.  Library work with rural schools.  P L 16: 83-5.

-- C. A.  An Ohio county library.  A L A Bull 5: 146-8; Library Work 1912: 140.

Metz, S.  Notes on the bookbinding leather controversy.  L A
R 13: 395-8.

Meuser, E.  A neighborhood apprentice class.  A L A Bull 12:
217-8, 306.

Meyer, A.  Development of a circulating music collection.  A
L A Bull 14: 182-6, 332.

Meyer, A. B.  German view of American libraries and museums.
L J 26: 868-9.

Meyer, H. H. B.  Collection of war material: Library of Congress.  A L A Bull 13: 388-9.

--- H. H. B.  The Division of bibliography of the Library
of Congress as a clearing house for bibliographical information.  Special Libraries 4: 151-2.

--- H. H. B.  Government documents relating to the war.
A L A Bull 12: 202-10, 310.

--- H. H. B.  Libraries of Washington.  A L A Bull 8: 84-
9; L J 39: 507-11; Wis Lib Bull 12: 240-6.

--- H. H. B.  Library of Congress, Division of bibliography.
List of references on industrial courts.  Special Libraries 10: 19-21.

--- H. H. B.  Library of Congress--Division of bibliography.
List of references on public service rates, with special
reference to regulation (Cabs, electricity, gas, street
railways, telephones, water).  Special Libraries 7: 21-8.

--- H. H. B.  List of commercial yearbooks and similar publications.  Special Libraries 7: 86-8.

--- H. H. B.  List of dictionaries of commercial commodi-
ties and other books descriptive of the material used in
the arts, manufactures, and commerce.  Special Libraries 9:
46-50.

--- H. H. B.  List of references on advertising.  Special
Libraries 7: 61-76.

--- H. H. B.  List of references on business libraries, and the relation of the business library to the business man.  Special Libraries 8: 147-9.

--- H. H. B.  List of references on community centers: their organization and application to war work.  Special Libraries 9: 149-53.

--- H. H. B.  List of references on hat manufacture and trade.  Special Libraries 8: 107-8.

--- H. H. B.  List of references on organization.  Special Libraries 9: 97-8, 100-2 Business books.  P L 23: 289-90.

--- H. H. B.  List of references on the cost of selling.  Special Libraries 7: 47-9.

--- H. H. B.  List of references on the milk industry.  Special Libraries 8: 10-22.

--- H. H. B.  List of references on the real estate business.  Special Libraries 7: 151-5.

--- H. H. B.  List of references on the relief of dependent families of soldiers and sailors.  Special Libraries 8: 69-72.

--- H. H. B.  List of references on the trade of the United States as affected by the war.  Special Libraries 7: 120-6.

--- H. H. B.  Memorandum concerning the directing of sources of information in the District of Columbia.  Special Libraries 6: 117-8.

--- H. H. B.  On the co-operation of the state libraries and the Library of Congress in the preparation of reference lists.  A L A Bull 4: 713-5.

--- H. H. B.  Remarks regarding a universal catalog.  A L A Bull 13: 393-5.

--- H. H. B.  Trade catalogues, circulars, etc., in public libraries.  L J 29: 590.

--- H. H. B.  U S Government libraries at Washington.  Scientific American Supplement 82: 70-1; Wis Lib Bull 12: 240-5.

Meyer, J. A.  University extension and public libraries.  L J 42: 416-7; Am Lib Annual 1917-18: 85-6.

--- M. W.  Present status of library war service.  N Y L 6: 162-3.

Meyer, Oscar.  German view of library conventions and library examinations.  L J 16: 213-4.

Meyer, W.  Setting books in motion.  Survey 44: 304-5.

Michaely, G.  New York A. L. A. war service warehouse.  L J 44: 787.

Midleton, Viscount.  Free libraries for the blind.  Letter from Viscount Midleton.  L A R 4: 420; L W 5: 25.

Midworth, H.  The duties of a librarian in relation to the reader.  L 5: 130-5.

Miers, H. A.  The golden age of readers.  L A 7: 22-32, Discussion 32-5.

Miersch, E. E.   Reading list on decoration and furnishing.
    N Y S L Rept 83, Bibliography No 20: 661-76.
Milam, C.   Adult self-education.   A L A Bull 14: 300; P L 25:
    182-4.
Milam, C. H.   A. L. A. war service continuation work.   L J 45:
    170.
--- C. H.   A call for munitions.   L J 44: 765.
--- C. H.   Co-operation on part of commissions with public
    libraries in their efforts to reach the farmers.   A L A
    Bull 4: 746-51; Library Work 1912: 248.
--- C. H.   Libraries for industrial plants, prisons, hos-
    pitals, etc.   A L A Bull 13: 365-6.
--- C. H.   The library and community service.   Texas Libra-
    ries 2: 58-63.
--- C. H.   Library training in Birmingham, Alabama.   Wilson
    Bulletin 1: 261-2.
--- C. H.   More munitions: an appeal to those behind the
    firing line.   L J 45: 119.
--- C. H.   Publicity for the sake of support.   A L A Bull
    6: 120-4.
--- C. H.   Rural library extension.   Ia L C Q 6: 104-6; Li-
    brary Work 1912: 254.
--- C. H.   Township unit in rural extension.   P L 17: 278-9.
Milam, Carl H.   Acting director of A. L. A. war service.   L J
    44: 562.
--- Carl H.   What's left of library war service.   L J 44:
    755-6; P L 25: 19-20.
Mildren, N. L.   Rural school-teacher.   Ladies' Home Journal
    Oct 1912, 29: 70.
Miles, A.   Library conditions in Oklahoma.   L J 34: 434-7.
Miles, R. E.   A clearing house for civic and social activities.
    Special Libraries 7: 161; Am Lib Annual 1917-18: 32.
Milkau, F.   Belgian libraries in the war.   L J 41: 389-91.
Mill, A.   Reform in indexing methods.   L W 9: 408-9.
Millar, A. H.   Dual control of libraries and museums.   Libn 1:
    35-9, 75-7.
---- A. H.   The needs of Scottish libraries.   L (3rd series)
    5: 424-33.
---- A. H.   Notes on some library administrative work and
    legislation.   L A R 13: 431-7, 513-8.
---- A. H.   Scottish library administration: Presidential
    address to the Scottish library association.   L W 17: 89-
    92.
Millar, E. S.   The new Palaeographical society.   L (3d series)
    6: 97-114.
Millar, P.   Landscape bookplates.   Connoisseur 29: 235-7.
Millard, G. M.   Spencer library at Althorp.   L J 17: 384-5.
Millard, J. H.   Work with children in a small library.   Paci-
    fic Northwest Library Assn Proceedings 1910: 44-9.

Miller, C. W.  Annual tax levy.  Lib Occ Nos 1-4: 10.

Miller, E. H.  Librarianship in South Africa.  L A 1: 143-5.

Miller, E. L.  College entrance requirements from the high
school point of view.  Western Journal of Education 4: 193-
206.

---- E. L.  Literary study and character formation.  School
Review 8: 285-91.

---- E. L.  Selecting books for high school boys.  Nat Educ
Assn 1918: 449-50.

---- E. L.  Separating composition from literature in the
high school.  English Journal 3: 500-12.

Miller, E. M.  School libraries and reading.  Education Gazette
and Teachers Aid (Australia) March, 1912.

Miller, E. V. D.  Public library advertises books on all jobs.
American City (T and C ed) 20: 441-2.

Miller, G.  Book advertising: illumination as to attractions
of real books.  A L A Bull 6: 187-92.

---- G.  Current year's books in sociology for a small library.  P L 10: 11-4.

Miller, G. C.  Library buildings.  Ia L C Q 3: 1-8.

Miller, G. L.  Forestry and lumbering in the northwest from
the librarian's viewpoint.  Special Libraries 6: 109-12.

Miller, Mrs. G. L.  Co-operation in library work.  New Hamp
Bull (ns) 15: 151-2.

---- Mrs. G. L.  A plea for the special library.  L J 43:
246-8.

Miller, H. A.  The true Americanization of the foreign born
child.  A L A Bull 13: 130-2, 387.

Miller, H. W.  The United States working reserve.  A L A Bull
12: 198-9.

Miller, J.  Unifying for war.  Wis Lib Bull 14: 41-3; L J 43:
696-7.

Miller, M.  Schools and libraries.  P L 1: 89.

Miller, W. A.  The library as an educator.  Nat Educ Assn
1902: 799-804.

Miller, W. M.  Work with children at Madison, N. Y., library.
L J 28: Conf No 169-70.

Miller, Z.  North Dakota free traveling libraries.  North Dakota Magazine 3: 73-7.

Miller, Z. K.  Clover-Land libraries are doing splendid work.
Reprinted from "Clover-Land" April, 1916: Mich Lib Bull 7:
98-102.

---- Z. K.  Discipline.  Wis Lib Bull 12: 136-7.

---- Z. K.  Filing as a profession for women.  P L 25: 24.

---- Z. K.  Guarantors for county high school pupils.  Wis
Lib Bull 3: 65.

---- Z. K.  The librarian and the local book-dealer.  Wis
Lib Bull 9: 51-3; 10: 44-5.

---- Z. K.  A new publication on filing.  Special Libraries:
11: 101-2

---- Z. K. Pamphlet and magazine boxes. Wis Lib Bull 3: 49, 62.

---- Z. K. Plan for inter-library loans. Wis Lib Bull 3: 65.

---- Z. K. Tentative plan for vocational guidance. Wis Lib Bull 11: 45-7.

---- Z. K. Tradition versus common sense in the day's work. A L A Bull 14: 155-60, 328.

Milligan, F. A year of township extension at Tipton. Ia L C Q 6: 198-200.

Milliken, M. H. Library clubs for boys and girls. L J 36: 251-3.

Millington, F. A year of township extension at Tipton. Ia L C Q 6: 198-200.

Millis, W. A. The library as an educator. Nat Educ Assn 1902: 799-804.

Milman, H. Society of arts' universal catalogue. L J 4: 18.

Milman, W. H. Library of Sion college. L 2: 55-62.

Milner, A. V. Artistic advertising. P L 10: 356.

---- A. V. Cataloguing mounted pictures. P L 9: 115-6.

---- A. V. Inexpensive resources for small libraries. P L 11: 363-7.

---- A. V. Instruction in the use of catalogs and reference books in normal schools. P L 4: 324-6.

---- A. V. Library resources at low cost and high value. N Y L 1: 173-7.

---- A. V. Magazines for small libraries. P L 17: 219-20; New Hamp Bull 8: 128-30.

---- A. V. Organizing a school library. School News 22: 448-9.

---- A. V. Reference sheets. P L 2: 87-8.

---- A. V. What is the best encyclopedia? P L 18: 104-5.

---- A. V. What shall we do with the book agent? P L 16: 390; 17: 45-6.

---- A. V. What the normal school can do for teachers on the library side. P L 8: 95-6.

Miner, L. B. Voluntary reading in the English high school. School Review 13: 180-8.

Miner, S. H. The two-book system. P L 2: 173-5.

Minot, J. C. Maine's contribution to literature. Maine Lib Bull 8: 104-6; 9: 6-8, 31-4, 57-61.

Minto, J. Anglo-American cataloguing rules. L A R 11: 289-302, Discussion 335-8.

--- J. Bibliography of local literature. L A R 4: 37-44.

--- J. Exemption of libraries from local rates. L (ns) 3: 256-60.

--- J. The library situation in Scotland. L A R 22: 367-71.

--- J. A notable publishing house: the Morisons of Perth. L (ns) 1: 254-63.

--- J. Public libraries and museums: a discussion of the
connection between libraries and museums and art galleries
and their inter-relationship. L A R 5: 261-4, Discussion
289-93.

--- J. Recent attacks on public libraries. L A R 5: 559-
68; Discussion 479-80.

Mitchell, A. C. The case against the librarian: public service corporation, New Jersey. Special Libraries 11: 75-6.

------ A. C. Library of the Public service corporation,
New Jersey. Special Libraries 9: 200-1.

------ A. C. List of references on street lighting. Special Libraries 10: 22-7.

Mitchell, D. Municipal reference work. Pacific Northwest
Lib Assn Proceedings 1913: 47-54.

Mitchell, E. C. European libraries. L J 2: 12-3.

Mitchell, J. M. The borough librarian's criticisms. L W 23:
559-61.

Mitchell, J. T. Indexing portraits. L J 13: 333.

Mitchell, M. E. Report on public libraries in 1876. P L 11:
246-7.

Mitchell, W. A. Use of the library. University Cynic 5: 75-7.

Mitter, E. Librarian's relations to his readers. L N (U S)
3: 379-85.

Moa, E. The Rural and social science library of the University of North Carolina. N C Bull 4: 46-8.

Moe, M. W. Magazine poetry in the class room. English Journal 4: 523-5.

Moffett, H. A. How the money was spent at Elwood (Ind.) library. P L 14: 349.

Moffett, J. C. Books as tools. Nation 91: 99-100.

----- J. C. Development of the Sunday library. L J 32:
112-3.

----- J. C. Information clearing house. P L 23: 273.

----- J. C. Why public libraries should be advertised.
L J 37: 263.

Moffitt, H. E. Real life geography. N C Bull 4: 8-9; Vt L
Bull 14: 34-5.

Moir, E. List of books on Canadian bibliography in the reference department of the Toronto public library. L W 13:
111-3.

-- E. Popular reference books--how to use them. Ontario
Lib Assn Proceedings 1911: 69-81.

Molesworth, M. L. S. Story reading and story writing. Chamber's Edinburgh Review 87: 772-5.

Monroe, W. S. Impressions of some European libraries. L J
32: 161-2.

Montgomery, L. County extension work in Union county. Am
Lib Annual 1917-18: 34.

-------- L. A county library in Illinois. P L 22: 65.

-------- L.   County library work (Stinson Memorial Library).
L J 42: 73-4; P L 22: 65.
Montgomery, T. L.   Civilization.   A L A Bull 12: 45-8; L J 43:
548-51.
-------- T. L.   Discusses the duties of trustees.   A L A
Bull 13: 375-7.
-------- T. L.   Duty of trustees as to legislation.   A L A
Bull 8: 245-6.
-------- T. L.   The new place of the public document in
the field of research.   A L A Bull 3: 313-5.
-------- T. L.   Relation of the state library to library
extension.   A L A Bull 8: 338-41.
-------- T. L.   Report of the co-operation committee.   L
J 24: Conf No 92-4.
-------- T. L.   Report on public libraries and university
extension.   L J 19: Conf No 64-7.
-------- T. L.   Survey of Pennsylvania libraries.   Penn
Lib Notes 6 No 4: 45-9.
-------- T. L.   The trustee.   L J 25: Conf No 42-3; P L 5:
291-4.
-------- T. L.   What may be done for libraries by the city.
L J 26: Conf No 5-7.
Montmorency, J. E. G. de.   Literature of the war; economics
and international law.   L A R 17: 461-5.
Moody, K. T.   Library reports from a frivolous point of view.
L J 38: 263-7.
Moody, L. B.   American college girls' ignorance of literature.
Journal of Pedagogy 18: 257-64.
Moon, R. C.   Books and libraries for the blind.   L J 30: 269-
74.
Moon, Z.   School children and public libraries.   L A 2: 83-6.
Moor, A. P.   Libraries of Truro.   L C 3: 105-7.
Moore, A. C.   Bookshop for boys and girls.   A L A Bull 11: 168-
9: 344.
--- A. C.   Children, libraries, and the love of reading.
Annals of American Academy 67: 123-9.
--- A. C.   Children's book week in New York.   P L 25: 25-7.
--- A. C.   Children's libraries in France.   L J 45: 831-2.
--- A. C.   The children's library in Stockholm.   L J 38:
145.
--- A. C.   Children's room.   P L 2: 125.
--- A. C.   Library membership as a civic force.   A L A Bull
2: 372-80; L J 33: 269-74; P L 13: 264-6; Minn P L C N 2:
127-9; Ia L C Bull 2: 128.
--- A. C.   Library visits to public schools.   L J 27: 181-6.
--- A. C.   Making picture bulletins.   Wis Lib Bull 2: 11.
--- A. C.   Place of pictures in library work with children.
L J 25: 159-62; P L 5: 281-2.
--- A. C.   Special training for children's librarians.   L
J 23: Conf No 80-2, Discussion, 134; P L 4: 99-102.

--- A. C.  Story hour at Pratt institute library.  L J 30: 204-11.

--- A. C.  Story telling in libraries.  L J 33: 401-2.

--- A. C.  Story telling in the New York public library. A L A Bull 3: 410-3.

--- A. C.  Suggestions for a children's room.  New Hamp Bull 4: 2-6.

--- A. C.  Training for the work of a children's librarian. A L A Bull 8: 238-43.

--- A. C.  What the community is asking of the department of children's work in the public library.  L J 38: 595-9; P L 18: 415-20.

--- A. C.  What the public libraries are doing for children. Ia L C Q 4: 17-23.

--- A. C.  The work of the children's librarian.  L J 28: 160-4.

--- A. C.  Work with children from institutions for the deaf and dumb.  L J 35: 158-9.

Moore, E.  Annotated catalog cards.  P L 6: 151-2.

Moore, E. G.  Children's book week in Detroit.  P L 25: 27-8.

Moore, E. L.  Departmental work in a library.  P L 12: 122-3.

--- E. L.  Library exhibits.  P L 4: 148-52.

--- E. L.  Picture work in children's libraries.  L J 25: Conf No 67-8.

--- E. L.  Reference work and special lists.  P L 2: 290-3.

--- E. L.  Reference work in a small public library.  L J 28: 653-7.

Moore, F. N.  Art of leather making.  L J 32: 367-70.

Moore, H.  City children and the library.  L J 25: 170.

Moore, H. H.  Wanted: a book for every man over there.  Outlook 20: 250-1.

Moore, H. K.  Municipal reference libraries.  L A R 19: 497-502.

--- H. K.  Open access in public lending libraries.  L (ns) 1: 49-62.

--- H. K.  University extension lectures and libraries.  L W 6: 117-23.

Moore, M. P.  Traveling library in Colorado.  P L 2: 54-5.

Moore, S.  General aspects of literary patronage in the middle ages.  L (3d series) 4: 369-92.

Moore, W.  Problem of the junior assistant.  L A 10: 203-4.

Moorhead, P. G.  Libraries at every crossroad.  Technical World Magazine 22: 679-80

More, P. E.  A prime function of the library.  N Y L 4: 34-5.

Morel, E.  Municipal libraries of France.  L W 14: 109-11.

Morgan, A.  Monastic book-making.  L A R 11: 303-20.

---- A.  Monastic libraries.  L A R 6: 290-7.

Morgan, E.  Township extension at Spencer, Indiana.  Lib Occ 3:2.

Morgan, E. S.  High school libraries in California.  Nat Educ
 Assn 1915: 1071-3; P L 21: 8-9.
---- E. S.  High school library and history teaching.  Nat
 Educ Assn 1916: 555-6.
Morgan, H. H.  Library co-operation.  L J 16: 39-40.
Morgan, J. E.  Camp library advertising.  L J 43: 407-8.
---- J. E.  County libraries for Kentucky.  L J 45: 497.
---- J. E.  County libraries: Utah makes a record.  P L 25:
 205-6.
---- J. E.  The high school library and the teacher-libra-
 rian movement.  School and Society 11: 188-91.
---- J. E.  How the camp library reaches every man.  A L
 A Bull 12: 233-6.
---- J. E.  Libraries and the nation.  L J 44: 714-5.
---- J. E.  The library and the home.  Education 40: 340-2.
---- J. E.  Library renaissance and the American Library
 Association.  Outlook 124: 609-11.
---- J. E.  Some notable publicity.  L J 45: 642.
---- J. E.  Standard library organization.  L J 45: 1021-2.
Morgan, J. H.  College libraries: how best made available for
 college uses.  Assn of Colleges and Preparatory Schools of
 the Middle States and Maryland, Proceedings 1892, 6: 44-9.
Morgan, L. L.  Concerning standard library service.  Mich Lib
 Bull Sept-Oct 1917: 82-4; L J 45: 295-6.
Morgan, T. J.  School and the library.  Nat Educ Assn 1887: 192-
 5.
Morgan, W.  The card catalogue of the Brussels institute.  L
 A 9: 46-9.
---- W.  Special reference work and the municipal reference
 library.  L A 12: 85, 157-63, 176-8.
Morison, H.  Progress versus difficulties.  New Hamp Bull (ns)
 11: 136-8.
Morison, M.  The need of an active library commission in New
 Hampshire.  New Hamp Bull (ns) 12: 215-7.
Morley, John.  On public libraries.  L 10: 208-11.
Morningstern, W. B.  Technical department of the Free public
 library of Newark.  L J 34: 104-6.
Morrill, G. H.  Education and culture for rural life.  Vt L
 Bull 7, No 4: 1-4.
Morris, C. S.  Need for trained librarians.  Wis Lib Bull 3:
 12.
---- C. S.  Plea for library training.  Wis Lib Bull 2:
 63-4.
Morris, E. C.  Teaching of English in secondary schools.
 Journal of Pedagogy 17: 56-76.
Morris, E. E.  Australian author and the libraries.  L A of
 Austral Proc lii-lv.
Morris, W.  The ideal book.  Bib Soc Trans 1: 179-86.
Morrisey, E. L.  Essentials of a good book for children.  P
 L 11: 548-9.

Morrison, G. W.  The value of traveling libraries.  N C Bull
1: 150-1.

Morrison, H. A.  Bibliography of the publications of the Confederate states of America.  Bib Soc Amer Proc 3: 92-122.

------  H. A.  Description of the Library of Judge Wickersham, delegate in congress for Alaska.  Special Libraries
4: 183-4.

Morrison, H. C.  The public library and the public school.  New
Hamp Bull (ns) 6: 215-7.

Morrow, E. A.  Wood block printing in schools.  Education Bi-
Monthly 5: 78-84.

Morse, A. L.  Reading list on Russia.  Bibliography No 15, N
Y S L Rept 81. 1898.

---  A. L.  Reuben McMillan free library, Youngstown, Ohio.
L J 36: 579-80.

Morse, E. S.  Distribution of government documents.  L J 19:
255, 263.

Morse, J. H.  The training of boys: books.  Harper's Bazar 34:
728-31.

Morton, A. H.  The reviewer reviewed.  Critic 39: 535-42.

Morton, Mrs. C. E.  The value of good books.  New Hamp Bull
(ns) 14: 94-6.

Morton, F.  What the librarian of a small library can do for
children.  Neb Lib Bull No 1: 3-7.

Morton, F. N.  Indexing and abstracting current literature for
the benefit of employees.  Special Libraries 2: 16-18.

----  F. N.  Public utilities references.  Special Libraries
2: 101-6; 4: 184-8; 5: 32-5.

----  F. N.  Technical literature abstracts and information
bureau work in the library of the United gas improvement
company.  Engineering Record 64: 398; Special Libraries 2:
68-9.

Morton, J.  The books in the state county traveling libraries.
Minn P L C N 2: 80-2.

----  J.  Exhibits and special days.  P L 8: 464-5.

Morvin, V.  Our printed treasures.  Canadian Magazine 37: 114-
9.

Moser, S.  Work with children in a small library.  Pacific
Northwest Library Assn Proceedings 1910: 44-9.

Moser, S. M.  An active small library.  P L 18: 114.

Moses, M. J.  The book line.  St. Nicholas 39: 740-6.

---  M. J.  The children's library and the home.  Outlook
87: 177-85.

---  M. J.  Draft army of books.  Bookman (N Y) 46: 625-9.

---  M. J.  Efficiency of the new New York library.  Independent 70: 1099-1105.

---  M. J.  The experimental temptation: or, the attractive
power of books versus the librarian's method.  New Hamp
Bull (ns) 9: 143-53; L J 34: 247-53.

--- M. J.  Halt! What book goes there?  Nation 106: 315.
--- M. J.  New York public library.  Review of Reviews 43:
     701-8.
Mosman, M. C.  Reference work at the Pratt Institute library.
     L J 16: 298-300.
Moth, A.  Danish terms used in bibliographies and by the book
     and printing trade.  Bull Bib 7: 157-62.
-- A.  Italian terms used in bibliographies, and by the book
     and printing trade.  Bull Bib 7: 106-10, 132-5.
-- A.  Spanish terms used in bibliographies and by the book
     and printing trade.  Bull Bib 8: 71-4, 102-5.
-- A.  Swedish terms used in bibliographies and by the book
     and printing trade.  Bull Bib 8: 10-4, 41-2.
Mould, A.  Some literary associations of Birmingham.  B A R
     15: I-VI.
Mould, R. W.  Efficient junior assistants.  L A R 11: 45-6.
--- R. W.  Local literature in public libraries.  L A R 1:
     582-8.
--- R. W.  Our work.  L A 3: 80-7.
--- R. W.  Princeton University scheme.  L A R 8: 131.
--- R. W.  Some library aids--other than mechanical.  L A
     R 5: 362-5.
--- R. W.  Symposium on public libraries after the war.  L
     A R 19: 229-30.
--- R. W.  Wanted--a classification.  L A R 8: 127-47, Dis-
     cussion 161-6.
Moule, H. F.  The Coverdale Bible of 1535.  L (3d series) 2:
     273-6.
Moulton, J. C.  Library bulletins: printing and distribution.
     L J 24: 473-4.
Moulton, J. G.  Duplicate pay collections.  L J 35: 397-400.
----- J. G.  The Haverill mounted picture collection.  Bull
     Bib 8: 32-3.
----- J. G.  Vocational guidance and education.  Mass L C
     Bull 4: 32-4.
----- J. G.  Work with schools in the Haverhill public li-
     brary.  L J 41: 652-3.
Moulton, R. G.  Many-sidedness of university extension.  L J
     23: Conf No 142-4.
----- R. G.  Study of literature.  Nat Educ Assn 1894: 210-
     20.
Mountjoy, J. C.  Schools and libraries.  P L 2: 368.
Mower, A. L.  Reference work in the small library.  Vt L Bull
     15: 15-9; N C Bull 4: 69-74.
Mowry, D. E.  Municipal reference libraries.  City Hall 10: 131-
     2.
--- D. E.  Reference libraries in cities: Baltimore as a
     type.  P L 12: 387-9.
Mowry, W. A.  Relation of the public library to education.
     L J 16: 301-3.
Moyer, J. A.  University extension and public libraries.  Mass
     Lib Club Bull 6: 84-6.

Mudge, I. G.   Reference books of 1910.   L J 36: 121-3.
--- I. G.   Some reference books of 1911.   L J 37: 125-8.
--- I. G.   Some reference books of 1912.   L J 38: 192-8.
--- I. G.   Some reference books of 1913.   L J 39: 100-10.
--- I. G.   Some reference books of 1914.   L J 40: 83-93.
--- I. G.   Some reference books of 1915.   L J 41: 82-92;
   Am Lib Annual 1916-17: 173-80.
--- I. G.   Some reference books of 1916.   L J 42: 175-82.
--- I. G.   Some reference books of 1917.   L J 43: 14-9.
--- I. G.   Some reference books of 1918.   L J 44: 11-6.
--- I. G.   Special collections in libraries in the United
   States.   L J 34: 546; P L 15: 20.
--- I. G.   Stimulation of general reading in the college
   library.   L J 31: 764-8.
--- I. G., and W. D. Johnston.   Special collections in li-
   braries in the United States.   Bureau of Education Bulletin
   No 23, 1912: 1-140; P L 18: 21.
Muhlenfeld, O.   Library schools of the Continent.   L A 10:
   154-7.
Mulheron, A. M.   Experiences with a book wagon.   Pacific North-
   west Lib Assn Proceedings 1920: 25-6.
------ A. M.   Savenay.   A. L. A. war service.   A L A Bull
   13: 322.
Mullen, B. H.   Plan for constant supervision of expenditure.
   L 8: 252-4.
---- B. H.   Salford and inauguration of public free libra-
   ries movement: a contribution to the history of free li-
   braries.   L A R 2: 183-9.
Muller, Mrs. J. Y.   The Gastonia public library.   N C Lib Bull
   3: 119-20.
Mullins, E. Y.   The value of books.   N C Bull 2: 76-7.
Mullins, J. D.   Birmingham newsroom.   L J 9: 101-2.
----- J. D.   Free library bye-laws.   L C 4: 163-5.
----- J. D.   Librarian and his work.   L A Trans 3: 69-76.
----- J. D.   Note on books suitable for lending libraries.
   1st Int Conf 59; L J 2: 152.
----- J. D.   Our newsrooms.   L C 1: 37-9.
----- J. D.   Some of the less pleasant duties of a libra-
   rian.   L A Trans 7: 61-5.
----- J. D.   Standard of library service.   L J 3: 52-3, 160.
----- J. D, J. Picton and E. C. Thomas.   The Royal visit
   to Newcastle-upon-Tyne, opening of the public libraries.
   L C 1: 137-42.
Mumford, E. W.   Choosing books for boys and girls.   New Hamp
   Bull 11: 81-3, 170-2; Texas Libraries 1: 21-4.
----- E. W.   Juvenile readers as an asset.   N Y L 4: 9-11;
   New Hamp Bull 8: 133-40; Publishers' Weekly 81: 1620-5;
   Wis Lib Bull 10: 45-6.
----- E. W.   The librarian and the bookseller.   L J 38: 136-
   42.

----- E. W.  Selling children's books.  Penn Lib Notes 7: 137-40.

Munro, W. B.  Bibliography of municipal government.  Bib Soc Amer Proc 1: 223-4.

Munroe, K.  The adventure book for boys.  A L A Bull 3: 267-9.

Munson, E. L.  Libraries and reading as an aid to morale.  A L A Bull 13: 184-7, 349.

Munsterberg, H.  Public library in American life.  L J 30: 925-7.

Murphy, C. D.  Getting the new idea first.  System ( N Y) 30: 170-9.

Murphy, D. C.  American history as a basis of literature.  Popular Educator 29: 62-4.

Murphy, T. J.  Newspaper files.  Greensboro, N C Daily Record Sept 4, 1911.

Murray, A. G. W.  The edition of the "Fasciculus temporum" printed by Arnold Ther Hoernen in 1474.  L (3d series) 4: 57-71.

Murray, D.  Bibliography; its scope and methods with a view of the work of a local bibliographical society.  Glasgow Bibliographical Society Records Vol 1, 1912-13: 1-105.

Murray, E.  Application of psychological methods to rating and differentiation of prospective library assistants.  A L A Bull 12: 305-6.

---- E.  Some experiments in secondary training.  A L A Bull 12: 305.

Murray, N.  International mind alcoves for libraries.  L J 43: 250.

Murray, W. R.  Traveling libraries.  Ontario Education Department, Report on public libraries 1910: 531-5.

Myers, D. P.  Bibliography of aerial law.  Special Libraries 5: 59-63.

Myers, G. C.  Wanted: a library for the masses.  Education 41: 264-7.

Myers, G. W.  Dusting the library.  Med Lib and Hist Journal 1: 135-6.

--- G. W.  Medical libraries for modern hospitals.  Modern Hospital Nov 1915: 341-3; L J 41: 153, 220; Am Lib Annual 1916-17: 60-1.

--- G. W.  Medical libraries in hospitals.  Med Lib and Hist Journal 3: 282-7.

Myers, Mrs. G. W.  War bibliography.  Bulletin of Medical Library Assn Oct 1917: 25-7; L J 43: 375-6.

Myers, I. T.  Report on the archives of Kentucky.  Am Hist Assn Rept 1910: 331-64.

Myler, M.  A code book.  Mich Lib Bull Jan-Feb 1916: 16-7.

Nadkarni, M. K.  A survey of Marathi literature.  Lib Miscellany (Baroda) 2: 95-102.

Narasimha, S. V.  A short history of the Andhra literature.  Lib Miscellany (Baroda) 3: 35-7.

Nash, G. R.  How one club maintains a library.  Ia L C Q 3: 22-4.

Nason, S. L.  Junior civic league.  Ia L C Q 6: 159-60.

Nathan, G. J.  Journalistic morgues.  Bookman (N. Y.) 31: 597-9.

Nearing, S.  Public library as an index of culture.  School and Society 4: 980-4.

Neesham, E. W.  Accession methods.  L W 8: 317.

----- E. W.  Care of books.  L W 11: 32-3.

----- E. W.  Cash receipts and petty cash.  L W 10: 248-51.

----- E. W.  Committee work (Specimen Agenda).  L W 10: 351-3.

----- E. W.  Registration of borrowers: some improvements.  L W 12: 341-3.

Neisser, E. R.  Books for the blind.  L J 31: Conf No 78-82; Discussion L J 31: Conf No 224-8.

----- E. R.  Work for the blind in Pennsylvania.  Penn Lib Notes 2 No 4: 5-8.

Nelson, C. A.  Bit of classification: treatment of Harvardiana by the Harvard club of New York.  L J 22: Conf No 47-8, Discussion 165.

---- C. A.  Choosing and buying books.  L J 12: 155-6.

---- C. A.  Criticism of the Peabody scheme.  L J 19: Conf No 71.

---- C. A.  Criticizes Mr. Rowell's scheme.  L J 19: Conf No 71-2.

---- C. A.  General catalogue of American literary periodicals.  L J 20: Conf No 30-1, 67-71.

---- C. A.  Harris collection of American poetry.  L J 12: 69-70.

---- C. A.  How books were bought in our library.  L J 15: Conf No 38-9.

---- C. A.  Libraries for specialists.  L J 12: 361-2.

---- C. A.  Library legislation.  Appleton's Annual Cyclopedia 1887: 318-20.

---- C. A.  List of articles noted in Library Journal since 1889.  L J 19: Conf No 69-77.

---- C. A.  Passing of the Astor and Lenox libraries.  P L 16: 296-300.

---- C. A.  Report on classification and catalogs.  L J 19: Conf No 69-77.

---- C. A.  Review of Mr. Olin's scheme for collective biography.  L J 19: Conf No 72.

---- C. A.  Reviews Borden's scheme.  L J 19: Conf No 71.

---- C. A.  Yearly report on cataloguing.  L J 10: 263-7.

Nelson, H. L.  American periodicals.  Dial 28: 349-52.

Nelson, M. O.  What is the library to the business man?  Minn P L C N 2, No 4: 49-50.

Nelson, W.  Suggestions for a New Jersey bibliography.  N J Lib Bull 2: 7-16.

Nesbitt, M.  Old time books, scribes and librarians.  Ave Maria
Sept 12, 1914: 328-34.
Nethaway, J. C.  Why library extension pays Washington.  Minn
Lib Notes 2: 82-4; Library Work 1912: 140; Cal News Notes
3: 131.
Neumann, F.  Cataloguing of early printing in the United States
prior to 1800.  L J 31: 669-71.
Neville, A.  Newspaper reading rooms.  L A of Austral Proc
XLVII-XLIX.
Newberry, M. A.  Macaulay: a maker and user of libraries.  L
J 44: 159-63.
------  M. A.  A normal budget for the high school library.
Nat Educ Assn 1914: 817-20.
------  M. A.  What should be the standard of admission to
the training class?  L J 44: 284-7.
------  M. A.  Women and library work.  Mich Lib Bull 7: 93-
4.
Newcomb, C. H.  School-room libraries.  Nat Educ Assn 1899: 527-
8; U S Bur of Educ Rept 1899: 718-9.
Newcombe, C. F.  Book-buying and book reading.  L A R 11: 147-
9.
------  C. F.  Book plates: their beauty and utility.  L A
R 11: 211-21.
------  C. F.  Debt of men of letters to libraries.  L A R
15: 502-21.
------  C. F.  District auditor and library lectures.  L A
R 12: 497-8.
------  C. F.  Edward Foskett, 1848-1901.  L A 3: 24-6.
------  C. F.  Library lectures and extension work.  L A 5:
61-4.
------  C. F.  On library readers' unions: their value and
possibilities.  L A R 2: 623-9.
------  C. F.  Presentation of the Leslie Stephens collection
to the London library.  L A R 10: 9-10.
------  C. F.  Raison d'être of library lectures.  L A R 9:
231-43, Discussion 261-6.
------  C. F.  Some aspects of the work of Henry Bradshaw.
L A R 7: 392-403.
------  C. F.  Training of library assistants.  L A R 12: 77-
8.
------  C. F.  Value of a knowledge of English literature to
library assistants.  L A 6: 261-5, Discussion 273.
------  C. F.  Prisoner-of-war library: being the history
of the British officers' library, Strabsund, Germany.  L
A R 21: 271-83.
Newcomer, A. G.  On teaching literature.  Dial 47: 276-8.
Newdigate, C. A.  Notes on the seventeenth century printing
press at Saint-Omer.  L (3d series) 10: 179-90, 223-42.
Newhard, M.  Use of the Victrola in the Virginia (Minn) public
library.  Wis Lib Bull 10: 76-7.

Newland, N.  The library and municipal betterment.  Minn P L
    C N 3: 56-8.
Newlon, J. H.  High school library standardization aims from
    the point of view of the school administrator.  Nat Educ
    Assn 1918: 383.
Newman, A.  Index to subject bibliographies in library bulle-
    tins.  N Y S L Rept 81.
Newman, F.  Dziatzko, Carl, 1842-1903.  L J 28: 105-110.
Newmark, M. R.  To keep faith with the fallen.  P L 25: 258-
    9.
Newton, A. E.  Amenities of book collecting.  Atlantic 115:
    336-47, 488-96.
Newton, H. W.  Elevating influence of public libraries.  L A
    R 6: 465, 519-31.
Neystrom, P. H.  Advertising the public library.  P L 17: 157-
    9, 199-202; New Hamp Bull 8: 95-101; Wis Lib Bull 8: 13-8.
------ P. H.  How to reach the working man.  Wis Lib Bull
    7: 168-71.
Nice, L. B.  Experiments in book disinfection.  Journal of the
    American Public Health Assn (Series 3) 1: 775-7.
Nicholl, M. W.  The college library in Nebraska.  L J 29: 294-
    7.
Nichols, F. F.  Bringing public and library together.  Wis Lib
    Bull 13: 258-63.
Nichols, F. J.  How to induce school reading.  P L 2: 9-11.
Nichols, J. B.  Indexing--Manual for librarians, authors and
    publishers.  L J 17: 406-19.
----- J. B.  Notes on geographical indexing.  L J 19: 330-
    1.
Nichols, M. A.  The need of a county library.  Pacific North-
    west Library Assn Proceedings 1920: 58-9.
Nichols, W. R.  On the deterioration of library bindings.  L
    J 4: 435-8.
Nichols, W. S.  The Palo Alto union high school.  Standford
    Illustrated Review 20: 184-5.
Nicholson, E. B.  Bibliography of libraries and librarianship.
    1st Int Conf: 248-9. 1877.
------- E. B.  Buckram - a palinode.  L A Trans 3: 117-9.
------- E. B.  Compendious cataloguing rules for the author
    catalogue of the Bodleian library.  L J 8: 298-301; L A M
    N 4: 5-9, 31-3.
------- E. B.  Consolidation and amendment of the Public
    libraries acts.  L A Trans 2: 21-7, 93.
------- E. B.  Drawback of English librarians.  L J 10:
    403.
------- E. B.  Exhibition of library designs, catalogues
    and appliances.  1st Int Conf 241-9. 1877.
------- E. B.  On buckram as a binding material.  1st Int
    Conf 124-6; L J 2: 207-9, 271-2.

------- E. B.  Rough list of some leading subjects connected with library formation and management.   1st Int Conf:
208-211.   1877.
------- E. B.  Size notation at the Bodleian.  L C 1: 191-3.
------- E. B.  System of classifying books on the shelves
at British Museum.  L J 2: 268.
------- E. B.  Use of buckram, linoleum and cretonne for
binding.  L A M N 1: 81-4.
Nicholson, F. B.  The Henry Watson music library and its found-
er.  L A R 17: 260-1.
Nicholson, F. W.  Recent changes in the rules of New England
college entrance certificates board.  Education 33: 261-5.
Nicholson, J. B.  What a librarian should know about binding.
L J 9: 102.
Nicholson, J. N.  Training of the trustee.  Minn P L C N 9: 14-
6.
Nilsson, E. B.  Scandinavian literature.  Minn P L C N 4: 183-
5.
Noa, E.  The rural and social science library of the Univer-
sity of North Carolina.  N C Bull 4: 46-8.
Nodal, J. H.  Special collections of books in Lancashire and
Cheshire.  L A Trans 2: 54-60; L J 4: 413-4.
Noe, A. C. von.  International institutes in Berlin for the
bibliography of the social sciences, medicine, jurispru-
dence and technology.  Bib Soc Amer Papers 5: 97-107.
Noe, A. C.  Our university libraries.  School and Society 10:
70-2.
Nordlinger, C. and W. E. Hoyle.  The concilium bibliographicum
at Zurich and its work.  L A R 1: 709-18.
Nolan, E. J.  Use of natural history books.  A L A Bull 1:
Conf No 123-8.
Nolen, J.  Aid from university extension methods.  L J 28:
225-7.
Norgate, F.  Book sales by R. H. Evans, 1812-1845.  L 3: 324-
30.
----- F.  Caxtoniana.  L 1: 264-8, 296-300.
Norman, O. E.  The library's part in the first food exhibit.
L J 43: 179-80.
Norman, P.  London topography.  L A R 2: 120-3.
Norrenberg, C.  Congress and the conferences of libraries in
Chicago.  U S Rept 1892-3: 575-83.
-------- C.  Libraries in Germany.  P L 9: 367-71.
-------- C.  Woman as librarian.  P L 6: 156-8.
Norris, H. E.  Cirencester booksellers and printers.  Notes
& Queries 20 Feb 1915, 141-3.
Norris, J.  Deterioration of newspaper paper.  P L 18: 63.
Norris, J. P.  Shakespeare bibliographies.  L J 10: 184, 379.
Norriss, O. O.  The social argument for the study of the clas-
sics.  American Schoolmaster 7: 1-19.

North, A.  Iowa libraries.  L J 16: 332-3.

North, Mrs. A.  A Western university library.  L J 10: 124-5.

North, E. D.  Publications of the Vale press: a bibliography.
Bookbuyer 20: 132.

North, M. G.  Shadow and the substance.  L W 14: 77-9.

--- M. G.  Unfrequented paths in classification.  L W 9:
437-40.

Northey, D.  County library system of Hood River.  Pacific
Northwest Lib Assn Proceedings 1913: 21-4.

----- D.  The school phase of county work.  Pacific Northwest Lib Assn Proceedings 1914: 68-71.

Northrop, B. G.  The reading of our boys and girls.  Connecticut Board of Education Report 1882: 1-6.

Northup, C. S.  Present bibliographical status of modern phil-
ology.  Bib Soc Amer Proc 5: 61-94.

Norton, E. S.  Some of the treasures in the library of Tran-
sylvania college.  L J 43: 269-71.

Norton, M. K.  A community library.  P L 21: 305-6.

---- M. K.  The library in co-operation with other interests of the community.  Vt L Bull 12: 4-5.

Norwell, C.  Norfolk and Norwich incorporated law society's
library.  L A R 22: 305-6.

Noss, T. P.  Library work in normal schools.  Nat Educ Assn
1904: 912-9.

Notz, W.  Important discoveries on fly-leaves of old books in
American libraries.  P L 16: 376.

Nourse, E. M.  Review of leather for binding during the last
eleven years in England and America.  A L A Bull 10: 472-5.

Nourse, H. S.  Free public library commission of Massachusetts.
L J 21: 10-3.

Nourse, J. H.  Naval observatory library.  U S Govt Rept: 267-
8.

Nowell, C.  The libraries of Norwich.  L A R 22: 290-306.

Noyes, E. C.  Ideal versus realities in high school English.
Nat Educ Assn 1908: 653-6.

Noyes, M. C.  Sketch of the library of the Medical and chir-
urgical faculty of the State of Maryland.  Med Lib and
Hist Journal 2: 317-20.

Noyes, S. B.  Cataloguing.  L J 8: 166-72.

--- S. B.  Classifying folklore and Shakespeariana.  L J
9: 156.

--- S. B.  Plan of the new catalogue of the Brooklyn mercantile library.  U S Rept 648-56. 1876.

Nunn, J. H.  Planning and equipping a high school library.
P L 20: 406-9.

-- J. H.  Some problems of a high school library.  P L 19:
432-5.

Nursey, W. R.  Trustee's duty to the public.  A L A Bull 6:
304-7.

Nuttall, P. E.   Literary history: a librarian's equipment.
  L A R 12: 625-9.
Nutting, M. O.   Please don't to bookbinders.   L J 12: 289.
Nyhuus, H.   Norwegian branch library.   L J 26: 864.
  ---- H.   Norwegian form of safe-guarded open access.   L
  J 25: 728.
  ---- H.   Organization of state-supported libraries in Nor-
  way.   L J 29: Conf No 60-3.
  ---- H.   Park libraries in Norway.   L J 26: 388.
Nystrom, P. H.   Business books.   Wis Lib Bull 11: 119-24.
  ----- P. H.   The business library as an investment.   L J
  42: 857-62.
  ----- P. H.   The relation of the public library to the
  private business libraries.   L J 43: 154-7; P L 23: 258-
  60; Special Libraries 9: 35-7.
Oakley, M. M.   Arranging and cataloguing scraps.   L J 32: 282.
Oberly, E. R.   Agricultural libraries section of the American
  library association.   Science (ps) 50: 167-8.
  ---- E. R.   Certification for librarians.   L J 45: 357.
  ---- E. R.   Circulation of periodicals.   Special Libraries
  10: 193-4.
  ---- E. R.   A difference of opinion.   P L 25: 436-7.
  ---- E. R.   The library service in the Report of the Con-
  gressional joint commission on the reclassification of
  salaries.   Special Libraries 11: May 18a-20a.
O'Brien, H. J.   Grievances of a free library reader.   L W 3:
  31-4.
O'Brien, N.   Our juvenile readers.   L A R 9: 506-9.
O'Connor, J. F.   Facts about bookworms: their history in lit-
  erature and work in libraries.   L J 23: 538.
O'Connor, M.   The next book.   P L 20: 158-9.
O'Connor, V. C. S.   Living pages from the East: the library
  at Patna.   Asia 19: 785-91.
Oehler, B. O.   Poster bulletins again--aesthetic principles.
  Wis Lib Bull 14: 146-9.
O'Flynn, J.   Woman suffrage: a reading list of books and parts
  of books on women suffrage.   Bull Bib 6: 119-22, 146-7.
Ogden, E. L.   Two important agricultural review journals.
  Special Libraries 10: 32-5.
  --- E. L. and W. H. Beal.   The contribution of the U.S.
  Department of Agriculture and the bibliography of science,
  with a list of the bibliographical publications of the
  department.   Bib Soc Amer Proc 3: 135-52.
Oger, H.   Plans for libraries in France.   L J 40: 414-5.
Ogle, H.   Book buying.   L A 1: 111-5.
  -- H.   An old town library.   L A 4: 141-5.
Ogle, J. J.   Annotations: some examples.   L A R 1: 115-7.
  -- J. J.   Assistants' training.   L A R 1: 338-40.
  -- J. J.   Edwards and Ewart and the select committee on
  public libraries of 1849.   L A R 1: 696-708.

-- J. J.  Hindrances to the training of efficient libra-
rians.  2nd Int Conf: 44-5.
-- J. J.  Library expenditure and salaries.  L C 5: 23-4.
--, J. J.  Library legislation in the United Kingdon.  L
J 29: Conf No 37-8.
-- J. J.  The mutual relationship of the public library
and technical school.  L A R 3: 567-71.
-- J. J.  Outlines of a new scheme of classification ap-
plicable to books.  L C 2: 160.
-- J. J.  Place of the free library in popular education.
L 3: 401-7.
-- J. J.  Proposal for establishment of district libraries.
L 6: 42-4.
-- J. J.  Public libraries and public education (a letter).
L A R 9: 47-8.
-- J. J.  Public library and the public elementary school:
a note and an experiment.  L 8: 93-5.
-- J. J.  Relationship of the public library committee to
other educational bodies.  L 7: 129-34.
-- J. J.  Some pitflals in cataloguing.  L 8: 150-6.
-- J. J.  Subject entries.  L 8: 580.
-- J. J.  Summer school of library science.  L 4: 319-23.
-- J. J.  Training of library assistants.  Greenwood's Yr-
Bk: 52-9.  1897.
O'Hara, J. C.  A library in chains.  P L 19: 430-1.
Ohlinger, F.  New journalism in China.  World's Work (London)
17: 66-71.
Ohr, C.  Value of library school training.  Lib Occ 5: 333-5.
Olcott, F. J.  The children's free library and city education.
American City 8: 257-64.
---- F. J.  The children's reading: review.  P L  18: 67-8.
---- F. J.  Fairy tales for children.  Bibliography No 13,
N Y S L Rept, 1898.
---- F. J.  Home libraries for poor children.  Chautauquan
39: 374-80.
---- F. J.  Pasadena exhibit of library work with children.
L J 36: 345-7, 362-3.
---- F. J.  The public library, a social force in Pitts-
burgh.  Survey 23: 849-61.
---- F. J.  Rational library work with children and the
preparation for it.  L J 30: Conf No 71-5.
---- F. J.  Story telling as a means of teaching litera-
ture.  N Y L 4: 38-45; P L 19: 141-6.
---- F. J.  Story telling, etc.  L J 25: Conf No 69-70;
Discussion, 129-31.
---- F. J.  Story telling, lectures and other adjuncts of
the children's room.  P L 5: 282-4.
---- F. J.  Training of the children's librarian.  A L A
Bull 2: 213-6.

---- F. J.  Work with children at Carnegie library, Pittsburgh. L J 25: 166-8.

Olcott, J. J.  Public library a social force in Pittsburgh. Survey 23: 849-61.

---- J. J.  Story telling: a public library method.  Child Conference for Research and Welfare Proceedings 1909, 1: 225-7; Pedagogical Seminary 16: 545-7.

Olds, F. A.  North Carolina's oldest library, James Hasell library at Wilmington.  N C Lib Bull 2: 62-3.

Olin, C. R.  Order table for collective biography.  L J 18: 144.

Oliver, T. E.  Impressions of some great European libraries. P L 19: 377-82.

Olrik, H.  Public libraries in Norway.  L A R 11: 131.

Olsen, J. W.  Library work among the children of Minnesota. Harper's Weekly May 15, 1909, 53: 24-5.

--- J. W.  School and the library.  Nat Educ Ass Proceedings (General Sessions) 1907: 117-25.

Olson, A.  Some books on occultism.  Mich Lib Bull 8: 103-7.

Olson, N. A.  The reading of the young person.  Minn P L C N 2: 57-62.

O'Mara, A. T.  Classification of public documents, pamphlets and miscellaneous matter.  Ontario Lib Assn Proceedings Ap 1912: 68-70.

O'Neill, J. J.  Irish theatrical history: a bibliographical essay.  An Leab 2: 115-22.

O'Neill, L.  The Insular library of Porto Rico: its history and development.  L J 38: 522-3.

Orcutt, W. D.  The art of the book in America.  "Studio" spring number 1914: 259-76.

Ormerod, J.  Library bureau visible index.  L A R 18: 212-4.

----- J.  Rand visible index: Revolving frame with transparent movable tube-holders for catalogue entries.  L A R 17: 18-23.

----- J.  The subject classification: suggested revision of C050 electrical engineering.  L A R 18: 109-12.

----- J.  Writings of Oliver Wendell Holmes.  L (ns) 9: 17-35.

Ormes, M. D.  Coburn library of Colorado college.  Colorado Lib Assn Occasional Leaflets 1: 55-6.

--- M. D.  Function of the librarian.  P L 18: 23-4.

Orr, C.  Book buying and trade bibliographies.  P L 3: 345-9.

Orr, W.  Connection of public libraries with schools and museums.  New England Mag (ns) 15: 242.

- W.  Co-operation in war work between the Y. M. C. A. and the A. L. A.  A L A Bull 11: 111-4, 327.

- W.  The co-operation of the Y. M. C. A. and the A. L. A. A L A Bull 12: 93-5.

- W.  Township extension of libraries; observations from experiences in Page county.  Ia L C Q 6: 65-8.

Orvis, M. B.  Wisconsin's package libraries.  Independent 73: 436-8.

Osgood, M.  System in a city engineer's office: methods in use in Ann Arbor, Mich.  American City Aug 1917: 136-8; L J 42: 921; Am Lib Annual 1917-18: 44.

Osgood, S. M.  The town library as an aid to the school.  New Hamp Bull (ns) 6: 223-9.

Osler, W.  The library school in the college.  L A R 19: 287-308; L J 43: 694-5.

--- W.  The "Religio Medici."  L (ns) 7: 1-31.

Ostler, W. H.  The public library and education.  L A R 11: 376-8.

Oswald, W. K.  Patience exerciser, or obstructor.  L W 10: 289-91.

Otis, B. N.  Books as carriers of scarlet fever.  L J 38: 27-8.

Otis, O.  Library future in New Orleans.  L J 17: 242.

Otis, W. A.  Library buildings from view point of the architect.  P L 8: 202-7.

Otlet, P.  The book: its world-wide use and international co-ordination after the war.  L J 43: 790-2.

--- P.  Pour une classification universelle.  L W 22: 232-6; L J 44: 907-8.

Overall, W. H.  Notes on broadsides and proclamations.  L A M N 2: 10-9.

Ovitz, D. G.  Course in reference work.  Wis Lib Bull 9: 144-5.

--- D. G.  Library instruction in normal schools.  American School 1: 76; L J 40: 753.

--- D. G.  Normal school training in library methods.  Nat Educ Assn 1914: 814-7; Minn Lib Notes 4: 112-4.

--- D. G.  Systematic training for obtaining information.  Western Journal of Education March 1912; L J 38: 150-2.

--- D. G.  Training rural teachers in the use of books.  Nat Educ Assn 1914: 802-7.

Owen, E.  Workmen's libraries in Glamorganshire and Monmouthshire.  L 8: 1-14.

Owen, E. B.  Notes on the Hartford library in relation to the schools.  L J 30: 217-8.

Owen, J. M.  Some student opinions on entrance requirements in English.  Education 25: 619-26.

Owen, T. W.  Library progress in Alabama.  A L A Bull 1: Conf No 75-6.

-- T. M.  Work and aspirations of the Alabama state department of archives and history.  A L A Bull 1: Conf No 101.

Owen, W. E.  Policy of the Library assistants' association to the individual assistant.  L A 8: 147-9.

-- W. E.  Variation on the staff time sheet illustrated in Brown's "Manual."  L W 13: 178-9.

Owens, B. M.  The use of war literature.  Minn P L C N 5: 51-3.

Owens, M. T.   Discussion of California county free library law. Cal News Notes 5: 378: California Lib Assn Proceedings 1911: 32.

Packard, F. R.   Early medical libraries in America; being an account of the origin and growth of the Pennsylvania hospital and of the College of physicians of Philadelphia. Med Lib and Hist Journal 5: 96-108.

Packer, B. G.   The Withes Farmers' institute and festival association.   Wis Lib Bull 7: 67-70.

Pacy, F.   Borrowing and rating powers under the Public libraries acts.   L 1: 132-6.

-- F.   The controlling authority: general effect of the recommendations of the Adult education committee upon future administration.   L A R 21: 395-8.

-- F.   The new opportunity.   L A R 22: 326-7.

-- F.   Possibility of mutual arrangement between county schemes and (a) borough libraries.   L A R 22: 385-90.

-- F.   Reference versus lending department.   L A R 3: 593-602.

-- F.   The Shakespeare Head press at Stratford-upon-Avon. L A R 18: 308-18.

-- F.   Sunday opening of London libraries.   L W 1: 92-3.

-- F.   Town libraries and surrounding districts.   L C 5: 45-8.

Paddock, A. M.   Alfred Dickey library.   Jamestown, South Dakota.   L J 44: 455.

----- A. M.   Make room for the documents.   P L 14: 126-7.

Padelford, F. M.   The decline in taste for good reading.   Washington Education Assn Proceedings, 1910: 83-9.

Page, M.   My attendance at the provincial library school, 1916. P L 23: 10-2.

Page, W. G. B.   Booksellers signs of Fleet street.   B A R 13: XIX-XXIV, XXXI-XXXVI.

-- W. G. B.   Notes on Hull authors, booksellers and stationers.   B A R 6: I-VII, 1909.

Page, W. H.   An intimate view of publishing.   World's Work (N. Y.) 4: 2561-5; L J 27: Conf No 166-70.

Paine, A. B.   Children's room in Smithsonian institution. Smithsonian Institution Rept 1901: 553-63; St. Nicholas 28: 964-73.

Paine, P. M.   Advertising the library.   New Hamp Bull (ns) 14: 122-4.

--- P. M.   American public as seen from the circulation desk.   A L A Bull 10: 283-6.

--- P. M.   Are we to have a free library?   Bookman (N Y) 49: 68-71.

--- P. M.   The "Books for everybody" campaign of the American library association.   New Hamp Bull (ns) 16: 23-4.

--- P. M.   The buying of books.   N Y L 3: 133-6.

--- P. M.  Library service is free.  N Y L 7: 12-3; Lib Occ 5: 383.

--- P. M.  The library's task in reconstruction.  A L A Bull 13: 117-20, 353; P L 25: 1-4; N Y L 6: 228-30.

--- P. M.  Overdue book day.  L J 41: 446.

--- P. M.  Reading for joy: its part in education.  N Y L 5: 51-5.

--- P. M.  The soldiers' branch of the Syracuse public library.  L J 42: 791-3; N Y L 5: 262-4.

--- P. M.  The use of print: its advocates in conference.  L J 44: 487, 507-9.

--- P. M.  What Americans read.  N Y L 7: 40-1.

Palmer, G. H.  Best books of 1902--Fine arts.  L A R 6: 206-12.

---- G. H.  Best books of 1903--Fine arts.  L A R 7: 113-33.

Palmer, M.  In the neighbourhood of the story hour.  Minn P L C N No 5: 12-4.

---- M.  Picture exchange for small libraries.  Wis Lib Bull No 3: 1-3; Neb Lib Bull 1, No 3: 1-3.

---- M.  Some collateral phases of library activity.  Wis Lib Bull 3: 29-30.

Palmer, M. B.  The public library and the state.  N C Bull 1: 104-5.

---- M. B.  Work with children.  N C Bull 1: 62-4.

Palmer, W. M.  The relationship of publishers, booksellers and librarians.  L J 26: Conf No 31-7.

---- W. M. and G. J. Gray.  Abstracts from the wills and testamentary documents of printers, binders and stationers of Cambridge from 1504-1699.  Bibliographical Society Publication, 1915.

Paltsits, V. H.  Plea for an anatomical method in bibliography.  Bib Soc Amer Proc 1: 123-4.

------ V. H.  Tragedies in New York's public records.  Am Hist Assn Rept 1909: 369-78.

Pardes, J.  Duluth and its advancement.  Wis Lib Bull 7: 76-9.

Parfitt, E.  Devon and Exeter institution.  L C 3: 107-9.

Parham, N. E.  The business man and the public library.  P L 24: 410-5.

---- N. E.  White list of periodicals for a public library.  P L 19: 451.

Parker, G.  Illuminated MSS. in the Ruskin museum, Sheffield.  L A R 11: 572-9.

Parker, J.  Browne charging system.  Vt L Bull 2: 1-2.

---- J.  Peabody Institute system of press marks.  L J 17: 233-4.

Parker, J. G.  On the leather question.  L A R 8: 489-91.

Parker, S. J.  Local prints.  L W 10: 278-80.

Parker, T. D.  Ships' libraries.  U S Naval Inst Proceedings
    Jan-Feb 1915: 143-9.
Parker, W. E.  Printed catalogue cards of Library bureau.  L
    J 19: 21, 256.
Parker, W. H.  Procedure in changing from a closed to an open
    library.  L A 9: 63-70.
Parkinson, H. O.  War libraries in action.  P L 23: 367-8.
Parlin, C. C.  Successful high school library at Wausau, Wis-
    consin.  Wis Lib Bull 3: 44-5; School Review 15: 251-4.
Parmelee, A.  Children's room, Richards free library.  New
    Hamp Lib Bull 12: 167-8.
Parnham, E.  Bugbears and how to overcome then.  P L 13: 382-
    3.
Parr, G.  Card ledger: a charging system without writing.  L
    A U K Trans 2: 73-5.
Parr, R. T. L.  The public library movement from the ratepayers'
    point of view.  L A 11: 4-14.
Parry, H. L.  Functions and possibilities of a library and mu-
    seum regarding the collection of local MSS. and seals.  L
    A R 12: 467-8.  Discussion 529-37.
Parshley, L. E.  The public library--theoretical and applied.
    New Hamp Bull 11: 143.
Parson, R. W.  Public library reform.  Libn 4: 313-6, 348-51,
    386-9.
Parsons, A. B.  The Randall library of social science.  Chari-
    ties 10: 549-50.
Parsons, A. J.  The division of prints of the Library of Con-
    gress.  Print Collector's Quarterly 3: 310-35.
Parsons, E.  Growth of the publishing industry in the United
    States.  World To-day 4: 97-108.
Parsons, F. H.  Care of maps.  L J 20: 199-201.
    ----- F. H.  Letter-pressing catalogue cards.  L J 19: 224.
Parsons, J.  First children's room.  L J 34: 552.
    ----- J.  The library and the school.  P L 1: 313.
Parsons, M.  The library and the working man.  New Hamp Bull
    8: 69-71; P L 13: 84-5.
Parsons, M. P.  Why catalog?  L J 44: 173-5.
Parsons, R. W.  Introduction to elementary bibliography.  Libn
    3: 43-50, 84-8, 192.
    ----- R. W.  Libraries and industries.  L A 12: 3-12.
    ----- R. W.  Library reform.  L A R 15: 101-2.
    ----- R. W.  Public library reform.  Libn 4: 313-6, 348-51,
    386-9.
Parsons, S. L.  Library work with schools.  Penn Lib Notes 5,
    No 4: 37-9.
Partridge, W. I.  Architectural competitions for library build-
    ings.  L J 29: 413-5.
Paton, J. B.  Public libraries and the National home reading
    union.  L A R 10: 488-97.
    --- J. B. and L. S. Jast.  New proposals in regard to the

public libraries by the National home reading union.  L A
R 9: 637-42.

Patrick, F. J.  The information bureau:  an undeveloped possibility.  L A 8: 10-6.

Patrick, M.  Tne library assistant and the library board.  A
L A Bull 14: 141-3.

Patrick, M. L.  Decoration of children's rooms in public libraries.  Mass Lib Club Bull 6: 48-9;  Am Lib Annual 1916-17:
41-2.

Patten, F. C.  Library and the lecture.  P L 11: 489-92.

---- F. C.  Library legislation.  P L 2: 3-5.

Patten, K.  Beginnings of an art library.  Ia L C Q 2: 32-3.

---- K.  Hospital liorary service at Fort Snelling.  Minn
P L C N 6: 2-3.

---- K.  Use of art books.  A L A Bull 1: Conf No 179-83.

Patterson, E.  How to keep books and information in the library
up-to-date.  Penn Lib Notes 5, No 4: 25-7.

Pattison, Mrs. F. A.  The library and the woman's club.  P L
15: 137-42.

Patton, A.  Cataloging economics:  the care of gift pamphlets.
A L A Bull 12: 249-50.

Patton, J.  Work of a library trustee from the trustee's point
of view.  L J 31: 656-7.

Patton, N. S.  Architects and librarians.  L J 14: 159-62.

---- N. S.  Designing of a college library.  A L A Bull 1:
Conf No 270-4.

---- N. S.  Heating, lighting and ventilation of libraries.
U S Rept: 717-24;  Discussion, L J 18: Conf No 28-9.  1892.

---- N. S.  Library architecture.  P L 6: 200-4.

---- N. S.  Lighting of libraries.  U S Rept: 722-4.

Paul, H. G.  On handling supplementary reading.  English Journal
3: 212-9.

Paulmier, H.  Getting in touch with our foreign readers.  P L
24: 295-6.

----- H.  Putting the library on the map.  P L 25: 445-7.

----- H.  The small town library as a community center.
L J 42: 376-7.

Paxton, E. T.  Municipal reference work.  Texas Libraries July
1916: 12-4.

Payne, E. G.  Safety education and the library.  Special Libraries 10: 209-10.

Payne, J. F.  English herbals.  Bib Soc Trans 9: 120-3; 11: 299-
306.

--- J. F.  On the "Herbarius," and Hortus sanitatis.  Bib
Soc Trans 6: 63-126.

Peabody, M. G.  Literature and reading.  Grade v. Teachers'
College Record 8: 55-60.

Peach, C. H. R.  Parliamentary commission of enquiry and their
reports.  L A 11: 91-8.

Peacock, A. L.   Library and the junior citizen.   Libn 9: 42-4.
Peacock, B. M.   A new labour-saver.   L W 16: 166-8.
----- B. M.   Trade unionism and library workers in America.
L W 21: 168-9
Peacock, M.   The L. A. A. as a trades-union.   L A 14: 182-3, 194.
----- M.   Nationalized public libraries.   L W 18: 196-9, 279-
80.
----- M.   Sex disqualification.   L W 22: 344-6.
----- M.   Trade unionism and library workers.   L W 20: 259-
61, 335-6.
Peak, E. E.   A trade catalog file.   L J 44: 442.
Pearce, J. G.   The future of documentation.   L A R 20: 162-6.
---- J. G.   The works library and its relation to the public
technical library.   L A R 21: 8-12.
Pearey, C. S.   Some reasons against purchasing subscription
books published in sets.   N Y L 1: 12
Pearse, C. T.   Library training in the normal schools.   Nat
Educ Assn 1915: 807-8;   American School 1: 266.
Pearson, E. L.   An amateur's notion of boys' books.   A L A Bull
2: 158-62.
----- E. L.   Books and the news.   Weekly Review 2: 372.
----- E. L.   The children's librarian versus "Huckleberry
Finn":  a brief for the defense.   L J 32: 312-4.
----- E. L.   Evil that books do.   P L 16: 188-91.
----- E. L.   How to discourage reading.   A L A Bull 7: 230-6;
New Hamp Bull 9: 209-14.
----- E. L.   Literary censorship and the library.   L J 42:
20.
----- E. L.   Of books and their keepers.   N J Lib Bull 3.
No 3: 14-6.
----- E. L.   Pestilent catalogue.   Nation 99: 130-1 July 30,
1914.
----- E. L.   Trade unionism in America.   L W 22: 243-4.
----- E. L.   Trials of librarians.   Nation 98: 750-1.
Pearson, J. B.   Emanuel college library.   L A U K Trans 5: 242-
3.
Peaslee, J. B.   Address to the Cincinnati A. L. A. conference.
L J 7: 206.
----- J. B.   Moral and literary training in public schools.
Nat Educ Assn 1881: 104-7.
Peck, A. L.   Adaptation of libraries to local use.   L J 20: 45-
8.
-- A. L.   Charging by means of baggage checks.   L J 13: 315.
-- A. L.   Correlation of a library and school on the part
of the library.   Univ of State of New York.   Regent's Bull-
etin 36: 103-8.
-- A. L.   Economical furniture and fittings.   N Y L 1: 41-2.
-- A. L.   What may a librarian do to influence the reading
of a community.   L J 22: 77-80.

Peck, E.  Legitimate aspirations of a village library.  L J
23: 522-4.
Peck, E. E.  Library of the Winchester repeating arms company.
New Haven.  Special Libraries 9: 41.
Peck, H. T.  New children's picture books.  Bookman (N Y) 4:
301-8.
Peck, N. L.  A summer reading course.  P L 23: 274.
Pecke, L. P.  Who and what is the library board?  Wis Lib Bull
9: 158 60.
Peckham, G. W.  The child and the book.  Wis Lib Bull 2: 90-3.
----- G. W.  Circular of information to teachers of Milwau-
kee.  Wis Lib Bull 2: 38.
----- G. W.  Public library and the public schools.  Educa-
tional Review 8: 358-62.
----- G. W.  Work with libraries and schools in Milwaukee.
L J 20: 123-4.
Peckham, S. P.  English reading in school and out.  School
Journal 73: 338.
Peddie, A.  Decimal classification and relative location.  L
9: 346-9.
Peddie, R. A.  Activities in bibliography.  L A 7: 43-6, Dis-
cussion 46-9.
---- R. A.  American newspapers in the British Museum.  L
W 13: 72-4.
---- R. A.  Cataloguing of periodicals.  L 3: 119-20.
---- R. A.  Copyright.  L W 13: 81-2.
---- R. A.  Best books of 1902 - Sociology.  L A R 6: 298-
300.
---- R. A.  Bibliography and copyright.  L A R 11: 517.
---- R. A.  Books on the practical side of printing.  1566-
1750.  Bib Soc Trans 9: 1-4.
---- R. A.  Decimal classificatin and relative location.
L 9: 346-9.
---- R. A.  English libraries:  a study in administrative
chaos.  L A 9: 17-9; L A R 13: 531-.
---- R. A.  Fifteenth century books:  an author index.  L
W 10: 166-74; 325-8; 11: 43-53, 144-54, 209-17, 267-71, 288-
300, 335-43, 374-82, 427-35, 455-62; 12: 10-8, 66-74, 102-9,
143-51, 192-200, 236-40, 280-92, 324-32, 364-72, 404-12,
436-44, 472-6.
---- R. A.  International conference at Brussels.  L (3d
series) 1: 442-4.
---- R. A.  List of bibliographical books published since
the foundation of the Bibliographical society in 1893.  Bib
Soc Trans 10: 235-311.
---- R. A.  Literature of the war;  bibliography and select
lists.  L A R 17: 478-80.
---- R. A.  Metallurgical bibliography, 1901-1906.  L W 9:
363-9, 411-5.
---- R. A.  National bibliographies.  L W 12: 301-4, 354-6,
379-80, 424-6 459-67; 13: 55-7, 165-8; 13: 273-4, 371.

---- R. A.  A note on the principal bibliographical authorities for the general history and topography of France.
L W 20: 202-3.

---- R. A.  Notes on provincial printers and booksellers --
Essex.  L W 7: 57-60.

---- R. A.  Notes on the history of the printed book.  L W
18: 164-7, 199-202.

---- R. A.  Past, present, and future of public libraries.
L A 3: 107-9.

---- R. A.  St. Bride typographical library:  its methods
and classification.  L A R 18: 235-58;  L A 13: 7-12;  L J
41: 787-8.

---- R. A.  Sale prices of incunabula in 1901.  L (ns) 3:
164-75.

---- R. A.  Sale prices of incunabula in 1903.  L (ns) 5:
318-35.

---- R. A.  Sale prices of incunabula in 1904.  L (ns) 6:
173-85.

---- R. A.  Some British libraries:  is there need of administrative reform?  L W 17: 162-5.

---- R. A.  Some possible bibliographical activities of the
Library association.  L A R 11: 187-93.

---- R. A.  Text-books on printing for public libraries.  L
W 20: 172-3.

---- R. A. and H. R. Plomer.  Stephen Bulkley, printer.  L
(ns) 8: 42-56.

---- R. A. and R. Steele.  English printed music to 1600.
Bib Soc Trans 5: 8-10.

Peet, H. E.  Co-operation between libraries and schools.  Elementary School Teacher 6: 310-7.

Peet, H. W.  Devonshire House reference library:  Quaker printing and the Society's treasures.  L A R 22: 229-31.

Pegan, P.  Teaching the use of books.  Colorado Library Assn
Occasional Leaflet 1: 69-70.

Peirce, B. K.  Probable intellectual and moral outcome of the
rapid increase of public libraries.  L J 10: 234-6.

Pence, R. W.  Chat with students about books.  English Journal
6: 667-85.

Pendleton, A. M.  How to start libraries in small towns.  L J
1: 161-2, 213-6, 249-50, 313-4;  355-9, 421-2.

Pendleton, A. M.  Notions wise and otherwise.  L J 5: 3-6.

------- A. M.  Warming libraries.  L J 5: 277.

Pendleton, E. S.  Library of the Children's aid society.  Special Libraries 2: 6-7.

Pendry, E. R.  A high school library club.  P L 25: 92-3.

Pennell, E. R.  Our national print room.  Nation 111: 512.

Pennell, J.  On English book-illustrators of 1860.  Bib Soc
Trans 3: 153-4.

Pennock, B. M.  The other side of "Paternalism".  L J 25: 61-3.

Pennock, B. W.    Browne charging system.  L J 22: 294-6, 340.
----- B. W.    Ordering books.  P L 2: 132-3.
Pentz, W. C.    Library campaign in Dubois, Pa.  Penn Lib Notes
    10: 47-8.
Peoples, N. T.    Relations of libraries to the book trade.  P
    L 7: 311-4.
Peoples, W. T.    How we choose and buy new books.  L J 14: 337.
----- W. T.    What we do about duplicates.  L J 14: 371.
----- W. T.    What we do with pamphlets.  L J 14: 471.
Pepcroy, B.    Tramcars as traveling libraries.  L W 9: 323-7.
Peplow, F.    Some tentative proposals for the compilation of
    catalogue of best books.  L A R 11: 222-8, Discussion 245-9.
Peplow, F. J.    Education and the diploma.  L A R 10: 319-20.
---- F. J.    Library planning.  L A R 11: 419-20.
---- F. J.    Literature of stamp collecting.  L A R 10:
    477-9.
---- F. J.    On the duties and qualifications of a librarian:
    an address delivered at the Sorbonne on December 23, 1870,
    by J. B. C. des Houssaves.  L (ns) 5: 182-91.
---- F. J.    Some tentative proposals for the compilation
    of a catalogue of best books.  L A R 11: 222-8, Discussion
    245-9.
Peplow, W. A.    Evaluative annotation.  L A 5: 211-3.
---- W. A.    Library lectures.  L W 12: 344-5.
---- W. A.    Local collections and the county collections.
    L A 5: 336-8.
Pepper, F. W. C.    Classification and the public.  L A 12: 69-
    74.
---- F. W. C.    The classification of biography.  L A R 15:
    328-34.
---- F. W. C.    Form classification.  L A 11: 167-74.
---- F. W. C.    Some problems of classification.  L A 11:
    27-30, 167-74.
Peppiette, E. A.    Registration of assistant librarians.  L
    A 13: 31-2, 36;  L W 18: 252.
------- E. A.    Some features of work in a college library.
    P L 18: 10-1;  L A 9: 230-7.
------- E. A.    Some reflections on modern librarianship.
    L A 14: 16-21.
Pereles, J. M.    What a trustee can do to help the librarian.
    Wis Lib Bull 2: 25-6.
Perkins, A. H.    Wasteful repetition in the study of English
    Texts.  Nation 86: 166-7.
Perkins, A. H.    Children's literature.  P L 10: 238-40
Perkins, F. B.    Best hundred novels.  L J 1: 166-7.
----- F. B.    The accession catalogue again.  L J 3: 336.
----- F. B.    Book indexes.  U S Bureau of Education Report
    1876: 727-32.
----- F. B.    Charging-card rack.  L J 10: 63.

----- F. B.   Classification in dictionary catalogues.  L J
4: 226-34.
----- F. B.   Free libraries and unclean books.  L J 10: 396.
----- F. B.   How to make town libraries successful.  U. S.
Rept 419-30.  1876.
----- F. B.   Movable location.  L J 7: 29.
----- F. B.   Public libraries of San Francisco.  L J 10: 223-
9.
----- F. B.   Schwartz mnemonic classification.  L J 4: 92.
----- F. B.   Young men's mercantile libraries.  U S Govt
Rept 1876: 378-85.
----- F. B. and J. Schwartz.  Dui-decimal classification and
the relative-index.  L J 11: 36, 37,68, 144, 156.
----- F. B. and M. Dewey.  Accession catalogue again.  L J
3: 336-8.
Perkins, N. C.   How to find periodicals.  L J 12: 354-6, 440.
Perry, B.   The American reviewer.  Yale Review (ns) 4: 3-24.
--- B.   Library criticism in American periodicals.  Yale Re-
view (ns) 3: 635-55.
Perry, C. R.   Books and contagion.  P L 6: 273-4.
Perry, E. M.   Experiment with children's book marks.  Wis Lib
Bull 1: 95.
Perry, E. R.   Aims and methods of library publicity.  L J 39:
259-66.
--- E. R.   Bulletins and library printing.  A L A Bull 9:
102-4;  P L 20: 301-3.
--- E. R.   Latin-Americana in the Los Angeles public library.
L J 44: 384.
--- E. R.   Reading list on Florence.  Bulletin No 106, Bib-
liography 41, N Y S L Rept 89 vol 1.  1906.
--- E. R.   Salaries in city and county libraries:  general
observations.  A L A Bull 13: 71-7.
Perry, F. M.   Dictionaries in the school room.  English Journal
4: 660-3.
Perry, W. A.   The association boys: Y.M.C.A. library.  L J 36:
182-3.
Peschke, M. D.   Motion pictures: a list of books and articles.
St. Louis Public Library Monthly Bulletin July 1920: 163-8.
Peters, H.   Delivery stations.  L W 10: 274-6.
---- H.   Show cases for books.  L W 10: 119-20.
Peters, O. M.   Fumigating books.  Lib Occ No 11: 8.
---- O. M.   Libraries in relation to citizenship and Amer-
icanization.  L J 44: 759.
---- O. M.   The rural-school library.  Nat Educ Assn 1917:
672-4;  L J 42: 495.
---- O. M.   What the public library can do for grade and
rural schools.  A L A Bull 10: 217-8, 432.
---- O. M. and Stern, R. B.   Rural school library.  Nat Educ
Assn 1916: 676-80.
Peterson, A. E.   A history teacher's use of a library.  Nat Educ
Assn 1910: 1000-2.

------ A. E.  New York's common council minutes, 1784-1831.
American City (C ed.) 19: 99-101.

Peterson, A. J.  Inter-library loans -- an experiement.  Wis
Lib Bull 2: 94.

Peterson, H. F.  Specialization in library collections.  P L
3: 249.

Petherbridge, M.  Albany library school.  L 7: 65.

---------- M.  American Library Schools.  L 7: 65-74.

Petherick, E. A.  Theoretical and practical bibliography.  2d
Int Conf 148-9;  1897.

Petrie, G.  The librarian as a statesman.  P L 25: 425-9.

Pettee, J.  Book marking with tools.  L J 35: 60-1.

---- J.  Classification for a theological library.  L J 36:
611-24.

---- J.  Graded catalogs: a suggestion for the "Librarian"
of the "Boston Transcript".  L J 40: 178-80.

---- J.  A projected information bureau of Cromwell's time.
L J 40: 660-2.

---- J.  Union list of Bibles by Dr. Gates of the Andover-
Harvard library.  A L A Bull 10: 449.

Pettee, J. E.  Library assistant once more, a plea for our professional ideal.  L J 29: 584-7.

Pettee, J. I.  Dissertations and program literature.  L J, 29:
297-300.

Petterson, G. S.  Books about new Americans.  Minn P L C N 5:
182-3.

Pettet, E.  Library in connection with the returning soldier
and sailor.  Wis Lib Bull 15: 41.

Pfoundes, C.  Japanese libraries and books.  L A M N 3: 178-80.

Phail, E.  Aids to magazine routing system.  Special Libraries
10: 165-6, 193-4.

--- E.  Library of the National cash register.  Special Libraries 8: 48-9.

Phail, E. A.  Clientele of men -- National cash register library.  L J 41: 265-7.

Phelps, A. R.  Evolution of a district library.  L J 21: 362-4.

---- A. R.  Evolution of a district library, second stage.
L J 27: 878-80.

Phelps, E. A.  Heating.  A L A Bull 1: Conf No 121.

---- E. A.  Library movement in Oklahoma.  A L A Bull 1:
78-9.

Philip, A.  Robert Pocock, of Gravesend.  L (ns) 8: 280-5.

Philip, A. J.  "Blacking out."  L W 7: 261-3.

---- A. J.  Bookbinding for lending libraries.  L A 4: 70-4.

---- A. J.  A British folk museum.  Libn 4: 46-8.

---- A. J.  Business of bookbinding: review.  Libn 3: 227-8.

---- A. J.  Card class register.  L W 7: 323-5.

---- A. J.  Cinematograph films: their national value and
preservation.  Libn 2: 367-70, 406-9, 447-9.

---- A. J. Co-operative exhibition. L W 11: 193.
---- A. J. Copyright and national registration. Libn 2: 384-7.
---- A. J. Decreasing issues. Libn 4: 48-50.
---- A. J. Defects of modern books as regards paper and printing, with suggestions for improvements. L A R 12: 34-6.
---- A. J. Heating of libraries. L A R 9: 225-30.
---- A. J. Inter-library loans. L W 11: 194-5.
---- A. J. Letter on the L. A. examination, 1910. L A R 13: 163-4.
---- A. J. Library classification, dealing more particularly with a scheme especially adapted to British libraries. L A 1: 152-5.
---- A. J. Mr. Carnegie's twelve million dollar dinner. Living Age 278: 58-60.
---- A. J. Mr. E. W. Hulme on cataloguing -- a letter. L A R 8: 125-6.
---- A. J. On the hiring of books. Libn 5: 243-6, 272-5.
---- A. J. The price of the novel. Libn 3: 361-4.
---- A. J. Profession and the press -- professional and other. L W 9: 353-6.
---- A. J. Proposed institute of librarians. L W 10: 294-5.
---- A. J. A reference library for London. Contemporary Review Sept 1912: 388-96.
---- A. J. Some notes on library lighting. Illuminating Engineer Nov 1915: 465-71.
---- A. J. Superannuation and the bill. L A R 9: 361-3.
---- A. J. Value of the linotype for catalogue printing. L A R 9: 400-1.
---- A. J. Ventilating of libraries. L A R 9: 225-30.
Phillimore, W. P. W. Contractions of forenames. L 1: 302-3.
Phillips, D. R. The collection of war records. L W 20: 35-9.
------ D. R. Literary and library activities in Celtic countries. L A R 17: 61-104; L J 41: 397-401.
------ D. R. Monastic libraries of Wales, fifth to sixteenth centuries (Celtic and mediaeval periods). L A R 14: 288-316, 374-98.
------ D. R. "Monastic libraries," review. L A 10: 60.
------ D. R. Public library policy and provision in Wales. L W 19: 117-20, 147-52.
------ D. R. Select bibliography of Owen Glyndwr. Welsh Bibliographical Society extra volume 1915, Glyndwr Centenary (1415-1915) p 48.
Phillips, E. M. Los Angeles State normal school library. P L 25: 89.
Phillips, I. C. Lights and shades of work in a town library. P L 24: 243-5.

Phillips, J. H.   History and literature in the grammar grades.
Nat Educ Assn 1892: 606-25.

Phillips, P. L.   Preservation and record of maps in the Library of Congress.   L J 25: 15-7.

Phillips, T.   Simple method of destroying insects which attack books and MSS.   British Assn Transactions 1837: 99.

Phillips, W. J.   Electrical energy in the library.   L W 11: 34-8;   12: 167-70.

------ W. J.   Library manuscript magazines.   L W 12: 4-7.

------ W. J. and T. O'B. Hubbard.   Books and periodicals on aeronautics: a buying list.   L W 12: 293-8.

------ W. J. and W. McGill.   Terms and phrases used·in library work.   L W 10: 354-60, 391-400, 429-40, 458-67.

Phythian, J. E.   Librarian and reader.   L A R 2: 305-12.

Pickering, J. E. L.   Electric light as applied to the lighting of the Inner Temple library.   L C 3: 173-7.

Picton, J.   Presidential address.   LA Trans 6: 11-5.

---- J., Mullins, J. D., and Thomas, E. C.   The Royal visit to Newcastle-upon-Tyne, opening of the public libraries.   L C 1: 137-42.

Pidgeon, M. K.   Argentine library conditions.   L J 44: 211-5.

Pier, F.   Tastes of bookworms.   Harper's Weekly 54: 27, June 11, 1910.

Pierce, A.   How one city school uses the library.   N C Bull 4: 48-53.

Pierce, B. K.   Probable intellectual and moral outcome of the rapid increase of public libraries.   L J 10: 234.

Pierce, F. M.   Cultivating a taste for something better besides fiction.   Vt L Bull 7, No 3: 3.

---- F. M.   Educational value of the library.   Vt L Bull 6: 6-7.

Pierce, I.   Reference work.   Lib Occ 2: 9-11.

Pierce, K.   On salaries of librarians and assistants.   L W 19: 184.

Pierce, K. E.   Education policy of the library association as affected by the suggestions in the Report of the Carnegie trustees.   L A R 19: 316-22.

---- K. E.   Women in public libraries: a reply to Mr. Chennell.   L W 4: 286-8;   5: 14-5;   9: 440-1.

Pierce, W.   Did Sir Roger Williams write the Marprelate tracts?   L (3d series) 3: 345-64.

Pierson, H. W.   Efficiency? -- On the changes in the title of the Efficiency society's journal.   L J 44: 369-70.

Pietschmann, R.   Dziatsko, Carl, 1842-1903.   L J 29: Conf. No. 87-8.

Pillsbury, M. M.   The general Theological library.   Special Libraries 9: 195-9.

Pilzgim, B.   Lord of creation in the library.   L W 10: 284-7.

Pincott, H. G.  The aims of our profession.  L A 13: 26-8.
Pink, J.  Advertisement circular of Cambridge public library.
   L A M N 3: 15-6.
   -- J.  After fifty years: a retrospect.  L A R 7: 513-26.
Pink, L. H.  Socializing the public library.  Survey 29: 675.
Pinney, M.  Boise children's librarian takes an active hand in
   movie situation.  L J 44: 47-8.
Piper, A. C.  Advisability of establishing county libraries.
   L W 14: 65-7.
   --- A. C.  Bibliography in relation to literature.  L W 18:
   79-83.
   --- A. C.  Book-trade in Winchester, 1549-1789.  L (3d
   series) 7: 191-7.
   --- A. C.  Contributions to the history of printing in Sussex
   B A R 13: I-IV.
   --- A. C.  Early printers and booksellers of Winchester.  L
   (4th series) 1: 103-10.
   --- A. C.  Libraries, museums and art galleries.  L W 10:
   419-21.
   --- A. C.  Library advertising methods.  L A R 15: 71-9.
   --- A. C.  Library exhibitions.  L W 12: 275-80.
   --- A. C.  Mr. John Burns and public libraries.  L W 14:
   353-4.
   --- A. C.  Music in public libraries.  L W 11: 78-9.
   --- A. C.  Non-resident borrowers.  L A 10: 45-52.
   --- A. C.  Note on the introduction of printing into Sussex
   up to the year 1850, with a chronology of Sussex printers
   to that date.  L (3d series) 5: 257-65.
   --- A. C.  A novel library experiement.  L W 15: 165-6.
   --- A. C.  The parchment making industry in Winchester and
   Hampshire.  L (3d series) 10: 65-8.
   --- A. C.  Private printing presses in Sussex.  L (3d series)
   5: 70-9.
   --- A. C.  Problem of the junior assistant.  L A 10: 234-6.
   --- A. C.  Some great printers and their work.  L W 15:
   239-371;  16: 3-204.
   --- A. C.  Technical training in librarianship in England
   and abroad.  L A R 14: 332-51.
   --- A. C.  Training for librarians in France.  L W 12:
   421-2.
   --- A. C.  Training for librarians in Germany.  L W 12:
   208-9.
Pite, B.  Architecture for librarians (Laurentian Library).
   L (ns) 1: 326-37.
   -- B.  Library architecture from architect's standpoint.
   2nd Int Conf 106-10.  Discussion 240-1.  1897.
   -- B.  On the Medico-Laurentian library at Venice.  2nd
   International Conference Proceedings 1897:  109-10.
Pitt, S.  Practical accession work.  L A R 6: 477-8;  7: 68-71.

Pitt, S. A.   Commercial libraries.  L A R 19: 467-72.
 --  S. A.   The Commercial library, Glasgow.  Special Lib-
   raries 8: 162-70.
 --  S. A.   The library rate in relation to the financial
   position of public libraries, with discussion.  L A R 21:
   103-13.
 --  S. A.   Memorandum on commercial libraries.  L A R 19:
   175-8.
 --  S. A.   Notes on the commercial library; with discussion.
   L A R 21: 49-60, 201-5, 310-3.
 --  S. A.   Notes on the disposal of duplicates.  L A R 12:
   393-5.
 --  S. A.   Possible co-operation in reference library work.
   L A R 15: 408-12.
 --  S. A.   Procedure in obtaining extension of rating power
   for public library purposes.  L W 13: 368-9.
Place, F.  Bibliographic style in medical literature.  Medical
   Record Jan 25, 1913: 157-60.
Place, F. Jr.  The pamphlet as a library tool.  Bulletin of
   Medical Library Assn Oct 1917: 17-22;  L J 43: 455.
 ---  F. Jr.  Verify your references:  a word to medical
   writers.  New York Medical Journal, Oct 7, 1916, 10p;  L
   J 42: 490;  Am Lib Annual 1917-18: 17-8.
Plaister, C. D.  Publicity.  Ia L C Q 8: 72-6;  L J 43: 636.
Plant, J.  Salford free public libraries and museum.  L A U K
   Trans 2: 117-8.
Plant, W. C.  Classified and dictionary forms of cataloguing
   compared.  L A R 1: 350-1.
 ---  W. C.  Disputed points in cataloguing.  L A R 5: 215-
   37, Discussion 251-6, Errata 300.
 ---  W. C.  John Dawson and his books; or, an exciseman's
   library of the 18th century.  L A 1: 165-73.
Platnauer, H. M., and E. Howarth.  Directory of museums in
   Great Britain and Ireland:  review.  Libn 2: 350.
Pleasants, L. L.  Author from the librarian's standpoint.
   Wis Lib Bull 4: 48-9.
 -------  L. L.  Place of the library in the social life of
   a small town.  P L 13: 7-8;  Wis Lib Bull 3: 84.
Plees, R. S.  Old prison broadsides.  Connoisseur Oct 1915:
   89-94.
Pleger, J. F.  Some inconsistencies in the bookbinding art.
   L J 36:  421-2.
Plomer, H. R.  Abstracts from the wills of English printers
   and stationers from 1492 to 1630.  Bibliographical Society
   Publication, 1903.
 ----  H. R.  Analysis of Civil war newspaper.  "Mercurius
   Civicus."  L (ns) 6: 184-207.
 ----  H. R.  An "anonymous" royalist writer:  Sir Edmund
   Peirce.  L (3d series) 2: 164-72.

---- H. R. Anthony Marler and the Great Bible. L (3d series) 1: 200-6.

---- H. R. Bibliographical notes from the Priory purse expenses of King Henry VII. L (3d series) 4: 291-305.

---- H. R. Bishop Bancroft and a Catholic press. L (ns) 8: 164-76.

---- H. R. Books mentioned in wills. Bib Soc Trans 7: 99-121.

---- H. R. Booksellers of London bridge. L A R 4: 626-9; L (ns) 4: 28-46.

---- H. R. A Cavalier library (Viscount Conway's library). L (ns) 5: 158-72.

---- H. R. A Charing Cross printer -- Robert Dyer. L 3: 6-11.

---- H. R. A Chester bookseller, 1667-1700: some of his customers and the books he sold them. L (ns) 4: 373-83.

---- H. R. The Church of St. Magnus and the booksellers of London bridge. L (3d series) 2: 384-95.

---- H. R. Dictionary of booksellers and printers who were at work in England, Scotland and Ireland from 1641-1667. Bibliographical Society Publication, 1907.

---- H. R. Edinburgh edition of Sidney's "Arcadia." L (ns) 1: 195-205.

---- H. R. Examination of some existing copies of Hayward's "Life and raigne of Henrie IV." L (ns) 3: 13-23.

---- H. R. An Exeter bookseller: his friends and contemporaries. L (3d series) 8: 128-35.

---- H. R. A glance at the Whittingham ledgers. L (ns) 2: 147-63.

---- H. R. Henry Bynneman, printer, 1566-83. L (ns) 9: 225-44.

---- H. R. Henry Denham, printer. L (ns) 10: 241-50.

---- H. R. Inventory of Wynkyn de Worde's house "The Sun in Fleet street." L (3d series) 6: 228-34.

---- H. R. James Abree, printer and bookseller of Cantebury. L (3d series) 4: 46-56.

---- H. R. The king's printing-house under the Stuarts. L (ns) 2: 353-75.

---- H. R. A lawsuit as to an early edition of "Pilgrim's progress." L (3d series) 5: 60-9.

---- H. R. Libraries and book-shops of Canterbury. B A R 14: I-VII.

---- H. R. Local records and free libraries. L 4: 137-40.

---- H. R. More petitions to Archbishop Laud, I-IV. L (3d series) 10: 129-38.

---- H. R. New documents on English printers and booksellers of the 16th century. Bib Soc Trans 4: 153-83.

---- H. R. Notes on books and work -- Bibliography and library work. L (ns) 1: 213-20.

---- H. R.  Notices of English stationers in the archives of the City of London.  Bib Soc Trans 6: 15-27.

---- H. R.  On Robert Wyer.  Bib Soc Trans 3: 1-3.

---- H. R.  On the value of publishers' lists.  L (ns) 3: 427-33.

---- H. R.  The Oxindeh letters.  L (ns) 6: 29-44.

---- H. R.  Plays at Canterbury in 1570.  L (3d series) 9: 251-4.

---- H. R.  A printer's bill in the seventeenth century. L (ns) 7: 32-45.

---- H. R.  Printers of Shakespeare's plays and poems.  L (ns) 7: 149-66.

---- H. R.  The Protestant press in the reign of Queen Mary. L (3d series) 1: 54-72.

---- H. R.  Richard Pynson versus Henry Squyr suit in the Star chamber.  Bib Soc Trans 6: 137-41.

---- H. R.  Robert Copland.  Bib Soc Trans 3: 211-25.

---- H. R.  Robert Wyer, printer and bookseller.  Bibliographical Society Publication 1897, 71p.

---- H. R.  St. Paul's cathedral and its bookselling tenants. L (ns) 3: 26-76.

---- H. R.  Secret press at Stepney in 1596.  L (ns) 4: 236-42.

---- H. R.  Secret printing during the Civil war.  L (ns) 5: 374-403.

---- H. R.  Some dealings of the Long parliament with the press.  L (ns) 10: 90-7.

---- H. R.  Some early booksellers and their customers.  L (3d series) 3: 412-8.

---- H. R.  Some notes on the Latin and Irish stocks of the Company of stationers.  L (ns) 8: 286-97.

---- H. R.  Some notices of men connected with the English book-trade from the Plea of Rolls of Henry VIII.  L (3d series) 1: 289-301.

---- H. R.  Some petitions for appointment as master printers called forth by the Star chamber decree of 1637.  L (3d series) 10: 101-16.

---- H. R.  Some private presses of the nineteenth century. L (ns) 1: 407-28.

---- H. R.  Stephen Vallenger.  L (ns) 2: 108-12.

---- H. R.  Thomas East, printer.  L (ns) 2: 298-310.

---- H. R.  Thomas Johnes's printing press at Haford, Cardigan, 1803-10.  In his  Some private printing presses of the 19th century.  L (ns) 1: 407-8.

---- H. R.  Two lawsuits of Richard Pynson.  L (ns) 10: 115-33.

---- H. R.  Westminster hall and its booksellers.  L (ns) 6: 380-90.

---- H. R., E. G. Duff and R. Proctor. Hand-lists of English printers, 1501-1556. Plates. 2 parts in 1. Bibliographical Society Publication, 1895.

---- H. R. and R. A. Peddie. Stephen Bulkley, printer. L (ns) 8: 42-56.

Plummer, H. Modern novels. P L 16: 399-400.

----- H. Personal impressions of America. L A R 11: 118-29.

----- H. Personal impressions of American libraries. L A R 10: 586-9.

----- H. Place of the public library in civic life. P L 16: 398.

Plummer, M. W. Apprentice classes. Wis Lib Bull 5: 46-7.

----- M. W. Beginnings of a library school. L J 37: 14-6.

----- M. W. The Christmas book exhibit. L J 36: 4-9.

----- M. W. Circulation of mounted pictures. P L 8: 107.

----- M. W. Columbia college library school from a student's standpoint. L J 12: 363-4.

----- M. W. Evolution of the Pratt institute library school curriculum. A L A Bul 2: 207-10.

----- M. W. International congress of librarians. L J 25: 580-2.

----- M. W. Librarianship as a profession. Wis Lib Bull 5: 48-9.

----- M. W. Library commissions. Wis Lib Bull 5: 47-8.

----- M. W. Library institute. Wis Lib Bull 5: 47.

----- M. W. The library of the future in "Light and Leading". L J 26: 63-5.

----- M. W. Library training. P L 7: 399-401.

----- M. W. Library publicity in general magazines. P L 19: 41-2.

----- M. W. Linotyping library catalogs. L J 19: 261.

----- M. W. Loan system. U S Rept 901-3. 1892-3; L J 18: 242-6.

----- M. W. Miss M. S. R. James. P L 8: 359; L A R 5: 326-7, 521; L A 3: 284.

----- M. W. National congress for the promotion of popular libraries in Italy. L J 33: 403.

----- M. W. Periodicals for the staff. P L 3: 97.

----- M. W. Personal reading of the librarian. L J 28: 5-7.

----- M. W. Photograph collection of Pratt Institute library. L J 24: 637; 25: 7-8.

----- M. W. Poetry in the children's room. L J 35: 463.

----- M. W. Pros and cons of training for librarianship. P L 8: 208-20.

----- M. W. The public library and the pursuit of truth. A L A Bull 10: 111-5; Discussion, 378-80; L J 41: 537-41; N Y L 5: 111-12; P L 21: 341-5; Wis Lib Bull 12: 343; School and Society 4: 14-9.

----- M. W.  Report of Committee on library training.  A
L A Bul 1: Conf No 108-10;  L J 28: 92-4.
----- M. W.  Sacramento public library tag system.  L J 16:
335.
----- M. W.  San Francisco mechanics' institute charging
system.  L J 16: 335-6.
----- M. W.  San Francisco public library wheel for borro-
wers' cards.  L J 16: 336.
----- M. W.  Some features of a booksellers equipment.
Publishers' Weekly June 1912: 1788-91.
----- M. W.  Specialization and grading in library schools.
A L A Bull 7: 343-7.
----- M. W.  Summer training schools, correspondence cour-
ses, etc.  Wis Lib Bull 5: 46-9
----- M. W.  Training for librarianship.  Wis Lib Bull 5:
45-9;  L J 26: 317-23.
----- M. W.  Value of a school for library training.  L J
16: 40-4.
----- M. W.  What can a children's department in a library
do for schools?  Journal of Education (Boston) 48: 94.
----- M. W.  Work for children in public libraries.  L J
22: 679-86.
----- M. W.  Work with children in the libraries of Greater
New York.  Survey 27: 1057-60.
----- M. W. and others.  Summer library schools.  P L 11:
131-4.
Plunkett, H.  McCarthy of Wisconsin.  Nineteenth Century, June
1915: 1335-47.
Plympton, C. W.  Select bibliography of travel in North Amer-
ica.  N Y S L Rept 80, Bibliography No 3.
Poe, C. A.  Rural school libraries in North Carolina.  Amer-
ican Review of Reviews 28: 338-9.
Poirier, L. M.  Popular library advertising.  Minn P L C N
No 5: 9-11.
Poland, M.  Biographical sketches of librarians and biblio-
graphers: IV.  H. P. James.  Bull Bib 8: 91-2.
Pollard, A.  Bibliography of manuscripts containing English
poetry, written before 1600.  Bib Soc Trans 7: 10-4.
Pollard, A. A.  Business end of a library.  L J 31: 311-5;
P L 11: 355-9.
----- A. A.  Speakers' training camp for education in pat-
riotism.  Mich Lib Bull 8: 80-1.
Pollard, A. W.  "Ad imprimendum solum."  L (3d series) 10:
57-63.
----- A. W.  Ames collection of title-pages.  Bib Soc Trans
7: 160-2.
----- A. W.  Arrangement of bibliographies.  L (ns) 10:
168-87.
----- A. W.  Authors, players and pirates in Shakespeare's
day.  L (3d series) 7: 73-101.

----- A. W.  Bibliography of Milton. L (ns) 10: 1-33.
----- A. W.  Book illustration in the fifteenth century. L (ns) 2: 190-209.
----- A. W.  The Central library for students. L A R 19: 372-8.
----- A. W.  Claudius Hollyband and his "French schoolmaster and French Littelton." Bib Soc Trans 13: 253-72.
----- A. W.  Copyright in Josephus. L (3d series) 8: 173-6.
----- A. W.  Division of rare English books between England and the United States. L (4th series) 1: 111-20.
----- A. W.  Dziatzko, Carl, 1842-1903. L (ns) 1: 353-5.
----- A. W.  Early English books -- different systems on which they may be arranged. L (ns) 2: 221-2.
----- A. W.  English bibliography before and after 1600. L A R 2: 3-12.
----- A. W.  English books printed abroad. Bib Soc Trans 3: 195-209.
----- A. W.  False dates in Shakespeare's quartos. L (3d series) 2: 101-7.
----- A. W.  The Franks collection of armorial book stamps. L (ns) 3: 114-34.
----- A. W.  French bibliography of first editions, and a plan for an English one. L 1: 64-8.
----- A. W.  The general catalogue of incunabula. L (3d series) 4: 105-8.
----- A. W.  Good printing and how to stimulate it. Printing Art 14: 165-70.
----- A. W.  Gutenberg, Fust, Schoeffer, and the invention of printing. L (ns) 8: 69-99.
----- A. W.  The improvers of Shakespeare. L (3d series) 7: 265-90.
----- A. W.  Letters of Henry Bradshaw to officials of the British Museum. L (ns) 5: 266-92, 431-42.
----- A. W.  Library association and its branches. L (ns) 8: 316-29.
----- A. W.  Manuscripts of Shakespeare's plays. L (3d series) 7: 198-226.
----- A. W.  Meditation on directories. L (ns) 2: 82-90.
----- A. W.  Melvil Dewey. L (ns) 2: 337-40.
----- A. W.  A new Oxford book of 1517. L (ns) 10: 212-3.
----- A. W.  Notes on bibliography and book collecting. L (ns) 1: 438-48.
----- A. W.  Notes on books and work. L (ns) 2: 100-7.
----- A. W.  Notes on books and work: Bibliography, literary history and collecting. L (ns) 1: 105-13, 337-47.
----- A. W. Notes on the history of book production in France, with especial reference to the French books exhibited at the Bibliothèque nationale. L 5: 102-8.

----- A. W.  Objects and methods of bibliographical coll-
ations and descriptions.  L (ns) 8: 193-217.
----- A. W.  On getting to work:  part of a paper read
before the Panizzi club, 24th June, 1914.  L (3rd series)
5: 325-6.
----- A. W.  On the exhibitions of facsimiles of rare
books in public libraries.  L 5: 260-4.
----- A. W.  On the supposed false dates in certain Shakespeare quartos.  L (3rd series) 1: 46-53.
----- A. W.  Our twenty-first birthday.  Bib Soc Trans 13:
9-27.
----- A. W.  The Panizzi club.  L (3rd series) 5: 95-102.
----- A. W.  Panizzi, Sir Anthony, 1797-1879.  L (ns) 2:
225-30.
----- A. W.  Practical bibliography:  a reply.  L (ns) 4:
151-62.
----- A. W.  Procter, Robert, 1868-1903.  L (ns) 5; 1-34,
192-205.
----- A. W.  Putnam, Herbert.  L (ns) 1: 241-4;  L J 20:
66;  L J 24: 51, 97, 129, 163, 172, 175, 694, Conf No 169.
----- A. W.  Recent Caxtoniana.  L (ns) 6: 337-53.
----- A. W.  Recent English purchases at the British Museum.
L (ns) 6: 1-28;  L (ns) 9: 323-32.
----- A. W.  Regulations of the book trade in the 16th cen-
tury.  L (3d series) 7: 18-43.
----- A. W.  Relations of bibliography and cataloguing.
2nd Int Conf 63-6.  1897;  L 9: 290.
----- A. W.  Richard Copley Christie.  L (ns) 1: 129-31.
----- A. W.  "Robeson Cruso."  L (3d series) 4: 204-20.
----- A. W.  The Rowfant books.  L (ns) 6: 309-26.
----- A. W.  Shakespeare at the Bodleian library.  L (3d
series) 7: 176.
----- A. W.  Siege of Rhodes.  L (ns) 7: 423-36.
----- A. W.  Sienese Tavolette -- Bibliographical forgeries.
L (ns) 9: 97-103.
----- A. W.  A sketch of the history of the printing of
the ends of books.  Printing Art 13: 273-80.
----- A. W.  Some notes on English illustrated books.  Bib
Soc Trans 6: 29-62.
----- A. W.  Two illustrated Italian Bibles.  L (ns) 3:
227-42.
----- A. W.  The two 1755 editions of Fielding's "Journal
of a voyage to Lisbon."  L (3d series) 8: 75-7, 160-2.
----- A. W.  Woodcuts in English plays printed before 1660.
L (ns) 1: 71-88.
----- A. W.  The work of Bruce Rogers, printer.  Bib Soc
Trans 1915-17: 9-22.
----- A. W. and Wilson, J. D.  What follows if some of the
good quarto editions of Shakespeare's plays were printed
from his autograph manuscripts.  Bib Soc Trans 15: 136-9.

----- A. W. and W. W. Greg. Some points in bibliographical descriptions. Bib Soc Trans 9: 31-51.

Pollitt, W. Collection and organisation of professional literature: a suggestion. L W 16: 225-8.

----- W. Duty of public library in relation to local literature and bibliography. L A R 16: 81. 119-26.

----- W. Municipal librarianship: a rational view. L A 11: 112-6, 142-6.

----- W. Pampering the public. L A 8: 235.

----- W. Principles of book-charging. L W 15: 340-3.

----- W. Readers and reading on active service. L W 21: 136-40.

----- W. Registration: a letter. L A 10: 80.

Pollock, F. Library of the Alpine club. L C 3: 136-40.

----- F. Uses and ordering of law libraries. L C 4: 11-7.

Pomeroy, E. Interlibrary visits. Mich Lib Bull 7: 23-4.

Pomfret, J. Reading circles. L W 13: 289-94.

----- J. Some essential points in the development of libraries. L W 20: 228-31.

Pond, G. G. Graded supplementary reading. Penn Lib Notes 3, No 1: 7-10.

Pond, M. E. Cleaning library furniture. Wis Lib Bull 10: 119.

-- M. E. Evening work with children. L J 39: 891-3.

-- M. E. Planning the year's work. Wis Lib Bull 8: 195-7.

Poole, E. W. Classification of recent books. P L 17: 272-3.

Poole, F. and Winsor, J. Proceedings of 1st Int Conf: 178.

Poole, R. B. Bookbinding memoranda. L J 14: 261-4, Conf No 281-2.

Poole, R. B. British Museum cataloguing system in the New York Y.M.C.A. L J 12: 338, 436.

--- R. B. Co-operative cataloguing report. L J 1: 289-90.

--- R. B. Elements of library binding. L J 17: Conf No 15-8.

--- R. B. Fiction in libraries. L J 16: 8-10.

--- R. B. Fires, protection, insurance. U S Rept, 1892-93: 724-33; L J 18: 223-4.

--- R. B. How we choose and buy new books. L J 14: 338.

--- R. B. Indexing portraits. L J 13: 313, 333.

--- R. B. Librarian and his constituents. L J 11: 229-32, Discussion 376.

--- R. B. Libraries of the Y.M.C.A. L J 10: 221.

--- R. B. The manuscript age. L J 18: 71-5, 109-12.

--- R. B. New York library law regarding mutilation of books. L J 11: 118.

--- R. B. Specialization in New York. L J 15: 69-70.

--- R. B. What we do with pamphlets. L J 14: 470-1.

Poole, W. F. Being a librarian. L J 15: 202.

--- W. F. Binding. U S Rept 491, 1876.

--- W. F.  Card catalogue. U S Rept 496, 1876.
--- W. F.  Catalogues. U S Rept 497-8, 1876.
--- W. F.  Cataloguing. U S Rept 489-90. 1876.
--- W. F.  Classification. U S Rept 492-3. 1876.
--- W. F.  Classification and shelf arrangement. U S Rept:
492-3. 1876.
--- W. F.  Construction of library buildings. L J 6: 69-77;
Discussion 123-6.
--- W. F.  Desks and counters. U S Rept: 487-9. 1876.
--- W. F.  Fiction in free libraries. L J 2: 256.
--- W. F.  Finding lists. U. S. Rept 496-7, 1876.
--- W. F.  Free town libraries. U S Govt Rept 445. 1876.
--- W. F.  History of the American library association. L
J 11: 199.
--- W. F.  Index symposium and its morals. L J 3: 178-85.
--- W. F.  John Gutenberg and the early printers. L J 18:
474-5.
--- W. F.  Lectures on the use of books. L J 8: 51-2.
--- W. F.  Library architecture. L J 13: 204.
--- W. F.  Methods of delivery. U S Rept 498-9. 1876.
--- W. F.  Movable system of classification. L J 6: 122.
--- W. F.  Newberry library plan for assisting readers. L
J 15: Conf No 107-11.
--- W. F.  Organization and management of public libraries.
U S Rept: 476-504. 1876.
--- W. F.  Plan for the new Poole's Index. L J 3: 109-10,
111-2, 119.
--- W. F.  Popular objections to public libraries. L J
1: 45.
--- W. F.  President's address. L J 12: 311-20.
--- W. F.  Progress of library architecture. L J 7: 130-6,
Discussion 196-7.
--- W. F.  Public library and public school. L J 8: 281.
--- W. F.  Public library government. L J 2: 20, 292.
--- W. F.  Purchase of books. U S Rept 481-3. 1876.
--- W. F.  Record of circulation -- description of an auto-
matic appliance for recording book issues. U S Rept: 502-4.
1876.
--- W. F.  Register of books borrowed. U S Rept 499-502.
1876.
--- W. F.  Report on library legislation. L J 12: 117-9.
--- W. F.  School and the library: abstract of an article
in the "Inter-Ocean," February 13, 1883. L J 8: 51.
--- W. F.  Selection of books. U S Rept: 179-81. 1876.
--- W. F.  Shelf lists. U S Rept 495-6. 1876.
--- W. F.  Shelf lists versus accession catalogue. L J 3:
324-6.
--- W. F.  Shelf marks. U S Rept 493-4. 1876.
--- W. F.  Shelving. U S Rept: 485-7. 1876.

--- W. F.  Small library buildings.  L J 10: 250-6, 328-35.
--- W. F.  Some popular objections to public libraries.  L
J 1: 47-51.
--- W. F.  Spread of contagious disease by circulating lib-
raries.  L J 4: 258-62, 292.
--- W. F.  Stamping and labelling.  U S Rept 491-2, 1876.
--- W. F.  Supplement to Poole's Index.  L J 8: 5, 194-8.
--- W. F.  Tags.  U S Rept 495.  1876.
--- W. F.  University library and university curriculum.
L J 18: 470-1.
--- W. F.  Why wood shelving is better than iron.  L N (U S)
2: 95-7.
--- W. F. and W. I. Fletcher.  Supplement to Poole's Index.
L J 9: 61, 70.
--- W. F. and others.  Discounts on book purchases.  L J
2: 26.
--- W. F. and others.  The twenty per cent discount rate.
L J 1: 134-9.
Pooley, M. H.  Problems met in reorganizing a high school lib-
rary.  A L A Bull 11: 180-3, 348;  L J 42: 866-8.
Pope, M.  Some problems in budgets.  Wilson Bulletin 1: 316-8.
Poray, A.  Extension work in the Detroit public library.  Mich
Lib Bull Dec 1911.
--- A.  Factory stations.  L J 33: 83-6: P L 13: 73-7.
--- A.  The foreign child and the book.  L J 40: 233-9.
--- A.  Library work in factories.  P L 13: 73-7.
Porter, A.  Deposit stations.  Pacific Northwest Library Assn
Proceedings 1913: 30-4.
Porter, C. F. and C. E. Rusk.  Mr. Jooley on the library
school.  L J 33: 141-3.
Porter, C. P.  Cambridge libraries.  B A R 4: XXV-XXX.
Porter, H. P.  Scientific management in the printing industry.
Printing Art 18: 17-20.
Porter, R. N.  Under the Orange sign:  county library service
in Santa Barbara.  Survey 44: 21-4 Ap 3, 1920;  Lib Occ 5:
370-4.
Porter, W. T.  Cincinnati.  In Galbreath, C. B. "Sketches of
Ohio Libraries" 1902: 96-104.
---- W. T.  County libraries:  Ohio and Wisconsin.  L J
26: 203.
---- W. T.  Do workmen's compensation acts apply to lib-
raries?  A L A Bull 8: 254-5.
---- W. T.  First county library in Ohio.  P L 6: 208-9.
---- W. T.  Library buidlings and their use.  P L 13: 271-4.
---- W. T.  Library privileges for rural districts:  a fur-
ther word.  Dial 30: 223-4.
Pospishil, L.  Personal element in library work with children.
Ia L C Q 3: 35-6.  Discussion, 36-7.
Post, W. L.  Author headings for U.S. public documents:  a de-
fence.  L J 33: 227-8.

-- W. L.  Centralization a needed reform in public document
distribution.  L J 34: 43-8;  P L 14: 49-51.
-- W. L.  Outlines for a working collection of public doc-
uments and aids to its use.  L J 34: 538-45.
-- W. L.  Output distribution and cataloging of government
documents.  A L A Bull 1: Conf No 135-45.
-- W. L.  United States documents and their bibliography.
A L A Bull 3: 315-27.
Potter, A. C.  Selection of books for college libraries.  L
J 22: Conf No 29-44.
Potter, A. E.  Handbook of descriptive and historical notes
on the library of Harvard university.  P L 8: 440.
---- A. E.  The ordering department of the Harvard college
library.  P L 2: 389-90.
Potter, A. L.  Latin-Americana collection in Harvard college
library.  L J 44: 225.
Potter, E. G.  Distribution of the book fund.  Wis Lib Bull
8: 197-8.
---- E. G.  Headquarters library.  A L A Bull 13: 316-8.
Potter, Mrs. E. G.  Library war work at Oakland free library,
Cal.  Cal News Notes 13: 169-71.
Potts, M. E.  Suggestions for library interest.  P L 22: 169-
70.
Poulson, M. W.  Conditions and needs of secondary school lib-
raries in Utah.  University of Utah Bulletin 10, No 4, 1919.
Powell, C. A.  The boy and the library.  P L 19: 241.
Powell, J.  Loaning more than one book at a time.  Minn P L
C N No 9: 25-7.
---- J.  Loaning reference books.  Minn P L C N No 9: 27-8.
Powell, M.  Art work that can be done in small libraries.  P
L 24: 192-4.
Powell, S. H.  Children's room plus the attic.  L J 45: 833-5.
Powell, S. P.  The public library in British reconstruction:
Third interim report of the Adult education committee.  L
J 44: 699-703.
Powell, W.  Birmingham Cervantes collection.  L A R 18: 296-7.
---- W.  Birmingham city libraries.  L W 19: 173-7.
---- W.  Birmingham commercial library.  L A R 21: 172-3.
---- W.  The Birmingham Shakespeare memorial library:  a
tercentenary memorial.  L A R 18: 282-97, 328.
---- W.  Book production in Great Britain.  L J 29: Conf
No 50-4.
---- W.  Book selection.  L A R 17: 176-8.
---- W.  Indexes wanted.  L A R 7: 105-12, Discussion 93-6.
---- W.  Librarianship in the future.  L A 5: 135-9.
---- W.  Libraries and reconstruction:  the financial pos-
ition.  L A R 21: 198-200.
---- W.  Library bookbinding.  L W 5: 171-7.

---- W. Publishers and publishing. L A R 4: 523, 590-601.

---- W. Symposium on public libraries after the war. L A R 19: 197-9.

---- W. Training of library assistants: a neglected aspect. L A R 12: 165-72, Discussion 208-13.

Power, D. A. Walter Bayley and his works. L (ns) 8: 370-407.

Power, E. L. Library co-operation with the Junior Red Cross. Nat Educ Assn 1918: 461-3.

--- E. L. Library in its relation to elementary schools. P L 11: 544-8.

--- E. L. Report of Committee on elementary school libraries. Nat Educ Assn 1915: 1073-5.

--- E. L. Report of Elementary school committee. Nat Educ Assn 1917: 671-6; L J 42: 490-1; Am Lib Annual 1917-18: 38.

--- E. L. St. Louis public library: children's opening. L J 37: 145.

--- E. L. Standards in children's literature. N J Lib Bull Jan 1915: 10-5; L J 41: 935-6; 1916: 10-5.

Power, R. L. The Brompton Oratory library, London. P L 25: 263-4.

--- R. L. Business education for business librarians. Special Libraries 8: 135-9; L J 43: 59-60.

--- R. L. Business literature in public libraries. Texas Libraries 2: 94-100.

--- R. L. The college of business administration library and supervised employment (Boston university college of business administration) L J 42: 13-4.

--- R. L. Commercial libraries of London. L J 44: 304-6.

--- R. L. First aid in business. N C Lib Bull 3: 117-8.

--- R. L. The insurance library maintained by the Insurance library association of Boston. Special Libraries 8: 49.

--- R. L. The library and museum in commercial education: library of College of business administration, Boston. P L 22: 93-5.

--- R. L. La Musée et bibliothèque de la guerre, Paris. L J 44: 303-4.

--- R. L. Secretarial laboratory of the Boston university College of business administration. L J 42: 431-3.

--- R. L. Special libraries of Boston and their uses. L J 42: 296-8, 373-4, 540-2, 728-32.

--- R. L. The special library and the student of business. Special Libraries 7: 147-50; L J 42: 574-5; Am Lib Annual 1917 18: 79-80.

--- R. L. Women in special libraries. L J 45: 691-5.

Powers, E. L. What the public library can do for grade schools. A L A Bull 10: 215-6.

Powers, W. H. Camp Cody library. South Dakota Lib Bull 4: 78-9.

---- W. H.  Current magazines: an appraisal of Century, Harper's and Scribner's.  P L 19: 245-7.

---- W. H.  President Eliot's book-shelf again.  P L 15: 186.

---- W. H.  Scope and current cost in the Land grant agricultural libraries.  A L A Bull 8: 192-7;  L J 39: 545.

Pratt, A. M.  Care of unbound material in libraries.  South Dakota Lib Bull Sept 1919: 172-4;  L J 45: 230-2.

Pratt, E. B.  The work of the New Jersey public library commission.  Bul Bib 9: 4-5.

Pratt, E. E.  Literature on foreign trade.  Special Libraries 10: 169-72.

Pratt, J. A.  Library and the children.  P L 3: 77-9;  4: 77-9.

Pratt, L. W.  Public library work.  Wash L A Bull 1, No 1: 7-8.

Pratt, M.  Preservation of local history.  Main Lib Bull 4, No 3: 8-9.

Pratt, O. C.  What the public library does for us.  Lib Occ 3: 104-6.

Prendergast, F. E.  Suggestion for library architecture.  L J 10: 35.

Prentice, M. H.  Myth and history in elementary schools: the use and limits of each.  Nat Educ Assn 1902: 447-54.

Prentice, M. L.  Vitalizing the relation between library and school: I -- The school.  L J 26: Con No 78-80.

Prentiss, M. E.  Book selection and purchase for small libraries.  P L 11: 55-9.

------ M. E.  Illustrative exhibits of library methods at annual meeting of the California library association.  Cal News Notes 2: 84-6.

Prescott, D. R.  Americanization through foreign print.  L J 43: 884-5.

------ D. R.  What Americanization is not.  L J 45: 216.

------ D. R.  Work with foreign newspapers in Newark free public library.  L J 44: 77.

Prescott, F. C.  Teaching literature.  Nation 83: 240.

Prescott, H. B.  Bibliographic apparatus in colleges.  Columbia Univ Q 13: 224-9.

Presnell, H.  Library legislation in United States.  U S Govt Rept 2: 523-99.  1895-96.

Pressfield, H.  The county library in California.  Outlook 21: 131;  Sierra Educ News 13: 397.

Preston, J. C.  The country child in the rural library.  Nat Educ Assn 1914: 796-7.

Preston, N. K.  The library visitor.  Mich Lib Bull 7: 157-8.

----- N. K.  Michigan school for the deaf library.  L J 43: 749-50.

----- N. K.  Some institutional libraries in Michigan.  L J 43: 748-50.

----- N. K.  Work of a library visitor (state control).  Michigan Board of Library Commissioners Report, 1915, 41-2.

Pretlow, M. D.  Opening day -- and after -- in a children's library.  L J 33: 177-9.

Pretsch, K.  Additions and corrections to author entries in the catalogue of the Peabody institute library and the British Museum.  L J 18:  37-40.

Prevost, M. L.  Citizenship and civics.  L J 43: 466, 484-6.

Price, A. M.  John Rylands library.  P L 19: 382-5.

--- A. M.  Library administration as affected by commission form of government in Illinois.  P L 17: 216-8.

--- A. M. Special library training.  P L 14: 338-42.

Price, C. M.  Design of the Avery architectural library.  Architectural Record 33: 533-49.

--- C. M.  Haddington branch of the free library of Philadelphia.  Architectural Record 40: 44-62.  1916.

Price, H. L.  Stories to read to children.  Wis Lib Bull 4: 59.

Price, H. N.  Possibilities for work with children in small libraries.  P L 14: 121-3.

Price, H. U.  The making of Pennsylvania libraries.  A L A Bull 4: 715-21.

Price, H. W.  Story hour in libraries.  P L 12: 347-9.

Price, R. R.  Co-operation.  Wis Lib Bull 9: 209.

Price, W. H.  On selecting economic literature.  Wis Lib Bull 6: 57-69.

Prideaux  S. T.  Bibliography of bookbinding.  L 4: 15-24, 50-6, 90-5.

Prideaux, W. R. B.  Bishop Selwyn's library.  L A R 13: 88-9.

------ W. R. B.  Library association diploma.  L A 6: 205-6.

------ W. R. B.  Library economy.  L A R 6: 129-38.

------ W. R. B.  Library economy in the 16th century.  L A R 11: 152-74.

------ W. R. B.  Medical libraries of London.  L A R 8: 405-22.

------ W. R. B.  Personal relations between staff and readers.  L A 5: 199-201.

------ W. R. B.  Professional education and registration.  L A R 8: 1-6, Discussion 20-7.

------ W. R. B.  Staff training in Scotland.  L A R 12: 391-2.

------ W. R. B.  Training of assistants.  L A R 12: 390-2.

Prince, F. F.  Book repairing.  Vt L Bull 5, No 2: 7.

---- F. F.  Materials for mending books.  Vt L Bull 5, No 2: 7.

Prince, H. L.  On facilities for examination of patent literature.  A L A Bull 1: 166-8.

Pringle.  Reference work with the rural districts.  Minn P L C N 3: 188-9.

Pringle, G. C.  The teaching of literature in schools.  Journal of Education (London) 25: 258-61, 318-20.

Proctor, R.   Berthelet's editions of the statutes of Henry
   VIII.   Bib Soc Trans 5: 255-62.
----- R.   Classified index to the Serapeum, 101-47, Bib
   Soc Publication, 1897.
----- R.   Earliest printers of Greece and their types.   Bib
   Soc Trans 5: 174-7.
----- R.   Early Pestblatter,  L (ns) 3: 3-12.
----- R.   Early printers of Koln.   L (ns) 4: 392-402.
----- R.   Experience of a Vermont library.   Vt L Bull 4:
   2-4.
----- R.   French royal Greek types and the Eton Chrysostom.
   Bib Soc Trans 7: 49-74.
----- R.   The "Gutenberg" Bible.   L (ns) 2: 60-6.
----- R.   Incunabula at Grenoble.   L (ns) 1: 215-24.
----- R.   Jan van Doesborgh, printer at Antwerp:   an essay
   in bibliography.   Bibliographical Society Publication No
   II, 1894.
----- R.   Marcus Reinhard and Johann Gruninger.   Bib Soc
   Trans 5: 143-60.
----- R.   Notes on signatures:   being additional notes to
   Blades' "Bibliographical miscellanies."   L 3: 177-80, 267-9.
----- R.   On two Lyonnese editions of the "Ars Moriendi."
   L (ns) 3: 339-48.
----- R.   Printing of Greek in the fifteenth century.   Bib-
   liographical Society Illustrated Monographs No VIII, 1900.
----- R.   Ulrich von Ellenbog and the press of S. Ulrich at
   Augsburg.   L (ns) 4: 163-79.
----- R., E. G. Duff and H. R. Plomer.   Hand-lists of Eng-
   lish printers, 1501-1556.   Plates.   2 parts in 1.   Biblio-
   graphical Society Publication, 1895.
Proctor, W.   Educational value of fiction.   L A R 13: 309.
----- W.   Public libraries:   their place in education.   L
   A 10: 230-4.
Prosser, R. B.   Bibliography of bookbinding and binding pat-
   ents.   L 4: 228-9.
----- R. B.   Henry Carey as a librarian.   L A R 3: 28-9.
----- R. B.   Origin of the card catalogue, a brief note.
   L A R 2: 651.
Prothero, G. W.   Bradshaw, Henry, 1831-1886.   L 1: 41-5.
Prouty, E.   American public as seen from the circulation desk.
   A L A Bull 10: 279-80.
Prouty, L. Gievres.   A. L. A. war service.   A L A Bull 13: 320.
Pryne, M.   Library work in the high school.   Sierra Educational
   News 9: 373-7.
Pulling, A. C.   Law libraries of the future.   L J 40: 704-7.
Pullman, J. M.   Sunday opening.   L J 7: 44, 231.
Purinton, E. E.   Building an office library.   Independent 96:
   214.

------ E. E. How the local library may make itself an efficient factor in serving the state and nation in the present crisis. N Y L 5: 222-3.

Purnell, C. J. Some seventeenth and eighteenth century catalogues. L A R 15: 349-59.

----- C. J. Subject-index of the London library. L A 9: 190-3.

Purnell, H. R. Development of notation in classification. L A 8: 25-33, 44-50.

----- H. R. Local literature and its collectors. L A 6: 36-41, Discussion 34-5.

----- H. R. National and international librarianship. L A 10: 26-33.

Purry, E. R. Bulletins and library printing. A L A Bull 9: 102-4.

Purtill, E. F. Formulas for cleaning books. Lib Occ 2: 140-1.

Purves, J. W. C. Library ideals: work and legislation in Canada. L A R 14: 439-61.

---- J. W. C. A reply to Mr. Jast's address to the N. C. L. A. on branch work. L A R 14: 327-31.

Purves, W. L. Literary output of Daniel Defoe. L (3d series) 3: 333-5.

---- W. L. "Robeson Cruso" -- a rejoinder. L (3d series) 4: 338-52.

Putnam, G. H. Copyright in relation to libraries. L J 34: 58-60.

Putnam, H. Access to the shelves: a possible function of branch libraries. L J 16: Conf No 62-7.

---- H. Address at Ottawa conference. A L A Bull 6: 59-66; L J 37: 423-9.

---- H. A. L. A. War service committee. A L A Bull 12: 106-62, 180, 182-3.

---- H. Advocating that state libraries be formed into reservoir libraries. A L A Bull 3: 161-2.

---- H. American libraries and the investigator. North American Review 197: 312-24; L J 38: 273-7.

---- H. Analysis of the new copyright law. Publishers' Weekly 75: 1100-5.

---- H. Application forms for foreign book importations. L J 41: 105-7; P L 22: 8.

---- H. Are you a modern librarian. Lib Occ 4: 89-90.

---- H. Bibliographical bureaus. L J 12: 409-13, Discussion 450-2.

---- H. Books and the people. Ia L C Q 2: 21-2.

---- H. A College library in war time; address at the dedication of the Converse library building at Amherst college. L J 43: 5-10.

---- H. Co-operative work of the Library of Congress. L J 28: Conf No 162-4.

---- H. Education for library work. Ia L C Q 1: 17-9.

---- H. Foreign book importations: Further regulations.
L J 41: 188-9, 338.

---- H. How to use the library. Springfield Lib Bull 26:
368-70.

---- H. Inter-library loans (Regulations). L J 23: 61.

---- H. The Library of Congress. Atlantic Monthly 85: 147-8.

---- H. The Library of Congress -- and you. Independent
82: 245.

---- H. The Library of Congress as a national library.
L J 30: Conf No 27-34.

---- H. The library war service. A L A Bull 12: 103-5,
277-8, Discussion 286-7, 288.

---- H. Local library associations in the United States.
2nd Int Conf 129-34, Discussion 243; L 9: 293. 1897.

---- H. On the Library of Congress. L J 25: 53-65.

---- H. "Per contra." A L A Bull 9: 119-24; L J 40:
471-6; P L 20: 290-6.

---- H. Presidential address. L J 23: Conf No 1-7; L J
29; Conf No 23-7.

---- H. Printed catalogue cards of the A. L. A. Publishing
board. L J 26: 752.

---- H. The prospect. L J 37: 651-8.

---- H. Public libraries -- their need for expert counsel.
Ia L C Q 4: 26-8.

---- H. The quick in the "dead." L J 37: 235-45; New
Hamp Bull 9: 185-96.

---- H. Relation of the state libraries and the Library of
Congress. L J 25: 729-33; P L 6: 13-28.

---- H. Report on cost of service in Library of Congress.
Rept of Libn of Cong 27-40. 1899.

---- H. The service of books in a democracy. L J 37: 59-
63.

---- H. Statement of the General director, A. L. A. war
service. A L A Bull 13: 261-5.

---- H. Whay may be done for libraries by the nation. L
J 26: Conf No 9-16; L J 27: Conf No 212-5.

Putnam, W. H. Duties of library directors. Minn P L C N 2:
43-6.

Pyle, J. G. Newspaper and the library. Minn P L C N 2: 52-5.

Pyle, W. Durability of leather in bookbinding. L J 26: 386-7.

Quaife, M. M. A difference of opinion. P L 23: 423-4.

Quayle, W. A. Books as a delight. Wis Lib Bull 9: 187-92.

Quick, H. Librarian of to-day. Ia L C Q 5: 210-1.

Quigley, M. Flaws in book-wagon service. P L 25: 130-3.

Quigley, M. G. Can we use war stories to train children for
peace? P L 20: 402-4.

----- M. G. How to interest mothers in children's reading.
P L 20: 165-6.

----- M. G. Systematic instruction in the use of the library at Grand Rapids. L J 31: 166-7.

----- M. G. Telling stories to children. P L 10: 351-3.

Quigley, S. University extension lectures. Minn P L C N 4: 16-7.

Quincy, J. P. Free libraries. U S Govt Rept: 389-402. 1876.

Quinn, J. H. A card-charging system for lending libraries. L 5: 34-9.

--- J. H. Developments in cataloguing. Greenwood's Yr-Bk 1900-01: 37-45.

--- J. H. Dictionary versus classified catalogues for public libraries -- The classified catalogue. L A R 3: 514-20, precis and discussion 487-9.

--- J. H. Library cataloguing: review. Libn 4: 60-3; L A 10: 242-3.

--- J. H. Manual of library cataloguing: a review. L J 24: 265-6.

--- J. H., and J. D. Brown. Classification of books for libraries in which readers are allowed access to the shelves. L 9: 75-82.

Quire, J. H. Legislation of the 1919 California legislature. Cal News Notes 14: 296-7.

--- J. H. Library war service at Camp Kearny, Cal. Cal News Notes 13: 17-8.

--- J. H. Suggested reading for the state bar examination. Cal News Notes 15: 35-9.

Rabb, K. M. Mental diet. P L 12: 392-3.

Radford, J. T. Sketch of the North Midland library association 1890-1893. L 6: 145-6.

Rae, W. S. C. Access to files of current periodicals in reading room. L W 13: 356-8.

- W. S. C. Class lists. L W 2: 298-9.
- W. S. C. Library lecture courses. L W 10: 81-3.
- W. S. C. Newsrooms. L W 2: 325-6.
- W. S. C. Popularizing the best books. L A R 5: 623-29.
- W. S. C. Reading for the blind. L W 4: 316-8.

Raine, W. M. The formula of the western novel. A L A Bull 14: 210-5.

Raines, M. D. A library Christmas tree for the birds. Ia L C Q 8: 141-2.

Raitt, W. Paper preservation in India. Lib Miscellany (Baroda) July and October, 1918: 41-6; L J 45: 232.

Ralph, G. S. Child welfare exhibit in retrospect. L J 36: 157-61.

Ramage, A. Public library's contribution to adult education. L A 14: 246-7.

Rambler, L. C. Embossed music for the blind. L J 40: 585-6.

Rammelkamp, C. H. Legislation for archives. Am Hist Assn Rept 1914, 1: 361-73.

Ranck, B.  The future university library.  Nation 84: 263.

Ranck, H. H.  The seminary library.  College Student 15: 39-42.

Ranck, S. H.  Books for the citizen.  Grand Rapids News, March 1912: 1-8.

--- S. H.  Conference on books for the blind.  L J 30: 799-800.

--- S. H.  Discusses valuation of books in a library.  A L A Bull 11: 2-4.

--- S. H.  Forgotten traveling libraries.  L J 26: 261-5.

--- S. H.  Functions of a professional association.  A L A Bull 12: 17-8.

--- S. H.  How to make the library of greater service to the student of school age.  L J 34: 52-4.

--- S. H.  Humanizing library work.  L J 45: 205-6, P L 25: 127-30.

--- S. H.  Leather for bookbinding.  L J 25: 332-3.

--- S. H.  A librarian's job in base section, No 1 France.  A L A Bull 13: 297-302, 348.

--- S. H.  Library administration on an income of from $1,000 to $5,000 a year.  L J 30: Conf No 58-63;  P L 10: 397-401.

--- S. H.  The library and the school in Grand Rapids.  L J 32: 162-4.

--- S. H.  Library at a city show.  L J 45: 353-5.

--- S. H.  Library branches in schools.  L J 37: 676-7.

--- S. H.  Library work in vocational guidance.  L J 39: 662-5.

--- S. H.  Library's opportunities in vocational guidance.  A L A Bull 7: 296-7.

--- S. H.  Making a library useful to business men.  A L A Bull 7: 210-5;  L A R 15: 536-8.

--- S. H.  Medical departments in public libraries.  Med Lib and Hist Journal 5: 210-20.

--- S. H.  Municipal reference libraries.  L J 34: 345-50.

--- S. H.  The Municipal reference library and the city library.  A L A Bull 10: 21-5;  Discussion: 48-50.

--- S. H.  Need of additional copyright depositories.  L J 20:  Conf No 43-5, 78.

--- S. H.  Proposed library laws for Michigan.  L J 45: 840.

--- S. H.  Public library as a factor in civic development.  National Conference for Good City Government, Proceedings 1910: 385-94; L J 36: 116-21.

--- S. H.  Public library as a part of the municipal government.  L J 32: 432-3;  P L 12: 385-7.

--- S. H.  Public use of college libraries.  L J 20: 235-9.

--- S. H.  Question of library renewals.  Dial 50: 82-3;  Lib Work 5: 4-5.

--- S. H.  Railroad or traveling libraries.  L J 22: 10-3.

--- S. H.  Relation of the public library to technical education.  Ontario Lib Assn Proceedings 1911:  83-91;  L J
36: 279-85.

--- S. H.  Relative shelf space occupied by books published
in England and the United States.  L J 29: 533-4.

--- S. H.  Right start, or don't be a quitter:  leaflet
issued by the Grand Rapids library.  P L 12: 65-6.

--- S. H.  The risk of loss in a public library.  L J 40:
651-3.

--- S. H.  Rural library extension.  Mich Libs 1: 39-46;
Michigan State Board of Library Commissioners.  13th Annual
Report 1912: 41-3.

--- S. H.  Use of library lecture room.  L J 36: 9-14.

--- S. H.  Use of medical books.  A L A Bull 1: Conf No
169-75.

--- S. H.  Welfare of librarians.  P L 25: 127-30.

--- S. H. and B. C. Steiner.  Replacements.  L J 21: 397.

--- S. H. and B. C. Steiner.  Report on access to the
shelves.  L J 19: Conf No 87-96.

Ranck, Mrs. S. H.  Books on the care of babies.  L J 38: 600-
2;  New Hamp Bull 10: 9-11.

Rand, T. R.  Relation of the public library to the public elementary school.  L A 14: 305-6.

-- T. R.  Some considerations of the relations between the
public library and public elementary schools as suggested
by the Third interim report of the Adult education committee.  L A R 22: 36-41, 64-70.

Randall, I. M.  Breaking into business.  Special Libraries
10: 67.

----- I. M.  The case against the librarian:  The manufacturing house library.  Special Libraries 11: 76-9.

Randall, J. M.  The Smith family and the Department of agriculture.  P L 25: 241-6.

Randall, S. W.  Revision of the library of the University of
Pennsylvania.  L J 26: 383-6.

Randall, W. J.  English literature for librarians.  Libn 3: 155.

----- W. J.  Library routine in the 1918 examination.  L
W 21: 8-13.

----- W. J.  Section VI of the 1917 professional examination.  L W 19: 317-20.

----- W. J.  Statistics and "statistical curves."  L W 18:
41-4.

Raney, M. L.  The A. L. A. Diplomat.  L J 44: 588-92.

--- M. L.  The A. L. A. follows the flag overseas.  A L A
Bull 12: 81-93;  L J 43: 552-62.

--- M. L.  Cataloging while you wait:  Longmans, Green &
Co. cataloging card service scheme.  L J 45: 735-6, 742.

--- M. L.  Censorship board lifts ban on foreign periodi-
cals.  L J 44: 186.
--- M. L.  Foreign book exchange:  cost of importing books.
L J 45: 255-7, 451.
--- M. L.  German periodicals for 1919.  L J 44: 113-4.
--- M. L.  Multigraph and flexotype in cataloging work.
L J 36: 629-32.
--- M. L.  A personal statement regarding importations.
L J 43: 667-8.
--- M. L.  Shipments of foreign books arrive in this coun-
try.  L J 43: 823-4.
--- M. L.  A time-saver in the Johns Hopkins University
cataloguing department.  L J 35: 256-8.
Rankin, Mrs. E. J.  The Oteen library.  N C Lib Bull 4: 84-6.
Rankin, F. H.  Agricultural libraries.  U S Dept of Agricul-
ture, Office of Experiment Stations, Washington, 1908, Bull-
etin 199: 57-63.
Rankin, J. F.  Printed cards from the Library of Congress.
A L A Bull 1: Conf No 286-8.
Rankin, J. T.  Story hour in the Carnegie library of Atlanta.
L J 36: 181.
Rathbone, F.  Magazines for a small library.  P L 14: 377-8.
Rathbone, F. L.  American library statistics -- an answer.
L J 33: 506-7.
------ F. L.  Borrower and his book.  N Y L 1: 228-32.
------ F. L.  Coloured covers for special subjects.  L J
26: 738-9.
------ F. L.  An experiment in fiction (improving the read-
ing).  Ia L C Q 6: 7-8.
------ F. L.  Library guides.  P L 11: 313.
------ F. L.  Magazines for a small library.  P L 14: 377-8.
------ F. L.  Necessity of staff meetings.  L J 34: 301-4.
------ F. L.  Picture bulletins practically applied:  New
York state library school scheme.  L J 32: 434.
------ F. L.  Results from staff meetings.  L J 33: 398-9.
------ F. L.  Some suggestions for fiction purchase and
circulation.  L J 28: 110-2.
------ F. L.  Successful experiment in directing the reading
of fiction.  L J 32: 406-7.
------ F. L.  Trained person in charge of condition of
books.  P L 12: 236-7.
Rathbone, J. A.  Classification of fiction.  L J 27: 121-4.
------ J. A.  Co-operation between libraries and schools:
an historical sketch.  L J 26: 187-91.
------ J. A.  Fiction in Pratt Institute library school.
P L 7: 72-3.
------ J. A.  Histories for children.  N C Bull 1: 120-1.
------ J. A.  Instruction in the use of reference books and
libraries in high schools.  L J 23: Conf No 87-91.

------ J. A.  Library school course as training for business men.  Special Libraries 8: 133-5;  L J 43: 61.

------ J. A.  Library school work at Pratt institute.  A L A Bull 7: 182-3.

------ J. A.  Modern library movement.  P L 13: 197-201.

------ J. A.  Opportunity of the library assistant.  P L 14: 333-8.

------ J. A.  A projected normal course at Pratt institute School of library science.  A L A Bull 6: 297-300.

------ J. A.  The proposed code for classifiers -- a discussion.  A L A Bull 9: 254-7.

------ J. A.  Recruiting for librarianship.  L J 45: 450.

------ J. A.  Requests sent to one library school.  P L 20: 116-8.

------ J. A.  Salaries of library school graduates.  L J 39: 188-90.

------ J. A.  Some aspects of our personal life.  P L 21: 53-6.

------ J. A.  Some bibliographical schemes.  P L 2: 178-9.

------ J. A.  Some points in the code of professional etiquette.  A L A Bull 8: 14-5.

------ J. A.  The training of assistants for lending department work.  A L A Bull 13: 173-5, 400.

------ J. A.  Views of library school directors.  P L 23: 13-4.

------ J. A.  What college librarians can do for library schools.  A L A Bull 7: 319-20.

Ratnaswami, H.  Mackenzie collection of Oriental manuscripts.  Lib Miscellany (Baroda) 2: 116-8.

Rawles, W. A.  University extension and the local libraries.  Lib Occ 3: 146-9.

Rawlins, C. M.  Margins in library service.  P L 15: 47-50.

Rawlinson, E. V.  Use of the library in the grades.  L J 37: 163-9.

Rawnsley, Canon.  Recent pernicious literature.  Libn 2: 38-9; L A R 14: 479-82.

Rawson, H.  Duties of library committees.  2nd Int Conf 28-9, 1897.

---- H.  Presidential address.  L 8: 421-3, 1896.

---- H.  Public free libraries of Manchester: their history, organization and work.  L 4: 288-94.

Rawson, P. W.  Appointment of non-professional and untrained assistants.  Libn 3: 379-82.

Raymond, E.  An old engineering library.  L J 39: 285-6.

Raymond, W.  On the value of fiction.  L W 17: 327-8.

Read, J. M.  Selection of children's books.  New Hamp Bull 13: 62-5.

Read, W. A.  The student in the foreign library.  P L 18: 14-5.

Reagan, I. M.  Library work in Humboldt county.  California Lib Assn Proceedings 1916: 50-1.

Reagan, M.  An evening at the public library.  N Y L 7: 101-2.
Recht, C.  Working man and the library.  P L 13: 303-4.
Redfield, W. C.  Where the special library is a necessity.
  Special Libraries 5: 1.
Redgrave, G. R.  The Abbe Domenech and his critics.  L (3d
  series) 6: 133-41.
  ------ G. R.  An ancient pilgrimage to the holy land.  L
  (3d series) 10: 69-72.
  ------ G. R.  Authors' own copies.  L (ns) 6: 251-6.
  ------ G. R.  Daniel and the emblem literature.  Bib Soc
  Trans 11: 39-58.
  ------ G. R.  "De re metallica."  L (3d series) 4: 199-203.
  ------ G. R.  Erhard Ratdolt and his work at Venice.  Bib-
  liographical Society illustrated Monographs No 1, 1894.
  ------ G. R.  Evelyn's essays on "Publick employment and
  an active life."  L (ns) 2: 349-52.
  ------ G. R.  First editions of modern books.  L (3d series)
  10: 26-33.
  ------ G. R.  First four editions of "English bards and
  Scotch reviewers."  L (ns) 1: 18-25.
  ------ G. R.  Inscriptions in books.  Bib Soc Trans 4: 37-
  46.
  ------ G. R.  Lady Dilke's gift to the National art library.
  L (ns) 7: 263-74.
  ------ G. R.  The Privy council in its relation to liter-
  ature and printing.  Bib Soc Trans 7: 92-5.
  ------ G. R.  Some books by Sir Samuel Morland.  L (4th
  series) 1: 165-9.
  ------ G. R.  Some early book illustrations of the Oppen-
  heim press.  Bib Soc Trans 3: 71-80.
  ------ G. R.  Some illustrated sermon books.  L (3d series)
  7: 44-52.
  ------ G. R.  Water-marks in paper.  L (ns) 5: 91-2.
Redgrave, J. J.  Public library book extension service.  L A
  5: 290-2.
Redway, J. W.  Dust problem in public libraries.  L J 45: 347-
  9, 657.
Reece, E. J.  The libraries of Hawaii.  L J 39: 15-9.
  --- E. J.  State documents for libraries.  A L A Bull 12:
  333-4.
Reed, A. L.  Special training of staff members of university
  and college libraries.  L J 43: 96.
Reed, A. W.  The canon of John Heywood's plays.  L (3d series)
  9: 27-57, 116-31.
  -- A. W.  John Heywood and his friends.  L (3d series) 8:
  240-70, 289-314.
  -- A. W.  John Rastell, printer, lawyer, venturer, drama-
  tist and controversialist.  Bib Soc Trans 15: 59-82.

-- A. W.  John Rastell's plays.  L (3d series) 10: 1-7.
-- A. W.  Regulations of the book-trade before the King's proclamation.  Bib Soc Trans 15: 135, 157-84.
-- A. W.  The Wydow Edyth.  L (3d series) 9: 186-99.
Reed, G. E.  Printed catalogs for the state library.  P L 6: 36-7, Discussion 37.
Reed, L. B.  Best novels of 1898.  P L 4: 62-4.
Reed, L. I.  The public library and the rural schools.  Ia L C Q 7: 54-7.
Reed, M.  The past, the present, and the future.  Libn 10: 40-1.
-- M.  Salaries and the status of women assistants.  Libn 2: 32-3, 76-7.
-- M.  Status of the lady librarian.  Libn 4: 278-9.
-- M.  Women and libraries in the new age.  Libn 9: 133.
-- M.  Women, libraries, and the war.  Libn 5: 75-6.
-- M.  Women's work in libraries.  Libn 2: 32, 76, 115, 149, 185, 228, 269, 307, 348, 388, 426, 466;  3: 19-20, 64-5, 235-6;  4: 9-10;  5: 170-1, 254-5.
Reed, T. B.  Bibliography of printers and printing in England.  Bib Soc Trans 3: 90-151.
-- T. B.  Invention controversy.  Bib Soc Trans 3: 88-90.
-- T. B.  List of books and papers on printers and printing under the countries and towns to which they refer, compiled by the late Talbot Baines Reed, edited by A. W. Pollard.  Bib Soc Trans 3: 81-152.
-- T. B.  On the use and classification of a typographical library.  L 4: 33-44.
Reeder, C. W.  Popularizing public documents.  A L A Bull 44: 368-75.
---- C. W.  Recall of public officials:  a select list of references.  Bull Bib 7: 5-8.
---- C. W.  Statistical comparison of thirty university libraries.  School and Society 4: 107-10.
Reely, M. K.  Selected list of current books.  Wis Lib Bull 16: 232-9.
--- M. K.  Selected list of new novels.  Wis Lib Bull 16: 193-9.
--- M. K.  Selected lists of children's books.  Wis Lib Bull 16: 197-9.
Rees, E. G.  Educational needs of library assistants.  L A R 5: 81-7, Discussion 101-7.
Rees, G.  Summer school of library service.  Aberystwyth.  July 30th - August 11th 1917.  L A 14: 98-106.
-- G.  Symposium on public libraries after the war.  L A R 19: 230-3.
Reese, R.  Exchange of service.  P L 22: 364-5.
--- R.  Libraries and schools.  P L 18: 29-30.

--- R.  The Odyssey of the local author:  a futurist exped-
ition.  L J 44: 319-20.

--- R.  Relation of the library and the school.  Colorado
Lib Assn Occasional Leaflet 1: 100-4.

--- R.  What is a local author?  L J 44: 43-4.

Reeves, Dr.  Memoir of the Public Library of Armagh.  L A U K
Trans 7: 32-44.

Reeves, P.  Books in relation to libraries.  L A 6: 211-4, Discussion 214-5.

Regnart, Mrs. O. M.  Santa Clara county free library.  Cal News
Notes 15: 7-12.

Reid, B. and J. J. Marshall.  Donaghadu printing.  Irish Book
Lover, Oct 1915: 46.

Reid, E. A.  Fiction old and new;  as advertised.  Minn P L C
N 3: 58-61.

Reid, H. W.  Hints on bookbinding.  P L 12: 63-4.

Reid, J. E.  Fines and charges for overdue, damaged and lost
books.  Ontario Lib Assn Proceedings Apl 1912: 71-3.

Reid, M.  Our new Americans.  Mass Lib Club Bull 2, No 2: 29-
56.

Reid, S.  Children's wonder house.  Independent 72: 30-6.

Reighard, K. F.  Books and the boy.  Outlook 65: 178-80.

Reinick, W. R.  Arrangement and cataloguing of U. S. documents.
P L 5: 83-7.

----- W. R.  Arrangement for Illustrations in periodicals.
P L 15: 376-8.

----- W. R.  Books as a source of disease.  American Journal of Pharmacy, Jan 1914: 13-25;  L J 39: 581-4.

----- W. R.  Cataloguing of United States government documents.  P L 5: 83-7.

----- W. R.  Checking serial publications.  L J 36: 416-20.

----- W. R.  Classifying and cataloguing public documents.
P L 11: 51-3.

----- W. R.  Insects destructive to books:  some pests that
play havoc with our libraries.  Scientific American Supp
70: 408-10;  73: 293-4, Dec 24, 1910, May 11, 1912;  L A R
14: 286-7;  English Mechanic March 24, 1911.

----- W. R.  Public documents as a commercial factor.  Special Libraries 4: 175-7;  L J 39: 207-9.

----- W. R.  Transmission of disease by means of books.  L
A 8: 237-8.

----- W. R.  Trials and tribulations of a document librarian.
L J 37: 504-6.

----- W. R.  Use of documents in the public library.  A L A
Bull 1: Conf No 146-9.

Reinsch, P. S.  Bibliography of colonial government.  Bib Soc
Amer Proc 1: 225-6.

Reissmann, G.  Kodak Park library.  Special libraries 10: 94-7.
Rendtorff, E. J.  High school physics library.  School Science
  and Mathematics 16: 139-44.
Renninger, E. D.  A library experiment in prison work.  L J
  41: 92-7.
------- E. D.  Organization of a library in a small town.
  L J 31: 112-7.
Reppelin, A.  What children read.  Atlantic 59: 23-32.
Resor, J. H.  The boy and the book; or, the public library
  a necessity.  P L 2: 282-5.
Rex, F.  The municipal library.  Education bi-monthly 4: 286-9.
  - F.  Municipal reference library as a public utility.
  Special Libraries 8: 23-37.
Reyburn, G.  Technical and commercial library movement in South
  Africa.  L A R 21: 229-31
Rever, E.  Library movement in Austria.  L J 29: Conf No 85-7.
  --- E.  Public libraries in Austria.  P L 9: 378-9.
Reynolds, G. F.  English literature in secondary schools.  Ed-
  ucation 32: 1-10.
Reynolds, G. H.  Traveling libraries:  their significance in
  our civilization.  Wash L A Bull 3: 4-7.
Reynolds, H. E.  Our cathedral libraries.  L A U K Trans 1:
  32-43, 144;  L J 4: 130.
Reynolds, J. H.  The technical library in its relation to ed-
  ucational and industrial development.  L A R 19: 250-61.
Reynolds, M. M.  Status of school libraries.  Wash L A Bull
  2, No 1: 9-10.
Rhoades, R.  The work of a library information desk.  L J 39:
  350-3.
Rhodes, J. V.  Library of the State board of visitors.  Minn
  P L C N 4: 12-3.
Rhodes, W. E.  Christie library, Owens college, Manchester.
  L A R 2: 73-81.
Ricci, S. de.  Colard Mansion (First printer of Bruges).  L
  (4th series) 1: 95-6.
Rice, Mrs. A. H.  Friends of my childhood.  Outlook 78: 835-6.
Rice, E. F.  Latin plays for schools.  Classical Journal 16:
  149-56.
Rice, F. V.  Towards the teaching of civic responsibility in
  and by librarians.  P L 25: 494-5.
Rice, O. S.  Normal school libraries.  Nat Educ Assn 1916:
  669-71.
  -- O. S.  Of interest to teachers.  Wis Lib Bull 8: 188.
  -- O. S.  Practicable library co-operation with Junior Red
  Cross associations in rural schools.  Nat Educ Assn 1918:
  450-2.
  -- O. S.  Rural-school libraries:  their needs and possibil-
  ities.  Nat Educ Assn 1913: 740-6
  -- O. S.  School librarian requirement in Wisconsin.  School
  Review 28: 733-5.

-- O. S.  Wisconsin high-school teacher librarian movement.
Wis Lib Bull 15: 248-9.
Rice, W.  Practical book reviewing and manuscript reading from
the inside.  A L A Bull 4: 630-3.
-- W.  Practical side of book reviewing.  P L 10: 291-2.
-- W.  Relation of city government to public libraries.
L J 12: 364-9.
Rich, L.  How can the beneficence of libraries be more succ-
essfully directed toward their assistants?  P L 25: 365-8.
Rich, W. A., Jr.  Centralization of merchandise catalogs.
Special Libraries 7: 128.
Richards, Mrs. C. E.  Indian legends of Colorado.  A L A Bull
14: 203-10.
Richards, E. H.  Sanitary construction and care of library
buidlings.  L J 28: 787-8;  P L 8: 427-8.
Richards, E. M.  Fiction in war time.  P L 23: 314-5.
Richards, H. C.  City libraries.  L C 2: 15-7.
Richards, H. H.  What school boys like to read.  Mass Lib
Club Bull 6: 57-8.
Richardson.  Librarianship as a profession for women.  L 6:
137-42.
Richardson, Mrs.  Davenport free library.  il Ia LCQ 1: 43.
Richardson, E. C.  The A. L. I. plan of co-operation by spec-
ialization.  L J 41: 163-5.
-------- E. C.  American libraries and the study of ancient
manuscripts.  L J 23: Conf No 102-3.
-------- E. C.  The American library institute.  Am Lib
Annual 1916-17: 12-3.
-------- E. C.  Antediluvian libraries.  L J 15:  Conf No
40-4.
-------- E. C.  Being a librarian.  L J 15: 201-2.
-------- E. C.  Bibliographical facilities of the British
Museum.  L J 9: 156.
-------- E. C.  Bibliothecal science and economy, Article
11 of the A. L. A. constitution.  L J 10: 244-5.
-------- E. C.  Book matters at home and abroad.  L J 34:
200-5.
-------- E. C.  Classification in books.  L J 26: 124-32.
-------- E. C.  Classification of theology:  critical study
of various schemes.  L J 8: 320-1.
-------- E. C.  Co-operation in lending among college and
reference libraries.  L J 24: Conf No 32-6, Discussion
156-7;  P L 14: 275.
-------- E. C.  Cumulative printed catalog for large libraries.  L J 41: 28-31.
-------- E. C.  Departmental libraries.  L J 28: Conf No
173.
-------- E. C.  Encyclopaedia and librarians.  L J 10: 211.
-------- E. C.  Essentials of public international co-operation.  L J 44: 207-9.

-------- E. C.  An expansive author-table:  a suggestion.
L J 18: 187.
-------- E. C.  Facts about old Egyptian librarians:  a
reply.  L J 37: 316-9.
-------- E. C.  Folk-lore classification.  L J 9: 177.
-------- E. C.  Franciscans new and old.  P L 15: 109-11.
-------- E. C.  Fundamental principles of cataloging.  A
L A Bull 6: 234-8.
-------- E. C.  The higher education of librarians.  L J
40: 333-4.
-------- E. C.  Hours of opening libraries.  L J 12: 402-6.
-------- E. C.  The Institute and its progress.  L J 43:
382-3.
-------- E. C.  Instruction in library schools.  L J 44:
622.
-------- E. C.  International bibliography.  L J 29: Conf
No 93-6.
-------- E. C.  International catalogue of current litera-
ture of social science.  Bib Soc Amer Proc 1: 194-202.
-------- E. C.  King Leo's classification.  L J 10: 208-11.
-------- E. C.  Lending library for libraries.  L J 24: 161.
-------- E. C.  Libraries the primary factor in human evol-
ution.  2nd Int Conf 158-9.  1897.
-------- E. C.  Library clocks.  L J 14: 378.
-------- E. C.  Library in the community.  L J 31: 107-11.
-------- E. C.  Linotype method.  L J 17: 377-8.
-------- E. C.  Linotyping library catalogs.  L J 19: 260-1.
-------- E. C.  Manuscript hunting.  Bib Soc Amer Proc 3:
14-28.
-------- E. C.  Mnemonics.  L J 10: 208-11.
-------- E. C.  National Library problem to-day.  L J 30:
Conf No 3-9.
-------- E. C.  Open shelves for university libraries.  A
L A Bull 2: 323-7;  P L 13: 241-3.
-------- E. C.  Place of the library in the university.
A L A Bull 10: 1-3, 45-8; P L 21: 86-7.
-------- E. C.  Presidential address.  L J 30: Conf No 1-9.
-------- E. C.  Princeton University Library and its reorg-
anization.  L J 25: 219-22.
-------- E. C.  The question of censorship in libraries.
L J 43: 152-4.
-------- E. C.  Reference books.  U S Rept 976-82;  L J
18: 245-7, Conf No 62-3, 1892.
-------- E. C.  Report of the Co-operation committee.  L J
25:  Conf No 71-3, 139-42.
-------- E. C.  Report on theological libraries.  L J 10:
269.
-------- E. C.  The return of co-operative indexing.  A L
A Bull 11: 222-6.

-------- E. C.  Scheme of classification of the International congress of arts and science at St. Louis.  L J 29: 528-9.

-------- E. C.  Some business aspects of the university library.  Princeton Alumni Weekly Apr. 21, 1915: 675-6; L J 40: 621-2.

-------- E. C.  Survival of the fittest among books.  L J 22 Conf No 45-7.

-------- E. C.  Systematic staff teaching:  Book arts and library schools.  A L A Bull 10:  10-1, Discussion, 45-8.

-------- E. C.  The travelling librarian.  L J 28: 58-64.

-------- E. C.  Treatment of books according to their use. L J 28: Conf No 173.

-------- E. C.  The university library.  Princeton University Bulletin 9: 73-92 New Princeton library.  P L 3: 270-1.

-------- E. C.  Why librarians know.  L J 11: 204-8.

Richardson, M. C.  Importance of the library in the school system.  P L 24: 334-5.

Richardson, M. K.  County libraries for South Dakota.  South Dakota Lib Bull 6: 59-64.

-------- M. K.  The reading of non-fiction:  how to increase it.  South Dakota Educ Assn Proceedings 1915: 308-15; L J 41: 940-1.

Richardson, R. T.  Classification and arrangement of local ′collections.  L A R 7: 12-8, Discussion L A R 6: 474-6.

Richberg, D. R.  Legislative reference bureaus for political parties.  Special Libraries 5: 38-42.

Richman, I. B.  American education and President Eliot's Five-foot library.  P L 15: 142-4.

Richmond, L.  What proportion of appropriation should be spent for books, periodicals, etc.  P L 6: 428-30.

Richmond, W.  Some art books in the Hammersmith libraries.  L A R 4: 110-27.

Richt, C.  Active library membership:  a suggestion.  L J 34: 263-4.

Ricker, S. W.  Periodical title-page record.  Bull Bib 8: 34.

Rickey, V. O.  Use of reference books.  P L 4: 364-6.

Rickman, I. B.  Value of local history.  L C Q 6: 121-4.

Riddell, W. R.  Use of a public library by a public man.  P L 21: 249-54.

Riddle, C.  Library movement in Bournemouth.  L A R 16: 109-18.

---- C.  Music in public libraries.  L A R 16: 1-10, Discussion, L A R 15: 645-8.

---- C.  Public library movement in Bournemouth.  L A R 15: 629-30.

Ridell, F. R.  Metal furniture versus wood.  L J 37: 436-7.

Rider, A. F.  Old classifications and the excuse for new ones. L J 35: 387-96.

--- A. F.  Bibliography on residential and industrial districts in cities.  Special Libraries 7: 2-7.

Rider, S. S.  What I saw in the free library at Pawtucket.  L J 14: 40-1.

Ridgeley, H.  Explanations of the library law.  Del L C Hdbk 1904: 16-21.

Ridington, J.  The challenge of the present days.  Pacific Northwest Lib Assn Proceedings 1919: 7-8;  P L 25: 175-8.

------- J.  Library development in British Columbia.  P L 25: 214.

------- J.  New needs and new responsibilities.  A L A Bull 14: 195-202.

------- J.  The poetry of the war.  Pacific Northwest Library Assn Proceedings 1917: 52-90.

------- J.  The university, the university library, and the returned soldier.  L J 43: 808-15.

Ridway, Mrs. F. H.  A classification for agricultural literature.  U S Bureau of Education, Bulletin 1917 No 41: Library books for high schools; L J 38: 561-3.

Ridway, Mrs. F. H.  On a book wagon in the Kentucky mountains.  L J 42: 520-1.

Rider, G. T.  Books for the blind.  L J 45: 119-20.

Riebenack, M.  Railway libraries.  L J 30: 927-8.

Riggs, E.  Library of the mosque of St. Sophia, Constantinople.  L J 10: 106.

Riggs, J. T.  Why does the school need the library?  P L 10: 507-9.

Rije, Miss T. van.  Organization and administration of the University library at Utrecht, Holland.  L A R 15: 597-603.

Ringwood, O. K. D.  "As the newcomer sees it":  The Bankers trust company library.  Special Libraries 10: 130-1.

Rintoul, R.  The control of industrial and scientific information.  Journal of Soc of Chemical Industry Feb 28, 1918; J L of industrial and engineering chemistry Feb 28, 1918: Special Libraries 11: 151-2.

Ripley, L. W.  County free library extension: the Sacramento plan.  Cal News Notes 3: 303-4;  L J 33: 445-6;  Library Work 1912: 136-7.

---- L. W.  County library system in Sacramento county.  Cal News Notes 4: 262-4;  California Lib Assn Proceedings 1909: 44-6.

---- L. W.  Discussion of county free libraries.  Nat Educ Assn 1911: 1029-30.

---- L. W.  Library conditions in Northern and Central California.  L J 30: 789-90.

Ripley, R.  Miss Kent on the library question.  L J 17: 489-90.

Ritchie, J. Jr.  Anent the Boston co-operative information bureau.  L J 40: 397-9;  Mass Lib Club Bull 5: 21-5.

----- J. Jr.  Boston Co-operative information bureau at work.
Special Libraries 3: 207-8.

----- J. Jr.  New library of the Massachusetts institute of
technology.  L J 42: 30-5.

Rittenhouse, J. B.  The new poetry and democracy.  A L A Bull
10: 137-43, 382.

Rivers, J.  Do public library books spread disease.  L W 5:
143-4.

---- J.  French utopia.  L (ns) 6: 265-73.

---- J.  From an old directory.  L (ns) 5: 173-81.

---- J.  Gutenberg missal controversy.  L W 6: 173-5.

---- J.  How great minds jump -- Literary forgeries.  L (ns)
4: 243-50.

---- J.  Shakespeare à la Française.  L (ns) 6: 78-85.

Rivington, C. R.  Notes on the Stationers' company.  il. L (ns)
4: 355-66.

Robarts, C. H.  University libraries as national institutions.
L J 2: 129-40, 249-51.

Robbins, F.  Medical literature as a specialty.  Medical Record
May 27, 1916;  L J 41: 939-40.

Robbins, G. E.  A library in a penal institution.  L J 38: 24-5.

Robbins, I. E.  Reading and literature.  Teachers' College
Record 8: 1-7.

Robbins, M. E.  Library schools.  Wis Lib Bull 12: 374-7.

----- M. E.  Life at New York state library school.  L J
21: 13-4.

----- M. E.  Our next of kin.  P L 15: 184-6.

----- M. E.  Training teacher-librarians in normal schools.
A L A Bull 13: 279-301, 397.

Robbins, M. H.  Ibarra edition of Sallust, 1772.  Printing Art
17: 453-9.

Robert, W.  Recent book sales.  19th Century 72: 1030-9.

Roberts, E. D.  Day of public documents.  P L 13: 408.

Roberts, F. B.  Being a citizen.  Minn P L C N 3: 171-4.

----- F. B.  Comparative importance of side lines in the
small library.  Penn Lib Notes Oct, 1913: 27-32.

----- F. B.  The library and the foreign citizen.  P L 17:
166-9.

Roberts, F. M.  Lectures in public libraries.  L A 2: 53-8.

Roberts, H. D.  Brighton public library, museum and art galleries: a retrospect.  L A R 10: 439-54.

----- H. D.  Education of the librarian: elementary stage.
L A R 8: 556-72, Discussion 504.

----- H. D.  Education of the library assistant.  L 9: 103.

----- H. D.  Educational work of the L. A.  Greenwood's Yr-
Bk: 57-60.  1900-01.

----- H. D.  Issue of periodicals in reading rooms.  L 10:
33-5.

----- H. D.  Library assistants and technical training.  L
A 2: 325-31.

----- H. D.  Library facilities for visitors to holiday re-
sorts.  L A R 16: 11-7, Discussion 15: 654-9.

----- H. D.  Library lectures (Letter).  L A R 5: 159.

----- H. D.  On the issue of periodicals.  L 10: 33-5.

----- H. D.  Question circulars.  L A R 15: 163.

----- H. D.  Relation between the public library and the
museum.  L A R 12: 361-7.

----- H. D.  Some remarks on the education of library assistants.  L 9: 103-12.

----- H. D.  Technical training of library assistants.  L
A 3: 175-9.

----- H. D.  Training for librarians in Great Britain.  L
J 29:  Conf No 39-46.

----- H. D.  Training of library assistants.  L A R 1: 274-
5, 352.

----- H. D.  A triple alliance:  the public library, museum
and art gallery.  L A 7: 182-91.

Roberts, K. L.  Club women and programs.  P L 14: 205-8.

----- K. L.  What the large library can do for the small
library.  L J 31:  Conf No 254-5.

Roberts, P.  The library and the foreign speaking man.  L J
36: 496-9.

----- P.  What can libraries do to aid the foreign speaking
people in America?  Penn Lib Notes 3, No 4: 16-23.

Roberts, R.  The museum of the Minnesota historical society.
Minn P L C N 6: 18.

----- R.  Relation of the public libraries to the present
system of education.  L A R 9: 1-14.

Roberts, W.  Recent book sales.  19th Century, 72: 1030-9.

Robertshaw, W.  How an increased library rate might affect library administration.  L W 17: 81-7.

-------- W.  Notes on popularizing a scientific library.
L W 22: 296-8.

-------- W.  Philosopher's public library.  L W 17: 16-7.

-------- W.  James Grant: military novelist;  a brief note
on some of his novels.  Libn 6: 2-3.

Robertshaw, W. S.  Classified or dictionary catalogue?  Libn
6: 29-32, 49-53.

Robertson, A.  School libraries in rural districts.  Nat Educ
Assn 1902: 818-24.

Robertson, A. W.  Arrangement for magazines at Aberdeen library.  L C 4: 111-3.

------- A. W.  Board school and its relation to the public
library.  L 8: 285-97.

------- A. W.  Classification in public libraries.  2nd Int
Conf 89-92, Discussion 235-6.

------- A. W.  The Duplex indicator.  L J 14: 42.

------- A. W.  Heating system at Aberdeen.  L 6: 95-8.

------- A. W.  Library indicators: with special reference
to the Duplex indicator.  L 2: 21-7.

------- A. W.  Note on fines for the damage of books.  L
4: 115-6.

------- A. W.  Public libraries of Aberdeen.  L 6: 1-2.

------- A. W.  Ventilating system of Aberdeen library.  L
6: 95-8 Greenwood's Public Libraries: 386.

Robertson, J. A.  Archives of the Philipines.  Am Hist Assn
Rept 1910: 421-5.

------- J. A.  Library work in Manila.  L J 35: 366-7.

------- J. A.  The Philippine library.  L J 37: 511.

Robertson, J. R.  College and school libraries in Oregon.  L
J 30: 149-50.

Robertson, L. H.  Lessons in library pictures for the children.
Greensboro (N. C.).  Daily Record, Sept 4, 1911.

Robertson, W. J.  Should the Education department issue a librarian's certificate.  P L 9: 209-12.

Robertson, W. S.  Short list of books on social science.  L J
42: 240-1.

Robins, A.  Paper that prevents eyestrain.  Technical World
Magazine 21: 882-3.

Robinson.  Progress of rural library extension work.  A L A
Bull 10: 56.

Robinson, A. L.  Commercial filing.  Filing Aug 1918: 49-51;
L J 43: 850.

------ A. L.  Filing.  Special Libraries 6: 147-9.

Robinson, D.  South Dakota literature.  South Dakota Lib Bull
4: 110-5.

Robinson, J. A.  Book influences for defectives and dependents:
helping those who cannot help themselves.  A L A Bull 7:
177-82.

------ J. A.  A few suggestions for stretching a small book
fund.  Wis Lib Bull 10: 237-8; Ia L C Q 7: 71-2; New Hamp
Bull 10: 23-4;  Lib Occ 3: 184-5;  Tex Lib 1, No 9: 6-7;
Vt L Bull 10: 27-8.

------ J. A.  The Iowa library commission: its purpose and
activities.  Texas Libraries 1: July 1916: 22-4.

------ J. A.  Libraries in Iowa state institutions.  Iowa
L C Q 6: 252-6.

------ J. A.  A library boys' club.  Wis Lib Bull 5: 5.

------ J. A.  Summary of county library laws.  L J 42: 127,
836;  P L 22: 17-9.

------ J. A.  Unification of state library activities.  A
L A Bull 12: 368;  Discussion, 282, 367.

------ J. A.  What the library commission is doing to help
win the war.  A L A Bull 12: 186-7.

Robinson, O. H.  Access to shelves in college libraries.  U
S Rept 516-20, 1876.
------ O. H.  Cataloguing for college libraries.  U S Rept
512-4, 1876.
------ O. H.  Classification for college libraries.  U S
Rept 509-10, 1876.
------ O. H.  College libraries as semi-public libraries:
the Rochester university library.  L J 2: 57-61.
------ O. H.  College library administration.  U S Govt
Rept 505-25, 1876.
------ O. H.  Description of the sheaf catalogue invented
by Professor Robinson.  il. U S Rept 666-72.  1876.
------ O. H.  Indexing periodical and miscellaneous liter-
ature.  U S Rept 663-72, 1876.
------ O. H.  Notes from Rochester university.  L J 5: 142-3,
480-2.
------ O. H.  Relation of libraries to college work.  L J
6: 97-104.
------ O. H.  Titles of books.  U S Rept 715-26, 1876.
Rockwell, A. G.  Fiction again:  Where shall we draw the line
of exclusion?  P L 8: 307-13.
------ A. G.  What's the use of a public library.  L J 31:
808-11.
------ A. G.  Ruts and how to avoid them.  P L 10: 339-43.
Rockwell, W. W.  Library of the Union theological seminary.
Columbia University Quarterly 13: 211-3.
Rockwood, E. R.  The Forest service library of Portland.  Pac-
ific Northwest Lib Assn Conference Proceedings 1914: 24-7.
------ E. R.  International government and the League to
enforce peace.  Bull Bib 10: 30-4.
------ E. R.  Things not worth while.  Pacific Northwest
Lib Assn Proceedings 1914: 43-5.
Roden, C. B.  Book-buying for public libraries.  Wis Lib Bull
11: 312-3.
--- C. B.  Care and distribution of public documents.  P
L 9: 285-8.
--- C. B.  Civil service administration in Chicago.  L J
45: 620.
--- C. B.  German library spirit.  P L 19: 439.
--- C. B.  Library as a paying investment.  P L 17: 111-4;
Wis Lib Bull 8: 5-8.
--- C. B.  Library extension in Chicago.  Papers presented
at the conference held during the Chicago Child welfare ex-
hibit.  Chic Sch Civics and Philanthropy, 1912 Part 7.
--- C. B.  On cataloguing -- some glittering generalities.
P L 9: 116-7.
--- C. B.  A question of business ethics.  L J 45: 515-6.
--- C. B.  Thoughts on reference libraries by a cataloguer.
A L A Bull 2: 361-4, Discussion 364-70.

Roden, C. R.  Book advertising:  information as to subject and
    scope of books.  A L A Bull 6: 181-7.
Roebuck, G.  Parliamentary return relating to public libraries
    in Great Britain.  L A R 14: 581-3.
Roebuck, G. E.  Are newsrooms a desirable adjunct to libraries.
    L A 4: 168-9.
----- G. E.  Argument against affiliation.  L A 5: 71-7,
    78-9.
----- G. E.  Books for the blind.  L A R 11: 611-2.
----- G. E.  The child in the library.  L A 2: 9-10.
----- G. E.  A consideration of the opportunities of the
    minor public libraries.  L A R 15: 110-21.
----- G. E.  How I would organize and administer a public
    library having a gross income of  800 a year (prize essay).
    L A 2: Supp VII-X.
----- G. E.  Library assistants' association:  a statement
    of its use and objects.  L A 5: 170-3.
----- G. E.  Literature for the blind.  L A R 15: 218-9.
----- G. E.  Literature for the blind and the public lib-
    rary movement connected therewith.  L A 3: 253-60.
----- G. E.  Newsroom question.  L A 4: 226-33.
----- G. E.  Newsroom reform.  L W 9: 273-82.
----- G. E.  On the need of a lecture bureau.  L A R 11:
    47-8.
----- G. E.  Opportunities of minor public libraries.  L A
    R 15: 119-21.
----- G. E.  Present conditions and possibilities of public
    library service to the blind.  L A R 13: 455-60.
----- G. E.  Professional etiquette.  L A 5: 252.
----- G. E.  Public libraries of the United Kingdom:  stat-
    isical returns, 1919.  L A R 21: 128, 161-71.
----- G. E.  Registration:  the means, difficulties, and
    the first step.  L A R 9: 418-20.
----- G. E.  Short review of the statistical tables and
    summaries in the Report to the Carnegie United Kingdom
    Trust by Prof.  W. G. S. Adams.  L A R 17: 516-22.
----- G. E.  The situation before us.  L A 14: 280.
----- G. E. and Thorne, W. B.  "Primer of library practice":
    Review.  L A 11: 198.
Roesler, F. E.  Co-operative subject index.  L J 1: 183-4, 222,
    226-7.
Rogan, O. F.  How small libraries can help state legislation:
    some practical suggestions.  P L 24: 3-5.
--- O. F.  Library advertising:  the Association.  Texas
    Libraries 1 Nos 10-11: 107-10.
Rogers, B.  The most beautiful type in the world.  Dial 47:
    36-9.
Rogers, F. H.  Co-operative index for public library.  L J 1:
    62-3, Discussion 113-7.

Rogers, J. M.  Collection of local history.  L J 35: 368-9.
Rogers, T. H.  Subject references wanted.  L J 10: 403.
Rojas, L. M.  National library of Mexico.  L J 44: 216-8.
Rollins, W. H.  Public library:  the people's university.  Ia
    L C Q 6: 23-5.
Ronan, Mrs. E.  Jennings county library, North Vernon, Indiana.
    Lib Occ 5: 374.
Rood, A. C.  Americanization at Sumner branch library.  Minn-
    eapolis.  Minn P L C N 6: 6-7.
Rood, E.  Library work in schools.  Neb Lib Bull 4: 2-5.
Rood, H.  What your gifts of books have accomplished.  Delin-
    eator 94: 30.
Roose, P. W.  Children's books.  Book Lore 5: 131-5.
Root, A. S.  College and university library salaries.  A L A
    Bull 13: 77-80.
    -- A. S.  Dziatsko, Carl, 1842-1903.  P L S: 159-60.
    -- A. S.  Future development of college and university lib-
    raries.  L J 39: 812-5.
    -- A. S.  Lecture.  Wis Lib Bull 9: 92-3.
    -- A. S.  The library school of the future.  A L A Bull 11:
    157-60.
    -- A. S.  Rules.  Wis Lib Bull 9: 93.
    -- A. S.  Scope of an American bibliographical society.  Bib
    Soc Chic Yr-Bk 1901-2: 41-52;  L J 27: Conf No 61-2.
    -- A. S.  To the would-be library school student.  P L 23:
    3-5.
Root, M. E.  Library work with children.  P L 20: 28-9.
    -- M. E. and Maltby, A. B.  Picture bulletins in the child-
    ren's library.  L J 27: 191-4.
Root, M. E. S.  Children and library tools.  L J 40: 24-7.
    -- M. E. S.  Children's library work.  L J 45: 827-31.
Rose, A. L.  National city financial library, New York.  L J
    45: 305-6.
Rose, E.  Vital distinctions of a library apprentice course.
    A L A Bull 10: 189-94, 429-31.
Rose, G. D.  Apprentice class in the medium sized library.  A
    L A Bull 4: 783-6.
    -- G. D.  The efficient library.  Ia L C Q 6: 241-5.
    -- G. D.  An Iowa librarian in a southern camp.  Iowa L C
    Q 8: 137-40.
Rose-Troup, F.  Two book bills of Katherine Parr.  L (3d series)
    2: 40-8.
Roseberry, Lord.  On public libraries.  L 8: 314-8.
Rosenau, N. S.  Co-operation of libraries in collecting annual
    reports.  L J 14: 473-5.
    ----- N. S.  Library exchange:  scheme for exchange of dup-
    licates.  L J 14: 473-4.
Rosenberg, I.  Directing the taste of casual readers.  P L 13:
    294-9.

Rosenberg, I. L.   Problems of a reference librarian.   L J 29:
  120-3.
Rosenberg, J. M. B.   Your future calling and what it means.
  Wis Lib Bull 13: 230-4.
Rosenberg, T.   Directing the taste of casual readers.   P L 13:
  294-9.
------- T.   To what extent can the public library direct
  the taste of readers.   L J 32: 401-6.
Rosenberry, J. M. B.   Your future calling and what it means.
  Wis Lib Bull 13: 230-4.
Ross, A. S.   Library progress in North Carolina since 1899.
  A L A Bull 1: Conf No 71-2.
Ross, J.   Book selection: local collections (has a biblio-
  graphy).   L W 10: 71-6.
-- J.   Librarianship after the war.   L A 13: 94-5.
-- J.   The Library assistants' association and its work.
  L A 13: 90-5.
-- J.   Library association examinations:  the L. A. Educa-
  tion committee's report.   L A 12: 141-3.
-- J.   Select bibliography of the art of printing to 1640.
  Libn 10: 28-31, 42-5.
-- J.   Technical training in librarianship in England and
  abroad.   L A R 12: 99-117.
Rossiter, W. S.   The individual in the printing office.   Print-
  ing Art 15: 25-7.
Roswell, P.   Flower library, New York state veterinary college,
  Cornell University.   L J 43: 332.
Routzahn, E. G.   A. B. C. of exhibit planning.   Wis Lib Bull
  14: 235.
------ E. G.   Concerning social and civic material.   L J
  38: 27.
------ E. G.   Exhibit material and units.   P L 18: 65.
Rowan, J. M.   Reading rooms and libraries for the blind.   Young
  Woman's Journal, April 1909;  L J 34: 221.
Rowe, L. S.   The need for more bibliographical data on Latin-
  America   L J 42: 375-6.
Rowe, M.   Classification of agricultural bulletins.   South
  Dakota Lib Bull 4, No 3: 94-6; L J 43: 907.
Rowe, T. W.   Public libraries in New Zealand.   2nd International
  Conference Proceedings 199-200, 1897.
Rowell, J. C.   Circular explaining method adopted at the lib-
  rary of the University of California.   L J 23: 104.
---- J. C.   Classification of pure mathematics.   L J 17: 447.
---- J. C.   College libraries and their relation to the
  people.   L J 19: 50.
---- J. C.   Departmental libraries of the University of
  California.   L J 41: 710.
---- J. C.   The first public library in California:  Monte-
  rey Library Association, 1850.   Cal News Notes 13: 39-40.

---- J. C.  On the distribution of income in the college
library.  L J 30: Conf No 84-6.
---- J. C.  Purchase of books for departmental libraries.
Am Lib Annual, 1916-17: 133.
---- J. C.  A retrospect of reading.  Cal News Notes 5:
382-4.
---- J. C.  Schemes of classification of law books.  L J
31: 147-8.
---- J. C.  Subject index to science.  L J 20: Conf No 27-8.
---- J. C.  University of California library.  P L 4: 212-4.
Rowlatt, H.  The provision of books for the blind.  L A R 4:
87-9;  Discussion 89-91.
Rowswell, B. T.  Story of the Guille-Alle's library in the Is-
land of Guernsey.  B A R 17: I-VII.
Ruby, E. E.  Library work in the Army of occupation.  Pacific
Northwest Lib Assn Proceedings 1919: 22-7.
-- E. E.  Third army headquarters.  A L A Bull 13: 318-9.
-- E. E.  A year of camp library work.  Pacific Northwest
Lib Assn Proceeding 1918: 9-16.
Rudolph, A. J.  Blue-print process for printing catalogues.
L J 24: 102-5, 560, 574, 608.
----- A. J.  The Newberry genealogical index.  L J 24: 53-5.
Rudwin, M. J.  Passion play literature.  Bull Bib 9: 66-7, 90-3,
10: 6-10.
Rugg, H. G.  Vermont books.  Vt L Bull 12: 29-34.
Rullman, F.  Library science:  a special study at the German
universities.  U S Rept: XXIII-XXVI, 1876.
Runkle, E. W.  The psychology of reading.  Penn Lib Notes 4:
11-29.
Runyan, M. D.  Stories and story telling for kindergarten and
primary school.  Teacher's College Record 5: 32-48, 438-48.
Rupp, J.  Non-fiction reading:  how to increase it.  Mich Lib
Bull July-Sept, 1915: 53-4.
Ruse, R.  A few general principles in library training.  New
Hamp Bull (ns) 14: 111-3;  Ia L C Q 8: 129-32;  Lib Occ 5:
105-8.
-- R.  Place of the training class in library service.  L
J 42: 872-4.
Rush, C.  List of children's books.  Wis Lib Bull 10: 46-7.
Rush, C. E.  Co-operative saving:  some examples of publicity
material.  P L 21: 85.
-- C. E.  Expanding its activities.  P L 24: 166-7.
-- C. E.  Greater publicity.  A L A Bull 13: 363-5.
-- C. E.  Home publicity.  P L 25: 23.
-- C. E.  The man in the yards.  A L A Bull 7: 154-8;  P L
18: 313-7.
-- C. E.  Moving pictures:  stereopticons.  Bull Bib 8: 34.
-- C. E.  One hundred books on business.  Bull Bib 9: 160-2.
-- C. E.  Practical problems in reorganization work.  L J
35: 3-6.

-- C. E.  Reference function of a small library.  A L A
Bull 8: 353-6;  New Hamp Bull 11: 100-3;  N Y L 4: 118-22;
Minn P L C N 4: 114-6;  Lib Occ 3: 196-9;  P L 19: 283-4.
-- C. E.  Two good books a year for my child.  Lib Occ 5:
421-2.
-- C. E.  Why I believe in advertising the public library.
Associated Advertising April 1918: 15;  L J 43: 456, 877-8.
-- C. E.  Working men's branch.  Wis Lib Bull 7: 109.
Russell, C. P.  Filing of newspapers.  L A Trans 1: 97-8.
----- C. P.  Note on the preservation of bindings.  L A
Trans 1: 99-100.
Russell, E. H.  Voluntary reading in elementary schools.  School
Review 13: 159-67.
Russell, J. A.  Presidential address.  L A Trans 4: 11-2.
Russell, J. B.  Department of Agriculture library.  U S Govt
Rept: 272-3, 1876.
Russell, J. E.  Observations upon children's reading.  L J
22: 194.
Russell, Lord.  The Lord chief justice on libraries at the
opening of Putney library.  L A R 1: 395-7.
Russell, T. O'N.  Knowledge is power.  An Leab 1: 136-9.
Ryan, E. V.  Games at the library.  Wis Lib Bull 3: 32-3.
Ryan, J. V.  Library conditions in American cities.  Educational
Bi-Monthly 7: 157-72.
Ryan, M. J.  Some notes on the libraries and book trade of
Dublin.  B A R 4: XLV-XLIX.
Rye, R. A.  A library policy from a university point of view.
Libn 1: 3-8.
Rye, W. B.  Leather for bookbinding.  L A R 3: 532-3.
Sabin, H.  Rural school libraries.  U S Bureau of Education
Report 1901-2: 579-81.
Sacconi-Ricci, G.  Observations on the various forms of cata-
logs used in modern libraries.  L J 18: 423-7.
Sackett, G.  Children's librarians.  P L 7: 303-5.
----- G.  Home libraries and reading clubs.  L J 27:  Conf
No 72-5.
Sadler, M.  Address at the opening of Rastrick branch of Brig-
house public library.  L A R 15: 29-35.
Sage, L. H.  Arrangement of law books.  A L A Bull 2: 296-8.
St. John, E.  Combinations in color-printing.  Printing Art
16: 463-6.
------ E.  Practical hints for color users.  Printing Art
15: 28-30;  16: 117-24.
Salford, Bishop of.  More about the Louvain library.  Tablet
30 Jan 1915: 138-9.
Salisbury, Mrs. E. C.  Development of extension work in the
north and west.  U. S. Department of agriculture.  Cal News
Notes 14: 140-1.
Salisbury, G. E.  Library work in a state normal school.  P L
8: 93-4.

------- G. E.   Library work in our normal schools.   Wis Lib
Bull 2: 70-1.

------- G. E.   Picture collections in small libraries (Instructional Dept No 3) 20p.   Wis Free Lib Commission.   1908.

Sally, A. S., Jr.   The first presses of South Carolina; with
a list of South Carolina imprints from 1735 to 1771.   Bib
Soc Amer Proc 3: 28-69.

Salmon, L. M.   Examinations in theory and in practice.   P L
10: 90-1.

---- L. M.   Instruction in the use of a college library.
A L A Bull 7: 300-9.

---- L. M.   On the college professor.   L J 36: 51-4.

---- L. M.   Vacation reading.   P L 19: 233-8.

Saltmarsh, E.   West Indianapolis library boys' club.   Lib Occ
2: 208-10.

Sampson, H. A. C.   Public library, lectureship.   L W 7: 212-4.

Samuel, B.   Mutual book lending between libraries.   L J 17:
373-4.

---- B.   Philadelphia library company.   Century 4: 81.

---- B. and S. S. Green.   Mutual book lending between libraries.   L J 18: 123.

Samuelson, J.   A famous industrial library.   L 4: 188-9.

Sanborn, A. E.   Filing posters.   L J 44: 545.

Sanborn, A. S.   Method of keeping statistics of expenditure
for books.   L J 27: 1007-8.

Sanborn, H. N.   Books for men.   L J 41: 165-9.

----- H. N.   Commission helps in book selection.   A L A Bull
10: 57-8;  P L 21: 90-1.

----- H. N.   Co-operation of small libraries.   New Hamp Bull
(ns) 14: 118-22.

----- H. N.   Indiana library commission's work with schools.
L J 42: 452-3.

----- H. N.   Library trustees association.   Vt L Bull 13:
3-4.

----- H. N.   Outlook in Indiana.   Conference of National
Charities and Correction.   Proceedings, 1916: 367-71.

----- H. N.   Present condition of rural library extension
in Indiana.   Lib Occ 4: 86-9.

----- H. N.   Principles underlying commission work.   L J
42: 121-2.

----- H. N.   Report on county libraries.   L J 41: 603-5.

----- H. N.   Scholar and the libraries.   Nation 97: 232-3.

----- H. N.   Standardization of library service.   L J 44:
351-8.

Sanborn, K. E.   A word on cataloguing.   L J 22: 13.

Sanborn, M. E.   The pupil's reading.   Vt L Bull 11: 14.

Sanders, M. A.   Possibilities of public libraries in manufacturing communities.   L J 12: 395-400.

----- M. A.   Relation of the public library to the school.
L J 14: 79-83.  .

----- M. A.  Report on reading for the young.  L J 15: Conf No 58-64.

----- M. A.  Special training for children's librarians. L J 23: Conf No 134.

----- M. A.  Value of local history in a public library. L J 20: 40-1, 78.

Sanders, M. R.  Reading rooms:  what a woman may do in them. L J 17: Conf No 92.

Sanders, W. H.  The high school student and the dictionary. Educational Review 50: 175-83.

Sanderson, E. M.  Some helps for librarians published during the past two years.  N Y L 4: 105-8.

------- E. M. and E. M. Smith.  Circulation of single numbers of periodicals.  L J 33: 86-94.

Sanderson, E. W.  Some library helps published in 1915-16.  N Y L 5: 198-200.

Sanford, O. M.  Librarians and reading.  L J 11: 188.

Sano, T.  Public library in Japan.  P L 14: 214-5.

Sargent, A. L.  Books for children: Fairy tales.  L J 26: Conf No 66-9.

----- A. L.  Children's books and periodicals.  L J 25: Conf No 64-5;  P L 5: 280-1.

----- A. L.  Reference work among school children.  L J 20: 121-2.

Sargent, G. H.  Collectors and dealers.  Bookman ( N Y ) 50: 239-44.

----- G. H.  New fashions in rare books.  Bookman (N Y) 49: 238-43.

----- G. H.  Rare books in wartime.  Bookman (N Y) 48: 303-8.

----- G. H.  Should collectors read books?  Bookman (N Y) 49: 744-9.

Sargent, M.  Report on reading of the young.  L J 14: 226-36.

Sargent, M. E.  How to interest schools in the library.  P L 6: 9-11.

----- M. E.  Library work with schools.  L A R 3: 205-8.

----- M. E.  Woman's position in the library service.  L J 17: Conf No 92-4.

Sargent, R.  Reading for the young.  L J 14: 226-36.

Saunders, H. J.  Rating free public libraries.  L A 7: 82-7.

Savage, A.  Bookworms.  L J 10: 131-2.

Savage, E.  The cost of education and its effect upon the library movement.  L A R 14: 603-13.

Savage, E. A.  Amalgamation of lending and reference departments.  L A 5: 106-7.

---- E. A.  Are public libraries becoming unnecessary?  L A R 15: 491.

---- E. A.  Birmingham commercial library.  L A R 21: 290-1.

---- E. A.  Book selection.  L A 4: 190-5.

---- E. A.  Care of books in early Irish monastic libraries. L (ns) 10: 362-70.

---- E. A.   Classification guides and indexes.  L W 8: 261-6.
---- E. A.   Co-operative annotation (a letter).  L A R 7:
375-6, 428.
---- E. A.   Co-operative book buying.  L A R 6: 229-40.
---- E. A.   Delivery stations and town traveling libraries.
L A R 6: 119-28.
---- E. A.   Descriptive annotation:  a review.  L W 9: 55-6.
---- E. A.   Development of classification.  L A R 8: 501-3.
---- E. A.   Difficulties of the selection of scientific and
technical books.  L A R 10: 162-74.
---- E. A.   Education of assistants.  L A R 9: 411-2.
---- E. A.   Examinations in war-time.  L W 18: 223-4.
---- E. A.   Form and alphabetic book classification.  L A
R 9: 375-83.
---- E. A.   Functions of technical libraries.  L A R 21:
200-1.
---- E. A.   L. A. refusal to increase the capitation grant
to the Northwestern branch.  L A R 10: 528-9.
---- E. A.   The librarian of the future.  L W 6: 4-7.
---- E. A.   Librarianship and literature.  L A R 11: 389-97.
---- E. A.   Library advertising methods: a letter.  L A R
15: 163.
---- E. A.   The library of the future.  L A 3: 29-32; 4:
239-45.
---- E. A.   Literature of the war;  origins, causes and
inspiring ideas.  L A R 17: 446-52.
---- E. A.   Manual of descriptive annotation:  a review by
E. McKnight.  L A R 8: 381-2;  L W 9: 55-6.
---- E. A.   Memorandum on future work of the Technical and
commercial libraries committee.  L A R 20: 219-22, 226-7.
---- E. A.   Memoramdum on the organization of library ex-
change areas.  L A R 19: 328-9; Special Libraries 11, May
No: 9a.
---- E. A.   A minimum for certificated library assistants.
L W 16: 228-32.
---- E. A.   A monastic humanist of the fifteenth century:
a study in English renascence book collecting.  L A R 22:
185-97.
---- E. A.   Municipal library's most expensive and least
useful department.  L A R 7: 429-42.
---- E. A.   Nationalization of libraries.  L A R 21: 63-4.
---- E. A.   New method of registration of borrowers.  L W
6: 45.
---- E. A.   Notes on some extensions of the Dewey classifi-
cation.  L A R 21: 137-40.
---- E. A.   Overdue books.  L W 2: 154-5.
---- E. A.   Periodicals check.  L W 3: 291-3.
---- E. A.   Practical work of annotation.  L W 7: 313-21.
---- E. A.   Principle of annotation.  L A R 6: 575-90, Dis-
cussion 479-80.

---- E. A.  Reading lists.  L W 2: 259-62.

---- E. A.  Report on libraries and museums by the Adult education committee of the Ministry of reconstruction.  L A R 21: 153-9.

---- E. A.  Representation of science and technology in public libraries.  L W 12: 1-4.

---- E. A.  Review of Mr. Brown's subject classification. L W 9: 48-55.

---- E. A.  Salaries of librarians and their assistants. L W 14: 33-6.

---- E. A.  Samuel Pepys' library.  L (ns) 4: 286-91.

---- E. A.  Scientific and technical literature.  L A R 11: 285.

---- E. A.  Some difficulties in the selection of scientific and technical books.  L A R 10: 163-74, Discussion 190-4, 251-2.

---- E. A.  Stock register.  L W 3: 11-3, 84.

---- E. A.  The summer school.  L A R 11: 4-5.

---- E. A.  Symposium on public libraries after the war. L A R 19: 161-2.

---- E. A.  Technical and commercial libraries.  L A R 20: 159-60.

---- E. A.  Technical libraries: a comment on the Third interim report of the Adult education committee.  L A R 21: 264-70.

---- E. A.  Union register of borrowers.  L W 5: 75-6;  L A R 5: 307-12.

---- E. A. and E. McKnight.  How the branch associations may help the library association.  L A R 9: 109-19.  Discussion 143-54.

Savage, E. V.  A few recent books on travel in the United States.  Minn P L C N 5: 53-7.

Savage, H. J.  Selected list on the drama.  Mass L C Bull 3, No 1: 15-9.

Sawin, J. M.  Some successful methods of developing children's interest in good literature.  L J 20: 377-9.

Sawtell, H. C.  Blacking out of betting news.  L A 5: 234-5.

Sawtelle, H. A.  College librarianship.  L J 3: 162.

Sawvel, F. B.  Aims in the study of literature.  Education 17: 290-3.

Sawyer, A. L.  The model library of the future.  Mich Lib Bull 11: 21-6;  L J 45: 1013-7.

Sawyer, E.  Inspiration in war literature.  Pacific Northwest Library Assn Proceedings 1917: 39-52;  P L 23: 105-12.

---- E.  The training class of the library association of Portland.  Pacific Northwest Library Assn Proceedings 1916: 33-5.

Sawyer, E. R.  Library extension teaching.  Pacific Northwest Library Assn Proceedings 1920: 27-8.

---- E. R.  Questionable books.  Pacific Northwest Library
Assn.  Proceedings 1913: 28-43;  L J 40: 691-9.

---- E. R.  The relation of the librarian of the small library to professional training.  New Hamp Bull (ns) 15:
145-8.

Sawyer, H. B.  Questions and answers about cataloguing.  Wis
Lib Bull 5: 11-3.

Sawyer, H. P.  Comparison of the curricula of library schools
and public library training classes.  A L A Bull 10: 185-9,
Discussion 429-31.

---- H. P.  Disinfection of books.  Wis Lib Bull 6: 110.

---- H. P.  Fines on non-fiction books.  Wis Lib Bull 6:
110.

---- H. P.  How to care for books in a library.  Wis Lib
Bull 5: 6-8.

---- H. P.  Method of filing newspapers.  Wis Lib Bull 3:
64-5.

---- H. P.  Outline for recataloguing a library.  Wis Lib
Bull 6: 78.

---- H. P.  Professional training section.  L J 42: 650-2.

---- H. P.  Question about cork carpets.  Wis Lib Bull 5:
15.

---- H. P.  Recasing books (recasing glue).  Wis Lib Bull
6: 109-10.

---- H. P.  Shellac for labels.  Wis Lib Bull 3: 97.

Sawyer, Mrs. H. P.  Salaries in state, mercantile and endowed
libraries.  A L A Bull 13: 80-1.

Saxby, Mrs. D. G.  Supplementary reading in the school.  Vt
L Bull 13: 12-3.

Saxe, M. S.  Assistants duties.  Lib Occ 4: 150.

-- M. S.  Books and classification.  P L 16: 323-7.

-- M. S.  Classification of books.  Ontario Lib Assn Proceedings 1911: 59-64;  P L 16: 323-7.

-- M. S.  Important aspects of the work of public libraries
to-day.  L J 42: 801-3.

-- M. S.  One hundred years ago, relatively speaking.  A
L A Bull 10: 299-301, 385.

-- M. S.  Popularizing the library.  L J 35: 363-6.

-- M. S.  Westmount public library.  P L 9: 209.

-- M. S.  With the children in Canada.  A L A Bull 6: 247;
L J 37: 433-5.

Saxton, M. L.  Work with schools: Keene public library.  New
Hamp Bull (ns) 12: 159-60.

Sayers, W. C. B.  The A. L. A. catalogue.  L A R 9: 401-2.

---- W. C. B.  Amalgamation of lending and reference departments.  L A 5: 89-93.

---- W. C. B.  American libraries.  L A 7: 51-4.

---- W. C. B.  Anglo-American cataloguing code.  L W 11:
467-72.

---- W. C. B.  Argument for affiliation.  L A 5: 68-71, 77-8.

---- W. C. B.  The assistant librarian:  present and future. L A 7: 103-9.

---- W. C. B.  Book war:  a further comment.  L W 9: 267-8.

---- W. C. B.  Cataloguing rules:  author and title entries compiled by the committees of the A. L. A. and L. A. U. K.: a review.  L. W. 11: 467-72.

---- W. C. B.  The classification of war books:  a few notes. L W 18: 132-4.

---- W. C. B.  Correspondence classes and the public.  L A R 14: 372-3.

---- W. C. B.  Decline in the reading of fiction.  L W 12: 453-5.

---- W. C. B.  Delivery stations.  L A 5: 288-90.

---- W. C. B.  The Dewey decimal classification after thirty years.  L A R 12: 314-34, Discussion 353.

---- W. C. B.  Discussion of Mr. Willcock's paper.  L A R 9: 401-2.

---- W. C. B.  An Easter holiday school at Brussels.  L A R 12: 611.

---- W. C. B.  Education of the librarian.  L A R 10: 146-7.

---- W. C. B.  Efficient junior assistants.  L A R 10: 639-40.

---- W. C. B.  Elements of notation:  a possible supplement to H. R. Purnell's "Development of notation in classification."  L W 15: 226-31.

---- W. C. B.  The expansive classification.  L A R 11: 99-117.

---- W. C. B.  Federation of London public libraries.  L A R 13: 330-3.

---- W. C. B.  A few necessary considerations.  L A R 11: 417-9.

---- W. C. B.  First steps in annotation.  L A 14: 136-43.

---- W. C. B.  Graded examinations.  L A R 10: 479-81.

---- W. C. B.  Grammar of classification:  review.  Libn 2: 290-1.

---- W. C. B.  How shall we take statistics of prints, photographs, etc.  L W 20: 14-5.

---- W. C. B.  The immediate programme of librarianship. L A 14: 229-37.

---- W. C. B.  In defence of the crank.  L A R 12: 41-3.

---- W. C. B.  Is affiliation with the Library association desirable?  L A 4: 216-7.

---- W. C. B.  Is the printed catalogue desirable for open access libraries.  L A 7: 209-13.

---- W. C. B.  Is the story hour within the librarian's province?  The affirmative.  L A 7: 72-3.

---- W. C. B.  The L. A. examinations.  L A 10: 229.

---- W. C. B.  Lending of reference books.  L W 20: 43-5.
---- W. C. B.  A letter on the L. A. exams.  L W 13: 94-5.
---- W. C. B.  Librarian as a lecturer to children.  L W
12: 23-7.
---- W. C. B.  Library assistants and the study of litera-
ture.  L W 8: 72-5.
---- W. C. B.  Library bulletins.  L A 4: 256-61.
---- W. C. B.  The Library committee: its character and
work.  L A 11: 205-11.
---- W. C. B.  Library council.  L W 9: 6-10.
---- W. C. B.  Library finance.  L A R 19: 17-29.
---- W. C. B.  Library lectures: their preparation and
delivery.  L A 8: 162-9.
---- W. C. B.  Library staff guilds and meetings.  L A R
11: 175-8.
---- W. C. B.  Local collection problem.  L W 18: 287-9,
340-3;  L W 19: 60-3, 177-80.
---- W. C. B.  Mania for bricks and mortar.  L A R 10: 223-
31.
---- W. C. B.  Methods of popularizing reference libraries.
L W 10: 4-6, 102.
---- W. C. B.  Model questions in classification.  L W 14:
43-5.
---- W. C. B.  The new prospect: a plea for a policy.  L
A R 22: 12-8.
---- W. C. B.  Newsroom question: a reply to Mr. Roebuck.
L A 4: 233-7.
---- W. C. B.  A note on privilege issues in connection with
lectures.  L A R 18: 63-7.
---- W. C. B.  An old question once more.  L A R 11: 561-2.
---- W. C. B.  On library publicity.  L A R 19: 199-201;
L J 42: 812.
---- W. C. B.  On the work of the Grand Rapids library.  L
A 7: 51-4.
---- W. C. B.  Our branches.  L A 11: 164.
---- W. C. B.  Past and present professional training:  its
results and prospects.  L A R 15: 585-96.  Discussion, 660-8.
---- W. C. B.  Place of fiction to-day in libraries.  L A
R 16: 273-9.
---- W. C. B.  Professional conduct.  L W 17: 109-10.
---- W. C. B.  Professional etiquette and the L. A. council
election.  L W 17: 210-1.
---- W. C. B.  The professional examination, 1910.  L A R
12: 357-60.
---- W. C. B.  Proposed professional classes in the Midlands.
L A R 12: 498-9.
---- W. C. B.  Proposed report on non-municipal libraries.
L A R 14: 435.
---- W. C. B.  Publishers and public libraries: a comment
on the "Book war."  L A 5: 187-8.

---- W. C. B.  Salaries of assistant librarians.  L A R 11: 207-9.
---- W. C. B.  Short course in practical classification, with special reference to the decimal and subject schemes. L A R 14: 545-61, 587-602;  15: 1-12.
---- W. C. B.  Short course in practical classification: review.  Libn 3: 465-6;  L A 10: 182;  Correspondence, Libn 4: 4-6.
---- W. C. B.  Should libraries advertise, and, if so, to what extent:  the affirmative.  L A 7: 100-3.
---- W. C. B.  Should library assistants be apprenticed? L W 12: 419-21.
---- W. C. B.  Some canons of classification applied to the Subject classification.  L A R 9: 425-42, Discussion 468-75;  L J 32: 442.
---- W. C. B.  Some notes on story telling in libraries.  L W 20: 288-90, 314-6.
---- W. C. B.  Some principles of classification.  L A 6: 82-8, Discussion 88-90.
---- W. C. B.  A suggestion:  A Library association club. L A R 17: 225-6;  L W 18: 64.
---- W. C. B.  Survey of the month.  L A 6: 11-3, 42-4.
---- W. C. B.  Symposium on public libraries after the war. L A R 19: 199-201.
---- W. C. B.  Things we may expect.  L A 4: 317-9.
---- W. C. B.  Thoughts on staff relationship.  L A 4: 153.
---- W. C. B.  The type of a public library.  L A R 22: 371-2.
---- W. C. B.  A word more about American libraries.  L A 7: 51-4.
---- W. C. B. and J. D. Stewart.  Abridged Jast code of rules for classified cataloguing.  L W 7: 326-30; 8: 1-4.
---- W. C. B. and Stewart, J. D.  The card catalogue.  L W 14: 162-5, 205-11, 236-9, 265-70  290-8, 325-9, 358-64; 15: 39-44, 77-83, 107-10.
---- W. C. B. and Stewart, J. D.  Card catalogue: a review. Libn 4: 85-9.
---- W. C. B. and Stewart, J. D.  Card catalogue reviewed. L A 10: 181-2.
---- W. C. B. and Stewart, J. D.  Catalogues for children: with code of rules.  L A R 7: 377-91.
---- W. C. B. and J. D. Stewart.  Cataloguing materials and technique.  L W 7: 288-90.
---- W. C. B. and J. D. Stewart.  Library magazines:  their preparation and production.  L W 7: 229-32, 257-61, 285-90, 326-30;  8: 1-4, 36-9, 91-4, 147-52, 180-3, 208-12.
---- W. C. B. and J. D. Stewart.  The magazine and card catalogue.  L W 8: 211.

---- W. C. B. and J. D. Stewart. Methods and examples. L W 8: 36-9, 91-4.

---- W. C. B. and J. D. Stewart. Reading lists. L W 8: 147-52.

---- W. C. B. and L. S. Jast. Scheme of re-classification of members of the library association. L W 10: 302.

Sayle, C. Annals of Cambridge university library. L (3d s) 6: 38-76, 145-82, 197-227, 308-405.

--- C. Cambridge fragments. L (3d series) 2: 338-55; 3: 336-9.

--- C. Initial letters in early English printed books. Bib Soc Trans 7: 15-47.

--- C. Reynold Wolfe. Bib Soc Trans 13: 171-92.

--- C. Vatican library. L 6: 327-43, 371-85.

Scarse, C. E. Standard book scale. L J 5: 13.

Scarse, S. E. The Birmingham library. 1779-1897. L 10: 68-75.

Schaefer, N. C. Relation of libraries to the schools. L J 31: Conf No 196-200.

------ N. C. The teacher and the librarian. Nat Educ Assn 1906: 355-61.

Schafer, J. Sources of Northwestern history. L J 30: 790-3.

Schaffner, M. Wisconsin legislative reference library. Iowa Journal of History and Politics 4: 475-9.

Schaper, W. A. The place of the public library in the administration of a city. National Municipal Review 3: 672-81.

Scheltema, J. F. Muhammadan books and libraries. Libn 1: 258-64, 290-4.

Schenk, F. W. Law libraries of Chicago. L J 41: 332-3; P L 21: 185.

---.- F. W. Statement on indexing legal periodicals. A L A Bull 1: Conf No 255.

Scherer, J. A. B. Books and the efficient life. A L A Bull 5: 179-85.

Schermerhorn, E. M. Literary Digest in the English class. Literary Digest 50: 383-4.

Scheuber, C. The library question. Texas Lib 1, No 7; 8-11.

Schinz, A. French newspapers and periodicals: some helps to American subscribers. L J 45: 927-30.

Schmidt, D. C. Library for students of business. University of Chicago, School of commerce and administration. Special Libraries 9: 171.

Schmieding, D. The relation between the local bookseller and the local library. Texas Libraries 1, Nos 10-1: 104.

Schnitzer, M. Supplementary reading for schools. Southern Education Assn Proceedings 1911: 660-3.

Schoble, F. Notes from library work for the blind. A L A Bull 14: 143-5.

Schoch, P. The library in the secondary school. Pennsylvania

Department of Public Instruction Report 1920: 141-2.

Scholderer, J. V.  Albrecht Pfister of Bamberg: a review of
Dr. G. Zedler's 'Dis Bamberger Pfisterdrucke'.  L (3d series)
3: 230-6.

-------- J. V.  Basel and Cologne printing in 1484 and 1485.
L (3d series) 4: 441-2.

-------- J. V.  Michael Wenssler and his press at Basel.
L (3d series) 3: 283-321.

-------- J. V.  Wenceslaus Brack's "Vocabularium rerum."
L (3d series) 4: 87-104.

Scholderer, V.  The author of the "Modus legendi abbreviaturas."
L (3d series) 2: 181-2.

-------- V.  The Chur breviary of 1490 and its printer Adam
von Spier.  L (3d series) 5: 44-59.

-------- V.  Development of Shakespeare's fools.  L (ns)
10: 201-7.

-------- V.  Early English translations from the Greek and
Latin.  Bib Soc Trans 9: 123-6.

-------- V.  A German diatribe against book sales.  L (3d
series) 10: 117-22.

-------- V.  The Haebler Festgabe:  Review.  L (4th series)
1: 52-6.

-------- V.  Jacob Wimpheling, an early Strassburg humanist.
Bib Soc Trans 13: 69-96.

-------- V.  Ludwig Hohenwang's second press at Basel.  L
(ns) 10: 98-100.

-------- V.  The petition of Sweynheym and Pannartz to Sixtus IV.  L (3d series) 6: 186-90.

-------- V.  Sixtus Reissenger's first press at Rome.  L
(3d series) 5: 320-4.

Scholefield, E. O. S.  Libraries in the British Northwest.  L
J 30, Conf No: 14-16.

--------- E. O. S.  Libraries of British Columbia.  Pacific
Northwest Library Assn Conference Proceedings 1909: 17-8;
1911: 52-9;  L J 36: 573-7.

Scholl, K.  Advertising the library.  N J Lib Bull 2, No 3:
12-5.

Scholz, R. F.  The forming of public opinion.  Pacific Northwest Library Assn Proceedings 1920:  36-9.

Schooley, A. J.  Bulletin material.  L J 42: 439-40.

------ A. J.  Making the most of storefront windows.  L J
43: 36-7.

------ A. J.  More library posters.  L J 42: 536-7.

Schrage, J. T.  How to be a secretary.  Wis Lib Bull 14: 12-4.

Schreiber, M. E.  How to direct children in their reading.  Nat
Educ Assn 1900: 636-40.

-------- M. E.  Literature in grades below the high school.
Nat Educ Assn 1901: 288-92.

-------- M. E.  Training of teachers so that they may co-
operate with librarians.  Nat Educ Assn 1897: 1008-14.

Schriber, M. E.  Co-operation between librarian and teacher.
   P L 2: 12-3.
Schroeder, T.  Our prudish censorship of literature, art and
   drama.  The Comstock law.  Forum Jan 1915: 87-99.
Schrote, L. C.  Order among the magazines.  Wis Lib Bull 4: 14.
Schulke, R.  New catalog indicator.  P L 11: 275, 319.
Schultz, W. H.  Relation of the school to the public library.
   Wis Lib Bull 4: 93-5.
Schultze, E.  Public library movement in Germany.  L A R 1:
   277-85.
Schuyler, H.  A plea for emphasizing the human element in our
   public libraries.  New Hamp Bull 7: 41-5;  P L 12: 167-70.
Schuyler, M.  The new Library of Congress.  Scribner's Mag
   21: 709-27.
Schuyler, W.  English as an art study.  School Review 12: 290-
   3.
Schwab, J. C.  Bibliography of the social sciences in the Yale
   University library.  Bib Soc Amer Proc 1: 203-4.
   ----  J. C.  The use of the teleautograph at Yale university.
   A L A Bull 3: 371-2.
Schwalbach, H. B.  The get together movement.  Wis Lib Bull
   7: 66-7.
Schwan, C. P.  Duties of a trustee.  Cal News Notes 2: 94-6.
Schwartz, J.  Alphabetical classification:  an anti-criticism.
   L J 11: 156-8.
   ------  J.  Alphabetical versus logical classification.   L
   J 7: 229, 272.
   ------  J.  Alphabetico-mnemonic classification and number-
   ing.  L J 10: 25, 77, 149, 174, 371.
   ------  J.  Apprentices' library charging system.  L J 14:
   468-9.
   ------  J.  Binding advertisements in magazines.  L J 14: 76.
   ------  J.  Brief description of a charging system.  L J
   4: 275-7.
   ------  J.  Business methods in libraries.  L J 13: 334.
   ------  J.  Charging systems.  L J 5: 73-4, 108, Discussion
   75.
   ------  J.  "Combined charging system."  L J 22: 428.
   ------  J.  A "combined" system of arranging and numbering.
   U S Rept 657-60;  1876;  L J 3: 6-10;  4: 3-12.
   ------  J.  Co-operative cataloguing report.  L J 1: 328-9.
   ------  J.  A dozen desultory denunciations of the dictionary
   catalogue.  L J 11: 470-4.
   ------  J.  Francis Bacon and the Athenaeum classification.
   L J 13: 12-3.
   ------  J.  Gas and binding.  L J 13: 278.
   ------  J.  Government publications muddle.  L J 14: 431-2.
   ------  J.  History of library charging systems.  L W 2:
   1-5, 29-31.

------ J. How we choose and buy new books. L J 14: 337-8.
------ J. Indicator-catalogue charging system. 2d Int Conf 142-5 246.
------ J. King Aguila's library; a sequel to King Leo's classification. L J 11: 232-44.
------ J. Librarian an educator. L J 14: 5.
------ J. Library exhibit of the Columbian exposition. L J 16: 238-9.
------ J. Mr. Cutter's numbering plan. L J 3: 302.
------ J. Mnemonic system of classification. L J 4: 1-7, 37.
------ J. Mnemonics. L J 11: 232-44.
------ J. New classification and notation. L J 7: 84-5, 148-66, 229, 251, 272.
------ J. New form of shelf list. L J 7: 251-3.
------ J. New method of size notation. L J 10: 394; 11: 9.
------ J. New York Apprentices library catalogue. U S Rept 657-60. 1876; L J 10: 178; 11: 419.
------ J. New York library law. L J 13: 279.
------ J. Schwartz's classification and notation. L J 11:9.
------ J. Three little maids from library school. L J 12: 511.
------ J. Twenty-five plus ten versus thirty-five or ten. L J 7: 84-5.
------ J. What we do about duplicates. L J 14: 369-70.
------ J. What we do with pamphlets. L J 14: 434.
------ J. and C. A. Cutter. Scraps from script. L J 7: 6.
------ J. and F. B. Perkins. Dui-Decimal classification and the relative index. L J 11: 36, 37-43, 68-74, 144, 156-60.
Schwill, R. Impressions of the conditions of Spanish-American libraries. L J 32: 72-4.
Scofield, F. A. Teaching high school students the use of the library. Wilson Bulletin 1: 260.
Scoggin, G. C. As to bibliomania. Unpartizan Review 12: 311-27.
Scott, A. Is it best for libraries to buy light fiction in paper covers? L J 19: 227-9.
--- A. Librarian and the patriotic societies. L J 22: 80-1.
--- A. Perplexities of gifts. L J 27: 129-32.
Scott, C. A. Suggestions on forming a professional library for teachers. L J 31: 168-9.
Scott, C. E. Good books for children's Christmas gifts. Lib Occ 1, No 10: 6-9.
--- C. E. How about the motor boys? Lib Occ 2: 190-1.
--- C. E. Indiana young people's reading circle. Lib Occ 3: 64-5, 135-7.
--- C. E. Keeping Indianapolis at the front. P L 24: 366-8.
--- C. E. Library section of Indiana teachers' association. Lib Occ 3: 106-8.

--- C. E.  Library work with children:  reading selected
from A. L. A. papers.  Lib Occ No 12: 6-8.

--- C. E.  Nature books for children.  Lib Occ 2: 10-4.

Scott, D.  Reasonableness of free public libraries.  L 4: 298-
301.

Scott, Mrs. E. L.  Inspirational influence of books in the life
of children.  A L A Bull 9: 179-85;  P L 20: 348-51;  New
Hamp Bull 12: 182-8.

Scott, E. M.  Relationship of the branch library to the central
library.  L A 7: 36-7.

Scott, F. N.  College entrance requirements in English.  School
Review 9: 365-78.

--- F. N.  Report on college entrance requirements in Englis
a criticism.  Educational Review 20: 289-94.

Scott, F. W.  Newspaper files at Albany.  Nation 92: 623, June
22, 1911.

Scott, G. H.  The Schotts of Strassburg and their press.  Bib
Soc Trans 11: 165-88.

Scott, J. C.  The co-operation of local libraries.  Lib 8: 189-
91.

Scott, J. F.  Some aids in cataloguing.  Lib Occ 2: 30-1.

Scott, R.  Books for the asking:  proposed foundation for free
book supply to applicants, by "Home Counties."  World's
Work, June 1915: 92-4.

Scott, S. M.  The early humanists of Elsass.  L (3d series) 2:
363-78.

Scott, T.  India paper:  its use in bookmaking.  Printing Art
17: 181-4.

--- T.  Should you give people what they want?  Printing Art
14: 416-20.

Scott, W.  Cheap library post.  L J 26: 225.

Scovill, E. R.  Good books to give to children.  Ladies Home
Journal 17: 32.

Scripps, J. E.  Gutenberg.  P L 6: 3-5.

Scroggie, G. E.  Library publicity.  Ontario Lib Assn Proceedings 1911: 111-6;  L J 36: 289-92.

Scruton, W.  Bradford library and literary society.  L A R 8:
545-55.

Scudder, H. E.  College libraries a hundred years ago.  U S
Govt Rept 1876: 21-31.

----- H. E.  Literature in public schools.  Atlantic Monthly
62: 223-30.

----- H. E.  Place of literature in common school education.
Nat Educ Assn 1888: 57-70.

----- H. E.  Public libraries a hundred years ago.  U S Govt
Rept: 1-37, 1876.

----- H. E.  School libraries.  Atlantic Monthly 72: 678.

Scudder, S. H.  Arrangement of books in libraries of scientific
societies.  L J 12: 221-4.

Seaman, Dr.  A notable library.  Washington Lib Assn Bull 2 No
  2: 10.
Sears, M. E.  Cataloging for department libraries.  A L A Bull
  7: 325-30.
--- M. E.  Organization of a cataloging department.  A L A
  Bull 11: 207-11, 341.
Seerly, H. H.  Library and the school.  Nat Educ Assn 1908:
  1110-2.
---- H. H.  Use of good books in general education.  Harper's
  Weekly May 29, 1909, 53: 24-5.
Selby, W. L.  Prison libraries: an hitherto undeveloped field
  of English librarianship.  L A 1; 187-90.
--- W. L.  Women as librarians in Bristol.  L A 1: 217-9.
Seldes, G.  Making books as plentiful at home as they were at
  the front.  Collier's 65: 76-7 May 15, 1920.
Seligmann, L.  Signification of libraries past and present.
  L A Trans 1: 68-74.
Semple, S.  What women's clubs have done for libraries.  Penn
  Lib Notes 6, Oct 1913:  65-6.
Seng  S. Tsu-Yung.  Can the American library system be adapted
  to China?  L J 41: 384-9.
Sephton, J.  On the study of Icelandic literature.  L (3d series)
  3: 385-411.
Settle, G. T.  Good reading for negroes.  I.  The Louisville
  free library.  Southern Workman Oct 1914: 536-40.
Severance, H. O.  Certification of librarians.  P L 25: 124-6.
------- H. O.  Charging system of the University of Missouri
  library.  P L 17: 117-8.
------- H. O.  New library building.  University of Missouri.
  L J 40: 405-8;  P L 20: 256-7.
------- H. O.  Three of the earliest catalogues.  P L 10:
  116-7.
Sewall, H. W.  Library of the Department of Agriculture of the
  University of Minnesota.  Special Libraries 10: 51-2.
Sewall, W. F.  War department indexes.  A L A Bull 12: 242-3,
  300.
---- W. F.  Where the personnel records for the army are
  kept.  L J 43: 642, 664-6.
Seward, L.  Library housekeepers: books on household economy.
  P L 21: 213-5.
Seward, L. H.  Mobilizing the library.  P L 19: 392-3.
---- L. H.  Picture work for the small library.  L J 40:
  715-7.
---- L. H.  The social side of library work.  P L 21: 314-5.
Seward, W. F.  Books and democracy.  P L 17: 361.
---- W. F.  Leaves from a camp librarian's notebook.  Book-
  man, (N Y) 48: 272-81.
---- W. F.  The man and his book.  P L 15: 273-5.
---- W. F.  Men and the library.  N Y L 2: 54-6.

---- W. F.  Outline of methods used to make our library "go".
P L 18: 231.

---- W. F.  Possibilities of the New York library association.  N Y L 3: 174-8.

Sexton, C.  Welsh assistant's outlook.  L A 6: 114-8.

Seybold, S. V.  University extension and public libraries.  P
L 10: 512-4.

Seymour.  Book marking.  L N (U S) 3: 426-9.

----- Book numbers.  L N (U S) 3: 429-50.

Seymour, M.  Decimal classification.  A L A Bull 5: 227-30.

----- M.  Letter file economy.  P L 13: 403.

Seymour-Jones, A.  On the glazing of libraries, with reference
to the chemical action of light upon leather.  L A R 8:
641-6.

Shackford, M. H.  For better bibliographics.  Educational Review 57: 434-8.

------- M. H.  Literature for admission to college.  Educational Review 27: 410-6.

Shambaugh, B. F.  Collection and preservation of the materials
of war history.  Ia L C Q 8: 81-3.

------- B. F.  Historical function of the public library.
Ia L C Q 4: 5.

------- B. F.  Work of the State history society of Iowa.
Iowa L C Q 4: 1-5.

Shannon, M.  Effective library exhibits.  L J 45: 1023.

Sharp, H. A.  Cataloguing and description of maps: some problems.  L W 18: 256-61.

--- H. A.  The Dutch public library.  L A R 16: 86-7.

--- H. A.  Letter on the L. A. examination questions.  Libn
2: 468-9.

--- H. A.  Library administration: a plea for uniformity.
L W 14: 247-9.

--- H. A.  Library assistants' association third Easter
school.  Libn 3: 377-9.

--- H. A.  Notes on section II of the Library association
examination syllabus.  L W 13: 298-302, 327-36, 377-84.

--- H. A.  Pages from a Dutch notebook.  L W 16: 180-2.

--- H. A.  Popularizing of public libraries.  L W 15: 374-6.

--- H. A.  The preservation of historical records in Holland.
L W 16: 195-6.

--- H. A.  Process work.  L W 15: 44-5.

--- H. A.  A typical Dutch library: Public library of Utrecht.  L W 16: 245-9.

Sharp, K. L.  A. L. A. Library exhibit at the World's Fair.  L
J 18: 280-4.

--- K. L.  Department of library science of Armour institute.
L J 19: 162-6.

--- K. L.  History of the public school libraries in Illinois.  Univ of Illinois University Studies 2: 447-90.

--- K. L.   Home libraries for children.  2nd International
Conference of Librarians 1897: 239.
--- K. L.   Instruction in library economy through university
extension methods.  L J 23: Conf No 75-8.
--- K. L.   Librarianship as a profession.  P L 3: 5-7.
--- K. L.   Libraries in secondary schools.  L J 20: Conf No
5-11.
--- K. L.   Library recipes.  L N (U S) 4: 205-23.
--- K. L.   On special training for State commission library
organizers.  L J 28: Conf No 231-5.
--- K. L.   University of Illinois.  University of Illinois
Studies, 2 No 1: 85-96.
Sharp, R. F.  Travesties of Shakespear's plays.  L (4th series)
1: 1-20.
Shattuck, H.  Good books for librarians.  Vt L Bull 7, No 2: 5.
Shaw, A.  Minneapolis public library.  L J 10: 84-7.
Shaw, A. C.  Birmingham free libraries.  L A R 4: 492-518.
-- A. C.  Sunday opening of libraries.  L A R 7: 580-4.
Shaw, A. E.  Earliest Latin grammars in English.  Bib Soc Trans
5: 39-65.
Shaw, B. M.  Library exhibit in a small town.  Vt L Bull 3: No
4: 2-3.
-- B. M.  New children's room in Maclure library at Pitts-
ford, Vt.  Vt L Bull 6, No 2: 7.
-- B. M.  A new way to hang pictures.  Vt L Bull 6, No 1:
6-7.
Shaw, C.  New library building at Davidson college.  North Car-
olina Lib Bull 1 No 1: 5-6.
-- C.  What to read.  N C Bull 3: 80-1.
Shaw, G. T.  Co-operative cataloguing.  L A R 9: 423-4.
-- G. T.  How to improve the "Library Association Record":
a criticism and a few suggestions.  L A R 9: 120-7, Discuss-
ion 143-54.
-- G. T.  Is it necessary to print in reference catalogues
lists of the contents of the publications of learned soc-
ieties?  L A R 4: 540, 583-9.
-- G. T.  L. A. examinations.  L W 13: 359-60.
-- G. T.  Libraries and advertising.  L A R 19: 379-81.
-- G. T.  Liverpool commercial library.  L A R 20: 21-3.
-- G. T.  Liverpool commercial reference library.  L A R
19: 313-5.
-- G. T.  Open access: an experiment.  L A R 15: 13-21,
Discussion 203-6.
-- G. T.  Place of the public library in the government
scheme of state settlement.  L A R 19: 93-5.
-- G. T.  Position of libraries during the war and after:
the call for financial help.  L A R 21: 343-54.
-- G. T.  Training of library assistants.  L A R 1: 129-30.
-- G. T.  War finance and public libraries.  Municipal jour-
nal (London) Feb 4, 1916: 101-2;  L A R 18: 139-45.

-- G. T.  The work of the Library association branches.
L A R 17: 125-6.

Shaw, H. S.  What the public library means to Wilmington.  N
C Lib Bull 3: 22-44.

Shaw, M.  Useful documents.  P L 18: 121.

Shaw, R. K.  Bibliography of domestic economy in English, 1850-
1899.  Bulletin No 52, Bibliography No 22, N Y S L Rept 84.
-- R. K.  Is the establishment of a central reference bureau
desirable?  A L A Bull 6: 278-80.
-- R. K.  Librarians in Rotary.  L J 42: 460-1.

Shaw, W. B.  Traveling library.  American Review of Reviews
17: 165-70.

Shearer, A. H.  Historical sketch of the library war service.
A L A Bull 13: 224-34, 395.

Sheavyn, P.  Livelihood of the professional writer, circa 1600.
L (ns) 8: 1-29.
----- P.  Patrons and professional writers under Elizabeth
and James I.  L (ns) 7: 301-6.
----- P.  Writers and official censors under Elizabeth and
James I.  L (ns) 8: 134-63.
----- P.  Writers and the publishing trade, circa 1600.  L
(ns) 7: 337-65.

Sheffield, E. L.  University of Michigan library.  L J 14: 315.

Sheldon, A. E.  The legislative reference bureau as a factor
in state development.  Special Libraries 5: 2-8.
----- A. E.  Legislative reference department.  Nebraska
Lib Bull Nov 1906, No 3.
----- A. E.  Report on the archives of Nebraska.  Am Hist
Assn Rept 1910: 365-420.
----- A. E.  Wisconsin system and the Nebraska plan.  Neb-
raska Lib Bull 1 No 3: 3-5.

Sheldon, H. G.  Elementary talks on charging systems.  L J
22: 63-4.

Shellenberger, G.  A cycle of stories on Iowa history.  Iowa
L C Q 7: 241-5.
----------- G.  The library and occupational therapy.  L
J 44: 380.
----------- G.  Library service in a reconstruction hospital
Iowa L C Q 8: 150-2.
----------- G.  Suggestions for the beginning of a story
hour in a small library.  Ia L C Q 7: 100-2.
----------- G.  Value of reading aloud.  Ia L C Q 6: 218-20.

Shelly, J.  Notes on the public libraries of Plymouth and
Stonehouse.  L C 3: 1-8.

Shepard, A.  The training class in the City library, Springfield (Mass.)  Mass Lib Club Bull 5: 108-12.

Shepard, H. E.  Teaching of the English language and literature:  methods of study in English literature.  Education
9: 73-8.

Shepherd, J.  Topographical prints, drawings and maps in public libraries.  L 8: 69-72.

Shepherd, W. R.  Lessons of the Spanish archives.  Am Hist Assn Rept 1909: 361-4.

Sherborn, C. D. and B. B. Woodward.  Curiosities of cataloguing.  L 9: 70-3.

Sheriff, O. A.  Finger-posts to children's reading:  stories for children of 4th and 5th grades.  Ia L C Q 7: 29-31.

Sherman, C. E.  Book-buying among college students.  L J 42: 305-8.

----- C. E.  John Masefield: a contribution toward a bibliography.  Bull Bib 8: 158-60.

Sherwood, G.  Publications of legislative reference departments.  Special Libraries 3: 201-4.

Sherwood, H. F.  The motion picture as a subject for discussion in schools.  L J 43: 221-2.

Shields, C. E.  An indignation meeting: Note on care of books.  Penn Lib Notes 7, No 3: 7-11.

Shiels, A.  The immigrants, the school and the library.  A L A Bull 10: 257-64.

Shillinger, M. W.  Books that tell boys and girls how to make and do things.  P L 23: 153-5.

Shillington, E.  Auckland free library, 2nd International Conference Proceedings, 201-3, 1885.

Shillito, A.  Disinfection of books.  Libn 2: 110-2.

Shimer, Mrs. N. T.  The Agricultural index.  Special Libraries 10: 35-6.

Shinn, C. H.  Among district school libraries.  Education 10: 369-72.

Shinn, M. W.  School libraries.  Overland Monthly (ns) 27: 644-56.

Shirley, Mrs. B.  Suggestions for desk assistants.  New Hamp Bull (ns) 12: 167.

Shoemaker, W. D.  Patent libraries.  Special Libraries 11: 82-4.

Shore, T. W.  Libraries and ancient parish registers.  L A M N 1: 22-4.

--- T. W.  Old parochial libraries in England and Wales.  L A U K Trans 1: 51-3, 145-53.

Short, M.  Technical and scientific libraries.  L A R 20: 26-7.

Shotwell.  War work of historians.  L J 43: 94-5.

Show, A. R.  History reference library for high schools.  History Teacher's Magazine 3: 79-81.

Showerman, G.  Vocational education.  Wis Lib Bull 11: 303-4.

Shrum, M. C.  Technical or professional phase of co-operation.  P L 8: 98-100.

Shryock, M.  List of histories for small libraries.  Penn Lib Notes 1, No 1: 9-12.

Shueman, E. L.  What the American community is reading.  P L 11: 190.

Shufeldt, R. W.  The library of the Army medical museum.  Medical Rev Dec 15, 1917, 92: 1022-5.

Shum, F.  Early Bath books.  Bib Soc Trans 5: 6-7.

Shuman, E. L.  How to judge novels.  P L 14: 259-60.

---- E. L.  The librarian and public taste.  P L 18: 179-82,
223-7, 271-4;  N C Bull 2: 40.

Shute, K. H.  Ideals in literature.  Journal of Pedagogy 13:
371.

--- K.H.  Teaching of English in the elementary schools.
School Review 10: 332-50.

--- K. H.  Value of literature.  Journal of Pedagogy 11:
226.

Shutterly, A. M.  Short normal school course.  Penn Lib Notes
5, No 4: 47-9.

Sias, C.  Useful arts and the public library.  Ia L C Q 5: 247
-9.

Sibley, H. O.  Syracuse university library.  University News
4: 876, 892, 900, 908, 916, 924, 932, 948, 972, 979, 996,
1006, 1014.

Sibley, J. L.  Address delivered before the A. L. A. at Boston.  L J 4: 305-8.

Sickley, J. C.  Completing sets of periodicals.  L J 8: 105-
6.

----- J. C.  Course of reading for pupils of the Poughkeepsie public library.  L J 12: 372-7.

----- J. C.  Is the A. L. A. too big?  L J 43: 463.

----- J. C.  Plan for a course of reading for pupils of the
public schools.  L J 12: 372-7.

----- J. C.  Women in war library service.  P L 23: 315-6.

Sickley, J. E.  The library AEsop: four foolish fables.  L
J 44: 117.

Sidener, M.  Books and the advertiser.  Special Libraries 7:
59-60;  Am Lib Annual 1916-17: 27.

----- M.  Library advertising.  P L 25: 299-305.

Siebert, Dr.  Disadvantages of wire-sewing and the necessity
for prohibiting it.  L 10: 255-9.

Sikes, L. M.  Advertising the children's rooms.  Lib Occ 10:
1-2.

Silliman, H. C.  Catalog system of the office of the Superintendent of documents.  A L A Bull 8: 207-8.

Silverthorn, B. B.  Library advertising.  Vt L Bull 6, No 1:
5-6.

--------- B. B.  Removing material no longer useful.  Vt
L Bull 7, No 3: 3.

--------- B. B.  Some good collections of children's songs.
Vt L Bull 9, No 2: 7-8.

--------- B. B.  Special material in libraries.  Cal News
Notes 14: 157.

Simkhovitch, V. G.  Columbia University library collections:
monumenta and rariora.  Columbia University Quarterly 13:
173-82.
Simmet, W. E.  Technical libraries and intelligence.  L A R
22: 124-40.
Simms, G. A.  The printing salesman.  Printing Art 17: 125-6.
Simons, S. E.  American literature and the modern magazine and
high school library course.  English Journal 2: 357-61.
Simonson, I. S.  Literature for children:  a course for normal
school students.  English Journal 2: 305-11.
Simpson, F.  Recent library aids.  P L 10: 296-9.
----- F.  Some problems in cataloguing a normal school lib-
rary.  P L 6: 152-4.
----- F.  Standardization of librarians.  Ia L C Q 8: 65-8;
L J 43: 555.
----- F.  Where shall I look?  Illinois Assn Teachers of
English Bulletin April 1912: 1-8.
Simpson, P.  The play of "Sir Thomas More" and Shakespeare's
hand in it.  L (3d series) 8: 79-96.
Sinclair, S.  Australian museum library.  2nd International
Conference Proceedings, 207, 208.
Sindall, R. W.  Manufacture of wood pulp for paper-making.
L A R 10: 336-41.
----- R. W.  Physical qualities of paper.  L A R 10: 24-
35, Discussion 60-2.
Singer, D. W.  Hand-list of scientific mss. in the British
Isles dating from before the sixteenth century.  Bib Soc
Trans 15: 185-99.  L (3d series) 10: 91-100.
Singleton, J. W.  Bookbinding:  a suggestion.  L W 8: 289-90.
------- J. W.  L. A. Northern counties branches.  Libn 7:
170-1.
------- J. W.  Libraries and registration.  L W 19: 28.
------- J. W.  Library bulletins.  L W 7: 118-20.
------- J. W.  The library in fiction.  L A R 20: 210-8.
------- J. W.  Symposium on public libraries after the war.
L A R 19: 233-4.
------- J. W.  Three phases of librarianship.  L A R 16:
280-5.
------- J. W.  Weeds in library work.  L A R 12: 261-6,
Discussion 285.
Sinker, R.  Trinity college library.  L A U K Trans 5: 144-8.
Sioussat, St. G. L.  The need of the library for best results
in teaching history.  Southern Education Assn Proceedings
1912: 400-8.
Sisson, E. O.  The high school's cure for souls.  Educational
Review 35: 359-72.
Sisson, F. H.  Value of a library in a financial house.  Spec-
ial Libraries 10: 121-2.
Skarstedt, M.  Children's war work exhibit in Evanston public
library.  L J 43: 333.

Skeer, T.  Series cards.  P L 6: 150-1.
Sketchley, R. E. D.  English book illustration of to-day.  il.
(with bibliography).  L (ns) 3: 54-91, 176-212, 271-320,
358-97.
Skinner, D. A.  Library of the Chamber of commerce of the
United States of America in its relation to foreign trade.
Special Libraries 6: 41-2.
Skinner, E.  How to acquire a taste for good reading.  Nat
Educ Assn 1899: 1148-50.
Skinner, H. M.  Literature and history.  Educational Founda-
tions 18: 287-92.
Skinner, N.  The Agricultural index.  Special Libraries 7:
49-50.
Skinner, R.  An hour or two in the college library.  Yale
Literary Magazine  27: 41-52.
Slade, W.  The school and the traveling library.  Vt L Bull
5: 4-5.
Slade, W. A.  Books and debarkation.  Weekly Review 1: 174-6.
Slater, G.  Concerning children's books.  Journal of Education
(ns) 19: 21-2.
Slater, J. H.  Some books on magic.  Bib Soc Trans 3: 171-93.
Slauson, A. B.  Co-operation in exchange for duplicates through
the Library of Congress.  L J 28: 773-4.
Sleneau, K.  First county library in Michigan.  P L 22: 365.
----- K.  Staff meetings.  Mich Lib Bull Jan-Feb 1916: 14-6.
Slobod, A.  Bibliographic material available in the publica-
tions of the United States Bureau of mines.  Special Lib-
raries 8: 88-90.
---- A.  Mine accounting:  reference list to books and
magazine articles.  Special Libraries 7: 172-7.
Slosson, E. E.  Books no public library should be without.
Independent 65: 1559-62.
----- E. E.  The fine art of reading current literature.
Wilson Bulletin 1: 67-8.
----- E. E.  How a journalist looks at the library.  N Y
L 5: 10-1.
----- E. E.  Library lunchroom: Dewey system.  Indepen-
dent 81: 440.
Smail, A.  Remarks on the public and private libraries of
Glasgow.  B A R 5 XXXV-XL.
--- A.  Some notes on libraries of Edinburgh.  B A R 5:
I-V.
--- A.  Some notes on Scottish printing.  B A R 5: II-V,
1907.
Smail, P.  Early printers of Glasgow.  B A R 5: XXXV-XL, 1907.
Smails, H.  Reading to get results at the State public schools.
Minn P L C N 4: 98-9.
Small, A. J.  The Iowa state library.  Special Libraries 11:
98-9.

--- A. J.  Law department of the State library of Iowa.
Iowa L C Q 6: 35-8.

--- A. J.  State library legislation in 1916 and 1917.  A
L A Bull 12: 354-61.

Small, J.  Historical sketch of the library of the Edinburgh
university.  L A U K Trans 3: 95-105.

--- J.  Presidential address.  L A Trans 3: 17-21.

Small, M. N.  Methods and materials used in library binding.
L J 33: 512.

Smalley, G. W.  Auction prices in books.  L J 10: 36.

Smetley, R. L.  Importance of good reading in the business of
finance.  Special Libraries 10: 123-4.

Smiley, M. H.  Relation of the library to art education in
schools.  Nat Educ Assn 1897: 1038-43.

Smit, D.  On Dutch libraries.  P L 9: 389-91.

Smith.  Library hours (and discussion).  P L 4: 349-56.

Smith.  Rules and regulations.  P L 10: 546-8.

Smith, A. M.  The instruction of students in the use of agricultural and scientific literature.  A L A Bull 4: 790-1.

Smith, B. S.  Joint administration of the high school library
by the board of education and the public library.  Nat Educ
Assn 1916: 656-60;  L J 41: 639-41.

--- B. S.  Library and high school:  Democratic agencies.
P L 23: 64-6.

--- B. S.  List of war books for high school use.  L J 43:
224.

--- B. S.  Methods of securing better reading.  P L 10:
171-3.

--- B. S.  Rules and regulations governing borrowers.  P L
10: 547.

--- B. S.  What a club woman has a right to expect from a
public library.  Ia L C Q 5: 34-9.

Smith, C. H.  Address at Proctor free library dedication.  Vt
L Bull 9 No 2: 3-5.

Smith, C. W.  Co-operation of libraries of the northwest.  Pacific Northwest Library Assn Proceedings 1909: 18-9.

--- C. W.  An expansion of the Dewey decimal classification
for the history of the Pacific Northwest.  Washington Historical Quarterly 2: 146-60.

--- C. W.  The library as a teaching institution.  Pacific
Northwest Lib Assn Proceedings 1920: 13-6.

--- C. W.  Library conditions in the Northwest.  L J 30:
Conf No 9-14;  Wash L A Bull 1: 1-6.

--- C. W.  Library conditions in Washington.  L J 30: 787-8;
Wash L A Bull 1 No 2: 1-2, 12-3;  Bull 2 No 1: 14-5; No 2:
12-4;  No 3: 12-3;  No 4: 12-6.

--- C. W.  Library legislation in the Northwest.  L J 30:
Conf No 10-2;  Wash L A Bull 1: 1-6.

--- C. W.  Methods of preserving clippings and small pamphlets.  Pacific Northwest Library Assn Proceedings 1910: 61-2.

--- C. W.  Notes on the historical literature of the Pacific northwest.  Pacific Northwest Library Assn Proceedings 1917: 25-35.

--- C. W.  Public documents as a library resource.  L J 32: 195-8.

--- C. W.  Public libraries and allied agencies.  Wash L A Bull 2: 1-2.

--- C. W.  Public library plans.  L J 29: 535-7.

--- C. W.  Seattle charging case.  L J 30: 350-1.

--- C. W.  Traveling libraries of Washington.  Wash L A Bull 2: 1-2.

--- C. W.  What the community owes to the public library.  L J 32: 315.

Smith, E.  Instruction in agricultural literature.  P L 17: 126.

Smith, E. A.  Some heresies.  A L A Bull 9: 264-6.

Smith, E. G.  Book-buying for small libraries.  Pacific Northwest Library Assn Proceedings 1915: 11-4.

--- E. G.  What the library can do for the schools.  Pacific Northwest Library Assn Proceedings 1909: 14-5.

Smith, E. M.  Library course of study for teachers.  Educational Foundations 20: 552-62.

--- E. M.  Picture bulletins: a reply to Mr. Dana's article in the "Wisconsin Library Bulletin" for Sept-Oct 1907.  A L A Library Bulletin 2: 8;  Wis Lib Bull 4: 16-7.

--- E. M. and E. M. Sanderson.  Circulating single numbers of periodicals.  L J 33: 86-94.

--- E. M. and L. E. Fay.  Library militant: a drama in blank verse.  L J 33: 95-7.

Smith, E. R.  Avery library of architectural literature at Columbia.  Columbia University Quarterly 13: 195-205.

--- E. R.  Special collections in American libraries -- The Henry O. Avery memorial library of architecture and allied arts at Columbia University.  L J 28: 277-85.

Smith, F. E.  Best catalog for a small library.  P L 6: 147-50.

--- F. E.  Changing conditions of child life.  A L A Bull 7: 184-8;  New Hamp Bull 9: 223-7.

--- F. E.  How to take care of pictures when not in use.  P L 12: 51.

--- F. E.  Interesting college women in library work.  L J 40: 263.

--- F. E.  Library work for children.  P L 12: 79-83.

--- F. E.  Theory of the training class in the large library.  A L A Bull 5: 269-71.

Smith, F. T.  Pupil's voluntary reading.  Pedagogical Seminary 19: 208-22.

Smith, G.  Dr. Thomas Bray.  L A R 12: 242-60, 282-5.
--- G.  Frankfort book mart:  a chapter in European literary history.  L (ns) 1: 167-79.
--- G.  Old newspapers.  L A R 7: 329-42.
Smith, G. S.  Methods of securing better reading.  P L 10: 171-3.
Smith, J. B.  Books for the blind:  their production and circulation.  L A R 22: 257-9.
--- J. B.  Library work with the blind.  L A R 22: 257-9, 377-9.
Smith, J. F.  Functions of a research library in the dyestuff industry:  Library of the National aniline & chemical company, Buffalo, N. Y.  Special Libraries 10: 100-2.
Smith, J. G.  Small library's solution of public documents.  P L 11: 514.
Smith, K. L.  Provision for children in public libraries.  Review of Reviews (N Y) 22: 48-55.
Smith, K. S.  Library and industrial education.  Ia L C Q 7: 119-22.
Smith, L.  Administration of a catalog department from the cataloger's point of view.  A L A Bull 7: 271-4.

--- L.  Helpful points in cataloguing and analysing.  P L 9: 103-6.
--- L.  List of books for librarians.  P L 13: 407.
Smith, L. G.  A library in Illumina.  L J 41: 805-8.
Smith, L. H.  Co-operative work of the museum and the library.  L J 27: 889.
Smith, L. P.  Classification of books.  L J 7: 172-4.
--- L. P.  Qualifications for a librarian.  L J 1: 69-74.
Smith, L. W.  Literature and pedagogue.  Poet Lore 21: 311-21.
Smith, M.  Children and consideration for others.  Wis Lib Bull 9: 94.
--- M.  Work with clubs in a county library.  Pacific Northwest Library Assn Proceedings 1914:  71-4.
Smith, M. A.  Business training.  Wis Lib Bull 11: 103.
--- M. A.  Care of cork carpets.  Wis Lib Bull 12: 216-7.
--- M. A.  Library instruction in schools.  Wis Lib Bull 7: 134-7.
--- M. A.  One trial at co-operation between library and continuation school.  Wis Lib Bull 11: 99-103.
--- M. A.  Progress at La Crosse. Wis Lib Bull 1: 48.
--- M. A.  Reading list on domestic science.  Wis Lib Bull 11: 100-3.
--- M. A.  What the librarian needs from the school.  L J 37: 169-74;  Wis Lib Bull 8: 22-7.
--- M. S.  How to utilize the school library.  History Teachers Magazine May, 1914.
Smith, N. A.  Training the imagination.  Outlook 64: 459-61.

Smith, O. I.  Method of accession used in the library of the
Wisconsin Historical society.  Wis Lib Bull 12: 443-4;  L
J 42: 221.
Smith, R.  An alphabetical mnemonic classification.  L W 21: 4-
8, 36-9;  Criticism 55-6;  Reply 82-4.
--- R.  Classification for rural libraries.  L W 23: 541-2.
--- R.  Objections to mnemonic classification.  L W 248-50.
--- R.  A universal classification -- The Yale library
scheme.  L W 21: 185-7.
Smith, R. E. and Webb, A.  Is a printed catalogue necessary in
an open access library.  Libn 3: 270-4.
Smith, R. L.  Some bibliographies of the European war and its
causes.  Bull Bib 10: 49-52.
Smith, S.  Brief note on an experiment in connection with a
subscription library.  L A R 10: 19-23.
--- S.  Club and institute libraries.  L C 2: 28-33.
--- S.  An English library in 1486.  L J 13: 76-9.
--- S.  Library pests.  L A Trans 6: 66-70.
--- S.  The public librarian:  his help and hindrances.  L
8: 157-67.
Smith S. H.  How the commission may help small libraries in
the choice and purchase of books.  Vt L Bull 6, No 1: 3-4.
Smith, T. L.  Public library and the mechanic.  P L 15: 6-10.
Smith, W. E.  The great "She" Bible:  historical account.  L
2: 1-11, 96-102, 141-53.
Smith, W. M.  Instruction in agricultural literature.  P L 17:
126.
--- W. M.  The libraries of Wisconsin.  Wis Lib Bull 12:
12-5.
Smith, W. P.  Responsibility of the State to the rural commun-
ity.  Vt L Bull 7, No 1: 3-6.
--- W. P.  State library commissions and traveling libraries.
L J 26: 56-8, 171-3.
Smither, R. E.  Information bureaus in public libraries.  L W
13: 99-106.
----- R. E.  Library of Congress classification.  L W 16:
130-6.
----- R. E.  Modern methods of book storage.  L W 14: 260.
----- R. E.  Treatment of pamphlets, maps, photographs and
similar items.  L W 15: 195-9.
Smithmeyer, J. L.  National Library building.  L J 6: 77-81,
126-7;  7: 270-1;  9: 29, 31, 72.
Smythe, A. H.  Libraries in bookstores.  L J 34: 266-9.
Snipes, M. C.  The township as a unit for library extension.
A L A Bull 11: 234-7, 360.
Snodgrass, R.  Legislative assistance.  Pennsylvania Bar Assn
Report 1908: 3-29.
Snook, V. J.  Getting films for small children.  L J 44: 157-8.
Snouck-Hurgronje, N.  Libraries of Holland.  L A R 16: 305-15.

Snow, C. T.   What is reading?  Education 12: 422-30.

Snow, K. M.   Aims and objects of organizing local war museums and collections of war literature in public libraries.  L A R 20: 167-72.

Snow, W. B.   Special collections: Engineering.  Special Libraries 2: 4-5.

Snowsill, W. G.   Library work as a career.  L A R 12: 153-62.

Snushall, M. M.   National library and library progress in Chile.  P L 14: 174-6.

Snyder, G. B.   Ridgeway public library.  Ontario education department report on public libraries, etc., 1910: 513-6.

Snyder, M. B.   The business library.  Special Libraries 9: 65-7.

Sohn, H. B.   Publicity for village libraries.  L J 40: 866-9.

Solberg, T.   Book copyright.  L J 26: Conf No 24-31.

----- T.   Charles Ammi Cutter, 1837-1903.  L J 28: 768-9.  L A R 5: 582-4.

----- T.   Copyright in Congress, 1837-1886.  L J 11: 418, 468.

----- T.   Copyright in England.  Library of Congress, 1902.

----- T.   Copyright law of the United States of America in force July, 1901.  Library of Congress, 1901.

----- T.   Directions for the registration of copyright under the laws of the United States.  Library of Congress, 1904.

----- T.   Hearing on the U. S. Copyright bill.  L J 31: 320-3.

----- T.   International copyright in Congress, 1837-1886.  L J 11: 250-80.

----- T.   List of foreign copyright laws in force, with citations of printed texts and translations, etc.  Library of Congress, 1904.

----- T.   Report on legislation, January, 1889 -- June, 1890.  L J 15:  Conf No 50-8.

----- T.   Rules and forms for copyright registration in Canada, together with copyright laws of Canada, Newfoundland, New Brunswick, Nova Scotia and Prince Edward Island.  Library of Congress, 1903.

Soldan, F. J.   Directions for binding.  P L 9: 259-60.

---- F. J.   Specifications for binding.  L J 8: 106-7.

Solis-Cohen, L. M.   Library work in the Brooklyn Ghetto.  L J 33: 485-8.

Sollenberger, Mrs. D. H.   Co-operation with women in community affairs.  Lib Occ 5: 362-4.

Somerville, Mass., public library.   Sunday schools and the public library.  L J 27: 972-3;  P L 7: 439.

Sonneck, O. G.   Bibliography of American music.  Bib Soc Amer Proc 1: 50-64.

----- O. G.   Library of Congress music division.  New Music Review 9: 74-8.

----- O. G.  Music division of the Library of Congress.
Music Teachers' National Association.  Papers and Proceed-
ings 30: 260-87;  L J 40: 587-9.
----- O. G.  Music in our libraries.  Art World and Art
Decorations 2: 242-4.
Soper, H. T.  Co-operative work between urban and rural lib-
raries.  L A R 22: 331-7;  Discussion, 337-8.
--- H. T.  Exeter libraries.  B A R 5: XXI-XXIII.
--- H. T.  Exeter printers and booksellers.  B A R 5: XXI-
XXIII, 1907.
--- H. T.  Exeter public library: an historical essay.  L
A R 13: 55-69.
--- H. T.  Library book clubs.  L A R 20: 103.
--- H. T.  My opinion of open access.  L W 10: 243-5.
--- H. T.  Open access and the theft of books.  L W 6: 259-
60.
--- H. T.  Royal Albert Memorial, Exeter: an example of
what can be done by co-operation.  L W 10: 411-5.
Soule, A. G.  Ye architect and ye librarian.  L J 13: 338.
Soule, C. C.  Amateur administration.  L J 17: 92-3.
--- C. C.  Articles on the administration of the Boston
library.  L J 17: 54-5, 88-94, 124-5.
--- C. C.  Boston public library.  L J 17: 88-94; 425-6.
public library.  L J 17: 425-6.
--- C. C.  Brooklyn branch library buildings.  L J 28: 113-
4.
--- C. C.  Co-operation of libraries with schools.  L J 17:
89-90.
--- C. C.  How to plan a library building for library work:
review.  Libn 3: 258-9;  P L 18: 65-7.
--- C. C.  Law books for general libraries.  L J 19: Conf
No 103-4.
--- C. C.  Library and the industrial classes.  L J 17:
90-2.
--- C. C.  Library architecture.  L J 17: Conf No 73-5.
--- C. C.  Mnemonics.  L J 14: 286.
--- C. C.  Need of an A. L. A. collection of plans of lib-
rary buildings.  L J 31: Conf No 45-6;  P L 11: 429-31.
--- C. C.  Newberry library plans.  L J 16: 11-3.
--- C. C.  On the value of delivery stations.  L J 17: 88-9.
--- C. C.  Points of agreement among librarians.  L J 16:
Conf No 17-9.
--- C. C.  Report on library legislation.  L J 10: 276-8.
--- C. C.  Shelves around reading rooms.  P L 14: 134.
--- C. C.  Trustees of free public libraries.  L J 15:
Conf No 19-24.
--- C. C.  Work of the American library institute.  P L
17: 10.
South-Cliffe, M.  A protest -- "Subordinate" versus "Assis-
tants."  L J 39: 198.

Southern, J. W.  Municipal libraries and their development.
L A R 1: 607-18.
------ J. W.  Presidential address.  L A R 1: 607-18.
Southward, J.  Technical literature in free libraries.  L A
Trans 6: 82-7.
Sparke, A.  Bolton authors and Bolton books.  B A R 12: XXXIX-
XLIV.
---- A.  Bury juvenile library.  L W 5: 231-3.
---- A.  Cataloguing association books.  L A R 20: 261.
---- A.  Co-operation for librarians.  L A R 20: 150-6.
---- A.  Co-operative work for a branch association.  L A
R 20: 57-63.
---- A.  Cycle accommodation in public libraries.  L W 2:
288-90.
---- A.  Extension of borrowing privileges to non-residents.
L W 10: 349-50.
---- A.  Library assistants and the future.  L A 14: 184-8.
---- A.  Local collections in public libraries.  L W 2: 185-
7.
---- A.  Minor recommendations of the Third interim report
of the education committee.  L A R 21: 402-6.
---- A.  Newspaper rack for bound volumes.  L W 3: 127-8.
---- A.  Some unfinished books.  L A R 18: 150-6.
---- A.  Symposium on public libraries after the war.  L
A R 19: 201-2.
---- A.  Town bibliographies.  L A R 15: 366-71.
---- A. and A. R. Corns.  Bibliography of unfinished books
in the English language:  Review.  L W 18: 319-20.
Spaulding, F. B.  "For Sailors, they be honest men."  L J 45:
313-5.
------- F. B.  The librarian's muse.  L J 41: 469-74.
------- F. B.  Library at Camp Dodge.  Iowa L C Q 8: 53-4,
69-70.
------- F. B.  A special library that encircles the globe:
American Merchant marine library.  Special Libraries 11:
94-5;  Wilson Bulletin 1: 457-8.
Spears, R. B.  On the catalogue of Glasgow university library.
1st Int Conf 84-5;  L J 2: 176-7, 185-7.
Speck, L.  Technical training and the personal element in lib-
rary work.  L J 23: Conf No 135.
Spencer, A. L.  Books for the American rural hinterland.  L J
44: 241-3.
----- A. L.  Library books through rural delivery.  P L 24:
297.
----- A. L.  Penny post for books in rural districts:  Re-
port of a tryout of the plan.  L J 44: 373;  P L 24: 79-80.
----- A. L.  Penny post for library books.  Steuben Courier
(Bath) Oct 20, 1916;  L J 42: 411-2;  Am Lib Annual 1917-
18: 60.

Spencer, A. P. and C. C. Warner.  Views of trustees regarding
library construction.  Ia L C Q 4: 23-6.
Spencer, F.  Filing systems of the National bank.  Filing Aug
1918;  L J 43: 850.
----- F.  Financial library of the National city bank.  Spec-
ial Libraries 3: 170-2;  L J 42: 282-3.
----- F.  What a public library cannot do for the business
man.  Special Libraries 8: 117-8.
Spencer, L. A.  Advertising in street cars.  Wis Lib Bull 8:
133-4.
----- L. A.  Common sense in binding and replacing.  Wis
Lib Bull 8: 200-2.
----- L. A.  The South Dakota free county library law.  L
J 42: 383-4.
----- L. A.  Traveling library plan in Richardson county.
Neb Lib Bull 6: 8-10;  Cal News Notes 3: 132.
Spencer, Mrs. M. C.  On the need of a new state library for
Michigan.  P L 22: 108.
Spender, H.  What do the children read?  Littell's Living Age,
August 1905.
Sperry, E. E.  Books on the war.  N Y L 5: 266-7.
---- E. E.  Views of library school directors.  P L 23: 17-
18.
Sperry, H.  Reading list on Venice.  Bibliography No 7, N Y S
L Rept 80.  1897.
Spielmann, M. H.  Art exhibitions and art catalogues.  L (ns)
1: 118-22.
------- M. H.  John Ruskin.  L (ns) 1: 225-40.
Spilman, E. A.  Catalog system of the Department of Justice
library.  A L A Bull 8: 208.
----- E. A.  The government directory in the Service bureau
at Washington.  L J 43: 733-7.
----- E. A.  Need for correspondence school courses.  P L
11: 503.
Spinney, G. F.  Newspaper methods yesterday and to-day.  Pear-
son's 23: 599-611.
Spivak, C. D.  Novel reading: make it of more value.  P L
4: 135-7.
Spofford, A. R.  Aids to library progress by Government of
United States.  U S Govt Rept: 704-8.  1892;  L J 18: 248-
9.
------ A. R.  Bibliography of bibliography and literature.
U S Rept 688-710, 1876.
------ A. R.  Binding and preservation of books.  U S Rept
673-8, 1876.
------ A. R.  Book auction catalogues and their perils.  L
J 3: 53.
------ A. R.  Copyright in its relation to libraries and
literature.  L J 1: 84-9, 139.

------ A. R.  Library bibliography.  U S Rept: 733-44.
1876.
------ A. R.  Library of Congress, or National Library.
U S Govt Rept: 253-61, 1876.
------ A. R.  List of reference books.  U S Rept 686-714,
1876.
------ A. R.  The mental and mechanical in libraries.  L
J 28: 10-2.
------ A. R.  The Nation's Library: I.  The new building;
II.  Special features of the Congressional Library.  Century
31: 682-94.
------ A. R.  Periodical literature and society publications.
U S Rept 679-85.  1876.
------ A. R.  Periodical literature in libraries.  L J 11:
189.
Spofford, E. P.  Catalog system of the Bureau of mines.  A L
A Bull 8: 206-7.
Sprague, H. H.  News from Utah.  Pacific Northwest Library
Assn Proceedings 1920: 24-5.
Sprague, L. W.  Americanization by indirection.  Special Lib-
raries 10: 175-6.
Sprague, W. R.  Information as to the possibility of using
fountain pens on the catalog desk.  L J 41: 439-40;  Am
Lib Annual 1916-17: 55-8.
Springer, R. W.  The advantage to the community of a public
library.  N C Bull 2: 4-6.
Squires, T.  Masculine versus feminine librarians.  P L 25:
435-6.
Stabbs, A. J.  Fire.  Libn 2: 236-9.
Staley, G. F.  Book exhibitions.  L W 10: 106-8.
---- G. F.  Ledger charging.  L W 10: 35-7.
Stallwood, S. S.  Public Libraries bill, 1913.  L A R 15:
298;  Libn 3: 383-4.
Stanford, C. T.  Presidential address at Brighton conference.
L A R 10: 432-8.
Stanley, H. H.  Discipline in a children's room.  P L 12:
362-3.
----- H. H.  Reading list on out-of-door books.  N Y S L
Rept 80, Bibliography No 8.
----- H. H.  Reference work with children.  L J 26: Conf
No 74-8;  P L 6: 398-400.
----- H. H.  School reference room in the Brookline library.
P L 6: 398-400.
----- H. H.  Summer library schools and classes.  L J 23:
Conf No 74-5.
Stanley, H. M.  Cumulative cataloguing.  L J 23: 184.
----- H. M.  Library specialization.  L J 13: 179.
----- H. M.  List of books for model libraries.  L J 17:
233.

----- H. M.  Methods of cataloging.  L J 13: 318-9.
----- H. M.  Suggestion for annotation of books.  L J 25: 104.
----- H. M.  University library buildings.  L J 14: 264-5.
Stansbury, A. L.  Library buildings from a librarian's standpoint.  P L 11: 495-9.
Stanton, A. C.  Reading room that succeeded in a small town.  Woman's Home Companion 38: 53.
Starch, E. F.  Cataloging and classifying Swedenborgia.  Journal of Educ of the Academy of the New Church Jan 1914: 141-63.
Starr, E. G.  Tooling or finishing.  Industrial Arts Magazine 5: 97-103.
Staton, F. M.  Reference libraries and reference works.  Ontario Lib Assn Proceedings 1911: 64-9.
Stearns, E.  Reference work with children.  Ohio Lib Bull 4, No 4: 1-3;  No 5: 1-3.
Stearns, E. J.  Library building.  Minn P L C N 1: 5-6.
Stearns, H. J.  Library extension work in Hawaii.  Minn P L C N 4: 227-8.
Stearns, L.  Recent tendencies in book production.  Wis Lib Bull 6: 24-9.
Stearns, L. E.  Advertising a library.  L J 21: Conf No 37.
----- L. E.  Agricultural collections in public libraries.  A L A Bull 4: 788-9.
----- L. E.  A bas the library basement.  Wis Lib Bull 7: 43.
----- L. E.  The book for the girl.  P L 7: 408.
----- L. E.  The books of 1910.  Wis Lib Bull 7: 24-7.
----- L. E.  Books of 1911.  Wis Lib Bull 8: 19-22.
----- L. E.  The child and the small library.  Wisconsin Free Library Commission, Biennial Report 1897-98: 12-20.
----- L. E.  Date of return of books.  Wis Lib Bull 3: 65.
----- L. E.  Disputed dates of renewal.  Wis Lib Bull 3: 64.
----- L. E.  An Eastern library tour.  Wis Lib Bull 1: 24-5.
----- L. E.  Educational force of children's reading.  P L 2: 6.
----- L. E.  Experiences of a free lance in a western state.  A L A Bull 3: 345-8.
----- L. E.  How to organize state library commissions and make state aid effective.  L J 24: Conf No 16-8, 181.
----- L. E.  Innovation in library meetings.  L J 31: 55-7.
----- L. E.  Is the public library fulfilling its function?  Minn P L C N 4: 217-8.
----- L. E.  Librarian, assistant and the public.  L J 21: 489-92.
----- L.'E.  Library extension.  Ontario Library Assn Proceedings Ap 1912: 114-21.

----- L. E.  The library militant.  Ontario Library Associa-
tion Proc.  April, 1912: 88-94;  Wis Lib Bull 7: 107-8.
----- L. E.  Library and the social center.  Wis Lib Bull
7: 84-5.
----- L. E.  Library and war and peace.  Minn P L C N 4:
209-12.
----- L. E.  Magazines and morals.  Wis Lib Bull 7: 172-3.
----- L. E.  New York City budget:  a suggestion to librar-
ians.  Wis Lib Bull 6: 123-4.
----- L. E.  Problem of the girl.  L J 31: Conf No 103-6,
Discussion 200-3.
----- L. E.  The problem of public leisure.  Wis Lib Bull
9: 162-3.
----- L. E.  Qualifications of a librarian.  L J 30: Conf
No 68-71.
----- L. E.  Question of discipline.  L J 26: 735-7.
----- L. E.  Question of library training.  L J 30: Conf No
68-71, Discussion 164-70.
----- L. E.  Report on reading of the young.  L J 19: Conf
No 81-7, 136-7.
----- L. E.  Rural free delivery and the library.  L J 26:
274-5.
----- L. E.  Rural free delivery for library books.  L J 30:
Conf No 162-3.
----- L. E.  Shellac for book covers.  Wis Lib Bull 3: 62-4.
----- L. E.  Some recent phases of library development.
Chautauquan 56: 116-22.
----- L. E.  Study club work.  Wis Lib Bull 9: 178-9.
----- L. E.  Traveling libraries.  P L 10: 76-81.
----- L. E.  Traveling libraries:  League of library com-
missions.  A L A Bull 2: 305-6;  P L 13: 276-7.
----- L. E.  Travels of the book wagon.  Wis Lib Bull 1: 14;
L J 30: 346-7;  P L 10: 76-81.
----- L. E.  Trustee's responsibility for the library in-
come.  Wis Lib Bull 6: 117-20;  8: 151-3.
----- L. E.  What state library associations should do for
the small library.  L J 31: Conf No 251-2.
----- L. E.  Wisconsin library association.  L J 21: 189-91.
----- L. E.  The woman on the farm.  A L A Bull 7: 173-7;
Texas Libraries 1, No 6: 2-6;  L J 38: 449-53;  Wis Lib Bull
9: 124-9.
Stearns, L. H.  Library activities in the Hawaiiam Islands.
P L 24: 189-92.
Stebbing, W. E.  Correspondence classes for the general reader.
L A R 14: 173.
Steele, Mrs. B.  The colored supplements.  P L 17: 265-6.
Steele, H. G.  A note on alphabetical order.  L W 15: 247-8.
---- H. G.  Practical library problems.  L A 10: 194-9;
L A R 15: 294-5.

Steele, L.   Iowa documents for libraries.   Ia L C Q 5: 21-4.
Steele, R.   The Casket sonnets.   L (ns) 9: 422-8.
  ---- R.   Chaucer and the "Almagest."   L (3d series) 10:
  243-7.
  ---- R.   Earliest English music printing.   Bib Soc Illus-
  trated Monographs No XI.   1903.
  ---- R.   Early printed English books on arithmetic.   Bib
  Soc Trans 4: 5-8.
  ---- R.   Hans Luft of Marburg: a contribution to the study
  of William Tyndale.   L (3d series) 2: 113-31.
  ---- R.   Materials for the history of the Lithuanian Bible.
  L (ns) 8: 57-62.
  ---- R.   Notes on English books printed abroad, 1525-48.
  Bib Soc Trans 11: 189-236.
  ---- R.   Spanish proclamation in English against Elizabeth.
  L (ns) 8: 303-8.
  ---- R.   What 15th century books are about (Divinity).   L
  (ns) 5: 337-58.
  ---- R.   What 15th century books are about (law).   L (ns)
  6: 137-55.
  ---- R.   What 15th century books are about (literature).   L
  (ns) 8: 225-38.
  ---- R.   What 15th century books are about (scientific
  books).   L (ns) 4: 337-54.
  ---- R. and R. A. Peddie.   English printed music to 1600.
  Bib Soc Trans 5: 8-10.
Steele, R. L.   Humphrey Dyson.   L (3d series) 1: 144-51.
  ---- R. L.   The Oxford university press and the Stationers'
  company.   L (3d series) 3: 103-12.
  ---- R. L.   Printers and books in chancery.   L (ns) 10:
  101-6.
Steenberg, A. S.   Agricultural libraries in Denmark.   L J 29:
  550-1.
  ------- A. S.   A Danish charging system.   L 6: 78-9.
  ------- A. S.   Libraries in Denmark.   2nd International
  Conference Proceedings: 138-40;   P L 7: 410-1.
  ------- A. S.   Libraries in Finland.   2nd International
  Conference Proceedings: 140-1.
  ------- A. S.   Libraries in Norway.   2nd International Conf-
  erence Proceedings 137-8.
  ------- A. S.   Libraries of Sweden.   2nd International Conf-
  erence Proceedings, 135-7.
  ------- A. S.   Library of the working men's institute.   2nd
  International Conference Proceedings, 137.
  ------- A. S.   Public libraries in Denmark.   L A R 12: 96-8.
  ------- A. S.   Public libraries in the northern states of
  Europe (Sweden, Denmark, Norway, Finland) 2nd International
  Conference Proceedings: 135-41.
  ------- A. S.   Recent progress in the popular libraries of

Denmark, and their present condition. L J 29: Conf No 63-6;  P L 9: 379-82.
------- A. S.  Royal library of Stockholm.  2nd International Conference Proceedings 135-6.
------- A. S.  Royal university library at Lund.  2nd International Conference Proceedings p 136.
------- A. S.  Royal university library of Upsala.  2nd International Conference Proceedings p 136.
------- A. S.  Town library of Gothenburg.  2nd International Conference Proceedings, 136-7.
Steiner, B. C.  Cost of preparing books in public libraries for the use of the public. L J 25: Conf No 32-3.
----- B. C.  Importation of books.  A L A Bull 10: 88, 102-4.
----- B. C.  The legal status of the public library in the United States.  American Law Review 43: 536-46.
----- B. C.  Librarian as literary critic.  Dial 59: 480-1.
----- B. C.  Library as a continuation school.  Nat Educ Assn 1915: 1081-5.
----- B. C.  Linotyping library catalogs.  L J 19: 259-60.
----- B. C.  Maryland library law.  P L 15: 241.
----- B. C.  Rev. Thomas Bray and his American libraries.  American Historical Review 2: 59-75.
----- B. C.  Some problems concerning prose fiction.  L J 28: Conf No 33-5.
----- B. C.  Specifications for a librarian.  Wis Lib Bull 12: 5.
----- B. C.  Sunday school library.  L J 23: 276-7.
----- B. C.  Transmission by mail of books for the blind. L J 30: 962.
----- B. C. and G. H. Ranck.  Replacements.  L J 21: 401.
----- B. C. and S. H. Ranck.  Report on access to the shelves. L J 19: Conf No 87-96.
Steiner, L. H.  Future of the free library.  L J 15: Conf No 44-7.
----- L. H.  Should uniformity mark the arrangement and administration of our libraries, or should individuality be permitted to assert itself in each?  L J 16: Conf No 57-61.
Stephen, G. A.  Application of exact classification to shelf arrangement.  L W 11: 251-5, 325-31.
----- G. A.  Book cloths.  L A R 11: 5-7.
----- G. A.  British Museum cataloguing rules.  L W 10: 401-10.
----- G. A.  Commercial bookbinding: review.  L A 7: 154-5.
----- G. A.  Edition binding.  L A 6: 326-30.
----- G. A.  English decorative endpapers.  Printing Art 16: 433-4.
----- G. A.  The examination essays.  L A R 12: 46-8.
----- G. A.  Fee for the diploma.  L A R 10: 522-3.

----- G. A.  First provincial town library, Norwich, established 1608.  L A R 19: 193-4.

----- G. A.  How to catalogue a novel by its title:  with a suggestion for a new rule.  L A R 1: 432-40.

----- G. A.  The Library association diploma.  L A 6: 188-9.

----- G. A.  Library rate limit removal.  L A R 20: 271-2.

----- G. A.  Machine book sewing, with remarks on publishers' binding.  L A R 10: 261-80, Discussion 305-10;  Lib Work 1: 72-5.

----- G. A.  Norfolk bibliography.  L A R 22: 352.

----- G. A.  Notes on materials for library bookbinding. L A 5: 143-6, 162-4;  Lib Work 1: 4-5, 72-5.

----- G. A.  One hundred book collectors arranged in chronological order of their decease.  L W 10: 194-200, 225-36.

----- G. A.  Publishers' bindings:  illustrated lecture. L A R 11: 526, 530;  12: 11-3;  L W 12: 380-1.

----- G. A.  Regulations affecting the loan of books in libraries.  L A R 9: 173-83.

----- G. A. and H. T. Coutts.  Manual of library bookbinding: review.  L A 8: 72-3;  L W 13: 363-4.

Stephens, E.  American popular magazines:  a bibliography. Bull Bib 9: 7-10, 41-3, 69-70, 95-8.

Stephens, J. A.  How I would organize and administer a public library having a gross income of  800 a year (prize essay). L A 2: Supp XI-XIV.

Stephens, T. E.  Rise and growth of public libraries in America.  L A U K Trans 6: 16-30.

Sterling, E. M.  Lessons from the methods of the Curtis publishing co.  L J 44: 333-6.

Stern, R. B.  Chicago libraries.  Wis Lib Bull 12: 117-27.

--- R. B.  Long distance reference work of "Mother's Magazine."  L J 41: 747-50.

--- R. B.  The rural-school library.  Nat Educ Assn 1917: 674-6;  L J 42: 494.

Sternberg, Count von.  Music in libraries.  L J 26: 207.

Sterneck, O. von.  Looking the gift horse in the mouth.  P L 14: 290.

Sterner, M.  Everyday problems.  Minn P L C N No 9: 29-30.

----- M.  German bibliography of the history and methods of arithmetic.  U S Rept 1893-4, vol. 1: 314-23.

----- M.  Library advertising.  Minn P L C N No 5: 11-2.

Sternheim, E.  The public library of tomorrow.  L J 44: 429-36.

Stetson, W. K.  An A. L. A. card catalogue.  L J 9: 71.

----- W. K.  Being a librarian.  L J 15: 231-2.

----- W. K.  Bookbinding from the librarian's standpoint. P L 11: 300-1.

----- W. K.  Charging by day-books.  L J 11: 121.

----- W. K.  Co-operation again.  L J 7: 106, editorial comment 103-4.

----- W. K.  Co-operative cataloguing -- a suggestion.  L J 9: 177, 191.

----- W. K.  Co-operative indexing of current periodicals. L J 8: 5-6.

----- W. K.  Delinquent borrowers.  L J 14: 403-4.

----- W. K.  Economical, educational, select catalogs for public libraries.  L J 16: Conf No 26-7.

----- W. K.  The leading of catalog type.  L J 20: 302.

----- W. K.  Linotyping library catalogs.  L J 19: 259-60.

----- W. K.  Planning for efficiency in library buildings. L J 36: 467-8.

----- W. K.  Shelf-pins and some other devices.  L J 44: 465.

----- W. K.  Typewriters in libraries.  L J 25: 104.

----- W. K. and W. A. Borden.  Printed cards for catalogues. L. J. 16: 209.

Stetson, W. W.  Rural communities and centres of population. Journal of Education 63: 3-4.

Stevens, A. D.  County work of the Logansport (Ind.) public library.  Lib Occ 5: 407-9.

----- A. D.  Pay duplicate collection at Logansport.  Lib Occ 2: 76-7.

Stevens, E. F.  Criteria for selection of technical literature. A L A Bull 3: 259-63.

----- E. F.  An honorable and lasting peace.  L J 42: 851-6.

----- E. F.  Industrial literature and the industrial public at the Pratt institute library.  L J 34: 95-9.

----- E. F.  The stranger at Liverpool.  L J 37: 600-2.

----- E. F.  Technical literature for the average library. Mass L C Bull 6: 86-7.

----- E. F.  The working library for the artisan and the craftsman.  A L A Bull 7: 170-3.

Stevens, H.  English bibliography before 1640.  L A Trans 4: 17-22.

----- H.  Ink maker as a spoiler of new English books.  L A Trans 4-5: 178.

----- H.  Panizzi, Sir Anthony, 1797-1879.  L A Trans 7: 117-24.

----- H.  Photo bibliography;  or, a central bibliographical clearing house.  1st Int Conf 70-81;  L J 2: 162-73, Discussion 258-9.

----- H.  Universal postal union and international copyright. L A Trans 1: 108-20.

----- H.  Who spoils our new English books.  L A Trans 5: 173-9.

Stevens, N. E.  Obligation of the investigator to the library. Science (ns) 53: 323-5.

Stevens, R. E.　Report on reading for the young.　L J 19: 81-7.

Stevens, T. W.　On some American bookmakers.　Bib Soc Chi Yr-Bk 1900-01: 25-31.

Stevens, W. F.　Decimal classification for railroad books.　L J 28: 114-5.

----- W. F.　Fiction reading at the Homestead Carnegie library.　L J 27: 326-7.

----- W. F.　How to interest working men in the use of the library.　P L 16: 93-5.

----- W. F.　Library and study clubs.　L J 33: 181-2.

----- W. F.　The library as a civic and social center as illustrated by the Homestead, Pa., library.　P L 17: 362.

----- W. F.　Outline for a library report.　L J 28: 297.

----- W. F.　Use of the library by foreigners as shown by the Carnegie library of Homestead, Pa.　L J 35: 161-2.

Stevenson, B. E.　How to be well posted.　P L 22: 281-3.

------- B. E.　Statement of European representative.　A. L. A. war service committee.　A L A Bull 13: 218-21.

Stevenson, O. J.　The old and the new in literature teaching.　English Journal 3: 69-77.

Stevenson, R.　Binding of serials.　L W 3: 266-7.

Stevenson, W. E.　Reserved books.　L W 10: 276-8.

Stevenson, W. M.　Weeding out fiction in the Carnegie library, Allegheny, Pa.　L J 22: 133-5.

------- W. M. and J. Thomson.　Proposed classification of fiction.　L J 27: 946-7.

Stewart, C.　Libraries in relation to settlement work.　L J 31: Conf No 82-5, Discussion 231-2.

Stewart, C. D.　Common sense study of Shakespeare.　Wis Lib Bull 12: 100-3.

Stewart, H. G.　Interchange of library assistants.　Pacific Northwest Library Assn Proceedings.　1911: 61-4.

----- H. G.　Regional and county libraries in British Columbia.　P L 25: 587-8.

----- H. G.　The situation in British Columbia.　Pacific Northwest Library Assn Conference Proceedings 1920: 22-4.

Stewart, J. D.　Advertising a library.　L W 13: 69-71.

----- J. D.　Brief alphabeting number.　L A R 9: 244-5.

----- J. D.　Cemeteries of workshops?　L W 14: 129-30.

----- J. D.　Compilation of reading lists.　L A 4: 181-3.

----- J. D.　Cult of the child and common sense.　L A R 10: 281-8.　Discussion, 310-2.

----- J. D.　An early chapter in the history of book annotation.　L W 13: 74-7.

----- J. D.　Guiding an open access lending library.　L W 7: 113-8.

----- J. D.　International librarianship versus the village pump.　L W 13: 374-6.

----- J. D.　Is the story hour within the librarian's province?　The negative.　L A 7: 73-4.

----- J. D.  Librarian as a human being:  a review of Mr. Edmund L. Pearson's "Library and the librarian".  L W 13: 266-8.

----- J. D.  Mechanism of book selection and ordering.  L W 14: 151-4.

----- J. D.  On theory and practice.  L W 17: 36-8.

----- J. D.  Oversize books.  L W 9: 208-11.

----- J. D.  Principles of library organization.  L A 6: 98-103.

----- J. D.  Rules for an author and title sheaf catalogue. L W 10: 364-7.

----- J. D.  School libraries.  L W 8: 173-7.

----- J. D.  Sheaf catalogue.  L W 10: 41-4, 85-8, 123-8, 204-6, 281-3, 364-7;  11: 15-7, 136.  Published in book form, 1909.

----- J. D.  Some points of contact.  L W 7: 70-2.

----- J. D.  Technical education and public libraries in England.  P L 10: 455-7.

----- J. D.  Terminological dictionaries.  L W 12: 87-92.

----- J. D.  Two government enquiries into public libraries. L A 7: 87-95.

----- J. D.  Work of a library commission -- a note on the Wisconsin Free library commission.  L W 12: 63-6.

----- J. D. and O. E. Clarke.  Book selection.  L A 7: 115.

----- J. D. and O. E. Clarke.  Guides to book selection. L W 11: 409-17, 445-50.

----- J. D. and O. E. Clarke.  Terminological dictionaries. L W 12: 87-92.

----- J. D. and W. C. B. Sayers.  Abridged Jast code of rules for classified cataloguing.  L W 7: 326-30;  8: 1-4.

----- J. D. and W. C. B. Sayers.  The card catalogue.  L W 14: 162-5, 205-11, 236-9, 265-70, 290-8, 325-9, 358-64; 15: 39-44, 77-83, 107-10.

----- J. D. and W. C. B. Sayers.  Card catalogue: a review. Libn. 4: 85-9.

----- J. D. and W. C. B. Sayers.  Card catalogue reviewed. L A 10: 181-2.

----- J. D. and W. C. B. Sayers.  Catalogues for children. L A R 7: 385-91.

----- J. D. and W. C. B. Sayers.  Cataloguing materials and technique.  L W 7: 288-90.

----- J. D. and W. C. B. Sayers.  Library magazines:  their preparation and production.  L W 7: 229-32, 257-61, 285-90, 326-30;  8: 1-4, 36-9, 91-4, 147-52, 180-3, 208-12.

----- J. D. and W. C. B. Sayers.  The magazine and card catalogue.  L W 8: 211.

----- J. D. and W. C. B. Sayers.  Methods and examples. L W 8: 36-9, 91-4.

----- J. D. and W. C. B. Sayers. Reading lists. L W 8: 147-52.

Stewart, K. L. Schools and libraries. Vt L Bull 9, No 1: 2-4.

Stickley, Mrs. B. F. Division of authority from the trustee's point of view. Colorado Lib Assn Occasional Leaflet 1: 179-81.

Stiles, G. Book-binding as a school craft. Elementary School Teacher 8: 29-35.

Stillman, B. W. An experiment in teaching reading. Atlantic Education Journal 6: 7.

Stillman, G. J. Oriental newspapers of San Francisco. Sunset 24: 197-201.

Stillman, M. L. Telephones in branches. L J 23: Conf No 166.

Stillwell, H. W. Should public schools have libraries? Texas Libraries 2: 24-9.

Stimson, F. From a loan desk. P L 18: 13.

Stimson, F. J. Legislative reference of the future. A L A Bul 3: 301-8.

Stimson, H. A. Boys and books. L J 9: 142.

Stinchcomb, H. Influence on children of war pictures. P L 20: 405.

Stingley, G. Studying a community in order to render better library service. Lib Occ 5: 156-62; Vt L Bull 15: 25-30.

Stirling, E. M. Lessons from the methods of the Curtis Publishing Co. L J 41: 333-6.

Stitt, E. W. Management of libraries in public schools. Educational Foundations 21: 272-81.

Stockbridge, F. P. American library association libraries in camp. Overland (N Y) 72: 451-3.

--------- F. P. Giving the soldiers books to read. World's Work (N Y) 37: 83-6.

--------- F. P. The library war service fund campaign. L J 43: 643-8.

--------- F. P. Publicity for libraries. L J 44: 31-2, 111-3, 171-2, 311-2, 391-3, 459-61, 596-8.

--------- F. P. Special libraries for our fighting forces. Special Libraries 9: 185-8.

Stockdale, F. Getting business books read. L J 42: 290-1.

Stockett, J. C. Checklist of the A. L. A. Booklist. Wis Lib Bull 11: 347-8.

------ J. C. Combination of schools and public libraries. Wis Lib Bull 11: 187-8.

------ J. C. Some popular methods of raising library funds. Wis Lib Bull 12: 436-9.

------ J. C. Suggestions for books and references on costume. Wis Lib Bull 11: 314-7.

------ J. C. Window displays. Wis Lib Bull 12: 246-8.

------ J. C. Working man's reading room. Wis Lib Bull 11: 220-2.

Stockwell, G.  Report on gifts and bequests.  1899-1900.  L J
    25: Conf No 92-105.
    ------- G.  What periodicals should be purchased -- a per-
    sonal opinion.  P L 7: 13-7.
Stokes, C. W.  Classification and filing of photographs.  Print-
    ers Ink Aug 3, 1916: 82-6;  L J 41: 857-8.
Stone, A. H.  Proprietary library's excuse for being.  L J 31:
    Conf No 274-5.
Stone, E. L.  Catalog system of the library of the Bureau of
    railway economics.  A L A Bull 8: 209-10.
Stone, J.  Library buildings and their use.  A L A Bull 2: 357-
    8;  P L 13: 271-4.
Stone, R. B.  Library legislation.  Penn Lib Notes 4: 56-63.
Stone, W. F.  Chemical literature and its uses;  Review of
    Marion E. Spark's work.  P L 24: 421.
Storer, T. I.  Care of pamphlet collections.  Science Nov 24,
    1916;  735-9;  L J 42: 412-3;  Am Lib Annual 1917-18: 66-7.
Stork, C. W.  Teaching of literature.  Nation 91: 440.
Storrs, R. S.  Libraries.  L J 12: 258.
Stosskopf, G.  Library bookbinding.  P L 14: 87-9.
Stote, A.  Goudy:  the craftsman and his work.  Printing Art
    17: 205-12.
Stoutemeyer, J. H.  The reading problem.  Tex Lib 1, No 7: 1-4.
    --------- J. H.  Texas school and the reading problem.  Texas
    Libraries 1, No 7: 4-8.
Stoutenborough, B. M.  What women's clubs can do to further the
    work of the library.  L J 26: Conf No 192-4.
Strachan, D. L.  Inter-relation between the library and museum.
    L A 14: 41-3.
    ------ D. L.  Public libraries and the care of local records.
    Libn 3: 322-4, 365-7.
Strachan, L. R. M.  An historic Bible at Heidelberg.  L (3d
    series) 2: 260-72.
Straight, M. W.  Repairing of books.  P L 5: 88-9.
Strange, E. F.  Chief bibliographical works published during
    the last 18 months.  Bib Soc Trans 2: 81-6.
    ----- E. F.  Decorative work of Gleeson White.  L (ns) 1:
    11-7.
    ----- E. F.  Early pattern-books of lace, embroidery and
    needlework.  Bib Soc Trans 7: 209-46.
    ----- E. F.  Writing-books of 16th century.  Bib Soc Trans
    3: 41-69.
Strange, J. G.  Library by-products.  A L A Bull 10: 540-1.
Strange, J. L.  Advertising methods used by libraries.  Penn
    Lib Notes 3, No 4: 2-7.
Straus, E.  Critical moments in the children's room.  L J 35:
    147-9.

---- E.  Reference work with children.  Ohio Lib Bull 4 No
4: 1-3;  No 5: 1-5.
---- E.  Some recent tendencies in children's literature.
P L 17: 252-6.
---- E.  Three essentials in the equipment of the children's
librarian.  Ohio State Lib Bull 3, No 12: 1-2.
Strauss, R.  The historical aspect of fine printing.  Book-
lovers Magazine, v 6.
Streeter, M. E.  Newspaper advertising.  Lib Occ 2: 225-6.
Stroher, G. W.  The future and the public library.  L A 8:
215-7.
Strohm, A.  Being fit:  address delivered before the library
schools of Illinois and Wisconsin.  P L 22: 135-8.
---- A.  Efficiency of the library staff and scientific
management.  P L 17: 303-6;  A L A Bull 6: 143-6.
---- A.  First European summer school in library science
at Stockholm.  L J 33: 504-5.
---- A.  Is camp library service worth while?  A L A Bull
12: 196-8.
---- A.  Is it worth while?  N Y L 6: 99-100;  P L 23: 263-4.
---- A.  Laying our course.  L J 44: 691-4.
---- A.  Some phases of popular education.  Wis Lib Bull
10: 172-6.
Strohm, A. J.  Do we need a post-graduate library school?  P
L 15: 54-5.
---- A. J.  Trenton public library.  L J 27: 752, 771-2.
---- A. J. and J. Jahr.  Bibliography of co-operative cata-
loguing, and the printing of catalogue cards (1850-1902).
Reprinted from the report of the Librarian of Congress,
1902.
Strong, G. F.  An A. L. A. book service.  L J 44: 374.
---- G. F.  Shall a permanent endowment be undertaken for
peace-time work of the A. L. A.?  A L A Bull 13: 92-4.
---- G. F.  Student access to book collections:  extent
and methods.  L J 44: 437-9.
Strother, G. W.  Library assistant's outlook from a provincial
point of view.  L A 6: 156-60, Discussion 161-2.
Strudwick, N.  Rural literature.  NC Bull 2: 98-9
Struthers, J.  Reading of public school children.  Religious
Education 4: 468-78.
Stuart, G. H.  Selected bibliography for League of nations.
Wis Lib Bull 15: 32-4.
Stuart, H. B.  The Doves press.  Booklover's Magazine 8: 83-5.
Stubbs, L.  The library in industry.  L A 14: 219-22.
Stuckey.  Selection of public documents in small libraries.
P L 13: 25.
Stuhlman, F.  Small library and the fiction problem.  N Y L
1: 78-9.

Sturges, J. V.  Training of teachers in the use of books and
the library and in a knowledge of children's books.  Nat Educ
Assn 1910: 1003-13;  New York State Teachers' Assn Proceedings 1910: 310-5;  American Education 14: 255-8;  L J 36:
194-5;  P L 16: 163.

Sturgis, J. V.  The library.  Univ of State of New York, Education Dept Bull No 472: 37-47.

Sturgis, R.  The Avery collection of modern printing.  Scribner's Magazine 31: 253.

Sullivan, E. C.  Instruction of all prospective teachers in
the contents and use of libraries.  Nat Educ Assn 1907:
967-72.

Sullivan, J.  Care of public records.  Am City 19: 33-6.

------  J.  The library, the hope of democracy.  N Y L 6:
156-9.

Sullivan, M.  Library administration.  Nat Educ Assn 1916: 546-
7.

Sullivan, M. D.  A report from El Paso, Texas.  P L 24: 314-5.

Sully, J.  Child study and education.  L J 27: 195-6.

Sulzer, W.  A congressman's estimate of the public library.
P L 15: 295.

Sumner, C. W.  Demand for the teacher-librarian.  University
of North Dakota School of Education Review Jan 1917: 30-2;
L J 42: 226;  Am Lib Annual 1917-18: 83-5.

----  C. W.  Hospital library service:  a new department of
public library work at Sioux City, Iowa.  Wilson Bulletin
1: 480-2.

----  C. W.  The state university library and state educational co-operation.  P L 19: 92-101.

----  C. W.  State-wide use of the university library.  Quar
Journal of Univ of North Dakota Oct 1915: 60-4.

Sumner, J. S.  Theological libraries in the United States.
U S Govt Rept 1876: 137-60.

Sumner, W. G.  Political economy and political science:  a
selected list of books.  L J 5: 17-21.

Sureties, H. G.  An appeal to Mr. Carnegie to pay off mortgages
on older libraries.  L A 4: 201-3.

------  H. G.  Branch libraries.  L A 5: 285-8.

------  H. G.  Display and filing of periodicals.  L A 4:
322.

------  H. G.  Library assistants' association in Paris.
Libn 2: 394-5.

------  H. G.  Negative:  discussion on library extension:
do lectures forward library work?  L A 7: 64-8.

------  H. G.  A note on some library problems and tendencies.  L A 14: 159-61.

------  H. G.  Those without:  a discussion of the membership of the L. A. A.  LA 10: 34-7.

Sutcliff, M. L.  Library training in California.  A L A Bull
5: 263-8.

Sutherland, J. T.   Books on India and Indian periodicals.   L J 33: 229-30.

Sutherland, L. A.   The children's department of the public library, Kansas City, Missouri.   Texas Libraries 2: 100-3.

Sutliff, H. B.   Things not mentioned in the curriculum.   A L A Bull 9: 266-7.

Sutliff, M. L.   Book numbers for popular libraries -- problem set for library school students.   N Y S L Rept 85, Bull No 75: 105-9.

----- M. L.   Library training in California.   A L A Bull 5: 263-8.

----- M. L.   Use of card catalogue -- questions set for library school students.   Bull No 75, p. 101, N Y S L Rept 85.

Sutton, C. W.   Bible Christian church library, Salford.   L A U K Trans 2: 125.

---- C. W.   Branch libraries:  their number and cost.   L A R 6: 67-71, Discussion 501-5.

---- C. W.   Edward Edwards.   L A R 14: 615-24.   Libn 3: 37-8.

---- C. W.   Judicious advertising.   L A R 12: 611-2.

---- C. W.   Lancashire independent college.   L A U K Trans 2: 126.

---- C. W.   Manchester libraries.   L A U K Trans 2: 126-129.

---- C. W.   Manchester libraries and booksellers.   B A R 6: LXV-LXX.

---- C. W.   Preservation of local newspapers.   L A R 3: 121-5, Discussion 157.

---- C. W.   Some of the institutions of Manchester and Salford.   L A R 1: 550-63.

---- C. W.   Subscription libraries and public libraries.   L A R 12: 2-3.

---- C. W.   What our readers will read.   L C 3: 140-1, 152-4.

---- C. W. and G. L. Campbell.   Statistical report on free libraries.   L A U K Trans 2: 138;  L J 3: 23-4.

Sutton, H.   Children and modern literature.   Littell's Living Age 192: 287-94.

Suzzallo, H.   The story and the poem.   Nat Educ Assn Proceedings 1907: 478-82.

Swan, C. H.   Alphabetic order table for names and places.   L J 11: 118.

Swan, F. M.   Preparing men for better jobs.   Special Libraries 9: 114-5;  System 33: 207-9.

Swan, R. T.   Paper and ink.   L J 20: 163-7.

Swann, J. H.   Training of library assistants, from the assistant's point of view.   L W 1: 164-6.

Sweet, B.   On reserve books.   Pacific Northwest Library Assn
   Proceedings 1911: 29-30.
Swem, E. G.   Some government libraries.   P L 12: 146-7.
   -- E. G.   State and local bibliography.   L J 26: 677-81.
Swezey, A. D.   Binding records.   P L 14: 5-7.
   ---- A. D.   Library reports and statistics.   Pacific North-
   west Lib Assn, Proceedings 1916: 6-12.
Swift, L.   James Lyman Whitney.   Bull Bib. 8: 152-4.
   --- L.   Pamphlets and continuations of serials.   L J 12:
   350-4, 440.
   --- L.   Paternalism in public libraries.   L J 24: 609-18.
   --- L.   Propaganda of the printing press.   Printing Art 15:
   17-20.
   --- L.   Proprietary libraries and public libraries.   L J
   31: Conf No 272-4.
   --- L.   Public library in its relations to literature.   L
   J 25: 323-7.
   --- L.   Question of public library expansion.   L J 28: 713-6.
Swift, L. B.   Essentials of library equipment.   P L 4: 72-6.
Swingle, M. K. and W. T.   Utilization of photographic methods
   in library research work.   A L A Bull 10: 194-9, 422;   L J
   41: 801-4.
Swingle, W. T.   Chinese books and libraries (Library of Congress
   collection).   A L A Bull 11: 121-4 828;   L J 42: 104-5;   P L
   22: 110-1.
   ----- W. T.   Difficulties attending research in Chinese pub-
   lications in Washington.   P L 15: 56.
   ----- W. T.   Orientalia.   Rept Libn of Congress 1920: 187-94.
   ----- W. T. and M. K.   Utilization of photographic methods
   in library research work.   A L A Bull 10: 194-9, 422-8;   L
   J 41: 801-4.
Switzer, C. F.   Love stories for children.   P L 22: 49-53.
Switzer, G. E.   Bellingham public library.   Wash L A Bull 1 No
   3: 7-8;   Bull 2 No 4: 8.
   ----- G. E.   The library budget.   Pacific Northwest Lib Assn
   Proceedings, 1913: 63-5.
   ----- G. E.   Value of traveling libraries.   Wash LA Bull 3,
   No 1: 7.
Sykes, F. H.   English in the secondary schools.   School Review
   14: 157-63.
Symington, J. A.   Value and utility of a local collection.   L
   A 7: 20.
Tafel, L. A.   Library service of the New Jersey zinc company.
   Special Libraries 10: 97-8.
Tafuris, M.   The immigrant: a composite portrait.   Wilson Bull-
   etin 1: 349.
Taggart, R. C.   Ventilation of a library.   L J 35: 253-5.
Tait, A.   Public library in its relation to the technical school.
   L W 6: 201-3.

-- A. Some of the public institutions of Leeds. L A R 5: 341-52.

Talbot, H. Library and the League of municipalities. Special Libraries 10: 175.

Tandy, F. D. Question of indexes. L J 22: 88, 303.

--- F. D. Some suggestions in regard to the use of the Dewey decimal classification. P L 4: 139-41.

Taner, M. E. Traveling library of pictures. P L 2: 263-6.

Tanner, G. B. Library situation in the Chicago high schools. Educational Bi-Monthly 7: 9-15.

Tanner, H. B. Niche devoted to local history. Wis Lib Bull 1: 90-1.

Tanner, H. G. A boys' nature club at London, Ontario. L J 45: 641.

Tanner, M. E. Traveling library of pictures. P L 2: 263.

Tapley-Soper, H. Charging system in use at Exeter public library. P L 16: 328-30.

---------- H. Custody of parish registers. L A R 14: 583-6.

---------- H. Distribution of government publications and documents. L A R 13: 373-83, 528-9.

Tappan, E. M. Reading for children. P L 16: 351-2.

Tapper, T. Public library in the community. Musician 22: 338, May, 1917.

Tappert, K. Base hospital library, U. S. Camp Upton, N. Y. Iowa L C Q 8: 107-8.

----- K. Books at work in Washington county, Maryland. American City (T & C ed) 23: 25-7 Jan 1920.

----- K. The point of contact. Ia L C Q 7: 199-201.

----- K. A suggestion for the story hour. P L 24: 373.

Taylor, A. R. The library of the Kansas State normal School at Emporia. L J 41: 27.

Taylor, C. F. Relation of the school to the library. Journal of education (Boston) 63: 678.

Taylor, E. A. The art of the book in France. Studio, spring number 1914: 191-200.

Taylor, F. B. Building a library. Ia L C Q 5: 192.

Taylor, F. J. Organization and administration of school libraries. L A 9: 54-8.

Taylor, G. Civic value of library work with children. A L A Bull 2: 372-82; P L 13: 247-8; Minn P L C N 2: 129.

---- G. Services of folk-lore in education. P L 13: 266-7.

Taylor, I. and J. McKillop. Best books of 1904 - sociology. L A R 7: 640-57.

Taylor, I. M. Co-operation between public libraries and Y. M. C. associations. L J 23: 518.

Taylor, J. Earliest free libraries. L C 3: 155-63.

---- J. First Protestant free library in England. L J 14: 477.

---- J. Monastic scriptorium. L 2: 237-44, 282-91.
Taylor, J. R. M. Device for handling books at the shelves.
Am Lib Annual 1915-16: 107.
Taylor, J. W. How to use the library. Maine Lib Bull 6: 62-3.
Taylor, L. A. Bibliographical aids in the public libraries of
Bristol. L A R 8: 218-9.
---- L. A. Reference library. L A R 6: 532-7.
---- L. A. Shelf classification: ways and means. L A R
4: 45-7.
---- L. A. Some of the public institutions of Bristol. L
A R 2: 459-68.
Taylor, L. H. The county medical society library. Medical Lib
Assn Bull July 1917: 1-4; L J 43: 454.
---- L. H. Medical libraries in smaller cities. Med Lib
and Hist Journal 2: 187-92.
Taylor, W. C. A word to cataloguers. L J 22: 180.
Taylor, W. L. Books for children: fiction. L J 26: Conf No
63-5.
Taylor, W. P. Patent Office library. U S Govt Rept: 271-2,
1876.
Teal, W. Arrangement and binding of British blue books. A L
A Bull 13: 177-8, 388; L J 44: 776-8.
Tedder, H. R. The Barkers and the early history of the'Bible-
patent. L C 2: 161-6.
---- H. R. Bibliography and classification of French his-
tory. L 1: 15-23.
---- H. R. Bibliography in 1882. L A M N 4: 22-30.
---- H. R. Bibliography of modern British history since
1485. Bib Soc Trans 12: 101-1.
---- H. R. Biographies in English. L A R 6: 611-3; 8:
57-60.
---- H. R. British Museum catalogue of English books printed
before 1640. L C 2: 57-63.
---- H. R. Catalogue of English literature scheme. L 8:
325-34.
---- H. R. Classification of Shakespeariana. L J 11: 441-2,
449 - L C 4: 105-7.
---- H. R. Doctor O. Hartwig's scheme of classification.
L 1: 21.
---- H. R. Evolution of the public library. 2nd Int Conf:
12-8.
---- H. R. Few words on the study of bibliography. L A
Trans 7: 128-31.
---- H. R. The librarian in relation to books. L A R 9:
604-18.
---- H. R. Librarianship as a profession. L A Trans 5:
163-72.
---- H. R. Mr. Melvil Dewey's work at Columbia college. L
C 1: 186-91.

---- H. R.  New Anglo-American joint code of cataloguing rules.  L A 6: 228-33, Discussion 233-5;  L A R 10: 690-2.

---- H. R.  New subject index of the London library.  L A R 11: 476-85, Discussion 521-3;  L J 34: 492.

---- H. R.  Official record of current literature.  Bib Soc Trans 1: 147-58, Discussion 159-63.

---- H. R.  On the study of bibliography.  L A Trans 7: 128-31.

---- H. R.  Place of bibliography in primary, secondary and higher education.  L A R 14: 504-12;  L J 37: 680-1.

---- H. R.  Presidential address.  L 9: 213-29.

---- H. R.  Progress of the free library movement in 1882. L C 1: 8-12.

---- H. R.  Projected bibliography of national history.  L A R 13: 510-2;  14: 209-15.

---- H. R.  Proposals for a bibliography of national history. L C 3: 185-94.

---- H. R.  Public records and the reports of the latest royal commission on the subject.  L A R 22: 342-8.

---- H. R.  Report of Committee on public education and public libraries.  L A R 7: 611-7.

---- H. R.  Shakespearean literature and its classification. L A R 18: 275-81.

---- H. R.  Women as librarians.  2nd Int Conf: 18, 1897; L A Trans 5: 171-2.

---- H. R.  Young librarians and self-improvement.  L A 1: 75-81.

---- H. R. and E. C. Thomas.  Library association of the United Kingdom: Hdbk and prospectus.  L J 8: 336.

Teggart, F. J.  Access to shelves.  L J 24: 667-79.

----- F. J.  Contribution towards a bibliography of ancient libraries.  L J 24: 5-12, 57-9.

----- F. J.  Criticism of Stein's "Manuel de bibliographie generale."  L J 24: 73-5.

----- F. J.  Handbook of American libraries.  L J 22: 741-3.

----- F. J.  International bibliography of humanistic literature.  A L A Bull 13: 360, 371-2.

----- F. J.  An international catalogue of technological literature.  P L 10: 114-5.

----- F. J.  Librariana: an outline of the literature of libraries.  L J 25: 223-5, 577-9, 625-9.

----- F. J.  Library literature in England and the United States during the 19th century.  L J 26: 257-61.

----- F. J.  On the literature of library history.  L J 22: Conf No 35-8.

----- F. J.  Plea for an international catalog of scientific literature.  P L 10: 114-5.

Telling, A. E.  Efficient assistants.  L W 7: 311.

Temmis, W. S.  Printing machinery.  Printing Art 17: 195-6.

Temple, A. G.   Art galleries in relation to public libraries.
 L A R 3: 13-21.
Temple, M.   A selected library for children.   P L 6: 406-9.
Templeton, C.   Possibilities of direct service to individual
 farmers.   A L A Bull 4: 742-6.
------- C.   With the prairie dwellers of Nebraska.   A L A
 Bull 3: 348-50.
Tepper, J. G. O.   Relation of the heating arrangements in lib-
 raries, museums, etc., to the conservation of books, speci-
 mens, etc., and the natural laws underlying their influence.
 L A of Austral Proc: LXXI-LXXIV.
Terry, H. L.   Two lines of high school reading.   School Review
 20: 476-82.
Tessier, C. F. G.   The junior assistant and the Library assoc-
 iation certificate.   L A 7: 103-9.
Thackeray, F. S. J.   Notes on the libraries at Windsor Castle
 and Eton college.   L 3: 54-8.
Thatcher, L. E.   Lead school library.   South Dakota Lib Bull
 5: 130-3.
Thayer, A. M.   How some teachers use school libraries.   L J
 43: 709.
Theiss, L. E.   The morgue man.   Outlook 102: 83-8.
Thelberg, E. B.   The home and the library.   L J 24: 145-7.
Thimm, F.   Goethe collection in the British Museum.   L C 4:
 116.
--- F.   Shakespeare in the British Museum.   L C 4: 41-5.
Thomas, A. C.   Some dangers of technical knowledge.   L J 25:
 328-9.
Thomas, C. E.   English for industrial pupils.   English Journal
 2: 241-6.
---- C. E.   Highgate and its literary associations.   B A R
 13: X III-L.
---- C. E.   Sion college library, London.   B A R 12: I-XII.
---- C. E.   Some booksellers' advertisements.   B A R 17
 XXI-XXV, 1920.
---- C. E.   Some old-time bookselling and printing ballads.
 B A R 15: XXXV-XLIII.
---- C. E.   Some recent schemes of classification.   L A Trans
 4-5: 184.
---- C. E.   Was Richard de Bury an impostor?   L 1: 335-40.
Thomas, D. C.   Organization of the library board.   Lib Occ 2:
 127-30.
Thomas, E. C.   Bradshaw, Henry, 1831-1886.   L C 5: 179-88.
---- E. C.   Classed catalogues and the new classed catalogue
 of the German Reichsgericht.   L A M N 4: 42-5.
---- E. C.   Classification of literature.   L C 1: 181-2.
---- E. C.   Edward Edwards, 1812-1886.   L C 3: 54-7.
---- E. C.   English legal bibliography.   L A Trans 4: 23-6.
---- E. C.   The libraries of London in 1710.   L C 2: 41-7.

---- E. C.  Libraries of Oxford.  L A U K Trans 1: 24-8.
---- E. C.  Manuscripts of the Philobiblon.  L C 2: 129-37.
---- E. C.  New building at the British Museum.  L C 1: 16-8.
---- E. C.  Popular libraries of Paris.  L C 1: 12-5.
---- E. C.  Proposed index to collectaneous literature.  L
A Trans 1: 88-9.
---- E. C.  Public libraries and the "promulgation list".
L A M N 4: 87-92.
---- E. C.  Richard de Bury and his editors.  L C 1: 148-53,
170-3.
---- E. C.  Scrutton's Laws of copyright.  L C 1: 194-5.
---- E. C.  Some recent schemes of classification.  L A Trans
4-5: 182-4.
---- E. C. and H. B. Wheatley.  Proposed subject index to
bibliologies and bibliographies.  L A M N 1: 89-95.
---- E. C. and H. R. Tedder.  Library association of the
United Kingdom:  Hdbk. and prospectus.  L J 8: 336.
---- E. C., J. D. Mullins and J. Picton.  The Royal visit
to Newcastle-upon-Tyne, opening of the public libraries.
L C 1: 137-42.
Thomas, H.  Cervantes collection in the British Museum.  L (ns)
9: 429-43.
---- H.  The Emblemata amatoria of Philip Ayres.  L (3d ser-
ies) 1: 73-95.
---- H.  Output of Spanish books in the sixteenth century.
L (4th series) 1: 69-94.
---- H.  The Palmerin romances.  Bib Soc Trans 13: 97-144.
---- H.  The romance of Amadis of Gaul.  Bib Soc Trans 11:
251-97.
Thomas, H. M.  Outline for the study of Alaska.  Mich Lib Bull
7: 146-50.
---- H. M.  Outline for the study of the war countries of
Europe.  Mich Lib Bull 7: 114-21.
---- H. M.  Outlines on twentieth century literature:  Mich-
igan and South America.  Mich Lib Bull 7: 52-78.
Thomas, J. C.  Conglomerate in periodicals.  L J 31: 817.
Thomas, J. M.  The public library: a community necessity.  N Y
L 5: 46-51.
---- J. M.  The value of the library.  Vt L Bull 6, No 4:
6-7.
Thomas, L. I.  Some whys and whats of our library, and a few
don'ts:  Factory magazine library.  Special Libraries 10:
167-9.
Thomas, M. R.  Library of the Safety institute of America.
Special Libraries 10: 218-9.
Thomas, T. H.  National museum and library for Wales.  L (ns)
6: 212-20;  L W 8: 6-7.
Thomas-Stanford, C.  Extension of the library movement to the
country districts.  L A R 10: 432-8.

Thompson, A. E.   The library period.   Popular Educator 32: 365-6.

Thompson, C. S.   Abolish the non-essential acknowledgment.   L J 43: 704.

------ C. S.   The dividend paying public library.   L J 38: 315-9.

------ C. S.   Labor-saving devices.   L J 39: 361-2.

------ C. S.   Library school requirements in Germany.   L J 36: 349.

------ C. S.   Report on labor-saving devices.   A L A Bull 10: 53-6, 345-6;   L J 41: 244-9, 584-5.

------ C. S.   Savannah, Georgia, public library.   L J 42: 456-7.

------ C. S.   To determine space typewritten copy will fill in print.   Bull Bib 8: 63.

Thompson, E. C.   Classics in grade work.   Education 12: 489-96.

Thompson, E. M.   Arrangement and preservation of manuscripts.   L C 4: 33-9.

------ E. M.   The autograph manuscripts of Anthony Munday.   Bib Soc Trans 1915-17: 325-53.

------ E. M.   History of English handwriting, A. D. 700-1400.   Bib Soc Trans 5: 109-42, 213-53.

------ E. M.   Presidential address.   L 2: 365-78.

------ E. M.   Some hints on the future of free libraries.   L 1: 402-10.

------ E. M.   Two pretended autographs of Shakespeare.   L (3d series) 8: 193-217.

Thompson, G.   High school reading:   the Newark plan.   School Review 21: 187-90.

------ G.   Selection of books for children.   L J 32: 427-31.

Thompson, H. M.   Relations between public education and public libraries.   L A R 5: 452-66;   Discussion 496-7.

Thompson, H. S.   Colour printing.   Printing Art 14: 273-5.

Thompson, J.   Dundee branch libraries:   Coldside branch.   Builder 25 June 1915: 31.

Thompson, Mrs. J. A.   What the library will mean to the returning soldier.   P L 25: 62-4.

Thompson, J. B.   University extension.   L J 17: Conf No 39-41.

Thompson, J. D.   Handbook of learned societies.   L J 29: Conf No 114-6.

Thompson, J. W.   Some suggestions concerning the needs and methods of historical bibliography.   Bib Soc Chic Yr-Bk 1899-1900: 26-37.

Thompson, L. A.   The Federal children's bureau.   A L A Bull 8: 215-8.

------ L. A.   The Kansas court of industrial relations:   a list of references.   L J 45: 887-9.

Thompson, P. E.   Essential qualities of a librarian.   L W 22: 392-4.

Thompson, S. P.  Peter Short, printer, and his marks.  Bib Soc
    Trans 4: 103-28.
Thompson, W. O.  Librarianship as a profession.  P L 5: 415-8.
Thomsen, Mrs. G. T.  The practical results of story telling in
    Chicago's park reading rooms.  A L A Bull 3: 408-10.
----- Mrs. G. T.  Story hour in Hawaii.  L J 43: 551.
Thomson, J.  Book stealing in Philadelphia.  L J 33: 445.
----- J.  Free library movement in Philadelphia.  L J 19:
    166-7.
----- J.  How to secure a state library commission.  L J 26:
    Conf No 191-2.
----- J.  Library work amongst the blind.  A L A Bull 1:
    46-7.
----- J.  Plan for a co-operative list of incunabula.  L J
    24: Conf No 131-2.
----- J.  Report on open shelves.  L J 23: Conf No 40-2.
----- J.  Suggested plan for an American bibliographical
    society.  Bib Soc Chic Yr-Bk 1901-2: 27-30, 53-6.
----- J.  Supplying of current newspapers in free library
    reading rooms.  L J 19: Conf No 47-8.
----- J.  Traveling libraries.  L J 21: Conf No 29-31.
----- J.  The working man and the library.  Penn Lib Notes
    3, No 4: 8-10.
----- J. and W. M. Stevenson.  Proposed classification of
    fiction.  L J 27: 946-7.
Thomson, J. B.  Display of magazines.  L W 10: 112-3.
----- J. B.  Research work in public libraries:  a word for
    information desk assistants.  L W 9: 320-3.
Thomson, O. R. H.  Budget for the library.  P L 16: 430-1:  Penn
    Lib Notes 4: 46-56.
----- O. R. H.  Classification and shelving of magazines in
    large branch libraries.  L J 28: 68.
----- O. R. H.  Classification of fiction.  L J 28: 770-2;
    P L 8: 414-8.
----- O. R. H.  Library budget.  L J 37: 16-7.
----- O. R. H.  Library statistics again.  P L 19: 187-90.
----- O. R. H.  A normal library budget.  Wis Lib Bull 8:
    161-3.
----- O. R. H.  Why not face the facts?  P L 21: 397-400.
Thorne, B.  How to deal with books from their accession to their
    delivery to the borrower (Prize essay).  L A 2: Supplement.
Thorne, E. G.  Infection through books.  P L 8: 55.
---- E. G.  Reading list on the Netherlands.  Bibliography
    No 9, N Y S L Rept 81, 1898.
Thorne, H. S.  Changes hoped for in library administration.
    P L 9: 173-4.
---- H. S.  Fiction reading.  P L 6: 15-6.
---- H. S.  Health in library work.  P L 9: 8.
Thorne, R. J.  Industrial library activity.  P L 23: 254.

Thorne, W. B.    Aids to readers:  printed and mechanical.  L A
5: 196-9.
---- W. B.    Bibliographical collections of the late William
Blades and the late Talbot Baines Reed.  L (ns) 3: 349-57.
---- W. B.    A famous printer:  Samuel Richardson.  L (ns)
2: 396-404.
---- W. B.    First steps in library cataloguing.  L A 14:
51-60.
---- W. B.    First steps in library routine.  L A 12: 135-41.
---- W. B.    Fourth international school, April 1914.  L A
R 16: 300-4.
---- W. B.    A full discussion needed.  L A R 11: 93.
---- W. B.    The Library assistants' association:  an outline
of its development and work.  Libn 2: 124-7, 163-6, 207-11.
---- W. B.    The Library association in relation to the pro-
gress of the public library movement.  L A R 12: 86-95.
---- W. B.    The next step.  L A R 11: 469-70.
---- W. B.    Our students and literary history.  L A R 10:
641-3.
---- W. B.    Policy of the library assistants' association
in its relation to the public library movement.  L A 8: 147-
9.
---- W. B.    Problem of the junior assistant:  the economic
standpoint.  L A 10: 104-5.
---- W. B.    A rejoinder.  L A R 11: 91.
---- W. B.    Seventeenth century cookery book.  L (ns) 4:
180-8.
---- W. B.    Simple card charging system.  L W 2: 212-3.
---- W. B.    Symposium on public libraries after the war.
L A R 19: 161.
---- W. B.    William Blades.  L A 1: 61-2 -- William Blades:
the man and his library.  L A 2: 155-62.
Thorne-Thomson, G.    Children's literature.  Wis Lib Bull 7:
129-32.
----------- G.    How to tell a story.  Minn P L C N 4: 128.
Thornsby, F.    Unification of public libraries.  L W 1: 263.
Thum, M. D.    Selection and proper use of periodicals;  partic-
ularly for smaller libraries.  Pacific Northwest Library
Assn Proceedings 1914: 50-7.
Thurber, C. H. and F. E. DeYoe.    Where are the high school boys?
School Review 8: 234-43.
Thurber, S.    An address to normal school teachers of English.
School Review 8: 129-45.
----- S.    An address to teachers of English.  Education 18:
515-26.
----- S.    English in secondary schools.  School Review 2:
468-77, 540-9.
----- S.    English literature in girls' education.  School
Review 2: 321-36.

----- S.  English literature in the schools.  Academy (Syracuse) 6: 485-98.

----- S.  The English situation.  School Review 11: 169-86.

----- S.  Voluntary reading of high school students.  School Review 13: 168-80.

Thurlow, M. C.  Encouragement of reading by women's clubs.  L J 28: 227-9.

Thurston, E. P.  Common novels in public libraries.  L J 19: Conf No 16-8.

------ E. P.  How can the character of the reading be improved?  L J 16: 47-9.

Thwaites, R. G.  Apprenticeship as a means of library training.  L J 23: Conf No 83-4.

------ R. G.  Bibliographical activities of historical societies in the United States.  Bib Soc Amer Proc 1: 170-5.

------ R. G.  Directories in public reference libraries.  L J 20: 341-2.

------ R. G.  Gathering of local history material by public libraries.  L J 22: 82;  Wis Lib Bull 1: 89-90.

------ R. G.  Historical publications of the state of Wisconsin.  Wis Lib Bull 7: 142.

------ R. G.  How to get Parkman read.  A L A Bull 2: 162-5.

------ R. G.  Library of the State historical society of Wisconsin.  L J 16: 203-7.

------ R. G.  Local history collections.  Minn, Ia and Wis L C Hdbk 30-1, 1902.

------ R. G.  Local history in the library story hour.  L J 32: 158-9;  Wis Lib Bull 3: 43-4.

------ R. G.  Local public museums in Wisconsin.  Wis Lib Bull 4: 34-6.

------ R. G.  Presidential address.  L J 25: Conf No 1-7.

------ R. G.  Relation between state and municipal libraries.  A L A Bull 2: 285-90.

------ R. G.  Some material in the Bancroft library.  P L 11: 60-1.

------ R. G.  Sphere of the library.  P L 11: 1-5.

------ R. G.  Ten years of Americna library progress.  L J 25: Conf No 1-7.

------ R. G.  Wisconsin books for Wisconsin men.  Wis Lib Bull 8: 98-100.

------ R. G.  Wisconsin state historical society library.  L J 16: 203-7.

------ R. G.  Bibliographical activities of historical societies in the United States.  Bib Soc Amer Proc 1: 170-5.

Ticer, F. W.  My friends the teachers.  Lib Occ 3: 131-3.

Ticer, W. F.  Library publicity.  Lib Occ 4: 55-6.

Tickell, A. H.  The Dun Emer press.  Booklover's Magazine 8: 6-14.

Tiefenthaler, L.  Municipal reference library and municipal work.  P L 17: 162-4.

Tighe, R. J.  Relation between libraries and schools from the school side.  A L A Bull 1: 90-2.

Tilling, A.  A Paris bookseller of the 16th century, Galliot du Pre.  L (ns) 9: 36-65, 143-72.

Tilling, A. E.  Assistants' ideals.  L A 2: 5-6.

Tillinghast, W. H.  Field of work in state and local clubs.  L J 23: 519-21.

--------- W. H.  Report of the co-operation committee.  L J 22: Conf No 81-3.

--------- W. H.  Rules for the preparation of the catalogue of the Imperial library, Vienna:  a review.  L J 28: 29-30.

--------- W. H.  Sketch of Mr. Winsor's life.  Harvard Graduates Magazine 6: 188-91.

--------- W. H.  Some general rules and suggestions for a library staff.  L J 27: 873-5.

--------- W. H.  Treatment of pamphlets in Harvard college library.  A L A Bull 3: 400-3;  P L 14: 309.

Tilton, A. C.  Davis memorial library.  New Hamp Lib Bull 9: 144-5; L J 38: 94-5.

---- A. C.  Printed series cards for public documents.  P L 15: 181-4.

Tilton, E. L.  Architecture of the small library.  P L 16: 341-3;  P L 17: 40-4.

---- E. L.  Scientific library planning.  L J 37: 497-501.

Tilton, F. T.  A good banking asset:  the financial library. Special Libraries 4: 113-5.

Timmins, S.  Special collections of books in and near Birmingham.  L C 4: 157-63.

Tindale, J. L.  Good musical habits.  Musician 25: 6, Nov 1920.

Tisdal, A. P.  Functions of the proposed library information service.  A L A Bull 14: 169-72.

Titcomb, M. L.  A county library.  A L A Bull 3: 150-2;  Library Work 1912: 137.

----- M. L.  A day at Fort Leavenworth.  A L A Bull 12: 241-2.

----- M. L.  The first county library.  L J 42: 232.

----- M. L.  Hagerstown-Washington county free library. Maryland State Library Comm, 7th annual report 1909: 123-4.

----- M. L.  How a small library supplies a large number of people with books.  L J 31: 51-5;  Library Work 1912: 139;  Cal News Notes 3: 132.

----- M. L.  Library wagon.  Wis Lib Bull 1: 70-1.

----- M. L.  Use of book wagon in library field work.  A L A Bull 3: 151-2, 354-5.

----- M. L.  What the county and rural library is doing to help win the war.  A L A Bull 12: 187-9, 282, 283.

Titus, G. M.  Duties of library trustees.  P L 7: 63-5;  Ia
L C Q 2: 19-21.
Tobey, C.  Story telling in the high school.  Story Hour 1:
8-11.
Tobin, J. F.  The ordering of engravings and designs.  Printing
Art 16: 445-6.
Tobitt, E.  American public as seen from the circulation desk.
A L A Bull 10: 276-9.
---- E.  Essentials of a good library school.  A L A Bull
4: 776-9.
---- E.  Plan of a course of instruction in the use of lib-
raries.  Nat Educ Assn 1909: 842-52.
---- E.  Type of assistants.  A L A Bull 6: 138-42;  L J
37: 439.
---- E.  What a librarian should know about binding.  Ia
L C Q 5: 18-21.
---- E.  What the librarian may expect from the trustee.
P L 12: 73-4;  Neb Lib Bull No 4: 17-20.
Toby, C.  Story-telling in the high school.  Story Hour 1: 8-11.
Todd, D. P.  South African public library, Cape Town.  L J 15:
Conf No 48-50.
Todd, M. A.  Use of pictures in a public library.  Minn P L
C N 3: 121-4.
Todd, M. E.  The Einstein theory:  a selected list of refer-
ences.  L J 45: 25-6.
Todd, R. H.  A library co-operative cooking club.  P L 20: 51-
3.
Todd, W. C.  Free reading rooms.  U S Rept 460-4.  1876.
Tolman, F. L.  Bibliography and cataloging.  P L 10: 119-22.
---- F. L.  The library's aid to the camp as a melting pot.
N Y L 6: 126-8.
---- F. L.  Making full use of the state library.  N Y L
7: 62-4.
---- F. L.  Mobilization:  a next step in organization of
a state library service.  A L A Bull 10: 497-502.
---- F. L.  New York state library in its relations to the
libraries of the state.  N Y L 1: 68-70.
---- F. L.  Notes on some recent state publications of in-
terest.  N Y L 1: 210-2, 239-40;  2: 35-6;  N Y L 2: 69-70,
105-6, 137-8, 198-200.
---- F. L.  Reference problem of the state library.  A L A
Bull 2: 334-8.
---- F. L.  War service of the local library and the state
library:  how they should co-operate in this service.  N
Y L 5: 223-5.
Tolman, W. H.  Library of Brown university.  U S Bureau of
Education, Circular of Information 1894 No 1: 190-4.

Tomlinson, E. T.  The historical story for boys.  A L A Bull
     3: 270-4.
     ------- E. T.  Reading for boys and girls.  Atlantic 86:
     693-9.
Toole, W.  Rural library service.  Wis Lib Bull 8: 46-7.
Topley, W. W.  Photographic survey and record work in its rel-
     ation to public libraries.  L A R 14: 69-72.
     ---- W. W.  Report of the Net books committee.  L A R 10:
     566-68.
Torrance, M. S.  Value of the county library to the city lib-
     rary.  Lib Occ 5: 215-7.
Torrey, C. A.  State supervision of public libraries.  P L 6:
     271-3.
Torrey, E. C.  Special collections in American libraries:  The
     Landbery collection of Arabic manuscripts at Yale University.
     L J 28: 53-7.
Towner, H. M.  Obligation of the citizen to the library.  Ia
     L C Q 2: 25-7.
     ---- H. M.  Trustees' problems.  Ia L C Q 5: 189-90.
Towner, I. M.  Catalog system of the Bureau of education.  A
     L A Bull 8: 208-9.
Townsend, E. E.  Apprentice work in the small public library.
     New Hamp Bull 9: 152-4;  L J 34: 8-10.
Townsend, R. D.  The American publisher and his service to lit-
     erature.  Outlook 81: 740-7.
Tracey, A. E.  The child and the library.  Maine Lib Bull 3, No
     4: 14-20.
Tracey, C. S.  Bibliography on library work with foreigners.
     A L A Bull 10: 263-4.
Tracy, J. P.  Something new in library service.  Wis Lib Bull
     10: 70-1.
Traill, J. W. H.  Classification of books in the natural sci-
     ences.  L 6: 13-8.
Trams, A. F.  Literary Digest in the classroom.  Literary Digest
     50: 381-2.
Trask, M. D.  Bulletins for children.  L J 31: 708-9;  Vt L Bull
     2, No 3: 6-7.
Treliving, N.  The junior assistant and his environment.  L A
     10: 106-7.
     ------- N.  The public library and the cheap book.  L A 9:
     225-30.
     ------- N.  The staff and the reader.  L A 8: 153-4.
Trent, W. P.  Books as a source of culture.  A L A Bull 1: Conf
     No 24-5.
     --- W. P.  Teaching literature.  Sewanee Review 12: 410-9.
     --- W. P.  The teaching of English literature.  Nat Educ
     Assn 1896: 104-11.

--- W. P.  Teaching the spirit of literature.  Atlantic
Monthly 78: 414-9.

Triepel, E. M. V.  United States treasury department library.
Special Libraries 10: 127-8.

Triggs, O. L.  Study and teaching of literature.  University
of Chicago Record.  1: 337-9, 364-6.

Trimble, A. L.  Popularizing a library in a small town.  Lib
Occ 2: 192-3.

Tripp, E. J.  The chamberlains' account of Stratford-upon-Avon.
L A R 18: 328-9.

Tripp, G. H.  Can the public library and the public school be
mutually helpful.  L J 29: 173-5.

--- G. H.  Improper inducements to buy books.  P L 25: 249-
50.

--- G. H.  The library as a social force.  L J 33: 241-2.

--- G. H.  Literature of the whaling industry.  Mass L C
Bull 2, No 1: 7-8.

--- G. H.  Use of library lecture rooms.  P L 21: 307.

Tripp, S. H.  Newspapers in libraries.  P L 14: 298-9.

True, A. C.  Co-operation between agricultural libraries.  Association of American Agricultural Colleges and Experiment
Stations Proceedings Atlanta 1912: 16-7.

-- A. C.  Suggestions as to a policy of administration of
agricultural college and experimental station libraries.
A L A Bull 6: 216-22.

True, E. I.  Phases of rural extension in Iowa.  P L 16: 99-102;
Library Work, 1912: 392.

-- E. I.  Rural extension under the township.  Ia L C Q 6:
152-5;  P L 16: 99-102.

True, J. P.  Juvenile literature: so-called.  Atlantic 92:
690-2.

True, M. A.  Impressions of a transplanted librarian.  Penn
Lib Notes 6, No 4: 70-5.

True, R. H.  Beginnings of agricultural literature in America.
A L A Bull 14: 186-94.

Trumball, J.  Otis library.  L J 18: 469-70.

Tuck, C. H.  How to reach the rural communities.  L J 37: 12-4.

Tuck, L. C.  The library at the School for the deaf.  Minn P L
C N 4: 5-6.

Tucker, S. M.  The Drama league of America:  its aims and methods.  N Y L 4: 178-80.

Tufts, J. H.  Notes on the bibliography of the history of philosophy.  Bib Soc Chic Yr-Bk 1902-3: 20-31.

Tuomey, H. R. P.  County free libraries.  Sierra Educ News 8:
170-3.

Turnbull, J.  Purchase of current fiction for libraries of small
means.  L J 27: 132-3.

Turnbull, T. E.  Are newsrooms desirable?  L A R 9: 510-5.

------ T. E.  Effect of an increased rate on library administration.  L A 9: 120-1.

------ T. E.  The initial stock of a library.  L A 7: 118-23.
------ T. E.  L. A. Exam., 1910:  a criticism of the papers.
L W 13: 42-4.
------ T. E.  L. A. Exam., 1911:  a criticism of the papers.
L W 14: 53-5.
------ T. E.  L A examinations:  a causerie.  L W 8: 152-4.
------ T. E.  L A examinations, 1908: a criticism of the
papers.  L W 10: 452-4.
------ T. E.  L. A. examinations, 1909, a criticism of the
papers.  L W 12: 130-2, 189.
------ T. E.  L. A. examinations, 1913: a criticism of the
papers.  L W 16: 56-8.
------ T. E.  Libraries of France.  L W 12: 125-7.
------ T. E.  Local records in libraries:  a reading list.
L A 8: 70.
------ T. E.  Reference library:  Plan and arrangement.  L
W 10: 37-40.
------ T. E.  Review of the Pittsburgh library catalogue.
L W 10: 48-54.
Turner, E. T.  Stories of American life which have been made
into motion pictures:  a selected list.  L J 44: 457.
Turner, F.  Defence of fiction reading.  L W 1: 113-5.
---- F.  Interesting development in library work -- Bulle-
tins.  L 10: 58-64.
---- F.  Place of the public library in relation to elemen-
tary, secondary, and higher education.  L 6: 168-76.
Turner, F. M., Jr. and Berolzheimer, D. D.  The chemical eng-
ineering catalog.  Special Libraries 10: 105-7.
Turner, I. M. C.  Book buying from agents and sets of books.
Penn Lib Notes 5, No 4: 31-3.
Turner, M. L.  Rural school libraries.  School and Home Educa-
tion 20: 295-6.
Turrill, C. B.  An early California photographer, C. E. Wat-
kins.  Cal News Notes 13: 29-37.
Turvill, H.  The average budget.  Wis Lib Bull 8: 160-1.
----- H.  Book labels.  Wis Lib Bull 6: 77-8.
----- H.  Influence of librarian's own reading.  Wis Lib
Bull 10: 185.
----- H.  Inventory.  Wis Lib Bull 8: 95-6, 163-4.
----- H.  Keeping up the library's book supply.  Wis Lib
Bull 16: 202-8.
----- H.  Numerical errors in records.  Wis Lib Bull 8: 98.
----- H.  Progressive libraries.  Wis Lib Bull 13: 73-4.
Tweedell, E. D.  Books for self culture.  P L 16: 389-90.
------ E. D.  John Crerar library and the business libraries
of Chicago.  Special Libraries 10: 70-1.
------ E. D.  Special libraries and the general reference
library.  Special Libraries 10: 162-4.

------ E. D. State documents for libraries. P L 20: 363.

Twiss, G. R. Relation of the science department to the high school library. P L 25: 47-9.

Twort, H. A. Collections of illustrations in public libraries. L A 5: 195-6.

Tyler, A. C. Library reading clubs for young people. L J 37: 547-50.

--- A. C. A live bookworm: a nature study. L J 33: 311-2.

--- A. C. Transition period in a girl's reading. New York State Teachers' Assn Proceedings 1911: 86-9; P L 17: 17.

--- A. C. Accessioning. P L 4: 383-4.

Tyler, A. S. Classification. P L 4: 377-80.

--- A. S. Department of education, United States. A L A Bull 13: 372-3.

--- A. S. Effect of the commission plan of city government on public libraries. A L A Bull 5: 98-103, Discussion 103-5; L J 36: 328-33; P L 16: 281-4.

--- A. S. An experiment in extension. Wis Lib Bull 7: 121-3.

--- A. S. Form of library organization for a small town library beginning. N C Bull 3: 3-7; Texas Libraries 1, Ap 1916: 24-7; L J 31: 803-6; 41: 444-5.

--- A. S. Instructional work of library commissions. P L 10: 60-1.

--- A. S. League of library commissions. L J 30: 27, 274; Ia L C Q 5: 11, 25.

--- A. S. Library commission, the small library and the card catalog. A L A Bull 2: 370-2; Discussion P L 13: 268-9.

--- A. S. Modification of subject entries for card catalogs. L J 28: 21-2; Ia L C Q 3: 48.

--- A. S. Plans for a national organization. L J 29: 483, Conf No 247-8.

--- A. S. The public library in commission governed cities. National Municipal Review 2: 255-9; L J 38: 403-5; Ia L C Q 7: 37-40.

--- A. S. Tolerance and co-operation: a message from the President of the A. L. A. L J 45: 890.

--- A. S. The widening field and the open book. Ia L C Q 7: 129-33.

Tyler, A. W. Book agent baffled. L J 14: 464.

--- A. W. Specimen of application slip. L J 13: 320-1.

Tyler, M. C. Historic evolution of the free public libraries in America. L J 9: 40-7, 171.

Tylor, D. Hospital libraries. L 7: 347-52.

Tyrrell, E.  Starting the picture habit.  Wilson Bulletin 1: 447-8.

Uhler, P. R.  Sketch of the history of public libraries in Baltimore.  L J 15: 334-7.

Umbaugh, O. F.  Value of magazines and newspapers in English classes.  Illinois University High School Conference Proceedings 1920: 203-5.

Underhill, A.  Exhibitions in Vassar college library.  P L 20: 417-8.

Underhill, C. M.  Accessioning.  P L 8: 147-8.

------- C. M.  Book ordering and buying.  P L 8: 142-4.

------- C. M.  Staff meetings: their organization, methods and results.  L J 32: 553-4.

Underhill, E. P.  Crumbs of comfort to the children's librarian.  L J 35: 155-7.

Underwood, H. K.  The teacher of literature for the elementary school.  Education 30: 174-83.

Underwood, J.  The public library, verses from "Processionals".  L J 40: 721-2.

Upham, W.  Duty of the public for preservation of local history.  Minn P L C N 3: 24-5.

Upton, G. E.  Best reading for the young.  P L 6: 88-90.

Usher, E. P.  The library from a citizen's point of view.  Wis Lib Bull 14: 229-32.

Utley, G. B.  A. L. A. work at headquarters.  A L A Bull 10: 67-9.

--- G. B.  Books for the public.  Survey 37: 367-8.

--- G. B.  California county free library statistics.  U S Commissioner of Education Report 1914, 1: 482.

--- G. B.  Financial responsibilities of the trustees to the communities.  Lib Occ 4: 77-8;  P L 21: 93-4;  P L 22: 261-8.

--- G. B.  Library conditions in Florida.  A L A Bull 1: Conf No 73-5.

--- G. B.  More members for the A. L. A.  L J 44: 379-80;  P L 24: 205-6.

--- G. B.  National association as a national helper.  Wis Lib Bull 7: 111-2.

--- G. B.  Reaching the public.  Minn P L C N 3: 115-21.

--- G. B.  Reinforced binding.  P L 14: 300.

--- G. B.  Scrap-book specifications for wounded soldiers.  P L 22: 375-6.

--- G. B.  Shall a permanent endowment be undertaken for peace-time work of the A. L. A.  L J 44: 382-3.

--- G. B.  Some impressions: three weeks at the A. L. A. exhibit, San Francisco.  P L 20: 415-7.

--- G. B.  Statement on library extension.  A L A Bull 13: 366.

--- G. B.  What should a public library mean to a community?  N C Bull 2: 31-4.

--- G. B. What the public library is doing for public education in America. Touchstone 6: 39-41, Oct 1919.

--- G. B. Work of the American library association. Texas Libraries Vol 1 July 1916: 31-2.

Utley, H. M. Books for the blind. L J 23: Conf No 93-5, 148-9.

--- H. M. Catalogue printing from cards. L J 14: 466-7.

--- H. M. Government, constitution, by-laws and trustees. U. S. Rept, 1: 743-7 (1893); L J 18: 225-7, Discussion, Conf No 31-3.

--- H. M. How the re-classification and re-numbering of 60,000 volumes was done in the Detroit public library without closing or stopping the circulation of books. L J 16: Conf No 20-2.

--- H. M. How to plan a library. L J 24: Conf No 21-2.

--- H. M. Newspaper volumes in a library. L J 12: 349-50, 438-40.

--- H. M. Presidential address, A. L. A. conference. L J 20: Conf No 2.

--- H. M. Relation of the public library to the public school. L J 11: 301-5, Discussion 373.

--- H. M. Report on library architecture. L J 15: Conf No 12-4, 75-85.

--- H. M. Report on library legislation (U. S.). L J 14: 190-4.

--- H. M. Responsibility of librarians for warning the public against untrustworthy books. L J 23: Conf No 150-2.

--- H. M. Selection of books. L J 19: Conf No 39-41.

--- H. M. State in relation to public libraries. L J 20: Conf No 1-4.

--- H. M. Supplying of current daily newspapers in free reading rooms. L J 19: Conf No 44-5.

--- H. M. Work between libraries and schools at Detroit, Michigan. U. S. Bur of Educ Rept 1897-98, pt 1: 676-7; L J 22: 184-5.

--- H. M. Work of a library trustee from the librarian's point of view. L J 31: 657-60.

Utter, R. P. Ship's library. Weekly Review 2: 404-6.

Uychara, G. E. The Judicial system in Japan. A L A Bull 9: 390-3.

Vail, H. S. Public library as a factor in public education. Educ Bi-Mo 4: 149-53.

Vail, R. W. G. What then! a reply to Mr. Compton. L J 44: 188.

Vaile, E. O. Reading for thought. Educ Review 41: 71-81.

Vale, G. F. Juvenile libraries. L A 4: 262-5.

-- G. F. On the track of the defaulter. L A 5: 251-2.

Van, L. What children read. P L 11: 183-5.

VanBuren, M. Children's magazines. Wis Lib Bull 8: 35-6.

------- M.  Children's reading.  Vt L Bull 2, No 3: 5-6.
------- M.  Civic pride in the library.  Wis Lib Bull 8: 37.
------- M.  Cleaning up Mankato, Minnesota.  Wis Lib Bull 7: 71-3.
------- M.  Junior civic league.  Wis Lib Bull 6: 133-6.
------- M.  The librarian and her apprentices.  P L 15: 369-72.
------- M.  Library and civic work.  Minn P L C N 4: 52-3.
------- M.  Library statistics and reports.  Wis Lib Bull 8: 96-8.
------- M.  Necessity of publicity.  Wis Lib Bull 7: 117-8.
------- M.  Newspaper publicity.  P L 25: 264-6.
------- M.  Periodicals for the children's room.  P L 17: 121.
------- M.  Popular practical books.  Wis Lib Bull 9: 93-8.
------- M.  Popularizing standard novels.  N Y L 1: 186.
------- M.  Reading for culture.  Minn P L C N 7: 4-8;  Vt L Bull 2: 5-6.
------- M.  Reference work in a small library.  Minn P L C N No 2: 1-4.
------- M.  Re-registration.  P L 18: 229-31;  Wis Lib Bull 9: 14-5.
------- M.  Small library and art.  P L 14: 18.
------- M.  Social side of the librarian's life.  Minn P L C N 9: 3.
------- M.  Some publicity methods.  New Hamp Bull 9: 199-202.
------- M.  Useful books for useful boys.  Wis Lib Bull 9: 97-8.
------- M.  What's it about?  Minn P L C N 2, No 4: 55-7.
Van den Bosch, J.  The library.  Anchor 9: 40-1.
Van Duzee, E. P.  Technical books in public libraries.  P L 6: 631-2.
Van Dyke, H.  Books that I loved as a boy.  Outlook 78: 833-5.
------ H.  The reader, the book and the library.  P L 15: 108-9.
Van Dyke, J. C.  Making of catalogues.  L J 10: 126-7.
Van Dyne, C.  American public as seen from the circulation desk.  A L A Bull 10: 280-3.
------ C.  Why continue the fines system?  L J 41: 322-3;  Ia L C Q 8: 40-1.
Van Laer, A. J. F.  Lessons of the catastrophe in the New York state capitol at Albany on March 29, 1911.  American Historical Assn Report, 1911, v 1: 331-6.
------ A. J. F.  Work of the International congress of archivists and librarians at Brussels, 1910.  Am Hist Assn Rept 1910: 282-92.
Van Liew, C. C.  Duty of the normal school toward the problem of school literature.  Nat Educ Assn 1894: 832-43.

Van Metre, S.  Ideals versus realities in high school English.
   Nat Educ Assn 1908: 656-8.
Van Name, A.  Report on library architecture.  L J 14: 162-74.
Van Rensselaer, M. E.  The art museum and the public.  Bulletin
   of the Metropolitan Museum of Art Mch 1917, pp 57-64;  Am
   Lib Annual 1917-18: 62-3;  L J 42: 572-3.
Van Sant, C.  Planning a county library campaign.  Pacific
   Northwest Library Assn Proceedings 1920: 59-62.
Van Sickle, J. H.  Children and literature.  Nat Educ Assn
   1897: 1006-8.
-------- J. H.  Libraries in the schoolroom.  L J 21: 152.
Van Valkenburgh, A.  Classifying and cataloguing a small lib-
   rary.  P L 3: 199-201.
------------- A.  Common sense in cataloguing small libra-
   ries.  L J 31: Conf No 127-9, Discussion 237-9.
------------- A.  How far should we help the public in refer-
   ence work?  Mass L C Bull 5: 102-8.
------------- A.  Margarita's soul.  Wis Lib Bull 6: 95-100.
------------- A.  A plea for the cataloger.  L J 39: 679-81.
------------- A.  Selection of fiction for a small library.
   P L 2: 123-5.
------------- A.  State normal travelling cataloguer.  L J
   21: 174.
------------- A.  Training or teaching.  A L A Bull 6: 295-7.
Vaughan, Cardinal.  On free church libraries.  L 5: 77-8.
Vaughan, J.  Bishop Morley's library in Winchester cathedral.
   Fortnightly 100: 338-46.
Vaughan, J. H.  Preliminary report on the archives of New Mex-
   ico.  Am Hist Assn Rept 1909: 465-90.
Veditz, C. W. A.  Bibliography of sociology.  Bib Soc Amer Proc
   1: 213-5.
Veitch, F. P.  Leather and paper.  A L A Bull 8: 512.
Venable, E.  Oral reading as an aid in the interpretation of
   literature in the high school.  School Review 13: 337-41.
Venable, W. H.  Books and reading.  L N (U S) 1: 255-60.
Venner, B. M. and F. W. T. Lange.  Standard books on the war.
   Libn 9: 59-62, 79-82, 93-8.
Verney, Sir E.  Public libraries act of 1892 in a small lib-
   rary.  L 7: 353-8.
Vincent, C. W.  On the libraries of the London school board.
   2nd International Conference Proceedings 1897: 238.
Vincent, G. E.  Individualizing duty of the library.  P L 13:
   391-7.
----- G. E.  The library and the social memory.  L J 29:
   577-84;  P L 9: 479-85.
----- G. E.  State supervision of library extension in Ill-
   inois.  P L 13: 430.
Vincent, J. H.  Meaning of Chautauqua.  L J 23: Conf No 131-4.

Vine, G.   National library of Ireland:   a short account of the building and its contents.  L A R 4: 95-109.
-- G.   On the construction of the subject catalogue.  L A R 11: 486-507, Discussion 523.
-- G.   The personality of the librarian.  L A R 12: 615-24.
-- G.   Typewriter and its employment for cataloguing.  L A R 3: 117-9.
-- G.   William Caxton, the printer.  L A R 17: 212-3.
Vine, W. K.   Selection of periodicals.  L W 11: 483-4.
Vinton, F.   Chief need in libraries.  L J 3: 49-50.
---- F.   Discussion on shelf classification.  L J 6: 116.
---- F.   Hints for improved library economy drawn from usages at Princeton.  L J 2: 53-7.
---- F.   New Astor catalog.  L J 11: 215-6.
---- F.   Registration of books borrowed.  L J 2: 55-7.
---- F.   Shall borrowers go to the shelves.  L J 11: 67, 74.
---- F.   Training of assistants in a library.  L J 7: 290-1.
Virgin, E. H.   Bodleian regulations.  Nation 89: 568-9.
---- E. H.   What the A. L. A. can do.  P L 18: 192-3.
Virtue, E. B.   Principles of classification for archives.  Am Hist Assn Rept 1914, 1: 373-84.
Vitz, C. P. P.   Cleveland experience with departmentalized reference work.  A L A Bull 9: 169-74.
-- C. P. P.   Meeting the demand for a printed catalog.  N Y L 2: 124-8.
Vivian, H.   Buonaparte's library at Elba.  L (3rd series) 7: 103-14.
Vöge, A.   Suggested classification for chemistry.  L J 34: 304-6.
Voge, A. L.   Certification of librarians and standardization of library work.  P L 22: 176.
-- A. L.   Chronological arrangement of subject cards in a dictionary catalog.  L J 42: 441-3.
-- A. L.   Classification making.  A L A Bull 11: 190-5, 340.
-- A. L.   The decimal classification (9th edition): a refutation of Mr. Bay's article in Public Libraries, v 21: 261.  P L 22: 10-1.
-- A. L.   Indexing of periodicals and the work of the Concilium bibliographicum, Zurich.  Bib Soc Amer Proc 2: 116-34; P L 13: 42-3.
-- A. L.   Why books fall.  P L 21: 137-8.
Volland, P. F.   Better books for children.  P L 24: 113-5.
Vought, S. W.   The state of New York and the school library.  Wilson Bulletin 1: 444-6.
Voynich, W.   On the study of early printed books: Notes from a lecture.  L (ns) 4: 189-99.
----- W.   Reference books.  L J 12: 184.

W. F.  Financial condition of German libraries.  L J 31: 274.

W. R. H.  Letter re membership.  Libn 3: 103-4.

Wade, E. I.  Cataloging in the future.  L J 20: 71, Conf No 21-4.

Wade, M. A.  How the Public library commission of Indiana works with the small public libraries of the state.  A L A Bull 13: 146-9, 405.

-- M. A.  How to interest the men of the community in the public library.  Lib Occ 5: 329-33.

-- M. A.  Magazines for men.  Lib Occ 5: 240-1.

Wadleigh, H.  Relations between the city libraries and the county free libraries in California.  California Lib Assn Proceedings 1914: 33-6.

Wadlin, H. G.  Branch reference work in the Boston public library system.  A L A Bull 3: 364-6.

---- H. G.  Ought public libraries to radically restrict their purchases of current fiction?  L J 29: 60-3;  P L 9: 170-3.

---- H. G.  Public library and the man who earns.  Special Libraries 5: 55.

---- H. G.  Public library as a municipal institution from the administrative standpoint.  L J 31: Conf No 30-4.

---- H. G.  The quality of fiction.  A L A Bull 7: 246-53.

---- H. G.  Report of committee on social education congress.  A L A Bull 1: Conf No 116.

Wagenseller.  The story hour.  P L 15: 437-8.

Wagner, G.  Method of preserving pamphlets.  L J 23: 685.

Wait, M. F.  Library work in the preparatory school.  L J 29: 182.

Waite, J. K.  Rating of free public libraries.  L C 1: 167-9.

--- J. K.  Subscription library in connection with a public library.  L 5: 40-7.

Wakefield, G. W.  Iowa library legislation.  L J 19: 331-3.

Wakeman, E. F.  The small library as a library center.  P L 11: 9.

Walcott, J. D.  Library extension in the United States.  U S Comm Educ Rept 1910: 161-219.

Waldo, R. H.  Business in print.  L J 42: 267-9.

Waldron, J. S.  Directories and time-tables.  L W 10: 239-40.

Wales, E.  Story of conditions down in Missouri.  A L A Bull 3: 350-2.

Wales, E. B.  Library commissions and the high school or rural school library.  A L A Bull 13: 149-52, 405.

Walford, C.  Books I have seen;  books I have not seen;  books I should like to see;  books I never expect to see.  L A M N 1: 41-7.

----- C.  Destruction of libraries by fire considered practically and historically.  L A Trans 2: 65-70, 149-54;  L J 4: 415-6.

----- C.  Early laws and regulations concerning books and
printers.  L A Trans 6: 88-99.
----- C.  New General catalogue of English literature.  1st
Int Conf 101-3, 1877;  L A Trans 1: 54, 154;  L J 2: 188-90.
----- C.  Notes on cataloguing.  1st Int Conf 86-7;  L J 2:
161-2, Discussion 259-62.
----- C.  On binding of books for public and private lib-
raries.  1st Int Conf 116-8, 193;  L J 2: 201-3.
----- C.  On special collections of books.  L J 2: 140-5.
----- C.  On the longevity of librarians.  L J 5: 67-71.
----- C.  Outline of the plan for the preparation of a cata-
logue of (British) periodical literature.  L A Trans 4:
43-50.
----- C.  Practical points in the preparation of a general
catalogue of English literature.  L A Trans 1: 55-64, 154.
----- C.  Proposal for applying a system of "clearing" in
duplicates in private libraries.  L A Trans 3: 104.
----- C.  Some account of early book fairs.  L A Trans 5:
129-43.
Walker, F. K.  The war and library training.  A L A Bull 12:
98-103, Discussion, 306;  L J 43: 728-32.
Walker, G.  Aberdeen: its literature, bookmaking and circu-
lating.  L 6: 238-45, 265-73.
Walker, H.  Reference libraries in small towns.  L A R 4: 327-
32.
Walker, I. M.  The book peddler glorified.  P L 25: 55-61.
---- I. M.  New selections for declamation contests.  Wis
Lib Bull 15: 99-101.
---- I. M.  On the program:  Platform selections for declam-
ation contests, community entertainments, Y. M. C. A., K.
C., and American league meetings.  Wilson Bull 1: 515-20.
---- I. M.  Why they do not tat.  Wis Lib Bull 15: 257-60.
Walker, J.  Public library in a small town.  Wash L A Bull 2:
10-2.
Walker, J. E.  The school library.  L A 6: 319-21.
---- J. E.  Some thoughts on Dewey.  L W 17: 23-6.
---- J. E.  Suggested rearrangement of Dewey classes 100
and 200.  L W 16: 163-5.
Walker, J. M.  Public library in a small town.  Wash L A Bull
2, No 4: 10-2.
Walker, K.  Co-operation between libraries and the engineering
profession.  Special Libraries 7: 167-70.
Walker, K. C.  Co-ordination of technical literature.  L J 43:
312-4.
---- K. C.  Handbook for the operation of clearing houses
of information.  Special Libraries 6: 152-4;  L J 41: 370-1.
---- K. C.  The pipe organ: a bibliography.  Bull Bib 10:
121-2, 139-40;  11: 24-8, 43-7.
---- K. C.  The safety first exhibit of the New Haven public
library.  L J 41: 31-3;  P L 21: 17-8.

Walker, R. C.  A library recorder.  L J 4: 203, 375.
Walkley, R. L.  "All in the day's work."  L J 43: 159-63.
----- R. L.  Business methods in libraries.  Minn P L CN
5: 47-51;  P L 21: 401-5.
----- R. L.  Increasing the library appropriation.  P L 21:
451-3.
Wall, A. J.  Collection and preservation of war literature.
A L A Bull 13: 391-2.
Wallace, A.  Library movement in the South since 1899.  A L A
Bull 1: Conf No 62-7;  L J 32: 253-5.
----- A.  Staff meetings:  their organization, methods and
results.  L J 32: 543.
Wallace, C. E.  The Browne and the Newark charging system.
Pacific Northwest Library Assn Proceedings 1910: 29-35.
----- C. E.  Bulletin work for children.  L J 26: Conf No
72-4.
----- C. E.  Limitation of reference work in branch libra-
ries.  A L A Bull 3: 362-4.
----- C. E.  Value of kindergarten training in library work
with children.  Pratt Institute Monthly 8: 195-9.
Wallace, J. W.  Librarians in the United States.  L J 1: 92-5.
Wallace, L. E.  Filing in the Metropolitan museum of art.
Filing Feb 1919: 219-22;  L J 44: 335.
Wallace, R.  Staff meetings.  P L 21:60-3.
Wallace, S. E.  Development of a trust company's statistical
and information files.  Filing July 1918: 11-3.
Wallar, J.  Uses of public libraries.  L W 7: 65-70.
Waller, F.  War impetus to technology.  Pacific Northwest Lib-
rary Assn Proceedings 1919: 8-11;  P L 25: 6-9.
Wallis, A.  Bookbinding in the 16th and 17th centuries.  L 3:
181-4.
Wallis, C. W.  Connection between free libraries, art galleries
and museums.  L C 5: 6-11.
Wallis, I. H.  Statutory laws:  official lists by states and
territories.  L J 13: 277.
Wallis, M. S.  Legislative reference work in Baltimore.  L J
32: 562-3.
---- M. S.  The library side of the department of legisla-
tive reference, Baltimore Special Libraries 1: 73-5.
Walsh, J. J.  What our libraries should supply.  America Feb
13, 1915: 430-2;  Am Lib Annual 1915-16: 31-2.
Walter, A. H.  Bird study.  Wis Lib Bull 6: 32-4.
Walter, F. L.  Care of school libraries.  New York State Teach-
ers' Assn Proceedings 1910: 296-302;  N Y L 2: 256-60.
Walter, F. K.  The coming high school library.  N Y L 5: 78-81.
---- F. K.  Free and inexpensive reference material.  L J
38: 8-12.
---- F. K.  The library in industry.  L J 44: 760-1.

---- F. K. New York state library school. N Y L 2: 103-5.
---- F. K. A plea for the teacher. P L 16: 141-2.
---- F. K. Reading list on Arthur Wing Pinero. Bull Bib
6: 298-300.
---- F. K. Reading list on Henry Arthur Jones. Bull Bib
6: 273-5.
---- F. K. Reference work in the small library. P L 18:
100-3.
---- F. K. Relation of the librarian to the trustee. L J
44: 694-8.
---- F. K. Report of A. L. A. Committee on training courses
for school librarians. A L A Bull 9: 282-7; 10: 219-27,
429.
---- F. K. A rising or a setting sun. L J 41: 793-7; N
Y L 5: 150-3.
---- F. K. The small library and reference material on the
war. N Y L 6: 100-1.
---- F. K. Some Latin abbreviations and terms occasionally
used in book catalogs and bibliographies. Bull Bib 7: 37-
41, 64-7.
---- F. K. Selective function of library schools. A L A
Bull 8: 234-8.
---- F. K. Specialization among library schools. P L 18:
227-9.
---- F. K. Teaching library use in normal and high school.
A L A Bull 6: 255-60.
---- F. K. Training for the librarian of a business library
or a business branch. A L A Bull 13: 273-6, 395-6; L J
44: 310, 578-80; Special Libraries 10: 3-4.
Walter, W. Interior decoration of libraries. L A R 10: 648-59.
Walters, A. Old children's books. Strand 15: 32-40.
Walton, G. M. The friendly book. A L A Bull 7: 224-30; New
Hamp Bull 9: 218-23.
---- G. M. Library ethics. P L 10: 181-3.
---- G. M. Usefulness of libraries as an aid to teacher
training. American Schoolmaster 13: 57-60.
---- G. M. What the library can do for the teacher. Mich-
igan Board of Library Commissioners Report 1909: 43-5.
Waltons, J. Concerning practical bibliography. L A 7: 7-15,
40.
----- J. Literary history and registration. L A R 11: 3-4.
----- J. Parliamentary publications. L A R 20: 242-50.
Wandell, C. As to catologing: a review of T. Hitchler's
"Cataloging for small libraries." P L 21: 43-6.
----- C. Typewriter for card catalogues. L J 27: 268-9.
Ward, A. T. Cripplegate institute and West city free libraries.
L A 2: 143-6.
Ward, C. C. Pictures for use in teaching literature. English
Journal Oct 1915, 4: 526-30 (DeCoverley Papers): Dec 1915,

4: 671-4 (Coleridge); April 1916, 5: 274-80 (Ivanhoe, Robin Hood); April 1917, 6: 267-9 (Irving).

Ward, E. J.  Summary of the report of the school extension committee.  National Municipal League Proceedings 1910: 353-74.

Ward, E. W.  Work of the camps libraries.  L A R 18: 588-9; 17: 433-8.

Ward, E. W. D.  Books for the armies.  L W 18: 250-2.

Ward, G. O.  Cleveland public library and Safety week.  Special Libraies 10: 222.

-- G. O.  The Cleveland solution of the problem.  Wis Lib Bull 8: 32-3.

-- G. O.  Elementary library instruction.  P L 17: 260-2.

-- G. O.  High school branches of public libraries.  A L A Bull 6: 266-8.

-- G. O.  High school library.  New York State Teachers' Assn Proceedings 1910: 304-10; L J 36: 193-4; P L 16: 161-3.

-- G. O.  Report on high school branches of the Cleveland public library.  Cleveland Public Library Report 1911: 90-2.

Ward, H. L.  Library and the museum.  L J 32: 307-11.

Ward, J. W.  Public libraries and the public.  L J 7: 167.

Ward, L. L.  Branch libraries -- functions and resources.  L J 27: Conf No 42-6; P L 7: 338-41.

Warner, C. C. and A. P. Spencer.  Views of trustees regarding library construction.  Ia L C Q 4: 23-6.

Warner, C. D.  The novel and the common school.  Atlantic Monthly 65: 721-31.

Warner, E. G.  Historical sketch of periodicals.  Wash L A Bull 3, No 1: 12-5.

Warner, G.  Notes on the architecture of libraries.  P L 6: 607-9.

Warner, J.  First year of reference work.  L A 5: 84-5.

---- J.  Holiday literature and picture exhibitions.  L W 12: 49-54.

---- J.  Photographic surveys in connection with public libraries.  L A 6: 244.

Warner, M. F.  Bibliographical opportunities in horticulture.  A L A Bull 13: 178-84, 373.

---- M. F.  The literature of horticulture.  L J 44: 766-76.

Warren, A. H.  The library's part in reconstruction.  P L 24: 151-3.

Warren, C.  Centennial library exhibit.  L J 1: 18-9.

---- C.  The place of libraries in a system of education.  L J 6: 90-3.

Warren, E. E. K  Culture system of first reading.  Kindergarten Mag 3: 101-2.

Warren, I.  Educational conference of secondary schools in
relation with the University of Chicago.  School and Soc-
iety l: 719-20.
---- I.  Filing and indexing.  Special Libraries 10: 8-9.
---- I.  Instruction in the use of books and libraries.  Ed-
ucation 35: 157-63.
---- I.  Instruction in the use of books in a normal school.
P L 3: 151-3.
---- I.  Library school problem.  P L 11: 541-3.
---- I.  Mutual needs of schools and libraries in Illinois.
P L 20: 486-8.
---- I.  Notable characteristics of school libraries in Chic-
ago.  Wis Lib Bull 11: 307-10.
---- I.  Opportunities for study in the high school library.
Wilson Bulletin 1: 139-41;  L J 41: 937-8.
---- I.  Relation between libraries and schools as shown by
current educational publications.  L J 40: 446;  P L 20:
54-6.
---- I.  Relation of the organized library to the school.
Classical Journal Nov and Dec 1915;  v 11: 115-9, 174-80.
---- I.  Some high school problems of interest to teachers
and librarians.  Wilson Bulletin 1: 20-3.
---- I.  A teacher's professional shelf.  P L 17: 422.
---- I.  Teaching the use of books in libraries.  Education
35: 157-63.
---- I.  Three-foot shelf for a teacher's professional lib-
rary.  P L 17: 422.
---- I.  Vitalizing the relation between library and school:
II -- The library.  L J 26: Conf No 81-2.
---- I.  What the normal schools can do for teachers on the
library side.  Nat Educ Assn 1901: 841-7.
Warren, K.  List of references on labor turnover.  Special Lib-
raries 10: 198-203.
Warren, S. R. and S. N. Clark.  College libraries in the United
States.  U S Govt Rept 60-126, 1876.
---- S. R. and Clark, S. M.  Common school libraries (covers
legislation, history and administration of these libraries
in 21 states)  U S Govt Report 38-58. 1876.
---- S. R. and S. N. Clark.  Copyright, distribution, ex-
changes and duties.  U S Rept 279-91, 1876.
---- S. R. and S. N. Clark.  Free town libraries.  U S Govt
Rept: 445-59;  Library reports and statistics, 745, 1876.
---- S. R. and S. N. Clark.  General statistics of all pub-
lic libraries in the United States.  U S Govt Rept: 1010-
1174, 1876.
---- S. R. and S. N. Clark.  Legislation respecting duties
on books for public libraries.  U S Rept 290-1. 1876.
---- S. R. and S. N. Clark.  Libraries for soldiers and
sailors.  U S Govt Rept 273-6, 1876.

---- S. R. and Clark, S. N.  Libraries in prisons and reform-
atories.  U S Govt Rept: 218-9, 1876.
---- S. R. and S. N. Clark.  Libraries of the general govern-
ment.  U S Govt Rept:  252, 1876.
---- S. R. and S. N. Clark.  Sketches of individual societies
U S Govt Rept 1876:  332-77.
Warrington, James.  Music for the non-musical.  L J 29: 129-30.
Washburn, E. A.  Caring for war posters.  P L 25: 569.
Waterman, I. D.  Relation of the librarian to the community.
Penn Lib Notes 2, No 3: 5-6.
Waters, C.  Library exhibits in Los Angeles.  Bindery Notes
Sept-Oct 1913: 11-2.
Waters, C. S.  San Bernardino library at the Orange show.  Bind-
ery Notes Sept-Oct 1913: 12-3.
Watkins, H. E.  Relation of the high school to the public lib-
rary.  Wis Lib Bull 8: 30-2.
Watkins, M.  The possibilities of the social service library.
Special Libraries 7: 129.
----- M.  Reference work.  P L 18: 29.
Watson, C. D.  Law of Vermont relating to Free public libraries.
Vt C Bull 5, No 3: 1-3.
Watson, D. M. B.  Stationery department publications and public
libraries.  L A R 3: 332-3.
Watson, F.  Curriculum and text-books of English schools in
the first half of the 17th century.  Bib Soc Trans 6: 161-
267.
Watson, M. G.  What the traveling library has done for Elmer.
N C Bull 1: 149.
Watson, P. B.  Bibliography of the pre-Columbian discovery of
America.  L J 6: 227-44.
Watson, S. M.  Size of newspapers.  L J 12: 116.
---- S. M.  Yearly indexes to magazines.  L J 12: 116.
Watson, Mrs. W.  Library work of the Vermont state federation
of women's clubs.  Vt L Bull 7, No 2: 4-5.
Watson, W. R.  Certification of librarians and standardization
of libraries.  A L A Bull 12: 367-8.
---- W. R.  County library legislation -- Montana.  A L A
Bull 8: 346.
---- W. R.  Library interests of a state.  A L A Bull 1:
Conf No 196-200.
---- W. R.  The New York state certification system.  L J
44: 482.
---- W. R.  Promoting the use of good books.  N Y L 4: 69-
72.
Watterson, H. M.  The library and history teaching.  P L 18:
136-8.
Watts, F. A.  Books for commonplace people.  Penn Lib Notes
July 1912: 6-10.
Watts, M. O.  Shakespeare society of Wellesley College.  Wis
Lib Bull 12: 106-7.

Way, S. J.   Presidential address.   L A of Austral Proc 1901:
VII-XII.

Waybur, J. R.   List of music for libraries.   Cal News Notes
15: 316-27.

Wayne, M. A.   Children's week at the library, Anderson, Indiana.
Lib Occ 4: 122.

Wead, K. H.   What the children of to-day are reading.   Smith
Alumnae Q Oct 1914;   New Hamp Bull (ns) 11: 105-8;   Vt L
Bull 11: 10-3;   Wis Lib Bull 11: 42-4.

Weale, W. H.   Early printing at Bruges.   Bib Soc Trans 4: 203-
12.

Weale, W. H. J.   Classification and cataloguing photographs of
paintings.   L (ns) 1: 365-72.

--- W. H. J.   History and cataloguing of the National art
library.   2d Int Conf 97-8, 1897.

--- W. H. J.   Newly discovered "Missale speciale."   L (ns)
1: 62-6.

--- W. H. J.   Subject classification of books on architecture.   L (ns) 1: 368-72.

--- W. H. J.   Two notes for art libraries.   L (ns) 1: 365-
72.

Webb, A.   Checks for periodicals.   L W 10: 320.

-- A.   Display of periodicals.   L W 10: 318-20.

-- A.   Modified Kennedy indicator.   L W 11: 281-4, 364.

-- A.   Newsroom methods.   L W 10: 317-20.

-- A.   Prints in public libraries.   Libn 3: 402, 443-7;   L
A R 15: 295.

-- A.   Problem of the junior assistant.   L A 10: 236-7.

-- A.   Some early dates in colonial printing.   L W 16: 236-
41, 272-8.

-- A. and R. E. Smith.   Is a printed catalogue necessary in
an open access library.   Libn 3: 270-4.

Webb, M. A.   Exhibits in children's room.   Fort Wayne (Ind.)
public library.   Lib Occ 2: 191-2.

-- M. A.   Shall we have a story hour?   Lib Occ 3: 26-8.

Webb, S.   Function of the public library in respect to political
science, with some particulars of the British library of
political science.   L 9: 230-8.

-- S.   How to improve the library service.   L A 4: 178-1.

-- S.   Library service of London: its co-ordination, development and education.   L A R 4: 193-203;   Discussion:
231-6.

-- S.   On the subject of librarianship.   L A R 9: 208-15.

Webb, W.   New York state publications of interest to libraries.
N Y L 5: 201-3, 237-9.

Webster, C.   Library extension in New York state.   N Y L 3:
63-4.

----- C. The organization of hospital library service. A
L A Bull 12: 231-3;  L J 43: 563-5.

----- C. Two inspiring chapters in recent library history
of New York. N Y L 4: 209-11.

----- C. Ways of increasing local interest in the village
library. N Y L 2: 166-8.

Webster, C. E.  What the district superintendent can do for
the school library.  New York Teachers' Assn Proceedings
1912: 138-40.

Webster, C. F.  Is hospital library work worth while?  L J
45: 167-8.

----- C. F.  Library work with foreigners.  A L A Proceedings, 1915: 192-5.

----- C. F.  Local history story hour N Y L 3: 178-80.

Wedenkampf, F.  A cataloging short-cut.  L J 43: 760-1.

Wedin, J.  Co-operation between public libraries and the traveling library and department.  Wis Lib Bull 15: 22.

--- J.  Problems of the rural reader.  Wis Lib Bull 13:
263-5.

Weeks, M. H.  Stories and story telling.  Child Welfare Magazine 5: 111-4.

--- M. H.  Stories and story telling for children.  National
Congress of Mothers.  Report of Proceedings, 1898: 87-90.

Weeks, R.  The "Chancun de Willame," a French MS. preserved
in England.  L (ns) 6: 113-36.

Weeks, S. B.  Select bibliography of North Carolina, for schools,
libraries and amateurs.  N C Bull 2: 11-6.

Weil, M. F.  School duplicate collection in the Madison free
library.  Wis Lib Bull 6: 136-8.

Weisse, H. V.  Reading for the young.  Contemporary Review 79:
829-38.

Weissenborn, L.  What an assistant expects of a librarian.
P L 21: 73-5.

Weitenkampf, F.  Accession book - why?  L J 28: 296-7, Discussion 251.

--------- F.  Art in the college library.  A L A Bull 7:
315-9.

--------- F.  Art in the school.  L J 40: 650-1.

--------- F.  Caricatures:  their use in the library.  L J
28: 112-3.

--------- F.  Cataloging of prints.  L J 32: 408-9.

--------- F.  Eighth conference of German librarians.  L J
32: 445-6.

--------- F.  Extraordinary art library in Paris (Bibliotheque Doucet).  L J 40: 337-8.

--------- F.  Illustrated books of four centuries.  L J
44: 383-4.

--------- F.  Institut international de bibliographie.  L J
33: 403-4.

--------- F.  Library and the graphic arts.  L J 41: 479-81.

--------- F.  The museum and the small library.  Art and Progress 4: 1069-72.

--------- F.  Need of a scientific bibliography of incunabula. L J 33: 358.

--------- F.  Ninth meeting of German librarians.  L J 33: 446-7.

--------- F.  Note on the artistic side of picture bulletins. L J 33: 183.

--------- F.  Notes on the cataloguing of prints.  L J 32: 408-9.

--------- F.  The print collection of the New York Public Library.  Print collector's Quarterly 1: 437-63.

--------- F.  Print made useful.  L J 30: 920-1.

--------- F.  The problem of the applied and decorative arts. The Museum May 1917: 10-2;  L J 42: 564.

--------- F.  The Royal library, Berlin.  L J 34: 552.

--------- F.  Special collections in American libraries -- The S. P. Avery collection of prints and art books.  L J 29: 117-9.

--------- F.  What is an illustrated book?  P L 25: 362-4.

Welch, B. J.  Inspiring a love of literature.  School Journal 78: 462-3.

Welch, C.  Bibliography of the livery companies of London.  L 2: 301-7.

--- C.  Brief outline of the life of Sir Thomas More, showing the periods at which the different works were written. Bib Soc Trans 5: 178-80.

--- C.  Children's reading at home.  L J 27: 196-7.

--- C.  The city printers.  Bib Soc Trans 1915-17: 175-241.

--- C.  Classification of municipal literature.  L J 20: 279.

--- C.  Economical suggestions in the preparation of printed catalogues.  L J 4: 439-41.

--- C.  Guildhall library and its work.  L 1: 320-34.

--- C.  Guildhall library and museum.  L (ns) 4: 68-84.

--- C.  Notes on London municipal literature.  Bib Soc Trans 2: 48-80.

--- C.  Public library movement in London: a review of its progress and suggestions for its consolidation and extension. L 7: 97-109.

--- C.  Scheme of classification for London literature.  Bib Soc Trans 2: 50-1.

--- C.  Training of librarians.  2nd Int Conf: 31-3.

--- C.  Young librarian:  his training and possibilities. L A 3: 19-23.

Welden, A. P.  Books and libraries (extracts from an address). L J 18: 512-3.

Welles, J. Apprentice class in a large library. A L A Bull
4: 780-3.
---- J. Dating outfit and its functions. Wis Lib Bull 13:
293-5.
---- J. A flexible book collection. A L A Bull 11: 239-41,
355.
---- J. Secondary education in library work. A L A Bull
11: 148-53; P L 23: 5-10.
---- J. Twentieth century lending methods. Wis Lib Bull
16: 42-3, 45-51.
---- J. We buy more rent books. Wis Lib Bull 16: 208-10.
---- J. What do the people want? A L A Bull 6: 132-3.
Wellman, E. C. The library's obligation. P L 20: 285-9.
Wellman, H. C. Advertising the library. Mass L C Bull July
1912: 94-9.
----- H. C. American libraries. Wis Lib Bull 12: 426-36.
----- H. C. Branches and deliveries. L J 23: Conf No 8-12.
----- H. C. Improving the quality of the circulation. N
Y L 1: 161-2.
----- H. C. Library and industrial workers. P L 13: 83-4.
----- H. C. Library as an investment. P L 16: 277-80.
----- H. C. Library should be known. P L 13: 83-4.
----- H. C. The library's obligation. P L 20: 285-9.
----- H. C. The library's primary duty. A L A Bull 9: 89-
93; L J 40: 467-71.
----- H. C. Practical economics of publicity. L J 33: 240.
----- H. C. Presidential address, A. L. A. Conference. L
J 40:  467-71.
----- H. C. Prime function of the public library. N Y L
4: 236-9.
----- H. C. Reference work with children. L A R 3: 400-7.
----- H. C. Some points in library ethics. L J 40: 116,
Discussion 116-9.
----- H. C. What the city Library is doing to help win the
war. A L A Bull 12: 57-60.
----- H. C. What the libraries are doing for children. At-
lantic Monthly 90: 402-9.
----- H. C., W. R. Eastman, and C. Marvin. Report of the
committee of library administration. L J 27: Conf No 86-91;
L J 29: Conf No 163-7;  L J 30: Conf No 102-6.
Wellman, H. O. Roof reading rooms in the branches of New York
Public Library. L J 35: 259-60.
Wells, C. Writers of juvenile fiction. Bookman (N Y) 14: 348-
55.
Wells, G. F. Select bibliography of the country church. N Y
L 3: 107-10.
Wells, H. G. Public libraries and serious reading. L J 28:
768-9.

Wells, H. W.  The U. S. Boys' working reserve.  A L A Bull 12: 198-9, 297.

Wells, J.  Teaching of English in schools.  Educational Review 6: 277-87.

Wells, K. G.  Responsibility of parents in the selection of reading for the young.  L J 4: 325-30.

Wells, M. E.  American international corporation library.  Special Libraries 11: 132-4.

Welsh, C.  Children's books that have lived.  L (ns) 1: 314-23.

--- C.  Early history of children's books in New England. New England Magazine (3rd series) 20: 147-60.

--- C.  Evaluation of children's books from the point of view of the history of literature for children.  L J 27: Conf No 76-9.

--- C.  Fairy tales and the trained imagination.  Dial 56: 412-3.

Welsh, R. G.  Modern drama as an expression of democracy.  A L A Bull 10: 143-9, 382.

Wendell, C.  Typewriter for card catalogues.  L J 27: 268-9.

Wendell, F. C. H.  Stranger within our gates: what can the library do for him.  P L 16: 89-92, 121.

Wenley, R. M.  Pleasures of reading.  P L 16: 321-3.

Wentland, Mrs. W. H.  County library: extracts from a talk given in South Texas.  Texas Libraries 2: 106-8.

Wenzel, F.  Music in the small communities.  Cal News Notes 15: 153-9.

Wert, W.  Utilization of the school plant.  P L 17: 78-9.

Wesivell, L. O.  School libraries in New York state.  N Y L 2: 192-6.

West, C. J.  Chemical warfare.  Special Libraries 10: 225-6.

-- C. J. and Greenman, E. D.  A reading list on industrial research.  Special Libraries 11: 19-28.

West, E. H.  What has the library worker to do each day?  Texas Libraries Ap 1 1916: 27-30.

West, J. L.  Princeton university library.  Harper's Weekly, June 1897, 41: 591-2.

West, K.  Aids in teaching Irving's "Sketchbook."  Wilson Bull 1: 483.

West, T.  Milwaukee library-museum building.  L J 21: 177-81.

West, T. H.  Improper books: methods employed to discover and exclude them.  L J 20: Conf No 32.

-- T. H.  Report on library architecture.  L J 19: Conf No 96-100.

-- T. H.  Usefulness of libraries in small towns.  L J 8: 237.

Westerfield, W.  Library for the blind.  L J 10: 399.

Weston, J. L.  Perceval legend in literature.  L (ns) 5: 59-90.

Westwood.  The juvenile defaulter.  Libn 5: 289.

Westwood, Prof.  Insect pests.  British Assn Transactions 1879: 371-2.

Whale, G.  Public library legislation.  L 2: 454-7.

Wharey, J. B.  Modern teaching and the library.  L J 32: 153-6.

Wharton, L. C.  Bibliography of Byzantine studies.  L A R 16: 324-6.

----- L. C.  Imprints in modern books.  L A R 10: 91-102, Discussion 126-7.

----- L. C.  An interesting relic of the Slavonic press at Fiol at Cracow.  L W 17: 117-8.

----- L. C.  The Jagellon library at Cracow.  L W 17: 165-6.

----- L. C.  Miscellaneous notes on Slavonic bibliography. L W 17: 323-6, 385-62;  18: 9-12.

----- L. C.  The next international congress.  L A R 13: 86-8.

----- L. C.  Some forms used in the Reading Room of the British Museum.  L A R 12: 396-403.

----- L. C.  Terminology.  L A R 15: 360-5;  16: 345, 441, 495, 550.

----- L. C.  Union catalog of Slavonic books in the metropolitan area.  L A R 20: 117-20.

Wharton, M. B.  The apprentice class in the small library.  Ia L C Q 7: 9-11.

----- M. B.  Binding in a small library, Ia L C Q 7: 133-6.

What, J. A.  What can the League of library commissions do for its members?  A L A Bull 13: 291-2.

Wheat, H. C. and F. W. Wilcox.  Modern methods of indirect lighting.  Libn 3: 300-3, 348-51, 407-10.

Wheatley, B. R.  Classification for college libraries.  1st Conf of Libns 128.

------ B. R.  Desultory thoughts on the arrangement of a private library.  L J 3: 211-6.

------ B. R.  Hints on library management.  L J 2: 210-6.

------ B. R.  Index society and its field.  L J 3:105-7, 154-5.

------ B. R.  On an "Evitandum" in index making principally met with in French and German scientific literature.  1st Int Conf 88-92;  L J 2: 178-85.

------ B. R.  On the question of authorship in "Academical Dissertations."  L A Trans 4: 37-42.

------ B. R.  Specimens of forms and account books used in the circulation of books.  1st Int Conf 195-8.

------ B. R.  Thoughts on the cataloguing of journals and transactions.  L A Trans 5: 190-6.

------ B. R.  Thoughts on title-taking, trite, trivial, or tentative.  L A M N 1: 25-32;  L J 5: 133-8.

Wheatley, H. B.  Bibliography of Chaucer.  Bib Soc Trans 2: 11-3.

------ H. B.  British Museum revised rules for cataloguing: a criticism.  L (ns) 1: 215, 263-73.

------ H. B.  Dr. Johnson as a bibliographer.  Bib Soc Trans 8: 39-61.

------ H. B.   Dryden's publishers.  Bib Soc Trans 11: 17-38.
------ H. B.   English illustrated books, 1480-1900.  Bib
Soc Trans 6: 155-8.
------ H. B.   Entry of anonymous books.  L J 7: 63-4.
------ H. B.   How to catalogue a library.  Reviewed in L J
15: 72-4.
------ H. B.   Leather for bookbinding.  L (ns) 2: 311-20.
------ H. B.   On the alphabetical arrangement of the titles
of anonymous books.  1st Int Conf 97-9, 159, 1878;  L J 2:
186-7, Discussion 263-4.
------ H. B.   Place of folk-lore in a classification.  L J
9: 188-9.
------ H. B.   Portraits in books.  Bib Soc Trans 4: 129-36.
------ H. B.   Post-Reformation quartos of Shakespeare's
plays.  L (3d series) 4: 237-69.
------ H. B.   Present condition of English bibliography, and
suggestions for the future.  Bib Soc Trans 1: 61-90;  L J
19: 336-8.
------ H. B.   Proposed subject index to bibliologies and
bibliographies.  L A M N 1: 89-95.
------ H. B.   Seventy years of cataloguing.  Bib Soc Trans
12: 25-37.
------ H. B.   Shakespeare as a man of letters.  Bib Soc Trans
1915-17: 109-32.
------ H. B.   Shakespeare's editors, 1623 to the twentieth
century.  Bib Soc Trans 1915-17: 145-73.
------ H. B.   Signs of booksellers in St. Paul's churchyard.
Bib Soc Trans 9: 67-106.
------ H. B., and E. C. Thomas.  Proposed subject index to
bibliologies and bibliographies.  L A M N 1: 89-95.
Wheatley, L. A.  Assyrian libraries.  L A U K Trans 3: 87-90.
Wheaton, H. H.  An Americanization program for libraries.  A
L A Bull 10: 265.
----- H. H.   Libraries and the "America First" campaign.
L J 42: 21-2.
Wheeler, C. T.  Collections of poetry for children.  N Y L 1:
141-2.
Wheeler, H. F. B.  Library of Mr. W. B. Slater.  Bibliophile
3: 228-37.
----- H. F. B.   Mr. G. A. Aitken's library.  Bibliophile
3: 282-5.
Wheeler, H. J.  Why a county law for Missouri.  L J 43: 472-3.
Wheeler, H. L.  Statistical department of the Boston· public
library and what it offers the business and professional
man.  Special Libraries 2: 3-4.
Wheeler, J. L.  Binding specifications for schools.  L J 42:
35;  P L 22: 13.
----- J. L.   Co-operative book-buying.  A L A Bull 13: 357,
61.

----- J. L.  Co-operative library lists.  L J 36: 24;  P L
18: 428-9.
----- J. L.  The county library.  L J 42: 83-9.
----- J. L.  The county library:  California and Ohio.  Ohio
Lib Bull 12: 3-4.
----- J. L.  Home reading with school credit.  L J 45: 679-
82.
----- J. L.  Industrial libraries.  Special Libraries 2:
10-2.
----- J. L.  The larger publicity of the library.  A L A Bull
10: 175-80, 385.
----- J. L.  The library and the business man.  L J 45: 13-
8, 19-24, 57-62.
----- J. L.  The library situation in Ohio.  L J 45: 877-
82.
----- J. L.  Los Angeles public library new quarters.  L J
39: 823-7.
----- J. L.  Suggestions for a library exhibit at San Fran-
cisco.  Bindery Talk Nov-Dec 1913: 4-5.
----- J. L.  Trades index.  Special Libraries 2: 93.
----- J. L.  Useful arts department of the Washington public
library.  Special Libraries 1: 33-6.
Wheeler, M. T.  Advance titles of "Best books."  N Y L 3: 105-6,
141-2.
----- M. T.  Aids to selection of books for children.  N Y
S L Rept 85: 139-43.
----- M. T.  Most excellent "Blood and Thunder."  N Y L 3:
311-2.
----- M. T.  New editions of standard books for children.
N Y L 3: 140-1.
----- M. T.  Reading for invalids.  N Y L 1: 203-6.
----- M. T.  Recent books relating to the state of New York.
N Y L 2: 157-63.
----- M. T.  Sunday school library.  Library Notes (U S) 3:
391-401.
----- M. T. and E. L. Bascom.  Indexing, principles, rules
and examples.  N Y S L Rept 88: Bull No 94, 1904.
Wheelock, J. H.  The librarian and the book-store.  P L 17: 7-9.
Wheelock, M. E.  Attractive picture books for children.  Ia L
C Q 5: 194-5.
------ M. E.  Bookbinding problem P L 25: 309-10.
Wheelwright, W. B.  Strength factors in papers as related to
binding.  Printing Art Jan 1913: 352-6.
Whelpley, A. W.  Common novels in public libraries.  L J 19:
Conf No 21-2.
------ A. W.  Supplying of current daily newspapers in free
reading rooms.  L J 19: Conf No 42-4.
Whipple, A. H.  The place of the public library in our system
of education.  L A R 21: 387-92.

Whitaker, A. E.   College library in education.  P L 2: 347-9.
Whitaker, J. V.   On the use of the printing press in libraries.
    L J 4: 114-7.
Whitbeck, Mrs. A.   Work with children in a county free library
    system.  Cal News Notes 6: 432.
Whitbeck, A. G.   Book-lists and bulletins in the children's
    room.  L J 31: 316-7.
    ------ A. G.   Business methods in the library.  New Hamp Bull
    (ns) 12: 160-3.
    ------ A. G.   Reading of older boys and girls.  A L A Bull
    9: 185-9;  P L 20: 343-8;  N C Bull 2: 120-5.
Whitcomb, A. F.   Children's book week in Chicago.  P L 24: 420.
Whitcomb, A. L.   One syllable versions of the classics.  Ia L
    C Q 6: 140-1.
Whitcomb, J. W.   Prairie sod house and the Kansas traveling lib-
    rary.  Craftsman 26: 452-4.
White, A. D.   My favorite books.  N J Lib Bull 5, No 1: 9-12.
    --- A. D.   "Safety-first" literature for libraries.  P L
    21: 211-3.
White, B.   What the neighbors did.  Country Life 23: 64-6.
White, C. H.   Literature of agriculture.  L J 35: 359-62.
White, E.   County and township libraries.  New Jersey Lib Bull
    2: 17-20.
    --- E.   High school library as a branch of the public lib-
    rary.  Mass Lib Club Bull 6: 49-50;  L J 41: 524-6.
    --- E.   Reaching the parents thru the children: an experi-
    ment in publicity.  L J 42: 522-3;  Vt L Bull 13: 16-8.
White, E. H.   Library instruction in a high school.  N J Lib
    Bull 5, No 1: 13-6.
White, F. M.   Men who made the Astor library.  Harper's Weekly
    55: 23, May 27, 1911.
White, G.   At the sign of the Dial:  Mr. Ricketts as a book
    builder.  Magazine of Art 20: 304.
White, G. F.   Catalog game played in the young people's room.
    L J 31: 815.
    --- G. F.   Library children.  New Hamp Bull 11: 103-5;  P L
    20: 9-11.
White, H.   On the value of home libraries.  L J 24: Conf No
    27-9.
    --- H.   On the value of prison libraries.  L J 24: Conf No
    27-9.
White, J. D.   An account of Marsh's library.  L A R 1: 132-45.
White, M. O.   Democracy in modern fiction.  A L A Bull 10: 126-
    36, 381.
White, N. J. D.   Treasures in Marsh's library.  Irish Book Lover
    Feb 1915: 108-10.
White, P.   Child in the library.  An Leab 1: 100-8.
White, W. F.   New Paltz system of treating pamphlets and art
    materials - illustrated by specimen card catalogue entries.
    P L 8: 301-6.

Whiteford, R. N.   Fate of English literature in secondary schools
    Dial 38: 35-7.
Whiteman, E.   Story telling bibliographies.   N J Lib Bull 2, No
    1: 3-5.
Whitham, R. A.   American college girls' ignorance of literature:
    a second point of view.   Journal of Pedagogy 19: 13-25.
Whiting, L.   As we are seen.   Libn 2: 155-6.
Whitley, C. F.   The Aberdeen association.   P L 9: 204-5.
Whitmore, F. H.   Delivery desk suggestions.   P L 18: 68.
    ------ F. H.   Reading list on ethics.   Bulletin No 93, Bib-
    liography No 38, N Y S L Rept 88.
Whitmore, J. H.   The need of a library interpreter.   P L 21:
    16-7;   Am Lib Annual 1916-17: 65.
Whitmore, T. H.   Methods of bookbuying.   L J 31: 16-7.
Whitney, A. W.   What does safety mean?   Special Libraries 10:
    221-2.
Whitney, H. M.   Public library and its critics.   Conn P L C
    1: 3-12.
Whitney, J.   Selecting and training library assistants.   L J
    7: 136-9.
Whitney, J. L.   Accents used in French books.   L J 14: 259-61.
    ----- J. L.   Catalogue of the illustrations and plans of
    library buildings in the Boston public library.   L J 11:
    409-17;   13: 291-5.
    ----- J. L.   Catalogues of town libraries.   L J 4: 268-75.
    ----- J. L.   Considerations as to a printed catalogue in
    book form for the Boston public library.   L J 24: Conf No
    8-13.
    ----- J. L.   Cost of catalogues.   L J 10: 214-5, Discussion
    322-5.
    ----- J. L.   Estimate of the comparative cost of setting
    catalogue matter.   L J 4: 268.
    ----- J. L.   Incidents in the history of the Boston public
    library.   L J 27: Conf No 16-24.
    ----- J. L.   A modern Proteus.   L J 8: 172-93, Discussion
    265-8.
    ----- J. L.   Pseudonyms and anonyms.   L J 1: 375-6.
Whittaker, J. V.   On the use of the printing press in libraries.
    L J 4: 114-7.
Whitten, R. H.   Classification of the library of the (New York
    state) Public service commission for the first district.
    L J 33: 362-3.
    ----- R. H.   Development of special libraries.   L J 34:
    546-7.
    ----- R. H.   Digest of governors' messages of the United
    States, 1905.   N Y S L Rept 88 vol 2, Bulletin No 101, Leg-
    islation No 27.
    ------ R. H.   Index to legislation, 1905.   Bulletin No 103,
    Legislation 28, N Y S L Rept 88, vol 2.   1905.

----- R. H.  Legislation reference list, 1906.  Bulletin No
111, Legislation 30, N Y S L Rept 89, vol 2.

----- R. H.  The library of the New York Public service commission.  Special Libraries 1: 18-20.

----- R. H.  List of references on street railway service.
Special Libraries 2: 61-3.

----- R. H.  Proposed library of municipal affairs and city
department libraries.  L J 33: 224-6.

----- R. H.  Review of legislation, 1906.  Bulletin No 113,
Legislation 33, N Y S L Rept 89, vol 2, 243p.

----- R. H.  Special libraries.  L J 31: 12-4.

----- R. H.  Taxation of corporations in New York, Massachusetts, Pennsylvania and New Jersey.  N Y S L Rept 84, Appen-
dix 2.  1901.

----- R. H.  Two decades of comparative legislation.  A L A
Bull 3: 296-301.

Whittlesey, W. L.  Notes on some books on American history and
politics.  P L 15: 112-4.

Whitton, M. O.  Craft of bookbinding as practiced in America.
Touchstone 3: 367-8.

Whitwell, C.  Musee Plantin:  Moretus (Home of Christopher
Plantin).  L A 5: 102-4.

Whyte, F. H.  Routine of work in the small library.  Wis Lib
Bull 15: 126-30.

Wickens, W. C.  The child, the book and the public library.
L A R 15: 247-8;  Libn 3: 394-5.

Wickersham, W. B.  Brief sketch of some of the libraries of
Chicago.  L J 20: 274-9.

Widdemer, M.  Bibliography of books and articles relating to,
children's reading.  Bull Bib 6: 240-3, 270-3, 301-3;  7:
9-12.

Wiener, L.  The transliteration of Russian.  L J 23: Conf No
174.

Wigginton, M. W.  Accession methods in cataloging economies:
meeting the demands of war service cataloging.  A L A Bull
12: 245-7, 300.

------- M. W.  A new music index.  L J 41: 323-5.

------- M. W.  Scheme of classification for military science.
L J 43: 264-5.

------- M. W.  Short-cuts.  A L A Bull 14: 162-3, 328.

Wightman, L. I.  Preparation of selling literature.  Printing
Art 16: 104-8.

Wilbur, E. M.  A scheme of classification for a theological
library.  Special Libraries 8: 74-8;  L J 42: 675-7.

Wilbur, M. G.  Index to reference lists published by libraries.
Wash L A Bull 2, No 1: 16.

Wilbur, W. A.  Lyric influences in the poets' corner of the
Library of Congress.  P L 14: 230-2.

Wilcox, A. R.  A mistaken judgment.  P L 22: 366-7.
Wilcox, F. W. and Wheat, H. C.  Modern methods of indirect
    lighting.  Libn 3: 300-3, 348-51, 407-10.
Wilcox, M. E.  Use of the immigrants guide in the library.
    Mass Lib Club Bull 4: 69-73.
Wilder, E.  Popularizing a library.  P L 11: 114-7.
Wiley, E.  Eighteenth century presses in Tennessee.  Bib Soc
    Amer Proc 3: 70-83.
    --- E.  The scope of the U. S. Naval war college library
    at Newport, R. I.  Special Libraries 9: 37-8; L J 43: 409-
    10.
    --- E.  Some sidelights on classification.  L J 44: 288-93,
    359-64.
    --- E.  The story of "The House that Jack built".  L J 43:
    750-1.
Wiley, S. L.  Show window exhibits.  Minn P L C N 4: 216.
Wilkinson, J. N.  Duty of the normal school in relation to dis-
    trict school libraries.  Nat Educ Assn 1904: 919-23.
    ------- J. N.  Librarian as a teacher.  Journal of Education
    (Boston) 66: 121-2; School Journal 75: 115;  Nat Educ Assn
    1907: 972-4.
Wilkinson, M.  Establishing libraries under difficulties.  A L
    A Bull 10: 161-9, 384.
    ------- M.  The St. Louis playground wagon.  L J 41: 653-4.
Wilkinson, M. S.  The children's year in library service.  Minn
    P L C N 5: 184-6.
    ------- M. S. and Frantz, C.  Shall there be a story hour in
    the small library?  P L 17: 122-3.
Willard, A. R.  College libraries in the United States.  New
    England Magazine 23: 422-40.
Willard, J. F.  Public archives of Colorado.  Am Hist Assn Rept
    1911, 1: 365-92.
Willard, W. B.  Picture books:  good and bad.  P L 11: 562.
Willard, W. D.  Training of the trustee.  Minn P L C N 9: 13-4.
Willcock, W. J.  Are children's reading rooms necessary?  L A
    R 9: 184-5.
    ------ W. J.  Classed catalogues and their indexes.  L W
    3: 261-2.
    ------ W. J.  Disposal of worn-out books.  L W 4: 91-3.
    ------ W. J.  How the rate limit affects public libraries
    of the smaller towns.  L A R 10: 153-61.  Discussion 194-5.
    ------ W. J.  Is the printed catalogue doomed?  L A R 9:
    384-9, Discussion 400-6.
    ------ W. J.  Ladies' reading rooms, L A R 15: 80-4.
    ------ W. J.  Library lectures:  a retrospect and a sugges-
    tion.  L A R 4: 394-400.
    ------ W. J.  Notification of infectious disease and the
    public library.  L W 2: 89-91.
    ------ W. J.  Proportionate representation of literature
    in libraries.  L A R 6: 336-44.

------ W. J.  Recording, replacing and disposal of worn-out
books.  L W 4: 91-3.

------ W. J.  What should an annual report contain?  L A R
8: 363-71, Discussion 392-7.

Willcocks, M. P.  Analytical library catalogue.  L A R 13: 91-7.

Wilcox, E. S.  Open shelves and the loss of books.  A L A Bull
2: 249-53, Discussion 253-4;  P L 13: 244-6, 262-3.

---- E. S.  Open shelves for large libraries.  L J 25: 113-5;
P L 5: 150-6.

---- E. S.  Proposed amendment of Illinois state library
law.  P L 13: 306.

Willcox, E. S.  Two-book system again.  P L 3: 44.

Willett, G. W.  The reading interests of high school pupils.
English Journal 8: 474-87.

Williams.  Reference work.  P L 19: 117-8.

Williams, B.  Reconstructing the community.  Wis Lib Bull 15:
42-3.

Williams, C.  Thomas Love Peacock.  L (ns) 7: 397-422.

Williams, C. H.  Publicity work for the county agent.  A L A
Bull 8: 362-7.

Williams, F. W.  Cataloguing women's names.  L J 13: 364.

------ F. W.  Gladstone's library.  L J 12: 116-20.

Williams, H.  College libraries in the United States:  contribution toward a bibliography.  N Y S L Rept 83, Bibliog No
19: 609-55.

Williams, H. H.  A brief course of reading from Chaucer to the
year 1780.  L A 8: 174-6.

Williams, H. R.  Branch libraries for rural schools.  Journal
of Education 69: 10-2.

Williams, J. B.  The earliest English Corantos.  L (3d series)
4: 437-40.

------ J. B.  Henry Cross-Grove, Jacobite journalist and
printer.  L (3d series) 5: 206-19.

Williams, L. A.  Cataloguing - a word to beginners.  L J 12:
121-3.

Williams, M.  Meeting called to consider special training for
school librarians, by the officers of the School library
section of the A. L. A.  L J 45: 695-6;  P L 25: 415-6.

Williams, M. C.  How can the town library serve the country
community?  Southern Educational Assn Proceedings 1914:
339-42.

Williams, M. F.  Reading for children's librarians.  N Y S L
Bulletin 62, Bibliography 27:  N Y S L Rept 1901: 750-69.

------ M. F.  Suggestions for library architecture.  P L
6: 385-7.

------ M. F. and B. M. Brown.  Furnishing of children's
libraries.  Ia L C Q 1: 21.

------ M. F. and B. M. Brown.  Reading list for children's
librarians.  Bibliography No 27, N Y S L Rept 84, 1901.

Williams, M. S.  Library work of the Bureau of Education.  L J
12: 64-8.
Williams, N.  Commission publicity.  A L A Bull 14: 343.
Williams, O.  Boy scouts and the library.  Lib Occ 3: 21-3.
------  O.  Pictures for an exhibit.  Lib Occ 3: 62-3.
Williams, R. G.  A graded course of reading divided into three
parts;  elementary, advanced and works of reference;  with
notes on each book dealing with the French revolution, 1789-
1795.  Libn 5: 126-8, 158-60, 190-3.
------  R. G.  A graded course of reading divided into three
parts:  elementary, advanced and works of reference with
notes on each book, dealing with the great Civil war.  Libn
5: 2-5, 45-8, 77-80.
------  R. G.  Principles of book selection.  Libn 9: 112-5,
131-2.
------  R. G.  Some notes on the Library association examination:  Bibliography.  Libn 7: 84-7, 102-6, 125-9;  64-6,
182-5;  8: 4-6, 23-6, 44-6, 62-5, 81-5, 103-8, 173, 193,
206-10.
------  R. G.  Some principles of book selection.  L A 13:
133-6, 140-4.
Williams, S.  High school library problems.  N Y L 4: 174-8,
192.
------  S.  In regard to reading.  P L 4: 57.
------  S.  Reading lists for public schools.  Nat Educ Assn
1898: 1022-8.
------  S.  Reading lists (graded).  U S Rept 666-8.  1899-
1900.
------  S.  Relation of public libraries to public schools.
Nat Educ Assn 1899: 270-6;  U S Bur of Educ Rept 1899-1900:
665-6.
------  S.  School and public libraries:  their part in public
education.  Minn P L C N 6: 142.
------  S.  School libraries.  New York State Teachers' Assn
Proceedings 1912: 216-20;  Univ of State of New York, Re-
gents' Report, 1900: 247-54.
Williams, S. J.  Building up a safety library.  Special Lib-
raries 10: 210-2.
------  S. J.  Fire protection in libraries.  Wis Lib Bull
12: 343-6, 391-3.
------  S. J.  Proposed fire prevention and protection code.
A L A Bull 11: 310-2.
Williams, S. R.  The libraries of Paddy's Run.  Ohio Archaeol-
ogical and Historical Q Oct 1912: 462-5.
Williams, T.  Address at the opening of the library.  L J 16:
108-12.
------  T.  Libraries and a public press.  L J 38: 227-8.
------  T.  Newspaper exclusion.  L J 13: 288.
------  T.  Plans for the library building of the University
of Pennsylvania.  L J 13: 237-43.

Williams, T. W.  Mediaeval libraries:  with special reference
to Bristol and its neighbourhood.  L A R 5: 353-61, 389-99.
------ T. W.  Wells cathedral library.  L A R 8: 372-7.
Williams, W. and Firth, S. A.  Should public libraries come
under the control of educational authorities?  L A R 15:
105-6;  Libn 3: 279-80;  L W 15: 253-4.
Williamson, C. C.  Discusses municipal reference library.  A
L A Bull 10: 49.
-------- C. C.  Efficiency in library management.  L J 44:
67-77;  Lib Occ 5: 148-54.
-------- C. C.  Importance of special libraries to the public
library.  Special Libraries 4: 115-6.
-------- C. C.  Library service.  Wis. Lib Bull 16: 90-2.
-------- C. C.  A look ahead for the small library.  A L A
Bull 13: 141-6;  Ia L C Q 8: 164-9;  N Y L 6: 223-8;  Lib
Occ 5: 201-6;  Wis Lib Bull 15: 191-7.
-------- C. C.  Need of a plan for library development.  L
J 43: 649-55.
-------- C. C.  The public official and the special library.
Special Libraries 7: 112-9.
-------- C. C.  Some aspects of the work of the New York
municipal reference library.  L J 40: 714-5.
-------- C. C.  Some present-day aspects of library training.
A L A Bull 13: 120-6, 351, 404;  L J 44: 563-8.
Willis, J.  Hours of opening for a village library.  N Y L 7:
111.
---- J.  Organizing small libraries.  P L 25: 506.
---- J.  Twentieth century lending methods.  Wis Lib Bull
16: 46.
---- J.  Unifying for war.  Wis Lib Bull 14: 241-5.
Willmer, J. C.  The commercial library: its organization, ad-
ministration and service.  L A R 18: 98-108.
Wilson, A.  Work of the Edinboro normal school.  Penn Lib Notes
6, No 4: 77-80.
Wilson, B.  Parody on Hamlet's soliloquy addressed "To the cat-
aloguer."  Ia L C Q 5: 121.
Wilson, C. A.  Publishers' slips for librarians and others.
L J 1: 14-5.
Wilson, E. A.  Book selection.  Colorado Lib Assn Occasional
Leaflet 1: 31-5.
Wilson, E. B.  Books of travel (travel hour).  Ia L C Q 6:
59-60.
Wilson, E. D.  Relation of trustees and librarian.  P L 8:
402-4.
Wilson, G. G.  Bibliography of international law.  Bib Soc Amer
Proc 1: 227-8.
Wilson, H.  Classification for public libraries.  L A Trans
2: 79-84, 156;  L J 4: 415.
---- H.  French provincial library: Tours.  L A M N 2: 46-
50.

---- H. Remarks on facsimile reproduction. L A M N 1: 33-40.

Wilson, H. W. The Agricultural index. A L A Bull 10: 405-6.

---- H. W. Clearing houses. A L A Bull 3: 165-6.

---- H. W. Co-operatively printed catalog. Lib Work 2: 1-2, 143-7;  Bib Soc Amer Proc 3: 29-42.

---- H. W. Problems of printed indexes in special fields. Special Libraries 4: 148-51.

---- H. W. Subject indexes: a criticism on Mr. Hawkes' article on "Subject hunting." L W 10: 332-5.

Wilson, J. D. The copy for "Hamlet," 1603. L (3d series) 9: 153-85.

---- J. D. A date in the Marprelate controversy. L (ns) 8: 337-59.

---- J. D. Did Sir Roger Williams write the Marprelate tracts? A rejoinder. L (3d series) 4: 92-104.

---- J. D. Euphues and the prodigal son. L (ns) 10: 339-61.

---- J. D. The "Hamlet" transcript, 1593. L (3d series) 9: 217-47.

---- J. D. Martin Marprelate and Shakespeare's Fluellen: a new theory of the authorship of the Marprelate press. L (3d series) 3: 113-51, 241-76.

---- J. D. A new tract from the Marprelate press. L (ns) 10: 225-40.

---- J. D. Richard Shilders and the English puritans. Bib Soc Trans 11: 65-134.

---- J. D. and A. W. Pollard. What follows if some of the good quarto editions of Shakespeare's plays were printed from his autograph manuscripts. Bib Soc Trans 15: 136-9.

Wilson, J. M. Library of printed books in Worcester cathedral. L (3d s) 2: 1-33.

Wilson, L. L. Characteristics of books which instill patriotism. P L 23: 420-2.

Wilson, L. M. The library and the teaching profession. P L 15: 93-8.

Wilson, L. N. Classification for the European war collection, Clark University, Worcester, Mass. P L 21: 408-9;  Libn 7: 63-5.

---- L. N. Common sense in library matters. P L 14: 168-73.

---- L. N. Correlation of the library and other departments of colleges and universities. P L 12: 220-1.

---- L. N. A fiction library. P L 13: 411.

---- L. N. Instructing students in the use of the library. P L 18: 251-3.

---- L. N. Is the public library doing all it can for the teacher? P L 4: 329-31.

---- L. N. The library and the teaching profession. P L 15: 93-8.

---- L. N. Some new fields of library activity. P L 16: 183-8.

---- L. N.  War literature.  P L 20: 252, 303.

Wilson, L. R.  Can our school libraries render a larger service?  North Carolina Education 6: 3.

---- L. R.  A constructive library platform for southern schools.  L J 37: 179-85.

---- L. R.  County library:  an agency to promote general reading.  American City (T and C ed) 30: 340-2.

---- L. R.  A decade of progress.  N C Lib Bull 1: 123-5.

---- L. R.  The high school library.  North Carolina High School Bulletin 1: 176-83.

---- L. R.  Libraries for schools and rural communities.  Southern Educational Assn Proceedings 1911: 669-71.

---- L. R.  North Carolina libraries:  their improvement.  N C Lib Bull 1: 80-3.

---- L. R.  Organization and administration of the college library.  L J 36: 560-5.

---- L. R.  Public library as an educator.  L J 35: 6-10.

---- L. R.  Satisfactory method of arranging pamphlets.  P L 15: 278-9.

---- L. R.  Second-class postal rates on Commission bulletins.  P L 16: 289.

---- L. R.  A system of traveling libraries.  N C Bull 1: 144-6.

---- L. R.  University libraries of Virginia, Carolinas and Georgia.  A L A Bull 1: Conf No 266-70;  L J 34: 550-1.

Wilson, L. W.  Some new fields of library activity.  P L 16: 183-8.

Wilson, M.  Books for high schools.  U S Bureau of Education Bulletin 41.

---- M.  Library military auxiliary.  A L A Bull 11: 321-2.

---- M.  School libraries in Minnesota.  Minnesota Dept of Public Instruction, Report, 1911-12: 33-40.

---- M.  School library management.  P L 24: 395-6.

---- M.  The school library room.  School Education 35: 29-30.

Wilson, M. C.  Reading list on colonial New England.  N Y S L Rept 80 Bibliography No 2.  1898.

Wilson, M. M.  Annual state aid to libraries.  Vt L Bull 6 No 1: 2-3.

Wilson, M. V.  The movement for better rural school libraries.  L J 39: 677-9.

---- M. V.  Possibilities of the rural school library.  A L A Bull 7: 291-5.

---- M. V.  School libraries in Minnesota.  Minnesota Department of Public Instruction, Report 1911-12: 33-40.

Wilson, M. Z.  How the school and library may help each other.  Wash L A Bull 2, No 1: 7-8.

Wilson, P.  The writings of Sir James Ware and the forgeries of Robert Ware.  Bib Soc Trans 15: 83-94.

Wilson, R. E.  Functions of a branch library.  P L 8: 275-7.
Wilson, W.  Desirable extensions and reforms in educational
    work.  L A R 10: 531-2.
---- W.  Impressions of the Liverpool conference.  L W 15:
    66-9.
---- W.  A word to assistants.  L W 2: 331-2.
Wilson, W. D.  The small library from the bookman's point of
    view.  Pacific Northwest Library Assn Proceedings 1913: 65-7.
Winchell, F. M.  A message from the Commission.  New Hamp Bull
    14: 74-6.
Winchester, G. F.  Danforth library building.  L J 16: 306-9.
-------- G. F.  Some statistics of thirteen libraries and a
    suggestion for an A. L. A. Statistical handbook.  L J 38:
    556-8.
Windeyer, M.  China and the far east, 1889-99.  A contribution
    towards a bibliography.  Bulletin No 59, Bibliography No 25,
    N Y S L Rept 84, 1901.
------ M.  Libraries in New South Wales.  P L 9: 412-3.
Windrem, H. H.  All in the day's work.  P L 25: 246-9.
Windsor, Lord.  Presidential address.  L 7: 293-9.
Windsor, P. L.  The association of American library schools.
    A L A Bull 11: 160-2.
----- P. L.  College and university libraries in the South-
    west.  A L A Bull 1: Conf No 277-8.
----- P. L.  Inter-library loans in the Middle West.  L J
    37: 326-7.
----- P. L.  Library situation in Texas.  A L A Bull 1: 77-8.
----- P. L.  A new vertical file for maps.  L J 35: 509;
    P L 15: 388-9.
----- P. L.  Problems for the certification of librarians,
    with discussion at mid-winter meeting of the A. L. A. coun-
    cil in Chicago, Dec 28-29, 1916.  A L A Bull 11: 41;  L J
    42: 121;  P L 22: 70-1.
----- P. L.  Problems of the A. L. A. analytical cards.  L
    J 36: 70-1.
----- P. L. Relation of the state university library to the
    other libraries of the state.  A L A Bull 4: 765-7.
----- P. L.  Some American university libraries we should
    know.  Wis Lib Bull 12: 196-9.
----- P. L.  Standardization of libraries and certification
    of librarians.  A L A Bull 11: 135-40, 329;  L J 42: 121.
----- P. L.  State supervision in Texas.  L J 34: 175;  P L
    12: 181.
Winfield, J. M. T.  Brief account of the library of the Medical
    society of the County of Kings.  Med Lib and Hist Journal 1:
    27-32.
------ J. M. T.  Medical library as a factor in medical ed-
    ucation.  Med Lib and Hist Journal 2: 183-7.
------ J. M. T.  Presentation of the Library of the physi-
    cians to the German hospital and dispensary, New York, to

the library of the Medical society of the County of Kings.
Med Lib and Hist Journal 2: 46-8.

Winks, W. E.  An attempt to solve the school library problem.
L A R 2: 190-9.

Winkler, E. W.  Place of the library in the educational system
of Texas.  Southern Education Assn Proceedings 1911: 663-9.

----- E. W.  Reference work and periodicals.  Texas Libraries
2: 71-3.

Winser, B.  Acknowledgment of library reports and bulletins
abandoned at Newark.  L J 44: 346.

---- B.  A. L. A. catalog of 1904.  L J 27: 1012.

---- B.  A camp library is a "man's job."  P L 23: 267.

---- B.  Current aids to book selection.  P L 10: 263-7.

---- B.  Delivery department.  L J 31: Conf No 267.

---- B.  Encouragement of serious reading by public libraries.  L J 28: 237-8.

---- B.  Making maps available.  A L A Bull 10: 245-8, 407.

---- B.  The realtion of the catalog department to other
departments in the library.  A L A Bull 7: 268-70.

---- B.  Simplifying methods.  L J 31: Conf No 266-7.

Winship, A. E.  Pernicious literature:  Sunday school books.
L J 16: 46.

Winship, G. B.  A library tonic.  New York Public library Bull
21: 451-6 July 1917;  Am Lib Annual 1917-18: 56-7.

Winship, G. P.  Bibliography of Spanish press of California,
1833-1845.  L (4th series) 1: 51.

----- G. P.  Bibliotheca Americana of the John Carter Brown
library.  L (4th series) 1: 49-50.

----- G. P.  Census of fifteenth century books owned in
America.  Edited by a committee of the Bibliographical
society of America.  Bulletin of the New York Public Library.  Ap-Dec 1918 Nos 4-12.

----- G. P.  Collection of books relating to the stage in
the public library of city of Boston.  L (4th series) 1:
50-1.

----- G. P.  Instruction in the history of books.  Am Lib
Annual 1916-17: 23.

----- G. P.  Thackeray library: catalogue of the private
collection of Mr. H. S. Van Duzer.  L (4th series) 1: 47-8.

----- G. P.  University press in relation to the library
world.  A L A Bull 11: 241-2.

----- G. P.  Widener collection of the John Carter Brown
library.  L (4th series) 1: 48-9.

Winslow, A.  Reading list for prospective librarians.  L J
45: 931-3.

Winslow, E. H.  Selection and purchase of juvenile books.  Vt
L Bull 8, No 1: 2-4.

Winslow, J. B.  The gospel of social service.  Wis Lib Bull
8: 119-26.

Winslow, M. E.  A children's librarian.  Vt L Bull 15: 23.

Winslow, W. C.  Library of Vermont university.  University Quar-
  terly, July 1861, 4: 30-48.
Winsor, J.  Address at the opening of the Orrington Lunt lib-
  rary.  L J 19: 370-5.
---- J.  Cathedral and other English libraries.  L J 15:
  332-3.
---- J.  Charging system at Harvard.  L J 3: 338-9.
---- J.  Classing and arranging maps and charts.  L J 12:
  442.
---- J.  Class-room libraries in colleges.  L J 14: 127-8.
---- J.  College library and the classes.  L J 3: 5-6.
---- J.  Days and hours of opening.  1st Inc Conf: 171-2;
  L J 2: 274-5.
---- J.  Development of the library.  L J 19:370-5.
---- J.  Discussion on shelf classification.  L J 6: 116.
---- J.  Free libraries and readers.  L J 1: 63-7.
---- J.  Harvard college shelf guide.  L J 6: 9-10, 54, 116.
  L J 9: 50-1;  L J 10: 259-60.
---- J.  Inaugural address.  1st Int Conf 1-21, 1877.
---- J.  Library buildings.  U S Rept: 465-75, 1876.
---- J.  Library memoranda.  U S Rept 712, 1876.
---- J.  Library pests.  L J 4: 448-9.
---- J.  On the Harvard scheme.  1st Int Conf: 164, 1877.
---- J.  President's address.  L J 2: 5-7, 99-119;  4: 223-
  5;  6: 63-4;  7: 123-4;  8: 163-5.
---- J.  Reading in popular libraries.  U S Govt Rept: 431-3.
  1876.
---- J.  Reference books in English.  U S Rept 715:  L J 1:
  247-9, 1876.
---- J.  Report on general library interests.  L J 8: 163-5.
---- J.  Scheme for automatic delivery of books.  L J 2: 22.
---- J.  Shelf lists versus accession catalogue.  L J 3:
  247-8.
---- J.  Small library buildings.  L J 13: 279.
---- J.  Statistics.  U S Rept: 714.  1876.
---- J.  Telephones in libraries.  L J 2: 22.
---- J.  What we do with pamphlets.  L J 14: 434.
---- J.  Women librarians in America.  1st Int Conf: 178.
---- J. and F. Poole.  Proceedings of 1st Int Conf: 178.
Winston, Z. T.  Library progress in North Carolina.  A L A Bull
  1: Conf No 3-4.
Winter, C.  How to use a library.  Bookman (N Y) 34: 504-8.
---- C.  Libraries on the transatlantic liners.  Bookman
  33: 368-75.
Winter, W.  Newspaper and the theatre.  Pacific Monthly 25:
  42-7.
Winterburn, F. H.  The child's taste in fiction.  New England
  Mag 27: 325-30.
Winterrowd, G.  Des Moines public library council.  L J 43:
  639-40.

Winton, G. E.   Business libraries of Detroit.   Special Lib-
   raries 10: 181-5.
   ----  G. E.   The high school library as a special library.
   Special Libraries 10: 193.
Wire, G. E.   Autobiographies of childhood.   Bull Bib 9: 121-2.
   --  G. E.   Binding of law books.   P L 9: 265-8.
   --  G. E.   Book selection, buying and binding.   L J 24: Conf
   No 63-5; P L 4: 261-2.
   --  G. E.   Expert advice, which is not expert.   L J 24: Conf
   No 523-4.
   --  G. E.   How should a librarian read.   L J 20: Conf No 16-9.
   --  G. E.   Ink for book labels.   Am Lib Annual 1916-17: 68.
   --  G. E.   Medical books for small public libraries.   L J
   20: Conf No 37-9.
   --  G. E.   Organization.   L J 24: Conf No 70-3.
   --  G. E.   Preservation of leather and cloth bindings.   New
   Hamp Bull 8: 85-91.
   --  G. E.   Reclassifying a library without stopping the cir-
   culation.   P L 1: 299-300.
   --  G. E.   Report on classification and cataloguing.   L J
   23: Conf No 18-22.
   --  G. E.   Review of Mr. Brown's adjustable classification.
   L J 24: 121.
   --  G. E.   Review of Brown's Manual of library economy.   P
   L 8: 466-8.
   --  G. E.   Some heresies about cataloguing.   L J 22: Conf
   No 62-3, Discussion 123-6;  P L 2: 391.
   --  G. E.   Some principles of book and picture selection.
   L J 26: 54-6.
   --  G. E.   State reports, digests and statutes.   L J 25:
   Conf No 57-9.
   --  G. E.   Subject classification of textbooks in law lib-
   raries.   A L A Bull 1: Conf No 258-60.
   --  G. E.   Summary of a paper on library assistants in the
   United States.   L A 1: 214-7.
Wise, S. S.   Moral power of the press.   Homilectic Review 60:
   408-12;  Pacific Monthly 23: 437-40.
Wishart, A.   The making of a citizen.   P L 16: 348-9.
Wishart, J. W.   University library at Aberdeen.   L W 2: 141-4,
   173-5.
Wissler, C.   The interests of children in the reading work of
   the elementary schools.   Pedagogical Seminary 5: 523-40.
Wister, O.   Subjects fit for fiction.   L J 31: Conf No 20-4.
Wiswell, L. O.   School libraries in New York State.   N Y L
   2: 192-6.
Witham, E.   Brooklyn public library:   neighborhood and exhibit
   reports.   L J 35: 62-4.
   ----  E.   Making a library useful.   L J 28: 604.
   ----  E.   Reference work in a branch library.   L J 35: 206-7.
Withington, G. B.   Forming a village improvement society.   New
   Hamp Bull (ns) 11: 71-2.

Withington, L.  Housing of federal archives.  Nation 92: 165-6.
Withington, M. C.  Latin Americana collection in Yale univer-
    sity.  L J 44: 228.
Witte, E. E.  Industrial problems to-day.  Wis Lib Bull 15:
    38-41.
Wolcott, J. D.  California.  U S Commissioner of Education
    Report 1911, 1: 163-5.
----- J. D.  California county free library system.  U S
    Commissioner of Education Report 1915, 1: 519-20.
----- J. D.  County extension.  U S Commissioner of Educa-
    tion Report 1912, 1: 385-7;  1915, 1: 521-22.
----- J. D.  County library law -- Oregon.  U S Commissioner
    of Education, Report 1911, Vol 1: 199-200.
----- J. D.  How the library of the Bureau of education may
    serve the schools.  L J 39: 676-7.
----- J. D.  Legislation.  U S Commissioner of Education
    Report 1915, Vol 1: 513-8.
----- J. D.  Library activities, 1916-1918.  U S Bureau of
    Education, Bull 1919, 64: 1-28.
----- J. D.  Library extension in the United States.  U S
    Bureau of Education Report 1911, pt 1: 161-219.
----- J. D.  Library service to immigrants.  U S Bur of Educ
    Report 1915, 1: 527-31.
----- J. D.  Rural library extension in Indiana.  U S Com-
    missioner of Education Report 1911, 1: 172.
----- J. D.  Washington county free library, Hagerstown, Md.
    U S Commissioner of Education Report 1911, 1: 180.
Wolf, E. C.  Collected information in  print and the training
    of employes of the Curtis publishing company.  Special Lib-
    raries 5: 96-7.
Wolfe, F.  A little tin station, Cedar Rapids, Iowa.  P L 22:
    186-7.
Wolfe, L. E.  How to make the library more serviceable to stud-
    ents of school age.  Nat Educ Assn 1908: 1104-10.
--- L. E.  The many versus the few books course of study.
    Educational Review 45: 146-54.
Wolfson, A. M.  The library in the teaching of commercial sub-
    jects.  Journal of Education 84: 97.
----- A. M.  Some bibliographical notes on Italian communal
    history.  Bib Soc Chic Yr-Bk 1902-3: 47-78.
Wolfstein, D. F.  Value of the medical library to the community.
    Med Lib and Hist Journal 3: 198-207.
Wolfstieg, A.  The organization of the library profession in
    the U. S.: trans. from the German by B. B. Winser.  P L 11:
    11-2.
Wood, A. A.  De Morgan's novels.  Minn P L C N 3: 63-6.
Wood, B.  Infectious disease and circulating libraries.  L C
    5: 24.
-- B.  Juvenile libraries.  L 4: 111-2.

-- B. Relative functions of reference and lending libraries. L A R 6: 29-39.

-- B. Rural libraries in the Report to the Carnegie U. K. Trust by Prof. Adams. L A R 17: 533-9.

-- B. Selection of books for a reference library. L 8: 522-30.

-- B. Thomas Gent: printer, bookseller and bookmaker. L A R 2: 235-45.

-- B. Three special features of free library work. L 4: 105-14.

-- B. Women's reading rooms. L 4: 108-11.

-- B. Yorkshire village libraries. L 6: 37-41.

Wood, E. Small libraries and small incomes: what can be done with them. Libn 3: 162, 204-7.

-- E. A small library's opportunities. L W 7: 32-5.

Wood, G. W. Literature in the Manx language to the middle of the nineteenth century. L A R 13: 343-53.

Wood, H. The public library and the school library: a joint opportunity. L J 45: 631-4.

Wood, H. A. Administration of high school libraries as branches of public libraries. Pacific Northwest Library Assn Proceedings 1914: 35-41; L J 39: 659-62; Ia L C Q 7: 164-7.

-- H. A. Ample space and durable equipment essential in high school libraries. P L 25: 87.

-- H. A. Book side of things. P L 13 40-1.

-- H. A. Cedar Rapids public library. L J 30: 914, 931-2.

-- H. A. Impressions of foreign libraries. Iowa L C Q 5: 145-9.

-- H. A. Librarians as educators. Ia L C Q 8: 213-6.

-- H. A. Librarians as educators: the possibilities of the county library. Minn P L C N 6: 59-62.

-- H. A. The library and the school. P L 18: 384.

-- H. A. Library course of study for elementary schools. Minn P L C N 6: 137-9.

-- H. A. The library hour in the school. Nat Educ Assn 1913: 736-40.

-- H. A. Outline of course given by the school librarian in Portland, Oregon: Library training in high schools. P L 23: 79-80.

-- H. A. A plan for the certification of librarians. A L A Bull 14: 342-3.

-- H. A. Problems of work with children. A L A Bull 5: 247-9; P L 17: 86-7.

-- H. A. The public library and the shcool library: a joint opportunity. A L A Bull 14: 141, 330; L J 45: 631-4.

-- H. A. Report of Committee on university and college libraries. Nat Educ Assn 1917: 651-2; L J 42: 570; Am Lib Annual 1917-18: 51.

-- H. A. Results in school reading. P L 23: 82.

-- H. A.  Sets for children.  P L 18: 138-41.
-- H. A.  Use and value of pictures in the library.  Ia L C
   Q 1: 49-52.
Wood, H. M.  Charging systems.  P L 4: 375-7.
-- H. M.  Keeping an index that finds clippings.  Factory
   Jan 1917: 136-44;  L J 42: 338;  Am Lib Annual 1917-18: 32-3.
Wood, J. L.  Who's who in the library.  P L 14: 81-4.
Wood, L.  From the other side of the counter.  L A 4: 270-3.
Wood, M. E.  Library work in a Chinese city.  A L A Bull 1:
   Conf No 84-7.
Wood, M. O.  Resources of the small library.  New Hamp Bull
   (ns) 15: 149-50.
Wood, P. W. ed.  Hand list of English books in the library of
   Emmanuel College, Cambridge, printed before 1641.  Bib Soc
   Publication 1915.
Wood, W. C.  High school and the county library.  California
   Blue Bull 1: 37.
-- W. C.  The high school library.  Cal Blue Bulletin 1:
   34-8.
-- W. C.  High schools may use county library.  Cal Blue Bull-
   etin 1: 6-7.
Woodard, G. E.  Notes on bookbinding.  L J 23: 231-7.
Woodbine, H.  Essay on modern methods of book storage.  L A R
   12: 446-54.
Woodford, C.  Digging our executives out of the ranks.  System
   36: 63-5.
Woodford, J.  Public documents for schools.  P L 24: 459-60.
Woodford, J. M.  How a little booth helped a big movement.  L
   J 45: 217.
------ J. M.  A venture in document publicity:  an experiment
   worth while.  A L A Bull 14: 163-8, 338.
Woodruff, C. R.  Correlation of municipal information.  L J 40:
   393-6.
------ C. R.  Economic conditions of the twentieth century.
   A L A Bull 10: 465-9, Discussion 469-70.
------ C. R.  Education through free lectures.  P L 10: 346-
   50.
------ C. R.  Legislative reference work and its opportun-
   ities.  A L A Bull 2: 278-83;  P L 13: 300-3.
------ C. R.  Municipal periodical literature.  L J 36: 183-
   4.
------ C. R.  Report of the Committee on a national center
   for municipal information.  Special Libraries 6: 114-6.
------ C. R.  Sources of municipal material with reference
   to a clearing-house of information.  Special Libraries 2:
   112-4.
Woodruff, E. B.  Reading list on Eugene Brieux (1858) Bull Bib
   2: 5-6.
------ E. B.  Reference work.  L J 22: Conf No 65-7, Discussion 127-9.

Woodruff, E. H.   Birmingham lectures.   L J 12: 253-4.

------ E. H.   Fiction in public reference libraries.   L J 20: 342-5.

------ E. H.   List of abbreviations used in book catalogues. L J 12: 187-92;  16: 141.

------ E. H.   University libraries and seminary methods of instruction.   L J 11: 219-24.

Woodruff, J. L.   A labor-saving method.   P L 15: 58.

------ J. L.   State supervision of library extension in Illinois.   P L 13: 383-4.

------ J. L.   Who's who in the library.   P L 14: 81-4.

Woods, E. A.   How the library helps the librarian.   P L 12: 297-8.

Woodward, B. B.   Symposium on public libraries after the war. L A R 19: 330-2.

------ B. B. and C. D. Sherborn.   Curiosities of cataloguing. L 9: 70-3.

Woodward, C. J.   Action of gas on leather bookbindings:  preliminary experimental enquiry.   L C 5: 25-9;  L J 12: 321, 428.

Woodward, G. E.   Device for card cataloguing -- use of rubber type in duplicating catalogue card entries.   L J 23: 606.

Woodworth, F.   A. L. A. exhibit at Paris exposition.   L J 25: 116-9;  P L 5: 96-100.

Wooley, E. C.   Students' use of the dictionary.   Educational Review 1912: 492-501.

Woolston, W. P.   Utility of libraries:  a bookseller's point of view.   L A R 14: 121-6.

Wooster, H.   Supplying of books to the fleet at Guantanamo Bay, Cuba.   L J 44: 386-90.

Wooten, K. H.   Library development in the South since 1907. A L A Bull 8: 158-66;  P L 19: 288-90.

Worden, R.   Picture bulletins at the May day fete, library school.   Wis Lib Bull 11: 190-3.

Working, D. W.   The county agent in relation to rural library work.   A L A Bull 8: 358-62.

----- D. W.   The relation between the agricultural college libraries and the extension work of the county as developing under the Smith-Lever act.   A L A Bull 9: 153-6.

Worman, E. J.   Alien members of the book trade during the Tudor period:  being an index to those whose names occur in the returns of aliens, letters of denization, and other documents published by the Huguenot society.   Bibliographical Society Publication 1906.

Worts, G. F.   What books are doing to Americanize soldiers of many races.   Outlook 20: 186-7.

Wray, E.   Business information service.   Special Libraries 11: 150-1.

Wright, C. C.   Rural libraries in Wilkes county.   N C Bull 2: 37-8.

Wright, C. T. H.   Books for the Russian prisoners of war in
    Germany.  A L A Bull 11: 108-11;   P L 22: 275-7.
    ---- C. T. H.   Early nineteenth century readers and the
    origin of the London library.  L A 8: 50.
Wright, D.   Book sizes.  L J 5: 177-8.
Wright, E. C.   Use of the Victrola in the story hour.  Minn
    P L C N 4: 126-7.
Wright, H.   Posters and war work:  Library of Congress.  Inter-
    national Studio 64: 121-4.
Wright, H. S.   The gracious time.  P L 17: 408-11.
    ---- H. S.   Miss Hewins and her class in children's reading.
    L J 38: 210-1.
Wright, I. F.   "The Gifts of the Nation."  L J 45: 215-6.
Wright, J.   Classification scheme for the Library of municipal
    research at Harvard university.  Special Libraries 8: 96;
    L J 42: 675;   Am Lib Annual 1917-18: 29-30.
    ---- J.   Early Bibles of America (Review).  L 5: 146-7.
    ---- J.   Plea of the art librarian.  P L 13: 348-9.
Wright, J. H.   The library as a workshop.  Vt L Bull 15: 19-20.
Wrigley, M. J.   Enquiry assistants:  a library waste.  L W 15:
    124-5.
    ----- M. J.   Library staff:  a plea for its recognition and
    organization.  L W 15: 211-3.
    ----- M. J.   Problem of the junior assistant.  L A 10: 202-3.
    ----- M. J.   Registration of periodicals.  L W 11: 33-4.
Wright, M. R.   Public reference library and higher education.
    L A R 6: 433-7;   Discussion 465-7.
Wright, P. B.   Branch libraries in schools.  Am Lib Annual 1916-
    17: 25.
    ---- P. B.   Buildings for small libraries.  Ia L C Q 3: 29-
    31.
    ---- P. B.   Character of permitted access to closed shelves.
    L J 25: 35-6.
    ---- P. B.   Duplicate pay collections of popular novels.
    L J 28: Conf No 40-1, Discussion 156-9.
    ---- P. B.   High school branches in Kansas City.  L J 39:
    673-6.
    ---- P. B.   High school branches of public libraries.  Nat
    Educ Assn 1914: 820-3;   L J 39: 790.
    ---- P. B.   How far should the demand of the public for pop-
    ular books be supplied?  P L 13: 122-3.
    ---- P. B.   Library and the mechanic.  L J 34: 532-8.
    ---- P. B.   Library legislation unprogressive.  L J 37:
    675-6.
    ---- P. B.   Reaching the people.  L J 31: Conf No 86-8;
    Discussion Conf No 258-9;   P L 11: 237-40.
    ---- P. B.   Relation of the library to the public school.
    P L 4: 11-3.
    ---- P. B.   Some book-buying and other library problems.
    PL 13: 120-3, 165-8.

---- P. B.  Some methods of library advertising.  L J 31: Conf No 86-8;  P L 11: 237-40;  Ia L C Q 4: 33-6;  5: 159.

---- P. B.  Staff meetings: their organization, methods and results.  L J 32: 553.

---- P. B.  Sunday opening.  P L 10: 518.

---- P. B.  A thought or two on library legislation.  P L 17: 430-1.

---- P. B.  Universal library card.  P L 23: 21.

---- P. B.  Work of libraries in civic campaigns.  L J 36: 3-4.

---- P. B.  Work of the Kansas City (Mo.) library.  L J 42: 454.

Wright, R.  Brown versus Dewey.  L A 7: 134-5;  227-37.

---- R.  Some principles of rural library economy.  L W 23: 537-40.

---- R.  Staff guilds, clubs and reading circles.  L A 6: 216-8.

---- R.  Technological classification.  L W 18: 312-6, 344-7;  L W 19: 9-10.

Wright, R. H.  How to make the library useful to high school pupils.  Nat Educ Assn 1905: 864-7;  P L 10: 480-2.

Wright, R. M.  Library situation in Oregon, Pacific Northwest Library Assn Proceedings 1910: 36-7.

Wright, R. W.  Glimpses of U. S. army hospital library, No 24, Parkview, Pa.  Vermont Lib Bull 15: 3-4.

---- R. W.  How to select books for the small library.  Vt L Bull 11: 31-3;  New Hamp Bull (ns) 12: 164-6.

---- R. W.  Liberal rules.  New Hamp Bull Sept 1912: 109-11.

---- R. W.  Picture-books versus the colored supplement.  Vt L Bull 8, No 1: 5-6.

Wright, T. W.  Relationship of the public library to local societies.  L A R 15: 413-7.

---- T. W.  Revival of printing.  L A 12: 129-30;  L A R 17: 325-6;  Libn 5: 335-6.

---- T. W. and Hamer, H.  An emendation of the Dewey classification 790-9.  L W 17: 232-3.

Wright, W.  Remarkable Bibles.  L 7: 250-61.

Wright, W. H.  Is library censorship desirable?  A L A Bull 5: 59-60.

Wright, W. H. K.  Best means of promoting the free library movement in small towns and villages.  1st Int Conf: 22-8.

---- W. H. K.  Censorship of fiction.  L A R 12: 4-6.

---- W. H. K.  An indicator-catalogue and charging system.  L A Trans 2: 76-8.

---- W. H. K.  Lending libraries and board schools.  L 1: 166-70.

---- W. H. K.  Librarians and local bibliography.  L A Trans 4-5: 197-201.

---- W. H. K.  Library association, 1877-1897, a retrospect.
L 10: 197-207, 245-52.

---- W. H. K.  Local collections:  what should be collected,
and how to obtain material.  L A R 7: 1-11.

---- W. H. K.  London school libraries.  2nd International
Conference Proceedings 1897: 239.

---- W. H. K.  Municipal libraries and suburban districts.
L C 4: 39-43.

---- W. H. K.  On the best means of promoting the free library movement.  L J 2: 119-25.

---- W. H. K.  Public library and the board school.  L A
Trans 2: 38-41;  L J 4: 410-1.

---- W. H. K.  Special collections of local books in provincial libraries.  L A Trans 44-50.

Wyche, B.  The lend-a-volume library:  private lending of books.
L J 40: 40-2.

Wyche, R. T.  Experiment in story telling in school.  Education
28: 76-9.

--- R. T.  The national story teller's league.  Child Conference for Research and Welfare Proceedings 1909, 1: 217-21;
Pedagogical Seminary 16: 537-41.

--- R. T.  Story teller's league.  World's Work (N Y) 25:
588-90.

--- R. T.  What stories shall we tell?  Kind M 34: 47-50.

Wyer, J. I.  A. L. A. exhibit at the Chautauqua conference.
L J 23: Conf No 184.

-- J. I.  Collecting local war material for the New York
state library.  A L A Bull 12: 336-7, Discussion 338-9.

-- J. I.  Factors in the development of the library school
curriculum.  A L A Bull 2: 205-6.

-- J. I.  How to treat public documents in a small library.
N Y L 1: 53.

-- J. I.  Library schools at the Chautauqua conference.  L
J 23: Conf No 183.

-- J. I.  Selected author headings for U. S. government documents.  Bull No 102, Library School No 21: 45-52, N Y S L
Rept 89.

-- J. I.  Some useful New York state public documents.  N
Y L 1: 10-1.

-- J. I.  United States government documents.  Bull No 102,
Library School No 21: 41-56, N Y S L Rept 89: V 1, 1906.

-- J. I.  United States government documents:  a list that
should be in even the smallest library.  N Y L 1: 43-5.

Wyer, J. I., Jr.  Agricultural libraries.  A L A Bull 4: 786-7.

-- J. I., Jr.  College and university library salaries.
School and Society 11: 351-3.

-- J. I., Jr.  Commission aims and achievement.  L J 41: 129.

-- J. I., Jr.  Discusses library architecture.  A L A Bull
10: 37.

-- J. I., Jr.  "Everyman's library."  L J 41: 797-801.
-- J. I., Jr.  First $100 for reference books.  N Y L 1:
8-10.
-- J. I., Jr.  Infection thru circulation of books.  L J
44: 683-4.
-- J. I., Jr.  Library planning.  L J 39: 747-52;  N Y L
4: 130, 134-9.
-- J. I., Jr.  Library reform in France.  L J 31: 215-7.
-- J. I., Jr.  Net fiction and the libraries.  Publishers'
Weekly 79: 1104-5;  L J 36: 185-6.
-- J. I., Jr.  New York state library and its relation to
schools and teachers.  New York State Assn Proceedings 1911:
16-21;  N Y L 3: 37-9;  P L 17: 15-6.
-- J. I., Jr.  New York State library and the college and
reference libraries of the state.  N Y L 2: 188-92.
-- J. I., Jr.  New York state library:  its present poss-
essions.  P L 16: 207-8.
-- J. I., Jr.  Objections to metal furniture.  L J 37: 328.
-- J. I., Jr.  Outside the walls.  N Y L 2: 213-8;  N Y L
3: 90; L J 36; 176.
-- J. I., Jr.  The poetry of the Great war.  N Y L 6: 159-62.
-- J. I., Jr.  Province of the state library in library
extension.  A L A Bull 3: 294-5.
-- J. I., Jr.  Recent state library surveys.  ALA Bull 11:
397-400.
-- J. I., Jr.  Responsibility of the American library assoc-
iation to discharged soldiers, sailors and marines.  L J
44: 758.
-- J. I., Jr.  Some talks to the library school.  Wis Lib
Bull 7: 163-4.
-- J. I., Jr.  State library and its librarian.  P L 19:
338.
-- J. I., Jr.  State reference work through the small lib-
rary and the traveling library station or small club.  A L
A Bull 8: 357-8.
-- J. I., Jr.  A visit to the camp libraries.  N Y L 6:
54-7.
-- J. I., Jr.  War service of the A. L. A.  N Y L 6: 23-6.
-- J. I., Jr.  What Americans read.  P L 16: 392-3, 450;
N Y L 3: 94-102;  N C Bull 1: 135-42;  Vt L Bull 8 No 1:
3; New Hamp Bull 9: 161-70.
-- J. I., Jr.  What the community owes the library.  A L
A Bull 5: 55-9;  N Y L 2: 253-6;  L J 36: 325-8;  P L 16:
244-5;  Minn P L C N 3: 91-2;  New Hamp Bull (n s) 7: 33-41.
Wyer, M. G.  Additional books for reference use.  Ia L C Q
6: 2-4.
-- M. G.  Book auction sales and secondhand catalogues.
P L 12: 53-6.
-- M. G.  Government documents in the small library.  P L
15: 38.

-- M. G.   Instruction in the use of books in a college library.  L J 39: 439-41.
-- M. G.   Reference books for a small library.  Ia L C Q 5: 205-7.
-- M. G.   Right reading in childhood.  Ia L C Q 6: 177-82.
-- M. G.   Some magazine editors.  P L 14: 212-3.
-- M. G. and C. E. Groves.  Index of New York governors' messages, 1777-1901.  Bulletin 100, Legislation No 26, N Y S L Rept 88, vol 2.
Wyer, W. I.  What the state library is doing to help win the war.  A L A Bull 12: 189-92.
Wynkoop, A.  Adequate state aid for libraries:  a plea.  L J 45: 70-1.
----- A.  Expensive books and the small library.  N Y L 2: 251-2.
----- A.  Free lending libraries in New York State.  Nation 98: 80-1.
----- A.  How libraries are growing in New York State.  N Y L 5: 55-60;  L J 41: 183-7.
----- A.  Libraries -- Legislation Bulletin 29h N Y S L Rept 88 vol 2, 1905.
----- A.  The library and the war.  N Y L 6: 58-67.
----- A.  The library as a factor in present-day education.  N Y L 6: 193-204.
----- A.  Library extension in 1906.  L J 32: 7.
----- A.  Library institutes in New York.  N Y L 5: 118-22, 131-6;  A L A Bull 10: 250-4, 452.
----- A.  Library legislation in 1905 -- Legislation Bulletin No 33 L, 129-33.  N Y S L Rept 89 vol 2;  L J 31: 57-9.
----- A.  Library legislation in 1906.  L J 32: 70-1.
----- A.  Library progress in the State of New York.  L J 40: 263-7.
----- A.  Outlines and references for library institutes: I -- Stocking the library:  Part 1, selecting books.  N Y L 4: 82-8.
----- A.  Selection for all the people in the community.  N Y L 4: 2-5.
----- A.  Waiting for bargains.  N Y L 2: 156.
----- A.  Weak points in village libraries.  N Y L 1: 185-6.
----- A.  What we may expect of the trained librarian in village libraries.  N Y L 4: 239-45;  Am Lib Annual 1916-17: 72-3.
----- A.  Where should state aid end and local responsibility begin in library extension work.  A L A Bull 1: Conf No 238-43.
Yarros, V. S.  The library and the book in Russia's revolutionary movement.  L J 43: 147-51.
Yates, A. H.  Need of a connection between the public library and the theatre.  L A 5: 253-6.

--- A. H.  Weeding out of obsolete books.  L A 6: 318-9.

Yates, J.  Indicators.  L A Trans 1: 76-8.

--- J.  The Leeds indicator.  L J 1: 255-6, 443.

--- J.  On public historiography and printing.  L A Trans
5: 158-62.

--- J.  Our town library:  its success and failures.  L C
3: 36-9.

--- J.  Progress of the Library association.  L J 11: 368.

--- J.  Public library system of England.  L J 1: 122-3.

Yates, M. S.  A plea for school libraries.  N C Bull 4: 3-4.

Yates, R.  Library progress in the northern counties.  L A R
11: 279-84.

Yeaxlee, B.  Libraries and adult education in rural areas.  L
A R 22: 379-80.

Yerby, C. K.  Good reading for negroes.  II. A Memphis library.
Southern Workman Oct 1914: 541-3.

York, F.  The training of the library assistant.  L A 14: 27-30.

Yost, E. W.  Some suggestions on school libraries, with recommended lists.  Michigan Board of Library Commissioners Report 1910: 32-8.

Young, C. C.  The public library and the public school.  L J 21:
140-4.

--- C. C.  Use of the library.  Nat Educ Assn 1899: 1150-5.

Young, E. F.  Literature in elementary schools.  Nat Educ Assn
1896: 111-7.

Young, F. R.  Public health nursing and its literature.  Vt L
Bull 14: 35-6.

Young, H.  Memorandum on some incunabula in the Toronto university library.  L J 32: 118.

--- H.  Subject headings.  Ontario Lib Assn Proceedings Ap
1912: 73-5;  P L 17: 405-8.

Young, J. D.  Are printed catalogues desirable for open access
libraries.  L A 7: 123-9.

--- J. D.  Book selection and discarding.  L W 10: 108-12.

--- J. D.  Fugitive bibliography in relation to book selection.  L A 6: 192-6.

--- J. D.  Newsrooms, their requirements and service.  L A
5: 57-60.

--- J. D.  Present conditions of library legislation.  L A
5: 222-6.

--- J. D.  Should libraries advertise, and, if so, to what
extent:  the negative.  L A 7: 100-3.

--- J. D.  Theory of book selection.  L A 10: 64-71;  L A
R 15: 60.

Young, J. H.  Romance of book-buying.  B A R 8: I-III.

Young, J. W. A.  Concerning the bibliography of mathematics.
Bib Soc Chic Yr-Bk 32-43.

Young, R. M.  An account of some notable books printed in
Belfast.  L 7: 135-44.

Yule, E. S.   Philippine library.   Bookman (N Y) 50: 511-4.
Yust, W. F.   Abstract of Wyoming legislation for county li-
braries.   L J 27: 24; P L 7: 56.
-- W. F.   Branch library rooms of Rochester, N. Y. public
library.   Wilson Bulletin, 1: 476-7.
-- W. F.   County libraries.   P L 9: 81.
-- W. F.   County library legislation in 1901.   Wisconsin.
P L 7: 56; Cal News Notes 3: 133.
-- W. F.   County libraries in Wyoming.   L J 27: 4; P L 7:
56; Cal News Notes 3: 133.
-- W. F.   County libraries: Oregon.   P L 8: 81; Cal News
Notes 3: 133.
-- W. F.   County library legislation in Ohio.   P L 7: 55.
-- W. F.   The dream of Tomus.   N Y L 6: 124-6.
-- W. F.   Industrial possibilities of Southern libraries.
L J 33: 99.
-- W. F.   Libraries and library movement in Kentucky.   A
L A Bull 1: 82-3.
-- W. F.   Library legislation.   L J 27: 22-4; P L 7: 55-7;
L J 28: 16-8; P L 8: 18-20; L J 29: 69-72; P L 9: 80-4.
-- W. F.   Library legislation in Georgia.   L J 27: 308.
-- W. F.   Library legislation in 1901.   Wisconsin County
Libraries.   P L 7: 56.
-- W. F.   Library legislation of 1904.   L J 30: 81; P L 10:
72-3, 83-7.
-- W. F.   Louisville library building.   L J 34: 398-401.
-- W. F.   The park, the museum and the library.   P L 15:
296.
-- W. F.   Public library section of Rochester child wel-
fare exhibit.   L J 38: 344-5.
-- W. F.   Publicity in library work.   Mass L C Bull 2, 4:
85-93.
-- W. F.   Shall the A. L. A. remain democratic.   P L 14:
132-3.
-- W. F.   Staff meetings: their organization, methods and
results.   L J 32: 518-9.
-- W. F.   Sunday school library, its nature and functions.
P L 4: 20-2.
-- W. F.   That girl stuff.   L J 43: 35.
-- W. F.   What of the black and yellow races?   A L A Bull
7: 159-67.
Zachert, A. B.   Children's librarian as social worker.   A L
A Bull 10: 421.
----- A. B.   Creed of the children's librarian.   P L 17:
257-9.
----- A. B.   Grade libraries in Rochester, New York.   L J
43: 219-20.
----- A. B.   The small library and the children.   N C Bull
1: 131-3.

----- A. B.   What our children read and why.   L J 39: 21-4.
Zaehnsdorf, J.   Practical suggestions on bookbinding.   L C 4: 107-11.
Zenodotus.   The true national library.   L J 27: 318-9.
Zimand, S.   Guild socialism: a bibliography.   L J 45: 258-64.
Zimmerman, O. B.   Collection of industrial catalogs by the public libraries.   L J 29: 63-5.
Zimmerman, W. F.   Some remarks on the net price system.   P L 8: 220-3.
Zivny, L. T.   Libraries in Czecho-Slovania.   P L 24: 381.
Zon, R.   Russian scientific literature.   Special Libraries 8: 157-59, 170.